The Hotel and Restaurant Business

**RELATED BOOKS WRITTEN OR CO-AUTHORED
BY DONALD E. LUNDBERG:**

The Management of People in Hotels and Restaurants, Wm. C. Brown
   Publishers, Dubuque, IA., 1993.

The Restaurant: From Concept to Operation, co-author, John R. Walker, John
   Wiley & Sons, New York, 1993.

Human Relations for the Hospitality Industry, co-author Robert Martin.
   Van Nostrand Reinhold, New York, 1991.

Understanding Cooking, co-author, Lendal Kotschevar, Marcus Printing,
   Holyoke, MA. 1988.

Understanding Baking, co-author, Joseph Amendola, Van Nostrand
   Reinhold, New York, 1992.

The Tourist Business, Van Nostrand Reinhold, New York, 1990.

International Travel and Tourism, co-author, Carolyn B. Lundberg, John
   Wiley & Sons, New York, 1993.

Tourism Economics, co-authors, Krishmory, M. and Stavenga, Mink, John
   Wiley and Sons, New York. To be published.

The Hotel and Restaurant Business

Sixth Edition

Donald E. Lundberg
Professor Emeritus, California State
Polytechnic University
Pomona

 VAN NOSTRAND REINHOLD
An International Thomson Publishing Company

New York • London • Bonn • Boston • Detroit • Madrid • Melbourne • Mexico City
Paris • Singapore • Tokyo • Toronto • Albany NY • Belmont CA • Cincinnati OH

I(T)P™ Van Nostrand Reinhold is a division of International Thomson Publishing, Inc.
     The ITP logo is a trademark under license

Printed in the United States of America

For more information, contact:

Van Nostrand Reinhold   Chapman & Hall GmbH
115 Fifth Avenue   Pappelallee 3
New York, NY 10003   69469 Weinheim
                                        Germany

Chapman & Hall   International Thomson Publishing Asia
2-6 Boundary Row   221 Henderson Road #05-10
London   Henderson Building
SE1 8HN   Singapore 0315
United Kingdom

Thomas Nelson Australia   International Thomson Publishing Japan
102 Dodds Street   Hirakawacho Kyowa Building, 3F
South Melbourne, 3205   2-2-1 Hirakawacho
Victoria, Australia   Chiyoda-ku, 102 Tokyo
                                        Japan

Nelson Canada   International Thomson Editores
1120 Birchmount Road   Campos Eliseos 385, Piso 7
Scarborough, Ontario   Col. Polanco
Canada M1K 5G4   11560 Mexico D.F. Mexico

   97 98 99 MNG 10 9 8 7 6 5 4 3

Library of Congress Cataloging-in-Publication Data

Lundberg, Donald.
    The hotel and restaurant business / Donald E. Lundberg. — 6th ed.
        p.   cm.
    Includes bibliographical references (p.   ) and index.
    ISBN 0-442-01246-2
    1. Hotels.   2. Restaurants.   I. Title.
TX911.L785   1993   92-28353
338.4'76479—dc20   CIP

Contents

Acknowledgments

This is one of those books that the author can only partially claim as his own. It has drawn heavily on the experiences and work of dozens of hospitality business practitioners and on articles and information written and compiled by others.

Many of the hotel business statistics come from the American Hotel and Motel Association and two international accounting firms: Laventhol and Horwath and Pannell Kerr Forster. Unfortunately, both accounting firms have disbanded because of financial difficulties.

Statistics for the restaurant business largely come from the National Restaurant Association. Numerous hotel and restaurant managers and hospitality management companies have generously provided photographs, charts, and other information.

Professor Stanley Davis, Ph.D, Professor Emeritus, School of Hotel Administration at Cornell University, contributed the chapter on management.

David K. Hayes, University of Houston, and Larry Yu, Northern Arizona University, reviewed the book at various stages. To them—many thanks!

Karen Eich Drummond, F.M.P., R.D., contributed much of the chapter on institutional foodservice. She also helped reorganize and edit other chapters.

To all the others who have made the book possible, my gratitude.

Preface

The sixth edition of *The Hotel and Restaurant Business* continues in the same vein as previous editions. It is a descriptive analysis of the hotel and restaurant business, from early inns to megahotels, from family taverns to multibillion-dollar restaurant corporations. An attempt is made to identify the determinants of the business, including changing socioeconomic conditions and especially the people who have shaped its style and direction. Brief biographical sketches of some of these superstars are included.

Statistical, biographical, financial, and ownership information has been updated. New technical developments are covered. But because of the rapid changes occurring, revisions are dated the day the book is published. The conceptual background of some chapters has been improved. New chapters on management of people and institutional foodservice are included. The book, however, remains largely descriptive in character, an attempt to present the extent and nature of the business. Specialized subjects such as hotel and restaurant accounting, engineering, and marketing are touched on briefly.

We in the hotel and restaurant business can take satisfaction from being engaged in activities that help make life pleasing and comfortable for our guests. Whereas the conflicts of nationalism, terrorism, religious differences, and economic rivalries rock the world, travel and tourism—of which the hotel and restaurant business is a part—bring people together under mostly agreeable conditions, in that way mitigating hostility and smoothing the rough edges of life.

1

Introduction: An Overview

What is hotel and restaurant management? It is a field that applies principles and information derived from a number of disciplines to the problems of selling food, beverages, and lodging to persons away from home. Practices and techniques learned from experience have their place as well.

Closely related to serving the public in this way is the field of institutional foodservice—in schools, colleges, hospitals, industries, and the like. The management of city and country clubs is also within the broader range of the profession.

Hotels and motels (Fig. 1-1) employ approximately 1.6 million people (including full-time and part-time) and enjoy annual sales approaching $65 billion. On an average day the industry accommodates over 2.6 million guests in 3 million available rooms in 44,300 properties. By comparison, the foodservice industry employs over 9 million people; 60 percent are female, and over half are under 30 years of age. Total sales approach $250 billion each year, equal to about 5 percent of the country's gross national product—generally defined as the value of all goods and services sold. Foodservices serve lunch or dinner every day to between 25 and 30 percent of U.S. adults.

Inextricably bound together with the hotel and restaurant business is travel and tourism, a business that provides services to travelers. These services include hotels, restaurants, and convention centers, as well as airlines, rental cars, or other forms of transportation; travel agencies and tour operators; and recreation and entertainment facilities. It is a burgeoning business.

The World Travel and Tourism Council states that travel and tourism is the world's largest industry. In 1992 it was expected to generate more than $3.1 trillion in gross output, 14 percent of the world gross national product. Over 400 million international visits will result in the employment of 130 million people. travel and tourism maintain an employment growth rate of 5.2 percent, far surpassing the world employment growth rate of only 2.45 percent.

1

Figure 1-1 The Feathers Hotel of Ludlow, Shropshire, England. The hotel first opened for business in 1600.

According to the World Tourism Organization, the world in 1989 inventoried about 11.2 million rooms suitable for international travelers, a number that was growing about 3.4 percent a year. Of the so-called megahotels, those with 1000 rooms or more, 99 of the 151 that existed in 1991 were in the U.S. Europe had 14 of them, 12 were in Japan. The number of U.S. hotels and motels were declining, smaller properties being replaced by larger ones.

Restaurant and hotel management is interdisciplinary. It draws on economics, psychology, management theory, food technology and chemistry, microbiology, physics, engineering, architecture, accounting, marketing, and law. From these disciplines, a set of approaches, systems, and analytical tools are formulated to make lodging and foodservice satisfying experiences for people away from home.

Much of hotel and restaurant supervision is an art. Relations with people—guests, patrons, employees, purveyors, and the community at large—are closer and often more sensitive than in

most fields. For example, retailers are concerned with customer relations, but their customers are not eating, drinking, and often sleeping under the same roof.

Hotel and restaurant managers must deal with a wide range of personalities. A patron or guest may be on his or her best behavior. On the other hand, the guest may be depressed and drunk and present all sorts of problems.

Clear systems and efficient practices help simplify the job of managing a hotel or restaurant, but the human element is difficult to systematize. Generally speaking, hotel or restaurant managers need a high energy level to be able to live with the long days and the multitude of demands on their nervous systems.

Joe Garvey, vice president of marketing for the Hyatt chain, compiled a humorous list of specifications for a hotelier. He or she must be:

A diplomat, a Democrat, an autocrat, an acrobat and a doormat. He or she must have the facility to entertain prime ministers, princes of industry, pickpockets, gamblers, bookmakers, philanthropists and prudes. He or she must be on both sides of the political fence and be able to jump that fence on occasion . . . . To be successful the hotelier must keep the bar full, the house full, the wine cellar full, and not get full himself.[1]

LIFE AS A HOTEL GENERAL MANAGER[2]

In a large hotel the general manager's (GM's) job is characterized by high intensity and extensive verbal communication, both face to face with a variety of people and by telephone. A 1987 study of ten highly successful GMs of large hotels in New Orleans tracked one GM as having 35 phone conversations in one day. Little wonder when you consider the size of their organizations (Fig. 1-2). Another GM in the study had face-to-face discussions with 25 people and 20 phone calls during a day. These interpersonal contacts lasted 10 minutes or less. Compared to verbal interactions, written communications were few. An interesting sidelight: Interruptions were expected.

---

1. Robert C. Lewis and Joseph Garvey, *The Practice of Hospitality Management II: Profitability in a Changing Environment* (Westport, Conn.: AVI Publishing Co.), 1986, p. 451.
2. Information for this section was taken from the study that appears in Eddystone C. Nebel III, *Managing Hotels Effectively: Lessons From Outstanding General Managers* (New York: Van Nostrand Reinhold), 1991.

One of the GMs, who is now a corporate vice president, kept a bowl of apples and grapes on his desk and invited his department heads to drop in whenever they wanted some fruit. The GMs indicated that during a typical day they were involved in a series of decisions, but few of them could be called major.

A GM's workday is long, often starting before 7:30 AM and continuing after supper to catch up on paperwork, a fact that corroborates the reputation of "long hours" for hotel executives.

Six of the ten GMs surveyed had served as resident managers on their way up the career ladder, and six had been in charge of the food and beverage operations of a hotel. Two came up by way of the accounting department. Only one each had been in sales, rooms, and housekeeping.

Contrary to what is commonly believed, only one of the executives tried to structure a very tight schedule and stick to it. Rather, GMs were highly adaptable to the pressures of the moment. Much of what they did in the course of a day seemed to depend on what was happening at the time; walking about from department to department and discussing problems of the moment occupied a lot of their time.

As might be expected, each of the GMs studied had a high level of confidence, a necessity for anyone having to make the dozens of quick decisions required for effective hotel operation. The GMs surveyed were star performers, men who reached the top position in less than 10 years. Nine of them were under 40 years of age.

As is customary in medium and large hotels, the GMs worked with and through an executive operating committee (EOC) made up of senior department heads. In medium-size hotels (about 300 rooms), the EOC consists of the Rooms Manager, Controller, Food & Beverage Director, Sales and Marketing Director, and Personnel Director (often called the Director of Human Resources). In large hotels three more executives join the EOC: the persons who head Convention Services, Engineering, and Public Relations.

Necessarily, GMs have their own management styles. Some tend to be autocratic, others democratic in involving department heads. Some GMs in the study delegated considerable responsibility and authority to individual subordinates and the EOC. Whatever his or her management style, a GM has final responsibility for the business success of a hotel. According to Nebel, GMs are well aware that they are "on stage" whenever they are in their hotels and consequently they are engaged in leadership in every contact with their subordinates.

The textbook recommendation that planning be done separately in an isolated setting was not practiced by these GMs. Instead, planning took place concomitantly while attending to current and specific issues. Dr. Nebel believed that planning probably took place as much on a subconscious as a conscious level.

The GM is ultimately responsible to the hotel guest, who evaluates the GM's performance by word of mouth, comment card, and returning (or not returning) to the hotel as a guest. As part of a hotel chain, the GM may report to a regional vice president or chain president, who in turn is responsible to the hotel owner(s). The owners may be a pension fund, bank, insurance company, savings and loan, airline, or some other business institution. Owners are currently taking a more active role in the oversight of hotel operations and may act through an asset manager to participate in budgeting, marketing, and operating policy. Their scrutiny and oversight have increased since hotel losses escalated in the 1980s.

Nearly all managers in a foodservice/lodging operation receive meals at no cost while at work. In large hotels, an entertainment account is set up that may run several hundred dollars a month. If a hotel/resort manager is expected to live on the premises, he or she receives complete maintenance: food and living quarters for themselves and their families.

LIFE AS A RESTAURATEUR

Restaurant owner/operators enter the restaurant business because they want to take control of their own lives and gain satisfaction from the exercise of their own skills—not necessarily kitchen skills, as might be expected, but skills in customer relations and dining room management. They need, according to a doctoral dissertation on entrepreneurship in restaurants, independence and control.[3] Customer orientation and an emphasis

---

3. Robert M. Small, "A Discriminant Analysis of Restaurant Entrepreneur Types and Restaurant Classifications," unpublished dissertation. Claremont Graduate School, Claremont, Calif., 1986.

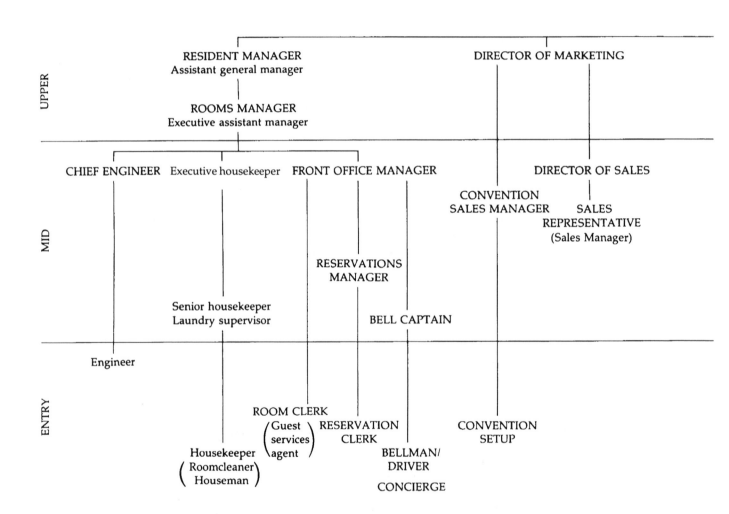

Figure 1-2 Organization of a large hotel.

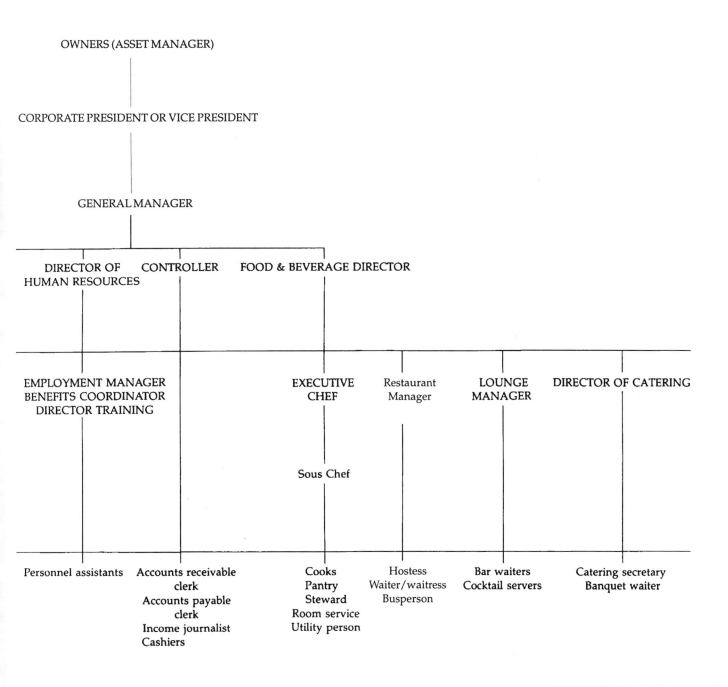

OWNERS (ASSET MANAGER)

CORPORATE PRESIDENT OR VICE PRESIDENT

GENERAL MANAGER

DIRECTOR OF   CONTROLLER   FOOD & BEVERAGE DIRECTOR
HUMAN RESOURCES

EMPLOYMENT MANAGER   EXECUTIVE   Restaurant   LOUNGE   DIRECTOR OF CATERING
BENEFITS COORDINATOR   CHEF   Manager   MANAGER
DIRECTOR TRAINING

Sous Chef

Personnel assistants   Accounts receivable   Cooks   Hostess   Bar waiters   Catering secretary
                       clerk   Pantry   Waiter/waitress   Cocktail servers   Banquet waiter
                    Accounts payable   Steward   Busperson
                       clerk   Room service
                    Income journalist   Utility person
                    Cashiers

on product quality are valued for the opportunities they afford for making money.

Those operating upscale restaurants—the dinner houses and luxury restaurants—form a group somewhat different from other restaurateurs. For them, income and profit are often of less importance than for owners of other kinds of restaurants. They are involved more for the love of it than for money.

Restaurant owners/operators are entrepreneurs by definition. They create, they innovate, they take risks, and they do their own thing. Some independent business people not in the restaurant field are entrepreneurs in order to avoid working for someone else. This is not so with restaurant owners/operators. They enjoyed their earlier work in the business and identified with the boss. Their memories of past employment are overwhelmingly positive. They also have a strong need for independence and control.

Stamina and the ability to work long hours characterize the restaurateur. Of the respondents to the dissertation questionnaire, 82 percent said they worked at least 50 hours a week. More than a quarter reported working 80 hours or more.

Several studies of hospitality management students have shown that relatively few are attracted to careers in fast food. Reasons include a feeling that fast food lacks glamour, demands long working hours, and leaves little room for innovation. District or regional manager jobs should hold more appeal, but they often require several years of experience as a unit manager.

District and regional managers supervise a number of unit managers within a geographical area. Their time is taken up in monitoring what is done by unit managers, in marketing and promotion, in facilities and safety management, and in trying to meet budget targets set by top managers or owners. Compared to hotel managers, fast-food district and regional managers make fewer family moves to new locations.

The ready availability of food and beverages has its hazards. There is the tendency to overeat, since food is free, as well as to drink too much. Coffee is bad enough, but the manager must be continually on guard to avoid visiting the bar too frequently with the guests.

Some managers are thrust into their positions before they have been tempered by experience;

their new power "goes to their heads." Now the center of attention, at least to their employees, some managers get carried away.

CHARACTERISTICS OF THE WORK

Long Hours

Long hours and work during evenings and weekends are the rule rather than the exception. A new manager may have to stay on the job 60 or 70 hours a week. In larger hotels the manager may not leave the property for days at a time. In the seasonal resort, the first few weeks just before and after opening are particularly exhausting; all time and effort must be focused on getting the hotel ready in time, usually with a large number of inexperienced personnel.

The unpredictable nature of the work looms as a distinct disadvantage to the person who prizes a weekend of leisure, long hours with the family, or a routine that fits in with the habits of neighbors. But the unusual hours are no handicap at all to other types, for whom the excitement of the job more than compensates for its inconveniences. Some hotel and restaurant managers speak with pride of the excessive numbers of hours they work, perhaps considering it evidence of their stamina.

All too often, hardworking managers see the long hours as a model for others to follow and justify it in terms of economic necessity.

The truth is actually different. For the average manager, efficiency drops after 44 to 48 hours of work. Decision-making ability suffers. The person who works extremely long hours in reality is handicapping the enterprise. It has been found repeatedly that reducing a work week from 50 to 44 hours or from 48 hours to 40 hours, increases the efficiency per hour worked. Overall productivity is not markedly reduced in most cases.

Unskilled Employees

The managers of hotels and restaurants usually work with a large percentage of employees who are relatively unskilled, uneducated, and disadvantaged. For well over a hundred years a large portion of the employees in hotels and restaurants in the eastern U.S. have been recent immigrants; in the last few years the majority have been from Puerto Rico and other Latin American countries. In New York City over 40 percent of the employees in the industry are Spanish-speaking.

Working with newly arrived or disadvantaged groups can be a challenge and a problem. It can also be an opportunity for many of these minorities to rise to supervisory and management positions.

It should be pointed out that academic achievement as such is not as important for many entry-level jobs as emotional stability, personal organization, energy, and tact.

Status

Ellsworth Statler, the famous hotelman, envisaged the hotelier ideally as owner manager and a pillar of the community. Many have achieved such status and recognition. More often, the status of managers varies widely, depending in part on the status of the establishment itself and their own position in the community.

Generally speaking, managers of large, luxurious hotels have the most status, whereas the small-restaurant operator, even with an income superior to the morning-coated hotel manager, has less status.

Restaurant operators improved their image as they grew in size and quality. Before the turn of the century, most of the restaurants in this country were relatively small and many were family enterprises. A few restaurant chains existed before then, but rapid chain growth took place only after World War II.

Club management as a "respectable" field of work is also of recent origin; until 1912 the Harvard Club contract called its manager a steward.

Range and Style

The range and style of operation within the hotel and restaurant arena are tremendous. It is not realistic to think that a "hotelier" or a "restaurateur" can step in and manage any hostelry or foodservice operation well. The skills and social poise needed to manage an elite club are also fairly rare. A highly successful person in such a club might not do well at all as the director of a college food service.

The manager of a large urban hotel must necessarily rely on department heads who are specialists in their own right. Such a manager is primarily an administrator and coordinator; he or she does not need to be particularly knowledgeable in all of the specialties found within the hotel. This same manager might not do well at all as a country innkeeper with no expert department heads to call on.

The manager of a small operation must have more "nuts and bolts" knowledge than the manager of a large one because he or she has fewer department heads on which to rely. The owner/operator of a highly successful restaurant, because of his or her knowledge of operations, may find it impossible to work within the confines of an organization of which he or she is not the boss.

Many restaurants are the reflection of the personalities of their owners, whereas the personalities of some chain enterprises are the result of the thinking of a number of specialists—site experts, food specialists, architects, decorators, financial planners, and so on.

In some cases, presidents of large and successful hotel operations have been failures when they struck out on their own as owners. Ralph Hitz, the well-known hotel operator of the 1930s, was able to make impressive profits when he operated for other owners. Yet, according to his son, Ralph Hitz, Jr., he was never able to make a profit in the hotels he owned himself. He seemed to cast aside caution when it came to investing his own money in a property or an idea.

Hotel managers normally are not owners. As might be expected, they place high value on maintaining friendships with the accounting firms and individuals who can help them into better positions. The owner/investor is keenly interested in improving his or her operation to increase profits; the professional manager may be less so.

Remuneration

Salaries for top hotel managers have always been high. The salaries in hotels of 250 or more rooms range from about $40,000 to $160,000 annually (plus a number of perquisites). Restaurant managers whose income includes bonuses make as much as $100,000 a year. Most, however, receive less than $40,000 annually. Department head salaries are much less.

The big incomes in the hospitality field go to developers, corporate executives, franchise owners, and owners of independent properties. Numerous restaurant franchisers have become millionaires.

College graduates will find salaries are average when compared to similar jobs in other industries, such as retailing. Salaries for middle and upper management are often quite good. Large organizations often pay more and offer more benefits than smaller organizations. Pay in affluent urban areas is generally better than in rural areas.

Skills Required

Hotel and restaurant management draws on several other disciplines, especially economics, nutrition, psychology, marketing, engineering, insurance, real estate, law, accounting, statistics, and data processing.

Closely related to general business, many of the skills useful in hotel and restaurant management are transferable to any area of management. Evidence of that transferability can be seen in the career of Edward Carlson. He grew up in the hotel business, became president of Western International Hotels, and then president of United Airlines, of which Western International (now called Westin) was a subsidiary. Carlson did an outstanding job of management in both positions.

To be successful in any business requires that a person have highly developed skills in time and money management, social management, and strategic planning. These are useful in any undertaking, not only in business. But hotel and restaurant management requires certain specific technical skills as well: professional background knowledge, such as some understanding of nutrition, food preparation and service, understanding of food and beverage cost controls, and knowledge of wines and spirits, along with specialized information about hotel, restaurant, travel, and property management. Knowledge of marketing principles and the ability to apply them to the field are also necessary.

RECENT DEVELOPMENTS

The travel and tourism business and its component, the hotel and restaurant business, are rap-idly becoming more international in character. Holiday Inns are owned by a British company, Motel 6 by a French firm, Westin hotels by a Japanese company. Eight major hotel chains originally American-owned are owned by non-American parent companies. Hotels may be owned by nationals of one country and managed by people from another, the employees may represent a dozen or more ethnic groups. The Best Western name appears on hotels in close to 1500 properties outside the U.S. Franchising has spread McDonald's, KFC, and other fast-food restaurants around the world.

In 1992, U.S. hotels were experiencing another of the overbuilt cycles that plagued the U.S. hotel business over time. A study by Smith Travel and the Arthur Anderson accounting firm showed that the U.S. hotel industry had 10 straight years of pretax losses on a per-room basis.[4]

Easy money made it possible for hotel developers to borrow vast sums for construction, and too many hotels and resorts were built. Many were overleveraged: too much debt for the earning capacity of the property. Leveraged buyouts made possible by the sale of junk bonds made fortunes for a few, but put unwary investors who were attracted by high yields on the bonds at risk. Many hotel companies had such large debts that, even with relatively high occupancies and good management, interest payments were difficult to meet. Small drops in occupancy were enough to place the properties in financial jeopardy.

A recession beginning in 1989 resulted in hotel occupancy rates—many below 50 percent—insufficient to meet operating costs and debt liabilities. Banks and other lending institutions would or could not make loans to distressed properties. Savings and loan institutions were forced to foreclose on hundreds of hotels, and it was estimated that half or more of U.S. hotels were financially stressed. By 1994 the U.S. economy was recovering and the hotel/motel business was reviving.

As for restaurants, their sales were experiencing little or no growth, and restaurant operators were using "value pricing" and discounting to

---

4. "Hotel Slump Is No Bar to Luxury Projects," *Wall Street Journal* (Dec. 12, 1991) p. 3.

keep sales from slipping. The basic conditions for hotel and restaurant growth had not changed much, and it was safe to predict that a return to growth in restaurant sales and hotel occupancy would take place.

UNIVERSITY EDUCATION FOR THE HOTEL AND RESTAURANT BUSINESS

Until the 1920s, education for the hotel manager was largely through experience. Most managers, like those of other enterprises at that time, did not have the advantage of a university education. The American Hotel and Motel Association (AHMA), then called the American Hotel Association, was responsible for initiating a program of instruction for hotel management at the college level.

Frank Dudley, president of the AMHA in 1917 when it became a truly national trade association, appointed Lucius Boomer, president of the Waldorf-Astoria, to chair an education committee to study the industry's needs.

Undergraduate Programs

One of the committee's recommendations was to establish a school of hotel management at Cornell University in Ithaca, New York. The financial support pledged by hotel operators did not materialize, however. Ellsworth Statler, the leading hotelier of his time, stepped in to underwrite $70,000 of the association's indebtedness if the other members would pay off the remaining $30,000.

Statler, who at that time did not favor college education for hotel managers, visited Cornell in 1925 as a personal favor to an old friend. At one of the classes on his first day, he was asked to say a few words and dropped this bomb: "Boys, you're wasting your time here. You don't have to learn this stuff to be a hotelman. When I have an engineering problem, I hire an engineer. I don't know a damn thing about the British thermal units, and there's no reason for you to, either. Go on home and get a job."[5]

By the end of his second day on the campus, however, Statler had changed his mind. At a banquet that marked the end of the two-day "Hotel Ezra Cornell" (an annual celebration at the school), he was asked to speak again. His second speech was as startling as the first: "I am converted. Meek [the school director] can have any damn thing he wants." Statler tried to make sure that would happen. In his will, he left 10,000 shares of Statler common stock (then worth $10 a share) to set up the Statler Foundation for the benefit of the school. By 1975 the Cornell hotel school had received more than $10 million, which it had used for the construction of teaching facilities, faculty salaries, research projects, and student scholarships. Additional millions have been given to the school by the foundation since then.

Under Howard B. Meek, Cornell became the best known of the hotel schools. It began offering master's and Ph.D. programs in 1927, open only to those who had completed the undergraduate program in hotel administration at Cornell. Its Statler Hall, completed in 1950, pointed the way for hotel training facilities elsewhere. With Statler Foundation sponsorship, several hotel research projects were begun in the early 1960s.

A number of other universities ventured into hotel management education after Cornell, with varying degrees of enthusiasm and persistence.

In 1928 Michigan State University started a hotel program under Bernard "Bunny" Proulx. In the late 1930s, the University of Massachusetts, Pennsylvania State University, the University of New Hampshire, and Washington State University began hotel curriculums. After World War II, Florida State and Denver universities introduced similar programs. A master of business administration (MBA) with a hotel and restaurant major was offered at Michigan State in 1962. By 1987 about 130 colleges and universities were offering 4-year degrees and 375 junior and community colleges had programs in hospitality management. A total of some 60,000 students were enrolled.

Do college grades predict career success in the hospitality business? Research conducted with hospitality students at Michigan State University showed a positive correlation. Performance in elective courses correlated higher than in

---

5. Floyd Miller, *Statler America's Extraordinary Hotelman* (Ithaca, N.Y.: The Statler Foundation), 1968.

required courses. On the other hand, there are examples of dropouts and poor students who went on to do exceptionally well. Some were so ambitious that long hours in outside jobs left little time for academic achievement. Yet, on the whole, grades seem to make a difference.

Most of the 4-year degree programs offered in American universities can be broken down into three parts: two years devoted to general education as required by the university, one year of business education, and one year of specialized hotel and restaurant courses.

The curricula usually include blocks of instruction in food preparation and service, accounting, hotel engineering, management, finance, marketing, and business law. These are in addition to the usual university-required blocks in the basic sciences, humanities, mathematics, and English. More recently, courses in computers have been added.

Graduate Programs

By 1992, 16 U.S. universities were offering graduate degree programs in hotel and restaurant education at the master's degree level, programs that in several instances were similar but at a higher level than those offered at the bachelor's level. A survey of 46 company recruiters, 15 representing the lodging industry and 31 the foodservice industry, found that a majority of the lodging recruiters believed that human resource management and higher management skills, such as decision making and delegation, were the most important subjects in a graduate program. Foodservice recruiters showed a preference for finance and accounting. The recruiters indicated that master's-level graduates should not expect higher starting salaries than the bachelor-level graduates. About two-thirds of the lodging recruiters said they expected master's-level graduates to have greater maturity and more practical experience than recent graduates with bachelor's degrees.[6]

Graduate-level work is almost a prerequisite for students who plan a career in teaching, and those who wish to teach in a university should consider a doctoral program. To advance within universities, research competency and the willingness to write are important.

Whether or not holders of a master's degree perform better than those with a bachelor's degree is not clear. Probably for corporate-level jobs involving research and analysis, graduate-level work is valuable. Master's-level work possibly gives the student greater competence and confidence in such skills as computer application, problem analysis in human resource management, and accounting and control.

Certification Programs

The Educational Foundation of the National Restaurant Association (NRA), offers undergraduate hospitality programs the option to adopt the Management Development Diploma Program— a complete foodservice management preparation program. Students who complete at least eight of the management development courses receive a management diploma from the National Restaurant Association.

Once students are actively working full-time in the hospitality field, certification programs are available from the AHMA and the NRA. These programs generally require a combination of work experience and courses, as well as an application and exam, to become certified. The AHMA offers the following certification programs for department-level managers and directors.

Certified Rooms Division Executive

Certified Human Resources Executive

Certified Food and Beverage Executive

Certified Engineering Operations Executive

Certified Hospitality Housekeeping Executive

The AMHA also offers a prestigious certification program for general managers, owner operators, and corporate executives—the CHA or Certified Hotel Administrator. The NRA offers the Foodservice Management Professional (FMP) Certification program to individuals who work in the foodservice field.

6. Hubert B. Van Hoof, "Entering the Job Market with a Master's Degree in Hospitality Management," *Hospitality & Tourism Educator*, Washington, D.C., Nov. 1991.

What Recruiters Look For

Criteria for hiring graduates vary with the recruiter and by industry segment. A study of management recruitment done at Florida International University and Purdue University found different selection emphases in food service, cafeterias, fast food, table service restaurants, and hotels.[7]

As might be expected, all recruiters ranked "articulateness, confidence, eye contact, and poise" at or near the top of their list of desirable traits. Recruiters for hotels and fast-food operations listed "articulateness" as the most important criterion. They also placed "eye contact" and "poise/confidence" near the top of the list. Contract food and cafeteria operators placed the applicant's "interest in the company" as the most important criterion. Fast-food recruiters ranked it second in importance.

"Work experience in industry" was number one in importance for table service restaurants. Age and athletic participation were ranked as unimportant by recruiters from all industry segments.

It might come as a disappointment to hospitality educators that "faculty recommendations," "program curriculum," and "quality of college attended" were of average to low importance.

Contrary to what is often reported—"ten jobs for every graduate"—this study showed that of 305 graduating students from the two universities involved, only 85 were hired by the recruiters, who represented 39 companies. The moral for the hospitality management graduate seems clear: Do not depend on being hired by the recruiters who appear on campus. Rather, build contacts and develop employer interest by any legitimate means: summer or part-time employment, help from friends and parents, and help from people in power positions.

The study bore out what hospitality faculty have observed for a long time: The hotel industry looks for management people who are highly presentable and personable, who speak well, are secure in interpersonal relations, and display a lot of self-confidence.

ROADS TO THE TOP

Which jobs are most likely to lead to a general managership in a hotel? An overview of hotel operations is best gained in the rooms department, starting as a desk clerk and moving through rooms manager and resident manager. Figure 1-2 shows the entry-level, mid-level, and upper-level jobs in a large property (job titles vary somewhat among hotels and hotel chains). Students should also acquire experience in the food and beverage department.

Anyone aspiring to restaurant management should work in not only the front of the house in service, but also the kitchen.

THE HOTEL/RESTAURANT FUTURE

Hotel and restaurant sales have a high correlation with discretionary time and money and with the amount of business travel. Pleasure travelers must have the time to travel as well as the disposable income to pay for that travel. Business travel reflects the economy: Travel increases when businesses prosper and declines during recessions. Foreign travel to a country also depends on currency exchange rates. A cheap currency tends to increase the number of foreign visitors. In 1992, 45.5 million visitors to the U.S. spent $71.2 billion. This enormous number of visitors to the U.S. was caused, in part, by the low value of the U.S. dollar compared to European and Japanese currencies and helped offset the reduced spending by Americans caused by a recession.

International conferences, meetings, and trade shows are particularly important for hotels and restaurants located in cities with convention centers and tourist attractions. Cities such as Orlando, Los Angeles, and Las Vegas attract millions of both domestic and foreign travelers. Hawaii is especially attractive to the Japanese and other East Asian nationals.

Convenience and cost of travel also correlate highly with the amount of travel. Airfares are comparatively cheap and flight schedules frequent, which stimulates travel. Most international travel in

---

7. Mary L. Tanke, "Recruitment Success: A Decision-Making Model for the Selection of Hospitality Management Graduates." *Conference Program and Proceedings, 1986 Annual Conference Council Hotel Restaurant Institutional Education (CHRIE),* Washington, D. C.

the early 1990s was occurring within and between North America and Western Europe. As Eastern Europe moves into a market economy and the economies of some third world countries rise, international travel to the U.S. and elsewhere will increase. East Asian travel is forecasted to grow at twice the rate of the rest of the world.[8]

International travel is a two-way street: Foreign visitors patronize U.S. hotels and restaurants and spend billions of dollars. Americans are also going to Mexico, Europe, the Caribbean, and nearly every other country for pleasure and business purposes, spending money and time that might have been otherwise spent in U.S. hotels and restaurants. In the past the U.S. has experienced a travel deficit—more money spent in travel outside the U.S. than received from foreign visitors. In 1990 tourism became the U.S.'s largest export and the travel deficit a surplus.[9] This was good news for hotels and restaurants, especially in the states of California, New York, Florida, and Hawaii that have huge numbers of foreign visitors.

No one can predict recessions with a high degree of accuracy, but history clearly shows a pattern of economic cycles, with periods of prosperity and inflation followed by recessions and reduced inflation or deflation. The hotel business is characteristically overbuilt in times of prosperity and then must wait for demand to

catch up to supply. The restaurant business has been said to be recession-proof because people "have to eat." Even in prosperous times, however, restaurants have a high failure rate. In times of recession, the failure rate increases.

Overall, the factors of demand, such as greater education, productivity, and consumer expectations, for travel and hotel and restaurant service are on the rise. Other factors, like facsimile services, teleconferencing, videophones, cost of travel, the decline of manufacturing in the U.S., and the need to service the huge national debt, are negatives for travel growth.

Although it is true that alternative leisure-time activities, such as cruising, spending time at second homes, parks, and time-share apartments, are all part of tourism, these alternatives mostly compete with hotels and restaurants.

Cruising is reported to be the fastest growing segment of travel, with some 5 million people selecting the closed, predictable, and safe environment of the ship as a way to vacation, and as of 1994 about 6 percent of the 70 million Americans who can afford to cruise have done so. Hotels do gain occupancy from before-and-after cruise stays, but the cruise itself competes directly with the resort hotel. Many Disney World and Disneyland customers split their vacation between a Disney visit and a cruise.

The time-share apartment is another direct competitor of the resort hotel, although here again hotels may benefit as the time-share owner travels to and from the time-share apartment.

8. Somerset R. Waters, *Travel Industry World Yearbook, The Big Picture—1991*, (New York: Childs & Waters, Inc.), 1991.
9. *Ibid.*

Questions

1. The hotel and restaurant business is fast becoming a science. What parts are likely to remain an art?

2. Name at least three personality requirements of a successful hotel or restaurant manager.

3. In what way does the large chain partially eliminate the need for "mein host?"

4. Owning and operating a hotel or restaurant calls for several skills not required of the nonowner/manager. Name three of them.

5. It is often said that the hotel and restaurant business gets "into your blood." Analyze the statement and name the factors that could make this true.

6. What are some of the temptations for a hotel or restaurant manager that can lead to failure?

7. What qualities would be necessary to manage an elite country club successfully that would not be necessary in a small hotel?

8. Who would need more detailed technical knowledge—the manager of a 150-room hotel or the manager of a 500-room hotel?

9. The qualities of affability and good taste would probably be more important in which of these operations: a private club, restaurant, or medium-sized hotel?

10. Tight cost controls are probably most important for which one of these: a hotel, restaurant, or club?

11. If you are seeking high status, you would probably which one of these: a large hotel, prestige restaurant, or country club?

12. Which one of these operations would probably demand the least personal energy: a country club, large hotel, or highly successful restaurant?

13. Which one of these would require the most personal time: a highly successful restaurant, hotel, or club?

14. Why has foreign travel to the U.S. increased so much in the last few years?

15. Graduate hotel and restaurant programs have increased in number. Would it be important for you to enroll in such a program?

Discussion Questions

1. In the future, what subjects will take on greater importance for success in the hospitality field?

2. How important is it for a student of hospitality management to have a basic course in chemistry? In physics? In psychology? In computer technology? In food preparation? In accounting? In travel and tourism? Substantiate your arguments with examples and reasons.

3. Some people say that the hotel and restaurant business promotes world peace and understanding. What is your opinion? Substantiate your opinion with reasons.

4. Given the several factors that affect hotel and restaurant sales, what is your sales forecast for hotels over the next few years?

Ellsworth Milton Statler

(1863–1928)*

Ellsworth Milton Statler is considered by many to be the premier hotelman of all time. He brought luxury, or at least a higher standard of comfort and convenience than ever before, to the middle-class traveler at an affordable price.

His life story is that of a man overcoming adversity. At age 15, with two years of experience as a bellboy at a leading hotel in Wheeling, West Virginia, Statler became head bellman. Noting the oversized profits gained from the hotel's billiard room and railroad ticket concession, he persuaded the owner to lease him these concessions. A studious promoter, he billed special billiard exhibition games and brought in the crowds.

Soon he had launched a bowling alley, then a restaurant—the Pie House. It was the best in town. Mother Statler's chicken sandwiches and pie were served on the finest china and with quadruple-plate silver. By 1894, at the age of only 31, Statler was making $10,000 a year and was ready for new fields to conquer.

Buffalo, New York, was the setting for his next venture, one that almost proved his undoing. Underwritten by a friend and the equipment supplier that had furnished his Pie House, Statler opened a restaurant in the basement of the Ellicott Square Building—a new office building billed as the "largest in the world." But there were no large restaurant crowds; Statler found that Buffalo was an eat-at-home town. Despite a brass band and an efficient operation, his creditors closed in.

Undaunted and with incredible imagination and energy, Statler then proceeded to change the eating habits of Buffalo's downtown business people. He advertised "All you can eat for twenty-five cents." Six meals were sold for the price of four, and prizes were given to lucky ticket holders. He tightened his operations, bought supplies on a day-to-day basis, fired his expensive chef, and when beans were cheaper than

peas on a certain day, beans appeared on the menu. Always efficiency-minded, he developed a service table for the dining room where waitresses could pick up napkins, glasses, butter chips, ice, silver, and linen without making a trip to the kitchen. The service table had ice water on tap—the first on record. To seat more people, he designed octagonal dining tables. In three short years the tide had turned. Statler was in the black and ready for bigger and better things.

He opened a 2100-room hotel, the Outside Inn, a temporary structure built to house visitors to the 1901 Pan American Exposition in Buffalo. The Exposition was a dismal failure, but fortunately Statler had learned from his restaurant venture to buy with cash so he was not in debt.

Three years later he plunged in again, this time at the World's Fair in St. Louis. The Inside Inn of 2257 rooms was described as the biggest exhibit at the World's Fair. At the end of the season, Statler found himself with $300,000 net profit and a yearning for a "big hotel."

In 1908 he opened a 300-room, 300-bathroom hotel in Buffalo. Statler's genius was seen in many details. Back-to-back rooms used common shafts for plumbing (later known as the "Statler plumbing shaft") and electrical conduits. He brought ice water on tap into every guest room. (According to Statler, "Ninety percent of the calls for a bellboy are to bring ice water. With ice water already in their room, we can cut down on the service staff. Also the guest avoids the annoyance of having to tip the bellboy.") A telephone in every room was another innovation. Also, every guest room included a full-sized closet with its own light. A towel

*Information adapted from Donald E. Lundberg, *Inside Innkeeping* (Dubuque, Iowa: William C. Brown, 1956), and Floyd Miller, *Statler, America's Extraordinary Hotelman* (Buffalo: the Statler Foundation, 1968.)

hook beside each bathroom mirror made it easy for the guest to hang up a used towel rather than to throw it on the floor, which resulted in savings in linen and laundry. Little wonder the place made $30,000 profit the first year of operation. From then on, the Statler story was one of successive successes.

Simplification and control were ever on his mind. He installed a food-cost control system in 1907, and in 1915 he hired C. B. Stoner, a professor of business administration at the Carnegie Institute of Technology, to sharpen standards and controls. Stoner found a lack of uniform auditing systems. The resultant cost-accounting methods became standard for the industry.

Anticipating the coming expansion of the convention business, Statler built the Cleveland Statler in 1912, a property that could handle large business groups. Here it was that the Statler policy of "a free newspaper every morning" began. That policy necessitated another one—cutting 1 inch off the bottom of each guest room door so that the newspaper could be shoved underneath it.

The kitchens at the Cleveland Statler were planned for unhindered traffic flow of food and personnel. The dining rooms were located around the kitchen instead of on a lower floor, the common practice of the day. One kitchen served the dining room, coffee shop, and a café, all of them operating off and around the kitchen. Guest rooms were decorated with variety but always with related colors so that draperies, bedspreads, and rugs could be interchanged from room to room throughout the hotel.

The Detroit Statler was built in 1915, followed by the St. Louis Statler in 1918, and the Pennsylvania Statler in 1922. Here, Statler introduced the Servidor, a bulging panel in the guest room door in which the guest could hang clothes that needing cleaning or pressing. A bellman could pick up and return the clothes without the guest being confronted by the need for a tip. The Pennsylvania Statler was also the first hotel to offer on-premise medical services.

Other Statler innovations included posted room rates, attached bed-headboard reading lamps, radios at no extra charge, and a liberal quantity of towels and writing supplies in all rooms.

As the premier hotelman of his day and with his interest in standards and controls, it was logical for Statler to chair the American Hotel Association's Proprietor's Committee that with an accountants committee put together the first edition of the *Uniform System of Accounts for Hotels* in 1926.

Statler is credited with being one of the first hotelmen to be concerned with employee relations and benefits. He offered group insurance on no other condition than a year's service and devised a profit-sharing plan that allowed many a maid and bellboy to eventually retire with dignity and security.

"EM," as Statler signed himself, was a dynamo of energy, and no detail of construction or operation was too small for his attention. He might be found lying down in a bathtub, fully clothed, gazing around the room to see what the guest would see in a similar position. If he spotted plaster smeared on the underside of the washbowl, he invited the manager of the hotel to assume a similar position; the smeared plaster was quickly removed. He could be seen on the top floor of a new hotel, stopwatch in hand, timing to the second how long it took the toilet to flush or a bath to fill.

Statler was continually preaching the theme of service to the public. "The Statler service code" was a formal company policy, each employee being required to memorize it and to carry a copy of it on his person during working hours.

The Statler Foundation today has assets of many millions. The School of Hotel Administration at Cornell has received millions for teaching facilities—Statler Hall and the Statler Inn—and for scholarships, faculty salaries, and research. San Francisco City College has a Statler Library. The Statler Foundation matches funds raised by regional hotel and restaurant educational foundations, funds that have also totaled many millions of dollars.

"Life is service. The one who progresses is the one who gives his fellow human being a little more, a little better service." Such a philosophy, public or private, fits the hotel business perfectly and Ellsworth Statler in particular. Statler service became world famous, and through the Statler Foundation, his contributions to U.S. hotel development will continue to be effective.

2

The Early Inn/Tavern

References to tavernkeeping have been found as early as 1800 BC; the Code of Hammurabi decreed death as the penalty for watering the beer.

Inns and taverns play an important role in history as one of society's safety valves. By supplying food, drink, and a place to sleep, they offer a respite from ceaseless competition, the pleasures of the table and the bed, a sanctuary for the weary, and titillation for the bored or frustrated.[1]

THE ANCIENT WORLD

The Ancient Greek tavernkeeper, like his modernday counterpart, offered food, drink, and sometimes a bed. The wine was both domestic and imported. The food served might have been goat's milk cheese, barley bread, cabbage, peas, broad beans, and lentils. Figs and olives were also available. Cheese cakes, honey buns, and sesame-seed cakes were favored. If there was meat, it was usually goat, pork, or lamb. A banquet might include thrushes, finches, and hares. Stuffed paunch of ass was considered a delicacy in Athens. Sausages and hog puddings might also have been offered. Fish and eel were common. Coriander was the most popular seasoning, but cumin, fennel, and mint were also used.

For a very practical reason, the early tavern might be located near a temple. After being sacrificed in a religious rite, animals were taken to the tavern and eaten (after the sacrifice, a feast; after the feast, drinking). Each guest lay on a couch with a cushion or bolster under the left arm.

Musicians, usually young girls, exercised their talents during the meal. Some of the taverns had a small stage for theatrical entertainment. When the meal was finished, it was the Athenean custom to pour three libations: one to the gods, one to the departed heroes, and one to Zeus. Garlands and, on occasion, perfumes were handed

1. Page, Edward B. and Kingsford, P.W. *The Master Chefs* (New York: St. Martins Press), 1971.

out. Then the drinking began. Some taverns had cubicles into which the worshipers of Aphrodite might retire.[2]

In Ancient Egypt, the poor ate mainly dried fish and whatever bread they could afford. For the rich, the menu was based on bread, birds, beef, fish, and fruit. Roast goose was a particular favorite. At banquets, the guests wore wigs; they might also wear a small cone of ointment placed on their heads, which melted and ran down over the wigs or hair. The serving girls and guests were provided collars of flowers.

Ancient predecessor to the stagecoach inn and, later, the motel was the caravansery, which served the caravans and other travelers as early as the fifth century BC. Each about a day's ride from the other, they were located throughout what today is Turkey, Iran, Afghanistan, and northern India. The typical caravansery consisted of an enclosed courtyard for animals and simple rooms for the traveler. From present-day Istanbul to the Moghul capital of Agra in north-central India (home of the Taj Mahal), the traveler had a place to rest and protect himself from bandits. In some cases, quarters could be rented for a fee.

The Seljuk Turks, who built many of the caravanseries, were social-minded. Every traveler of whatever nationality or religion was entitled to three days' lodging with food, medical care, and, for the poor, new shoes, all at the expense of the state. Over a hundred caravanseries are still intact in Turkey, but no longer used.

By the time Rome had conquered the then known world, inns and taverns were well established. A segment of a military road map of the Roman Empire in the time of Emperor Theodosius Magnus (AD 347–395) is a kind of guide to the accommodations of the time (Fig. 2-1). The symbols on the map indicate the type available at each place. An accurate picture of what they were like can be seen at Pompeii and Herculaneum, small Ancient Roman resort towns in southern Italy that had the misfortune to be located near Mt. Vesuvius. In AD 79 the mountain erupted as a volcano. Ashes, lava, and hot mud smothered these towns, killing all the inhabitants but preserving them and the towns for modern times.

Today's traveler can wander about Pompeii and see the hospiteum, caupona, popina, thermopolia, and tabernas. The caupona and hospiteums were inns or hotels providing lodging and, in some cases, a basic menu of wine, bread, and meat. They are much as they were, even the graffiti, "Serena hates Isadore," written on a town wall.[3]

The reputations of the operators, the caupones or innkeepers, were even worse than those of the tavernkeepers. All were often accused of fraudulent or immoral dealings, and the female caupones occasionally achieved a reputation for sorcery. Nearly every block of houses had its own bar, in much the same way that cafés are found in every downtown block of American cities. In Pompeii alone, a relatively small town in its day, 118 bars or restaurant bars are identifiable.

The thermopoliums, the snack bars of the day, sold wine from a "hot drink and food counter" that faced the street. Pottery jars were set into a marble counter and held snacks such as olives, dried vegetables, and probably pickled appetizers. Some of the counters were fitted with a small furnace that heated water for the caldum, a hot drink made of wine and boiling water. Thermopoliums had a room behind the counter that served as a dining area, which is how they differed from the popina, predecessor of our modern restaurant. The popina sold hot restaurant food, whereas the thermopoliums sold only snacks.

Tabernas, forerunners of the bar of modern times, might also sell food and offer such attractions as gambling and prostitution (not too different from some bars and B-girls of today). In Rome, taverns were identifiable by their pillars, "girt with chained flagons," and the red, thyme-flavored sausages hung around the walls. Floors were bright with mosaics and the walls were enlivened by paintings; the decor was similar to that found in the trattorias of modern Italy.

In the country were rustic pubs where the owner might grow his own grapes and make his own wine. Small dried cheeses that hung around the room in rush baskets were also available.

Hospitality terminology owes much to the Romans. The word *hospitality* is derived from the

2. William Younger, *Gods, Men, and Wine* (London, England: The Wine and Food Society), 1966.

3. Howard Luxton, *Pompeii and Herculaneum* (London, England: Spring Books), 1966.

Latin *hospitium.* Related words are "host," "hospice," "hostelry," and "hotel."

CHURCH HAVENS FOR TRAVELERS

With the fall of the Roman Empire in about AD 500, the inn went into decline for several hundred years. Trade was largely at a standstill and travel was infrequent. Since there were few travelers, there was little need for innkeeping.

The church came to play the dominant role in society and was the only authority recognized from one country to another. Monasteries and other religious houses took in travelers (and welcomed donations). Many monasteries made guests welcome, with the rich and noble sitting with the head prelate, while the poor were housed and fed in separate quarters. There were no room rates, although donations were ex-

pected. Often, the monastery porter, whose primary function was that of gatekeeper, also managed the guest house. It might be said that the church operated the first hotel chain.

The Crusades, beginning in 1095 and lasting over the next 200 years, encompassed a great social revolution. Among other things, they helped create the trade that led to the rise of a middle class. Indirectly, the crusades revived innkeeping, starting in Northern Italy. Innkeeping there became a solid business. Guilds of innkeepers (similar to mutual benefit societies) flourished, establishing rules and regulations for themselves and their guests.

In Florence, for example, the innkeepers guild in 1282 controlled business to the extent that city officials interviewed all strangers to the city at the gates and directed them to officers of the guild, who in turn assigned the travelers to designated inns.

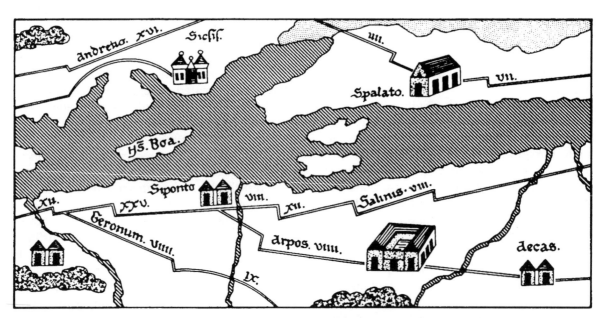

A segment of a military road map of the Roman Empire in the time of Emperor Theodosius Magnus (347–395 A.D.). The symbols on the map indicate types of accommodation:

 1. the simplest roadside accommodations suitable only for rest

 2. better accommodations than the places uninhabited

 3. better quarters for larger units but no service (no live-in slaves or local vassals)

 4. good shelter, a place for longer rest, recuperation, and refurbishing of supplies.

Figure 2-1   Artist's rendering of a military road map from the Roman Empire, AD 347–395.

Source: Map privately printed in Vienna in 1753. Used here courtesy of Chef Louis Szathmary, The Bakery, Chicago, Ill.

THE OLD ENGLISH INN

English common law declared the inn to be a public house and imposed on the innkeeper social responsibilities for the well-being of travelers. The innkeeper had not only the right to receive travelers, but the duty as well. He was required to receive all who presented themselves in reasonable condition and were willing to pay a reasonable price for accommodations.

The earliest English inn followed in the tradition of the ghildhus, or ale house, of Saxon England. An evergreen bush attached to a pole was understood by everyone to mean that ale could be had inside. A form of the custom is still observed in some Austrian villages. A green bough or twig signifies that apple wine is available for sale. Here people gathered to socialize and discuss problems of the day. Armies were recruited in drinking establishments; Chaucer's pilgrims quenched their thirst with beer on their way to and from Canterbury.

It was in an inn over a glass of ale, according to one commentator, that the rudiments of self-government evolved from the feudal system; there, also, much of what meager pleasures life had to offer were to be found. By the thirteenth century, the inn had special significance, or so it seems from one Walter de Map, who said, "Die I must, but let me die drinking in an inn."

Though each parish had its ale house, those that rented rooms were few. Inns existed in the larger towns and at crossroads and ferry crossings. The buildings were often little more than shelters with a minimum of furnishings; rushes thrown on an earthen or stone floor acted both as a carpet and a convenient surface on which to throw bones or other food remnants. Mattresses placed along the walls of a main room were the extent of the sleeping appointments. Meals were an individual matter, as most guests brought their own food.

By the fifteenth century, some of the inns had 20 or 30 rooms. The George Inn, one of the better known, had a wine cellar, a buttery or pantry, a kitchen, and rooms for the host and for the hostler, the caretaker of the horses. The guest rooms or chambers were named after well-known people, cities, or prominent offices; they included the Earl's chamber, Oxford chamber, the Squire's chamber, London chamber, and the Fitzwarren chamber.

The inns or taverns were identified by signs with simple symbols, not words. Most people could not read, but they could say, for example, "Meet me at the sign of the Bull." There were many Lions, Golden Fleeces, White Hares, Black Swans, Dolphins, and similar signs.

In the later 1700s, names began to include the word "arms," such as the King's Arms or Dorset Arms. Display of a lord's arms at an inn often meant that the inn was in the territory of a particular noble family and was under its protection. Some heraldic signs were related to the original ownership of the land on which the inn stood, or a servant-turned-innkeeper might use the arms (or badge) of his former master. Even today there are said to be 400 pubs with the name King's Head, 300 with the name Queen's Head, and more than a thousand with the word "Crown" in the name.

Some early inns had open galleries that were approached by outside staircases. With time, these galleries were enclosed against the weather. Boxes or stalls for the horses and rooms for harness and hostler were in the courtyard. A mounting block in one corner helped the more portly customer climb aboard his horse. At the larger inns, quarters for the postboys, who carried the mail, were above the stables.

During the Tudor period from 1485–1603 (Fig. 2-2), and for some time thereafter, traveling troupes of players performed in the courtyards of some of the inns. The audience sat in the surrounding galleries.

Many inns had a garden and bowling green. Some had brewhouses for making their own beer. A long room, or assembly room, with a large fireplace at one end was the function room for banquets and dances.

From 1400 to 1800 the dietary regimen of the common people hinged on the word "monotony." The average person in Europe and England ate the same meal day after day, say the historians: "bread, more bread, and gruel." Adult males consumed two and three pounds of bread a day. Alcohol was used excessively; men and women often drank themselves into insensibility.[4]

Menus in the early English inn relied heavily on meat and ale; vegetables were relatively few.

---

4. Fernand Braudel, *The Structures of Everyday Life*, Vol. 1, 15–18th century (New York: Harper and Row), 1982.

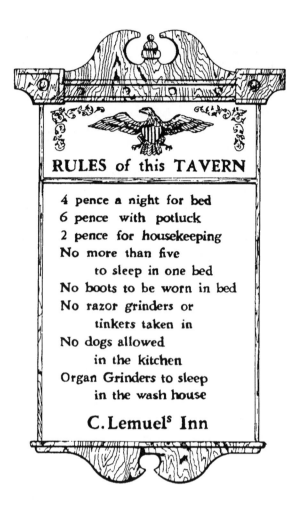

Figure 2-2 Sign for a local tavern of the Tudor period 1485–1603.

The vegetables familiar today were not available until the sixteenth century. The New World introduced such foods as tomatoes, sweet and white potatoes, pumpkin and squash, string beans, kidney beans, lima beans, peppers, cocoa, tapioca, corn, cranberries, blueberries, and strawberries.

Growth of Early Inns

Without intending to do so, Henry VIII fostered the growth of innkeeping when he suppressed the monasteries in 1539. These had played a major role in travel by maintaining the principal roads taken by pilgrims to the larger cathedrals. Pilgrims could stay for two days at the hostels built adjacent to an abbey or monastery, where they were accommodated and fed according to their rank. When Henry VIII decreed that church

lands had to be given away or sold, the church's function as host to the traveler disappeared. As a result, innkeeping flourished. A partial census of 1577 found 14,202 alehouses, 1631 inns, and 329 taverns in England and Wales.[5]

Long before a national postal system was established, selected inns and innkeepers were forced to retain stables and horses for the exclusive use of the Royal Post. This function also favored the development of inns.

In the middle 1600s some inns issued unofficial coinlike tokens that the innkeepers, men of repute, guaranteed to redeem in coin of the realm. Permission to issue such trader's tokens meant that the inn and innkeeper were of considerable importance at the time.

The early stagecoaches in England, first mentioned in 1635, were huge, lumbering vehicles. They were joyless affairs for the riders, especially since travel began early in the morning, usually before sunrise, and lasted until late at night. Later stagecoaches had such improvements as springs, seats for four inside, and seats for eight or ten on top. Outside passengers were treated as a superior race of Spartans, says one historian, the interior seats were left for whereas "anaemic spinsters and querulous invalids."

The English inn was headquarters for a variety of sports, both indoors and outdoors. A variety of dart and dice games, dominoes (called by such names as hazard, strutt, and shove groat), billiards, and bagatelle (a game like billiards) were played; cockfighting was also common, both indoors and out. The bloodthirsty could also enjoy bull and bear baiting—putting dogs on the animals—and throwing rocks at cocks. Those who liked active sports used the inns as headquarters for fishing, shooting, coursing (hunting with dogs trained to chase game by sight), hunting, and falconry. Dogfights and prizefights on rough ground were popular. Of course, the main pastime was drinking beer, ale, wine, and, later, gin.

The word "hotel" was used by the French to refer to a mansion or public building; large houses in which apartments were let by the day, week, or month were called *hotel garni*. In England, the word was borrowed by the Fifth Duke

5. Michael Brander, *The Life and Sport of the Inn* (New York: St. Martin's Press), 1973.

of Devonshire in about 1760 and applied to a crescent-shaped building in London. It housed three "hotels": the Grand, the Centre, and St. Anne's.

The Coaching Inns

The likely image of the old English inn is the coaching inn, which flourished during the eighteenth and early nineteenth centuries. The coaching era in Great Britain began in earnest in 1784, when Parliament commissioned government mail delivery by coach. Until then, mail had been carried by postboys riding horseback over the poor roads of the time. A nationwide posting system was established, with many inns used exclusively as posting inns.

Mail coaches soon made their appearance. They were easily identified by their scarlet wheels and underbody and black upper body. At one time, there were 59 large mail coaches in England and Wales, each pulled by four horses. Scotland had 16 and Ireland 29. More than 30,000 men and 150,000 horses were employed primarily in moving the mail.

At the height of the coaching era, 17 mail coaches assembled each evening at the General Post Office in London. Nine others left inns in Piccadilly and the West End of London each day of the week.

In the eighteenth century the mail coaches carried a maximum of seven passengers: four inside and three up in front with the coachman; the guard rode in the rear. Because of its security

Figure 2-3 The Swan, Lavenham, England. This half-timbered inn grew from three separate houses built in 1425. In its early days, it could stable 50 horses. Traveling apothecaries invited sufferers of diverse diseases to come to the inn to be cured. In 1607 John Girling, the innkeeper, issued a trader's token—a sure sign of a good reputation.

Source: Courtesy of Trusthouse Forte Hotels.

and small number of passengers, the traveler paid a little extra for riding in the mail coach. Private companies had their own stagecoaches and took as many passengers as could be squeezed in and on top of the vehicle. Sometimes, as many as 13 people rode: four inside, four up front, and five in back, with luggage piled on the roof.

A traveler with the money and desire for prestige and privacy could ride a post chaise, a private conveyance. This was drawn by two horses, one of which was ridden by a young post-boy. Although costs for such elegant travel were twice as much as the usual, many people used the post chaises.

Speed was the challenge; the coach company that could cut travel time got the business. Mail coaches originally averaged about 10 miles per hour. In 1830 the Birmingham Independent Tallyho raised that to 14.5 miles per hour on the trip from London to Birmingham. Competition was fierce. The time required to change horses was finally reduced to 45 seconds.

Coachmen were the athletic heroes of the day, many of them driving four horses and averaging 60 miles a day, three stages out and three stages back. Young gentlemen often bribed the coachmen to let them take the reins. A few noblemen went so far as to set up their own stagecoach companies to insure their participation in the sport of driving.

The country inns were largely dependent on the travel habits of their customers, and a large part of their business came from providing horses for the coaches. Several inns maintained as many as 50 horses; the Bow and Mouth in London kept 400. However, travel was slow. It took something like 34 stages and 42 hours to cover 400 miles.

When the English railroad began operation in 1825, most people were not aware of its implications for innkeeping; the innkeepers themselves were no exception. Travel time from London to Bath, a distance of 110 miles, took 11 hours by coach; by steam locomotive it took only 2.5 hours. The choice of travel was obvious.

When Parliament permitted the carrying of mail by railroad in 1838, the coaching era was over. It was not until the 1900s, when the country inns were rediscovered by cyclists and then later by motorists, that the beautiful inns of the countryside of England, Wales, and Scotland re-

turned to their former position of importance to the traveler.

Old English Inns Still in Operation

Approximately 200 of the old coaching and posting inns, together with some hotels, were operated in England and Wales as part of Trust Houses Ltd., which was organized in 1903 to prevent the old inns from becoming merely local taverns and to establish and maintain certain standards. Today, the level of cleanliness and the quality of food and service are excellent. The majority of these old inns are now managed by husband and wife teams, much as they were originally.

Today in Britain, some pubs claim to date back nearly a thousand years to earlier taverns on the same site. Others have been in the same building for centuries and are protected as national landmarks.

THE EARLY AMERICAN TAVERN

"With a heart full of love and gratitude, I now take leave of you. I most devoutly wish that your later days may be as prosperous and happy as your former ones have been glorious and honorable." This was General George Washington saying farewell to his top-ranking officers on December 4, 1783.

Washington spoke emotionally. "I cannot—I cannot come to each of you but shall feel obliged if each of you will come and take me by the hands."[6] The place was the old DeLancey mansion, the Fraunces Tavern at the corner of Pearl and Broad streets in New York City. The proprietor was a black man named Samuel Fraunces, known as Black Sam.

The Fraunces Tavern was an appropriate place for Washington to say farewell to his officers since it had been a meeting place for the Sons of the Revolution. Samuel Fraunces, a former West Indian, was later to be voted cash grants by the government for his services to American prisoners of war and for "other acts." He was one of America's first intelligence agents; when British officers frequented the tavern during the English

---

6. *American Heritage Book of the Revolution* (New York: Simon & Schuster), 1958.

occupation of New York, they apparently were unaware that Fraunces' sympathies remained unchanged. He later became the first chief steward of the Executive Mansion, again serving Washington, this time when he was president.

Early New England Inns

The first tavern in Boston, and probably the first in the colonies, was opened by one Samuel Coles in 1634. Called the Coles Ordinary, it later became known as the Ship Tavern. Coles eventually became one of Boston's first citizens, a deacon of the First Church, steward of Harvard University, and leading businessman.

The term "ordinary" comes from England. It was customary for eating places to offer a daily midday meal, which was called the ordinary. It was served to all guests at a common table at a fixed time and often consisted of a dish that was a

Figure 2-4 The Black Swan Hotel, Helmsley, North of York, England. This inn has been added to and renovated many times in 400 years. The rough stone walls are more than two feet thick. For many years, the Earl of Feversham held his annual Rent Dinner here, entertaining over 70 tenants. Venison from the Earl's deed park was served at least once a week in season.

Source: Courtesy of Trusthouse Forte Hotels.

Figure 2-5 Period table setting at an early American tavern (Ordinary at the Hall Tavern, Charlemont, Mass., 1700). Note the use of the wooden servingware and horn drinking cups. Dinner was served family style. In some taverns along the Eastern seaboard, the menu was fairly long. At the more primitive inland taverns, the menu might include corn in some form, bread, bacon, and whiskey.

Source: Courtesy of the Heritage Foundation. Photograph by Samuel Chamberlain.

specialty of the host. The tradition traveled to this country.

The meal was served at two in the afternoon. Guests were called together by a bell rung outside in the street. Customary fare was salmon in season, veal, beef, mutton, fowl, ham, vegetables, and pudding. Each guest had a pint of madeira at his or her place. The carving was done at the table, the guests helping themselves to what each liked best.

The ordinaries in the colony closely followed the establishment of churches. The courts at first recommended, and later required, that some kind of public house be set up in each community. Sometimes, land was granted and tax exemptions or other inducements were offered to encourage the establishment and upkeep of an ordinary.

The early New England taverns were under the strict guardianship of the Puritans. If a man was clocked drinking beer for more than a half hour on a weekday (when he was supposed to be at work), he was guilty of idleness and could be fined. In 1634 a Robert Coles (no relation to Samuel) of Boston was fined 10 shillings and enjoined to stand with a white sheet of paper pinned to his back that read "Drunkard." Prices were firmly regulated as well. In 1634, when the first taverns were built, they could legally charge no more than sixpence for a meal and a penny for a quart of ale or beer.

Luckily for us today, the Puritans were followed by the French Huguenots in 1685. They were everything that the Puritans were not—

merry, buoyant, cheerful, and music-loving. They loved dancing, theatricals, and entertainment. They also loved good food. Although French cuisine then and now has never been widely popular, it has strongly influenced our hotel and restaurant menus.

During the colonial period, a well-known hostelry was the City Tavern in New York City. Built on the docks in 1642 by the West India Company, it was meant primarily for the English traveling from New England to Virginia. The Blue Anchor, on the Delaware River in what is now Philadelphia, was where William Penn first stopped on his arrival in the New World.

In colonial Williamsburg, Virginia, some 30 inns, taverns, and ordinaries welcomed guests. The King's Arms offered a meal of some 15 courses. Four well-known taverns of the period have been reconstructed on their original foundations and reopened as distinctive colonial eating places: Christina Campbell's Tavern, the King's Arms Tavern, Chownings, and the Raleigh Tavern. They have been modernized to some extent and the menus are not completely authentic, but the overall pre-Revolutionary feeling is there.

It was in The Raleigh Tavern that Phi Beta Kappa, the collegiate honor society, was founded. The tavern's motto, *Hilaritas, Sapientiae et Bonae Vitae Proles* (Jollity, the offspring of wisdom and good living), is appropriate to any good hostelry, then or now.

Patrick Henry called taverns "the cradle of liberty." In Boston, the Green Dragon and the Bunch of Grapes had been the meeting places of the Sons of Liberty during the Revolution. The Boston Tea Party was planned in The Green Dragon.

Buckman Tavern had been the rallying point for the Lexington militiamen. Catamount Tavern was where Ethan Allen and the Green Mountain Boys met to plot their strategy against the New York Staters and against Gentleman Johnny Burgoyne. Generals Israel Putnam, Jethro Sumner, and George Weeden were former tavernkeepers. John Adams, our second president, owned and managed his own tavern between 1783 and 1789.

A Bill of Fare

Meals in a colonial tavern were simple but plentiful. Here is a bill of fare from an early Plymouth, Massachusetts, tavern:

Large baked Indian whortleberry pudding

Dish of saughetach (corn and peas)

Dish of clams

Dish of oysters

Dish of codfish

Haunch of venison

Dish of sea fowl

Dish of frostfish and eels

Apple pie

Course of cranberry tarts

Beverages flowed freely. At first, the only choice was between poor beer and rum. Later, beer and rum were combined with other ingredients to make the most popular drink in the Colonies, flip, which consists of rum, beer, cream, beaten eggs, and spices heated by plunging a hot loggerhead into the mixture. It was said to be both food and drink; if a guest drank enough, it was also lodging for the night. There were many drinks—bounce and sling, punch and shrub, eggnog, Tom and Jerry—some hot, some cold, but all basically rum.

Travel was on the rugged side. Travelers were wakened at 3:00 AM and rode until 10:00 PM. One pair of horses usually carried the stagecoach 12 to 18 miles (i.e., the stagecoach traveled by stages, horses being changed at the end of each stage). The first regular stagecoach route was established in 1760 between New York City and Philadelphia and later between Boston and Providence. As many as 40 coaches were on the road at one time.

The word "turnpike" came from the practice of placing a pike or staff across a toll road. The side facing the traveler was embedded with spikes; when the toll was paid, the pike was turned spikes down so the traveler could pass. The first turnpike was built between Philadelphia and Lancaster in 1792. By 1838 Pennsylvania had 2500 miles of turnpike.

In populous sections like Pennsylvania, where the 66-mile Lancaster Turnpike was located, there were 60 taverns of varying levels of acceptability. Wagon drivers slept on bags of hay and oats on the taproom floor. Cattle drovers stopped at drover stands, taverns that had lots into which the livestock could be turned and fed.

The 60 taverns were known by their signboards, such as "The Jolly Tar."

Accommodations follow travel. In the late 1820s, Pennsylvania began the development of what eventually became 1200 miles of canals. Canal taverns sprang up every 10 or 12 miles. New York State also developed a fairly extensive canal system; taverns and, later, hotels edged the canals.

Taverns as Homes

Many New England villages and towns today contain a home that was previously a tavern, thereby returning it to its original function. Most of the old taverns were originally constructed as large homes and so used by the tavernkeeper and his family. The early furnishings and equipment of these old taverns are preserved and still in use at a few of them. In Old Deerfield, Massachusetts, one can tour the Hall Tavern and see the long table set for guests with "treen," the name for wooden dishes, horn spoons, and cups. Pewter plates replaced wooden ones in later Colonial America. The barroom stands ready to serve the traveler. One can almost hear the tavernkeeper calling out, "Mind your p's and q's [pints and quarts]!" to permit another round of drinks before closing time.

The family of the tavernkeeper was kept busy making souse sausage (boiled pig's feet, ears, and skins pickled in vinegar); filling pork and corned beef barrels; preparing lard and tallow for candles; and making mince, apple, and cranberry pies. If this was not enough to keep the wife busy, she could make clothes for her family. In the cellar were barrels of cider, vegetables in bins, seed, and the apples of the time—golden pippins, greenings, russets, seek-no-furthers, and pumpkin sweets.

FACTORS IN THE GROWTH OF THE HOTEL AND RESTAURANT BUSINESS

Innkeeping and, later, the hotel and restaurant business has paralleled the growth of trade, travel, and industry. In modern times the growth correlates highly with the level of disposable income and the cost and convenience of travel.

During the approximate period 1775–1875, Northwestern Europe and North America became industrialized continents. Beginning about 1850, rapid economic and population growth in the world's industrial societies created enough disposable income for their population so that the masses could travel and stop at hotels and restaurants.

Modes of travel have also helped determine the growth of the hotel and restaurant business. As each new form of transportation brought down the cost of travel and increased its convenience—the steamship, the railroad, and then the automobile—travel became possible for more than the elite. The commercial jet ushered in the era of international travel in 1959.

Table 2-1 shows the growth and development of the hotel and restaurant in modern times.

TABLE 2-1   Chronology of Hotel and Restaurant Business to 1900.

ANCIENT PERIOD, 500 BC TO AD 500

Greek symposiums; Spartan and Roman military mess the forerunner of the private club.

Greek inns close to temples—"after the sacrifice, a feast…after the feast, drinking."

In the Middle East travelers stop at caravanseries and kahns, primitive inns.

Roman inns, caupona, and hospiteum provide rooms and sometimes a restaurant. Limited menu—by necessity, not choice—of bread, meat, wine, perhaps figs and honey. Popinas sell wine and restaurant food, thermopoliums wine and snacks; tabernas, essentially bars, serve drinks.

Nearly every block of houses has its own bar.

MIDDLE AGES, AD 500 TO 1300

Monasteries and other religious houses take in travelers; donations welcome.

Inns were primitive. In England, beer was the beverage and could be had at the sign of the bush, green bough, or bunch of leaves. (In Austrian villages today, a green bough over a wine cellar means apple wine is available.)

(continues)

TABLE 2-1 *(continued)*

First Crusades begin in 1095, stimulating trade and travel.

In approximately 1183 public cookhouses on London's river bank offer "dishes of roast, fried and boiled fish, great and small, venison and byrds."

RENAISSANCE, FOURTEENTH AND FIFTEENTH CENTURIES (ITALY); FIFTEENTH AND SIXTEENTH CENTURIES (NORTHERN ENGLAND)

Food sold at London's Westminster Gate in 1400 London includes "bread, ale, wyne, ribs of beefe, hot peascod, hot sheppes feet, macherel and oysters."

Trade revives; inns appear in northern Italy.

Selected innkeepers are forced to retain stables by Royal Act in Tudor England (1485–1603).

Some innkeepers act as unofficial postmasters and keep stables for the Royal Post.

Catherine de Medici in Italy marries the future Henry II of France in 1533 and brings brigade of chefs with her; is credited with initiating a concern with things gastronomic.

Henry VIII of England suppresses the monasteries in 1536, forcing the growth of inns. They serve meat, poultry, ale, bread. New World foods (turkey, cranberries, tomatoes, corn, potatoes, cocoa, coffee, and so on) not yet available. Mermaid Tavern, the first English Club, is founded by Sir Walter Raleigh; frequented by Shakespeare.

Catering established in France. Few inns, but private homes can be rented for special occasions.

Henry III of France (reigned 1574–1589) makes the fork fashionable.

EARLY MODERN, SEVENTEENTH AND EIGHTEENTH CENTURIES (EUROPE)

Louis de Bèchamel, Marshal Mirepoix, and Cardinal Richelieu, food-minded men of importance, have sauces and other culinary items named for them or create them.

1645.	First coffeehouse in Venice.
1650.	First coffeehouse established in England, at Oxford. Coffeehouses become greatly popular in late seventeenth and early eighteenth centuries. More than 200 in London by 1700.
1653–1658.	Oliver Cromwell in power, suppresses culinary and other pleasures in England.
1658.	Stagecoaches are introduced in England; travel gives taverns further prominence. Louis XIV of France (reigned 1643–1715) hated water (did not bathe) but loved food. A glutton with a tapeworm, made dining a state occasion and focused attention on food.
1669.	Coffee introduced to Paris by Turkish ambassador; served by beautiful slave girls.
	Louis XV of France (reigned 1715–1774) has great interest in love and food, in that order. *Hotelsgarni*—large houses from which apartments can be rented by the day, week, or month make their appearance in France.
1760.	Word "hotel" introduced in London about 1760 when Fifth Duke of Devonshire constructs a crescent-shaped building housing the Grand, the Centre, and St. Anne's hotels.
1765.	The first restaurant, as distinct from an inn, tavern, or food-specialty house, opened by Boulanger in Paris.
1784.	Coaching era begins in England with first government mail routes.
About 1790.	Count Rumford, born Benjamin Thompson in Woburn, Massachusetts, invents the drip coffeemaker, the kitchen range, and applies his knowledge of heat transfer to cooking. Invents portable steamers to cook food for armies on the move; creates cheap nutritious soups—boiled combinations of peas, barley, and potatoes—for the poor; adds croutons; helps make the New World potato popular in Europe.
1792.	Louis XVI, after being condemned to death, sups on six veal cutlets, a chicken, eggs, and three glasses of wine.
	After the Revolution in France, hotels, once residences of the rich and the nobility, become available as public houses because their owners, some of whom lost their heads, were absent.
	In England, posting and other inns become plentiful, usually built around a central courtyard (unlike American taverns). Many of these English inns are still operating today.

(continues)

TABLE 2-1 *(continued)*

MODERN, NINETEENTH AND TWENTIETH CENTURIES (EUROPE)

1800–1833.	Carème fashioned *La Grande Cuisine.*
1825.	*La Physiologie Du Gout*, by the world's best-known gourmet, Brillat-Savarin, appears.
1825–1858.	Alexis Soyer gains culinary eminence. He writes *Gastronomic Regeneration* and introduces steam cooking at the Reform Club, London, in 1840s; only chef to be mentioned in Britain's *Dictionary of National Biography.*
1841.	In England Thomas Cook begins the travel agency business.
1880–1900.	César Ritz entices the elite from their homes to hotels for entertaining; manages the Claridge, the Carlton, and the Savoy.
1907.	Ritz Development Company franchises the Ritz name to the Ritz-Carlton Hotel, New York City. Later the franchise is extended to Montreal, Boston, Lisbon, Barcelona, Madrid.
1880–1935.	Auguste Escoffier, known as "chef to kings and king of chefs," works with Ritz and writes *Le Guide Culinaire* in 1907, which is considered by many to be the bible of cookery.

INNKEEPING IN THE U.S.(FROM TAVERN TO MOTEL)

1634.	Ships Tavern, Boston, is opened by Samuel Cole.
1642.	City Tavern, New York City, is built by West India Company.
1670.	First coffeehouse in Boston; serves coffee and chocolate.
	American plan in use, although not called by that name. Similar to the French *table d'hôte*, in which the guests sit together at one table, with the host at the head. The meal was called the ordinary; some of the taverns were called ordinaries.
	Menu favorites: journey cake (johnny cake) dunked in cider, suppawn (cornmeal in milk or butter—the cornmeal sometimes boiled in molasses), and tipsy cake (cake with wine or liquor added).
	Beverages were rum and beer and variations of the two, such as flip—strong beer and rum sweetened with dried pumpkin; cherry bounce—rum and cherries sealed in a keg for at least a year; and other whimseys such as whistle belly vengeance—sour beer and molasses.
1775.	The Green Dragon in Boston becomes the meeting place of American revolutionaries. Patrick Henry calls the taverns of colonial America the "cradles of liberty."
	Most taverns are named for their proprietors, but there are also many with names such as "Red Lion," "Golden Bowl," *"White Horse," and "Black Horse." After the Revolution, a number quickly came to be called "George Washington," Washington's visage being painted over that of the British monarch, George III.
1785.	Jefferson named American minister to France, which began his interest in French cookery and wines; served French wines and crêpes while President.
1790s.	First use of "hotel" in the United States. 1790: Carre's Hotel, 24 Broadway, New York City.
1794.	The City Hotel (first known as the Burns Coffee House), 115 Broadway, New York City.
	The first canal opens, a modest affair; circumnavigates the falls of the Connecticut River at South Hadley, Massachusetts.
	French refugee opens a *restorator* in Boston; serves truffles, cheese fondue, and soups.
1801.	Francis Union Hotel, Philadelphia, in the former presidential mansion; later becomes an inn.
1801–1820.	Taverns rechristened "hotels" following a surge of popularity for all things French. The tavern then becomes a place with emphasis on drinking.
	A typical tavern of the early 1800s is a large, home-style building painted white, with green blinds and trim. It contains about 25 rooms and a combination dining room and bar.
1806.	The Exchange Coffee House in Boston, seven stories tall, contains 200 apartments; largest building in America.

(continues)

TABLE 2-1 *(continued)*

1817.	Forerunner of the Somerset Club forms in Boston.
1824.	The Mountain House, first of the large resort hotels in the Catskills; eventually has 300 rooms and accommodates 500 persons; American neoclassical architecture.
1825.	First recorded mention of gas stove.
	Erie Canal opens; links New York Harbor via the Hudson and Mohawk rivers with the Great Lakes; hotels built fronting the canal.
1826.	City Hotel of Baltimore (Barnum's) becomes the first "first-class" hotel; 200 apartments.
1827.	Concord Coach in use; travel becomes more bearable than before.
1829.	America's first restaurant opened, Delmonicos in New York City, with first female cashier; serves lunch. First of more than a dozen eating establishments that brings the name of Delmonico's to preeminence in the service of fine food.
	The Tremont House in Boston appears; designed from cellar to eaves to be a hotel; three stories, 170 rooms. (1) first bellboys (rotunda men); (2) first inside water closets; (3) first hotel clerk, complete with standard smile; (4) French cuisine on Yankee menu; (5) first menu card in this country; (6) annunciators in guest rooms; and (7) room keys given to the guests.
1830.	American Plan establishes itself when "Americans were churning around the West;" resembles the French *table d'hôte*.
	Tipping, originally considered undignified by the help, becomes part of the business as immigrants used to the custom are hired.
1834.	Boston and Worcester railroad opens.
	Hotel managers trained in New England are in demand in the nation.
	The Astor House, New York City, first palatial hotel; rooms furnished in black walnut and Brussels carpeting.
1836.	First private membership club with rooms of its own in New York City established in the City Hotel.
1846.	First centrally heated hotel, the Eastern Exchange Hotel in Boston.
1848.	Safety deposit boxes provided for guests by New England Hotel, Boston.
1855.	Original Parker House of Boston opens; offers the European Plan.
1856.	Baking powder is sold commercially for the first time.
1859.	First passenger elevator ("vertical railway") in a hotel; upper rooms sometimes more expensive than those on the lower floors.
1868.	Commercial yeast available.
1870s.	Sporting country and city clubs form in United States.
1875.	The Palace Hotel, San Francisco, "World's largest hotel;" floor clerks installed.
	The Hotel World, trade magazine, started; *The Hotel Red Book* first published.
1876.	Fred Harvey founds the company that by the 1880s establishes Harvey Houses every hundred miles along the Santa Fe Railway.
1881.	Louis Sherry opens his first restaurant in New York City; develops the art of catering.
1882.	Electric lights dazzle guests for the first time, in New York City's Hotel Everett.
1880–1890s.	Resort boom in Florida, New England, Virginia, Pennsylvania, and Atlantic City; Fred Harvey and John R. Thompson develop first large restaurant chains.
1884.	First co-op apartment in New York City (now Chelsea Hotel); forerunner of condominiums in this country.
1887.	*Stewards Handbook and Dictionary*, by Jessup Whitehead, appears.
	Ponce de Leon Hotel, St. Augustine, built; first luxury hotel in Florida.
1888.	Del Coronado Hotel built; first luxury resort in California.
1890s.	The John R. Thompson Company in Chicago operates first extensive commissary system.
1894.	*The Epicurean*, cookbook by Charles Ranhofer, chef at Delmonico's, "[gives] away Delmonico's secrets."

Questions

1. Tavernkeeping is an old business that goes back as far as __ BC.

2. The Ancient Greek tavern was often located near a temple for a very practical reason. What was it?

3. Fast-food services were seen in what ancient culture?

4. In Ancient Rome taverns were identifiable on the outside because their pillars were hung with what?

5. In what way was a monastery hospice similar to a hotel of today?

6. How would a passerby of an early English tavern know that ale was served inside?

7. The early inns and taverns of England had signs using symbols, such as a white hare or black swan, for a very good reason. What was it?

8. Besides being a place that offered food and lodging, the early English inn had other functions. Can you name two or three of them?

9. Why were stagecoaches called by that name?

10. Henry VIII had an influence on the development of the early English inn. In what way?

11. In 1825 something happened in England that drastically changed the hospitality business. What was it?

12. In what way did the Huguenots leave an imprint on the hospitality business of this country?

13. The Crusades had what impact on the development of the hospitality business?

14. Military roads were used both by the military and what other group of people during the Roman Empire?

Discussion Questions

1. Henry Ford at one point in his life said, "History is bunk." Do you agree or disagree? Why?

2. As a professional hotel or restaurant person, do you feel that knowing what innkeeping was like in the Middle Ages has any value or relevance? Defend your opinion.

3. What relevance, if any, do the innovations of César Ritz and Auguste Escoffier have to modern-day innkeeping?

César Ritz

(1850–1918)*

César Ritz's beginnings were anything but ritzy. When he was 15, he was apprenticed to a hotelkeeper in the town of Brig, Switzerland. He later headed for Paris, hub of the hotel universe at the time, and worked as a handyman in a small, undistinguished hotel. At the age of 19, he became a restaurant manager, no small accomplishment in the Paris of the 1860s.

The Voisin Restaurant was the most famous restaurant of the era, and it was to the Voisin that César went, starting over again as an assistant waiter so that he could learn the best methods and have the opportunity to serve the famous and the wealthy. He learned to deal with people so well and was so responsive to their wishes that before long customers were insisting on being served by him. It was the beginning of his rise to fame and influence. Serving the elite and the powerful, he learned their likes and dislikes, their habits, their vanities, and eventually, how to influence them. To cultivate fashionable society and make an impression on its leaders was for Ritz purely a career decision.

To be near the top of the social pyramid, Ritz traveled to Vienna to work in a restaurant near the Imperial Pavillion. Emperor Franz Josef entertained there on a grand scale; the waiters he used came from the restaurant where Ritz worked.

It was here that Ritz secured himself a most important and lifelong patron, the Prince of Wales, a frequent guest. Ritz studied the Prince and learned his tastes. The Prince told Ritz at one time, "You know better than I do what I like; arrange a dinner to my taste."

At the age of 27, Ritz was offered the managership of the largest and most luxurious hotel in Switzerland, the Grand National at Lucerne. Even though it was the most luxurious hotel in the world when it opened in 1870, it was losing money. Ritz sent out a large number of personal letters to former patrons and the social elite of Italy to whom the name of the owner,

Colonel Pfyffer, meant something. Ritz's diligence and imagination paid off. Before long, dukes, duchesses, Morgans, and Vanderbilts came to the Grand National. If honors and pomp were dear to any of them, they could be found at the Grand National. The Grand Hotel became the center of continental social life.

Ritz did not hesitate to spend money when necessary to achieve an effect. On one occasion, 10,000 candles were lighted to show off a beautiful mountain. A huge bonfire was built on a mountain peak. Later in his career, he flooded the lower dining room of the Savoy, turning it into a Venetian scene complete with gondolas and singing gondoliers.

For 11 summer seasons, Ritz reigned at Lucerne. Winters he spent managing or operating hotels and restaurants in France.

Much of Ritz's success can be attributed to his association with Auguste Escoffier. Both knew the importance of pleasing the rich. Ritz catered to them in furnishings and decor and saw to it that Ritz-operated hotels were to their social liking; Escoffier catered to their palates and their egos.

In 1887, at the age of 37, Ritz married the daughter of a hotelkeeper. Soon after, he reached the apex of his career. The Savoy Hotel of London had opened and, after six months of operation, things were not going well. Ritz had previously been paid to go to London for the opening of the Savoy and to make recommendations. He was now asked to take over the management on his own terms.

According to some commentators of the period, Ritz revolutionized dining out in London. He was even accused of breaking up home life by making dining out

---

*Information concerning Ritz was adapted from Marie Louise Ritz, *Cesar Ritz, Host to the World* (Philadelphia, Pa.: Lippincott), 1938 and Stephen Watts, *The Ritz* (London: The Bodley Head), 1963.

fashionable. London's social life changed; men who previously dined in their men-only clubs now took their wives out to dinner or supper at the Savoy.

How did he do it? He introduced orchestras to play during dinner, starting with composer-conductor Johann Strauss. Music lengthened the dining period and increased the sale of beverages. He made evening dress compulsory in the dining rooms and banned unaccompanied ladies. For the first time, the glamorous coquettes of the day dined with their lovers in the same room as the aristocracy and their families.

Ritz understood the power of women and recognized that they wanted to be beautiful. He decided to help them be so. Instead of lighting that was glaring and functional, he decided to make it romantic. He spent weeks experimenting with the effects of various colors and intensities of light on the clothing and complexion of his wife. Apricot peach, he decided, most complimented the skin. Alabaster urns were hung from the ceiling in the Paris Ritz, their lights reflected upward onto tinted ceilings. In the bedrooms, bowls suspended from the ceiling created similar indirect lighting effects. The soft and glamorizing quality was achieved. Rich, fashionable women traveled with many clothes; Ritz, therefore, placed king-sized closet and drawer spaces in the Paris Ritz.

Ritz "stayed on top" of new projects, checking out details that many of today's executives would delegate to others. In March 1898, three months before the opening of the Paris hotel, César moved with his family into one of the top-floor apartments in order to be on hand to supervise the finishing details in person.

Each day after the workers had gone, he walked through the hotel, noting what had been done that day and planning for the next. He took elaborate notes: a new lamp needed here; a tapestry for a wall was too thin; sheerer curtains for a window with a fine view; a room with a north light must have the pale blue curtains lined with pale rose. He personally taught the housekeeping staff the art of bedmaking.

Although hotels in America were being built with bigger and more plush lobbies, Ritz built a small lobby to discourage idlers. To reduce maintenance costs, he painted the walls rather than papered them. Ritz believed that the style of decoration was not as important as how well the decorations and furnishings were done. If the furniture was the best, harmonized perfectly, and arranged with a view to maximum comfort, in Ritz's opinion it created a good room. With all the changing fashions over time since then, his view has been proven correct: Subdued elegance and absolute comfort are goals to strive for in any hotel decor.

Service at the Ritz was dignified; servants served in silence but were always on hand when needed. Guests were escorted to their suites by an attendant. They could lay out their wrinkled clothes and go to breakfast; returning in the early evening to dress for dinner, they would find their clothes freshly pressed and hung, ready for wear. The food was epicurean, prepared by Escoffier or his disciples. In short, it was the Ritz; the term came to be used throughout the English-speaking world to mean the ultimate in hotelkeeping.

Once the Paris Ritz was successful, the master turned his attention to the Carlton in London. The house was renovated, and the Carlton became the first London hotel to have a bath in every room. The hotel opened one year after the Paris Ritz, and it was an immediate success. A 7 percent dividend was paid to the stockholders the first year.

Ritz ranked the ability to handle people well as the most important of all qualities for the hotelier. His imagination and sensitivity to people and their wants contributed to a new standard of hotelkeeping. His son observed that he would have made a great general, because he was logical, intuitive, and decisive. He thought quickly and devoted himself completely to the job at hand.

Ritz was a driven man, pushing himself often to the point of exhaustion. In fact, in 1902 he suffered a nervous breakdown.

The Ritz name has been carried on by the Ritz Development Company. In 1907 the company franchised the Ritz name to the Ritz-Carlton Hotel in New York City. Later, other franchises were sold to hotel companies in Montreal, Lisbon, Boston, and elsewhere. The Ritz-Carlton in New York is no more, but the Boston Ritz-Carlton remains active and is considered to be one of the "great hotels" of the world. The Chicago Ritz was completed in 1975 and the Ritz-Carlton in Laguna Niguel, California in 1985. The Ritz-Carlton Company, headquartered in Atlanta, is primarily a management company that operates deluxe hotels for investors, many of them Japanese. Ritz-Carlton standards in design and appointments would please César Ritz by their elegance. The company is also known for its outstanding personnel policies and posh service.

3

The Developing and Modern Hotel/Motel

Things French were popular in this country about 1790 because of France's aid to the Colonies during the American Revolution, and also because the early days of the French Revolution were regarded as a time of great democratic upsurge. The hotel thus emerged from the tavern by the simple expedient of a name change: The term "tavern" was changed to "hotel." That word had a more glamorous ring, since in France it was the city residence of a wealthy or prominent person or referred to a public building such as the "hotel de ville," the town hall, or better yet, the "Hotel de la Monnaie," the mint.

During the French Revolution, many private residences in France were converted into public houses and called hotels. Country houses that served as inns were known, and are still known, as *auberges*. "Hotel" shares a common Latin root with "hospitality," "hostelry," "hospital," "hospice," and "host." The Spanish word for guest, *huesped*, probably dates back to the same Latin origin.

The word "hotel" was well known in America at least as early as 1791; city directories of the 1790s show that many a tavern had become a hotel.[1] By about 1800, "tavern," "hotel," and "coffeehouse" were being used, but by 1820 "hotel" was the generally accepted term. From then on, the tavern became more of an eating and drinking place than the hotel, with emphasis on the drinking.

The early hotels continued the tavern custom of serving an "ordinary," the set meal served at a given hour and at a fixed price. Hotels from the beginning were known for their good tables, or lack of them.

The American Plan, the arrangement by which one charge covers both room and meals, was probably the extension of the practice of tavernkeepers offering room and board (also beer in many taverns) for a single all-inclusive price. The

---

1. Doris Elizabeth King, "Early Hotel Entrepreneurs and Promoters, 1793–1860," *Explanations in Entrepreneurial History, Vol. VIII* (Cambridge, Mass.: Harvard Research Center in Entrepreneurial History), Feb. 1956.

European Plan (first introduced in France) was offered in the U.S. in the 1830s. A New Englander visiting New York City reported that three hotels in that city were operating under the new system—food, beverage, and room being priced separately.[2] The American Plan especially suited the resort where families might stay for the season, and even today many resorts operate on the American Plan.

Hotels proliferated as the cities grew. New York City had only 8 in 1818; by 1836 there were 28; and 10 years later, in 1846, there were 108.

STATUS AND IMPACT OF HOTELKEEPING IN THE U.S.

From the outset in America, tavernkeeping and, later, hotelkeeping were usually in the hands of respected members of the community and enjoyed a status not found in Europe. George Washington owned several small public houses; Abraham Lincoln was part owner of a tavern in Springfield, Illinois.

In the 30 years before the Civil War, hotelkeeping came to be referred to as a "profession." Many managers strove to be hosts rather than proprietors, which puzzled the British visitor no end. Charles A. Stetson, manager of the Astor House in New York City, put the difference like this: "A tavernkeeper knows how to get to market and how to feed so many people at a public table. A hotelkeeper is a gentleman who stands on a level with his guests."[3]

Until recently, historians had little to say about the effect of the hotel in shaping our culture. Fortunately, that has changed. Daniel J. Boorstin has much to say on the subject in his book, *The American National Experience*.[4] The chapter on hotels is called "Palaces of the Public." Jefferson Williamson calls the hotel "the most distinctively American of all our institutions" in his book, *The American Hotel*.[5]

In England, the upper classes had enormous homes and large staffs of servants. When they traveled, they were likely to stop with friends. When they entertained it was in their homes. It was not until the turn of the century that they were enticed away from their homes to dine out with César Ritz and Auguste Escoffier in such places as the Savoy and the Claridge.

In America, hotels were the usual meeting places of civic committees, associations of businessmen, and in the frontier communities, the city council and other government agencies. Businessmen called many of the hotels exchange houses and used them somewhat as a stock exchange. Some secured bank privileges and issued paper currency. As late as the 1860s, the Burnet House in Cincinnati issued five-dollar bills, authenticated by its cashier, that carried an engraved likeness of the building. In New Orleans, the lobby of the St. Charles Hotel was used for public slave auctions.

Quite logically, the promoters of new American towns recognized the values of a good hotel, and in several instances a hotel was built standing alone before the town even existed. As Daniel Boorstin says, the hotels were both the creature and the creator of communities, as well as symptoms of the frenetic quest for community.

Even in the early nineteenth century, Americans gathered to do their politicking and conventioneering. The first national nominating convention of a major party met in 1831 to name Henry Clay for president, and where did it meet? Quite naturally, in a hotel—Barnum's City Hotel in Baltimore, a six-story building with 200 apartments, reputed to be one of the best in the country.

AMERICAN HOTELS DIFFER FROM ENGLISH AND EUROPEAN INNS

An English barrister, Alexander McKay, who traveled in this country in 1846, observed the differences between English and American hotels. He pointed out that in England hotels were regarded as purely private property, in appearance very much like the residences that surrounded them. In America, hotels were regarded as public concerns and even looked like public buildings. Often they were the most impressive and grandest buildings in the town or city. (This remains true today of many modern hotels.)

2. Dorsey and Devine, *Fare Thee Well* (New York: Crown Publishers), 1964.
3. Thomas Lately, *Delmonico's, A Century of Splendor* (Boston, Mass.: Houghton Mifflin Co.), 1967.
4. Daniel J. Boorstin, *The American National Experience* (New York: Random House), 1965.
5. Jefferson Williamson, *The American Hotel: An Anecdoted History* (New York: Alfred Knopf), 1930.

Figure 3-1 The Nicolett House was a structure that Minneapolis could well boast of in 1858: five floors and 70 spacious rooms. The first floor was rented to a bank and several stores, which gave the house an assured income. Ladies had a private entrance and separate "parlors." Speaking tubes led from the front desk to all floors, and bell pulls for service were in all rooms, a practice borrowed from early inns. Cooks and porters stoked the hotel's ranges with cordwood. Three complete meals and a room cost $2 a night. The building was used until 1923, when a new 13-story Pick-Nicollett was built on the same site.
Source: Courtesy of Albert Pick Hotels.

Indeed, the American hotel served a different purpose than the inn or railroad hotel in England. The class system did not really exist in the U.S., and the hotel was a place where all classes of people stopped and tended to mingle, the wealthy together with the workingman or frontiersman.

Another way in which the nineteenth-century American hotelkeeper was different from his European counterpart, "mein host," was in his self-concept and social standing. The innkeeper in England was supposed to be a genial, deferential individual, only one cut above a servant.

THE MOTEL EMERGES

When Henry Ford put the Model T in reach of the average pocketbook, travel from town to town and into the city became a peculiarly American diversion and preoccupation—almost a way of life.

The word "motel," an abbreviation of "motor hotel," was first used in 1926 in California. The motel met an obvious need. It became a quick stopping-over place for the traveler, and no attempt was made to provide food and beverage. Travelers away from the towns and cities who needed to stop overnight were pleased to find four walls, one dangling lightbulb, a bare floor, and an outside privy. Rates were low—$1 a night was the prevailing rate in the early 1920s—and it was all part of the sport of travel.

The growth of the motel business was spectacular. In 1935 the Bureau of the Census listed 9848 motels. The figure had increased to 13,521 in 1939. Then World War II placed a definite brake on expansion; for a time, with the shortage of tires and gasoline, many motels were hardpressed to survive.

After the war, a pent-up urge to travel burst forth and motels sprang up to help satisfy that urge. Husband-and-wife teams invested their savings and borrowed to build 10- to 20-unit motels, and were quite successful. Many of them made enough to pay back the entire cost of the motel in 5 years or less. By 1951 the *American Motel Magazine* estimated that there were 43,356 motels in operation.

About this time, a significant change took place in the character of the motel operation. Investors with several hundred thousand dollars available moved into the field, and soon the small "Mom and Pop" motel was no longer the typical operation. Motel operators kept up with the times by offering indoor plumbing, radio, TV, enclosed showers, carpeted floors, and tiled bathrooms.

As competition forced the issue, however, another style and pace were introduced. Large motels were built, with sizable swimming pools, luxurious lobbies, and restaurants of some size. They required investments running well over 1 million dollars.

Telephone and room service are standard services in what was called the motor hotel. Many motels take on the atmosphere of a resort as more recreation facilities such as playgrounds, putting greens, swimming pools, and shuffleboard and badminton courts are built. "Pleasure domes," central areas with a pool and transparent roof, are often found.

For the traveling family, the motel is ideal. It is more informal than the hotel, tipping is likely to be less often called for, restaurant prices are usually lower, and there is a swimming pool. No need to travel into the heart of the city to get to the accommodations; the newer motel is probably located near a super highway on the periphery of the city or town. It is also apt to be chain-affiliated, and the traveler can make a reservation the evening before at another unit of the same operation. The traveler is reassured by the affiliation, relatively certain that the place will be clean, safe, and attractive. The same can be said of most of the new budget motels that arose in large numbers in the 1970s, although in one way they are a return to the basic motel: rooms only, no food and beverage.

The Hotel and Motor Hotel Come Together

From the 1920s and 1940s, the motel operator had little in common with the hotel owner and operator. The motel was small; it usually lacked food

and beverage facilities. Its owners were amateurs. Their life savings were often tied up in the business. They wanted to hold what they had and maybe to expand a little.

Hotel managers, quite differently, had a tradition going back at least to hotels in the 1830s. The complexity of their job called for professional expertise. They enjoyed relatively high status. Managers of the larger hotels looked on their profession as a career field, and they were constantly on the lookout for bigger and better jobs.

In the eyes of the hotel owner and manager, motel owners were small potatoes, sometimes an object of fun. Hoteliers did not associate with motel people; they had separate trade journals and trade associations.

The Holiday Inns concept was a landmark in the lodging business, a marriage of the basic motel and some of the features of the hotel. Kemmons Wilson (see pages 152–153) kept the low-rise, park-near-your-room features of the motel and added no-frills food and beverage. The word *holiday* suggests leisure travel, attractive to the vast expanding market of the family on vacation, as well as to the business traveler on a small budget. Begun in 1952, Holiday Inns spread rapidly via the burgeoning franchise system.

Marketing and referral groups such as Best Western added to the efficiency and appeal of the motel by providing standards and reservation systems.

Hotels Outnumbered

Once established, motels soon outstripped the traditional hotel in number of properties, but not in number of rooms. Figure 3-2 shows the percentage mix of guest rooms in hotels as compared with motels in the period from 1939 to 1977.

By the early 1960s, motels were an accepted part of the hotel business. The American Hotel Association changed its name to the American Hotel and Motel Association (AH&MA). The larger motels, especially those affiliated with chains, became members of the AH&MA and were listed in the *Hotel and Motel Red Book*.

The larger motor hotels, similar in operation to hotels, were glad to join forces with the hotel fraternity. This was not true of the small-motel operators, who largely saw themselves as small-business people selling rooms along the highways. Most continued to maintain their own state and national trade associations.

Whether they are called motor hotels or motels, the larger ones are hotel operations and include most of the services offered by the large hotel. The atmosphere tends to be more relaxed than the hotel, and less emphasis is placed on group business. Foodservice is also likely to be less formal, more often than not a coffeeshop-style operation.

Indian Motel Owners

By the 1990s, a large number of the owners of motels with fewer than 50 rooms were from India. According to the AH&MA in 1989, 40 percent of these smaller properties were operated by Indian immigrants who, in effect, had bought themselves an immigration permit and a job by purchasing a small motel and operating it with the

help of their family. About a quarter of Days Inns franchise holders were of Indian origin. Many of these family enterprises did well, what with low labor costs and rising real estate values. This was especially true in Southern California and Arizona. Some of the owners had turned developers and were building hotels, and a few had moved into residential development.

CLASSIFICATION OF LODGING ESTABLISHMENTS

There are about 300,000 hotel and motel properties in the world, about 45,000 in the U.S. The average hotel or motel is getting bigger while the actual number of hotels declines. The total number of guest rooms keeps pace with the population growth.

Hotels and motels can be classified according to location, number of rooms, principal markets,

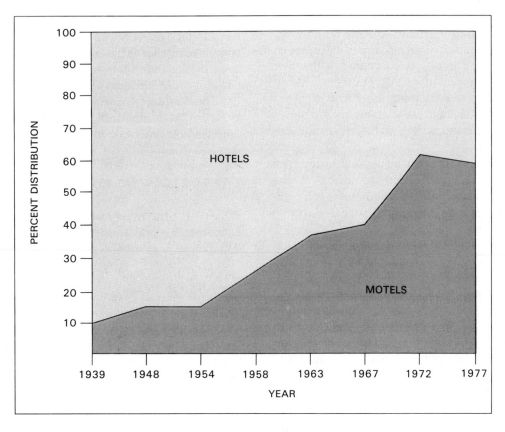

Figure 3-2 Percentage mix in hotels vs. motels (total guest rooms).

Source: Albert J. Gomes and Pannell Kerr Forster, *Hospitality in Transition* (New York: AH and MA).

and other criteria, such as room rate. Classification by location gives these groupings

Center city

Suburban

Highway motels

Resorts

Airport hotels

The distinction between hotel and motel was probably clear when small single- or two-story hotels were first built along principal highways in the late 1920s. Adjacent auto parking was provided, but no food and beverage service. Today, larger motels tend to be called motor hotels or motor inns and provide one or more restaurants. Motels generally offer a minimum of services, whereas hotels usually provide food and beverage services and bell service and, in some states, must do so.

The term "motel" seems to be fading. Properties that could be called a motel are called something else: inn, motor inn, budget inn, lodge, or chalet. The term "motor hotel" was popular for some time. Lodging chains assume that, by advertising, a property will be properly positioned in the public's mind, as compared with other lodging accommodations. Always there is the attempt to impute something more to a property, not merely rooms, but associations of cleanliness, efficiency, glamour, safety, status, or some other added value.

The term "resort" can be applied to any type of lodging accommodation according to the American Automobile Association if it has a vacation atmosphere and offers extensive recreational facilities.

Another way of classifying is to describe the principal market served by a hotel: convention, residential, transient, and resort (vacation). Hotels may fit more than one category. The large Hawaiian hotels are both resort and convention hotels. So too are many of the casino properties in Las Vegas. Most large hotels depend heavily on convention sales, but may also cultivate tours and pleasure travelers.

The average room rate is one key to hotel classification, but varies with location and time. In 1992 luxury hotels were defined as full-service properties charging $175 or more a night and costing more than $200,000 a room to build. Such properties usually have top-quality restaurants, exercise and health facilities, and business services, including office space and equipment like computers and in-room fax machines.[6]

THE FOUR TIERS

The hotel industry can be seen as a four-tier business: luxury, first class, midscale, and budget. The tiers are determined in terms of room rates, location, service, and prestige. At the top are the luxury hotels, with room rates of $150 a day and up. The next level down, the first-class hotel, has rates of $60 to $150. The next level down is the midscale motor hotel: Ramadas, Holiday Inns, Rodeways, and the like. On the bottom tier is the budget property, with rates of $30 to $50.

When it comes to the level of service, at the bottom is the budget property and many small motels, the Mom and Pop properties.

Many of the first-class hotels in this country have set aside their top one or two floors for a "hotel within a hotel," with private elevators, private check-in and checkout, and a concierge on hand to take care of hospitality and travel problems. The rate for these executive floors may be a third higher than that on the regular floors. Expense account travelers are the biggest market.

The Waldorf-Astoria opened its tower in 1931, but it was not until the 1970s that the hotel within a hotel was seen in any numbers.

TYPES OF LODGING ESTABLISHMENTS

Table 3-1 lists most types of lodging establishments. Several are described below in more detail.

The All-Suite Hotel

The all-suite hotel offers the transient traveler a suite of two rooms plus a small kitchen. An added attraction is a complimentary full American breakfast and a daily two-hour cocktail hour. The concept is a variation of the resort motel offering of a housekeeping unit and resembles the condo

---

6. "Hotel Slump Is No Bar to Luxury Projects," *Wall Street Journal* (December 2, 1991).

TABLE 3-1 Kinds of Overnight Accommodations

Transient hotels	Price is for room only.	Inexpensive to very expensive.
European Plan	No meals included.	
American Plan (AP)	All meals included in one price (usually resort hotels).	
Modified American Plan (MAP)	Dinner and breakfast included in one price.	
Resort hotels	Hotel with recreational activities and facilities.	
Casino/hotels	Cater to gaming customer, usually offer entertainment. Suites often complimentary to high rollers.	Inexpensive to expensive.
Conference centers	Similar to hotels, but catering to groups for educational meetings. Some are resorts or are attached to a university.	Moderately expensive.
Health spas	Hotels or resorts with emphasis on weight reduction or medical treatment.	Expensive to very expensive.
Rental condominiums	Found mostly in resort areas. Completely equipped apartments.	About the same as moderate- to high-price resort rooms.
Motels/motor inns	Provide bedroom, bath, and parking; rooms are usually accessible from parking lot. Convenient for auto travelers. Usually adjacent to highways.	Inexpensive to moderately expensive.
All-suite hotels	Apartment motels; breakfast often included in the room rate.	Moderately expensive.
Guest houses	Resemble small, inexpensive hotels. May have shared baths with breakfast included in the room rate.	Inexpensive.
Bed & breakfast	Guest lodged in private homes; breakfast included.	Inexpensive to expensive.
Pensions	Found in Europe; similar to boarding houses or guest houses.	Inexpensive.
Hostels	Appeal mostly to young travelers. Minimal amenities. Guest often required to help with work.	Inexpensive.
Campgrounds	Appeal mostly to families who travel in RVs.	Inexpensive.
Castles, chateaus, and mansions	Lavish accommodations and meals.	Very expensive.

rental. Expansion has been rapid via limited partnerships (the hotel company is the general partner and manages the property; the limited partners have no management rights and their risk is limited to their investment) with investors.

The all-suite bridges the gap between the traditional residential and transient hotel. Residential guests usually lease apartments for a month or more and may bring in their own furniture. All-suite guests may rent for up to a month, but typically do so for shorter stays. Housekeeping is done daily by the staff. All-suites are similar to rental condos but the suites are usually smaller, about 600 square feet (compared to the usual hotel room's 400 square feet).

Bob Wooley, a builder and founder of Granada Royale Hometels in the late 1960s, is credited with the prototype for most contemporary all-suites: limited public space, complimentary cocktails in the early evening, complimentary breakfast, suites centered around an atrium or courtyard. Some hotels add all-suite towers to existing properties. The cost of housekeeping increases (12 to 14 suites per day per maid vs. 16 to 18 standard guest rooms) and maintenance, utilities, and landscaping costs are higher. Other costs are lower. The all-suite provides a hedge for the owner: If it fails as a hotel, it can be easily converted into office space or rental apartments.

Labor cost is low, running between 12 and 20 percent of sales. That becomes possible because foodservice, except for breakfast, is provided by a separately leased restaurant. In addition, administrative personnel are kept to a minimum, usually employing only a general manager and sales director. Costs of the complimentary breakfast and cocktail hour run at less than 5 percent of sales. In a typical 260-room all-suite, breakfast is prepared by two cooks and offered for a 3-hour period. Serving ware is disposable. Only well (the well is where most served drinks are kept ready for pouring) drinks (less expensive) are available during the cocktail hour.

The Conference Center

The conference center appeared in the 1960s and 1970s. The Kellogg Foundation funded a number of these adult education facilities around the country, each connected with a university. Independent for-profit centers then appeared, designed to attract groups seriously intent on learning and wishing to be away from the convention hotels, mostly located in downtown areas.

Conference centers offer more and larger meeting rooms than convention properties. The typical conference center offers 1000 square feet of public space and two employees for each guest room. Convention hotels provide 700 square feet and one employee per guest room.[7] Rates usually include room, meals, and use of meeting rooms specially equipped as classrooms.

Bed and Breakfast Accommodations

Somewhat akin to the wayside inn of Colonial times and of the so-called tourist rooms rented for $1 a night during the 1930s depression, bed-and-breakfast accommodations (B&Bs) are springing up around the country, particularly on the West Coast and in New England and Canada.

Operators of B&Bs have taken their cue from the popular home accommodations found in villages, towns, and cities throughout Britain and Ireland, in which the traveler gets a pleasant room and a breakfast complete with eggs, bacon, orange juice, coffee or tea, and toast.

Most of the B&Bs in this country are much more elaborate than the basic British variety; the residences may be virtually small hotels (without a hotel license, bars, or restaurants as such). Even though room rates in many are as high or higher than in local hotels, travelers often find them more personalized and interesting than a competing hotel.

The more expensive ones may offer wine and cheese in the late afternoon and a lavish home-cooked breakfast. Because they are mostly found in private homes, however, the B&B bathroom may be down the hall.

Starting a B&B is relatively easy, especially for those who own a large home. Government regulation is minimal in most states. Operators have formed their own associations and in a few instances their own marketing groups. B&B's compete mainly with motels and resort properties. They are likely to spread rapidly in some areas and could in time become serious competition for hotel and motel operators.

---

7. Wall Street Journal (March 6, 1985).

The American Bed and Breakfast Association divides B&B's into three groups:

Homes. Private homes where one or more spare rooms are rented to paying guests.

Inns. Usually B&B lodgings that have several rooms and are operated as a business.

Country inns. Inns with restaurants that serve other meals in addition to breakfast.

The American Bed and Breakfast Association sends inspectors to each inn and rates it in five major areas: exteriors, common rooms, guest rooms, guest baths, and administrative procedure. The scoring is done with a 1-to-5 system, with 5 representing the highest score. In 1994 there were about 20,000 bed and breakfasts in the U.S. and supply exceeded demand.[8]

Budget Hotel and Motel

Budget properties offer low room rates. Sleep Inns, Quality International's entry in the budget category, features one queen-size bed, a 730-inch vanity desk, concealed fluorescent lighting, a mini-bar, a color TV with a built-in VCR, light-button telephone with data port, and oversized shower stall but no tub. Housekeeping time is minimized by wall-mounting all furniture, including a space for hanging clothes and luggage board. This minimal room can be cleaned in 20 minutes, as compared to the 30 minutes usually required for a regular hotel room.

The economy/budget, or limited-service, hotels represent about 22 percent of America's hotel rooms. Attractive to investors, the break-even occupancy rate is only 55 percent, compared with the industry's break-even average of 65 percent. Even so, in many areas the budget properties have been overbuilt.[9]

Personnel costs for the typical budget property are low. Often a husband-and-wife team manage and live in the property.

Rental Condominiums

Thousands of rooms have been added to the public-accommodations inventory by the construction of rental condominiums in resort areas. A typical owner of a vacation condominium is upper middle class or higher and regards the vacation condominium as an investment, as well as a vacation facility. The rule of thumb is that the annual income of the condo buyer is about the same as the price of the condominium. The buyer of a $100,000 condominium would probably have an annual income of at least $100,000. (The rule, however, is not followed by many buyers.)

The big appeal of the condominium is that in the past it may have appreciated two or three times in value over a 5-year period, an appreciation rate that in 1988 had declined or in some cases become negative.

Rental income is a different story, however. Condo experts point out that owners should not expect cash flow from rentals to reach the amount necessary to carry the mortgage and maintenance charges on a condominium.

The usual owner who rents a condominium does not occupy it for more than two or three weeks of the year. Under federal income tax regulations, if a condo is occupied for a longer period, the owner is not eligible for tax deductions resulting from maintenance and repair costs, interest cost, or depreciation allowances. Owners can avoid this restriction to a certain extent if, while they are occupying a condominium, they engage in maintaining and repairing it.

The management of condominiums for owners has become a business unto itself. Under a management contract agreement, a management company or individual arranges a separate contract for each owner. Management is then directly responsible to the owner. Continual communication between management and owner is necessary to maintain good relations. Owners are particularly keen on receiving current financial information.

In some ways, condo management is more difficult and in other ways less so than resort hotel management. Since most condominium enterprises have no restaurants, food and beverage problems are not present. On the other hand, condo management is similar to club management in that the manager has numerous bosses rather than one or a few.

A 100-room condominium resort may have 80 or 90 owners participating in a rental pool. Each owner is concerned with receiving the maximum return from rental income and maintaining the in-

8. Somerset R. Waters, *Travel Industry World Yearbook—1993–94* (New York: Childs & Waters, Inc.), 1993.
9. *Ibid.*

dividual apartment in the best possible manner. Furniture and equipment may not be uniform, and owners often install personal items that are sometimes a problem to care for and keep in place. Housekeeping takes on added importance since owners are much more critical than renters.

When a strike against an airline that serves a particular destination takes place, occupancy can drop sharply. When United Airlines employees struck in 1979, occupancy dropped sharply in hotel and rental condominiums in Hawaii. The cost of jet fuel is a factor, since it is reflected in air fares and hence the occupancy levels that are of immediate interest to owners.

Reserving space in a condominium may be particularly difficult, in that owners often do not specify long enough in advance the time that they wish to occupy their units. Management must then schedule around the owner's intended time of occupancy, which is often difficult when blocks of rooms are needed for groups.

Condo managers must be residents, which proves to be highly confining after a period of time. For this and other reasons, many who think condo management would be a fun job sooner or later find it to be otherwise.

Trophy Hotels

A new term entered the hotel vocabulary when, beginning in 1987, some luxury hotels with prestigious locations were bid up to prices that broke all valuation rules. These became the so-called "trophy" hotels; the Hotel Bel-Air in Beverly Hills and the Beverly Hills Hotel are examples of this category. The owners of the Bel-Air have received $1.1 million a room; the Sultan of Brunei paid $757,000 per room at the Beverly Hills Hotel. The reasons for these astronomical prices are said to involve the egos of the buyers and the fact that over time the buyers feel that the land they sit on will exceed the purchase price. Japanese buyers place a much higher value on real estate than do most Americans and have also paid exorbitant sums for hotels. Paying over a million dollars for a hotel room involves some of the same rationale at work as when one pays $50 million for a Van Gogh painting. Donald Trump, the New York real estate tycoon, paid $496,000 a room for the Plaza, a New York City landmark, probably as much for the gratification of owning this historic building as for its financial value. Whoever owns a trophy hotel assumes a certain prominence as well as social cachet. Like public stock buyers, such purchasers expect to sell their assets for an even higher price. Hotel chain presidents buy or operate trophy properties because they bring status to the entire chain.

Some developers and owners have made large profits by selling trophy hotels. The Bel-Air, for example, was purchased in 1982 for $23 million, and another $20 million was spent on renovations and the addition of 30 rooms and suites. Dallas-based Rosewood, the owners, sold the property (which included 11.5 acres of prime real estate) for $110 million to Tokyo-based Sekitai Keihatsu Company.[10]

A "different" classification of hotels exists in France, where travelers who crave quiet can go to one of 275 Relais du Silence, an association of individually owned hotels, explicitly dedicated to meeting "the deep need of nature and peace we all encounter in our frenzied world." Paris has three of them. The others are spread around France, with an average of 22 rooms each and cheap to moderate prices.

THE LODGING LEADERS

Until the 1980s, it was fairly easy to keep track of the large lodging chains worldwide. The names Sheraton, Hilton International, Intercontinental, Westin, Holiday Inn, and Marriott were well known and American-based. By 1992 lodging ownership had become much more international, and the list of "top" lodging chains changes frequently. British, French, and Japanese names are among the top 20 lodging chains.

The largest 20 lodging chains as reported by *Lodging Hospitality* (1991) are seen in Table 3-2. Motel 6, which was the typical American budget motel chain, is now part of Accor S.A., a French company that with the addition of the some 600 Motel 6 units makes Accor the largest of the lodging chains in terms of number of properties. Choice Hotels International franchises more than 3000 properties in 30 countries. ITT Sheraton is probably the largest of properties traditionally called hotels. It has more than 400 owned, leased, managed, or franchised properties worldwide.

---

10. "Was the Bel-Air Worth It?", *Lodging Hospitality* (Oct. 1989).

TABLE 3-2 Size of Largest Lodging Chains

Rank U.S. Lodging Chain	U.S. Properties		Status of Properties				Foreign Properties	
	Rooms	Number of Properties	Company Owned	Franchised Licensed	Management Contract	Other	Rooms	Number of Properties
1 Holiday Inn Worldwide								
Atlanta								
Holiday Inn Hotels	258,783	1350	0	1245	0	105[a]	43,674	198
Holiday Inn Crowne Plaza	8195	20	0	11	0	9[a]	8866	29
Holiday Inn Express	780	6	0	3	0	3[a]	0	0
Holiday Inn Garden Court	0	0	0	0	0	0	1174	12
TOTAL	**267,758**	**1376**	**0**	**1259**	**0**	**117[a]**	**53,174**	**239**
2 Choice Hotels International								
Silver Spring, Md.								
Comfort Inns/Suites	78,543	845	2	843	0	0	3633	45
Quality Inns/Hotels/Suites	56,808	435	7	428	0	0	13,632	112
Clarion Hotels/Suites/Resorts								
and Carriage House Inns	11,557	68	1	67	0	0	2580	25
Sleep Inns	2573	31	0	31	0	0	2723	30
Econo Lodges	58,706	787	0	787	0	0	362	6
Friendship Inns	6576	133	0	133	0	0	189	4
TOTAL	**230,729**	**2451**	**12**	**2439**	**0**	**0**	**23,426**	**224**
3 Best Western International								
Phoenix								
Best Western	164,861	1793	0	0	0	0	96,643	1457
TOTAL	**164,861**	**1793**	**0**	**0**	**0**	**0**	**96,643**	**1457**
4 Marriott Corp.								
Washington, D.C.								
Marriott Hotels/Resorts/Suites	96,556	226	29	54	143	0	8300	21
Residence Inn	20,996	172	65	64	43	0	0	0
Fairfield Inn	10,693	84	80	4	0	0	0	0
Courtyard	26,608	195	71	4	120	0	0	0
TOTAL	**154,853**	**677**	**245**	**126**	**306**	**0**	**8300**	**21**
5 Hospitality Franchise Systems								
Wayne, N.J.								
Howard Johnson	57,894	459	0	459	0	0	2378	19
Ramada	88,322	530	0	530	0	0	0	0
TOTAL	**146,216**	**989**	**0**	**989**	**0**	**0**	**2378**	**19**
6 Days Inns of America								
Atlanta								
Days Inn	128,664	1108	4	1081	23	0	2914	26
Daystop	2939	61	0	61	0	0	0	0
TOTAL	**131,603**	**1169**	**4**	**1142**	**23**	**0**	**2914**	**26**
7 Hilton Hotels Corp.								
Beverly Hills, Calif.								
Hilton Hotels	42,543	46	23	0	46	0	0	0
Hilton Inns (includes CrestHil)	49,833	203	0	203	0	0	0	0
Hilton Suites	1095	5	5	0	5	0	0	0
Conrad Hotels	0	0	0	0	0	0	2196	7
TOTAL	**93,471**	**254**	**28**	**203**	**51**	**0**	**2196**	**7**
8 ITT Sheraton Corp.								
Boston								
Sheraton Hotels	51,679	137	0	102	0	35[b]	38,577	103

(continues)

TABLE 3-2   *(continued)*

Rank	U.S. Lodging Chain	U.S. Properties		Status of Properties				Foreign Properties	
		Rooms	Number of Properties	Company Owned	Franchised Licensed	Management Contract	Other	Rooms	Number of Properties
	Sheraton Inns	22,464	123	0	120	0	3[b]	960	6
	Sheraton Resorts	9425	26	0	14	0	12[b]	6724	26
	Sheraton Suites	755	3	0	1	0	2[b]	0	0
	TOTAL	**84,323**	**289**	**0**	**237**	**0**	**52**	**46,261**	**135**
9	**Motel 6**								
	Dallas								
	Motel 6	70,340	618	618	0	0	0	0	0
	TOTAL	**70,340**	**618**	**618**	**0**	**0**	**0**	**0**	**0**
10	**The Promus Companies Inc.**								
	Memphis								
	Embassy Suites	22,949	94	8	43	18	25[c]	0	0
	Hampton Inn	33,384	265	15	230	1	19[c]	0	0
	Homewood Suites	2034	18	8	10	0	0	0	0
	Harrah's	4541	5	5	0	0	0	0	0
	TOTAL	**62,908**	**382**	**36**	**283**	**19**	**44[c]**	**0**	**0**
11	**Hyatt Hotels Corp.**								
	Chicago								
	Hyatt Hotels	57,137	105	0[d]	0	105	0	46	1
	Hyatt International	444	1	0	0	1	0	19,500	53
	TOTAL	**57,581**	**106**	**0**	**0**	**106**	**0**	**20,146**	**54**
12	**Super 8 Enterprises, Inc.**								
	Aberdeen, S.D.								
	Super 8 Motels	50,133	810	52	758	0	0	735	10
	TOTAL	**50,133**	**810**	**52**	**758**	**0**	**0**	**735**	**10**
13	**Carlson Hospitality Group, Inc.**								
	Minneapolis								
	Radisson Hotels International	39,299	160	n/a	133	27	0	11,219	52
	Colony Hotels & Resorts	7298	37	n/a	11	26	0	1371	5
	Country Lodging by Carlson	1906	20	n/a	20	0	0	584	8
	TOTAL	**48,503**	**217**	**0**	**164**	**53**	**0**	**13,174**	**65**
14	**Forte Hotels, Inc.**								
	El Cajon, Calif.								
	Travelodge	34,594	433	158	272	50	0	0	0
	Travelodge Hotels	6653	30	27	3	5	0	0	0
	Thriftlodge	237	4	4	0	0	0	0	0
	Forte Hotels	0	0	0	0	0	0	72,000	900
	TOTAL	**41,484**	**467**	**189**	**275**	**55**	**0**	**72,000**	**900**
15	**La Quinta Motor Inns, Inc.**								
	San Antonio								
	La Quinta Inns	26,458	207	203	4	0	0	0	0
	TOTAL	**26,458**	**207**	**203**	**4**	**0**	**0**	**0**	**0**
16	**Hospitality International**								
	Atlanta								
	Red Carpet Inn	12,800	127	0	127	0	0	150	2
	Scottish Inns	10,100	153	0	153	0	0	84	1
	Master Hosts Inns/Resorts	2600	19	0	19	0	0	170	2
	TOTAL	**25,500**	**299**	**0**	**299**	**0**	**0**	**404**	**5**

(continues)

TABLE 3-2 *(continued)*

Rank U.S. Lodging Chain	U.S. Properties		Status of Properties				Foreign Properties	
	Rooms	Number of Properties	Company Owned	Franchised Licensed	Management Contract	Other	Rooms	Number of Properties
17 R&B Realty Group								
Los Angeles								
Oakwood Corporate Apartments	24,761	46	32	0	14	0	0	0
TOTAL	**24,761**	**46**	**32**	**0**	**14**	**0**	**0**	**0**
18 Red Roof Inns								
Hilliard, Ohio								
Red Roof Inns	23,261	209	209	0	0	0	0	0
TOTAL	**23,261**	**209**	**209**	**0**	**0**	**0**	**0**	**0**
19 Westin Hotels & Resorts								
Seattle								
Westin Hotels & Resorts	20,439	33	13[e]	0	20	0	13,435	29
TOTAL	**20,439**	**33**	**13[e]**	**0**	**20**	**0**	**13,435**	**29**
20 Economy Lodging Systems, Inc.								
Warrensville Heights, Ohio								
Knights Inn	15,120	126	0	72	55	0	0	0
Arborgate Inn	1470	21	0	16	5	0	0	0
Knights Court	300	3	0	3	0	0	0	0
Knights Stop	200	2	0	2	0	0	0	0
TOTAL	**17,090**	**152**	**0**	**92**	**60**	**0**	**0**	**0**

[a]Co-owned or managed properties.
[b]Properties owned or under management contract.
[c]Joint ventures managed by Promus.
[d]Partial ownership in some hotels.
[e]Not all fully owned by Westin.
Source: Lodging Hospitality (August 1991).

Illustrating the transnational and shifting ownership of chain hotels was the purchase of Westin Hotels & Resorts from the parent company of United Airlines in October, 1987. The Westin chain was developed beginning in the 1930's and based in Seattle, Washington. Westin was bought in 1987 by the Aoki Corporation in partnership with the Bass Group of Texas for $1.53 billion, one of the largest hotel deals in history. In 1994 the Aoki company agreed to sell a large portion of the lodging chain to a Mexican conglomerate for $708 million. Under the deal, Westin's brand name and business and operations in North America, South America and Europe, will be owned by DSC, a large Mexico City based construction and real estate firm with interests in hotels and travel agencies. Aoki will retain Westin's properties in Asia, six hotels in Canada, and several minority investments in the U.S.

It is seen that the large chains represent a mixture of ownership, managed, and franchised operations. Many also operate hotels under management contract. Holiday Inn owns only 104 of the more than 1700 hotels that operate under its name. Neither does Days Inns of America. Most of the Choice Hotels International are franchisees. Best Western International is a marketing/referral organization whose members are independent owners. Hilton Hotels owns 21 hotels, partly owns 14, and manages or franchises 207 others, including 42 resorts.[11] It can be said that the larg-

11. Somerset R. Waters, *Travel Industry World Yearbook—1993–94* (New York: Childs & Waters, Inc.), 1993.

est hotel companies have largely moved out of ownership and become management, franchise, or marketing/referral companies.

Market Segmentation

Market segmentation emphasizes the importance of building and operating hotels for particular groups of people, according to what they want in the way of room rate, location, prestige, and amenities.

> Target markets for large hotels are:
>
> Business and corporate groups
>
> Meetings and convention groups
>
> Tour and travel, domestic and international
>
> Incentive groups

Luxury hotels such as the Four Seasons and Ritz-Carlton chains know that their clientele would not appreciate sharing breakfast with the members of a motorcoach tour. Luxury-market hotels appeal to the upscale business traveler and affluent vacation traveler and try to reach both. Budget properties are after the salesperson on a limited expense account, as well as the pleasure traveler on a tight budget. The large transient hotel may segment its markets into conventioneers, tour groups, and independent vacationers and sell its concierge floor to top executives and the affluent. The weekend market may be the middle-income husband and wife who want a brief holiday away from the routine of everyday life.

Choice Hotels International segments its markets by offering seven levels of prices and service:

> Comfort Inns/Suites
>
> Quality Inns/Hotels/Suites
>
> Clarion Hotels/Suites and Carriage House Inns
>
> Sleep Inns
>
> Rodeway Inns
>
> Econo Lodges
>
> Friendship Inns

Holiday Inn Worldwide has four categories of properties: Hotels, Crowne Plaza, Express, and Garden Court.

Airline Hotel Ownership

Hotel ownership by airlines would seem a natural marriage, especially for locations served by the airlines. Flight crews can be booked into hotel-owned properties. Tour packages sold by the airline can include hotel accommodations controlled by the airline. Destination advertising can be done jointly. Airlines feed hotels and vice versa. The airlines, it would seem, might have easy access to capital for hotel purchases. However, the probable reason that more airlines are not hotel owners is lack of money.

Pan American World Airways was the first to enter international hotelkeeping on a grand scale. During World War II, President Roosevelt met with Juan L. Trippe, then president of Pan Am. Roosevelt suggested that U.S. interests would be best served if Pan Am fostered the growth of first-class hotels in Latin America. Out of the meeting grew the Inter-Continental Hotels Corporation (IHC). Unfortunately, later financial pressures forced Pan Am to sell the highly profitable IHC.

Swissair is an example of the intermarriage of travel business segments. In a joint venture with Nestlé of Switzerland, the airline owns Swisshotel, an international chain of hotels. Swissair also controls Reisburo Kuoni, parent company of Kuoni Travel, which in turn owns Kuoni Hotel Management, a hotel company focused on managing hotels in the Caribbean and Mediterranean regions.

Exported Management Concepts

American hoteliers abroad brought a new sense of management to international hotelkeeping: a huge referral system in many cases and a flair for promotion and advertising. Of course, they would much rather spend somebody else's money—a local investor's or the local government's—in building the hotel abroad. Preferably, they would operate on a management contract, which removes many of the risks and tends to insure better treatment within the country.

The economic consequences of American-managed hotels abroad were much greater than would be indicated by the 60,000 or 70,000 rooms involved. The Istanbul Hilton, for example, realized a $13 million profit during its first year of operation in 1955 and played an important part in the 60 percent increase in tourism in Turkey that

Figure 3-3 Hoteldom's international character is well illustrated in Zimbabwe's new Harare Sheraton Hoted. Built with Zimbabwe government funds at a cost of $80 million, the hotel was constructed by a Yugoslav company and is managed by the Boston-based Sheraton Corporation. The 360-room hotel, which is finished in metallic gold, adjoins a 4,500-seat ultramodern convention center. Costs exceeded $200,000 a room, difficult to justify in a country as poor as Zimbabwe.

year. The Caribe Hilton is said to have been one of the great profitmakers after the casino hotels in the continental U.S.

In many countries, the American-managed hotel was the only hotel of any consequence, and it is almost always the newest, the biggest, and the best in the country (see Fig. 3-3). For example, in Caracas, the capital of Venezuela, the leading hotels are the Tamanaco and the Hilton. Before their construction, there was only one first-class hotel in the city, the Avila, and this was a Rockefeller hotel. There are only a few first-class hotels in Panama, one of which has been managed at different times by Hilton and IHC. Some of the developing nations have but one first-class hotel in the entire country; some have none.

American management abroad does not mean any considerable number of U.S. hotel management personnel abroad. In most countries, an agreement is reached between the management company and the local government to restrict the number of Americans employed. Except for a few top-level personnel, the rest must be nationals. In Mexico, for example, only foreigners with special skills unavailable in that country can obtain work permits, and even then arrangements must be made to train nationals within three years.

However, the few U.S. personnel are enough to install American business enterprise and methods and, most important, American marketing methods. Nearly all the American-managed hotels abroad are impressive, large, and beautifully designed. The local country usually sees them as a symbol of national prestige and builds accordingly.

INDUSTRY ANALYSES

In 1931 the accounting firm of Horwath & Horwath (later to become Laventhol & Horwath) began publishing annual studies. In 1936 Harris Kerr Forster & Company (later to become Pannell Kerr Forster) published its first study of the operating results for 100 hotels. Each year since then similar studies have been done by the firms, and they grow more comprehensive with time.

The annual studies and other publications of these two international firms helped to standardize accounting and control practices in the hotels of this country and the world.

The need for a uniform system of accounting that would provide guidelines for financial reporting and allow for comparison of operating results between hotels was first officially recognized in 1926. A group of hotel owners and accountants formed an accountants committee and prepared the *Uniform System of Accounts for Hotels*. The eighth revision of that book appeared in 1985. Revised editions appear about every 10 years.

Another result of the committee's work was the organization of the Hotel Accountants Association of New York City, which also became the founding chapter of what is now the International Association of Hospitality Accountants (IAHA).

Hotel accounting has to do with the collection, classification, and analysis of financial information, to be used in managerial decision making. Accounting and control are two sides of the same coin. Control is impossible without accounting. Forecasting revenues and budgeting are also based on information processed via accounting. Sizable hotels and motels have an accounting department headed by a controller (sometimes called a comptroller).

Unfortunately, Laventhol & Horwath went out of business in 1991, but some of its partners established a new firm. PKF Consulting publishes an annual survey of hotel trends around the world represented by 1,900 properties.

THE AMERICAN HOTEL & MOTEL ASSOCIATION (AH&MA)

The AH&MA is a federation of over 70 lodging associations in the U.S. and 33 foreign countries. More than 8800 lodging facilities around the world are members, representing over 1.25 million rooms. Membership in one of the various state lodging associations automatically confers membership.

The association had its origins in 1919, when hoteliers banded together for fraternity and mutual benefit as the American Hotel Association. As late as the 1930s and beyond, it did not accept the motel business burgeoning in this country. Today, however, the AH&MA provides membership services for every type of lodging operation,

including condominiums. The most active members are, still, generally associated with hotels.

The AH&MA Educational Institute, headquartered in East Lansing, Michigan, offers courses, seminars, and publications to improve the professionalism of hotel employees and those oriented toward a hotel career.

Published quarterly, the *Business Travel Planner* is the official lodging directory of the AH&MA which is headquartered in Washington, D.C. The publication includes hotel listings, room counts, fax numbers, and locations. Corporate and government rate availability and credit card acceptance information are included. General information covers such items as per diem guidelines, frequent guest/flyer awards, metropolitan area maps, and 800 numbers.

THE GUEST

Who stays at a hotel or motel? The answer varies according to the location, rate structure, and particular establishment's image. A number of studies have been completed in an attempt to identify the typical hotel and motel guest. One of the more recent of these brought out some interesting facts. Among them were the following.

Tourists make up about one-third of the typical hotel's business. Specialized staff have been added to larger hotels to work with tour groups. The Los Angeles Hilton, for example, has six employees assigned solely to this task. Conference participants seem to grow in number each year; they comprise nearly one-fifth of the typical hotel's house count. Government officials add up to about 5 percent of total guest registration.

The mainstay of the hotel, however, continues to be the business traveler. In the U.S. as a whole, the business traveler comprises 40 percent of the average hotel's occupancy. In some hotels, it is as high as 80 to 90 percent of the total registration.[12]

According to an AH&MA poll of travelers stopping at major hotel and motel chains, the most important factors bearing on the selection of a chain hotel or motel were cleanliness, reasonable prices, and comfort.[13] The most important

12. *Worldwide Lodging Industry* (1981).
13. *The American Hotel and Motel Association News* (July 1969).

reasons for selecting a hotel for the first time were location, convenience, rates, appearance and cleanliness, and recommendations by others, in that order. A different method of questioning and different questions might have brought out such other factors as prestige, the effect of advertising, and so on.

Several surveys have shown the conventioneer to be the biggest per-day spender, followed by the businessperson and the person traveling for pleasure. This is easy to understand when this question is asked: "Who is paying—the individual traveling or someone else?"

Broadly speaking, hotel guests fall into two groups: travelers for business purposes and those traveling for pleasure. A Hotel & Travel Index 1990 U.S. Hotel Guest Study gave this breakdown of travelers who stayed in hotels:

Personal and leisure   56 percent

Business travel   44 percent

Cutbacks in travel budgets by major corporations have reduced business travel and forced hotel marketers to increase their efforts to attract leisure travelers. Of the total business stays, 38 percent resulted from conferences and conventions. Of all stays including both business and leisure, conferences and meetings represented 17 percent of the total.

Of the leisure travel, weekend escapes accounted for 11 percent, visits to friends and relatives for 10 percent, and vacation travel for 25 percent. Couples represented 46 percent of all hotel stays; lone men 32 percent and lone women 22 percent.[14]

What about the number of international visitors who stay at hotels? Horwath & Horwath International reports that almost 21 percent of guests at North American resorts are foreign visitors. At city center hotels, the figure is 19.5 percent. International travelers overall account for 16.8 percent of hotels' business.[15]

Each hotel has, or should have, its own target markets, markets that change over time or can be changed if a hotel repositions itself in the public mind. One chain identified its typical guest as a 44-year-old male with a median income of $51,600. He traveled by air, rented a car, and spent 4.9 room nights per month in hotels. Either he was self-employed, a salesman, or a white-collar professional.[16]

Hotel markets differ widely. 80 percent of the guests at a Waikiki hotel may be "salary men" and honeymooners from Japan and 80 percent of the guests at a New York City property could be from Europe, whereas an Orlando hotel market is 100 percent pleasure travelers who are visiting Disney World. Some hotels cater to tour groups and some to conventioneers, while others depend largely on the highway traveler who takes only the recommendations published in American Automobile Association guidebooks. Hotels close to a convention center may get 80 percent of their business through the center. Resort hotels usually have both social and group business; the mix between the two varies according to the season.

Common Guest Complaints

The most common complaints relate to poor employee attitude, more so in this country than abroad. A Consumer Perception Study of the American Hotel Industry, conducted by Citicorp Diners Club, asked Diners Club cardholders to name their three biggest complaints about U.S. hospitality establishments. Of the responses, "poor employee attitude" topped the list. "Rooms not ready" was number two, followed by "No record of reservation."

An American Express survey showed that a supposedly guaranteed reservation was not honored for over one-quarter of their members. At least half of those said they would not stay at the hotel involved again. Hotel managers explain that a large percentage of people making reservations are no-shows. The Regency-Hyatt House of Atlanta reported that 18 of every 100 persons making reservations there do not show up. Naturally, hotels overbook—typically by 15 percent, especially if they can direct the overflow elsewhere. Once in a while, almost everyone appears "and you're in a bucket."

Another explanation is that many guests overstay their scheduled visits and later reserva-

14. Reported in Somerset R. Waters, Travel Industry World Yearbook—1991 (New York: Childs & Waters, Inc.), 1991.
15. Hotels (June 1990).

16. J.J. Vallen and G.K. Vallen, Check-In Check-Out (Dubuque, Iowa: William C. Brown), 1991.

tions sometimes cannot be accommodated. Miami hoteliers complained that this often happened when a cold snap up North spurred patrons to linger a while longer. The hotel manager tries to ease the overstayers out, sometimes by locking them out of their room.

Another guest complaint related to high prices. One patron said he was charged a high price at a new hotel and found his room so small, "I had to go out in the corridor to change my mind." Hotels often either tried to raise their quoted prices when conventioneers started showing up or put them in the worst rooms.

Travelers were generally displeased with slip-ups by inexperienced personnel. One said that telephone operators at a major hotel in Los Angeles had on three occasions told people calling for him that the hotel had never heard of him and that he was not registered. In fact, he was a convention manager of a medical organization and had been in the hotel for three days.

Complaints about banquet foodservice are common but understandable, since many banquet waiters are moonlighting postal workers, taxi drivers, police officers, and the like sent over for the evening by the union, with little or no interest in, or knowledge of, proper table service.

Guests mention convenience of location as a prime reason for staying at a hotel/motel for the first time. Repeat guests, on the other hand, place cleanliness and appearance in first place. Service holds a strong second place; the overwhelming reason for going elsewhere was its lack. Another major offender was the "don't-give-a-damn" front office treatment; so was inadequately made-up guest rooms.

GROUP SALES

"The Americans of all ages, all conditions, and all dispositions constantly form associations." The Frenchman Alexis de Tocqueville, a widely quoted commentator on the American scene, made this remark in 1831. The judgment is as valid today as it was then.

The real impact of group business did not hit U.S. hotels until the 1950s. By the late 1960s, most of the large downtown hotels were getting at least 40 percent of their business from conventions and corporate meetings. Some hotels receive as much

as 90 percent. The ease of travel and its tax deductions for business purposes make it easy for Americans to express their desire to get together with others or exchange information, look for a new job, buy new merchandise for their businesses, and have fun doing it.

Although more and more manufactured goods can be produced by fewer and fewer people, the number of persons engaged in management, finance, sales, higher education, and a variety of technical positions has grown steadily. Sales meetings, conferences, technical seminars, training sessions, and educational meetings have made Americans "the meetingest people in the world."

We have a special eagerness to exchange information and pass on, even to our competitors, ideas that in other countries are retained entirely for the benefit of the person who has them.

In 1989 some 93.7 million Americans attended about 1.07 million meetings and conventions and spent $39.59 billion in the process. Close to 60 percent were delegates to corporate meetings. Convention attendance totaled 13.59 million. Association meetings accounted for 21.72 million attendees. The big spenders were those attending association meetings. Although the number of association meetings represented only 1 percent of all meetings, the expenditures constituted 38 percent of all meeting expenditures. The average delegate to an association meeting spent $967 per convention. Little wonder hotel managers are eager to attract conventions.[17]

Group markets are the lifeblood of larger hotels and resorts and may account for half or more of sales. Marketing directors block off large numbers of rooms for group sales, depending on forecasts of transient or social guest occupancy. Group sales fill in nicely during off and shoulder seasons.

Since the mid-1960s, most new large hotels, including resorts and casino properties, were designed and built to accommodate group business. Large banquet facilities, escalators, and fast elevators are needed to expedite the passage of hundreds of convention guests from one area to another. The New York Hilton that opened in

17. Reported in Somerset R. Waters, *Travel Industry World Yearbook—1991* (New York: Childs & Waters, Inc.), 1991.

1963 was one of the first hotels especially designed as a convention hotel.

To service the sometimes thousands of conventioneers, everything possible is done to facilitate their reservations, rooms, food and beverage service, and often entertainment. Convention guests are often preregistered, and a group and convention coordinator is assigned to "live" with the group while they are in the hotel, seeing to it that functions occur on schedule, billings to the group are made correctly, and complaints are handled at once.

Convention properties necessarily work closely with convention centers and visitor bureaus. When thousands of conventioneers converge on a destination, hotel bookings are coordinated through a convention center and/or visitors' bureau. Visitors' bureaus often assist with personnel in the registration for meetings and entertainment.

For large hotels, those of about 300 or more rooms, the target markets fall into these major categories:

Business and corporate groups

Tour and travel, domestic and international

International and incentive groups

Meetings and convention groups

Business and Corporate Sales

Hotels catering to the business and corporate markets tend to provide at least some suites that will appeal to top-level executives or can be used as hospitality suites for corporate entertainment, public relations, and sales. These hotels are likely to include a health club in their facilities, including an exercise room and sauna.

Tour Groups

Every large hotel has a marketing department headed by a director of sales, regional salespersons, and often a director of conventions and tours.

Some hotels specifically go after tour groups and employ a tour director, who solicits such business and coordinates groups after they have arrived at the hotel.

Some of the larger hotels employ a director of public relations, who works with or is part of the marketing department. That person may be assigned in-house advertising and work with an outside advertising agency as well. Special promotions, such as those for holidays, can be part of the job. The public relations person may prepare routine letters of response to guest complaints for the manager's signature, conduct tours of the hotel, and work with photographers and travel writers.

Incentive Groups and Trade Shows

Group meetings for salespeople are likely to be a combination of entertainment and sales pitch. Philco-Ford charters 30 jets to carry 5000 appliance and electronic dealers and their spouses to such places as Puerto Rico, Hawaii, Las Vegas, and Paradise Island in the Bahamas. Entertainment may cost as much as $300,000 for the group. A resort hotel like the Princess in Acapulco can rely on groups for more than half of its sales.

Trade shows and exhibitions are closely related to the convention business. Many trade associations make the bulk of their income from such shows held each year. The National Restaurant Association receives much of its budget from this source.

Conventions

Conventioneering means big money to hotels. Some national gatherings are attended by as many as 100,000 delegates—enough to fill rooms for miles around. What makes conventions even more interesting to hotel managers is that they can often be scheduled to fill low-occupancy periods, weekends, and off seasons. Also, once a convention has checked in, the majority of the guests take most of their meals in the hotel.

Much of the convention business has quietly merged into the vacation business. The executive going to a business meeting has his or her expenses paid. The independent businessperson's spouse may be an officer in the company; both travel to a meeting as a business expense, which is tax deductible. The small extra cost for double occupancy makes the trip for both relatively inexpensive.

With group airfares, today's convention is likely to be a family affair. Spouses accompany over half of the conventioneers to New York City and about 75 percent of those who go to Florida.

The top cities for conventions, meetings, and exhibitions in 1989 were:[18]

1.	New York	2,934,000
2.	Dallas	2,472,644
3.	Chicago	2,273,763
4.	Atlanta	1,800,792
5.	Orlando	1,675,681
6.	Las Vegas	1,508,842
7.	New Orleans	1,314,000
8.	Washington, D.C.	1,248,973
9.	San Francisco	1,204,000
10.	Anaheim	1,062,000

The U.S. competes with the Caribbean, Canada, Mexico, and Europe for the convention trade and incentive travel.

Convention service organizations. Convention business has grown to such an extent that several organizations to serve conventions have been established. They handle many of the details of a convention other than lodging or events that take place within the hotel. The people who work behind the scenes to see that everything runs smoothly provide practical services—transportation, tours, activities for traveling companions, delegate registration—and in general arrange for free-time activities. These personnel are often dressed in distinctive costume for better recognition. In Los Angeles, for example, some 700,000 people attend conventions and spend close to $300 million a year. A sizable portion of that money goes to convention planning services. Disneyland, Beverly Hills, and golf or tennis tournaments are part of the arrangements. Some companies are geared to the "incentive market," those visitors being sent by their companies.

One convention company alone hires some 70 part-time tour guides and staff members; they obtain tickets for theatrical or sporting events, set up sightseeing tours, and arrange special parties. Some of the convention service companies have an office within a leading hotel and work closely with that hotel's personnel. Many large corporations have their own convention planning staffs.

Convention centers and visitors' bureaus. Attracting conventions is a specialized business; to further it, some 330 towns and cities have set up specialized convention and visitors' bureaus. Competition for business is keen. In Southern California, convention bureaus in Palm Springs, Anaheim, Los Angeles, Long Beach, and San Diego often vie to serve the same groups. Bureau budgets can exceed $1 million a year. Funding for conventions and visitors often comes from a tax on hotel rooms, typically 6 percent. The Las Vegas bureau's budget of $13 million a year is generated by such a tax. Of the 60 principal convention centers, reports show that most have operated at a financial loss that was offset by public funds—local, state, or federal.

The bureaus' primary purpose is attracting visitors to the area they represent. Those from large cities with several thousand guest rooms compete for the large conventions and meetings: groups from such professions as teaching, medicine, and law; governmental groups such as city councilmen or tax collectors; trade groups such as plumbers or junk dealers; and union groups. Political conventions, especially on the national level, bring thousands of visitors to an area.

Convention bureaus often act as housing bureaus and assume complete responsibility for accommodating a large group, allocating rooms among various properties in a given area. A bureau may also manage a convention center and sell exhibit space, arrange for registration and side trips, provide for buses between hotels and the center, help with the news releases, and work with the media of the area.

Within a bureau, such as the Anaheim Convention and Visitors' Bureau, a number of salespersons are employed, each responsible for up to 1000 groups. A large convention bureau often may employ 30 to 60 persons full-time and double that number part-time. They keep files with information on meeting dates, names of association executives, and other information of value in soliciting groups to come to an area. Convention bureau work is closely related to hotel sales work and calls for alertness, a pleasant personality, and the ability to relate easily to association executives. The work can be highly rewarding financially and otherwise and offer a more stable career than hotel management.

Cities that at one time were not considered convention towns have gotten into the act. About

---

18. Business Travel News, 1990.

200 towns and cities in the U.S. have built convention centers.

Other large convention cities are Chicago, New York City, Anaheim, Las Vegas, Los Angeles, San Francisco, San Diego, Dallas, Atlanta, Honolulu, Detroit, Houston, New Orleans, Denver, and Washington, D.C. The top states in convention activity are California, Texas, Florida, New York, and Illinois, in that order.

In-hotel convention management. Within the hotel, the sales department personnel have the responsibility for not only attracting a convention, but also seeing to it that the convention runs smoothly once it has checked in. This is a full-time job for at least one person, and in the large hotels it requires several people. Within a large hotel there may be a director of sales, three more national sales managers, and a director of tours and conventions. The latter person is first-line liaison between a group and the hotel, seeing to it that all functions move as planned and all facilities and services within the hotel work to satisfy the group guests.

Rooms assigned to the officers of a large convention are often compliments of the hotel; sometimes meeting rooms also are made available without charge. The convention group can then rent to purveyors and others as it wishes.

Chain hotels and conventions. A sizable part of the convention business is controlled by the larger chains, those with large hotels in the principal cities. Hilton, Hyatt, Ramada, Loews, Sheraton, and a few of the other larger chains can afford a big convention sales staff—specialists whose principal business it is to cultivate and sell key people in the large national associations.

Some of the large national groups, such as the National Education Association and the American Medical Association, plan their conventions at least five years in advance, sometimes even earlier; the American Chemical Society selects its convention sites 10 years in advance. Most of these associations move the annual meeting from place to place to equalize travel distance for members from all parts of the country. A change of place also adds interest and fun to the national meeting. Some go out of the country to Canada, Mexico, or the Caribbean.

Only the larger chains have the budgets necessary to make and continue the contacts needed to influence the location decisions of these associations. It should be pointed out that the very large hotels that can accommodate large national groups are mostly managed by the chains; because this is so, the chains are not competing with the smaller or independent hotels as much as they are with each other.

With careful development many seasonal hotels can fill their low spots and extend their seasons with group and convention business.

Once booked, groups and conventions hold to the convention date, regardless of the weather. The convention segment itself, however, is somewhat seasonal, depending on location. For the country as a whole, the high months for major conventions are March through November. December through February are low months. Any one property, however, may experience a different pattern. Conference centers that cater to educational meetings have another pattern: low periods around major holiday periods and a low August. The usual problem is low weekend occupancy, so an effort is made to convince groups to start their meetings on Saturday or Sunday.

Management can draw an occupancy curve showing expected occupancy and then push for filling the valleys with group and convention business. The shaded area in Figure 3-3, drawn for a particular hotel, shows those periods where the major sales effort should be focused on such sales.

HOTEL OCCUPANCY

Following World War I, the hotel business boomed. In 1920 hotel occupancy peaked at 85 percent. Then, even as numerous hotels were built, occupancy fell off through the 1920s. With the beginning of the Great Depression in 1929, occupancy dropped sharply and bottomed out at 51 percent during 1932 and 1933. Chicago commercial hotels had a 35 percent occupancy rate in 1932. It was said that some 80 percent of the hotels were in receivership.

With the National Recovery Act, business and occupancy rates picked up gradually through the rest of the 1930s (Fig. 3-4). America's entrance into World War II in 1941 brought a surge in business that prevailed through the war years—hotel occupancy peaked in 1946 at 93 percent. The figure for that year has never been topped. After 1946, occupancy trailed downward year after year to 60 percent in 1963. Another low, 54 percent, was reached in 1971. Since then, occupancy climbed gradually to about 69 percent, but then declined to about 62 percent in 1990.

The hotel occupancy figures are merely suggestive of what happened in the hotel business. Those percentage numbers, with their lows and highs, are also about the rise and fall of the well-being of thousands of hotel employees and investors. Highway hotels/motels were also dealt a severe blow during the 1974 OPEC oil embargo; because of its five-fold increase in gasoline prices, road travel dropped drastically.

These numbers point to a central fact of American business: It never goes up continuously. Individual hotels, even cities, can prosper mightily, other hotels and whole areas whereas fade economically.

Occupancy and room rates vary from place to place. In 1980 Philadelphia experienced a 60 percent occupancy, whereas San Francisco had an 80 percent occupancy. Within the greater Los Angeles area, occupancy rates can differ by as much as 25 percentage points from one district to another.

The annual occupancy rate, or even the weekly rate, can be very misleading. The majority of commercial transient hotels are likely to be filled Monday through Thursday night, with weekend occupancy dropping to 40 percent or less. On the other hand, resort hotels near cities usually fill up on weekends. A beach resort hotel in a warm climate may be filled around Christmas and again from about January 15 to March 15. But then the "shoulder" periods, early spring and early fall, can evidence very low occupancy rates, with a summer season somewhere in between. Any one hotel has a different weekly, monthly, and annual occupancy rate; averaged out, it may seem misleadingly low. Figure 3-5 shows typical variation in monthly occupancy.

Room Rates

National average room rates are less important as an indication than the average room rate for a specific kind of hotel in a given area. For example, the national average room rate may be $60 and the national room occupancy rate 62 percent. At the same time, the average room rate in a part of a city can be $100 with a 75 percent occupancy rate. In another part of the city, the average room rate could be $45 with an occupancy of 50 percent. Three hotels sitting side by side can experience widely different occupancy and room rates, depending on the markets to which they appeal.

There is a fairly close correlation between general business activity and hotel occupancy, a more or less commonsense observation. Figure 3-6 compares the growth of the gross national product (GNP) with that of lodging sales. As said earlier, occupancy can vary greatly by region or even city. With the reduction in oil prices in the mid-1980s, Texas hotel occupancy dropped sharply because of its dependence on the oil business. At the same time, the big California cities enjoyed a boom based partly on defense spending. Other wide differences in occupancy between cities and regions have occurred over the years. By

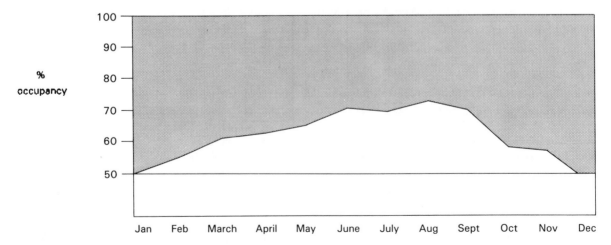

Figure 3-4 Percent occupancy for a given hotel for one year.

Figure 3-5 Percentages of occupancy 1920–1979.

Source: Adapted from Laventhol & Horwath, *U.S. Lodging Industry*, 1980. Prior to October 1927, no systematic monthly study was made of hotel business trends. The only figures available are those compiled by Horwath & Horwath in 1928, covering the years 1920–1926. They were based on the records of relatively few hotels; they did, however, include two of the largest chains of hotels existing at that time.

1987 the $200 room rate in this country and Europe was a fact in several luxury hotels. A few properties charged up to $300 a day. Today, that figure could be $400 in Paris or Tokyo. The national occupancy rate for hotels was in the middle 60s, due in part to overbuilding brought on by tax-motivated investment. Suite hotels and budget properties generally experienced higher occupancy rates than hotels and were being built in large numbers.

Overbuilding

Unfortunately, hotels take a long time to build—2 to 10 years. They tend to be planned and financed when business is good and opened when business is bad. This creates a room imbalance: too many rooms for too few customers. Excessive rooms must wait for demand to catch up. Overbuilding is also caused by decisions to build for reasons related to interest rates, urban renewal, government grants, or other financial factors unrelated to hardheaded projections of occupancy or income from operations. Land-development

schemes form a principal reason for much hotel construction, the object being to enhance the value of the surrounding property. Probably the biggest cause of overbuilding has been tax-motivated investment. Tax credits for new construction have been granted several times (later removed by Congress), and other tax deductions have spurred hotel construction often in the face of only mildly favorable occupancy projections.

One reason for hotel overbuilding was the low cost of borrowed money, which started a construction binge in the mid-1970s. Tax advantages combined with inflation, in effect, gave hotel builders an easy ride in financing new properties, in some cases at negative interest rates. In a study of 500 lending companies, Professors Avner Abel and Robert H. Woods found that hotels achieved the lowest effective financing costs among all industries. Inflation, which causes an increase in the value of real property such as hotels, helps the borrower. In periods of low inflation or deflation, the owners must rely on operational income to provide debt service. In the past, hotels were viewed as being able to increase room rates to

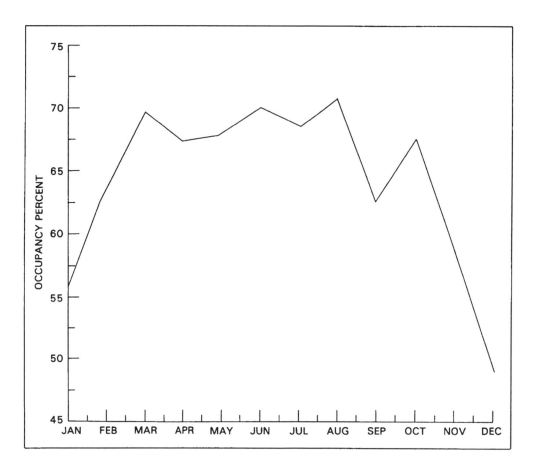

Figure 3-6 Variation in monthly occupancy for 1985. The curve varies only slightly from year to year, however. Occupancy variation has particular significance for personnel scheduling and for the employment of part-time personnel.

Source: Laventhol & Horwath, *National Lodging Trends.*

keep in step with inflation. In times of recession, both room rates and occupancies decline and hotel owners who rely on inflation or increasing room rates often find themselves in financial trouble. "The industry now is paying the cost of its free lunch by having to cope with all of the consequences of overbuilding and excess capacity—cut-throat competition, lower profitability, bankruptcies and the worst decline ever in hotel prices."[19]

HOTELS AND COMPUTERS

Today all but the smallest hotels use a computer for making reservations and for doing much or

most of their bookkeeping. Larger properties rely on a Property Management System (PMS), explained later, for performing a range of functions once done by hand. Computerization of hotels began in the late 1950s, proceeded in fits and starts until about 1985, and is now widespread. Hotel computerization continues to evolve as new programs are produced and costs continue down.

The advantages of belonging to a hotel or motel chain, franchise, or marketing system became apparent by the 1950s and 1960s. Western International Hotels (now Westin) installed a reservation system in their properties using teletype equipment in the 1950s. By the end of 1968, all of the eight largest hotel and motel groups in the country had similar reservation systems.

Sheraton Hotels introduced a centralized reservation system in 1956. Hilton Hotels, using

19. Reported in *CHRIE Communique* (Feb. 1, 1991).

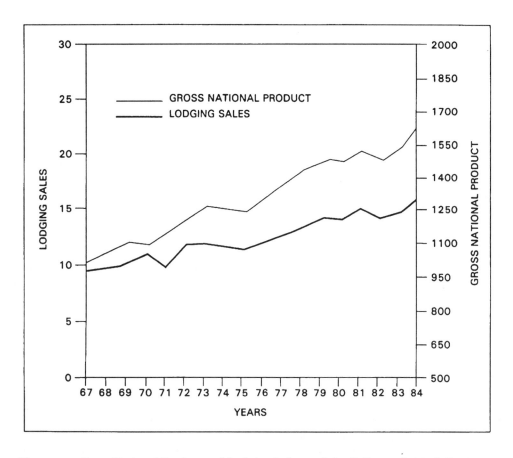

Figure 3-7 Gross National Product and Lodging Industry Sales (billions of 1972 dollars).

Source: The National Income and Product Accounts of the United States (Washington, D.C.: Bureau of Economic Analysis, U.S. Department of Commerce). Appeared in Albert J. Gomes and Pannell Kerr Forster, *Hospitality In Transition* (New York, AH & MA), 1985.

an IBM card sorting system were among the first to automate their payroll system. Seeing the success of the airlines in computerizing their reservation and other systems, a few hotels tried to follow suit. The New York Hilton hotel, in 1963 one of the largest convention properties, attempted to computerize its front office. The results were disastrous because suitable hardware (computer equipment) and software (computer programs) had not yet been developed. Other large hotels shied away for fear of having similar experiences. Cost was also a factor. As late as 1989 the cost to install a computer system in a large hotel exceeded $300,000. Vendors selling computer programs and hardware came and went. Computer breakdowns were commonplace.

Nonetheless the computer advantage was so great that hotel and motel computerization con-

tinued and was especially advantageous for the hotel chains and for chains like Holiday Inns, whose reservation systems were critical to growth. Holiday Inns developed its Holidex I, so large that at the time that it was designated a part of the strategic defensive reserve of the United States. In the 1980s computerized reservation systems using microcomputers were adopted by most hotels and motels of 50 rooms or more.

Sheraton Corporation's Reservation IV is located in Braintree, Massachusetts. It is online in 59 countries and has 15 toll-free telephone lines to Sheraton's 42 reservation centers. The system can quote six sets of single and double rates, plus tour packages and special-rate programs for groups such as corporations, retirees, teachers, students, and government, airline, and travel agency personnel. The number of rooms available in any category at a particular time can be found out easily using an inventory-depleting system.

Best Western's Star System has been made as simple as possible to operate. The system comprises several modules, all of which can be monitored through a telephone line at headquarters. If a module does not work properly, a new one is shipped to the property and can be installed by the motel operator. The Star System links the 3100 Best Western hotels in 30 countries.

Two major reservation centers—located in Phoenix, Arizona, and Winston-Salem, North Carolina—are linked to the reservation systems of five domestic and two international airlines. More than 90 percent of American travel agents are tied into one or another computer system and can book rooms in much of the world.

Hotel chain computer systems are being linked between properties, no matter where located. The Ritz-Carlton hotel chain headquartered in Atlanta, for example, requires all of its employees to carry a notepad and note guest preferences, whether it be a certain type of pillow or a particular newspaper. That information is immediately entered into the guest history database available to all Ritz-Carlton hotels. A guest may fly from the U.S. to Australia and find his or her preferences being realized at a Ritz-Carlton in Australia.

This kind of guest service is not new. The Ritz Hotel system in the early 1900s did the same thing. The necessary information arrived by mail. Now it is delivered electronically.

Among the computer applications found in mid-sized and larger hotels and incorporated in a PMS are room availability, room status, guest credit checking, accounting for guest calls (call accounting) work order status, night audit, accounts receivable, accounts payable, general ledger, payroll, profit and loss statements, personnel files, reservations, and guest history.

Point-of-sale terminals make instant accounting and information available to the front desk, for cooks and a variety of other personnel who have terminals interfacing with the PMS.

Microcomputers and off-the-shelf programs fostered the development of separate programs (e.g., one for the rooms divisions, one for reservations, and one for accounts receivable). Tying these various modules together allows them to operate as a total property management system. One module furnishes data to all of the others.

The same hardware interrelates them all into the PMS, which can be accessed instantly from any number of keyboards. Printers make hard copies of such things as guest folios (guest accounts), reservation confirmations, or spread sheets. The value of the PMS can be extended by adding modules (computer programs) as needed.

Property Management Systems

The most obvious and pressing need for hotel computers was the reservation system. Other uses became apparent and continue to grow. Dozens of computer software companies started up. Many failed. New programs (modules) became available. At first they operated as separate systems—one for reservations, one for accounts receivables, one for keeping a record of telephone calls (call accounting), and so on. As they were tied together electronically, a master system was possible, all modules tied together and communicating with each other. The PMS was born. All can be accessed from any keyboard within the total system. Additional programs can be added if the computer is large enough to handle them.

Hotel accounting and control is moving towards a paperless system, except for the need to make hard copies, such as letters and hard-copy reports. The manual room rack with metal pockets and array of room rates becomes a relic, replaced by the computer which when programmed provides the information on a cathode ray tube (video display terminal). The old National Cash Register machine, once widely used is no longer needed, accounts being posted electronically. Unpaid balances are electronically transferred to an accounts receivable (city ledger). The status of rooms, whether on change or ready for occupancy, can be called up by punching a computer keyboard.

The job of night auditor, that lonely task of posting and proving all income figures for the previous day, is being preempted by the computer.

VSAT Satellite Networks

Most reservation systems are connected using the services of AT&T and other long-distance phone companies. In 1987 Days Inns, using a small satellite dish called VSAT (standing for "very small operative terminals"), set up its own satellite network for handling reservations. Some 750 properties were linked using rooftop dishes to the central reservation headquarters in Atlanta. According to Days Inns executives, the VSAT has the advantage of using a Ku band, a frequency set aside for satellite transmission that is subject to less interference. The VSAT, they say, processes reservations four times faster than is possible using phone lines. Video conferencing, credit card verification, and in-room video entertainment can also make use of the satellite network. Holiday Corporation and other chains are planning similar systems.

800 Numbers

Hyatt Hotels offer a nationwide 800 number that enables a traveler to check in and receive a room assignment by phone. Sheraton does the same for frequent guests. Room keys may be picked up at the concierge's desk. Computer modules are available for a long list of functions, and more will be available in the future.

Point of sale of any item sold can be recorded electronically. For example, each beverage, food, or gift shop sale can be posted instantly. Guest sales information can be collected and analyzed. Advanced registration information can be analyzed and used to forecast the number of personnel needed at a particular time anywhere in the hotel. Point of sale input can be made from any number of wait stations, bars, storerooms, gift shops, spas, or any other terminal that links with the PMS system. Recipes can be stored electronically, and food and labor costs can be computed. An electronic guest history can be maintained. Computers are being used to turn off guest room air conditioning when there are no guests, turn them on when guests are roomed, and control off-on guest room door locks.

Computerization has changed hotel keeping and, as miniaturization of equipment and other advances come along, will make the job of hotel keeping easier and more sophisticated. Handheld computer terminals will be more widely used, replacing the telephone in many instances.

ANOTHER CONVENIENCE: PREREGISTRATION AND CHECKOUT

Responding to a major complaint voiced by travelers—they must wait in line to register, then wait in line again to check out—some hotel/motel chains have offered mail preregistration and checkout. The individual or group merely picks up room keys at the front desk. Tour groups' luggage is delivered to their rooms without face-to-face contact with a bellperson. On leaving, guests merely drop off their keys, and their company or credit card is billed by mail.

American Express offers its Assured Room Reservation Plan to innkeepers and cardholders. Members give their AMEX card number when making reservations, and their rooms are held until checkout time of the day after arrival date. If the card member does not arrive and does not cancel, he or she is charged for one night. If the person arrives and finds no room, the property involved must supply the individual with a free room at a comparable inn and pay for transportation there and for a phone call advising business or family of the change. The plan can help reduce the number of complaints involving overbooking if it starts an industry trend.

The latest easy checkout ties the TV in the room to a central hotel computer so that the guest can request his or her bill at any time and check out without the necessity of appearing at the front-desk cashier's station.

WRITERS AND HOTEL LIFE

Life in a hotel has interested writers and a sizable segment of the general public for centuries. Many observers saw the English inn as a place of good cheer, comfort, and a respite from the workaday world. Samuel Johnson, famous English lexicographer and author of the eighteenth century, made the widely quoted comment, "There is nothing that has been contrived by man by which so much happiness is produced as a good tavern." One can still relish steak and kidney pie in the very seat occupied by Johnson in the Cheshire Cheese Inn in London.

Modern-day writers have frequently set their plots in hotels, probably because the hotel is a natural place for things to happen, for strangers to meet, for passion to erupt; it is generally a place of excitement and ferment where deals are cut, jobs lined up, and contacts made and reinforced.

The hotel is many things, for it is life in a capsule. The place of the handshake, the quick smile, the setting for marital bliss and for illicit love. It is a place where deference can be bought, where a phone call brings food and drink. It can be a sanctuary from discouragement or a room relieved only by a TV; a place to flaunt one's ego or have it deflated; a place where a hotel employee may subtly dominate a guest or be dominated.

The hotel world is a microcosm of the larger world, compressed into a building where the hopes and fears of people can be readily observed. No wonder writers have used it as a setting for thousands of stories.

THE ELEGANT HOTEL

What makes for an elegant hotel? First and foremost, elegant people stay there. If the "right people" choose a hotel, it automatically gains status. The Brown Hotel in London is an example. Of dowdy-looking Victorian style, the place is not particularly attractive. But since bonafide aristocrats choose it, the place has genuine luster.

Next, the hotel must offer service and an abundance of service personnel. Whereas commercial and convention hotels almost always have less than one employee per room, the luxury hotel may have two and even three per room.

Americans still look to the British to define what is posh. An example is the afternoon tea, which is becoming *de rigueur* in the elegant American hotel. High tea is as much ritual as refreshment, as is what is traditionally served: cucumber and watercress sandwiches, scones with Devonshire-style cream (extra heavy with butterfat), strawberry preserves and French pastries, and tea or coffee, of course. It helps if somewhere in the background a dignified person is caressing a baby grand piano or plucking a harp.

At the elegant European hotel, the guest is usually seated while he or she registers and then is escorted to the room by an assistant manager. A porter follows, bags in hand, ready for the tip. Once the guest is ensconced in the room, a knock on the door announces the floor maid or a valet, who inquires if "the gentleman [or lady] requires his [or her] bags to be unpacked."

Guest room amenities become part of the steeplechase—which elegant hotel can come up with something a little more posh than another by way of amenities: eiderdown comforters, velour robes, scented soaps, brand-name bottled waters, sachets, shower caps, a small box of

Figure 3-8 Lobby of the Crown Center Hotel of Kansas City. This lobby contains a waterfall four stories high.

chocolates, splits of champagne, fruit, bathroom scales. Some little favor like a chocolate mint or an orchid should be placed on the pillows, especially if the hotel is in Hawaii.

The ultimate may have been reached in the penthouse suite of the Park Hyatt, Chicago: 13 telephones, five TVs, 14 bedside switches in the master bedroom, personalized stationery, a sunken marble tub, an 1898 Steinway piano, and an open bar with a butler completes the package.

Turndown service is a must at the elegant hotel. The maid (not the "room cleaner") taps discreetly on the door and, if invited in, turns down the covers at the top of the bed.

Posh hotels almost invariably come equipped with a team of concierges, those urbane ladies or gentlemen who can arrange almost anything a guest desires: a tuxedo, seat at the opera, or plane reservation. The concierge at the Imperial Hotel in Vienna will get you into the Spanish

Figure 3-9 Plaza Hotel seen from the vantage point of the picturesque duck pond in Central Park, directly across from the hotel on 59th Street in New York City. Considered by many to be the queen of hotels, the Plaza displays no sign. It is said that if a patron does not recognize the Plaza, he should not be going there. This has changed, no doubt, since the hotel was purchased by Donald Trump, the New York real estate tycoon.

Riding School. In Rome the concierge may get you an audience with the Pope or a seat for a sold-out performance of *Tosca*. In Dallas it may be a seat on the 50-yard line for a Cowboys' football game. In New York the concierge can arrange to have a guest greeted by the maitre d' of a famous restaurant and the bill sent to the hotel. In Paris the concierge may arrange a complete trip around the continent. The European concierge can be recognized by the golden crossed keys, *clefs d'or*, emblem of the concierge association on his lapel.

Some Examples

Robert Morley, the well-known British actor, declared the greatest hotel in the world to be the Ritz in Paris. There, the guest is a guest, and nobody forgets it for a single moment. Morley did not care for hotels that conserve space, likening them to batteries for hens. He hated to be attacked by the fast-moving doors of modern elevators. Too bad; slow-moving elevator doors mean slow elevators.

Morley graciously included an American hotel, the Century Plaza of Beverely Hills, in his list of greats. Designed by Minoru Yamasaki, the hotel is part of a "city within a city—a place to work, to live, to shop, and to participate in leisure activities." The hotel has 800 rooms, including 67 suites with private balconies and lanai. It has the largest hotel ballroom on the West Coast, seating up to 3000.

Aside from Morley's list, one of the great hotels of the world is the Caneel Bay Plantation in the U.S. Virgin Islands. Las Brisas in Mexico is architecturally unique. Built up the side of a small mountain, it has 200 villas with private pools. The Acapulco Princess, part of the Princess chain headquartered in New York City, is one of the most beautiful highrise resorts ever built. With 770 rooms, it employs about 1500 people, 70 alone to keep its magnificent landscaping and plants beautiful. Twenty flower-bedecked floors center on a breeze-swept patio. The floors are stepped to resemble a Mayan temple.

Many a person's secret desire is to run a small hotel like the 16 antique-filled rooms of the Mansion in San Francisco. Robert C. Pritikin, the owner, has tried to create an Edwardian fantasy world in his Queen Anne–style building, which was built by a Gold Rush millionaire. The owner, dressed in striped trousers, greets guests at the door and escorts them into the parlor for a glass of chablis while taped strains of Bach play. Breakfast is served in bed: coffee, orange juice, warm croissants, butter, and strawberry jam.

The ultimate in personal service can be found in the Orient. At some of the traditional Japanese inns called the *ryokan*, the guest is greeted by a woman in a kimono, bowing and on her hands and knees. Shortly after arrival, a chambermaid brings tea. Later there is the bath, the temperature at 99 degrees for foreigners, 104 for Japanese. At 6:00 PM or so, the chambermaid arrives with dinner, an array of small dishes artistically presented. Extensive dossiers are kept on repeat customers: favorite dishes, favorite types of pillows, and favorite chambermaids. At the best of the ryokan, each guest room has a private garden. There are no beds. (Not every guest, including many Japanese, likes to sleep on the floor, as is the custom.)

The Room Service

Some luxury hotels go all out for room service. Table tents are placed in every guest room. A few hotels advertise room service on commercial TV. Most popular of all breakfasts, of course, is the continental breakfast—a choice of juice, beverage, and breads. At the medium-priced property, room service comes via a tray. In the luxury hotels, it is wheeled in on a cart that becomes a table and is covered with fine linen. Coffee is served from a heated pot. Marmalades and berry preserves are offered in individual jars. Boiled eggs may be served in egg holders. The silver is spotless and the meal an experience.

At a few hotels, the room-service order taker keeps a guest list so the guest can immediately be addressed by name. In the posher places, each floor may be equipped with its own pantry, manned round the clock. Room-service waiters become stewards, able to appear quickly at the door of the guest room after being summoned by a special room-service button.

Feelings about room service vary among general managers. Those at Holiday Inns may offer it on a limited-hour basis and only as a necessity; they prefer guests to eat in their dining rooms. Some luxury hotel operators charge high prices, offer service around the clock, and make a profit in doing so. A few hotels have a separate room-service department; most operate as an adjunct of the main kitchen.

Prestige

The prestige of a hotel's clientele determines its overall rating. The Claridge of London gets high points for exclusivity, as do the Paris Ritz and the Beverly Wilshire in Beverly Hills, California.

The posh hotel should be ready to deal with any occasion. At Claridge's in London, it is told that one evening an elderly, titled lady marched out of the lift on her way to an important dinner, dressed only in her jewelry. She had simply forgotten to put any clothes on, a mistake that was instantly rectified by the manager. He at once stepped forward, covered the lady with his own coat, and accompanied her back into the lift as though nothing had happened.[20] The hotel ran into another problem when two kings arrived, both intent on staying in the Royal Suite. The solution: The manager ordered workmen to pull down half the ceiling in the Royal Suite, showed the unfortunate damage to the officials of both countries in question, and arranged for two smaller "royal suites" immediately. The Claridge, incidentally, is not much to look at from the outside. Nevertheless, it arranges for no fewer than six waiters, six chambermaids, two valets, a house porter, and three bathroom cleaners to be ready at the ring of the appropriate bell to come springing along the corridor to administer to the guest's slightest need. Even a simple whisky and soda arrives on a trolley covered with a white linen tablecloth, together with "crisps," black and green olives, and hot salted almonds. That hotel is also one of a very few with a number of courier rooms set aside for the personal servants of guests.

Good press must be maintained if a hotel is to be recognized for its name and greatness. Of course, the greater the prestige of the evaluator, the better for the hotel. César Ritz could do no wrong after the Prince of Wales, later Edward VII, was quoted as saying, "Where Ritz goes, I go."

The Paris Ritz, one of the best-known prestige hotels in the world as well as one of the most expensive, makes very little profit.[21] The Ritz philosophy of hotel operation places profit secondary to maintaining standards and service. According to Bernard Penche, general manager of the Paris Ritz, César Ritz's only interest in making money was to enable him to make more and better hotels, offering the ultimate in comfort and the best staff available, "to maintain the atmosphere of a private home" in the hotel. The Ritz offers 24-hour room service. All calls are placed through a switchboard, since dialing would constitute a "decrease in personal service." In 1980 the Ritz was taken over by a Middle Eastern investment group.

---

20. Christopher Matthew, *A Different World* (London, England: Paddington Press), 1976.
21. *Wall Street Journal* (Sept. 14, 1947).

HOTEL RATING SYSTEMS

Millions of travelers rely on hotel rating systems to provide information about location, price, facilities offered and level of service to expect. For the hotel and restaurant operator a favorable write-up and rating means thousands of dollars in added revenues; an unfavorable rating equates to a sharp drop in customer count. The loss of a star and a diamond can mean a loss of a million dollars or more in revenue for a well-established five-star and five-diamond resort.

In the U.S. two hotel rating systems stand out and are widely followed: the American Automobile Association Tour Book and the Mobil Travel Guide. Both grade hotels and restaurants in five categories. The AAA Tour Book is given free on request to its 30 million members. The book is published in 25 regional editions. AAA accepts

Figure 3-10 The Waldorf-Astoria is probably the best-known hotel in the world. It was completed in 1931 and carries the name of the older, now demolished Waldorf-Astoria, built in the 1890s.

TABLE 3-3   Salient Public Lodging Facts

Number of hotels and motels in U.S.: 44,300

Number of employees: about 1.5 million full- and part-time

Number of guest rooms: 3 million

Number of guest rooms per 100 U.S. residents: About 4.83

Annual gross revenues of hotels and motels: $57 billion

Gross revenues of hotels and motels as percent of Gross National Product: about 1.1

Food & beverage revenues as percentage of total hotel and motel revenue: about 32 percent

Kinds of hotels and motels: motels, motor hotels, commercial/transient hotels, residential hotels, all-suites, convention hotels, rental condos, conference centers, resorts

Kinds of lodging management operations:

  Independent

  Independent/marketing referral affiliation

  Independent/franchise

  Management contract

  Lease/management

  Chain ownership/operator

  Time-share

advertising but does not make it a condition for being rated.

The Mobil Travel Guide has seven regional editions. It is published by Rand McNally and can be bought at bookstores. Both guides contain an enormous amount of information: where to stay, to eat and geography, history and places of interest. Neither book has any governmental oversight or affiliation. Both books employ inspectors who visit the properties rated. Seen below are the criteria for achieving a 5-Star rating in the Mobil Travel Guide:

"The few five-star awards go to those places which go beyond comfort and service to deserve the description 'one of the best in the country'. A superior restaurant is required, although it may not be rated as highly as the hotel or motel. Twice-daily maid service is standard in these establishments. Lobbies will be places of beauty, often furnished in fine antiques. If there are grounds surrounding the building, they will be meticulously groomed and landscaped. Each guest will be made to feel that he or she is a Very Important Person to the employees."[22]

Although Mobil evaluates some 20,000 properties each year, only two to three dozen get the coveted five-Star rating.

Overseas many countries have set up required rating systems. The validity of the systems vary and in some countries the use of "luxury" and "deluxe" are used too freely.

In Europe four and five-star hotels always have restaurants. Two-star properties almost never do. "Garni" means that no restaurant is available but a continental breakfast is served. In England, "hotel garni" is the American version of bed-and-breakfast.

Guest Behavior

How guests behave relates to what they want. A Holiday Inn Corporation study of their guests revealed some interesting information.

Five percent of salesmen take baths.

Ninety-five percent of all guests take a shower.

The average guest spends two hours in the room when he or she is not asleep.

Ninety-two percent of all guests watch TV an average of one hour each night.

Forty percent ask for a wakeup call.

The vast majority, 81 percent, have made reservations.

22. Jerome J. Vallen and Gary K. Vallen, *Check-In   Check-Out*, (Dubuque, Iowa: Wm. C. Brown Publishers), 1991.

TABLE 3-4   Chronology of Hotel/Motelkeeping, 1900–1985

1900.	Statler builds the Inside Inn, a temporary hotel for the St. Louis World's Fair with 2,257 rooms, largest building of the time. The hamburger as Americans know it is introduced at the same fair.
1907.	Buffalo Statler opens. Each of the 300 rooms has a bathroom: "A room and a bath for a dollar and a half." The name changes to the Buffalo Hotel when a new Buffalo Statler is built in 1923. Some Statler firsts:
	Access plumbing shafts that serve two bathrooms and run from first floor to top floor
	Posting of room rates
	Built-in free radios
	Free newspaper under the door each morning
	Circulating ice water in guest rooms
	"Servidors" that eliminate tipping for cleaning and pressing service
	Free stationery for all guests
	Mail chutes connecting all floors.
1907.	The Plaza on Central Park in New York City opens for the elite. Pincushions and room telephones are provided in each of the 1000 rooms.
1910.	American Hotel Protective Association of the United States and Canada incorporated in Illinois. Forerunner of the American Hotel and Motel Association.
1912.	McAlpin opens in New York City, 1700 rooms, 25 stories. "World's largest."
1913.	Miami Beach is reached by causeway from Miami.
1918.	Pitco fry kettle marketed.
1919.	National restaurant and hotel associations take on their present form. Frank Lloyd Wright electrifies a hotel kitchen, The Imperial Hotel in Tokyo. Hotel Pennsylvania opens, 2200 rooms. "World's largest."
1920s.	The "drive-in" and "motel" appear on the edge of town.
1921.	The Pig Stand outside Dallas becomes one of the first drive-in restaurants. Child's becomes the largest restaurant chain. White Castle, the first hamburger chain, opens.
1922.	Cornell University offers the first degree in hotel administration.
1925.	*Hotel Management* by Lucius Boomer appears. First substantial book on hotel management.
1926.	First motel in San Luis Obispo, California, opens. First fastfood franchise, A&W in California.
	First U.S. commercial airline, Western Airlines, carries about 300 passengers.
1928.	The Stevens Hotel, now the Conrad Hilton, is built at a cost of $35 million. John Courtney, Cornell Hotel School student, initiates the exchange of accountancy information among 50 hotels. System is picked up by Harris Kerr Forster and Horwath & Horwath, major accounting firms.
1929.	Hotel New Yorker is built: 43 stories, 2500 rooms. First airport hotels go up at Croyden, England; Templehof, Berlin; Oakland, California.
1931.	Air conditioning provided on some rail trips in the U.S.
1932.	The new Waldorf-Astoria opens and becomes best-known hotel in the world; until 1967 also the largest in cubic space—47 stories, 2150 rooms.
1940s.	Sheraton and Hilton become major chains.
1942–1945.	World War II. Number of meals eaten in restaurants climbs from 20 million to 60 million per day.
1947.	Intercontinental Hotels, a subsidiary of Pan American Airways, begins operations in Latin America and becomes first large international hotel chain.
1948.	Raytheon introduces the first microwave oven, Radarange.
1949.	Shamrock Hotel, Houston, opens. First large hotel built since early 1930s. Hilton goes international, with management contract to operate the Caribe-Hilton in Puerto Rico.

(continues)

TABLE 3-4 *(continued)*

1950s.	Howard Johnson demonstrates profitability of large-scale commissary and long-distance distribution of frozen foods. Convention business grows in importance. Many hotels become convention-oriented. Beginning of computer application in hotels and restaurants. Beginning of the travel and entertainment credit-card boom. Large hotels develop specialty restaurants (HCA, later Sheraton, Hilton, and others). Large motor hotels built by hundreds, older hotels razed. Number of hotels declines but number of hotel rooms increases.
1952.	Holiday Inns, a marriage of hotel and motel, opens in Memphis, Tennessee. Franchising plans become popular for motels and restaurants.
1958.	The Boeing 707 jet airplane began transatlantic flights, setting the stage for rapid growth in international travel.
1954.	Federal tax law permits rapid depreciation that encourages hotel construction.
1959.	Gas-fired convection oven introduced. United States airlines begin shift to jet planes. Supreme Court rules that many hotels and restaurants are involved in interstate commerce and therefore under the jurisdiction of National Labor Relations Board.
1960s.	Era of mergers and franchising. Transportation companies enter the hotel and motel field. Cruise business takes over ocean liners—converts them to floating resort hotels.
1962.	Budget motel industry begins with Motel 6 in Santa Barbara, California.
1963.	New York Hilton tries to fully computerize—and fails.
1964.	Supreme Court ruling strengthens prohibition against racial discrimination in hotels and restaurants.
	American Airlines introduces the first computerized reservation system.
1967–1969.	The number of junior colleges offering hotel and restaurant courses of study increases from 40 to 98. Homotels, first all-suites, appear. Hotel and restaurant stocks boom. Price/earnings ratios of 35 to 50 become common.
1967.	TWA purchases Hilton International. Forty or more other airlines enter accommodations business. Federal minimum wage law applied to hotels, motels, resorts, and restaurants grossing $500,000 or more in sales annually.
1967.	Hilton permits guests to check out when they check in.
1967.	Hotel Rossiya in Moscow opens, takes over title of "World's largest," with 3182 rooms accommodating 5890 guests; can serve food to 4500 persons simultaneously. (Really three adjoining properties, each with own manager.) The Hyatt Regency of Atlanta opens and sets style for multistoried hotel lobbies—the atrium. Food manufacturers enter the restaurant business:
	Del Monte—Service Systems
	General Foods—Burger Chef
	United Fruit—A&W Root Beer
	Ogden Corporation—ABC Consolidated
	Pillsbury—Burger King
	Pet, Inc.—Schrafft's
	General Hosts—Uncle John's
1968.	Thirteen franchise food companies each have sales exceeding $50 million: Big Boy (Marriott), Burger Chef, Burger King, Castle Franchise, Denny's, Frisch's, McDonald's, Shakey's, A&W Root Beer, Howard Johnson, ITT, International House of Pancakes, Orange Julius.
1969.	About 2.5 million public guest rooms available, 270,000 public eating places. Federal minimum wage law applied to hotels, motels, resorts, and restaurants grossing $250,000 or more in sales annually. Travel to Caribbean exceeds 4 million tourists.
1970s.	Hotel management contract supplants the franchise: risk-free enterprising. Grows out of the lease— why lease when you can contract? Real Estate Investment Trusts (REITs) lend more than $1 billion for hotel and motel construction and become owners by default. In the mid-1970s a revitalization of central business districts includes new hotels, funded in part with government money. "Hotels within

(continues)

TABLE 3-4 *(continued)*

	hotels" provided by setting aside top floors with concierge and other special services at premium rates. Sharp increase in consumer and employee litigation against hotels, restaurants, and travel companies.
	AMTRAK formed to upgrade and increase efficiency of passenger rail service.
1976.	Of 20 largest hotel chains, 18 use data processing for at least part of their corporate accounting and reporting. Of the 18, 5 use outside computer services; the others have their own computer installations. Timesharing plans and right-to-use plans become popular in the vacation business. Interval ownership also popular: condominium purchasers acquire a fee interest in a unit for a week or more. Resort hotels offer the right to use a specified type of accommodation for a week or more over a period of 12 to 40 years. Condominiums built in large numbers in a number of resort destinations and rented out as hotel/apartments. The hotel guest room becomes an entertainment center; by 1981, 500,000 guest rooms provide in-room movies.
1980.	Hotels can install their own earth stations that communicate directly with satellites hovering 22,300 miles above earth and offer up to 24 hours of programming. Some 300 Holiday Inns offer teleconferencing facilities. The $100 a day rate becomes common in larger cities and in luxury resorts.
1984.	Cruising attracts 1.5 million Americans.
	Bed & breakfast operations spring up in private homes.
1985.	All-suites grow in number. The $200 room rate appears in luxury properties.
1988.	"Fantasy" resorts built in Hawaii by Japanese investors.
1989.	Boeing 747-400, with 8000-mile range permits nonstop flights between New York and Tokyo.
1990.	International travel passes the 400 million mark. A recession results in numerous restaurant failures. More than half of U.S. hotels are in financial difficulty.
1994.	MGM Grand Hotel opened in Las Vegas, the world's largest with 5005 guest rooms, and 8000 employees. (Although the number of employees will probably decrease as the hotel gets well into operation).

The Woman Guest

By 1985 up to one-third of hotel guests were unaccompanied women, mostly traveling for business reasons.[23]

Women traveling alone have probably always had certain problems revolving around sexism, amorous males, and fears for personal safety. Businesswomen claim that they are often treated like second-class citizens on planes and in restaurants. Some businesswomen get upset if a male insists on carrying their briefcase or in any way patronizes them. One female executive recalls a male executive who called her "honey;" she retaliated by calling him "sonny." Bars can be daunting, and some women travelers just do not go to bars alone. Westin Hotels teaches its bar employees to judge whether a woman is being harassed in a bar and to help "discreetly." Ramada Inns has turned its hotel lobbies into well-lighted areas with tables where a woman can feel comfortable sitting over a drink. In the matter of who pays when a woman is entertaining a man in a restaurant, Ramada Inns tells its waiters to place the dinner check halfway between the two.

To increase personal safety, a number of hotels place all single women guests on the same floor and increase the floor's security. Hilton's Lady Hilton program, introduced in 1966, included "women-only" floors, but it was later found that many women did not like this arrangement and the Hilton chain canceled the program. The Radisson Hotels provide extra security on its women-only floors, paint the rooms in pastels, and include feminine amenities such as blowdryers, skirt hangers, makeup mirrors, shampoo, and complexion soap.

Hyatt adds womens' magazines and perfumes to rooms reserved by women. Concierges contact women guests to ask if they would like reservations in the hotel's restaurants. Sheraton adds bath crystals, hand lotion, sewing packs, and cream rinse to rooms reserved by women.

23. "The Woman Traveler: A Special Report," *Lodging Hospitality*, (Dec. 1985).

Films on the right and wrong ways to deal with particular situations involving women guests are part of employee training programs in many hotel chains.

Women are reported to favor the all-suite hotels and executive floors (the concierge levels, tower rooms, regency clubs, and so on). Their focal points are the club rooms where guests can breakfast or socialize. Security is strong. The executive floors in some hotels require special keys and are staffed with receptionists or concierges.

All-suites provide two-room accommodations that permit some cooking. Many of the all-suites offer complimentary breakfast and evening cocktail receptions. The latter are nonthreatening compared to the usual cocktail lounge or bar.

Hotel operators are thinking security. Peepholes in guest rooms allow a 180-degree view of corridors. Receptionists are instructed not to call to a bellman, for example, "Take Miss Roberts to Room 510" for fear a potential intruder or thief nearby might hear the room number.

Surveys have found that women exert a strong influence in planning family leisure travel. They also appear to be the driving force behind honeymoon planning.

Table 3-3 lists salient public lodging facts and Table 3-4 is a detailed chronology of hotel/motel keeping.

Questions

1. The early hostelries of the U.S. were known as taverns, but later the name of many of them was changed to hotel. Can you explain how this came about?

2. Why have the larger city hotels been called "the palaces of the public"?

3. After about 1840 and until the 1940s, the best location for a downtown hotel was likely to be close to what?

4. How did the early American hotelkeeper compare in social status with the innkeeper of England?

5. Hotels can be classified in a number of ways—commercial or transient, resort, residential, and what other major classifications?

6. Can you name two organizations that rate hotels in this country?

7. Name five major "hotel cities."

8. Chain properties control what percentage of the total number of hotel and motel rooms in this country?

9. In the late 1940s, which hotel chain made a major commitment in Latin America and really started Americans in the international hotel business?

10. Which hotel in Puerto Rico acted as a model for large hotels in the Caribbean when it was built in 1948?

11. The Holiday Inn system has had a major impact on hotel keeping in this country. Name three factors that may account for the success of that company.

12. Observing the growth of hotels, is it safe to say that there are more hotels today than there were 30 years ago? Why or why not?

13. What does a person with the title "tours director" do in a hotel?

14. Why is it that the major hotel chains get the lion's share of the convention business?

15. Although the national occupancy may be 63 percent, does this occupancy level hold generally around the country?

16. Generally speaking, the highest hotel occupancy and lowest occupancy are experienced in which two months?

17. Travelers have complained about arriving at a hotel with reservations and finding no room available. American Express and some of the major chains are now doing something about this problem. Explain.

18. Name five "great" hotels in this country or abroad.

19. In Europe the term "deluxe hotel" is used widely. Who decides whether a hotel is in the deluxe category?

20. What factors increase the number of conventions and meetings?

21. Why is it so difficult to distinguish between a hotel and a motel?

Discussion Questions

1. Why should we care that British writers do not feel that our service is up to standard?

2. Many students studying hotel and restaurant management aspire to work abroad. Will opportunities for such work increase or decrease over the next 10 years? Identify the forces that helped determine your answer.

3. Will the bed-and-breakfast phenomenon ever become as widespread in this country as in Britain?

4. Is the cruise ship serious competition for the resort hotel?

5. How serious is time-sharing as competition to the resort hotel?

6. Comment on this statement: We'll always have either too many or too few hotel rooms.

Ralph Hitz

(1891–1940)*

Hitz does not rank with the other great hotelmen in the sense that he built an empire or left an estate. He did neither. His period in the limelight lasted only 10 years—a period when the hotel business was at its low ebb in American history. Hitz was a sales and promotion phenomenon, who was able to take ailing hotels, predict within a few dollars what their sales and profits would be, and then produce the sales he had forecast. During the 1930s, his was the largest chain of hotels, the National Hotel Company. In New York it included the New Yorker, the Lexington, and the Belmont Plaza. He had the Adolphus in Dallas, the Netherland Plaza in Cincinnati, the Nicollet in Minneapolis, the Van Cleve in Dayton, and one in Chicago.

Ralph Hitz had early struggles similar to Statler's. In his teens he ran away from home in Austria, came to the U.S., and worked at any job he could get as a busboy, waiter, and cook. He learned rapidly and at the age of 30 became manager of Cleveland's sedate Fenway Hall.

He spent $20,000, a large sum in the Depression year of 1930, to change a delicatessen into a coffee shop, which was an instant success. Against the owner's wishes, name bands were brought to the Cleveland hotel. Ice shows were also a favorite with Hitz in his New York City hotels. He saw to it that his shows and performances were well attended even if 30 to 40 percent of the guests at first night performances were "deadheads," nonpaying guests. His explanation: "Business brings business."

According to his son, Ralph Hitz, Jr., Hitz was the first to air-condition a hotel dining room. Again, a simple explanation: "People eat more when they are cool."

By 1932 he was able to sign a contract for the operation of the 1200-room Book-Cadillac Hotel (now Sheraton-Cadillac) in Detroit. It was the beginning of the National Hotel Company, which grew rapidly as word of the Hitz service and promotional skills spread.

*Information adapted from Albert J. Gomes, *Hospitality in Transitions* (New York: Pannell Kerr Forster), 1958, p. 58.

During the registration procedure, the word loved most by any guest, his or her name, was used at least three times. The bellman continued to use it. This "strange music" of one's name did not stop until the guest was cozily settled in his or her room.

First-time guests could expect even more of the red-carpet treatment: A few moments after settling down in their room, they were called by the so-called hospitality desk and a solicitous inquiry was made to see if "anything further can be done to make your stay comfortable."

Statler started the idea of slipping the daily newspaper under the guest room door, "compliments of the management." Hitz went a step further and provided a hometown newspaper for the guest (provided he came from one of the cities from which much of the hotel's business was derived).

Tall people were given rooms with seven-foot beds. Sick patrons were personally visited by the floor managers. Guests leaving on an ocean trip were sent bon voyage messages. Also, whereas most hotels were requiring guests without luggage to pay in advance, a no-luggage guest at a Hitz hotel was provided with an overnight kit containing pajamas, toothbrush, toothpaste, and, for the men, shaving gear.

Hitz hired a seven-passenger plane to salesblitz all cities of 100,000 and more in population. Everyone in his hotels was trained and expected to be a supersalesperson. Room clerks were sent out over the country for one or more months each year to pick up business and become acquainted with their customers firsthand. A Hitz employee was supposed to give his all for the hotel, and room clerks were expected to make calls within their own city during their off hours. To insure compliance, each salesperson kept a file card on each prospect and noted the time of the contact.

Selling went on all the time the guests were in the hotel. If they opened a closet door, there staring them in the face was a placard advertising one of the hotel services or a dining room. Even the mirrors in the bathroom medicine cabinets held advertisements. Should the guests settle down on the bed to listen to the radio, they were still within the masterseller's voice range; programming was interrupted at set intervals so that the hotel services might be extolled and called to the guests' attention.

Hitz is credited with being the first to develop and exploit a guest history. Before the turn of the century, Ritz sent private letters to his hotels describing the idiosyncracies and special likes and dislikes of his guests. Hitz systematically collected the information he wanted on each guest and set up a guest history department. This department, manned by a separate staff, kept guest records and followed the Hitz system of enticing a guest back to the hotel. Color signals on the record showed if there was to be no publicity, if the person was undesirable and not to be welcomed, or if the address given was questionable.

The system also kept track of each guest's birthday and wedding anniversary date, his or her credit standing, and other information of value to the hotel. It was also routine to send a letter to all first-time guests, to each guest who had stopped with the hotel 25 times, 50 times, and 100 times.

On the 50th visit, the guest received a complimentary suite. With the hundredth visit, an appropriate gift with a letter was sent; the guest became a member of the Century Club and his or her name was engraved in gold on a gift notebook. Birthday greetings and wedding anniversary felicitations went to all regular guests.

Any complaints were also recorded, and personal explanations were made by one of the hotel's traveling representatives to the guest involved. When guests returned, they would be given the same room they occupied on their previous visit—another personal touch to increase one's ego. Special credit cards for people important to the hotel were developed by Hitz management.

To insure that guest rooms were really clean and in immaculate order, a full-time room inspector went from room to room to check on everything. His inspection was in addition to the "O.K." placed on the room by the regular inspector.

Hitz demanded much from his employees, and because he was a leader and it was a time of economic depression, he got superior performance. He also paid higher wages. The prevailing wage was $85 a month for a room clerk; Hitz paid $135. His department heads were the highest paid in the business because he knew it was through them that his systems would be effected.

In 1927 he was offered the management of the Cincinnati Gibson Hotel, which was having financial difficulties. No one was more surprised than the board of directors when Hitz promised to earn $150,000 in profit during his first year of operation. The directors were more astounded than surprised when his first year's profits were $158,389.17.

Not one to hide his light, Hitz publicized his methods and cost accounting system to the entire hotel industry. In 1929 the Hotel New Yorker made its debut, simultaneously with the Depression. Undismayed, Hitz, as its manager, went on to use the hotel as a laboratory where all operations were done by the book.

Because he gave the type service usually associated only with deluxe rates to a person paying $3 to $5, his hotels ran high occupancies. During the Depression, when hotel occupancies across the nation were at 50 percent and lower, such an operator was in great demand.

Hitz did more than promote; he introduced all-out standardization to hotel keeping. His kitchens were fine examples of efficiency and uniformity. Controls of all kinds were installed and thorough accounting practices followed. Hitz memorized standard operating ratios and then set about to exceed them. The income from his restaurants and such services as valet and guest laundry was so high as to confound his contemporaries. What others had done, he could do better.

Like others before him, he could make money for other people—but not for himself. With friends, he bought the Belmont Plaza, across the street from the Waldorf-Astoria, ran out the prostitutes, and put in the Hitz systems. Nothing seemed to work. According to his son, if an idea failed, he would not admit failure, as he would have done if spending other people's money. Instead, if an ice show failed to bring in the crowds, Hitz would spend another $50,000 to promote the show. This did not prove to be the answer for the Belmont Plaza.

A hard-driving man, he was also known for quick thinking and a well-developed sense of humor. It is said that he craved friendship and had a genius for hospitality. To get a true picture of him, one had to see him making daily tours of his house, busily taking copious notes, and later, during check-in hours, to see him in the lobby, a short, ebullient man, personally greeting new arrivals in an almost incomprehensible Viennese accent. He also had his failings; drinking and gambling were problems. He died in 1940 at the age of 49, leaving behind a small estate.

Because he was the driving force of the company that operated 10 of the country's largest hotels, his death brought quick disintegration of the system. Hitz owned no hotels and left no institutions as his legacy. Surprisingly, his name is scarcely known to the younger generation; the memory of this great hotelman is almost lost.

4

Hotel/Motel Finance

The hotel business can be thought of as two businesses: finance and operations. Hotels, like all real property including office buildings, are subject to changes in tax laws that affect depreciation rates, which in turn encourage or discourage new building. The value of a hotel rises and falls depending on general economic conditions: Prosperity increases occupancy and room rates; recessions reduce the average daily rate and occupancy rate. There are also other factors to consider. Hotels typically carry large debt loads, the cost of which fluctuates with the rise and fall of interest rates. The value of a hotel is also influenced by investor demand, which can be driven up artificially by foreign investors, whose money may be overvalued in relation to the American dollar and who find hotels comparatively cheap to buy. This happened in the mid-late 1980s.

The rate of inflation greatly influences the value of hotels. Inflation increases the dollar value of real estate, including hotels. A hotel bought for $1 million may be valued at $2 million in 5 or 6 years, not because the hotel has been particularly profitable but because of inflation.

Illustrating how finance may be far more important and complex than hotel operation was the $2.25 billion purchase of the Holiday Corporation by Bass PLC, a company whose money had been made in operating British betting parlors. The purchase, the most significant lodging transaction in the 1980s, gave Holiday's chief officers and stockholders about $125 million in Bass stock, as well as one share of Bass stock for each share of stock they held in Holiday Corporation. Stockholders also received a one-time taxable $35-a-share dividend from a spin-off company left after the Bass purchase and paid for by taking on about $1 billion in debt. In addition, the Bass company assumed the $2.1 billion debt that had been accumulated by the Holiday Corporation.[1] Fortunately for Holiday Corporation stockholders, the sale took place before the financial crunch

---

1. *Lodging Hospitality* (Oct. 1989).

72

hit American hotels beginning about 1989, this would probably have devalued Holiday stock by at least one-half.

Figure 4-1 shows the lobby entrance of the Phoenician hotel in Scottsdale, Arizona. Its cost of $265 million, or about $456,000 a room for each of its 580 rooms and suites, make it almost impossible to operate at a profit without writing off much of its cost. Opened in 1988, it was one of the many hotels financed by savings and loan institutions, many of which were declared bankrupt. Federal regulators took over the Phoenician in 1989. In 1991 the Kuwait Investment Office, which was a 45% owner of the hotel, bought the government's share and is now the sole owner. A lavish hotel sitting on 130 acres at the base of Camelback Mountain, it has seven connecting swimming pools, the lowest, tiled in mother-of-pearl. A "Centre for Well-Being" keeps an exercise physiologist, a registered dietitian, and life-style management consultant on its staff.

HOTEL FINANCIAL HISTORY: BOOM AND BUST

As civilization spread westward in the U.S., the hotel went along, sometimes preceding most of the population. Real estate developers, quick to recognize the importance of a hotel for the growth of a community, often built a hotel before the community arrived. (The Gayoso Hotel in Memphis stood alone in a meadow for years.) A few hotels never acquired a town around them and fell into decay.

Hotels were built for a variety of reasons other than pure investment. Sometimes, they went up to satisfy an individual's vanity or as a monument to someone or something. In many towns, the hotel was built as an expression of civic pride and became the center of community activity. In some larger communities, it boosted a particular section of the city.

Overbuilding in the 1920s

In the early 1920s, hotel investment looked very tempting. Room occupancy had jumped from 14 percent in 1919 to 86 percent in 1920, and up until 1927 occupancy never dropped below the breakeven point for nearly all hotels. A great boom in hotel building resulted. Chicago, for example,

had 11,000 hotel rooms in 1920; by June 1926, the figure had increased to more than 22,000.

As mentioned, there were many reasons for all the building. In addition, it became clear that a valuable piece of land could be made more valuable by the addition of a hotel. Promoters, who had a considerable part in creating the boom, were able to do well for themselves financially. Investment houses were also interested, since a new hotel provided an outlet for the sale of securities.

Charles Moore, active during the 1920s as a hotel promoter, noted that the total cost of financing many hotels averaged between 12 and 20 percent. Borrowed money was as much as 88 percent of the total amount used for payments on construction. Often, very little of the owner's actual cash was put into a hotel right up to the time the building was completed. Then, if it was a success from the start, well and good; if not, trouble lay ahead.

Buying a large lot with a big mortgage, then dividing it up into small pieces, and selling it to the public was sound in theory, said Moore, but many people entered the field who did not know the business and too many hotels were built.

A hotel could be created out of "thin air"—that is, with no equity capital. An incident from Pittsburgh in the late 1920s is a good example. A contractor needed a job to keep his company busy. He purchased a large lot in exchange for a second mortgage, providing an equity behind the purchase in the form of securities or services. He then created a third mortgage for about twice his legitimate fee as a contractor, sold half of the third mortgage to subcontractors to build a hotel, and retained the other half for his fees.

A typical hotel was financed during this period with an equity equal to about 30 to 40 percent of the total cost of the land, building, and financing expense. The owner applied to one of the first mortgage houses for a combined building and permanent loan. If approved, construction would start at once, even though this method of financing was relatively expensive.

The Debacle of the 1930s and World War II

Hotels financed in this way made good investments as long as occupancy was high. High occupancy required a kind of monopoly in location. That was hard to come by, since overbuilding was

Figure 4-1 Lobby entrance of the Phoenician Hotel, Scottsdale, Arizona. (Courtesy of Phoenician Hotel)

rife. If a 100-room hotel was needed in a community, local enthusiasm often forced the building of a 200-room property.

With the Depression, occupancy dropped below 40 percent, and many hotel ventures sold for a few pennies on the dollar. It is said that over 80 percent of the country's hotels were in serious financial trouble during the 1930s; many of them were taken over by insurance companies and other lending institutions forced to foreclose on their mortgages.

What are debacles for some are opportunities for others. As the 1930s came to a close, Europe was at war and business in the U.S. Began to recover. Our entry into World War II against the Axis powers provided a windfall for hotel owners and operators, especially those located in cities. Hotel occupancy soared to heights never before equaled. So too did operating profits. Rooms in some hotels could be rented twice in a 24-hour period. Profits were high, but curbed by price controls. Hotel construction came to a halt. Hotel occupancy rates peaked in 1945 at 93 percent.

Post-War Period

As said, the hotel business is usually either under- or overbuilt. Equilibrium does not last for long. Following the war, motel construction boomed, but these were the Mom and Pop operations of 6 to 30 or 40 units described earlier. The money for construction came from savings, banks, and local savings and loan associations. The land and buildings were mortgaged as collateral.

Few hotels were built until the mid-1950s. From then on, especially during the 1960s, numerous large hotels went up, as did motor hotels with more than 100 units. Larger properties tended to replace smaller ones that became obsolete.[2] Typically, motor hotels were built on or near major highways leading to or around towns and cities, bringing obsolescence to the downtown hotel, typically an older property built in the booming 1920s.

Hotel construction was fostered in the late 1960s by investors discouraged with the bearish stock market who were seeking tax shelters. Such

investments produced significant losses as a result of allowable tax deductions. The losses were used to reduce tax liabilities attached to investors' other unrelated taxable income. A hotel/motel business seemed an excellent medium for realizing capital gains rather than straight income. Most tax-sheltered investments were possible because of tax laws passed by Congress; they were not the result of tax loopholes as many people believed.

Hotels offered tax advantages to owners another way as well. Of the total purchase price, a large portion could be allocated to personal property and depreciated over a relatively short period of time. The building itself must be depreciated over the estimated life of the building. Other tax advantages have been available in the past.

The Real Estate Investment Trust

Another factor in the rapid hotel construction of the period came as a result of a new type of trust made legally possible in 1968, the real estate investment trust (REIT), "a mutual fund of real estate loans." Such trusts acquired millions of dollars, which eager investors made available because of two features of the REIT:

1. By law, the REIT must pass 90 percent of its earnings on to its investors. (In the usual public corporation, the board of directors decides whether the investor receives anything at all.)

2. The trust, being a trust, was not taxed.

A number of REITs went public, attracting billions of dollars, and were able to borrow additional millions from commercial banks. A REIT with $10 million might borrow $90 million and invest $100 million in hotels and other real estate. At first, the REITs prospered mightily, lending money to developers at rates of 15 percent and more; a few REITs had millions of dollars to invest every day.

On the down side, many rushed into construction and development (C&D) loans for hotels and motels without proper investigation of the borrower's experience or a reasonable feasibility study of the site and project. Savings and loan associations, commercial banks, insurance

---

2. *Financing the Lodging Industry: A Survey of Lender Attitudes* (Philadelphia: Laventhol & Horwath), 1975.

companies, and mortgage bankers were guilty of the same thing, but to a lesser degree. A 1975 study found that 24 lending institutions had made $3 billion in loans and investments in the hospitality business in the previous few years.[3]

REITs had made C&D loans covering 82 properties, and 72 percent of them became "distressed"; the lenders were not being paid according to agreement or had foreclosed on the property. It was nothing like the conditions prevailing in the 1930s, but it was serious. The REITs lost millions of dollars of their investors' money.

Lenders in Trouble

Overbuilding, the energy crisis of the 1970s, increases in construction costs, higher interest rates, and reduced demand for all sorts of real estate were principal causes of the problem faced by the lenders. Unemployment increased, and travel, both pleasure and business, dropped. Developers, many of whom were highly leveraged and lacked backup capital, lost some or all of their equity in the hotels or motels they were constructing. Inexperienced operators failed to budget enough money to cover startup costs, which in a major downtown convention hotel could run up to $1500 a room before the hotel reached a breakeven point in sales.

Lenders pushed up the cost of money to 15 percent and more. Overly optimistic developers paid not only record interest rates, but also agreed to charges in addition to interest, the so-called front-end fees. Equity kickers were also demanded, the lender receiving 1 or 2 percent of gross room receipts—this on top of the high interest rates and front-end fees.

By 1975 lending institutions and borrowers were a chastened lot. Lenders had become extremely cautious, investigating borrowers very carefully and requiring at least 5 to 10 years of operational experience. C&D loans were not made unless the borrower had a firm commitment for long-term financing. Often, lenders would not get involved unless the borrower personally agreed to invest in the project and put up as collateral as much as 25 percent of the value in cash or land, placed in escrow.

When a property became distressed, the lender was reluctant to foreclose. What was true then still holds today. With foreclosure, hotel and construction costs continue even though the construction has halted. Capital is tied up in unproductive real estate, taxes continue, and guards must be employed to protect the property. In addition, once an operating hotel closes down, motivating travelers to come back after it opens again is difficult. Owner bankruptcy often means loss of liquor licenses, which can cost thousands of dollars to acquire. The lender usually tries to reach a "workout" agreement, perhaps granting a moratorium on the repayment of interest, even advancing money to keep the property operating. In return, the borrower usually agrees to various stipulations, provides monthly financial reports, and permits frequent inspections. Management is changed in some cases, and a consulting firm brought in to assist in turning around the property.

The failure of hundreds of hotels and motels owned by REITs became an opportunity for small management companies. Hundreds were formed. Most lasted only a few years. The successful ones turned around the properties financially and thereby worked themselves out of a job. Lenders (usually commercial banks that acquired the property when the REITs could not pay) sold the property once it was successful. Today, management companies protect their position by including an option to purchase in their contract.

Saving and Loans in Trouble

By 1989 numerous hotels were on the market, put there by savings and loan institutions (S&Ls) that were in serious financial difficulty and had outstanding loans to hotels that were defaulting on loan payments. This was particularly the case in Texas, Colorado, and other oil-producing states suffering from fallen oil prices. The S&Ls had made dozens of loans for hotel and motel construction, loans that in many instances were made by loan officers who lacked knowledge of the hotel business. Some proved later to be in cahoots with crooked developers. A number of S&L officers were convicted of malfeasance.

The plight of the S&Ls provided buying opportunities for hotel buyers who could buy troubled properties at huge discounts from their book value.

---

3. "Management Contract Pendulum Now Swinging in Favor of the Owners," *Hotels & Restaurants International* (March 1987).

Overbuilding During the 1970s and 1980s

Even though a number of hotels and motels had financial problems, overbuilding continued, stimulated by low interest rates. A construction binge started in the late 1970s when, according to one study, the hotel industry could borrow money at almost no cost.[4] Long-term funds could be borrowed at 9.25 percent in the period of 1974 to 1982, and because of an allowance for depreciation, the capital cost was reduced to 5.6 percent. Inflation offset most of the rest of the debt cost.

Hotels, it was believed, could quickly increase room rates to adjust for inflation. Although this belief may hold true over long periods of time, heavy debt loads can quickly overcome hotel borrowers in times of economic recession. Overbuilding was also stimulated by periods of rapid growth in the economy and in places like Hawaii, California, and the Southwest by the influx of foreign investment.

Toward the end of the period, hotels and motels scheduled to be built had to be completed even though the economy had turned down. Financing had been committed and the construction had to be concluded.

These were financial factors over which the professionals who manage hotels had little or no control. Yet debt load and other financial factors greatly influence whether or not a hotel can be profitable. No matter how well operated, a hotel with a heavy debt load may find profitability impossible.

Among the reasons that the hotel business was overbuilt in the 1980s were the following.

Most hotels in this country are built by developers, not hotel companies or owners. When credit and money are available, developers quite naturally borrow and build. If there are buyers for the hotels, the developers go on to build more hotels, whether needed or not. When the economy is in an inflationary period, hotels also inflate in value and this conceals the fact that there are too many hotels built at costs that are too high for them to operate profitably.

The low value of the American dollar was another factor in overbuilding. Foreign investors using their currency could buy land and build at prices that for them were low. This forced up the

valuation of hotels and increased debt loads that hotel operations could not support.

The real estate side of the hotel business placed an impossible cost burden on the operating side of the business. When the recession of 1991 hit, many hotel owners ended up in a no-win situation. Room rates were forced down because of a shrinking market to the point where debt charges could not be met, and hotel owners who lacked backup capital were forced to sell at fire-sale prices.

History Repeats Itself

By 1990 news headlines proclaimed: "Far Too Much Room at the Inn." Some 774,000 rooms were added in the 1980s, as much as 65 percent of them to create losses that could be deducted from investors' income. New tax laws in 1986 plugged that tax advantage for investors, but hotels already committed went forward, with the result that the percentage of occupied rooms dropped by 1990 to about 63 percent, below the 67 to 68 percent range that had prevailed. A generally accepted idea is that most hotels need close to 70 percent occupancy to break even. Investors felt the pain.

The Laventhol & Horwath chart in Figure 4-2 shows that the number of hotel rooms climbed to 3 million, while the number of occupied rooms held at less than 2 million. Consequently, the break-even point was not reached from about 1980 through 1992.

According to the New York–based accounting firm Coopers & Lybrand, 60 percent of hotels posted net losses in 1990 and almost 20 percent of hotels were at extreme risk of failure, having occupancy rates below 50 percent. Figures 4-3 and 4-4 show how room supply outstripped demand for the 1980–1990 decade and the annual profit per available room fell from when the profit per room was above $1000 in 1979. Losses per room beginning in 1981 and extending through 1989 are seen in Figure 4-2.

Going Through the Wringer

When a hotel is sold at a considerable loss, the buyer is more likely to experience profit because of its reduced cost and new tax base. Excessive cost and debt load have been "wrung out" of the hotel and the room rates charged can be reduced if necessary.

4. Robert W. Woods and Avner Arbel, "Hotels Borrowed Money at Little Cost Research Shows," *CHRIE Communique* (Feb. 2–11, 1991).

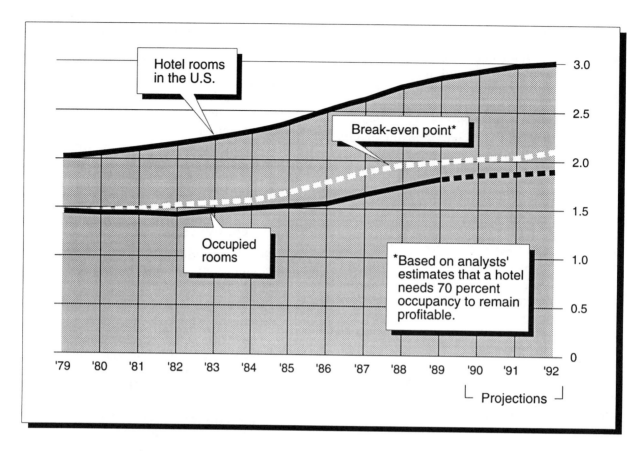

Figure 4-2   Hotel growth outpaces demand.

Source: Laventhol & Horwath.

The value of distressed properties is greatly reduced because of the risk the buyer assumes. To have any value, the buyer must believe that the operation can be turned around over time or sold at a higher price or for another purpose. The new owner must also have the capital available to cover operating losses for a two- to five-year period.[5]

A hotel with a low occupancy rate may have to be sold at a fire-sale price because the prospective buyer values the property based on its current occupancy rate, not the occupancy rate it can reasonably be expected to achieve in the future. The situation is favorable for a well-capitalized buyer, disastrous for the owner who is forced to sell.

Normal financing is generally unavailable for distressed hotels, and the so-called vulture funds seek returns of 25 to 50 percent of their in-

vestment. This high rate of expected return reduces the value of the distressed hotel only two to four times the cash flow being generated.[6]

There has been one good result of this trend: The U.S. became a travel bargain for foreign visitors, and visitors to the U.S. have soared. In 1990 38 million foreign visitors came to the U.S. and spent $51 billion, making tourism America's largest export.[7] Without the millions of visitors from foreign countries, the occupancies of many hotels would have been considerably lower than 65 percent, the national average for 1990.

As the recession continued, hotel and motel real rates declined as discounts, frequent flier programs, and other deals are offered. The $30 room rate has reappeared in many motels.

5. Stephen Rushmore, "Investment Today," *Lodging Hospitality* (March 1990).

6. *Ibid.*

7. Somerset R. Waters, *Travel Industry World Yearbook* (New York: Childs & Waters, Inc.), 1991.

BUDGETS AND BUDGETING

Defined simply, a budget is an itemized summary of expected expenditures and income for a given period. Budgeting is the process for arriving at a budget. Of all financial tools, budgeting is probably the most useful and can be the most formidable. Managers at all levels are usually asked to state in dollars what will be needed to operate effectively during the budget period. The budget is a set of financial targets that at the same time places limits on spending. Budgeting can be a cause of fear and anxiety for those working on a budget, especially when superiors set unrealistically high targets or when controls are so tight that they interfere with action. Budgeting includes:

Establishing financial goals

Forecasting revenues

Estimating expenditures

Monitoring and controlling expenditures

Noting variances from financial targets

Taking corrective actions

One value of budgeting is that it sets in motion a review of past performance and requires that

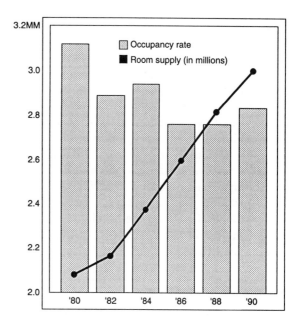

Figure 4-4 Room supply outstrips demand (seasonally adjusted occupancy rate vs. no. of hotel rooms).
Source: Coopers & Lybrand.

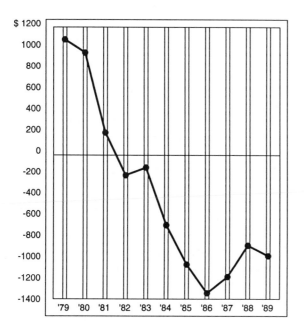

Figure 4-3 Hotels post eight straight years of losses (annual profit per available room).
Source: Coopers & Lybrand, Bureau of Economic Analysis.

thought be given to what is likely or may be expected to happen in the future, especially during the period covered by the budget. Budgets are usually set annually, but management often adjusts budgets weekly or monthly and sometimes daily. Last year's performance is the baseline for anticipating the future. Anything that will affect sales—conventions, tour groups, parties, and so on—are cause for adjusting a budget. Budgets reflect local, regional, and national conditions. Inflation or deflation are considerations. The availability of credit is a factor. Highway changes in the hotel's vicinity may be a factor, and the construction of a new hotel or motel in the area is likely to change the income forecast. A change in menu, a new chef, or higher or lower prices will be factors. Wage and salary increases are part of the forecast.

Conditions a great distance from a hotel can also be important. For example, a reduced airfare between Los Angeles and Australia or a new nonstop flight will affect forecasts for parts of Los Angeles. The flights on the polar route from New York City to Asian destinations have affected the number of guest nights in Anchorage, Alaska. The American dollar, purposely kept weak by federal administration policy, greatly increased tourist flow from Europe to the U.S. and changed what had been a travel deficit into a travel surplus for the U.S. In some hotels international arrivals account for as much as 25 percent of sales. For hotels in the Pasadena, California, area, the annual Rose Bowl game figures big in the fall sales forecast. Western Canadian weather is a factor in sales forecasts for San Diego, California. Central Florida hotel budgets may be highly correlated with Disney World events. Becoming a part of a marketing network, such as Best Western, can increase sales dramatically for some motels. Budgeting as a process looks at the environment that affects the hotel, even though part of the environment may be a thousand or more miles away.

Bottom Up or Top Down

Budget commentators say that budgets are set from "bottom up" or "top down," meaning the budget process is dominated by top management or is more democratic in nature, including input from all supervisory levels. Top-down budgeting can be exasperating and resented by lower echelon personnel. The mere fact that input has been invited may serve to blunt budget criticism. The budget process is more than "setting the numbers." It can act as a vehicle for organizational unity or resentment.

Operational, Capital, and Cash Budgeting

Budgets can be planned and written for any entity—personal, military, or the spending that will take place during a trip. For hotels, operational budgets include sales forecasts and departmental budgets, such as rooms, food and beverage, and marketing. Interest expense and depreciation are also planned for and itemized.

Cash budgeting is largely a control device, a plan that helps insure that the entity will always have cash (or credit) to continue in business.

"Flexible budgeting" takes into account that budgets, no matter how well planned, will encounter the unexpected. "Worst-" and "best-case" budgets are made—the former a fallback position if the worst conditions prevail, a "best case" if things turn out to be much better than expected. Computer spreadsheets can quickly change budget figures to account for changes. For example, a 10 percent unexpected increase in sales may mean the employment of a number of personnel throughout a hotel and the necessity of revising costs upward by a certain percentage. A recession can mean the opposite, reducing personnel and purchases. Flexible budgeting adjusts quickly for such changes and anticipates these changes within a range of possibilities.

Budgeting can be thought of as business planning set in definite time frames—a way of looking at the future, anticipating it, and setting about to control it.

RAISING CAPITAL FOR HOTELS AND MOTELS

Investors

Investors in hotel and motel real estate include individuals, partnerships, stock companies, real estate investment trusts, large insurance companies, and pension funds who in the past have seen hotels and motels as long-term investments that reflect inflation and offer a satisfactory yield. Albert J. Gomes, of Pannell Kerr Foster, found in a study of IRS statistics that hotel profitability for the years 1967 to 1981 was comparable to an investment in any other form of real estate. The average after-tax cash flow to total revenues was 16.7 percent for sole proprietorships, 11.5 percent for partnerships, and 26.3 percent for corporations.[8]

That finding, as stated, does not hold for more recent history, but long-term investors like insurance companies have been heavy investors in the hotel and motel companies. Prudential Insurance Company owns 35,000 rooms, representing an investment of $2 billion. John Hancock companies have $370 million in the hotel business. Equitable Insurance owns 20,000 rooms outright. Metropolitan Life has close to $2 billion invested. The Japanese are also big investors. All but one of the major hotels on Waikiki Beach in Honolulu are Japanese-owned, and elsewhere more have been bought and are being purchased. To them, American real estate looks cheap in comparison with Japanese real estate and because of the value of the dollar.

Many U.S. development companies have large hotel holdings as part of mixed-use devel-

---

8. Albert J. Gomes, *Hospitality In Transition* (New York: Pannell Kerr Foster), 1985.

opments. The Chicago-based VMS Realty has almost $2 billion in hotel investments. The company contracts with several chain management companies. Beacon Companies has hotel properties valued at $200 million. About 70 percent of Atlantic Hotels' holdings is in chains, such as Holiday Corporation, Hilton, Stouffers, and Best Western—hotels operated by Atlantic Hotels itself. The Pritzer family of Chicago owns Hyatt and Hyatt International Hotels, which are management companies, and is also owner of some properties. Sheraton Corporation is a subsidiary of ITT. Rodeway Inns are owned by Ladbroke Group, PLC, a British conglomerate.

Public Stock Offerings

Hotel and motel companies have also raised huge sums of money via public stock offerings, rare before the 1960s. Since about 1965, "going public" with a stock offering has been a means of raising capital for foodservice operations and for hotels and motels. Hotel and restaurant stocks suddenly became glamour stocks. Public investors were swept off their feet by anything that sounded like a hotel or foodservice business. By 1979 a number of hotels were listed on the New York and American stock exchanges.

A warning: Many companies making public stock offerings have little to offer but a marketing concept, neither tested nor modified by actual operating experience.

Syndication

Another way of raising capital for hotels and motels has been syndication. A syndicate is a group of investors joined together as limited partners in order to acquire property. The members own the property and receive rent from it. Part of the rent represents depreciation on the property; it is tax free and considered a return on the capital.

Funds are placed in the hands of syndicate organizers and managers. The latter usually receive 10 to 15 percent of syndicate shares. The managers then obtain a lessee operator, collect the rents, and distribute them among the syndicate members. The purchase of hotels and motels is left to the managers' judgment, thus giving them entire command of the syndicate's funds. The syndicate members maintain only minor control or supervision.

A weakness of this arrangement lies in the fact that the syndicate manager may have little or no money of his or her own invested, yet has complete authority to invest the syndicate's money. Since he or she is paid a percentage of the cash flow, the syndicate manager cannot lose, unless the entire plan collapses.

The syndication acquires high-leveraged properties with minimum cash down. The rest of the debt is financed through first and junior mortgages or by extended installment purchase contracts. The properties may be expected to produce more rent than they are capable of doing. The lessee might pay the rent but at the same time milk the property by eliminating maintenance and repairs. Should the lessee decide to walk away, the owners receive back the property in rundown condition.

Another means of rapid hotel growth has been via the merger or, more precisely in most cases, one company buying control in another.

Airlines bought into the hotel business; hotels and motels bought into free-standing restaurants. Some large oil companies began building and operating inns and restaurants. Huge food manufacturers bought into restaurant chains. In brief, conglomerates bought into just about everything.

Some of the more notable mergers: Litton Industries bought Stouffer's, and later Canteen, a large contract foodservice operator; Trans World Airlines bought Hilton International Hotels; International Telephone and Telegraph bought Sheraton Hotels; the Hawaiian conglomerate, AmFac, bought the Fred Harvey Corporation; the Carlson Hospitality Group owns a network of retail travel agencies, travel wholesalers, and tour operators, along with TGI Fridays, Country Kitchens, Colony Resorts, and Raddison Hotels.

Franchising as a Means of Growth

Franchising is also a means of financing growth, although it is indirect and not ordinarily thought of as a means of raising capital. In effect, the resources of each franchisee are used to expand the franchisor's business.

Franchising first became important with the growth of the Howard Johnson restaurants in the 1930s. During World War II, however, it almost came to a halt. In the 1950s the idea moved ahead again, with the rapid growth of Holiday Inns of America demonstrating franchising's advantages. In the late 1960s franchising spread across the country.

Well-known hotel companies such as Hilton Hotels franchise as well as operate. Hilton Inns are a case in point.

HOTEL AND MOTEL VALUATION

At a given time, the value of a hotel or motel is what the market will bring, which in the final analysis is usually what a buyer believes the property will generate in profit, what it can be sold for later at a profit, what favorable tax consequences it has for the buyer, or what other benefits it can bring, such as prestige to the buyer. Like those for most real property, hotel prices rise and fall. Hotel prices in the mid- and late 1980s were bid up by foreign buyers to unheard of levels for top hotels. Several prestige hotels sold to foreign investors at more than $500,000 a room. The Bel-Air Hotel in Beverly Hills, California, fetched the unheard of price of nearly $1 million a room. (To be profitable, the hotel would need an average room rate of about $1000 a day.)

Part of the reason was the cheap American dollar, which made hotels appear inexpensive in terms of the Japanese yen, British pound, and other European currencies. In the case of many motels located in California and the Southwest, hotel and motel prices were bid up by immigrants from Asia who needed to buy a business to be able to gain immigrant status to the U.S.

One measure of a hotel's value is its gross operating profit. Gross operating profit is the net profit before taxes, interest, and depreciation. The price paid can be determined as a multiple of the gross operating profit. In the late 1980s three large American hotel companies were sold to foreign buyers. The multiple paid was different for each chain. Motel 6 was sold to Accor S.A. at a multiple of 10.5 (10.5 times the gross operating profit). Bass PLC bought Holiday Inn at a 13.2 multiple, and Seibu Saison paid a multiple of 17 for Interconti-

nental. Each buyer no doubt felt it had made a good purchase, each for different reasons.[9]

Hotel values can change rapidly and drastically, as happened in the late 1980s and early 1990s when the stock market value of some of the leading U.S. hotel chains dropped by two-thirds, and following the insolvency of numerous S&L institutions, financing for hotel purchases was in very short supply. Numerous insolvent hotel properties were for sale. Hotel prices fell sharply. As Stephen Rushmore, a well-known appraiser, pointed out: "It is not unheard of for a hotel to suffer a 50 to 70 percent loss in value from factors unrelated to the property itself." A new hotel close by can siphon off sizable occupancy from an existing hotel. A general drop in the economy of a region is also quickly reflected in hotel occupancy.[10]

In placing a value on a hotel, a first step is to project income into the future, a tricky estimate because no one really knows what the future will bring in the way of interest rates, prosperity, or recession. New hotels may be built that compete in the same market. Foreign buyers of a hotel company may underprice their rooms to build market share, and hotels and motels regularly undergo cycles of overbuilding.

Once net income is projected into the future, the value of the hotel is discounted at a rate that reflects the cost of capital at the time. The present value of money is not the same as it will be a year from now. A dollar today is worth less a year from now because that dollar could have been earning interest. (In times of rapid deflation, the dollar gains in value.)

Hotel and motel appraisal is not an exact science and cannot be done using a computer program, although such a program can be used as a guideline. Hotel buyers may insist on more than one appraisal because no two appraisers are likely to come up with the same valuation, not surprising because of the many variables involved in an appraisal, including the assumptions made by the appraisers and their experience. Brokers involved also may influence an appraisal to further a sale. The availability of money at the time is a considerable factor. An in-

9. *Wall Street Journal* July 16, 1990.
10. "Misconceptions About Appraisals," *Lodging Hospitality* (June 1990).

surance company, for example, may have millions of dollars to invest daily and be looking for suitable investments. Past experience with hotel investments, however, may turn them against further hotel investment. Sometimes, hotels and motels have been popular with lending institutions. This may not be so at other times. And judging from past experience, lenders, large and small, have made egregious mistakes in where to place their loans.

Book Value vs. Market Value

Book value and market value are different from each other and are often confused. Market value tends to reflect closely the earning power of a property; book value is an accounting concept arrived at by subtracting the depreciation allowance over the years since the property was purchased. Book value in no way reflects inflation; market value usually does. In times of recession hotels may be undervalued as they were in 1994.

Depreciation vs. Reality

In 1977 the Hilton Hotels' book value based on cost less depreciation was $371 million, whereas the fair market value placed on the properties by the management was $717 million. Barron Hilton, president of Hilton Hotels, claimed that the Waldorf-Astoria, built in 1927, still had a useful life of 25 or 30 years in 1977. Thus, to replace it in 1977 would cost about $180 million, its market value, even though its book value was only $45 million.

What Ernest Henderson pointed out in the early 1960s remains just as true today: The real value of any business property is what it will produce in earnings. Both Henderson and Hilton have shown their stockholders that traditional accounting methods are unrealistic as related to hotel properties. These properties tend to appreciate rather than depreciate because the dollar, accountancy's basic unit of measure, has not been a stable standard. For these and other reasons, if hotels are well located and well managed, their market value may be greatly in excess of book value.

What is a reasonable depreciation period for the hotel or motel? The answer differs among experts and even among IRS spokespeople. Book

value and market value continue to be different matters.

INVESTMENT STRATEGIES

Financial managers and CEOs are continually faced with determining which investment and operational strategy is best. One strategy may be best at one time and unsuitable later.

Hotel management has several strategies from which to choose. Properties can be bought or built. Leverage can be small or large. Franchising is a choice. Management contract or leasing may be choices under some circumstances. Sales and leaseback can be useful. The big decision often hinges on the amount of debt that should be taken on at the time.

The management contract proved to be a good strategy to partially or wholly insulate the hotel company from the vagaries of finance by selling its properties to insurance companies, banks, saving and loan institutions, and pension funds. A management contract is set up that removes most risk, especially if the chain is not required to take an equity position. Management compensation, however, is usually tied to profitability. If there are no profits, there is little or no compensation for the hotel chain. Intercontinental Hotels, established in 1946 as a wholly owned subsidiary of Pan American World Airways, began in the 1950s to operate some of its hotels under management contracts. They were among the first.

Since the late 1970s and early 1980s, an increasingly popular strategy to reduce risks and optimize capital has been to sell off ownership and retain management. Most notably, Holiday Corporation, Marriott, Hyatt, Westin, and Hilton hotels use this technique.

Charles A. Bell, formerly executive vice president of Hilton International, observed that hotel owners are requiring the holders of management contracts to assume some of the risk by providing part of the equity capital and taking on some debt-service exposure. The management fee is likely to be 3 or 4 percent of gross sales. The "group services" fee may be limited to 1 or 1.5 percent for advertising and marketing. Management compensation is likely to be limited to a percentage of net profit after debt service, payable only when cash flow exists. The right of the management contractor to survive a sale of the property, added Bell, is being resisted.[11]

Bell noted that the first management contract was arranged by Hilton International, forerunner of dozens of similar contracts that were very favorable to the operator. Governments, eager to attract the Hilton name and management skills (particularly marketing), offered to build, furnish, and equip hotels, while the owners took full risk for debt service and the maintenance of working capital. The governments own the hotel and pay the operator a flat fee or percentage of income for management services.

The Sale and Leaseback

The sale and leaseback is a financial arrangement that has been used in hotel financing for some time. A motel owner, for example, who needs cash but does not want to give up his or her operation can sell the motel and at the same time negotiate a long-term lease with the new owner. The sale and leaseback usually gives the former owner greater legal assurance of remaining as the operator than would arise in a management contract. The old owner stays on as operator and, as a result of the sale, has a large sum of cash with which to do business. The new leaseholder pays all operating expenses and real estate taxes and maintains the property. The new owner pays the mortgage-carrying charges. The arrangement is helpful to both. The original owner may have needed cash or used up his or her depreciation. The new owner is assured a good return on his or her investment and has ownership of the motel as equity. The leases are usually arranged to last 15 to 25 years, with renewal options.

The Marriott Strategy

In the 1980s the Marriott Corporation chose to continue its growth using a different strategy, one that involved heavy investment. Marriott constructed its own hotels, thereby insuring a suitable location and design, and then sold the property to insurance companies or other investors who agreed to place the operation under management contract with Marriott. The plan

worked well until the recession beginning in 1989, when hotels built by Marriott found no buyers and Marriott was loaded with about $2 billion of debt incurred in building its hotels. Marriott stock plunged by as much as two-thirds, from about $36 a share to around $10. It has since recovered. The Marriott experience shows once again the risk that is involved in hotel ownership using leveraged money vs. operation under a management contract and minimizing risk. Of course, the Marriott plan of building, selling, and assuming a management contract probably would have been successful under a different economy.

High finance seems never to end. In 1992 Marriott split its company into two parts: Marriott International Inc. and Host Marriott Corporation. The latter carried most of the long-term debt, about $2.9 billion. Marriott International was left largely free of the huge debt, able to manage and franchise and with the ownership and management of the Marriott time-share properties. Finance again took precedence over operation. Marriott assets had not changed by splitting the company. Its value in the eyes of investors, however, had changed. Debt was shifted, and Marriott stockholders could choose to take on an additional liability by staying with the Host Marriott Corporation with the possibility of a higher yield or they could go with Marriott International, whose revenues would come largely from operations. Marriott bonds fell sharply. (The Marriott family owned about 25 percent of each company.) More than 200,000 people are employed by Marriott, and the company's revenues exceed $9 billion annually.

The Role of Leverage in Hotel Building and Finance

Leverage means making a little cash do a lot of work. It is the maximum use of credit. The investor acquires control of a business or property with a minimum of cash. It has many advantages and one major disadvantage. If things go well, a little cash controls a lot of assets. But if things go sour, the leveraged purchase still remains, carrying a big debt load and its expensive interest.

Ernest Henderson, founder of Sheraton Hotels, was a master at the use of leverage. According to him, if hotel investments are enhanced by "leverage" or mortgage financing, the normal re-

---

11. *Financing the Lodging Industry: A Survey of Lender Attitudes* (Philadelphia: Laventhol & Horwath), 1975.

turn was close to 14 percent per annum before taxes. Henderson began buying hotels for cash at a fraction of their value in the 1930s. Before his death in 1967, he had created the largest hotel chain ever known to the world.

As Henderson tells it in his autobiography,[12] he parlayed $1000 into $400 million. In 1933 he purchased the Continental, an apartment hotel, for one-third of its construction cost of about $1 million. Of that one-third, only $25,000 was offered in cash. A few years later, the Continental was seen as perhaps the most profitable hotel of its size in the country. He bought the Copley-Plaza in 1941. Shares of stock worth $100 each were bought at $1 a share.

Henderson was always ready to pay a higher price for a hotel in exchange for a smaller down payment. His purchase of The Beaconsfield Hotel in Brookline, Massachusetts, is an example. The owner wanted to sell, but the highest offer he had received was $150,000. Henderson offered $200,000, but with only $50,000 as a down payment. The owner began to show interest. He had in mind $330,000 as the price of the hotel. Finally, Henderson offered him the $330,000, but with the right to pay only $2500 in cash. A few years later, the hotel was resold for $1.25 million.

A Detroit hotel was purchased with no cash changing hands at all. The owner had not operated successfully and was impressed with the Sheraton record. Reputation alone made the sale.

At the time, control of hotels and office buildings was easy to obtain with a small amount of cash. The Park Square building in Boston, which was owned by the First National Bank of that city, had a sale price of $4 million; Henderson and his partner, Moore, acquired control for only $125,000 in cash. The bank was persuaded to approve a first mortgage of $3 million, and an individual put up $150,000 for preferred stock. The $125,000 went to buy half of the $250,000 in common stock that was created.

Henderson and Moore continued the process, as they took earnings from properties they owned to acquire loans against buildings bought from banks and insurance companies. The sellers were pleased to take back second mortgages, par-

ticularly after seeing the success these men were having with other Sheraton properties.

The Sheraton Corporation took a huge step forward in 1956, when it purchased 22 hotels from Eugene Eppley, who had acquired them all during the course of his lifetime.

Conrad Hilton's experience was similar. He purchased his first hotel in Cisco, Texas, in 1919, when the owner, who was doing capacity business, preferred selling his hotel for $50,000 down so he could go out in search of oil in the area.

These successful men and others like them established this rule: Borrow or otherwise acquire as much money as possible, buy properties with as little cash down as possible, take maximum depreciation, and when the depreciation has begun to run out, sell the property. Buy a new property, again with as little cash as possible, and repeat the cycle.

The system works, when it does, because people have confidence in a particular business and will buy bonds or stock in a business, the economy continues upward, the real estate appreciates, and the value of the dollar depreciates. Used many times in other businesses, the system is particularly effective in the hotel industry because of the central role of real estate.

As long as there is a rising economy and the property shows some profit, the entrepreneur can pyramid his or her holdings spectacularly. However, if the economy falters or some of the properties are losers, it is quite easy for the entrepreneur to become overextended; the system can collapse.

Leveraged Buyout

Leverage took on a new meaning in the late 1970s when the term "leveraged buyout" (LBO) appeared and the practice of using a company's own assets to buy it out was enthusiastically adopted by numerous entrepreneurs. Under the guidance of brokerage firms, huge sums of money were borrowed, using higher interest rates to attract investors. Insiders and brokerage houses were able to gain control of many companies. Those who took over often laid out little of their own money. In many cases, the amount borrowed was greater than warranted and the company was put at risk, possibly to fail. If the company that is bought out can service its increased debt, well and good. In any case, the in-

---

12. Ernest Henderson, *The World of Mr. Sheraton* (New York: David McKay Company), 1962.

dividuals putting together a leveraged buyout usually do quite well. Some have made huge fortunes.

Days Inns illustrates how an LBO enriched a few and cost others millions. An LBO was responsible for the decline of Days Inns of America Inc., a motel chain started by Cecil B. Day in the 1970s. Day, a former Baptist minister, maintained high standards, prohibited the sale of alcohol in his properties, and employed a chaplain on call 24 hours a day at each of the inns' units. The company owned and operated at least half of its motels and insisted on quality standards by its franchisees. Only about 10 percent of franchise applications were approved.

In 1984 an investor group assembled by Saul P. Steinberg's Reliance Capital Group paid $570 million to buy out Days Inns. Of the $570 million, only $30 million came from the buyout group. Most of the rest of the money was raised by Drexel Burnham Lambert, the well-known junk-bond firm. The buyout group profited handsomely and in 1989 sold the chain to Tollman-Hundley Lodging, Inc., the largest Days Inns' franchisee. The buyout group walked away with a $125 million profit. The sale was about $765 million, and Tollman-Hundley assumed about $620 million of debt. (Tollman-Hundley put up only a few million dollars of its own money.) Unable to make payments on its high-interest debt, Days Inns had to file for Chapter 11 bankruptcy.

Days Inns switched from being a quality motel operator of several hundred motels to being a franchisor of some 1200 properties, many of which could not meet the standards of other franchise operators. Days Inns owns not a single hotel but aggressively sells its sign, reservation, and marketing. Its income is exclusively from franchise royalties of between 6 and 10 percent. According to a *Wall Street Journal* some operating standards of some Days Inns have slipped.[13]

WILL THE INVESTMENT PAY OFF?

The bottom line and ultimate question in an investment decision is: Will the investment pay off?

The payoff can manifest itself in various forms: immediate return on investment (ROI) or appreciation over a specified time period. Return can be measured in terms of growth in stock price, growth in book value, profit as a percentage of sales, and so on. As said, the big ROI from hotels and motels has usually come from an appreciation of assets. Profits from operation have been forthcoming during some periods, but fortunes have been made from property or stock sales.

Hotels and motels are almost always available for purchase. Buyers want the minimum price possible; sellers the maximum price. The hotel buyer usually uses leveraged money, and the sophisticated lender wants to be sure that the money being loaned will be repaid. Both buyer and seller are almost certain to be biased. To help eliminate bias and arrive at a value that the lender will accept, a market and feasibility study can be called for whenever a hotel or motel is bought. The lender obtains an assurance that the property can generate enough income to service the debt. The buyer is shown that indeed there are a sizable number of potential guests and certainly enough of them to create a profit.

Consultants and accounting firms are employed to conduct market and feasibility studies to forecast occupancy, average daily rate, and net income. The studies and their forecasts have not been particularly accurate. A study of 35 hotel feasibility projections covering the period from 1981 to 1985 showed that 65 percent of them had first-year occupancies that were too high. Of the feasibility studies covering the period from 1986 to 1988, there was roughly a 50/50 chance that the occupancy forecast would be inaccurate. Holiday Inns had monitored the accuracy of over 300 feasibility studies done for the company both by outside sources as well as internally. The Holiday Inn results and those found in the study by John M. Tarras were similar.[14]

Hotel Feasibility Studies

Hotel feasibility studies are designed to forecast probabilities, not certainties, and are subject to analyst bias, information limitation, and in some cases distortions because of a desire to please a cli-

13. "How a Motel Chain Lost Its Moorings O's Buy-Out" *Wall Street Journal* (May 26, 1992).

14. John M. Tarras, "Accuracy of Hotel Feasibility Study Projections," *FSU Hospitality Review* (Spring 1990).

ent. In other words, consultants may signal a "go" when the recommendation should be a "no go."

In "doing the numbers," analysts consider debt structure (interest rate, loan-to-value ratio, and amortization period). The tax rate of the investor and the depreciation method to be used are considerations. Cash flow (the cash receipts or net income, reckoned after taxes and other disbursements) may be a critical figure in deciding on an investment.

Market analysis goes hand in hand with a feasibility study. Feasibility presumes markets, but they must be identified.

Market Analysis

Market analysis includes the following:

Identification of a potential market: the type of people who can be expected to patronize the proposed hotel or resort.

Quantification of the market: how many people can be expected to patronize the hotel or resort.

The kind of facility that will appeal to the market.

Estimation of the size of the facility needed for the market.

Estimation of the cost of the facility that will serve the market.

Existing or planned hotels in the same area that cater to the same market.

Cost of travel to the hotel—rising or falling.

Number of airlines serving the area.

Whether the area is growing as a destination.

Whether the area around the hotel is becoming more popular, more prestigious, and more appealing, and whether the hotel compatible with the neighborhood.

One of the most famous statements made about hotels was Ellsworth Statler's comment that the three most important factors in the success of a hotel were first, location; second, location; and third, location. The problem remains as to what is a good location because the definition changes with conditions and involves a number of physical and economic factors.

Havana, Cuba, was a desirable hotel location until Castro's revolution. The Disney company believed its EuroDisney location 20 miles outside of Paris was good, and it may be in the future, but did not prove so during the first year of operation. It lost a million dollars a day. Gasoline shortages in the mid-1970s made numerous highway motels losers for several months. The recession beginning in 1989 changed many highly capitalized hotels in Hawaii into poor locations. Cheap airfares improve the marketability and profitability of hotels that rely heavily on foreign visitors, places like Los Angeles, New York City, and Orlando. By becoming a part of a particular referral marketing system, the value of a motel's location can be increased as much as 20 percent. The recession of the late 1980s and early 1990s placed many locations and the investors who owned them at risk.

The Caribe Hilton's location is good, as long as there is fast and relatively inexpensive transportation to Puerto Rico from Miami and New York City.

Factors beyond the control of any individual or corporation can determine a particular location's value. A motel on a well-traveled highway had 95 percent occupancy—until a large and striking Howard Johnson Lodge was built across

Figure 4-5 The Cincinnati Terrace Plaza was built in the 1950s. The hotel begins on the eighth floor; it houses one of the first glassed-in "top" restaurants.

the street, whereupon the motel's occupancy dropped by 30 percentage points.

The construction of a complex of business buildings may increase the value of a location if it is on the intercept route to this complex. Highway changes of all kinds, of course, affect location value, either for better or worse. Hundreds of motels withdrew from the race after being bypassed by the interstate highway system.

Site or location experts are constantly searching for good locations for their companies. They do not necessarily only look for vacant lots; they also search for sites with existing buildings that might be replaced by a hotel or motel. Real estate brokers who specialize in hotel and motel building sales and sites evaluate potential locations. They pinpoint those that might be available and project the amount of business that could be attracted there given certain facilities. Usually, several alternative sites are available, but there may be only one.

The really prime sites are usually too expensive for the erection of a two- or three-story motel; the building must go straight up in order to return enough income to cover the cost of buying or leasing the land. One hotel/motel chain allocates 17.5 percent of the total expenditure to the cost of the land; others use different guidelines.

The cost of a building reflects such features as the type of soil on the site, the soil's drainage features, sewage disposal, water availability, and the amount of fill or excavation necessary. These factors are particularly important away from established communities and in countries less developed than America. Building costs in the Caribbean, for example, are usually at least 25 percent more than in the U.S. because almost every item used in the building, including the cement, must be imported.

Another factor acknowledged as important by experienced operators is the cumulative attraction of an area with several similar businesses. A group of motels becomes known as a motel area to travelers. Many travelers will head there rather than stop at an individual property, even though the latter may be as good as or better than many in the group. Proximity to well-known restaurants, department stores, or sporting facilities is another major consideration.

Location experts are much concerned about compatibility with the neighborhood. A rundown neighborhood or one or two unsightly businesses within the neighborhood reflect unfavorably on anything new, even if it is completely contemporary and pleasant.

A market study examines where the travelers originate and what they are doing in the area—whether they will be commercial, convention, or transient patrons. It studies the area's population trends and the existing hotels and motels. The personnel departments of major manufacturers and other large employers in the area are visited to learn the number of their visitors who need accommodations. Purchasing agents are asked where their visiting salespeople stop. A company's visitors' register, an excellent source of information, may be examined.

For a motel, the highway situation—what it is and what it will be—is critical. State highway departments usually have traffic counts for all major highways in the state, as well as data on the origin and destination of travelers. Service stations can be canvassed for information about the volume of gasoline pumped and the amount of credit card sales.

Distance from a market is not always a clearcut factor. It can be measured in air miles, road miles, or travel time. A resort's market distance may be 1000 or more miles. The ease and cost of travel can become prime considerations. Witness the New York City market's distance from Florida or the Caribbean, or the distance of Los Angeles from Hawaii. New air service can make a location highly desirable for a resort area.

The fact that operators in a particular community say that the area is already overbuilt means little. The established operators would think there were plenty of hotel rooms unless their occupancy was running at 90 percent year-round. A community may be overbuilt with tired, obsolescent rooms and desperately need a new hostelry. The luxury hotel does not necessarily compete with the commercial one.

Market and feasibility studies for new hotels and resorts are very difficult to conduct and are expensive when done in depth. Practical limits have to be established. For example, a 1500-room hotel might well attract guests from all over the U.S. and many foreign nations. To conduct a market study based on questioning potential guests in all of the possible places of origin would be impractical. Instead, the market analyst compares a proposal with the experience of similar, already existing properties.

Like so many businesses, hotels have life cycles: startup, midlife, and decline. A few properties, like the Willard Hotel in Washington, D.C., the Sheraton Palace in San Francisco, and the Plaza in New York City, have gone on with the help of renewals for some 80 years. Most, however, have much shorter life spans. Characteristically, new hotels experience rapid growth in occupancy and income during the first 5 to 10 years. According to Stephen Rushmore, the income then remains fairly level for 8 to 15 years after opening. After that the revenue-producing capacity declines. Studies show, says Rushmore, that a hotel's economic life averages about 40 years.

Many of the factors that play on the life cycle are beyond the control of management. Changing demographics and changes in neighborhoods, traffic flows, and hotel overbuilding are examples.[15]

15. Stephen Rushmore, "Hotel Life Expectancy," *Lodging Hospitality*

Questions

1. Describe what influences the value of hotels.

2. Summarize hotel financial history from the early 1920s to the present.

3. What does budgeting include?

4. In what way is a budget a system for controlling costs?

5. How does an operational budget differ from a capital budget?

6. Describe ways in which hotels and motels can raise capital.

7. What is the difference between book value and market value?

8. Describe investment strategies from which hotel managers can choose.

9. Explain the nature and use of feasibility studies and market analysis.

10. What did Statler state are the three most important factors in the success of a hotel?

Discussion Questions

1. In the period from 1989 to 1994 the hotel business in the U.S. suffered severe financial problems. Judging from past experience, is this likely to happen again? what can be done to avoid a recurrence of a similar experience?

2. Foreign investors have purchased many U.S. hotel and motels since about 1980. In what way will these investments influence the careers of hotel students in the 1990s?

3. In what way has leveraged money played a central role in the growth of the hotel and restaurant business?

4. A hotel manager may have almost nothing to say about the way his or her hotel is financed or its debt load. Why would it be important for the manager to have this information?

5. Why is the "present value" of money, a dollar in hand, worth more than money some time in the future?

6. How is it possible for hotel finance to be more important than hotel operation?

Ernest Henderson

(1897–1967)*

The person who built the largest chain in the world, Sheraton (the name Sheraton was given to the chain because one of the first hotels purchased had that name and it would have been costly to change it), never took any real interest in designing a hotel or building one, never managed a hotel, and probably never thought of himself as a hotelman. Ernest Henderson was 44 years old before he really took the hotel business seriously. Twenty-six years later at his death 154 hotels bore the Sheraton name, and Sheraton Corporation grossed about $300 million in sales annually. How did an investor from Boston create the largest hotel system the world has known in the space of about 26 years? The answer lies in Henderson's organizational and financial skills, and his hard-bitten New England common sense about investments, operations, and profits.

As a person, Henderson had a strong sense of duty and self-discipline. He was a capitalist in the best sense of the word, believing that there were few virtues greater than those found in ownership and the creation of new wealth. Energy, hard work, and keen analysis were combined with skepticism and shrewdness. He was also an opportunist—ready to buy or sell a hotel if the right deal could be worked out. Sentiment played little part in whether a hotel was bought or sold; the tax base against which depreciation could be taken was much more important. Some hotels were bought and sold as many as four times by the Sheraton Corporation.

The decalogue that he drew up for the Sheraton Corporation tells something about Henderson. He urged that decisions be made on the basis of facts and knowledge; he commended the merits of self-control and the virtues of probity, and insisted on employees keeping their word. The following is a paraphrase of the Sheraton Ten Commandments:

1. Do not throw thy weight around, however irresistible may be the urge to do so.

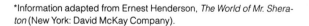

*Information adapted from Ernest Henderson, *The World of Mr. Sheraton* (New York: David McKay Company).

2. Thou shalt not take presents from those seeking thy favors; gifts so received must be passed on to a specified vice president for auction and the proceeds used for the employee fund.

3. Suffer not thy wife to gratify a yen to decorate a Sheraton Hotel.

4. Thou shalt not dishonor a confirmed reservation.

5. Thou shalt not give orders to an underling without fully making clear the exact purpose thereof.

6. Thou shalt duly recall that the virtues of those running small hotels may be the vices of those guarding larger establishments (for example, the desirability of delegation of authority and responsibility).

7. Thou shalt not demand the last drop of blood when effecting a business transaction.

8. Thou shalt not permit food to be served cold.

9. Thou shalt make decisions based on facts, calculation, and knowledge, not on a vague feeling.

10. Thou shalt not explode like a firecracker when an underling falleth into error (it may be your fault).

Henderson illustrated how an organization can rapidly acquire numbers of hotels, expand its equity ownership in hotels and motels, and yet show only a modest profit for tax purposes. As conducted by the Sheraton Corporation, chain hotelkeeping was as much a real estate venture as it was bedmaking, food-service, and advertising. Henderson put into practice a theory of "minimaxing"—minimizing costs and maximizing return on one's investment.

He believed in the use of leveraged money whenever possible and perhaps used it more successfully than anyone else in the hotel business. Leveraging money requires courage, confidence, and judgment. Henderson apparently had these qualities in abundance. One of the most daring major policies ever set in the hotel business was his decision in 1962 to reduce room rates drastically in the belief that greater occupancy and higher food and beverage revenues would more than compensate for the reduced room rates. Net income in that year for the Sheraton Company dropped from 60¢ to 17¢ per share.

Reducing room rates has always been an anathema to hotelmen and especially their accountants. Tables have been drawn up showing the impossibility of making a profit when rates are reduced. Yet Henderson, probably over the objection of his advisors, reduced rates in all the Sheraton hotels by as much as one-third or more. Perhaps equally daring was Henderson's decision to provide free parking at all Sheraton Hotels. The decision was necessary, he believed, to compete with the free parking of the motor inn. It cost the Sheraton Corporation millions of dollars a year.

The free parking plan is still in effect, but room rates have increased in Sheraton Hotels so that they are comparable to those charged by competing hotels. The lower rates did increase Sheraton occupancy to about 73 percent, which was slightly higher than the Hilton Hotels occupancy rate, but much lower than those for such chains as Holiday Inns and the Howard Johnson Motor Lodges. Even with the philosophy that life is full of opportunities and that our biggest regrets arise from a failure to grasp them, some mistakes are inevitably made.

One mistake committed by the Sheraton Corporation, according to Ernest Henderson III, was the failure to institute tight controls, budgetary and otherwise, over Sheraton managers during 1961 to 1964. Sheraton earnings fell off sharply between 1962 and 1965, and much of the loss was attributed to a lack of control over budgets and operations. Managers are now required to forecast sales and profits for each department a year in advance. Centralized management with area supervisors is part of Sheraton management policy.

What about Henderson's feeling about the guest? The hotel-guest relationship in a Sheraton Hotel is more likely to be something like that between a business firm and its customers. The customers are not necessarily right. They may be entirely unreasonable in their expectations. They may want more than they are entitled to.

At the same time, Henderson felt that one of the most effective management tools was the guest questionnaire. When the voluntary flow of complaints to the head office ran low, questionnaires were left in hotel bedrooms. Letters sent to Sheraton headquarters are answered promptly, and compliments and complaints are passed on to the manager concerned. The traveler, said Henderson, can run hotels better than the management.

He was no friend of bureaucracy and did not believe in a large headquarters staff. The training department consisted of one man, and the personnel department was hardly much larger. Every Sheraton employee, especially staff and executive-level personnel, was expected to contribute and every day; no prima donnas, please, and no juicy stock options for executives.

Henderson was definitely sales-minded. Though the "sales blitz" idea originated with Ralph Hitz, Henderson strongly favored such a plan. This resulted in a campaign to saturate cities with the Sheraton Hotels' promotion. Salespeople from a wide area converged on a city and in a team effort called upon hundreds of potential Sheraton customers. Sheraton credit cards were distributed in quantity and group business solicited. Several hotel chains still use the sales blitz successfully.

Henderson believed in national advertising. Franchising the Sheraton name brought in additional revenue, but of more importance to him was the fact that each franchise added another unit to the Sheraton referral system.

Henderson will probably be remembered largely for his ability to increase the equity value of the Sheraton Corporation from an estimated value of about $50 million in 1947 to close to $400 million in 1967 when he died. The increase was brought about with very little speculation in the usual sense of the word. Constant attention was given to avoiding the danger of financial overextension.

Sheraton guests might be a little surprised to find an announcement on their bedside table telling them of the merits of buying Sheraton bonds. Henderson explained why in his biography. Interest payments on the debentures were tax deductible to the company; it actually cost Sheraton less in interest than if preferred stock had been issued paying 3.75 percent interest. Unlike the bond, interest on preferred stock interest is not tax deductible for the corporation.

Because the Sheraton Corporation took the maximum depreciation allowable, the equity value of the company increased rapidly while earnings appeared comparatively small. In addition to net income, profits, depreciation, and cash flow, the company reported an "estimated value" of each common share. Also reported were an estimated net asset value and "adjusted earnings." These were theoretical estimates based on the judgment of the Sheraton officers and were presented to show stockholders their real holdings and the value of their stock. Sheraton had the highest cash flow of any hotel chain, taking the maximum allowable depreciation.

Henderson invested for profit, not prestige. One of his investment rules was that for every dollar added in improving a hotel, the hotel should be expected to increase in value by $2. Indicative of the company's financial orientation is the practice of posting the latest market value of Sheraton stock in the corporation office. What other hotel company would do this?

Unlike several of the real estate holding companies of the 1950s and 1960s, Sheraton Corporation never experienced any serious financial uncertainty. Yet some of Henderson's methods of financing and accounting were so unorthodox that the stock market took little notice of the company's real worth. He did not hesitate to offer capital income debenture bonds carrying a 7.5 percent interest rate when the going rate was 6 percent.

The financial community never really accepted the financial figures. Although it was obvious that the equity value of a share of Sheraton stock increased year after year, the market value of Sheraton dropped steadily, from a high of $22 a share in 1962 to less than $9 in early 1967. The fact that International Telephone and Telegraph Company offered to buy control of the Sheraton Corporation at $35 a share came as a surprise to the "smart money" crowd. The offer from ITT was consummated shortly after Henderson's death.

How can Henderson's career be summarized? He introduced no major innovations into hotelkeeping as a profession. He bought and sold; he built; he operated well. He gave the public fair value for its money. His goal was to create a billion-dollar organization, and he worked to that end diligently, quietly, and with amazing insight into the economics of hotelkeeping.

Perhaps it is more than enough to say, "He built the world's largest hotel chain."

5

Hotel/Motel Architecture and Design

From the humble inn by the side of the road to the 5000 room casino resort hotel, architecture has included everything from a single-story motel to the 70-story skyscraper reaching to the sky in Atlanta, Detroit and Singapore. Famous architects Frank Lloyd Wright, I.M. Pei, and John Portman have designed hotels along with hundreds of other architects less well known. The variety of design is incredible given the usual constraints of money and space. A high rise hotel, for example, must contain enough rooms to produce the revenue needed to cover costs and yield a profit. Land cost may in itself be 20 percent of total cost.

Economics drives most hotel design. A casino hotel is built to feature the casino and its hundreds or even thousands of slot machines where up to half of the hotel's revenue is produced. A Hawaiian beach hotel features the beach and ocean view. The landscaping of some beach hotels is more interesting than the structure. Lobbies and hallways may contain dozens of works of art that must be appropriately displayed. The archi-

tect of a high rise city hotel decides on the amount of space for the entrance and lobby. Some are indeed grand, others utilitarian. There is the problem of creating a place that is something other than hundreds of rooms connected by narrow, drab hallways.

Variety in design continues. The huge atrium in many hotels was first seen in a small version in St. Augustine, Florida before 1890. The apartment hotel has reappeared in the guise of the all-suite hotel, offering a common location for breakfast and later a beverage, both included in the room rate.

When Tremont House in Boston was completed in 1829, its Greek Revival architecture became the talk of the hotel world (Fig. 5-1). The design sketches themselves became a popular guide for hotel promoters and designers everywhere. Isiah Rogers, the architect, was at once established as the most important hotel designer of the day; soon his hotels could be found in Bangor, New York, Charleston, Richmond, Cincinnati, New Orleans, Mobile, Louisville, and Nashville.

Figure 5-1 Then: The Tremont House, Boston (inset), was generally considered to be the first "modern" hotel. It was built in 1829 by Isiah Rogers, who became an authority on hotel construction and strongly influenced hotel architecture in this country for the next 50 years. It featured private single and double rooms; doors with locks; every room equipped with a bowl and pitcher; and free soap. The Tremont was the first to employ bellboys. The architectural sketches of the hotel became a popular handbook for hotel promoters and designers everywhere. Now: A contrast in architecture, and bellboys, too, is the Century Plaza Hotel of Beverly Hills, part of a giant trade-living-entertainment complex. It is operated by Westin Hotels and is ranked among the best in this country.

Since America lacked royal palaces as centers for society, community hotels became what the *National Intelligencer* in 1827 called "Palaces of the Public."[1] The hotel lobby, like the outer rooms of a royal palace, became a gathering place and convenient vantage point for a glimpse of the great, the rich, and the powerful.

Hotels have been among the first public buildings to introduce the latest in facilities. For

example, the Astor House in New York City was the first to include plumbing on the upper floors. The water closets and bathrooms on each floor were fed from a roof tank to which water was raised by a steam pump.

The elevator, originally known as a "vertical railway," was introduced in Holt's Hotel in New York City in 1833; it was used for baggage. An elevator was first used for passengers in 1859 at the Fifth Avenue Hotel in New York City. Elevators changed the room rate structure by making it possible to charge more for rooms on the upper floors

1. Daniel J. Boorstin, *The American National Experience* (New York: Random House), 1965.

than for those lower down, the upper floors being away from the noise and busyness of the lobby.

Tremont House in Boston used gas light in all its public rooms and whale oil lamps in the guest chambers. American House, opened in Boston in 1835, was gaslit throughout. The Hotel Everett on Park Row in New York City was the first hotel to light its public rooms with electricity. Soon after, Palmer House in Chicago lighted its two dining rooms with 96 incandescent lamps powered by its own electrical plant. The first room phones were installed at the New York Hotel Netherland in 1894.

SOME BASIC ARCHITECTURAL DESIGNS

Hotels built before the twentieth century were likely to be block structures, as seen in the inset of Figure 5-1. That unimaginative design has continued to the present day. Many hotels are built around an open shaft, the court offering no better view than the window of a guest room on the other side of the court or a view of a dirty roof within the court. Inside, the hotel is one long corridor after another, usually unbroken by color, change of lighting, or any distinctive architectural feature.

During the resort boom of the 1880s and 1890s, New England resort hotels were likely to be block structures, to which porches were later added. The porch, extending at least the length of one long side of the building, was the distinctive feature of the summer resort. Here battalions of "rockers" relaxed between meals.

The Moorish or Spanish influence in resort hotel design began with the construction of the Ponce de Léon in 1888 in St. Augustine, Florida, with its minaret and open court. These features also appeared in the nearby Alcazar and in the giant Tampa Bay Hotel built by Henry Plant soon after. In far-off California in 1888, the minaret and the huge open patio could be seen in the Hotel Del Coronado.

The original Palace Hotel, built in 1875, occupied 2.5 acres in the heart of San Francisco. Its interior court was a famous meeting room. When the Palace burned during the 1906 earthquake, the rebuilt Palace incorporated a beautiful inner court, which was at first used as a carriage entrance. The present Garden Court of the Sheraton-Palace, as the hotel is now called, is a beautiful restaurant and has been declared an official landmark by the San Francisco board of supervisors.

Henry Boldt, who managed William K. Vanderbilt's Waldorf-Astoria, abolished the ladies' entrance; women arrived on the arms of their escorts. The Waldorf opened in 1893, the first to offer a room with a private bath. In 1896, John Jacob Astor IV tore down his mansion next door and a new structure was connected with the original Waldorf, giving the Waldorf-Astoria a total of 1000 rooms.

Like many grand hotels, the Willard (Fig. 5-2) in Washington, D.C., has had its ups and downs over the years since its opening in 1901. It finally closed in 1968 for 18 years. A near-record $113 million was spent to bring it back to its original condition, and it was reopened by Intercontinental Hotels in 1986.

Some American hotels were built to truly resemble palaces. The Willard and the Plaza in New York City exemplify that tradition, which has existed in the Western world since about 1900. Several hotels in Europe were actually originally built as palaces, not hotels.

The World's Largest

"The world's largest" has an awe-inspiring sound to it. Large hotels are usually among the largest buildings and, in many cases, are the largest buildings in our towns and cities. They constitute landmarks, centers of community activity, and objects of civic pride. The first building in the U.S. to be built as a hotel, The Tontine City Tavern, created something of a sensation because it had 73 rooms. Built in 1794, the name was changed quickly to The City Hotel.

The Fifth Avenue Hotel of New York, finished in 1859, was called the first great modern hotel. It captured the "largest" title and held on to it until the Palace was built in San Francisco. The Palace cost $5 million, a tremendous sum for those days, and had 800 rooms. The Palace burned to the ground following the San Francisco earthquake in 1906.

In 1994, where but in Las Vegas would there be a billion dollar MGM Grand Hotel, Casino, and Theme Park. It has 3500 slot machines, its life blood, and 8000 employees.

The "tallest hotel" title was shared by two of John Portman's 71-story designs, one in Atlanta

Figure 5-2 The Willard Hotel of Washington, D.C., was the prestige hotel of the city for many years. It has been refurbished and is part of the Ritz-Carlton chain.

and one in Detroit, until 1987 when a 73-floor Westin Stamford was completed in Singapore.

Megahotels

The large hotels of the twentieth century are almost towns in themselves. The Dallas Statler-Hilton Hotel has a capacity of 10,000 people, Palmer House 15,000, and the Conrad Hilton in Chicago 20,000. The Conrad Hilton switchboard has more equipment than is used in a city with a population of 35,000 because of the level of usage.

William B. Tabler, architect for many Hilton hotels, says it takes from 2 to 5 years, sometimes even 10, to put together a large hotel. There is the matter of land acquisition, architectural planning, financing, and finally the construction of the building. Nightclubs, ballrooms, shops, offices, laundry and valet rooms, barber and beauty shops, telephone rooms, refrigeration, incineration, and boiler plants are all part of hotel planning. Guest rooms make up only a minor part of designing a hotel; planning the dining facilities is a greater challenge and calls for a foodservice consultant to lay out the kitchen and identify needed equipment. Some of the larger hotels have medical departments with emergency rooms, isolation rooms, and laboratories.

It is little wonder that there are sometimes major planning oversights, as at the Sheraton-Philadelphia, with its insufficient elevator capacity. Elevators in the larger properties are likely to be computer controlled, but many hotels have elevator traffic problems. These can occur in the morning, when guests all decide to get up at the same time; in the evening when there is a check-in; and later when they all decide to move from floor to floor to visit friends or the public rooms.

Proper Room Mix?

Much attention is paid to developing a proper room mix—the right number of singles, doubles, twins, and suites—that would make it possible to offer a range of room sizes, quality of furnishings, and rates to the hotel guest. It has been found that in the usual transient hotel the suites are the last rooms to be sold. Suites also return the least revenue per square foot.

In convention hotels, however, suites are usually in demand by companies wishing to use them as hospitality suites. The newer convention hotels have a number of suites.

The motels offer a one-size room with two double beds and have demonstrated the value of such an arrangement. Unless a motor hotel is certain that its market will be largely for the single business traveler, most of the rooms will be doubles. A double room can be rented at a single rate to the single traveler and is also available for a couple or family.

RULES OF THUMB FOR HOTEL PLANNERS

William Tabler, designer of many of the newer Hilton hotels in this country, has listed eight "rules of thumb" for planners of commercial hotels. (He does point out that there are exceptions to these rules.)

1. The cost of construction per room should equal about $1000 per $1 of the average room rate. If the room can be sold for $50 on an average, no more than $50,000 can be spent per room. This includes the cost of the public and service areas. Per room cost in a hotel is total cost divided by the number of rooms.

The dollar-per-thousand rule of thumb has remained remarkably reliable over the years in spite of several factors that affect it. Food and beverage volume, management and marketing expertise, cost controls, payroll costs, energy costs, taxes, physical layout, and union agreements all influence whether or not the rule applies in unmodified form. It is based on the assumption that the hotel will maintain a 75 percent occupancy and debt cost (interest rate) of 12 percent. Higher interest rates or lower occupancies invalidate the rule. So too do any marked variations from other average operating figures. For example, labor costs in a country like Mexico may be 20 percent vs. 38 percent for the U.S., which could permit profit at less than a 75 percent occupancy rate and a lower room rate per $1000 invested.

2. At least 50 percent of the total space in a commercial hotel should be given over to bedrooms. It may seem strange that a hotel has more public and service space than bedroom space, but it is quite possible. Public and service space has been responsible for 60 to 65 percent of the construction cost in some hotels. In downtown areas, land costs and the cost of support facilities have forced a reduction in bedroom size.

Statler, recognizing the high cost of support facilities, seldom built hotels in the secondary cities that could not support a 1000-room hotel. When he built a hotel of fewer than 1000 rooms, he found that the public and service areas were proportionately higher and profits lower. Motels, built on less costly land and including less public space, can have larger bedrooms and bathrooms, as well as a small swimming pool.

3. The hotel should be planned so that it can be operated with less than one employee per room. Some luxury hotels located in countries with low labor costs employ two and even three employees per room. The Savoy of London has three employees per guest room and charges room rates accordingly. American hotels are making do with something like eight-tenths of an employee per room. In other words, a 100 room hotel can employ about 80 people.

4. The cost of land in most cases should not exceed 10 percent of the building cost. If land costs are exceedingly high, more rooms can be added by stretching the hotel skyward, thus reducing the per room cost of land.

Tabler points out exceptions to the 10 percent rule, one being Palmer House in Chicago, which has revenues of more than $1 million from ground-floor shop rentals. With such additional income, land costs can be higher than 10 percent.

5. What profit should be expected from each department in a hotel? Tabler believes that departmental profit should be 70 percent for rooms and 50 percent from the sale of beverages. Rentals should bring in 20 percent of the hotel's total revenue. No profit at all is expected from the sale of food.

Hoteliers are seldom outstanding restaurateurs. The hotel restaurant has traditionally found it difficult to compete with the good restaurant located nearby or one that, even at some distance from the hotel, has acquired a culinary reputation. Some restaurant operators say that the best location for a restaurant is directly across the street from a major hotel.

This may be the experience of hotels in general, but need not be. Specialty or theme restaurants in hotels have been much more profitable than the usual dining room or coffeeshop operations. The Hotel Corporation of America (now the Sonesta chain) opened its first Rib Room in 1952. Polynesian restaurants have been favored in Hilton and Sheraton hotels. Tabler's rule of thumb that the food contributes nothing to the profit of the hotel is gain-said by such instances of hotel foodservices making fairly sizable profits. In some of the smaller hotels, the food and beverage operation is the major reason for the existence of the hotel, the rooms being secondary to the restaurant business.

6. The hotel must have at least 60 to 65 percent occupancy to break even financially. Hotel design should allow for the reduction of operating costs when occupancy drops.

7. If room rates are to vary depending on the size of the bedrooms, to qualify for a higher rate, a room must be at least 20 square feet larger than the room being rented at the next lowest rate. Guests do not notice a smaller difference; they expect to see an appreciably larger room if they are being charged a higher rate.

8. The minimum size for a bedroom is 90 to 110 square feet for a single room; 130 to 150 square

feet for a double room; and 160 to 180 square feet for a twin bedroom.

Rooms

According to Jerome Vallen, the parallelogram is the favorite guest room shape, the depth of the room being about twice the width. For a bigger room, length is first added. Width is enlarged room the 12- or 13-foot minimum to 16 feet in luxury-class hotels. Guests, says Vallen, do not have a feeling of luxury until a room is larger than 400 square feet. The typical, standard-size room is between 325 and 350 square feet. Choice International's Sleep Inn, a budget property, is 210 square feet. The Ibis chain gets by with only about 130 square feet. Adding a full or false balcony and French or sliding doors creates a feeling of added spaciousness. Wall mirrors do the same.

The all-suite hotel rooms run in size from 380 to 650 square feet, one reason they are so popular. Corner rooms command higher rates.[2]

Lobbies

Hotel lobbies vary greatly in size and grandeur and have always done so. Few generalizations can be made about them.

Resort hotels are likely to have comparatively large lobbies because they are the gathering points for guests. Small motels tend to have lobbies only large enough to check guests in and out. César Ritz favored the small lobby to discourage idlers; he viewed the space primarily as a corridor to the dining room and guest rooms.

Statler, very cost- and space-conscious, built quite large and impressive lobbies. The one in the Pennsylvania Statler is tremendous, perhaps because the hotel was built with Pennsylvania Railroad money and leased by him.

Hilton, well known for his ability to carve revenue-producing space out of lobbies, did so by adding restaurants and bars. In some cases, he even lowered the ceiling to produce another floor above the lobby. The New York Hilton has immense lobby space but very few chairs; it seems designed primarily to move people from floor to floor, and to the function and dining room areas. The Summit, also in New York, has a lobby so small that the front desk is jammed with patrons during check-in and checkout.

Resort hotels typically have had large lobbies where guests can congregate. Some lobbies in Miami Beach have been grand; in Las Vegas they house slot machines by the hundred. The Portman-designed hotels, described later, contain lobbies awesome in scale and appointments, marking a new adventure in hotel design.

Dining Areas

The formal dining room has been out for some time; the specialty room is in. It is almost always built with direct access to the street, since patronage from hotel guests alone will not make it profitable.

The cost of transforming dining rooms or other spaces into specialty rooms can be remarkably high, often $500,000 or more. Usually, a remodeled dining room requires 6 months to a year of operation before it begins to be profitable.

Other Important Details

Beds are a major concern. More attention is given to firmness than in the past, and guests are often offered a choice of regular or extra-firm orthopedic mattresses. Platform beds, the so-called sandbox design, are more expensive than others, but they eliminate the need for carpet under them and for cleaning beneath the bed.

High energy costs have helped the return to windows that can be opened. Some Sheraton properties have sliding glass doors that can be locked in a partially open position to allow fresh air without being a security risk.

Hotels catering to businesspeople create the multiple-use guest room, one that can be used equally as a bedroom, office, meeting room, or living room.

The use of double-paned glass has permitted "glass walls" to be part of the building; the Flying Carpet Motor Inn opposite Chicago's O'Hare International Airport has an exterior 90 percent constructed of glass. The new silent and heat-resistant glass muffles up to 66 percent more noise than plate glass. Sound waves are converted into heat energy by absorption into a treated inner layer between the double glazing. Self-shading glass eliminates glare and heat. Made like a miniature Venetian blind, it is composed of thousands of tiny louvers sealed airtight and fixed between two panes of glass.

---

2. J.J. and G.K. Vallen, *Check-In Check Out*, 4th ed. (Dubuque, Iowa: William C. Brown), 1991.

Newer convention hotels usually include an assembly room and smaller meeting rooms, a banquet room and private dining rooms, a registration lobby, and an exhibition hall. Dining rooms and meeting rooms are near and on the same level as the kitchen, if possible, for reduction in wage costs. The beautiful Beverly Hills Hilton is built like a "Y"; three wings emanate from a central core, in which the kitchen is housed, allowing one kitchen easy access to more than one restaurant.

THE ALLOCATION OF SPACE

Sonesta Hotels' management has done a number of studies to establish guidelines for the allocation of space. Space allotted in foodservice areas is as follows: 18 to 20 square feet per seat in a dining room, 15 square feet per seat in a coffee shop, 12 to 15 square feet per seat in lounges and bars, and 10 to 12 square feet per seat in banquet facilities. These figures allow 25 to 33 percent of the total space for the free movement of service personnel within the facility.

A kitchen that serves both a dining room and a coffee shop should be about 60 percent of the total area of the dining room and the coffee shop combined. In other words, each seat should be reflected in 10 to 11 square feet in kitchen areas. If the kitchen serves only a coffee shop, the kitchen should be about 45 percent of the size of the coffeeshop serving area, allowing 6.75 square feet per seat. Food and beverage storage space should be about half that set aside for the kitchen, or about 5 square feet per seat.

Figure 5-3 In the effort to provide the kind of luxury and service offered by the prestige hotels of Europe, a number of American hotels offer "club floors," hotels within hotels. They usually offer concierge service and a number of amenities not found in the rest of the hotel.

Figure 5-4 The master bedroom of the Celestial Suite at the Astrodome Hotel, complete with Roman bath. Where else but in Texas and at $2,500 per night!

Banquet kitchens, of course, are much smaller; only about one-fifth of banquet facility space is needed for the banquet pantry and only about 8 percent for banquet storage.

Space allocated for housekeeping and general storage becomes smaller per guest room as the hotel gets larger, ranging from 8 square feet per guest room in a 1000-room hotel to 15 square feet in a 100-room property. The same relationship is seen in the space for hotel administration and the rooms department, ranging from 3 feet per guest room in a 1000-room hotel up to 5 feet per guest room in a 100-room property.

The needs of personnel are often overlooked in planning hotels and motor hotels. They require eating facilities, lockers and lounge space, showers, and so on. Approximately 7 square feet should be allotted per guest room in a 100-room property for employee facilities.

The location of something as simple as towel racks and hooks is also part of the architect's problem. Towel hooks are placed so that the guest

will use a towel an average of three times before throwing it into the hamper. The shelves for towels are located so that they can be reached from the tub, thereby cutting the laundering of bath mats by half.

Designers are forever attempting to maximize a "quality experience" in a minimum of space. Once a desirable room layout has been achieved, the room is then replicated tens and even hundreds of times in the same hotel or motel or in a chain of properties. The dollar savings can be considerable. For a time, bedrooms got smaller and smaller, but the trend now is toward larger and more comfortable bedrooms.

Room size and furnishings necessarily vary with the market being served, as seen in Table 5-1. In Japan, room sizes are often smaller than elsewhere; in fact, some are merely sleeping cubicles furnished with a small TV. Budget hotel prices usually mean budget-sized rooms with minimal furnishings and smaller beds. Twelve feet is considered the minimal width of a room in the U.S.

TABLE 5-1 Hotel and Motel Room Terminology

Hotel and motel rooms come in a variety of sizes, shapes, and decor. The number of beds and their sizes are important to the guests. Among the various classifications of rooms and bed sizes available in hotels and motels, are the following:

Adjoining rooms: two or more rooms side by side without a connecting door between them (in other words, rooms can be adjoining without being connected).

Cabana: a room adjacent to a pool area, with or without sleeping facilities; usually separate from hotel's main building.

Double: room with a double or queen-sized bed.

Double-double: room with two double beds.

Duplex: a two-story suite—parlor and bedroom(s) connected by a stairway.

Efficiency: an accommodation containing some type of kitchen facility.

Hospitality suite: a parlor with connecting bedroom(s) to be used for entertaining.

Junior suite: a large room with a partition separating the bedroom furnishings from the sitting area.

King: largest bed available; may be 80″ by 80″ or 72″ by 72″; can be formed by putting two twin mattresses crosswise on twin box springs.

Lanai: a room overlooking water or a garden, with a balcony or patio (found mainly in resort hotels).

Parlor: a living or sitting room not used as the bedroom (called a "salon" in some parts of Europe).

Queen: middle-sized bed—larger than double, smaller than a king; dimensions—60″ by 80″, or 60″ by 72″.

Roll-away bed: a portable, folding single bed that can be moved in and out of a guest room.

Sample: a display room that is used for showing merchandise. It may or may not be provided with sleeping facilities.

Single: a room with one bed for one person.

Studio: a one-room parlor setup with one or two couches that convert to a bed (sometimes called an **executive room**).

Suite: a parlor connected to one or more bedrooms.

Twin: a room with twin beds.

Twin-double: a room with two double beds for two, three, or four people; sometimes called a family room or double-double.

Source: Georgina Tucker and Madelin Schneider, *The Professional Housekeeper* (Boston: Cahners Books) 1975.

Luxury rooms take on the character of apartments, with artworks, upholstered bed headboards, sunken bathtubs, armoires, phones, and even TVs in the bathrooms. Suites sometimes occupy two and three levels with lots of glass facing choice views.

Guest rooms today tend to run to a standard of about 12 feet wide and 24 to 26 feet long, including the bathroom. Designers tend to make suites two or three times larger (Fig. 5-5).

According to Gregory Philis, the three categories of guest rooms are economy, first class, and luxury. Room widths vary from a little less than 12 feet in the economy property to 16 feet in a luxury hotel. Lengths range from 24.5 feet in the economy property to 28 feet in a luxury hotel. Total square feet may be as little as 290 in an economy motel to 450 in the luxury property.

In conserving space and "upscaling" rooms, many hotels have substituted the armoire, an ornate freestanding wardrobe, for the traditional clothes closet. Occupying a fraction of a closet's space, an attractive armoire adds a note of class and is quite suitable for the guest who travels with one or two suitcases.

Again to save space, combination sofa beds are used; in some cases, the old Murphy bed, which folds up into a wall space, has reappeared.

BASIC HOTEL DESIGN

Motels and hotels are characteristically built as horizontal slabs with rectangular buildings. In the beginning, they were one or two stories high, but with the development of structural steel and building expertise, they shot up into the sky. The 1920s downtown hotel was likely to be two to four slabs built around an open court. Later hotels took on all sorts of configurations: L-shaped, Y-shaped, and, finally, cylindrical (Fig. 5-6). In 1976 a cylindrical hotel designed by John Port-

Figure 5-5 With the great increase of business interchange with Japan, Japanese investors have bought a number of American hotels and, as in the New Otani in Los Angeles, offer the Japanese business traveler facilities similar to those found in first-class hotels in Japan.

man reached 70 stories into the sky of Atlanta, Georgia (Fig. 5-7); it was soon followed by another such hotel in Detroit. The three-sided motor hotel, which is featured by the Travel Lodge Corporation, allows two blocks of motel space to face an ocean or other scenic view. The elevator is located in the central core.

Some hotels are designed with a specific market in mind; it may be the upper-income group, business traveler, conventioneer, corporate training group, air traveler, and so on. In general, however, hotel markets are not nearly so well defined as restaurant markets.

The highway hotel and motel are probably appealing to wider markets—anyone within the price range of and with the inclination to stop at the hotel. A motel located in an industrial park area probably has identified its market as being a largely made up of people with business at the park. A resort hotel, which is by definition located some distance from its market, must define its market much more carefully than a motel, and its

design must be appropriate to that market. A hotel in the Virgin Islands, for example, necessarily caters to people in the middle- and upper-income brackets, at least at the height of the season. Only people in those brackets have the discretionary income and freedom to take vacations at that time.

Balconies can be built to project 4 to 6 feet from the guest room and provide a partial sunscreen. Vertical walls that separate each balcony unit are also helpful in excluding direct sunlight.

The rectangular motel built like a barracks is probably the least expensive of all designs. Most budget motels are constructed following such a plan. In temperate climates, most of these properties omit basements and inside hallways that add to costs.

A comparison of 27 high-rise hotels showed that the circular plan is the most efficient in terms of a surface-to-volume ratio.[3] The guest rooms

3. Clark and Benner, "Hotels and Life-Cycle Costing," *Cornell Hotel and Restaurant Administration Quarterly* (Feb. 1977).

Figure 5-6 The new generation of super hotel—glass, concrete, and steel cylinders around a giant atrium—is seen here in the Los Angeles Bonaventure Hotel. The principal owners are Japanese.

are necessarily at least partially pie-shaped. The rectangular slab design is more efficient than the more compact, nearly square tower. The corners of a pure square-shaped hotel are often left void because of the difficulty in providing direct corridor access to them. Figures 5-8 through 5-11 show individual floor plans for circular, slab, square, and deformed-square hotels.[4]

To avoid a slab-sided uninteresting exterior, the resort hotel or any hotel that commands a view is likely to have a balcony attached to each guest room. It adds glamor and architectural interest to the building, as well as access to the view.

4. *Ibid.*

Figure 5-7 In the Portman view of the new inner city, the hotel is seen as one habitat among several, an integral part of a living complex where business, entertainment, and residences come together. The cylindrical building in this picture is the hotel in a redevelopment project for downtown Atlanta.

Panel Walls

Panel wall construction began to be used in the 1950s. William Tabler is credited with the first use of a true curtain or panel wall in a hotel, in the construction of a Statler hotel. The curtain wall replaces masonry and is lightweight. It also has twice the insulating ability of masonry construction, a factor in reducing air-conditioning requirements. Panel walls allow the heavy columns required to support masonry to be moved from the outer wall to the interior, allowing more glass and open views.

The curtain wall is also more water-resistant than masonry. During the 1955 hurricane, 9 inches of rain fell in New York City in 24 hours; 17 ceilings dropped in the Hotel Statler, which had masonry walls. Two weeks later, about 14 inches of rain fell in Hartford in the same period of time. The Statler there suffered no damage; it had curtain walls.

Slab Construction

Tabler used cantilevered flat-slab construction in the Dallas Statler-Hilton. The slabs for each floor are raised along a central core and held in place by a central support. This brings down the number of support columns needed and reduces the depth of the foundation by 50 percent. Beams are not required, and less reinforcing steel is needed.

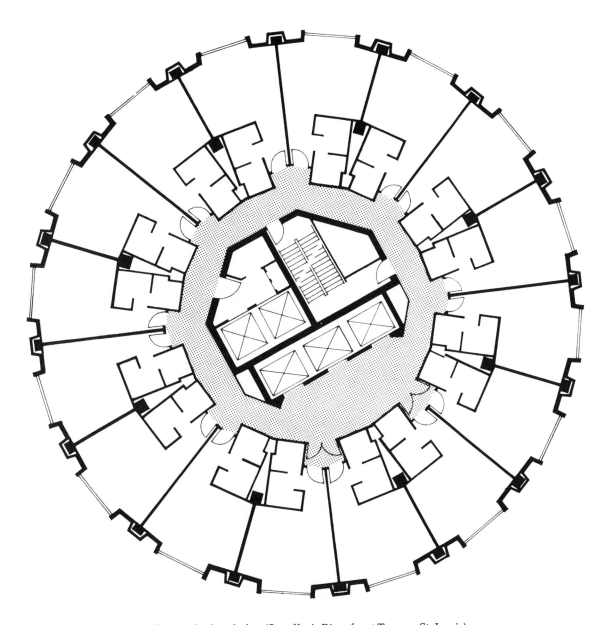

Figure 5-8 Rendering of a circular hotel plan (Stouffer's Riverfront Towers, St. Louis).

Only half the usual number of columns appear in the lobby space. Traditionally, these are the columns that usually get in the way and have to be disguised with expensive marble.

Optimal Size

How is the optimal size of a hotel or motel determined? The answer is probably best arrived at through a series of steps. Motel experts as a rule believe that a motel must have at least 50 rooms to be large enough to support a capable manager and also to produce enough profit for the motel to

be of interest to a big investor or chain operation. (A remote resort hotel, on the other hand, probably needs at least 150 to 200 units to stand on its own and be profitable.)

If the area can support it, the optimal motel size might jump to 100 or 150 rooms. Those with 100 who do capacity business might well add another 50. The additional rooms would show a higher percentage of profit on gross income than the rooms already in existence. Added labor costs are minimal. The only new personnel needed would be two bellmen, one clerk, and four maids. In other words, adding 50 rooms to a 100-room

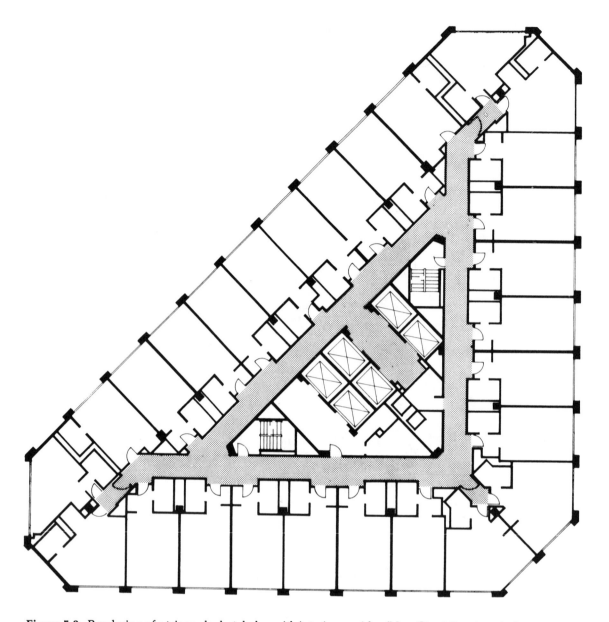

Figure 5-9 Rendering of a triangular hotel plan with interior corridor (New Otani, Los Angeles).

motor inn increases the basic payroll costs by only $2000 to $3000 a month. Computed on an 85 percent room occupancy, the additional labor costs for the added 50 rooms are only 11 to 15 percent of gross sales.

For maximum profit from rooms and service areas, the optimal size of the property depends on the market. An extremely large hotel may be needed to attract the largest conventions, for example; anything smaller would not be efficient.

If it is too large, the hotel begins to take on an impersonal character that mitigates against the kind of service expected in a luxury hotel. The de-

luxe-hotel operator is likely to feel that for maximum personal service the hotel property must be under 400 rooms, or perhaps even smaller. Some experts feel that a 225-room hotel is optimal.

To provide the intimacy of the smaller hotel, large-hotel operators may set aside two or more floors, usually the top ones, as luxury hotels-within-hotels. These floors are, in effect, operated separately from the rest of the property. They are reached by their own separate elevator. The guest is welcomed by a concierge. Complimentary breakfast, wine and hors d'oeuvres, and/or afternoon tea with sandwiches, pastries, and coffee

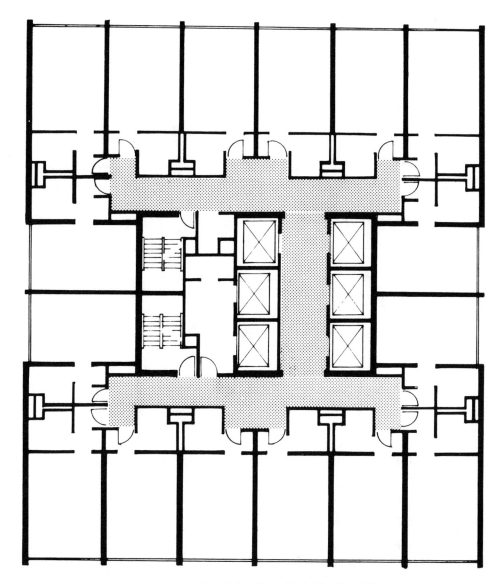

Figure 5-10 Rendering of a square hotel plan (Stouffer's Cincinnati Towers).

may be offered, along with some other special services, such as the turned-down bed. Room rates are considerably higher than in the rest of the hotel.

The concept was pioneered in the Waldorf-Astoria with the opening of the Waldorf Tower in 1932. Another Hilton property, Chicago's Palmer House, picked up the idea in the mid-1960s. Since 1975 these luxury accommodations rooms have proliferated, with such names as club Floors, Regency Club, Galleria, Executive Rooms, or VIP Floors. They range in size from one to eight floors, 22 to 300 rooms. Upper-echelon corporate travelers and, to a lesser degree, affluent leisure travelers constitute the market for these luxury enclaves.

Land cost may determine the number of rooms. The bigger the price, the greater the number of rooms needed to make the hotel financially feasible. The higher the cost, the higher up the hotel must go. Hong Kong, with its astronomically expensive land and limitations on building height, goes the other way: floors often go underground. One Hong Kong hotel built five floors into the ground.

In the last analysis, the optimal size for a hotel or motel depends on what the investor thinks based on a market feasibility study and the amount and cost of money available. How many rooms at what cost can a location justify? Stated in other terms, how much money can be invested profitably in a given location?

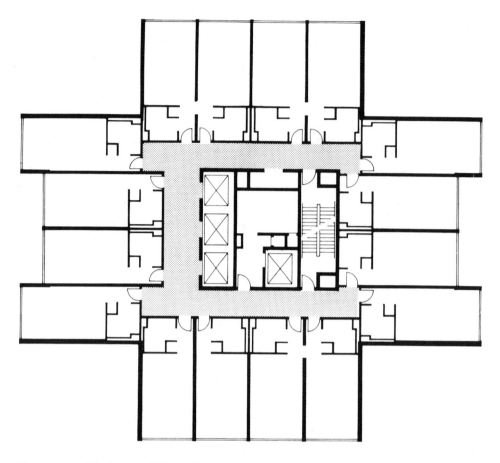

Figure 5-11 Rendering of the "deformed" square hotel plan (Holiday Inn, Quebec).

The Management and Design of Energy

Energy control has become one of the important aspects of the hotel and restaurant business, along with the control of food and labor costs, time management, financial management, and personnel management.

Energy management necessitates an emphasis on "present value analysis." Required capital should be viewed in terms of its value in years to come—its life-cycle cost—not only in terms of its present cost. From this point of view, a building that costs $1 million may actually be a much less desirable investment than one that costs $1.5 million if the added investment will result in lower energy and maintenance costs over the life of the building.

Energy management involves the design of the building. Some elements to be considered are minimal glass area, the use of solar screens that shut out unwanted sun, insulation, and perhaps even the possibility of a hotel built into the ground, guest rooms facing a central well or patio with clerestory windows to allow in light.

Equipment is purchased with particular consideration of the life-cycle cost. Controls are installed that reduce energy consumption during peak load hours when the cost of electricity is highest. Ice machines can be shut off between 5 and 8 PM, when there is peak load demand on electricity. Hot water need not be heated during that period either; instead, it can be heated during periods when energy cost is lower and stored for later use.

Solar Collectors

Solar collectors that convert the sun's warmth into energy began to receive serious consideration in 1975. They permit a large BTU input and reduction in oil consumption.

Several hotels and motels, particularly resorts, now use solar energy not only to heat water (up to 140°), but also to power air conditioning.

Frenchman's Reef, a luxury resort in St. Thomas, U.S. Virgin Islands, uses 13,200 square feet of solar collectors specially designed by Northrup, Inc. They track the sun across the sky, concentrating and focusing the rays on copper absorption tubes. Water in the tubes is heated almost to steam and can be used to heat or, with the proper equipment, air condition.

Roof solar collector panels are designed to allow maximum sunlight each day. In most systems, the piping holds a liquid that is heated by the sun and then carried to a large water tank, where the warmed pipes heat the water, which can be used whenever needed.

The Perennial Parking Problem

Automobile parking has been a problem for hotels ever since the automobile appeared in numbers. After about 1950, many a hotel succeeded or failed depending on its available parking.

The attractive Christopher Inn of Columbus, Ohio, solved its parking problem in a novel way. The first three floors of the circular inn form a parking ramp. The inn proper begins on the fourth floor and extends up 10 more stories. Elevators take guests to their rooms.

Experience has supplied the answer to how many parking spaces are needed in a hotel. In *Planning and Operating Motels and Motor Hotels*, Podd and Lesure give the requirements as follows:

One parking space for each guest room

One parking space for each five restaurant seats

One parking space for every three employees

Two additional parking spaces for service trucks

One unobstructed loading space

Figure 5-12 The La Fontaine Room of the Warwick Hotel, Houston. The room is not so large that it loses its charm and feeling of intimacy. This roof-top restaurant and bar is accessible by an outside elevator.

Figure 5-13 The Prudential Center of Boston has helped to change the face of the city. The center is a trade-educational-entertainment complex. At the top of the 52-story Prudential building is the Top of the Hub restaurant, operated by Stouffer's. The Sheraton-Boston Hotel, opened in 1965, was the first major hotel to be built in Boston since the 1920s. Twenty-nine stories high, it has 1012 guest rooms and can accommodate meetings of 2500. The complex also contains the Hynes Auditorium, where trade shows and educational meetings of considerable size are held.

An automobile requires between 300 and 400 square feet of space. The area allocated can include the driveway but not the entranceway. It can be seen that parking requirements add up fast as guest rooms increase.

Since the older hotels had no provisions for parking, most of them had to make arrangements with parking garages to house guests' automobiles. Sheraton has instituted a policy of providing free parking for all guests at their hotels, regardless of the cost to the hotel. However, getting a car out of a parking garage can sometimes take half an hour or more, not calculated to soothe the guest who is in a hurry.

Freestanding restaurants require at least one parking space for every two seats; a 100-seat restaurant will need 50 parking spaces. Some municipalities require a higher ratio of parking to seating.

HOTEL DESIGNERS

Modern hotel design has been greatly influenced by four men: Morris Lapidus, William Tabler, Emanuel Gran, and John Portman. Lapidus designed the lobbies of the Fontainebleau in Miami Beach and the Americana in New York; Tabler designed the new Statler Hotels; Gran has been the consulting architect for Hilton Hotels International; Portman, a designer, architect, and developer, first teamed up with Hyatt Hotels and later Westin Hotels.

Morris Lapidus

Morris Lapidus, originally a retail store designer, thought of the hotel, and especially its lobby, as a stage set that should convey luxury, excitement, and the possibility of the unexpected. The traditional grand hotel achieved an impression of luxury with numerous lounges, thick carpeting, dozens of service personnel, and ornate design and heavy furniture that Lapidus avoided.

The Lapidus-designed hotel and motor hotel offer a gala atmosphere that is lighthearted as well as functional. Color is important, and lighting is used for effect as well as illumination. He reintroduced the use of hanging light fixtures and chandeliers. He mixed classic design with contemporary, contrasted textures and made wide use of columns in his lobbies. Although the commercial hotel lobby was getting smaller and smaller, Lapidus designed huge lobbies like those at the Eden Roc and the Fontainebleau in Miami Beach and the Arawak in Jamaica, the West Indies. He is best known for the Fontainebleau design and for the Americana in New York.

Lapidus believed that nobody wants to go to a resort. Average vacationers are not tired and do not need a rest. They do not want peace and quiet. What they do desire is a change. Most people are too restless to spend even a week in a hotel; the average stay in a resort area is about four days. He contended that the commercial hotel has been married to the resort hotel and that every hotel is a resort.

Nobody, said Lapidus, wants a "home away from home," nor do guests want to do at a hotel what they would normally do at home. Business can be conducted in a holiday atmosphere that hardly separates it from pleasure.

The huge costs of the new downtown hotels are exaggerated, according to Lapidus. In some cases, publicly stated costs are almost double the real ones for reasons of publicity and to artificially create value.

Confirming Lapidus's idea that the downtown hotel is a kind of a resort, the Los Angeles Statler introduced reflecting pools and palm trees in the lobby of that large hotel to create a holiday atmosphere.

The spectacular in hotel design can be seen in the Mauna Kea, a Westin hotel in Hawaii, the Princess Hotel in Acapulco, and in a series of hotels designed by John Portman.

John Portman

In 1967 the Atlanta Hyatt Regency House, with its 21-story open lobby or atrium, established a new trend in hotel architecture. It was the first new hotel in years to create a special atmosphere within a large downtown property. Designed by Portman as part of a downtown renewal project, it initiated a series of similar huge-lobbied hotels, most managed by the Hyatt company.

Since that opening, Portman has come to have possibly the greatest impact on hotel design of any architect in history. The Regency concept, rooms surrounding an open lobby, is nothing new. What is new is the scale, the grandeur, the multistoried mobiles, the glass-sided elevators with their view of the lobby that are, in turn, in full view as they glide up and down.

One of the most spectacular Portman designs is the Hyatt Regency in San Francisco, with its 17-story lobby; it seems the perfect metaphor for San Francisco, an airy city built on hills. The Century Plaza Hotel in Los Angeles, designed by Minoru Yamasaki, was also a landmark in hotel construction. It created its own environment with a handsome garden, which the lobby overlooks. Its restaurant, glass-walled on the garden side, contributes to the ambience.

Figure 5-14 The River Front Inn of St. Louis was built in 1968. It is one of several inns operated by Stouffer's, a subsidiary of Litton Industries. An impressive part of its setting is the magnificent arch overlooking the Mississippi River.

The open lobbies, soaring to the top of the hotel, are called atriums, from the Roman patios of the same name. The lobbies, says Portman, are an explosion of space, an attempt to overcome the tight and cramped space of the central city. Forty-foot trees, lakes, open restaurants, waterfalls, "people spaces"—elevators and people moving on several different balcony levels—give the atriums a "live, or kinetic, quality." Birds, trees, reflecting pools, vines trailing down from guest room balconies within the atriums, and grounded and hanging sculptures add interest and warmth. The lobbies are not only filled with guests of the hotels, but also have become tourist attractions in their own right (Fig. 5-15).

When the Atlanta Regency was being built, Portman invited the officers of the major chains to discuss possible management contracts. They were not impressed. Portman recalls that Conrad Hilton, after looking down on the hotel construction, announced, "That concrete monster will never fly." When the hotel was offered for

Figure 5-15   The Hyatt Regency House in Atlanta is one of the most profitable and spectacular of modern hotels. Completed in 1967 at a cost of $18 million, it originally had 600 rooms; 400 rooms were later added. Each room has both an inside and outside balcony made possible by a 21-story center court. La Parasol Lounge has a parasol suspended over it hanging 23 stories above the lobby. The Polaris Revolving Lounge, 327 feet above the ground, revolves at the rate of one revolution every 58 minutes. The hotel also has three specialty restaurants.

sale, the Pritzkers, principals in Hyatt Houses, bought it.

Between 1967 and 1972, several Hyatt Regency Hotels—Portman-designed—were built and taken on by Hyatt in major cities, an association that helped considerably in making the Hyatt company the fastest growing large-hotel chain in the 1970s.

Portman-designed properties were soon in great demand around the world because their occupancy rates ran near capacity—this in 1975, when the industry rate as a whole was at a low 60 percent.

Unusual for an architect, Portman is also a developer and an investor in many of the properties he designs. The Portman Hotel Company has affiliated with Hong Kong's Peninsula Group, which is building properties in Atlanta and Shanghai. Portman has also "created" a small service-oriented hotel in San Francisco.

Portman is responsible for a major breakthrough in hotel design, which in effect means hotelkeeping. Portman sees the hotel as a part of a city complex, a rearrangement of inner city living, a closed environment with huge blocks of air-conditioned space.

It is reported that the costs of the energy required to heat and air condition such huge spaces can be excessive. Building codes require that fresh air be brought in from the outside for each recirculation, air that must be heated or cooled, usually at considerable cost.

Introducing symbols of rural life into the central city, Portman rearranges walls so that they surround large areas, producing a new geometry inside of the hotel and in its relation to the other parts of the complex that Portman envisions. Many architects have tried this in the past; Portman is doing it and, in the process, making a fortune for himself and those associated with him.

MEGAHOTEL DESIGN: PRO AND CON

The super hotel, represented by the Bonaventure in Los Angeles, is viewed by many as the hotel of the future; in fact, it has been used as the background in futuristic films. People seem to react strongly to the large-space lobbies, either for or against them. These giant glass, concrete, and steel structures with large atriums seem to be efficient places for conventions and large group meetings. They are not built on a scale that generates warmth and intimacy. Traditionalists have a difficult time identifying with the ambience. It contrasts so dramatically with that of the European personal-service luxury hotel that many travelers may indeed be uncomfortable or downright disoriented.

Because they are built many stories into the air, the high cost of the underlying land is reduced on a per room basis. Hundreds of rooms also justify extensive public space, lobbies, banquet rooms, and escalators between meeting-room floors. The megahotels have proved to be more profitable investments than other properties partly because of their popularity for large groups.

Megahotel negatives include the difficulty of escape from fires. Recent fires in megaproperties have caused the deaths of scores of guests. Some travelers now insist on being roomed no higher than the sixth floor, which is the highest floor that fire ladders can reach.

There can be no question of John Portman's impact on hotel architecture. Of course, there are critics. The 25th anniversary of the first Portman hotel, Atlanta's Hyatt Regency, elicited a cautious encomium by Herbert Muschamp, who remarked that Portman had shifted the controlled order of the suburban mall to the disordered downtown location. The vast, enclosed spaces of the Portman atrium are supposedly a symbol of how downtown architecture retreated from the public realm into enclosures of private luxury.[5]

Good hotels have always had that as an objective: to set off exclusionary space for the people who pay the tariff to eat, sleep, and fraternize in safety. Hotels are not public spaces, like parks, for anyone and everyone to enjoy. It is, says the writer, "a tightly controlled private environment outfitted with the trappings of public space." True, Portman's atriums and the sleek, highly visible elevators may not "maintain a constant emotional pitch by blending pleasure and terror, cocktails and vertigo." They do add a new dimension to large hotels, a dimension that may

---

5. Herbert Muschamp, "The Thrill of Outer Space for Earthbound Lives," *New York Times* (Sept. 20, 1992).

distract those who wish less excitement in a hotel, not more.

MOTEL/MOTOR HOTEL DESIGN

Today, the design of the larger motel is often indistinguishable from that of the hotel. The distinction is reduced even more with the motor hotel.

Most early motels were designed by the owners. When architects were used, they were cautioned to keep the structure simple and inexpensive. The early motel resembled a long row of boxes in which the tired traveler would enjoy the reverberations of passing traffic throughout the night. Indoor plumbing came as an improvement; the hanging light bulb was changed to a lamp. Every several years, progressive owners tore down existing units and replaced them with something more modern and permanent.

The first motels offered no food facilities, recognizing that business from guest food service was likely to be too small to create a profit; the guests were directed down the road to a good restaurant. Kemmons Wilson, who pioneered Holiday Inns of America, saw the necessity of a restaurant operation in the motel and, beginning in 1952, included one in each of his

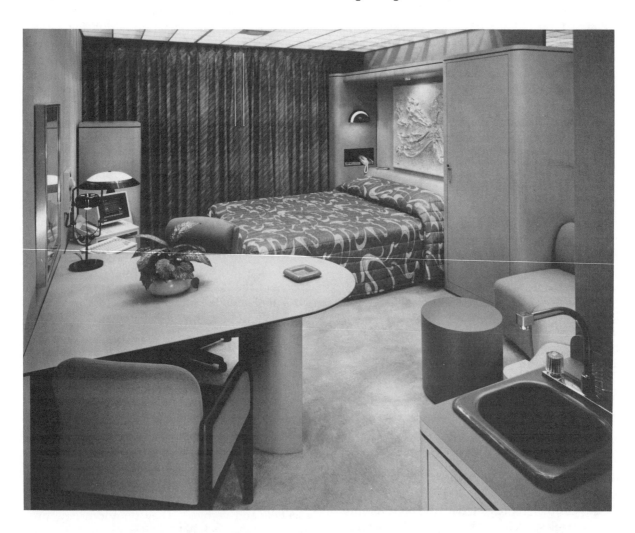

Figure 5-16 The Hi-Tech Guestroom designed by Holiday Inns fits a standard 12-by-18 guestroom and has such features as a video printer word processor and an electronically operated safe. Door locks are actuated by a plastic card rather than a key. Faucets are infrared actuated.

Source: Photo by Gary Walpole.

properties. Gradually, all the larger motels added food facilities.

The first motels comprised only a few units; for many years, the average was less than 20 rooms. In time, the motel grew larger, and today the usual motel—for example, one built by the Holiday Corporation—exceeds 130 units.

Because Kemmons Wilson and his partner, Wallace Johnson, were building contractors, they built their Holiday Inns well and efficiently. One of the reasons for the success of Holiday Inns is the fact that the average unit cost in 1969 was $10,000 a room. Even in high-cost Chicago, Holiday Inns built a property for $12,500 a room. In the South, where construction labor is cheaper, the per unit cost may be even less. One of the secrets of keeping building costs in a motel low, according to Wilson, is to omit the construction of a basement.

Motel Cost

What is the cost breakdown of building a new motel?

Land is likely to cost less than for a hotel because the motel is usually out of the expensive downtown area and takes up less acreage. It is not likely to have the public space of a hotel and can invest more in bedrooms. In fact, room size is usually bigger, running as high as 20 by 20 feet.

Podd and Lesure suggest a motel cost breakdown as follows:

Land 10 to 20 percent

Buildings 65 to 70 percent

Furnishings and equipment 15 to 20 percent

Standardized Elements and Structures

The computer has been put to novel use by William W. Bond, Jr., architect and vice president of Holiday Inns. He standardized many structural elements and developed optimum sizes for dining rooms and lobbies. Much of the information is then stored in a computer linked to a drafting machine. A rough sketch of a proposed new inn and standard bedroom is coded on tape. The tape activates the drafting machine, which in 25 minutes provides detailed plans and elevations accurate to 0.002 inches.[6]

The system saves a great deal of time and hence money. Each month's delay in building an inn raises the cost of, say, a $1 million building site by several thousand dollars.

TraveLodge Corporation has developed an unusual floor plan to reduce costs. Its 200-room "triarc" lodge in exists in the shape of a triangle with concave sides. Because it has no front or back, it can be placed on almost any site. Each lodge requires 8 to 12 months to build, about two-thirds the time needed to construct the usual 200-room hotel.

Space

The characteristic motel silhouette of the past was a single long line of one-story units stretching alongside the highway. The motel today comes in a variety of shapes and patterns, some exceedingly beautiful. A beachfront motel is shaped like a U, with the swimming pool in the center and the back of the property facing the beach. The highrise motel looks very much like a hotel; it is a hotel in everything but name.

The better motels have a room size of about 14 feet wide by at least 24 feet long, including bathroom. Because of the cost of land and construction, most good sites require a minimum of 60 rooms for economic feasibility; for absentee management, a 100-room minimum is recommended.

Expansion up or out should always be allowed for, if at all possible. At least 650 square feet are needed per room for a two-story motel; this includes the restaurant. The minimum average room size is 12 by 24, or 288 square feet. The remaining 362 square feet go outside—for driveways, parking, landscaping, pool, and other facilities. A 100-unit motel then would need a minimum of 60,000 square feet; a more generous 100,000 square feet permits larger rooms and a more attractive siting. Restaurants need between 40 and 60 square feet per person, including parking space and 100 feet of frontage.

Marriott, a highly experienced chain, recommends one parking space for every 2.5 seats in the restaurant. A 100-seat restaurant then needs about 40 parking spaces. Some city building codes require one parking space for every two seats.

---

6. "Reveille Sounds for the Hoteliers," *Fortune Magazine* (Sept. 1969).

The trend is toward larger lobbies in the motor hotel. When prestige is important, more money must be spent on the lobby, and it should be placed so that it is easily seen by the traveler on the highway. The larger the lobby, the more people seem to respect the motel. The bigger space can usually be paid for by a slight increase in the room rate.

Another trend is the creation of "fun domes." Their swimming pools, miniature golf, pool tables, table tennis, and other recreational facilities attract the weekend, as well as the commercial guest. Motels without foodservice require fewer personnel. A TraveLodge motel of 250 rooms, for example, employs only 55, with labor costing less than 25 percent of total sales.

Landscaping

In the past, experts recommended that motels be constructed on large plots easily seen for some distance on the highway. The large lot was used for a swimming pool, landscaping, and parking and for possible expansion in the number of guest rooms. The rising cost of land, however, has forced a change of design. The swimming pool is frequently located above a terrace or on the roof: sometimes, it is indoors. Parking is sometimes underground or on several levels reached by a ramp. At some motels, landscaping is also being moved indoors; plants are now placed in lobbies.

Most motels could do with more and better landscaping. It should relate to the region. Trees and other plantings that come from the same area as the motel are more likely to thrive and require less work. Stone walls and rambling roses, for example, are popular in New England.

Trees can screen streets from the buildings. A few properly placed trees effectively "break" or soften harsh horizontal building lines and make them more inviting. Low spreading plants at the base of motel entrance signs "tie them down" to Mother Earth.

Lighting can create a romantic glow for a motel. Lights cast interesting shadows on walls, emphasize beauty spots, and add color at night. A drive past Miami Beach motels after dark should convince anyone of the magic that lighting can cast on palms, pools, and other plantings.

Some motels have added sculptures and reflecting pools to their entrance areas. The Cabana Motor Hotels have beautiful landscaped grounds, including putting greens. A number of sculptures are set up in front of the motel, reminiscent of the grounds of an Italian villa.

Budget Motel Design

The so-called budget motel appeared on the American highway in 1962. The first of such chains, Motel 6, was started in Santa Barbara, California, and is now owned by Accor, S.A., an up-and-coming French company that at that time already owned the Sofitel and Novetel budget motels in Europe. By 1992 the company had grown to over 600 properties. That year marked the introduction of a reservation service for a fee of $1. Motel 6 rooms are minimal in size, an average of 12 by 12 feet, not counting the bathroom. Old hotels and motels on their way out are priced below the budget motels.

Accor, S.A., is also testing new roadside motels in France that opened without a receptionist, bellmen, or even a bathroom. Telephones, showers, and toilets are located down the hall. The rooms are offered at rock-bottom rates. Each contains a bed to sleep two and a sink. Guests gain entry by putting a credit card into a banking machine outside the motel that debits their accounts and spits out a code number that allows access to the building and the room. Accor's purchase in 1990 of Motel 6 made it the largest lodging company in terms of the number of hotels owned.

Budget properties are usually located near one of the established moderately priced national chains, such as Holiday Inn, Ramada Inn, or Howard Johnson's, where they can attract the price-sensitive traveler. The lower room rate is possible because of lower construction costs, sometimes the complete absence of public space and restaurants, and a minimum of land and landscaping. Management is often a retired husband and wife team. Management salary is usually supplemented by a bonus plan.

The rooms are quite adequate and well-furnished in most cases. There is likely to be pay television and sometimes a small pool to attract family trade. Most of the chains are regional and have not developed the more costly computer reservation systems.

The budget property may cost as little as half the amount of a full-service motor hotel. The two to three acres of land required is one to two acres less than for the motor hotel because lobbies are smaller, and no restaurant or bar exists as an integral part of the building. Operating costs are lower because of fewer employees: an average of 22 employees as compared with 58 for the full-service motor hotel.

There is little doubt that the budget motel will force a leveling or even decrease in motor hotel and other motel room rates in those areas where a number of them operate.

Questions

1. Give two reasons why people build hotels besides operating them for a profit.

2. Some of the most successful hoteliers have made excellent use of leveraged money in buying hotels. Give an example that will illustrate the term "leveraged money."

3. Ernest Henderson would prefer selling Sheraton bonds to selling Sheraton stock to the general public. What advantage did the bonds have over the common stock for the Sheraton Corporation?

4. In the late 1960s and early 1970s, real estate investment trusts (REITs) owned large numbers of hotels and motels. Was this from choice? Explain how this came about.

5. Why is it that insurance companies have seen fit to invest so heavily in hotels?

6. Large numbers of motels in California and the Southwest are owned by Indians and Orientals. Can you explain the reasons for such ownership?

7. At times, it is more to the benefit of the hotel owner to give away the hotel than to operate it. Can you explain the circumstances under which this might be true?

8. Often, a company with a high price/earnings ratio buys a company with a low price/earnings ratio, merging the two companies together. The per share earnings of the new company is higher than for the buying company. Can you tell why?

9. Suppose you and four of your friends decide to buy a motel. Could you rightly call yourself a syndicate?

10. What advantage would there be to leasing TV sets for a hotel rather than purchasing them?

11. Suppose a motel has a book value of $20 a share, but its market value is $30 a share. How can this be?

12. Suppose you owned a $1 million motel and your financial advisors suggest that you sell it, lease it back, and operate it. What advantages would there be for you in such an arrangement?

13. An excellent location for a hotel at one time may be a very poor one at a later time. Can you give an example where such a change has taken place?

14. In trying to establish whether or not a particular site is a good location for a hotel, is the fact that other hotels are close by necessarily negative? Explain why or why not.

Discussion Questions

1. What do you think the hotel of the year 2000 will look like, and how will it differ from the hotel built in the 1980s?

2. Futurists speak of hotels underwater, underground, and on the moon. Will these be built within your lifetime? Why or why not?

3. Over the last several years, most major hotel chains have switched from being owner/operators to being management/franchise companies. Why has this come about?

4. What are the advantages of being a motel owner/operator over being a professional, nonowner hotel manager?

5. Take a position for or against the statement: "In a particular city there will always be a condition of having too many or too few hotel rooms."

6

Hotel/Motel Organization and Operations

It's the little things that make the big things possible. The close attention to the fine details of any operation—restaurants, hotel, or what-not—make the operation first class.

—J. Willard Marriott, founder, Marriott Corporation

This chapter deals with hotel organization and touches the broad subject of hotel and motel operations. In doing so, it perhaps only touches on the topics of personnel and developments in the areas of marketing, management, and technical developments. Only enough will be said to provide a glimpse of what happens and the kind of management needed for effective hotel and motel operation.

PERSONNEL ORGANIZATION

From the days of the early inn to the modern megahotel, personnel have been and will continue to be the prime ingredient of good hotel and motel operation. The small, or budget, motel runs

well or not so well, depending on the know-how and attitudes of the owner alone. As size increases to that of the larger motor hotel, hotel and finally megahotel, the number of personnel grow. A few of the very large properties have well over 1000 employees. The employees who come into contact with guests combine with the appearance, reputation, and equipment of a property to create the guest's final verdict—a pleasant stay or an unpleasant one.

Figure 6-1 is the organizational chart for a typical 150-room motor hotel, the Downtown Motor Inn, and Figure 6-2 is that for the Sheraton-Boston Hotel and Towers. They both illustrate the wide range in structure within the industry. The 150-room hotel has a relatively simple structure; the organization of a large hotel is complex and can vary considerably from one property to another.

Each chain has its own job titles and organizational particularities. The assistant manager in a medium-sized Holiday Inn is also the food and beverage director. Front desk clerks are called

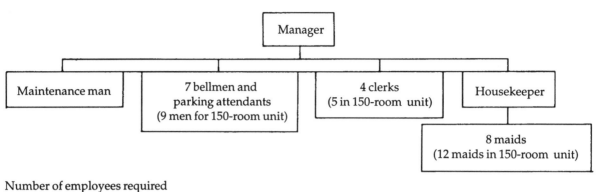

Number of employees required
for 100- and 150-room Downtown Motor Inn

Figure 6-1 Organization chart for a 100- to 150-room motor inn without food and beverage service.

guest services representatives, with a guest services manager in charge instead of the traditional front office manager. Figure 6-3 shows an organizational chart for a typical Holiday Inn of about 130 rooms. In the larger properties, there may be a resident manager and an executive chef, the latter reporting to the food and beverage manager.

Role of General Manager

Leading the personnel and sitting at the top of the hotel and motel organization is the general manager (GM), who necessarily has the responsibility, authority, and accountability granted him or her by the owners to manage the property so that guests are satisfied and will return. The GM also assures that the property will operate at a profit under ordinary circumstances and is not overloaded with debt.

The GM operates in an environment somewhat like that of a ship, where the captain is highly visible and at the helm much of the time in relationship to personnel, guests, people in the community, politicians, and owners. The GM sets tone and style and is in large part responsible for personnel's morale. He or she is assisted by department heads and in larger hotels by an executive operating committee (EOC) composed of senior department heads. The GM, in turn, reports to an owner or investment group or, in the case of a chain organization, a corporate regional vice president, as seen in Figure 6-4.

In a large hotel, the EOC would also include the directors of engineering, convention services, and public relations. Members of the EOC in some instances are considered to be in training for the position of GM, and at times when the hotel is not operating at capacity, they may function as the GM.

Role of Hotel Controller

In large hotels the accounting and control function is divorced from everyday management. The controller or finance officer, as the controller is sometimes called, is separate from line management. For example, the finance officer within a large Hilton hotel reports directly to the Hilton Hotels home office rather than the general manager of the property. Such an arrangement has advantages and disadvantages. The general manager may resent losing that element of the control function. The controller and general manager may clash, and one or the other may have to be moved to another property. The primary advantage is that a specialist is in charge of the cash and accounting and is responsible directly to headquarters. This decreases the possibility of thievery or manipulation by the general manager or immediate staff. In addition, the general manager is also freed from day-to-day concern over accounting and control procedures and, hence, can devote more time to concentrating on guest relations, overall hotel operations, and the marketing function.

A survey of 311 members of the International Association of Hospitality Accountants (IAHA) found that the typical hotel controller was responsible for his or her hotel's general accounting, payroll, accounts receivable (payments owed

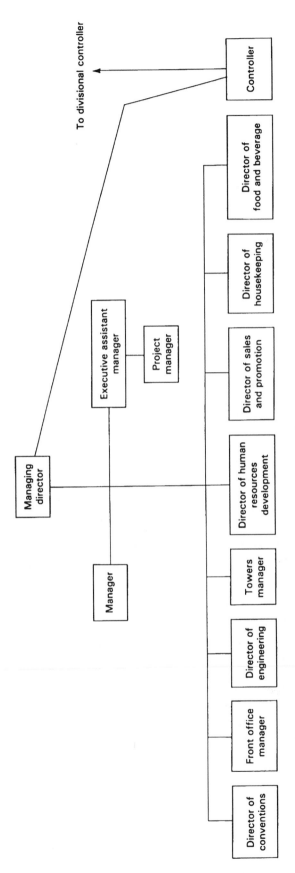

Figure 6-2 Sheraton Boston Hotel and Towers executive committee organization chart. With 1252 rooms, the Sheraton Boston Hotel and Towers is among the largest hotels. The managing director heads the management team. Directly under that person is the manager and executive assistant manager. There are nine departments, each with its own department head: conventions, front office, engineering, towers, human resources development, sales and promotion, housekeeping, food and beverage, and accounting. Together, the managing director, manager, executive assistant manager, and department heads make up the executive operating committee as seen above. (The director of training and director of human resources development also sit on the executive committee.)

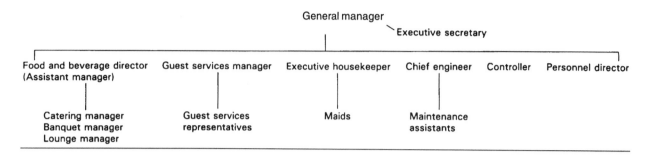

Figure 6-3 Organization chart of a Holiday Inn with about 130 rooms.

the hotel), accounts payable (money the hotel owed others), auditing (checking the validity and accuracy of accounting within the hotel), and cash control. (See Fig. 6-5.) The controller needs to know accounting principles, capital budgeting, cash management, statistical measurements, and internal controls. The typical controller answering the survey questionnaire held a bachelor's degree in accounting and was a member of the executive operating committee of a hotel and had the authority to sign checks, approve purchases, and extend credit. Some controllers could also set or change prices and borrow funds (presumably with the GM's approval). In some hotels, the controller also had responsibility for the personnel department. The controller may also have oversight of all of a hotel's computers.[1]

Budget preparation usually begins with the hotel controller. An estimate of future income and expense is a projection used to plan, control, and shape operations, especially personnel scheduling, capital outlays, and borrowing needs. Many hotels update the budget throughout the year, usually for 3 months in advance. In some hotel chains, annual budgets come down from a headquarter's financial president and are modified by the controller in consultation with the GM and department heads. In other chains, the budgeting begins at the hotel level and is modified at the chain headquarters.

Computerization of hotel and motel accounting has removed much of the drudgery of bookkeeping from accounting and eliminates the need for a room rack, rack slips, stock cards, guest bills, and the telephone and information rack. The

computer files the status of every room and can be asked to assign rooms. Once a guest is registered, an electronic in-house folio (guest account) is created and the guest's name and room number is entered into the switchboard computer terminal. The computer eliminates most of the night auditor's accounting functions and has revolutionized many of the routines associated with manual accounting. For example, on checking out a guest, the computer can produce itemized guest folios and transfer them to the proper city ledger account if the guest charges are not paid in full.

The hotel accounting system is set up to conform to the organization, nomenclature, and chart of accounts recommended in the *Uniform System of Accounts* and *Expense and Payroll Dictionary* published by the AH&MA. Without such a uniform system, hotels could not compare operating results. Accounting employees can move from one hotel to another and be assured that the accounts and systems will be the same.

Human Resource Manager

The human resource manager (also known as human resource director or personnel director) is responsible for recruiting personnel and assisting in their selection, placement and training, as seen in Figure 6-6. In a large hotel he or she may sit as a member of the Executive Operating Committee. Employee records and wage and salary administration are usually a responsibility. In some hotels the human resource manager hires new employees; in other properties he or she screens them; actual employment choices are made by department heads.

The person in charge does not direct or manage any employees as their job title might sug-

1. A. Neal Geller and Raymond S. Schmidgall, "The Hotel Controller: More Than a Bookkeeper," *The Cornell Hotel and Restaurant Administration Quarterly* (Aug. 1984).

Figure 6-4 The Executive Operating Committee.

gest, only those within his or her relatively small staff. In a small hotel the director may be the only employee or be assisted by a secretary. In large unionized properties, union relations may be a sizable responsibility.

Some of the personnel officer's work is defensive against the possibility of charges of violating government regulations or to prevent complaints of negligent hiring, negligent retention, and/or negligent entrustment. Negligent hiring is the failure by management to uncover a job applicant's incompetence or lack of fitness. Negligent retention is the failure to be aware of unfitness for a particular position or to take corrective action, such as training, reassignment, or discharge. Negligent entrustment refers to entrusting an unfit employee with the means of harming another person. An example would be entrusting an unfit person to drive a van owned by the hotel.

Management acting through the personnel office must be careful not to imply in any way that a job applicant is assured of a job or once given a job, has tenure on the job. Employee handbooks, which detail company rules and procedures, are carefully written to avoid establishing a contractual relationship and terms like "discharge for just cause" are carefully spelled out.

Determining what constitutes sexual harassment and the policies to uncover or stop harassment are part of the personnel function. Age discrimination against "protected" workers (those over age 40) is a continuing concern. Termination policy—when, how, and under what circumstances an employee should be discharged—is in part defensive in nature, done carefully to avoid legal charges.

How to deal with employees suspected of abusing or known to use illegal substances is also a part of personnel policy. So is the matter of how to react to a government investigation. Employment discrimination has become an important is-

sue as many lawyers have taken on cases of alleged discrimination on a contingency basis. This means that the complainant does not pay litigation costs, but that the lawyer who assumes the case receives a sizable amount of any settlement fee. Rather than risk the possibility of having to pay a huge award to a complaintant, hotels and restaurants often pay sizable amounts to settle out of court even though the complaint is groundless.

The Equal Employment Opportunity Commission (EEOC) and often a state agency with similar responsibilities for protecting employee rights are on hand to hear complaintants, and employee unions may also be ready to challenge management decisions or actions.

Job applicants or employees with disabilities must be treated fairly to avoid charges of discrimination. Job description detailing the qualifications and work performed on a job can help job placement so that there is less of a question about whether or not a handicapped person can perform a job satisfactorily. The defensive nature of the personnel officer's work may not be as rewarding as the functions of recruitment, selection, training, and management development; nevertheless, it is part of the job.

The Front Office: Hub of Human Relations

In physical terms, the front office (Fig. 6-7) of a hotel is its focal point, its nerve center, its command post, a crossroads, the conjunction where guests and hotel employees merge, interact, and move on. It is also an information center, a place for recording transactions and for recordkeeping and control. Psychologically, it is a human relations center where a guest meets and interacts with hotel personnel, each interaction evoking feelings that in the final analysis determines whether the guest enjoys the hotel experience. As a visible symbol of the hotel operation, at the nerve center, is the clerk. He or she is the subject of praise and focus of hostility when almost anything pleasant or unpleasant happens to a guest.

Figure 6-8 suggests some of the relationships that ebb and flow in and around the front desk. Personnel are interacting and communicating with guests who are checking in or out. The clerks react to and initiate actions with the housekeeping department, general management, sales-

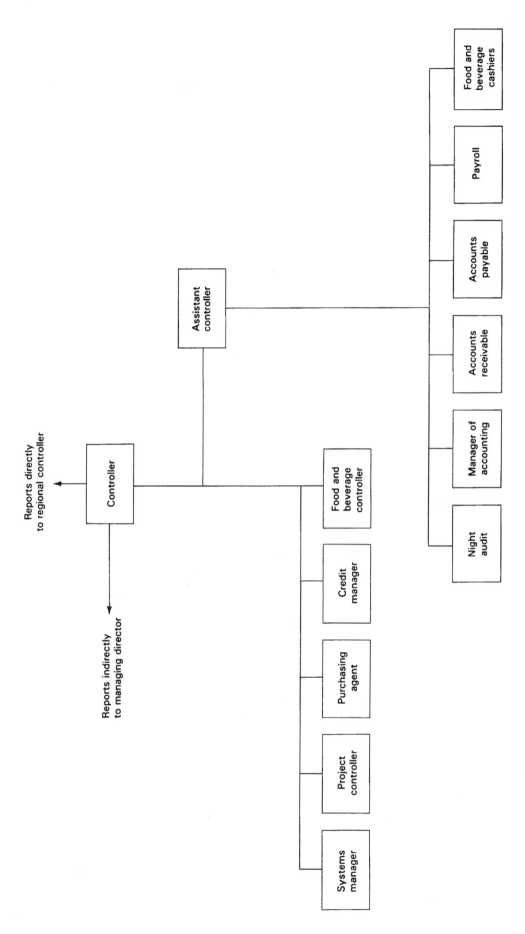

Figure 6-5 Sheraton Boston Hotel and Towers controllers department organizational chart. A controller heads the controller's (accounting and control) department. As shown in the figure, that person reports to both the managing director and the regional controller of the Sheraton Corporation. These positions report to the assistant controller: night audit, manager of accounting, accounts receivable, accounts payable payroll, and the several food and beverage cashiers. A systems manager (computers), project manager, purchasing agent, credit manager, and food and beverage controller report directly to the controller.

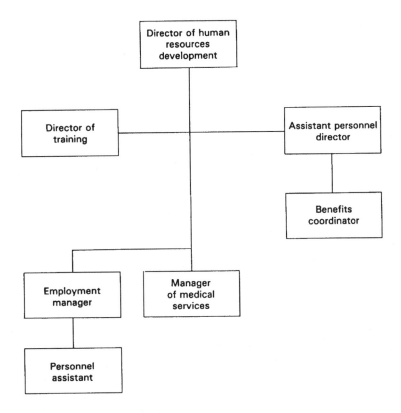

Figure 6-6 Sheraton Boston Hotel and Towers personnel department organizational chart. Over the years, what was the personnel department has become the human resources development department . The Sheraton Boston places a director in charge who works with an assistant director, director of training, employment manager, manager of medical services, benefits coordinator, and personnel assistant.

people, engineering, and accounting department. In brief, they maintain communications with personnel in all other departments.

The job title of desk clerk is inadequate and misleading, even a misnomer. It suggests only one aspect of the job, the clerical, which perhaps is the least important and least demanding of all. In fact, the job breaks down into three parts: clerical, human relations, and sales. The clerk plays several roles: management representative, problem solver, guardian of the public safety, social facilitator, creator of hotel image, salesperson, and friend of the traveler.

Of course, the clerk functions as a clerk—adding and subtracting (or working a computer), registering guests, and checking them out. The clerk often works also as night auditor, cashier, and even night watchman, but also much more. He or she is a dealer in human relations, almost a

psychologist. The clerk's presence, manner, and level of service define job effectiveness.

Human relations and sales are often two sides of the same coin. The effective salesperson "sells" himself or herself first and then tunes in to the needs of the client. In order to do this well, the first commandment is to know the product thoroughly, in this case, the entire hotel—its range of rooms, the appointments in each room and suite, the advantages and disadvantages of each room, and of course, the tariffs. To familiarize clerks with the hotel, management at some hotels ask them to spend a night in various rooms, to look over the swimming pool, to try the sauna, to relish the oversized towels, and so on.

Each room offers certain advantages over others, such as view, furniture, quietness, elevator access, or nearness to restaurant or bar. The perceptive clerk quickly identifies what kind of

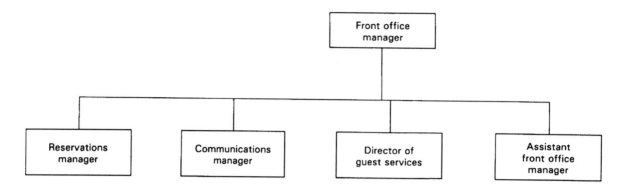

Figure 6-7 Sheraton Boston Hotel and Towers front office organizational chart. The front office is headed by a manager and backed up by an assistant front office manager. Guest services, communications, and reservations are each headed by a supervisor, all of whom report to the front office manager.

things a guest would prefer—for example, a quiet back room or one close to the bar.

The clerk is not just selling rooms; he or she is selling an experience, the experience of the entire hotel—its game room, its swimming pool, its fine restaurants, its 24-hour coffee shop, its accessibility to the highway, its proximity to the state house, its price, its clientele, its cheerful rooms, its status. The room is only one part of the total experience, and it may be negligible compared with the beautiful golf course, six tennis courts, afternoon tea service, and great personnel—not to mention "the courtesy cars available to pick you up and take you back to the airport."

MARKETING

The person in charge of sales is now usually the director of marketing, a change that implies a much broader role than sales alone. Marketing is concerned with not only selling, but also learning more about the product that is being sold, as well as the competitor's product, the customer, the customer's motivations and wants, and how the product can best be produced and presented to meet the customer's needs. Marketing implies research. In the hotel it involves carefully identifying who the present customers are, where they come from, what they earn, and what they want in the way of hotel services. A Los Angeles hotel may find that its principal source of customers, its market, is western Canada, San Francisco, and Chicago; promotion and advertising would then be concentrated in those areas.

Some hotels have a sharply focused market, perhaps the military, government employees, or airline employees. The marketing director wants to know what percentage of his or her guests are price-sensitive and what percentage are not. Will a "September Days" club that was established for Days Inns guests be effective? Should the market research be done in-house or contracted out to a professional marketing firm?

How valuable is membership in a marketing consortium, such as Best Western? For some locations, it is very valuable; for others, not much. Judging from the rapid growth of franchising and market referral groups, we can surmise that most independent hotels cannot afford to go it alone. Hotels worldwide are becoming affiliated with a franchise or marketing organization in one way or another. The advantages of group advertising and being part of a computer reservation system are great for most sizable hotels and motels.

The identification of *target* markets is a major concern of hotel management. Markets can be identified in terms of room rates that will be accepted, origins of travelers, purpose of traveling, and other classifications. Market segmentation is associated with room rates. Luxury hotels may target only travelers who can pay $150 or more on a room; budget properties are interested in anyone who will pay $30.

Classification according to the purpose of a trip is another common way of market identification. Most large hotels located in cities expect at least half of their guests to be business travelers, and in many hotels in gateway cities a sizable percentage of the guests are international travelers.

Overall, about 17 percent of the business of hotels comprise international travelers. Horwath and Horwath International reported the percentage of international guests in North America as seen in Figure 6-9.

A Few Marketing Devices

A motor hotel manager may be surprised to learn that 70 percent of the guests are traveling for pleasure, not business. A hotel or motel that is a member of a referral organization may find that it receives less than 30 percent of its customers through that referral system. The group marketing research and development section of Holiday Corporation found that Holiday Inns were not as successful as some other chains in attracting families traveling with teenagers simply because the other chains did not charge for teens. As a result, a "teens-free" policy was instituted in 1300 inns. The same company wondered how business travelers felt about the holidomes, their covered courtyards with pools and games. The business traveler thought that they were innova-tive and impressive and added to the appeal of the inn. Business travelers were asked about the chain's policy of "kids eat free." The program was seen as positive and seemed to influence the business traveler to stay at a Holiday Inn when traveling with his or her family.

Market analysis can determine where new investment is needed. Should it be spent in redesigning the lobby or improving the restaurant operation? Ask the customer. What effect will a severe winter have on summer business? In Harrisburg, Pennsylvania, for example, a severe winter caused the schools to close 3 weeks late, well into June. This affected the June business for a number of inns that depended on Harrisburg as a summer feeder market. As a result, the inns could accept group or meeting business that they normally would have turned away in June.

The Staff

The sales staff of hotels and motels varies in size from one place to another. In a small motel, the manager performs the sales function. A me-

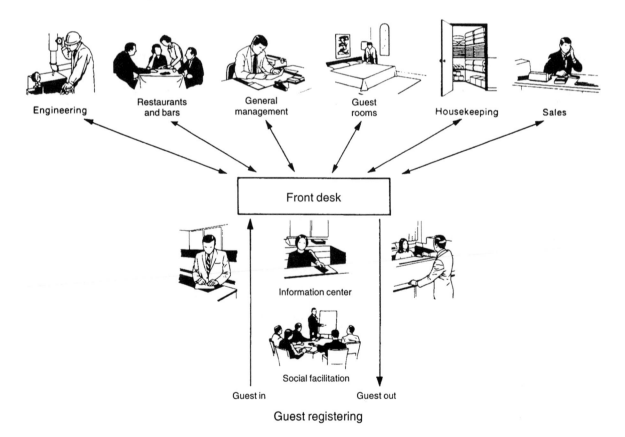

Figure 6-8 Guest and employee interactions with the front desk.

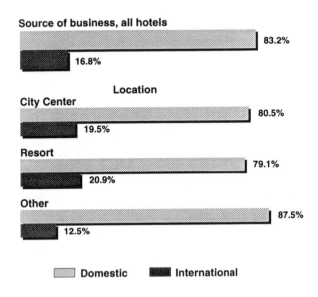

Figure 6-9 Hotel market in North America.
Source: Horwath & Horwath, International.

dium-sized hotel, such as the 408-room Radisson South in Minneapolis, may have a staff of five in the sales department. In a megahotel, a director of conventions (Fig. 6-10) or director of marketing may have a staff of eight or ten persons, plus the assistance of the corporate office sales staff. Most of the staff's effort is directed toward group sales.

Small hotels ordinarily do not employ a full-time salesperson. The owners have the choices of relying heavily on a referral system (such as Best Western) for business, periodically buying the services of an advertising and marketing company, doing no marketing and expecting word-of-mouth recommendations or location to attract guests, or the general manager may take on marketing responsibilities.

Whoever does the job or however it is done, current and potential target markets are identified and a promotion plan is then assembled. Promotion is carried out by direct mail, newspaper ads, and travel agent cultivation. All hotels, large and small, are engaged in marketing, whether they know it or not—be it systematic and logical, or haphazard and unplanned.

In one Radisson Hotel, the director of sales is primarily concerned with setting up game plans, establishing goals, budgeting, forecasting, and supervision. He also spends 20 percent of his time on the road.

With the general manager and executive assistant manager, the sales director develops an annual rooms sales forecast for group bookings for every day of the year. Day-to-day forecasting is done by the executive assistant manager.[2]

The assistant director of sales spends 20 percent of his time away, primarily at national conventions, and assists the director of sales in reporting, record keeping, and performing analysis and evaluation.

The sales manager spends 35 percent of his time away, primarily on convention sales with an emphasis on state and regional meetings.

A salesperson spends 70 percent of his or her time away, promoting corporate meetings and other multiple reservations. Another salesperson spends 90 percent of his or her time outside, visiting corporate offices.

Hotels customarily provide one complimentary guest room for every 100 rooms the group fills. Some hotels provide a suite.

Travel, Tours, and Public Relations

Travel management is closely related to hotel and restaurant management, both being a part of the broader field of hospitality management. Many hotels are dependent, in part, on travel agents for much of their business. Business travelers increasingly turn to travel agents to book hotel rooms as well as flights. Some resort hotels may get 90 to 100 percent of their bookings via the 30,000 travel agencies in this country.

Several hotels receive as much as 60 percent of their business from tour operators. Some large hotels have established a new job title in their marketing departments—travel or tour director. This person has direct responsibility for selling the hotel to tour operators and coordinating group tour service once they have arrived at the hotel.

Hotel managers are well aware of the impact of air schedules and fares on their business; markets change radically when air services and fares do. For example, West Coast hotels found large new markets developing from Australia and the Orient as Pacific airfares came down.

The large hotels, chains, and theme parks use public relations (PR) personnel, whose primary job is to create a favorable image for their proper-

2. "The Radisson South, a Case Study in Hotel Operation," *Lodging* (Nov. 1977).

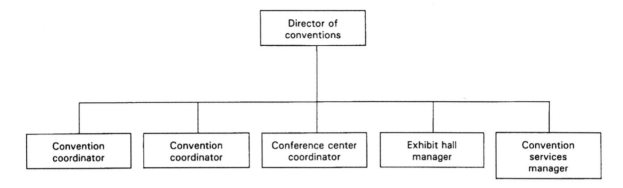

Figure 6-10 Sheraton Boston Hotel and Towers convention services organizational chart. Convention business is a large part —in many large hotels, the major part—of the total business. The Sheraton Boston places a director of conventions in charge of this segment, with five supervisors—two convention coordinators, a conference center coordinator, an exhibit hall manager, and a convention services manager—all reporting to the director.

ties. Special promotions, such as holiday or weekend packages, can be part of their role. They also prepare letters in response to guest complaints for the manager's signature and conduct tours of the property.

PR staff cultivate editors, travel writers, and other media personnel and encourage them to write about the property concerned. They also send out news releases designed to keep the hotel, theme park, or other attraction in the public eye.

PR employees are usually excellent writers, likable, and often highly imaginative. When the Six Flags Over Texas theme park introduced its new high-speed thrill ride called the "Runaway Mine Train," it broke down with a dozen newspaper writers and photographers and four television cameramen on board; the train came to a screeching halt on the high loops. The whole thing could have been a publicity disaster, but the quick-thinking public relations person suggested that the media people treat the incident from a different angle: "Safety Systems on New Runaway Train Work Perfectly."

A give-away guidebook for an area may increase the average hotel stay from 1 to 3 days, the guest having discovered a number of new things to do.

OPERATING ARRANGEMENTS

Hotels and motels are operated in a number of ways:

Owner operates and manages.

Owner sells and then leases back and operates.

Owner hires professional management.

Owner purchases franchise from companies such as Hilton or Holiday Inns and operates under own management.

Owner purchases franchise and franchise company operates.

Owner operates but under referral organization name, such as Best Western.

Owner leases property to an operating company or individual.

Owner employs a management company such as Hilton or Sheraton to operate.

Management Contracts

Since about 1960, management contracts have been particularly favored by such companies as Hilton, Sheraton, Hyatt, Marriott, and Westin because such contracts permit them to offer their management expertise without tying up large amounts of capital.

Large numbers of hotels were built in the late 1960s through 1986 as a result of easy money. Real estate investment trusts (REITs) attracted millions of dollars from investors, and REIT managers eagerly lent out the money. But as seen earlier, many of the hotels and motels they financed had to be taken back by the REITs. Since REITs are prohibited by law from managing and operating properties for more than 90 days, they were often desperate to find operators. As a result, they signed up reputable hotel operating companies under management contracts with little or no operator investment. The large chain operators, however, were not interested in bidding on properties with fewer than 300 to 350 rooms because the smaller properties could not afford their management fees unless the hotels were experiencing high-volume sales.

Several fee arrangements for the operators emerged. Basic fees were usually 3 to 6 percent of gross revenues. When an incentive fee was added, the basic fee typically ran 2 to 4 percent of gross revenue plus 10 percent of the gross operating profit. The fee could also be a fixed amount plus a percentage of gross operating profit. Or the operator would receive a basic or incentive fee, whichever proved to be greater.

However, as competition for management contracts grew, operators were forced to make investments in the property as a condition of obtaining the contract. Investment participation included money for such things as working capital; the purchase of furniture, fixtures, and equipment; supplying the preopening expenses; stock purchase; and partnerships.

Contracts usually run for 1 to 20 years. Chain operators are able to negotiate longer initial terms and renewal terms because of their reputation and financial stability.

Hotel owners who turn to hotel management companies to operate the owner's hotel(s) have tightened the terms of the contracts and reduced the fees paid the management companies to 3 or 6 percent of total revenue. In some instances, the fee percentage is less. Owners also negotiate veto power over the operating budget proposed by the management company. Owners may employ an asset manager who represents the owner and supervises the budget process and its implementation. Hotel owners insist on performance standards that must be met and want the right to terminate the contract. Moreover, owners are taking a much more active role in overseeing marketing, pricing, redecorating, and even labor negotiations.[3] Having to accept such involvement may be galling to some management companies and removes some autonomy from the GM. It could also make for a more conservative approach to management, leaning toward the Japanese style of management, which emphasizes consensus.

Owners of foreclosed properties usually want to be able to cancel a management contract quickly, since their intent is to sell the property as soon as possible. Experienced operators want contracts that can be cancelled with 90 days' notice.[4]

The Franchise

Franchised properties in the U.S. took in more than a third of all U.S. hotel sales in 1987, according to the U.S. Department of Commerce. Franchising in the hotel and restaurant business goes back at least to 1907, when the Ritz Development Company franchised the Ritz-Carlton name to a hotel in New York City.

A franchisor can expand business straight across the country by signing up hundreds of franchisees, who are then almost always largely or totally responsible for raising much of the necessary capital to start the business. The system can expand as rapidly as the franchisees sign.

The two principal problems of the franchisor are (1) maintaining the quality and standard of the product and services being franchised, and (2) seeing to it that few if any of the franchisees fail.

The more successful franchise organizations have arrived at the enviable position of being able to screen and select franchisees carefully. The financial capacity of a franchisee is carefully reviewed; the site for the motel or restaurant must be approved by the franchisor. In some cases, the franchisee has no voice in the selection of the site, but must take the one that has been analyzed by the site expert of the franchising organization.

Howard Johnson's. In 1927 Howard D. Johnson began franchising his stores, and the name Howard Johnson was to become a household word on the East Coast and later in the Midwest and West. By 1973 the company included more than 900 restaurants and 450 motor lodges nationwide.

TraveLodge. In 1948 Scott King of San Diego, California, began selling the TraveLodge franchise. It was an unusual franchise in that the company and franchise holder went into partnership. The franchise holder put up half the cost of the

3. Stephen Rushmore, "Negotiation the Name of the Game," *Lodging Hospitality* (Feb. 1992).

4. James J. Eyster, *The Negotiation and Administration of Hotel Management Contract* (Ithaca, N.Y.: School of Hotel Administration, Cornell University), 1977.

motel; the corporation built the motel with something less than the other half of the investment, since it received the contractor's fee. With the help of TraveLodge, people who had $60,000 or $70,000 in cash could get into the motel business on a much bigger scale than if they were to establish the motel themselves.

The new partner operated the motel and was paid a monthly salary for doing so. All the accounting was done in San Diego by the central office of TraveLodge, and profits were divided at the end of each month. Today, TraveLodge is owned by Trusthouse Forte of England.

Holiday Inn Worldwide (formerly Holiday Inns of America).   Owned by Bass PLC, a British firm, Holiday Inn Worldwide is headquartered in Atlanta, Georgia. Franchising, begun in 1952, made it possible. By 1978 there were more than 1700 Holiday Inns around the world, varying in size from 100 to 700 rooms. With more than 275,000 rooms in more than 50 countries, sales exceeded $2.3 billion, about $1.5 million for an average inn.

Two factors that contribute to the success of Holiday Corporation are a sizable number of rooms in all properties and on-premises dining facilities.

The typical inn is a one- or two-story brick structure, built in a square or U-shape around a central pool, with 100 to 150 rooms. Characteristically, each has large windows covered with heavy drapes.

Building costs vary with the cost of labor around the country. Holiday Corporation helps the franchisee arrange financing, usually 60 percent of the cost, and suggests an architect and contractor.

Fledgling hotel and restaurant managers or assistant managers attend the Holiday Inn University at Holiday City in Memphis for five weeks. There they learn about operations, the appropriate public manner, and the company philosophy.

To help maintain company standards, each inn receives four unannounced inspections a year that cover such things as the condition of the Great Sign, cleanliness, and the state of the boiler room. The inspector samples the specialty of the day in the restaurant and examines the kitchen. If an inn fails to pass such an inspection, a second inspection is given 30 days later. If the inn fails to pass the second inspection, the franchise is withdrawn.

In the accommodations field, the large hotel chains were slow to see the merits of franchising. The phenomenal success of Holiday Inns focused attention on what could be done, and in the 1960s Hilton and Sheraton began to franchise their names and referral systems to existing hotels and new inns and motels.

Hotel/motel franchisees have the advantage of national advertising, a national identity, access to training programs and materials, and most important, access to the national reservation system of the franchisor.

Costs and benefits.   Stephen W. Brenner and A. Carmi Gamoran, writing in the *Cornell Hotel and Restaurant Administration Quarterly*,[5] summarized the costs and benefits of a hotel or motel franchise to a franchisee. First, the costs:

1. Initial franchise or affiliation fees.

2. Royalty fees paid as a percentage of room sales or fees based on number of available rooms.

3. Advertising costs.

4. Unit cost per reservation or cost for reservation service.

5. Sign rentals.

6. Other costs (e.g., stationery and other guest supplies, forms, and menus with the trademark or logo of the franchise organization).

Next, the benefits are listed:

1. More room sales because of a network of reservation outlets within cities and along highways.

2. National advertising that gives greater exposure to the name of the franchise with which the operator wishes to be identified; also, all groups publish and distribute directories; the distribution and quantity of these are an important benefit.

3. More sales due to credit card affiliation.

---

5. Stephen W. Brenner and A. Carmi Gamoran, "The Quest for Identification," *The Cornell Hotel and Restaurant Administration Quarterly*, Vol. 8, No. 4 (Feb. 1968).

4. Stature that affiliation and identification with a recognized name offers.

5. Central purchasing and its savings may be offered.

6. Architectural plans may be offered.

7. Advice on planning, layout, decoration, and other critical areas.

8. Training—front office procedure manuals and similar training tools for housekeeping and other departments are available through some franchisors; in addition, some companies hold annual conventions during which members can discuss problems, exchange ideas, and get further help in securing business or solving operating problems; there are also regional sales and training meetings.

9. Borrowing costs may be reduced and mortgage money more readily available if the mortgagor knows that the property will be identified with a nationally recognized franchise organization.

The referral business that membership in a nationwide and well-known hotel or motel franchise system brings is a benefit. The same is true for restaurant franchises in terms of increased patronage when the restaurant is part of a nationally known group with a favorable public image. Not all hotel and restaurant locations benefit from being a franchisee.

The larger the franchise system, the greater the potential benefits to the individual unit. Each unit, if it is favorably received by the public, enhances every other unit. Motels have been known to increase their patronage as much as 30 percent the day the franchise sign was erected.

Every unit is theoretically tied to every other via a reservation system. National advertising, impossible for the individual unit, can be carried out by the franchise organization. Most of the contracts of the larger franchisors stipulate that a certain percentage, from 1 to 3 percent of gross sales, be paid by the franchisee into a national advertising fund. Pooling advertising dollars in this manner makes for advertising exposure otherwise impossible by the individual.

Costs to the franchisee include an initial fee plus an advertising/marketing fee based on a percentage of gross room revenues, plus a per reservation fee. *Lodging Hospitality* annually publishes a chart (Table 6-1) that includes a listing of fees and requirements for becoming a franchisee.

The franchise favors the franchisor. The terms of the agreement are drawn up by the franchisor; the franchisee is free to buy the franchise or reject it. Ordinarily, the agreement is fixed. Most agreements contain clauses that permit the franchisor to buy back the franchise or to cancel it should the franchisee fail to live up to the terms of the agreement.

When the franchise involves primarily the use of a name, as is the case with Sheraton Hotels, the parent company may quietly nullify the agreement, take back its sign, and remove the hotel or motel from the list of Sheraton Hotels that take part in the company's referral system.

From the point of view of the franchisor, the most difficult operating problem is the need for continuous control of the product and service standards in every unit. Every customer who frequents a poorly operated unit walks away with a less favorable image of the total organization. The bright orange roof of a Howard Johnson's or the Great Sign of Holiday Inns somehow becomes a little tarnished in the mind of the customer. Each unit reflects on all other units. The franchisor cannot afford to allow many units to fall below standard or to fail, otherwise he or she fails.

The franchise agreement is generally restrictive regarding the style of operation, product, and services offered. No room is left for imagination, no changes in menu, decor, furnishings, or equipment are permitted. Neither is there room for regional differences in taste or other customer preference. Some of the franchise fees add up to 15 percent of the gross sales and more; this can be a burden, especially during slow periods.

Inevitably, there are disagreements. Often, franchisees find that they are not cut out to operate a restaurant or motel. These businesses appear glamorous until the people involved learn that they must live, work, and think their business to remain successful. Those who think they can "retire" to a motel or restaurant are usually shocked to find that they have married a business. Babysitters for motels or restaurants are hard to find; Mom and Pop find they must march to the tune played by the operation.

TABLE 6-1   Franchise Fees

Name of Chain	Minimum No. of Rooms	Fees
Holiday Inns, Inc. (Atlanta, Georgia)		
Holiday Inns	100	Initial fee of $25,000 minimum or $300 per room. Advertising/ marketing fee of 1.5 percent gross room revenue. Reservation fee of 1 percent of gross room revenue plus $4.40 per room. Royalty fee of 4 percent of gross room revenue.
Crowne Plaza	100	Initial fee of $75,000 minimum or $300 per room. Advertising/ marketing fee is 2 percent of gross room revenue. Reservation fee of 1 percent of gross room revenue. Royalty fee of 4 percent of gross room revenue plus $4.40 per room.
Hampton Inns	80	Initial fee of $35,000. Advertising/marketing fee of 3.0 percent of gross room revenue. Reservation fee of $300 per room per month. Royalty fee of 4 percent of gross room nights.
Hilton Inns (Beverly Hills, Calif.)	100	Initial fee of $250 each for first 100 rooms and $150 for each additional room. Reservation fee of $6.50 per reservation plus an $4.87 access fee.
Sheraton Corp. (Boston, Mass.)	100	Initial fee of $30,000 deposit for first 100 rooms plus $150 per additional room for new construction. Reservation fee of 1.8 percent of gross room revenue with $17.75 maximum. Continuing fee of 5 percent of gross room sales per month. No ad fee.
Econo Lodges of America, Inc. (Charlotte, N.C.)	40	Initial fee of $20,000. Other combined fees totalling 6.5 percent.

Source: "Franchise Fact File," *Lodging Hospitality* (Dec. 1990).

Not many individuals have the energy and temperament needed to run the variety of franchised restaurants or motels. The operation demands long hours and constant attention. After a few months of being "locked in" to a motel or restaurant, many franchisees want out.

Getting out without financial loss is not always easy. The bickering between franchisor and franchisee begins. It may go on for months until both parties wish they had never heard of each other. The franchisor usually ends up buying back the unit or installing a company manager to operate it.

MARKETING AND REFERRAL GROUPS

Close relatives of the franchise concept are the numerous marketing and referral groups (also known as consortia) that provide a group image, group marketing, group purchasing, and often other chain services such as training and performance analysis. Most charge a marketing fee.

These marketing/referral groups are open to any hotel/motel owner who can meet the group's qualifications in regard to number of rooms, quality of the property, facilities offered and promise not to violate restrictions made by the group. The property owner whose property is accepted picks up the group sign, participates in the referral system, and may buy other services, such as training programs from the group. Some groups also offer furnishings and equipment at reduced prices. The major benefit of belonging to one of the marketing/referral consortia is the additional business that results from referrals from other members and the group advertising and marketing efforts. Like a franchisee, a member can be dropped for failure to abide by standards set by the group, such as standards of cleanliness, ethics, and the like.

These consortia are not franchisors, but they are similar. Some are membership-governed. Owners of one or several properties may join these marketing consortia, provided that they meet the criteria established. Like franchise groups, consortia members pay reservation and other fees to the consortia.

The largest of these groups is Best Western with about 3350 members, the world's largest in number of properties. Headquartered in Phoenix, Arizona, its reservation system is linked with seven major airlines. More than 1000 people are employed in its central office. It runs a school for its members, with such courses as front desk management and housekeeping. The company publishes and distributes 6 million copies of its maps, pinpointing member locations. Best Western is controlled by its members, who own hotels and motels that are part of Best Western.

Several consortia are international in scope. Leading Hotels of the World, headquartered in New York City, has members in 43 countries. SRS Hotels operating out of Frankfort, West Germany, exist in 40 countries. Some of the groups (Distinguished Hotels, for example) are operated by a private concern that acts as a marketing and sales representative. Some groups feature economy, as does Budget Host Inns, based in Fort Worth, Texas. The French Relais du Silence features two-to four-star European hotels. The Golden Tulip World Wide, owned by KLM airlines, has 320 member properties in 60 countries.

Membership can increase occupancy rates. The JAL Hotel System has members in Europe, the Mideast, and Africa. After joining Best Western, the now named Best Western Inn of Chicago mounted its five-story Best Western logo on the side of the hotel. Subsequently, its occupancy increased 58 percent.

Some consortia permit their members to belong to chains and other consortia; others restrict membership. Membership fees are computed and paid in several ways: a percentage of bookings, percentage of sales, flat fee per number of rooms, or retainer fee.

REMOTE CONTROL CHECK-IN, CHECKOUT

Using in-room video and computer assistance, Sheraton and Marriott have arranged for guests to bypass the cashier at the front desk and check out by using the TV set in their guest rooms. Having left a credit card imprint at the front desk, the guest can use a series of commands to bring his or her folio, or guest account, to the television screen. Digital prompts communicate through the master antenna TV system and the hotel's Property Management System (PMS). The PMS tells the host computer that the guest wishes to check out. The folio is printed at the concierge desk, where the guest picks up a copy on the way out.

Sheraton is experimenting with another remote check-in service, one that links the hotel and Avis rental counters at La Guardia, Newark, and Kennedy airports in the New York City area.

Low-Voltage Systems

As new hotels are constructed, a number of low-voltage systems can be installed in the same conduits as regular ones. These include equipment that will control peak power demand, room status, automatic wake-up systems, and electronically controlled guest room and storeroom access.

The automatic turnoff or turndown of heating, ventilation, air conditioning, and lighting when a guest checks out, along with an automatic turn-on when the guest checks in, is likely to become widely used. Energy-controlling equipment has a fast payoff—the investment is made up within 6 months to 2 years.

Room-status systems remove the need for constant phone calls between the front desk and housekeeping. If security continues to be a problem, electronic security systems are likely to be installed, with "forced-entry" alarms, motion detectors, and metal detectors.

Large convention hotels are likely to use other types of low-voltage technology, including:

Large-screen TV projection

Paging: audio and visual

Closed-circuit TV

Video recording equipment

Front- and rear-screen projection equipment

Automatic wake-up systems

IN-ROOM ENTERTAINMENT

As of about 1970, just about every hotel and motel room in this country contained a TV set; today, almost all of them are color sets. In-room movies through the TV set began being offered in 1971. From the start, these were relatively new movies without commercials; some are offered free, others for a fee.

Home Box Office (HBO), a satellite/cable subsidiary of Time Warner, is one of the largest suppliers of movies. Its programs are free to the guest. The hotels are charged on a per-room-per-month basis. Hotels can receive their programs direct from a satellite signal picked up by a roof dish. Just as the TV set has come to be seen as a basic service, now many guests perceive movies and other in-room entertainment as a standard amenity.

The next step seems to be to give the guest an even greater choice of movies by using video cassette recorders (VCRs). Guests can check out films on a complimentary basis through the front desk to enjoy as their schedule permits. Some hotels maintain 1000 titles in their cassette library. In general, VCR libraries are more appropriate for long-stay guests, such as those in all-suites, than for brief stopovers.

VIDEOCONFERENCES

Videoconferencing has entered the hospitality management scene in a significant way. Hilton Hotels and other chains are moving into conventioning via satellite.

Videoconferencing works by sending signals from a central conference site to a satellite thousands of miles in the sky and then back down to saucers set up on the roofs of or near the hotel property. The saucer relays the satellite signal to a screen in a conference room or auditorium in a way similar to TV projection. One-way video reception is common, and two-way video reception can be arranged at a greater cost. A corporation can reach literally thousands of its employees at the same time at a number of different locations. Total travel expenses are drastically reduced. Savings in time translates into savings in salary, since so little time must be spent traveling to a convention site.

Videoconferencing makes it possible to do things like introduce a new program or hold a press conference in several locations at the same time. M-G-M introduced the film *Pennies From Heaven* simultaneously to 16 cities in the U.S. and Canada. The 3M Company, headquartered in Minneapolis, was able to introduce a new program to 80,000 employees in a relatively short time.

How will videoconferencing affect the hotel business in the future? This question is being pondered by many hotel executives, and no one has a clear answer.

Hotel operators disagree about whether videoconferencing will increase both room sales and the sale of food and beverages. There is little argument that the latter will increase. The number of long-distance meetings and conventions will be reduced, but more regional meetings will be scheduled. Instead of only the top sales, management, and technical people going to conventions, large numbers of personnel at lower levels will attend the regional meetings. But just because they are regional, many of those who attend will come from the area and be able to go home at night, which is why many hotel operators believe room sales will go down.

All agree that videoconferencing will never completely substitute for the face-to-face exchange of ideas and feelings that goes on at large meetings and conventions.

Teleconferencing, in which several parties in different locations link up by phone, is already offered by Holiday Inns. Videoconferencing adds the next dimension—the big screen. Next will probably be the videophone, which may have much more drastic effects on the hotel business than videoconferencing. When it is easy to set up a conference with several people in which all involved can see each other's faces, the need for travel and hotel rooms will be greatly reduced.

Will more or fewer hotel rooms come with these technological advances? The chains are taking no chances. Holiday Inns offer videoconferencing as a hotel feature, just as the radio, the swimming pool, and the TV set in every room were once offered.

GUEST SECURITY

Guest security has been a problem in hotels since their beginning. But with rising crime, the courts and the general public have rising expectations as to what a hotel or motel should provide in the way of security, or perhaps the general public is more conscious of criminal activity and is becoming more wary and demanding.

In 1974 the well-known singer Connie Francis was raped while staying at the Howard Johnson Motor Lodge in Westbury, New York. She sued the restaurant and motel chain for $6 million, charging that the company had failed to provide her with a safe and secure room. The singer was awarded $2.5 million and her husband an additional $25,000 by the Federal District Court in Brooklyn. Howard Johnson's insurance company filed a motion, asking that the award be set aside as excessive. The parties settled out of court in 1977 for $1,475,000. The case alarmed the hotel and motel industry and focused attention on the necessity for providing greater guest security.

Large hotels have used plainclothes security personnel, often off-duty police officers, since before the turn of the century. In a large hotel, the security force headquarters itself in a guest room and changes rooms from time to time. Now hotel operators are strengthening their security forces and looking for new ways of insuring guest security within a room.

A number of new systems have been introduced. Some are not very convenient. For example, one system works this way: After a hard day, a guest unlocks the door, walks into the hotel room, turns on the light and the television, and flops down on the bed to relax. Two and a half minutes later, the television and lights go off and the air conditioner shuts down. To activate the electrical system again, the guest must throw a deadbolt in the lock on his or her door. System control is a metal box fitted under the desk in each room that is connected to the lock and electrical appliances.

Other systems are simpler. Some use plastic cards as substitutes for keys. Peepholes have been installed in guest rooms, and stronger locks are in use. Chain locks appeared in many properties a number of years ago; now closed-circuit television monitored by security personnel focus on corridors and stairwells.

One of the most successful security programs utilizes television monitors in all areas where large amounts of money are held. One person can monitor a number of places from one location, and if a problem arises, he or she can alert security personnel quickly. A few hotels provide personal safes, one in each guest room activated by punching in a six-digit code. (The problem is, the guest often forgets the code.)

Regardless of deadbolts and other systems, it is also necessary for hotel personnel to be able to enter the room in case of fire or any other emergencies whether the guest is present or not.

A principal ingredient in any security program's effectiveness is the ability to respond promptly. To this end, beeper systems and walkie-talkies are widely used in the larger properties. Maintenance personnel can be equipped with beepers and become a prominent part of the security system if they are properly trained.

A large hotel like the 1000-room Marriott at the Los Angeles airport may have a security force of 16 or more persons, plus a number of off-duty regular police officers who work on an hourly basis. None of the security people wear uniforms, and only the regular police officers may make police arrests; the others must make do with a citizen's arrest. All may use handcuffs when necessary, as when people are fighting or drunk and disorderly. By far the largest number of arrests in downtown hotels are of obvious prostitutes. Guests are also apprehended for carrying off hotel property, although items like stolen towels are overlooked.

PERSONNEL MANAGEMENT

Wages and Tips

In the typical 100- to 250-room hotel or motor hotel, only two to four people receive sizable salaries: the manager, the chef, and the food and beverage director. Among them, they are responsible for the complete operation of the hotel.

The manager at a Holiday Inn typically makes a good salary, plus free food and beverage while on the job. The live-in manager and family receive full maintenance, all meals, room service, laundry, and other benefits. The assistant manager is also the restaurant manager, with a salary approximating that of the manager. The salary is usually higher in the independent hotel or motel, where the manager has considerably more responsibility.

As the hotel or motel increases in size and complexity, the manager's salary increases. In a few of the major hotels, the salary exceeds $150,000 a year, plus a number of fringe benefits. Department heads, such as the housekeeper and engineer, might receive salaries in excess of $60,000 annually. Chefs at some of the prestige hotels may also be paid a salary of $60,000 a year.

The reputation of the hotel and restaurant business for comparatively low wages is widespread and of long standing. The reputation is well deserved among entry and semiskilled positions, but it is not true of wages and salaries paid to technical specialists and supervisory and management personnel.

Since a large number of hotels, motels, and restaurants are small, they are likely to be family enterprises. Wages and salaries in such instances are, in large part, the profit generated by the business. These can be relatively high.

In the larger establishments, 50 to 60 percent of all nonsupervisory personnel are low-paid, unskilled, untipped employees. These include room attendants, dish machine operators, housemen, washroom attendants, laundry workers, porters, and utility personnel. This situation is changing as employees from minority groups move into skilled and supervisory positions.

Area differences in hotel wages are large. Twice as much is paid in San Francisco, for example, as in Kansas City or the South. The spread between North and South has narrowed slightly with the minimum wage laws, but it is still great. The wage differentials only partly reflect different living costs in each area; union pressures are important as well.

Skilled and semiskilled workers, such as bartenders, cooks, desk clerks, and pantrymen and women, account for about 10 percent of nonsupervisory hotel employees. Their wages are high relative to those in the unskilled groups.

Productivity and wages are rising together as ways and products are found that reduce labor. No-iron linens, convenience foods, and direct-dial phones eliminate personnel, as do self-service elevators, vending machines, and shoeshine equipment in guest rooms.

Office personnel account for about 15 percent of nonsupervisory employment, and their wages are usually determined by the prevailing wage in the community for similar jobs. Front-desk personnel have traditionally been low-paid employees, especially in resort areas. Many people are eager for such jobs, however, since the position has a certain status and is relatively interesting. The job offers psychic income as well as a salary.

About 5 percent of hotel employees are maintenance employees—engineers, firemen, upholsterers, electricians, painters—who are paid at rates competitive for the area. Maintenance workers are often well organized and receive union-scale wages.

About 15 percent of hotel personnel receive tips. These employees—doormen, bellmen, bartenders, waitpersons—are a group unto themselves. In many cases, their income is much too high in relation to their contribution to the enterprise. Wages may be a relatively small part of total income. The class of restaurant, seat turnover, and average check determine to a large extent the income of the tip employee. It is not unusual for waiters and waitresses to make as much as $150 a night in tips. A Bureau of Labor Statistics report found that tipped employees' average income was 61 percent higher than that of their nontipped counterparts.

Income from tips went largely unreported for tax purposes until after 1982, when the Tax Equity and Fiscal Responsibility Act (TEFRA) was passed. Reported income from tips more than doubled. Employees of large hotels and restaurants must report all tips. If the total is less than 8 percent of gross food and beverage receipts, the employer must allocate an amount that brings the total to the 8 percent figure. Employers are unhappy with this arrangement because it forces them to become part of the income tax collection system.

Tipping practices vary widely throughout the country. The highest rates are in New York City and in cities on the West Coast. Tips are lower in the Midwest and South and are nonexistent in some rural communities. Wealthy people with "old money" are not necessarily big tippers; the nouveaux riches, generally speaking, do tip well. Tipping can be big in prestigious restaurants—something for the maitre d' for a choice table, a separate something for the captain, another something for the sommelier (wine steward). Tips can also be memorable. Once a group of Kuwaiti men with their wives and bodyguards left a $20,000 tip to be shared by the staff of Commanders Palace, a well-known New Orleans restaurant.

Impact of the Union

Unionization has played an important role in the hotel and restaurant business, but only in large cities outside the South. As of 1994, only about 8 percent of all hotel and restaurant employees were covered by collective bargaining agreements.

The Hotel and Restaurant Employees and Bartenders Union is the major union. Uniformed personnel, such as bellmen and elevator operators, may be members of the Building Service Employees International Union. Some technical personnel are represented by still other unions. The Disneyland Hotel negotiates with 24 separate unions.

Restrictive Union Practices

Some restrictive practices imposed by a number of union contracts push up the cost of labor unnecessarily. For example, a contract at the Condado Beach Hotel in San Juan, Puerto Rico, specified that the hotel may never employ fewer than 75 percent of the number of employees employed at the time the contract was negotiated no matter what economic conditions prevail.

Job classifications are zealously guarded by union representatives in many places. A glass washer may not wash dishes; do not ask a bellman to clean anything if his union contract does not permit it; a roast cook may not prepare soups; and so it goes.

The ultimate weapon in any union's arsenal—the one weapon that gives any employer or group of employers real pause—is the strike or the threat of one. The union gathers even more muscle when other nonhotel or restaurant unions, such as the Teamsters, back the strikes.

As wages and salaries go up, the cost of service climbs. The hospitality business is obviously labor-intensive. Consider the fact that about 80 personnel are needed to service 100 rooms in a full-service hotel, and it is easy to see why the room costs have increased so fast. Add to this the fact that the cost of the room itself in a downtown hotel, the capital investment, is anywhere from $50,000 to $200,000. It is understandable why room rates can climb to $175 or $200 a day.

As labor costs and capital costs increase in the industrially advanced countries, vacations to those countries are likely to be shortened because of rising room and restaurant rates. Destinations where cheap labor is available increase in appeal because of low cost and the fact that the cost of transportation via air for the pleasure traveler is going down relative to other costs. It is quite possible that it will be cheaper to fly 1000 people to Portugal, Spain, or Mexico and to live there more cheaply than at home. The British have been doing so for years in Spain.

THE RIGHT ROOM RATE

How to determine the right room rate has been the subject of much discussion and dispute. The idea, of course, is to optimize business by charging an amount that will generate the most profit, but that is not so high as to discourage a guest from coming or returning in the future. The starting point is to settle on a rate that will cover all costs and still provide a reasonable profit and then increase it as much "as the traffic will bear."

Room rates for a seasonal operation are based on the fact that about three-fourths of the resort's total revenue is usually taken in during the peak season, which may last only 3 or 4 months. High-season rates must be set accordingly.

Large hotels generally offer five rate categories based on location in the hotel, the view from the room, amenities, amount of service, and size of room (or suite). Location near elevators usually means a lower rate; rooms on upper floors are generally priced higher than those lower down. The categories in the Hilton Kona Hotel in Hawaii, for example, include: A for standard, the least expensive, and E for deluxe oceanfront, the most expensive. Those in between—B for medium, C for superior, and D for deluxe—are priced accordingly.

The Hubbart Formula

One way to determine a room rate is to work backward: Find the total revenue needed to break even, the expected profit, and divide by the projected number of rooms that will be sold in the coming year. This is the Hubbart formula, developed by two national accounting firms and named in honor of Roy Hubbart of Chicago, the major proponent of the plan. It is the best known formula for arriving at a room rate.[6]

---

6. *The Hubbart Formula* (AH&MA) 1953.

As an example, suppose that in a 100-room house the total income needed for expenses is $400,000. On a predicted occupancy of 70 percent, the number of rooms that will be sold in the year is 25,550. Suppose the house costs $4 million and that the owner expects to make a 15 percent profit on the investment, or $600,000. The owner needs to take in $1,000,000 in the course of the year to meet costs and make a profit. Dividing $1,000,000 by 25,550 gives him an average room rate of about $39.14.

Other factors may be more important than a mathematical computation, but the Hubbart formula is still worthwhile as a guide.

The Dollar per Thousand Rule

A rule of thumb for determining room rates is that $1 should be charged for each $1000 dollars invested per room. If a 100-room hotel costs $4 million, the cost per room is $40,000. The room rate necessary for a fair return on the investment would be $40.

The usual Holiday Inn costs $30,000 to $50,000 a unit, so the rate based on this formula would be $30 to $50.

Calculation of the dollar-per-thousand building cost assumes a 70 percent occupancy over the life of the hotel and management good enough to show a 55 percent house profit on room sales. House profit is defined as all profits except income from store rentals and before the deduction of insurance, real estate taxes, depreciation, and other capital expenses. It assumes that store rentals will offset real estate taxes and interest charges on the land. The calculation further assumes that the hotel will show a 6 percent return on the total investment.

The rack rate, or the posted rate, is quite different than the average room rate, the actual income from rooms divided by the number of rooms sold. The difference is one-third more. The average rate being discussed is not the rate advertised by the hotel. It is the average daily rate (room revenue divided by number of rooms sold). As the percentage of occupancy increases, so does the average rate. Less expensive rooms sell first, and as they are sold out, higher-priced rooms are rented, raising the average rate.

Several of the large city hotels built in the mid-1970s were part of the urban redevelopment plans of various cities. The developers were able to secure money at less than the going rate through the economic development administration of the cities involved and elsewhere. In some cases, the land cost them nothing. Feasibility studies and the determination of a room rate had to be tailored to the particular property, and the dollar-per-thousand rule of thumb was not relevant. That rule probably still applied to the motor hotels, which could still be constructed at somewhat reasonable cost on the outskirts of cities and towns.

Setting the right rate involves a combination of a number of factors, including general economic conditions, competitive rates, and what is necessary to sustain an acceptable rate of return. The expense account hotel, which caters to the business traveler, is likely to post much higher rates than the property catering to those who pay their own travel costs.

The dollar-per-thousand rule of thumb has been modified to include the cost of land, building, and equipment. A return of 10 percent on invested capital is considered a minimum goal.[7]

A rule of thumb is only a guide. Occupancy rate and the ratio of food and beverage sales to room sales vary widely from one hotel to another. Generally speaking, the greater the ratio of restaurant sales to room sales, the higher the occupancy or room rate needed to achieve a desirable return on the investment. The reason for this is that food and beverage sales do not produce the high percentage of profit generated by room sales.

In the final analysis, the room rate is what the market will bear.

Special Rates

The price-insensitive traveler prefers the established multiple-serviced hotel or motel and is not concerned with room rate. The same person, though, traveling at personal expense will often pick a budget property, especially if it is new, clean, and reputable. It is interesting to note the number of expensive automobiles, including Cadillacs, parked in the budget motel parking lot.

The international chains, many airline-owned, have also found it necessary to provide

---

7. Laventhol & Horwath, *The U.S. Lodging Industry*, Philadelphia, PA, 1980.

some rooms priced less expensively than others. Rates in such cities as Tokyo, Paris, and London skyrocketed during the early 1970s and 1980s.

Inter-Continental Hotels introduced their version of a budget hotel, Forum Hotels. Self-service was emphasized. There were vending machines on each floor, buffet breakfasts, and self-service restaurants.

The European Hotel Corporation—owned by Alitalia, British Airways, Lufthansa, Swissair, and TAP—is a similar chain of moderately priced hotels called Pentas. Room rates about 30 percent less than those of first-class international hotels are made possible by such cost-cutting practices as the absence of bellmen and automated room service.

The corporate rate, a reduced rate offered regular guests, started sometime before 1915. The traveler, usually a salesman, began asking for the lower rate as a repeat guest. He usually was charged a little less than the few tourists or other travelers who were in the hotel. Later, during the Depression, many hotels permitted the commercial traveler to bring his or her spouse along at no extra charge. As with today's family plan, cries of "rate cutting" were heard from those hoteliers not engaging in the practice.

Hotels in resort areas that cater to both commercial people and vacationers have a real problem identifying the bona fide corporate traveler. Experienced travelers may ask for the commercial rate while traveling as tourists during the peak season. The problem can be solved by requiring such people to have stayed in the hotel at least three times during the off-season.

When the motel first appeared, the practice was to rent the room at a given price regardless of the number of people who occupied it—the so-called family rate. Hotels did the opposite—they characteristically charged on the basis of the number of people occupying the room. The family rate became so popular in the motel that eventually most hotels had to offer special rates for family groups. The hotel is more likely to charge twice the usual rate for each room occupied by a family and add a small charge for setting up roll-away beds.

It is also customary to offer reduced rates to groups and provide a certain percentage of the rooms on a complimentary basis. Such "comp" rooms are usually occupied by the executive secretary of the group or some of the officers. Sea-

sonal resorts have an off-season rate that may be only half, or less than half, of the high-season rate.

Hilton, Sheraton, and a number of other chains offer reduced rates to students and faculty. They employ a student representative on many campuses to publicize their availability. The Sheraton student-faculty plan, for example, allows a slight reduction to students, faculty, administrative personnel, and athletic teams during the summer, weekends, and the low period between December 15 and January 1.

Package plan rates, which usually include transportation and lodging and sometimes meals, are likely to be arranged by a travel agent in cooperation with an airline and hotel or a group of hotels. The rate is often the same that the guests would pay if there were no package plan, but the guests do not know this.

Going Overboard

One of the biggest headaches of innkeeping is to maximize room sales without "going overboard." Going overboard is selling more rooms than are available in the house. The operator wants to get as close to 100 percent occupancy as possible, and when hotel rooms are in short supply, hotels have operated at 100-plus occupancy, beds being turned over more than once in a 24-hour period. Consequently, the typical hotel manager is likely to take more reservations than he or she has space for, anticipating that a certain percentage of the people reserving will be no-shows.

Rate Cutting

When business is slow, the inclination of the motel or hotel owner is to reduce room rates: "There's no business like slow business." A sign goes up outside the motel advertising, "$30 Monday through Thursday," or some other rate reduction. Resorts have always cut rates drastically during their off-season, and transient hotels have a number of special rates—weekend packages, groups, commercial travelers, students, and so on.

No less a person than Ernest Henderson believed that reducing rates was one way to increase occupancy. He reasoned that by increasing total occupancy, the extra profits from increased food and beverage sales would more than compensate for the loss in rates. In the early 1960s he did just that for all the Sheraton Hotels. Some of the less desirable hotels and blocks of rooms in some of the better Sheraton Hotels were labeled "Sherwyn," and their rates drastically reduced. Later, rates were quietly increased because the extra occupancy expected did not materialize. The accountants have likened the results of rate cutting to the wages of sin, and they can draw up charts to prove it. For example, to compensate for cutting room rates by 20 percent when the hotel has a 64 percent occupancy, the occupancy level must be raised to 77.2 percent.

Countering these statistics, of course, is the fact that "a room not sold tonight is revenue from that room lost forever." What actually happens to avoid that is the granting of discount rates to all who can be labeled in some way—the corporate traveler, weekend getaway, senior citizen, AAA member, military personnel, "package tour" traveler, and so on. Those people who could not plan their trip in advance or are not in the favored categories pay the posted, or rack, rate.

Then there is the flexible rate. It changes according to the time of day, the current occupancy level in the hotel, and how full other hotels in the general vicinity are at the time. The person who calls from the airport gets one rate and the walk-in gets a higher rate. In times of low occupancy, discounting disguises rate cutting, but it amounts to about the same thing.

Yield Management

Rate cutting, discounted rates, special rates—whatever they are called—have been given new respect under the label of "yield management" and made more systematic by the use of computers. Like the airlines, most large hotel chains use computers to expedite yield management programs that discount room rates for certain market segments at certain times. Seasonally adjusted room rates, group rates, special rates for airline crew members, increased rates when crowds are expected for a championship football game, reduced rates for seniors, military rates, and corporate rates are involved in yield management.

Yield management as a management tool was adapted from airline experience in adjusting fares to fit demand and began in the hotel business about 1987.[8]

A yield management program can be set up to automatically project room demand based on historical records. The "rules" for the computer program are made by management and sales personnel. The computer then chooses discount rates to sell room nights that would otherwise be lost during slack periods and selects high rates to maximize revenue during busy periods. Some yield management programs measure group room requests in terms of points and will suggest alternative dates for a group if the points calculated for a certain date are not high enough. High occupancy weekday reservations for a group may be rejected.

The difficulty is knowing when to raise or reduce rates and for how long, to maximize yield revenue. Figure 6-11 shows that if rates are lowered more rooms must be sold to achieve the same revenue. For a 1-month period, 48.75 percent occupancy at a daily room rate of $100 yields the same as 97.50 percent occupancy with a $50 room rate.[9]

Yield management calls for forecasting room sales by market segment: business travelers, tour groups, transients, government guests, convention groups, or other market segments. Rooms are blocked out for each segment for a three-month (or another appropriate) time period.

Room counts for each segment are tallied by computers, and discounted rates (or rate increases) are made to fill as many rooms as possible.

Some motels raise their rates for call-in customers if they are filling up toward 5 PM. If unsold rooms are few, a call-in customer may pay an increased room rate, and special rates for seniors, military, and other market segments are blocked out. Each property sets its own yield management policy. A computer program (algorithm) can be designed that will indicate when rates should move up or down according to a predetermined policy. Weekend bargain rates for pleasure travelers are commonly offered.

---

8. Jerry Breen, "Hoteliers Yield to Yield Management," *Hotels* (Nov. 1991).
9. Gary Vallen, "Yield Management—An Old Idea Revitalized by Technology," *Arizona Hospitality Trends* (Jan. 1991).

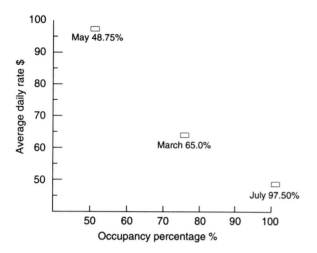

Figure 6-11 Three months attaining identical 48.75%

Source: "Yield Management—An Old Idea Revitalized by Technology," Gary Vallen *Arizona Hospitality Trends* (Jan. 1991).

Designing a computer program for a yield management program can be extremely complicated and is based on a management policy that relates to the level of service management wants to offer and the problems that come with "going overboard" (confirming more rooms than are available and having to handle guests who must be accommodated elsewhere). A yield management program assumes that the reservations and front-desk staff understand how the program works.

Yield management requires adjusting room rates up or down and doing so for the different markets of a hotel. The program tries to maximize multiple-night stays and avoid prematurely releasing rooms at discount rates. Information on which to base discounting depends on factors such as time of year, day of week, special events in the area, current reservations, and space available at competitive hotels.[10]

Hilton Hotels Corporation began a yield management system in 1988 that forecasts demand up to 120 days in advance. Room rates can be adjusted up to 4 months ahead of the actual date in question. If bookings are slow, the number of discounts are increased. If it appears the hotel will be sold out, bookings can be made at higher rates.[11]

---

10. Paul R. Gamble, "Building a Yield Management System—The Flip Side," *Hospitality Research Journal*, Vol. 14 (Nov. 2, 1990).
11. Somerset R. Waters, *Travel Industry World Yearbook, The Big Picture—1989* (New York: Childs & Waters, Inc.), 1989.

HOTEL FINANCE

The Lodging Dollar, Income and Outgo

While still in business, Laventhol & Horwath and Pannell Kerr Foster published a financial survey of lodging business in the U.S. each year. In all, these studies give a running account of the financial health of the business. However, the data collected are from the client hotels and motels of the two firms and therefore do not represent the entire industry; they are probably biased in favor of the more successful enterprises. An approximate percentage of income produced by each department is shown below:

Guest room rentals	55–60%
Food sales	23–25
Beverage sales	8–10
Rentals and other income	1.5–2.9
Telephone sales	2–3
Minor operated departments	2–3

For the typical property then, food and beverage sales constitute about 35 percent of the total income; the other departments aside from room rentals contributed about 6 percent. Of course, any individual hotel may have a widely different breakdown of income.

Percentages of the income dollar that were spent by each department are approximately as follows:

Payroll and related expense	36–40%
Rent, property, taxes, and insurance	7–10
Departmental expenses	10–13
Food costs	7–9
Depreciation	6–7
Administrative and general	4–5
Interest	4–6
Energy	4–6
Marketing	3–5
Property operation and maintenance	3–4
Beverage cost	2
Net Income Before Taxes	2–4

Revenue Projections

Hotel restaurant operators make projections of income based on a number of factors, such as the occupancy trend they have experienced recently and over the past years, the amount of competition in their area among hotels and restaurants catering to the same markets, and general economic trends for the region. In making projections, it is well to separate revenue and expenses that are relatively fixed from those that are relatively variable. Property taxes and insurance are considered fixed expenses: They do not vary with the volume of sales. The cost of food and beverage is highly variable: Their cost increases or declines with the volume of sales.

Stephen Rushmore presents an illustration of revenue and expense categories for a hotel.[12] The percentages in Table 6-2 show the portions of each category that are typically fixed and variable. The last column describes the basis for calculating the percentage of variability. Estimates

of the portion of revenues that are variable must be made for the individual property.

Operating Ratios

Hotel GMs must keep a close eye on financial operating ratios to learn how property is doing financially. Financial operating data in the mass are broken down into component parts and compared with those from similar properties. Comparisons are made in terms of ratios (percentages).

Two of the ratios often discussed when GMs get together are the average daily rate (ADR) received by a hotel (room revenue divided by the number of rooms sold) and the occupancy rate (the total number of rooms in the property divided by the number of rooms sold or rented).

The ADR reflects the number of rooms sold as doubles, the income from suites, and the various discounted room rates offered by the hotel.

12. Stephen Rushmore, "Forecasting Revenues and Expenses," *Lodging Hospitality* (April 1989).

TABLE 6-2 Revenue Projection Components

Revenue and Expense Category	Percent Fixed	Percent Variable	Index of Variability
Revenues			
Food	30–50	50–70	Occupancy
Beverage	0–30	70–100	Food revenue
Telephone	10–40	60–90	Occupancy
Other income	30–60	40–70	Occupancy
Departmental Expenses			
Rooms	50–70	30–50	Occupancy
Food and beverage	35–60	40–65	Food and beverage revenue
Telephone	55–75	25–45	Telephone revenue
Other income	40–60	40–60	Other income revenue
Undistributed Operating Expenses			
Administrative and general	65–85	15–35	Total revenue
Management fee	0	100	Total revenue
Marketing	65–85	12–35	Total revenue
Property operation and maintenance	55–75	25–45	Total revenue
Energy costs	80–95	5–20	Total revenue
Fixed Expenses			
Property taxes	100	0	Total revenue
Insurance	100	0	Total revenue
Reserve for replacement	0	100	Total revenue

Source: Stephen Rushmore, "Forecasting Revenues and Expenses," *Lodging Hospitality* (April 1989).

Occupancy rates indicate how efficient management has been in filling the rooms available. The ADR reflects the pricing policy and may suggest changes in room rates, up or down.

Room sales provide the largest gross profit per sales, and the manager wants to know the percentage of income provided by room sales. (Hotels that have large food and beverage sales show a lower ratio of room sales to total sales.)

A study of how GMs viewed an array of financial ratios[13] showed that, in addition to average room rate and the occupancy ratio, the GMs found the profit margin to be most useful. Not surprisingly, managers are most interested in profit margin (net income compared to total revenue). It is the single most useful ratio. Those cost control ratios considered most useful by GMs are:

Cost of labor percent

Cost of food sold percent

Cost of beverage sold percent

Other ratios that GMs find helpful are:

Total revenue percent change from budget (how revenues actually compared with the revenue figures forecast by the budget)

Room sales to total sales percent

Operating efficiency ratio

Total revenue percent change from prior year

Owners and lenders place emphasis on liquidity and solvency ratios, those ratios that indicate the financial soundness of a hotel. An example of a solvency ratio is the long-term debt to total capitalization. Current assets divided by total assets is an example of a liquidity ratio, indicating the amount of assets that can quickly be turned into cash, as compared to total assets (much of which may be difficult or will take time to convert to cash or other liquid assets).

The Break-even Point

Every hotel and motel has a break-even point, the percentage of occupancy necessary to pay all op-

erating expenses, including interest on indebtedness, calculated before projected or desired profits. Since the national average on occupancy for hotels and motels is between 60 and 70 percent, the break-even point for the average hotel or motel is obviously lower than 60 percent. Once the break-even point is reached, profit rises sharply.

Where the break-even point falls, of course, changes with wage rates, efficiency of operation, increases in costs, and room rates. The debt load being carried is a major factor; high interest costs push it up. Some hotels can reach it below 40 percent occupancy; others, given their debt load and competition, cannot break even at 100 percent.

HOTEL MONOPOLY

Can a hotel or group of hotels develop a monopoly and fix prices?

The answer is not quite no. Monopoly over a long period of time and wide area is not possible in the hotel business because of the relative ease of entry into the business by individual corporations. However, chains control a very sizable portion of local markets. Chains may also have competitive advantages not possessed by independent or smaller operations in their reservation systems, credit arrangements, national advertising programs, and extensive guest services.

If there is a shortage of hotel rooms within a particular area, a group of first-class hotels could exercise a limited monopoly. People not on expense accounts, or who are naturally frugal will not be affected by the monopoly. They will simply stay outside of town or in less expensive hotels or motels.

Indeed, hotels have been convicted of price fixing. In 1977 Sheraton Hawaii Corporation, the Hilton Hotel Corporation, Cinerama Hawaii Hotels, Flagship International, and the Hotel Association pleaded "No Contest" to criminal charges of conspiring to fix Hawaiian hotel room rates and were fined. Hilton and Sheraton were fined the maximum $50,000; Cinerama and Flagship $25,000; and the Hotel Association $10,000. The price fixing took place during 1971–1972 when visitor totals to Hawaii dropped at the same time that many new hotels had opened. Room rates had been cut to below break-even points, while tour operators and travel agents pitted hotels against each other and obtained net room rates that were

13. "Financial Ratios: Perceptions of Lodging Industry General Managers and Financial Executives," *FIU Hospitality Review*, Vol. 2, No. 5 (Fall 1989).

often 15 percent below rack rates (and lower) for groups. The hotel operators felt that some kind of price fixing was necessary to survive.[14]

NEW MANAGEMENT AND PLANNING TECHNIQUES

An emphasis on "management style" has found its way into the hotel and restaurant field. In the past and still generally today, hotel and restaurant management has been to a large extent autocratic. Planning was done only at the top. The manager presumably knew what should be done, how it should be done, and when it should be done and does not hesitate to tell all concerned exactly when and how. The boss orders; the staff obeys. The system works well if the employees are conditioned by their upbringing and temperament to respond to an autocrat. Many of the most successful restaurants and hotels in the world are run largely in this style.

Today's style of management, labeled "participative management," involves much more two-way communication between boss and employee. Work objectives are at least partly arrived at jointly by boss and employee. Participative management, however, is not democratic management. The manager involves most employees in problems and goal-setting, but his or hers is the final determination and the responsibility for profit. The boss retains the full burden of responsibility for final results.

Participative management lends itself to team building, where the emphasis is on change, challenge, and group goals. It conceivably can change the nature of innkeeping for the better.

Recently, some hotel and restaurant companies have adopted advanced management training methods and policies. Sonesta has developed an interesting management team approach to opening new properties. The six to ten people involved in the opening go off to a relaxed setting for a 2- or 3-day session and to determine the resources necessary for these actions. The general manager of the new property and all department heads are asked to describe their assigned role in the new hotel as they understand it. They state

their broad areas of responsibility and authority and agree on who is responsible for what. After the opening of the property, follow-up meetings are held to check results and review the various commitments made at the first meeting.

Planning

With change taking place at an unprecedented rate, a growing number of companies in the hospitality business are becoming involved in strategic, or long-range, planning. Typically, companies develop a strategy for a 5-year period. The main purposes are to specify the company's overall objectives and establish the main courses of action to achieve these objectives, because many security analysts request financial information pertaining to this particular time frame.

For different purposes, short-range plans covering 1- and 2-year horizons are also developed. The 1-year plan outlines specific tactics for the year and summarizes anticipated financial results. A 2-year plan is necessary in some cases because of the 18- to 24-month lead time associated with real estate and construction activities. James Crownover, a former long-range planner for Saga, outlined the strategic planning process in five major steps:[15]

1. Establishing a business definition

2. Setting long-range objectives

3. Diagnosing current company operations

4. Developing strategies for meeting long-range objectives

5. Determining implications of strategies:
    a. Financial resources
    b. Top management resources
    c. Organizational structure

The business definition. A hotel, restaurant, or foodservice company should be able to state in one sentence its overall purpose or mission. The statement will describe the services or products to be provided and the customer group or groups to be served. That statement is the business defi-

---

14. *Travel Weekly,* May 1977.

15. Much of this section is based on a lecture presented by James Crownover at California State Polytechnic University, Pomona, Calif., Nov. 1976.

Figure 6-12 One of the salons of the Ritz of Paris, considered by many to be the best hotel in the world. It has no television and does little advertising. Charles Ritz, son of César Ritz, says the place is not "ritzy." Rather, to its patrons it is a place like home, a townhouse for the wealthy. It has 210 rooms, 2 restaurants, and 3 bars. Every guest room has a golden clock and is kept cozy by a wood fire. It is now owned by a group from the Middle East.

nition. It is particularly important because it provides a foundation on which the corporate strategy is based.

The business definition should not be overly narrow; an example of that is railroads defining themselves as being in the railroad rather than transportation business. Nor should the definition be so broad that it fails to give the company proper direction in identifying and evaluating alternative strategies.

Three business definitions appropriate for different kinds of hotels might be:

1. To provide good but unpretentious accommodations that are clean, comfortable, and safe.

2. To offer excellent service and hospitality with well-landscaped grounds and attractive public spaces. Food service will be offered in an attractive coffeeshop-style restaurant.

3. To offer exceptional service and maintain luxury facilities presented with style and impeccable taste. The guest will feel important and pampered.

The business definition should not be changed on a year-to-year basis, but it can be modified if circumstances change dramatically inside or outside the company.

Long-range planning is covered more fully in the last part of the chapter on restaurant operations.

The definition of a business strategy points the way to its marketing and internal management structure. When Holiday Corporation redefined its company purpose from the motel business to the "travel business," the strategic change led to the acquisition of a number of diverse companies, such as Trailways and Delta Steamship Lines. When Kemmons Wilson, the chairman of the board, retired, the new management changed the focus from the "travel business" to viewing Holiday Corporation as a "hospitality company"; then the company divested itself of most of its acquisitions that did not bear directly on the lodging business.

The Hyatt organization's strategy calls for developing unique hotels with differentiated high-quality services that cater to sophisticated, affluent clientele in key market areas throughout the U.S. Its organization has been structured to permit managers the flexibility to adapt to the environments in which the hotels are located. Each manager is also allowed flexibility in management style. In fact, general managers and food and beverage directors operate their hotels as semiautonomous subsidiaries.

Best Western, a marketing/referral group, is made up of a number of separate hotel operations that control their own balance sheets. The group provides individual operators with centralized promotion and competitive reservation systems.

Robert Hazard, former chief executive officer, tried to centralize control and make the company into a for-profit organization, but he was forced out. His strategy was useful in building sales, but conflicted with the individual owner's ideas and values.

Like all specialized businesses, the hotel and motel businesses has coined a number of words and terms peculiar to the industry. The most important of the terms dealing with room rates are given below in Figure 6-13, followed by those that deal with hotel/motel operations (Fig. 6-14).

TERMINOLOGY: ROOM SALES

AP (Full American plan): rate includes three full meals and room; also called *full board* or *full pension*.

Bermuda plan: rate includes room with full American-style breakfast.

Cancellation procedure: reservation should be cancelled as early as possible but a minimum of forty-eight hours prior to scheduled date of arrival in a commercial hotel. In resort hotels, guests should verify cancellation policy at time of making reservations.

Commercial rate: rate agreed upon by company and hotel for all individual room reservations. Often given to any regular guests known to be commercial travelers.

Comp: complimentary, no charges for room.

Confirmed reservation: an oral or written confirmation by hotel that a reservation has been accepted (written confirmations are preferred). There is usually a 6:00 PM (local time) checkin deadline. If guest arrives after that and the hotel is filled, the assistant manager makes every effort to secure accommodations in another hotel. (This does not apply to guests with confirmed reservations where "late arrival" has been specified.)

Cutoff date: designated day when buyer, upon request, must release or add to function room or bedroom commitment. Certain types of groups should send rooming lists to the hotel at least two weeks prior to arrival.

Day rate: usually one-half regular rate of room if the guest during a given day vacates by 5:00 PM. Sometimes called a *use rate*.

Demipension (European term): rate includes room, breakfast, and either lunch or dinner.

Deposit reservation: a reservation for which the hotel has received cash payment for at least the first night's lodging in advance and is obligated to hold the room regardless of the guest's arrival time. Guest is preregistered.

EP (European plan): no meals included in room rate.

Farm out: sending guests with reservations that cannot be honored to other hotels with vacancies. Also called *walk*.

Flat rate: specified room rate for group, agreed upon by hotel and group in advance.

Full comp: no charges for anything taken in hotel, including room, meals, telephone, and valet.

Guaranteed payment reservation: room set aside by hotel at request of the customer; payment for room is guaranteed regardless of whether the guest appears unless reservation is properly cancelled.

Guaranteed reservation: a confirmed reservation with the promise to accommodate or, if unable, to pay for a room elsewhere, including transportation involved. Guest guarantees to pay if a no-show.

MAP (Modified American plan): rate includes breakfast, dinner, and room.

Preregistered: no-delay checkin, usually provided for guests who have stayed in hotel previously; often room assignments based on guest's previous preference.

Rack rate: current rate charged for each accommodation as established by hotel management.

Run of the house rate: an agreed-upon rate, generally between minimum and maximum, for group accommodations for all available rooms except suites; room assignments usually made on a "best available" basis.

Figure 6-13 Terminology: room sales.

Source: Georgina Tucker and Madelin Schneider, *The professional Housekeeper*, 2nd ed. (Boston, Mass.: CBI Publishing Company), 1982.

TERMINOLOGY: HOTEL/MOTEL OPERATIONS

Daily report: a management report prepared daily by the income auditor. The report's content varies, but will usually include: (1) source and summary of sales, (2) room statistics, (3) summary of cash receipts, (4) bank account analysis, and (5) accounts receivable analysis.

Daily room count report: a form prepared daily by the night room clerk from the room rack that indicates: (1) the rooms occupied, (2) the number of persons in each room, and (3) the rate charged for each room.

Due bill: a type of voucher issued by the hotel in exchange for purchased advertising that may be used as a credit against specified hotel charges.

Engineer's log: a record maintained by the hotel's chief engineer of periodic meter readings, inventories, and consumption of water, electricity, and fuel oil.

Front office: the office situated in the lobby, the main functions of which are: (1) control and sale of guest rooms, (2) providing key, mail, and information service for guests, (3) keeping guest accounts, rendering bills, and receiving payments, and (4) providing information to other departments.

Front office cash sheet: a form used daily by each front office cashier to record all cash receipts and disbursements, itemized as to name, room number, and amount.

Function: a prearranged, catered group activity usually held in a private room or area. It may be a cocktail party or a banquet, which includes food service.

Function room: a special room used primarily for private parties, banquets, and meetings; also called *banquet room*.

General cashier's daily summary: a form prepared daily by the general cashier summarzing all cash turned in by the departmental cashiers, which should be reconciled with the day's bank deposit. This report should show, for each cashier and in total: (1) total cash received, (2) paid outs, (3) cash over and/or short, (4) due backs or exchange, and (5) actual cash turned in. The cash receipts journal may be entered from this report.

Guest account: an itemized record of a guest's charges and credits, which is maintained in the front office until departure. Also called *guest bill*, *guest folio*, or *guest statement*.

Guest history card: a record maintained for each guest who has stayed in the hotel, with a separate entry for each visit. Among other things, it can be used as a valuable reference by the reservations and credit departments.

Guest ledger: the caption used for trade accounts receivable of guests in the hotel. These accounts are generally maintained in the front office and must be updated throughout the day to avoid undue delay when a guest checks out.

House: a synonym for *hotel*, commonly used within the industry. Examples: full house, house count, house income, house bank, and house charge.

Housekeeper's report: a report prepared each morning by the housekeeper, based on an inspection of each room by the maids, that indicates whether a guest room was occupied or vacant the previous night.

Information rack: a visible alphabetical index of guests in the hotel, used at the telephone switchboard and in the front office to facilitate delivery of mail and messages.

Linen control sheet: a record kept by the housekeeper of all linen and uniforms sent to and received from the laundry that will also account for shortages and damages.

Maid's report: a form used daily by each maid to report to the housekeeper the status of each guest room based on inspection. The *housekeeper's report* is prepared from all of the maids' reports.

Mail and key rack: a series of pigeonholes numbered for each guest room, used to hold room keys and guests' mail. Also, a series of alphabetized pigeonholes is used to hold mail for expected guests.

Master account: the guest account for a particular group or function that will be paid by the sponsoring organization.

NCR: a commonly used term to identify the National Cash Register Company, a major supplier of mechanical and electronic machines especially designed for hotels, restaurants, and clubs.

Occupancy, percentage of: the percentage of available rooms occupied for a given period. It is computed by dividing the number of rooms occupied for a period by the number of rooms available for the same period.

Officer's check: a special type of restaurant check used for gratis meals served to hotel staff in a public room.

Out of order: a guest room that is temporarily unsuitable for occupancy and is not to be sold. Generally used to designate rooms being rede-

Figure 6-14 Terminology: hotel and motel operations.

Source: A guide to Terminology in the Leisure Time Industries (Philadelphia, Penn. Laventhol & Horwath).

corated or in which some maintenance work is being performed.

Overbook: more reservations made than guest rooms available.

Point-of-sale equipment: mechanical or electronic devices that, in addition to serving as cash registers, generate sales, control, accounting and management reports; may or may not be part of a computer system.

Precost: a food-control technique used to establish a potential cost based on forecasts of menu items to be sold and predetermined menu item costs.

Preregister: to register guests before they check in. This is done to reduce delay and confusion at the registration desk for persons attending conventions and other organized groups expected to arrive at about the same time.

Prime cost: the combined cost of food and labor in a foodservice operation; usually expressed as a percentage of sales.

Public space: any area in the hotel that is accessible to the general public, including dining rooms, bars, lobbies, and function rooms.

Receiving clerk's daily report: a report prepared daily by the receiving clerk listing all merchandise received and showing cost distribution.

Registration card: a form on which arriving guests record their names and addresses and which the room clerk completes with room number, rate, and length of stay. Some form of guest registration is required by law in each state.

Reservation deposit: an advance payment required to obtain a confirmed guest room or function room reservation.

Restaurant cashier's sheet: a form used by each restaurant cashier on which all guest checks used are recorded. Separate columns for food sales, beverage sales, cover charges, and tips facilitate summarization.

Room change slip: a form filled out by the room clerk whenever there is a change in the status of a guest room other than a new registration or it is vacated.

Room rack: a special rack with a drop-pocket for each guest room bearing the corresponding number. Its purpose is to provide a visible record of the exact status of each guest room at all times.

Room rack card: a card or slip inserted in the appropriate pocket of the room rack when a room is sold. The card should show: (1) room number, (2) guest's name, (3) city of residence, (4) number of persons occupying the room, (5) daily rate, and (6) arrival and expected departure dates.

Room rate and inventory rack card: a card for each guest room that remains permanently in the room rack. It shows the fixed rate structure, bed capacity, and other pertinent information.

Rooming slip: a form filled out by the room clerk for each registered guest showing name, room number, and rate. A copy is given to the guest to avoid any subsequent dispute. Other copies are sent to the mail and information desk and the telephone switchboard.

Skipper: a guest who departs without checking out or paying the bill.

Store rentals: revenue derived from the rental of space, usually on the ground level with street access, for businesses not ordinarily a part of hotel service.

Telephone traffic sheet: a form used by the telephone switchboard operators to record all long-distance telephone calls.

Trading advertising contract: an agreement whereby the hotel agrees to purchase advertising space or time in exchange for hotel accommodations and, possibly, restaurant service. (See **Due bill**)

Transcript: the daily recapitulation of the guest ledger, prepared by the night auditor in a manual system.

Undistributed operating expenses: a group of operating expenses that are not distributed to the operated departments. The general captions for expenses are: (1) administrative and general, (2) marketing, (3) guest entertainment, and (4) property operation, maintenance, and energy costs; also referred to as *deductions from income*.

Uniform System of Accounts for Hotels: a manual outlining and describing a system of uniform accounts classification for hotels which has been adopted by the American Hotel and Motel Association.

Waiter's signature sheet: a form used by the food checker or cashier to control the issuance of guest checks to service personnel. Each server must sign for checks received (identified by number) and must account for their use.

Figure 6-14 *(continued).*

Questions

1. About how many employees are needed in a 100-room motor inn without a restaurant?

2. Hotels and motels are often built and operated by the same individual or group. Name three other ways in which a hotel or motel is operated.

3. The large hotel chains today favor which means of operation—ownership, management contract, or franchise? Explain why.

4. Around the turn of the century, the Ritz hotels were highly fashionable in several parts of the world. Were they all owned and operated by the Ritz Company or was there some other arrangement?

5. Name two advantages to the franchisor and two advantages to the franchisee in a franchise arrangement.

6. Name at least two disadvantages for the franchisee and two for the franchisor in a franchise arrangement.

7. The large hotel or motel of something over 300 rooms that installs computer equipment would probably first put it to use in what two areas of operation?

8. Explain a room status system and its advantages for a large hotel.

9. In a large hotel catering to business people, great numbers of guests want to be awakened at 7:00 AM. How can this be done without a large number of hotel personnel being used?

10. In large hotels a sales staff of several persons is on hand largely to solicit group business. What other functions does that staff perform?

11. Be able to define these commonly used terms dealing with room sales: rack rate, MAP, AP, EP, commercial rate, full comp.

12. Increased vigilance to insure guests' safety stimulated a number of new security systems, including plastic cards in place of keys, beeper systems, and television monitors. Explain the function of each.

13. Who are likely to be the three highest paid persons in a large hotel?

14. In some hotel chains, the auditor or financial officer in each hotel does not report to the general manager of that hotel. Why?

15. What is the name of the most prominent union that deals with hotel employees in the hotel and restaurant business?

16. In establishing a room rate, the Hubbart formula factors in all the operating costs,

    other costs, and one other important factor. What is that other factor?

17. An old rule of thumb for establishing a room rate is the dollar-per-thousand rule. Based on this, a hotel that has cost $50,000 per room to build would charge an average rate of what amount?

18. The dollar-per-thousand rule for deriving a room rate can be modified in light of certain operating experiences. Name some.

19. What can be done to alleviate the disappointment when a guest is "walked"?

20. How would you explain the meaning of the "break-even point" for a hotel?

21. Is it possible, or has it ever happened, that a group of hotels have formed a monopoly? Explain.

22. What is the value of the Uniform Systems of Accounts for hotels?

23. What ranks right after guest room rentals as the source of hotel income?

24. The largest cost in operating a hotel turns out to be what?

25. The allowance made for depreciation in a hotel runs about 7 percent of the income. Where does this 7 percent go?

26. Some of the major hotel chains are setting objectives for a long period of time. Usually, the period covers about how many years?

27. Yield management is a system being used to maximize room sales. How does it work?

28. Name three functions performed by personnel managers in larger hotels.

29. In a 300-room hotel, what department heads would serve on the executive operating committee?

Discussion Questions

1. Can we expect the Japanese to outcompete us in the world hospitality business and soon control major international hotel and restaurant companies? Give reasons for your answer.

2. Is videoconferencing good or bad for the hotel business?

3. The Tax Reform Act of 1986 required hotels and motels to extend the period of time over which depreciation for the building is taken. How did this affect the hotel business?

Kemmons Wilson

(1913–)

Holiday Corporation is the largest innkeeping operation the world has known. It incorporates more guest rooms than the Sheraton and Hilton corporations combined. Yet the man who created the company and initiated motel franchising is little known in hotel circles and considers himself more of a promoter, builder, and salesman than an innkeeper; more an entrepreneur than a professional hotelman.

Kemmons Wilson started Holiday Inns in 1952. By 1976 the company had more than 1700 motels in 50 states and 25 foreign countries. (About one-fifth of them are company owned; the rest are franchised.) Total rooms in 1986 numbered more than 340,000. Total revenues were $1.8 billion.

Wilson did for the motel business what Statler did for the hotel business. He brought relative luxury to the middle class at prices they could afford. He standardized motel keeping just as Howard Johnson standardized the roadside restaurant. All three men—Wilson, Statler, and Howard Johnson—insisted on cleanliness, relative uniformity, and careful attention to maintenance. Such practices endear a product or service to the middle class who want, above all else, predictability and safety in lodging and food.

Kemmons Wilson was born in 1913 in Osceola, Arkansas. A year later, when his father died, his mother took him to Memphis, Tennessee. He learned business early. At 14, he was a delivery boy for a Memphis drug firm and at 17 set himself up in the theater popcorn business—with a popper bought on $50 credit. He sold so much popcorn that the theater manager bought him out.

Wilson took those proceeds and bought five ancient pinball machines. Later, he purchased an old airplane, prevailed upon the seller to teach him to fly, and sold $1 rides around country towns. Dorothy, his future wife, sold tickets; his mother sold popcorn. Later, he went into the home construction business; eventually, he built and operated seven movie houses. He also had a Wurlitzer distributorship. In 1943 he sold his businesses for $250,000 and for the next two years served as a flight officer in the Air Transport Command.

The idea for Holiday Inns, he says, came as a result of a vacation trip with his family. It was "the most miserable vacation trip of my life." For poor accommodations he was charged $10 a day, plus $2 for each of his three children. Here, he thought, was "the greatest untouched industry in the country."

In 1952 Wilson borrowed $300,000 from a bank and built the first Holiday Inn* at a cost of $8000 per room, including the price of the land. It offered large rooms and two double beds in each room. Most important, it contained a restaurant when most motels of the day were too small to have one.

The first Holiday Inn was an instant success, and it still operates with an occupancy exceeding the national average. Three more were constructed the same year. From the beginning, the inns were geared for the family trade and commercial person. No charge was made for children under 12. This was more or less a standard practice in the motel business, but not the case with hotels. Franchise purchase was made easy: Put down $500, build a motel according to plan for about $300,000, and pay the company 5¢ per room each night.

Every Holiday Inn had to have a swimming pool, another appeal to the family and an added note of luxury. At the time, some motels offered free TV; Wilson included free TV, free ice, and a telephone in every room.

In 1952 motels were springing up all over the nation, but most were still relatively small, fewer than 30

---

*The name "Holiday Inn" was scribbled across the building plans by the draftsman, who had seen a Bing Crosby film of that name the evening before.

rooms. Wilson built large motels; the structures were imposing and attractive. By 1975 the average Holiday Inn motel exceeded 125 units. There were 10,000 requests for franchises each year; Holiday Inn accepted 200.

The "Great Sign" used as an entrance display by the Holiday Inns is enormous compared with the usual motel sign and expensive. The sunburst lighting and a huge lighted space, the part of the sign for posting advertising and welcome notices, made Holiday Inns stand apart from the many nondescript smaller motels that might be in the neighborhood.

From the outset, Wilson realized the tremendous advantage of a referral system. Once a customer stays at a Holiday Inn, he or she is likely to remain in the system for the rest of the trip. Holiday Inn makes it so simple that the guest follows the path of least resistance. At first, the innkeeper called long distance to the other Holiday Inns and the customer paid for the call. Today, the entire reservation and referral system is operated at no charge to the guest by a computerized system called Holidex.

A referral system increases in value as it enlarges. With each new franchised Holiday Inn, an additional 100 to 200 travelers are fed into the system. Each new inn also adds to the attractiveness of this system for the traveler, who has one more choice of a motel at which to stop. The more inns in the system, the more valuable it becomes to the traveler and the individual franchise holder. In peak months, 1000 reservations agents are on duty in the Memphis headquarters.

Someone in Holiday Inns, probably Wallace Johnson, saw the tremendous advantage of setting up a joint credit card with Gulf Oil Company, to the advantage of both companies. Gulf Oil advertises Holiday Inns; Holiday Inns advertises Gulf Oil. Gulf Oil has also made large sums of money available for Holiday Inns' growth. In addition, a number of Gulf service stations have opened adjacent to Holiday Inns.*

Key to the inns' phenomenal growth has been the franchising plan, which permits the company to grow as rapidly as there are people with the money and credit to buy a franchise. Investors of all kinds purchase a franchise to erect a Holiday Inn; they pay the company a daily operating fee and about 6 percent on their gross sales. As long as present franchise holders are successful and make a profit on their investment, more doctors, lawyers, and businesspeople seek to have a motel with the Great Sign at the entrance.

Holiday Corporation became a hospitality conglomerate in 1969, when it acquired by merger TCO Industries, Inc. That company controlled Continental Trailways, the second largest intercity bus system in the U.S., and Delta Steamship Lines, Inc. Operating 25 industry-related companies, Holiday Inns with TCO became a combined food, lodging, and transportation system. By the early 1970s it had also acquired a dinette maker, catering service, campground chain, meatpacking company, industrial park, and more.

By the 1970s some of the luster was lost as energy costs rose sharply, budget motels attracted some of the inns' market, and inflation and recession cut back travel.

The true Achilles heel of Holiday Corporation was the foray into conglomeration. It was too much to digest. The company has since backed away from most of these ventures.

In 1978 Wilson quietly sold a large percentage of his company stock, and in 1979 he suffered a heart attack followed by open-heart surgery. Soon after, he retired as chairman. The management style has changed drastically. Under Wilson, the executives had breakfast prayer meetings, motels had on-call chaplains, and franchisee conventions had Billy Graham as a speaker. Making money from gambling would have been repugnant to Wilson. Today, Holiday Corporation owns Harrah's casino hotels in Reno, Lake Tahoe, Las Vegas, and Atlantic City. In 1983 a quarter of all Holiday Inns' profits came from one hotel, Harrah's Marina in Atlantic City.

The new Holiday Corporation has segmented its properties. Its Hampton Inns compete with low-priced chains, such as Days Inns and La Quinta Motor Inns. Its Embassy Suites and Residence Inns offer three-room suites, plus complimentary breakfasts and cocktail hours. At the upper end of the rate scale are the Crowne Plaza properties. Harrah's are the company's casino hotels.

Holiday Inn Worldwide is a much different organization than envisioned by Wilson. In 1989 a U.K. brewer, Bass PLC, bought most of the company for $2.1 billion. Holiday continues to operate its newer brands—Embassy Suites, Hampton Inns, and Homewood Suites.

As for Kemmons Wilson, in 1987 at the age of 74, he was actively engaged in a huge resort development, Orange Lake Country Club, just west of Walt Disney World in Orlando, Florida, and also involved in putting together a minichain of hotels called Wilson World. His thoughts on retirement: "You can't play golf and make love all day; I'd rather wear out than rust out." To executives thinking about retirement, this curt advice: "Get out and get another job as quickly as you can."

---

*Wallace E. Johnson, *Work Is My Play* (New York: Hawthorn Books), 1972.

7

Hotel Food and Beverage Operations

In midscale and upscale hotels, food and beverage (F&B) is a major component of the hotel's customer appeal. Hotel restaurants help to create the overall ambience of a hotel by the decor, menu, and service offered. Lodging, food, and beverage sales were projected by the National Restaurant Association to be $15 billion in 1992. As a percentage of total hotel income estimated by the American Hotel & Motel Association, F&B constituted about 26 percent. F&B in many hotels comprises a third or more of total sales. For many hotels, perhaps most, the profit from F&B is negligible or nonexistent if the food outlets are charged their proportionate share of overall hotel operating costs.

In the midsize and larger hotels, the F&B department is headed by a director whose department has more employees than any other, with the exception of perhaps the housekeeping department. The F&B director is an active member of the executive operating committee and reports directly to the General Manager (GM). In smaller hotels with food service, an executive chef may be

in charge. Budget properties and motels usually have no food service and rely on a nearby restaurant for restaurant service. All-suite hotels offer a complimentary breakfast, but no regular restaurant service.

Of all hotel departments, F&B requires the most attention and expertise. Meal deadlines must be met, food sanitation standards followed, customer food preferences tracked, and costs carefully controlled. The kitchen itself is a place of pressure, and employee skill requirements are extensive. Any letdown in customer service can mean that a hotel guest will not return. Banquet service is an exercise in precision timing. Table setup (*mise en place*) must be ready, the food hot but not overcooked. Hundreds of guests may be involved.

BRIEF HISTORY

The tavern, the predecessor of the hotel in the U.S., was a center of community activity and likely to be the only place where the general public could eat away from home. Food, and sometimes beer or ale, were served as part of the total charge. Food service became definitely associated with taverns and later hotels so that today, by legal definition in some states, a property is not considered a hotel unless it offers food as well as rooms.

When the hotel displaced the tavern, the grander properties in the cities maintained several dining rooms and at least one ballroom. These "palaces of the people" were the scenes of public and civic entertainment, as well as a place where guests could eat and drink.

Much of a larger hotel's success depended on the promotional skill of the GM in attracting F&B functions to the property. Ceremonial banquets quite naturally were held in a community's leading hotels. Civic and fraternal clubs had their luncheon and dinner meetings there, and except for private clubs, the hotel became the logical place to meet for entertainment and business. Places like the Astor and the old Waldorf-Astoria in New York City became famous for their food as well as their rooms. The hotel dining room in the usual American town from the early 1900s to the 1930s was one of the few first-class eating facilities available.

Well-known restaurants operating independently of hotels were scarce even in large cities. Following World War II, this changed. Independent restaurants and restaurant chains flourished, and by comparison the traditional hotel dining room looked rather unexciting. It was not uncommon to find a large, high-ceilinged room in a hotel, well staffed and well appointed, having tables with white tablecloths and very few customers. Hotel guests wanted to get out of the hotel for a change and obtain a quick meal at a moderate price, rather than endure elaborate service with the high prices to be found in a formal dining room.

Specialty Restaurants Appear

Hotel management reacted to the growth of independent restaurants by installing coffeeshops, and it was not too long before nearly every hotel of any size in the country had one. Then came the theme restaurant. In the East, Sonesta Hotels opened their Rib Rooms in 1952. Others followed in other Sonesta properties, with rigid requirements regarding the quality of the rib served.

Weight, age, trim, fat marbling, and allowable shrinkage were part of the buying specifications. Steps for cooking, carving, and service were spelled out clearly and in detail.

Hyatt now fills each property with up to five different specialty restaurants, ranging from snack to gourmet. Hugo's Rotisserie specializes in roasts and offers a dish of lemon sherbet between courses. Hugo's Market features fanciful salad bars and self-service ice cream. There is also an Oyster Kitchen and a Ginsburg and Wong Restaurant. The latter offers such unexpected combinations as lox, bagels, and fried rice.

Large hotels found themes to incorporate into their different foodservices, and menus are slanted to fit them: Polynesian food for Polynesian atmosphere, French cuisine for French or international ambience, and roasted meat in a rotisserie. Roast beef continues to be the number-one seller in hotel restaurants.

Allen W. Hubsch, former F&B director for Sonesta Hotels, proposed a few rules for establishing a hotel specialty restaurant:

1. Establish an easily identifiable image.

2. Create an atmosphere that appeals to customers' "escapist desires"—period rooms, nationality rooms, steak houses, South Sea Island rooms, garden rooms, hearthside rooms.

3. Manage and promote the specialty rooms in the same manner as successful independent restaurants.

4. Provide direct access to the restaurants from the street or parking area.

5. Merchandise and advertise the specialty rooms separately from the hotel.

With these rules, Sonesta has produced departmental profits far and above those they had usually obtained:

Banquet sales (including beverages)—20 to 25 percent profit

Beverage sales in bars and cocktail lounges—40 to 50 percent profit

Specialty restaurants (including beverages)—20 to 30 percent profit

The specialty restaurants that require highly specialized knowledge are often run by persons or companies not directly connected with the hotel. A number of hotels lease them out to established foodservice companies. Recently, many budget and midpriced chains have gotten out of foodservice and turned it over to such chains as Red Lobster, Bobby McGee's, KFC, Wendy's, and Burger King.

Luxury hotels are expected to have at least one four-star-quality restaurant.

Most all-suite hotels are built without foodservice, except for a small hotel kitchen to produce the complimentary breakfast. Small motels, and some large ones, forego a restaurant, but like to be able to recommend "the restaurant just across the street."

F&B DEPARTMENT ORGANIZATION

The organization of F&B departments varies around the country as well as with chain policy.

Hotels with much group business usually separate the catering function from the regular restaurant operations (Fig. 7-3), the catering function being much more profitable. The organization for the Century Plaza Hotel of Beverly Hills, California, a Westin Hotel, represents the newer thinking in F&B organization (Fig. 7-4). The hotel has three restaurants plus a Yamados, a restaurant leased to an independent operator. Its ballroom seats 2000 people.

The director of F&B reports directly to the resident manager and GM. Responsible to him or her are the director of restaurants, director of catering, and executive chef. (Often, the executive chef is responsible to the director of restaurants.) Within the F&B department is an operations committee concerned with making suggestions for a profit plan.

The F&B controller prices each banquet menu daily and the restaurant menus twice a year. He or she produces sales forecasts for the department and conducts sales analyses and butcher and can-cutting tests (tests that deter-

Figure 7-1 The Garden Court of the Sheraton-Palace Hotel in San Francisco was originally the carriage entrance to the hotel and called the Grand Court. The original Place Hotel, opened in 1875, was built in the form of a hollow square surrounding the great Sun Court, filled with palms and flowers. The hotel was destroyed by fires caused by the earthquake of 1906. In the Garden Court today there are ten enormous chandeliers, each valued at over $50,000. The Gold Service, reputedly one of the oldest and the most complete in the world, adds grandeur when it is used for important foodservice functions.

mine costs per portion of edible food). He makes monthly reports and produces a profit and loss statement for each unit. He or she helps allocate expenses and assists in taking inventory. Half the hotel's total revenue is generated by the F&B department. More than half that department's business is from catering; about half of that is generated by conventions. The Century Plaza's organization is somewhat unusual in that a director of convention sales stays at the hotel with a registered group and sees to it that all of its needs are met. He or she becomes their "man [or gal] Friday" and, being completely familiar with the hotel and the various people on staff, can cut across department lines to accomplish whatever is necessary.

Food costs for the entire F&B operation of the Century Plaza run about 30 percent; in the catering department alone it runs 25 percent. Labor costs continue to escalate; the cost of fringe benefits is rising even faster, adding another 35 percent to the wage cost.

Unlike the large properties represented by the Century Plaza, typical hotels have 100 to 300 rooms. They are best represented by chains such as the Holiday, Roadway, and Ramada inns. An organizational F&B chart of the F&B department in such a property is seen in Figure 7-5. A typical

Figure 7-2 Terrace Dining Room of the Phoenician Hotel, Scottsdale, Arizona. The room features a marble dance floor, grand piano, and floor-to-ceiling windows. The menu features Italian-American cuisine. The hotel has a separate porte cochere entrance for meeting and event arrivals and provides six butlers and a convention concierge for group service. (Courtesy of the Phoenician Hotel)

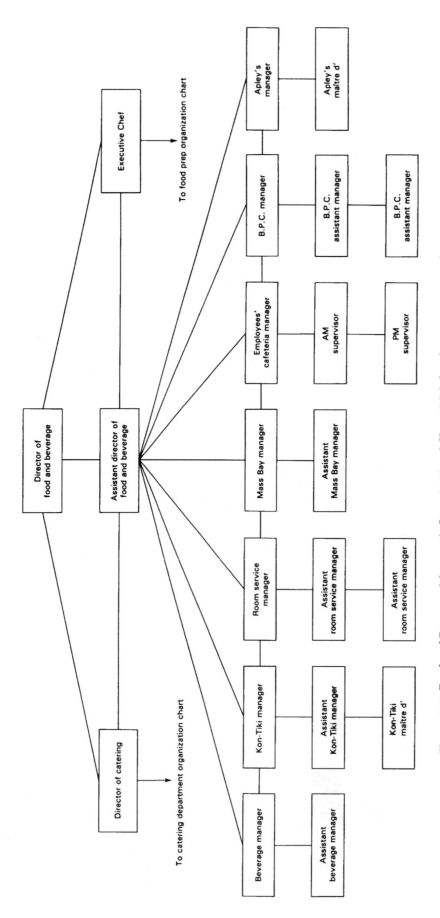

Figure 7-3 Food and Beverage Manager's Organizational Chart. With four large restaurants plus room service, an employees' cafeteria, and a catering department, the food and beverage department is a large endeavor. The director is head of the department. The director of catering, an assistant director, and the executive chef report directly to him or her.

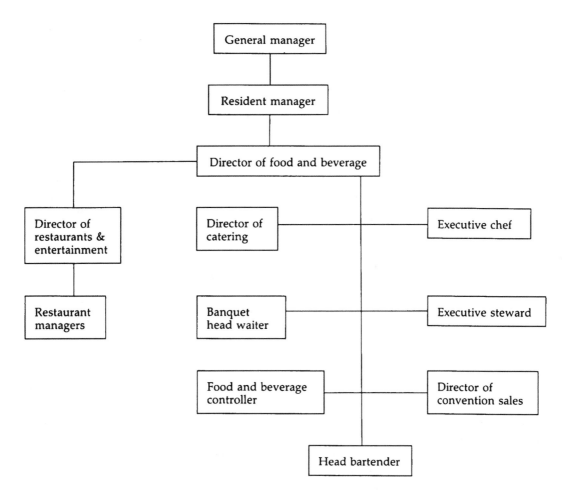

Figure 7-4 Organization of the food and beverage department of the Century Plaza Hotel. All total, the department employs about 400 people.

job description for a food and beverage manager appears in Figure 7-6.

Kitchen Organization

The organization of a traditional kitchen in a large hotel may include a number of specialized craftsmen and women, such as an oyster man, a garde manager (cold food preparation), a chicken butcher, roast and broiler cooks, vegetable cooks, bakers, sugar workers, ice cream makers, and pastry chefs. Reporting directly to the executive chef are a night chef, sous chef, and perhaps a pastry chef.

A kitchen steward in a traditional kitchen is in charge of sanitation and all personnel relating to that function. He or she might also act as purchasing agent for food and other supplies.

In large hotels with a resident auditor, who may be in charge of all bookkeeping and accounting taking place in the property, the night auditor and sometimes every cashier in every restaurant report to the auditor rather than the restaurant manager. All cash and accounting of the restaurant's sales go directly to the auditor's office in such instances. Each kitchen may use a food checker, who prices all food before it goes into the dining room. He or she inspects the food for appearance and determines if what is going out of the kitchen corresponds with what is written on a guest check. The practice of having a food checker, however, is fading in this country.

ROOM SERVICE

It is agreed that a first-class hotel must offer room service even if it constitutes a losing operation.

Room service is a hallmark of a fine hotel and can constitute up to 15 percent of total sales. Deluxe hotels may even maintain individual floor pantries; press a button and in seconds a room-service waiter appears.

Successful room service depends on delivering the food to a room as quickly as possible. To do a good job, proper equipment is necessary—equipment that will keep hot things hot and cold things cold. The person in charge must be a good organizer, someone who gets *mise en place* (set up) quickly so that the waiter has nothing to do but pick up and deliver the order.

Breakfast accounts for 70 to 90 percent of room service. Perhaps three-fourths of such orders are for the continental breakfast. "Doorknob" programs—guests check off breakfast items and the delivery time desired on a special card that is hung on the outside of the doorknob—work well. The cards are collected at night so that the service tables can be set up and some of the food prepared, ready for delivery in the morning.

Some hotels allocate a service elevator for exclusive use by room service during the morning rush. The elevator may contain heating and refrigeration units (a few carry a small microwave oven), plus space for bread, rolls, linens, and condiments. In some hotels, breakfast orders are phoned directly to the elevator operator, who

transports waiters and carts to the designated floors.

Room-service hours may be limited or may operate 24 hours a day. Menus may be for room service only, or guests can order either from those menus or the menus of any of the hotel's restaurants.

To keep room service as profitable as possible, the menus are usually higher priced than the restaurant menus. Some hotels add a service charge.

In large properties, captains oversee each room-service shift; in the small hotel, the bellman, busboy, or regular waiter makes the room-service delivery.

THE CATERING FUNCTION

In a large hotel, the catering function is a separate department with its own manager, to whom special-sales personnel report. At the operational level, a maître d'hotel may be in charge, with head waiters, banquet waiters, and sometimes room-service waiters reporting to him or her.

An American catering manager in a hotel usually deals strictly with group meals and has little to do with the restaurant operations. (In Britain the catering manager is equivalent to restaurant manager or F&B manager.) He or she mainly works with those who are arranging group func-

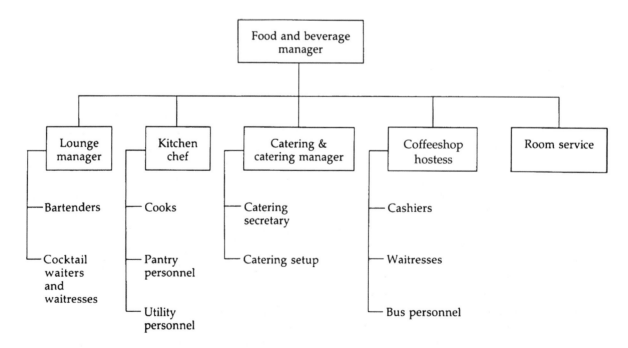

Figure 7-5 Organization of the food and beverage department in a 200-room motor hotel.

tions, such as weddings, banquets, bar mitzvahs, anniversary dinners, and so on.

Banquets as Theater vs. Menu Monotony

Over the years, imaginative hoteliers have produced banquet extravaganzas, as much drama as meal. History offers a wealth of examples, from the Roman orgy to the state dinners of Louis XIV of France. Louis, who centered the attention of France on himself, used his meals as public performances. The food was delivered to the Sun King (as he was known) by selected nobility. As it passed along the route from the kitchen across the

---

**JOB DESCRIPTION
FOOD AND BEVERAGE MANAGER
200-ROOM MOTOR HOTEL**

Supervise the coffee shop, dining room, banquet service, and lounge operation. Maintain an optimum of good service while assuring maximum profitability of all food and beverage outlets.

SPECIFIC DUTIES AND RESPONSIBILITIES

—Hire, train, and terminate cashiers, waitresses, hostesses, and personnel in room service, cleanup, the bar, and kitchen preparation.

—Account for the numerical sequence of all checks issued daily.

—Maintain a daily missing-check record. Take action, as recommended by the general manager, to correct any accounting problems.

—Test and verify the clerical accuracy on all checks for prices, state and federal taxes, and paidouts of tips.

—Keep a daily payroll record of all food and beverage employees.

—Assist the general manager in preparation of bimonthly payrolls.

—Assist the secretary to the general manager in preparation of all P-2 forms, on a daily basis, by forwarding all necessary information to keep personnel files up to date at all times.

—Assist the general manager in preparation of all F&B daily reports and deposits.

—Post a work schedule for all personnel one week in advance. Schedule coverage of all banquet functions.

—Issue cashier banks for each scheduled shift, including the lounge operation.

—Verify and reconcile the restaurant register machine tapes with total revenue reported.

—Maintain counts of total meals served, comparison of register tapes against reported revenue, etc., as directed by general manager.

—Make sure that a guest check is prepared and posted correctly for each F&B transaction, including employee and banquet functions.

—Assist general manager in taking the end-of-the month inventory of all sundry items.

—Assist the general manager in purchasing sundries and make sure that all items sold are posted on the proper cash register key.

—Maintain responsibility for appearance, cleanliness, and proper setup of the coffee shop and dining room. Check the maintenance of all equipment in the dining room, coffee shop, and lounge, and request immediate repair of all damages.

—Make sure that the guests receive immediate and proper attention and endeavor to rectify any complaints, conveying them immediately to the general manager if they cannot be solved on the spot.

—Direct the activities of all service personnel in the dining room, coffee shop, and lounge. Draw their attention to guests newly seated and make sure that orders are promptly and courteously taken; observe when guests are being neglected and urge employees to give prompt service.

—Ask departing guests if food and service were satisfactory and ask them to come back again.

—Replace, without charge, any unsatisfactory food or beverage item served to a guest.

(continues)

Figure 7-6 Job description—food and beverage manager in a 200 room motor Hotel.

—Direct premeal meetings with dining room and coffee shop personnel to relay information, policy changes, and to brief personnel on updates of operation.

—Call the security officer or general manager for help with disorderly guests or those apparently under the influence of alcohol.

—Insist on full and unprejudiced cooperation of all F&B service employees.

—Make sure that established service procedures are adhered to and correct any deviations discreetly, but immediately.

—Make suggestions to the general manager concerning possible improvements in the dining room, coffee shop, and lounge, which would tend to produce more satisfied customers, increase volume of business, cut payroll costs, etc.

RELATIONSHIPS

Report to: General manager

Supervise: Hostesses, cashiers, waitresses/waiters, bus help, room service, chef, cooks, preparation and service crew, lounge staff.

Work closely with: chef, sales, and catering departments, hotel assistant manager, and front office.

Figure 7-6　(continued).

courtyard and into the dining room, the food itself was bowed to by the people as it passed. Before the King would touch it, a marquis acting as guinea pig tasted it for flavor and, most important, ascertained if it had been poisoned. Anyone, including commoners, could attend the state dinners, provided they owned or could rent a hat and a sword.

Some banquets around the beginning of the twentieth century were pure theater. At one, all guests were served while seated on horseback; at another, guests sat in boats floating in a temporary lake in the dining room. Today's banquets are much more quietly produced, but some are still presented with fanfare.

Hotel banqueting today is often the butt of jokes because of menu monotony—"the rubber chicken circuit." After-dinner speakers tell of the "blahs" from having to "stare at the rear end of a rock cornish hen night after night" in hotels around the country. Catering managers reply that actually there are relatively few menu items acceptable to a large group; beef and chicken are favorites because of the average taste preferences, cost, and food preparation factors.

Quite naturally, when an item like Beef Wellington proves popular at one hotel, it will almost certainly be seen on a number of other hotel menus in the area very soon. Because of the relative ease and brief time it takes to prepare chicken, that item will probably remain inexpensive and a favorite for the banquet table. It is diffi-

cult to pick entrees that are acceptable to everyone at a banquet; there will always be someone who cannot stand veal, pork, or fish. Most people like lobster or crab, but are unwilling to pay the price. Veal is also expensive. Steak is difficult to cook and serve quickly to a large group. The consequence: Roast beef and chicken are the ubiquitous banquet choices. Even so, a multitude of choices in preparation and presentation can make these items interesting. Buffets can help: They are time-consuming to prepare and present, but they often offer something for everyone.

Profitability

Banquet sales, or catering sales as they are called in hotels, can be profitable for several reasons:

1. Banquets can be priced higher than restaurant meals. They are often included in a total package price for a group or as expense-account meals, and there is less resistance to a high-priced banquet meal than a high price for a restaurant meal.

2. The number of participants is guaranteed and income assured. This permits easy forecasting and less waste in food preparation and labor.

3. Labor costs are usually comparatively low because servers are hired for a limited period of time, no longer than needed.

Figure 7-7 The Praying Monk, a private dining room in the Phoenician Hotel, Scottsdale, Arizona. (Courtesy of the Phoenician Hotel)

Offsetting these factors are the following negatives:

1. The return on the investment of banquet space is often low, and some of the costs connected with banquets are high.

2. Groups holding banquets in the evening tie up the banquet space for the entire evening. Often, however, it is occupied only for one meal a day or not at all.

3. Unionized waiters and waitresses are employed for a minimum of 4 hours or must receive pay for 4 hours.

4. Compared to a restaurant, banquet-seat turnover is very low, once in about 4 hours. In the same four-hour period, a restaurant seat might turn over four to eight times.

BREAKING THE FAST

Breakfast reigns for many a traveler as the supreme test of a hotel's sensibilities, its speed, and its concern for its friends (and hang the cost). The veteran nondieting traveler in some of the really posh hotels will have none of the disembodied voice at the other end of the phone when ordering breakfast. How much better to press a little button on the wall and find a waiter at one's door three minutes later. The floor waiter then proceeds to inquire how one wants the coffee brewed, strong or light, and what else the guest needs in order to be fortified for the day.

Within a few minutes, the floor waiter reappears, pushing a trolley over which has been spread a white linen tablecloth and on which are placed croissants, Danish pastry, two types of rolls, Ryvita, two types of brown bread, butter on ice in a dish, and perhaps three individual dishes of such items as jam, honey, and marmalade, each with its own spoon. The single flower in a vase rounds out the morning ensemble.

How different this is from the room-service breakfast in a large convention hotel! There, the guest is urged to order breakfast the evening before by checking off items on a menu and hanging it on the outside doorknob. Even though one or two elevators have been set aside as mobile pantries, the breakfast may still arrive a half-hour late.

The Buffet Breakfast

For many people, breakfast is the best meal of the day. A theatrically presented buffet with a wide variety of foods has proved the best answer for many large hotels. It permits the display of an assortment of foods that would be almost impossible to manage even with complete wait service.

Hotels are gravitating to these breakfasts for an even simpler reason. A significant number of guests have appointments in the morning and descend en masse on the restaurant in a surprisingly short period of time, everyone in a hurry or at least eager to down some black coffee and clear the cobwebs. The breakfast buffet provides the quickest and least expensive method of service. Guests can help themselves and return as often as they desire. They are usually quite willing to pay considerably more for the help-yourself-to-all-you-want buffet than individual table service.

BEVERAGE OPERATIONS

Although the food business in the usual hotel may not be very profitable, the beverage business usually is. Bar and lounge operations can be highly profitable since the cost of goods sold and costs of labor to serve total a relatively small percentage of the sales dollar. Beverage costs usually run something under 25 percent of the sales. In convention hotels, the costs are often less than 20 percent. In a busy bar or lounge, labor costs are not likely to exceed 15 percent.

Profit in a popular bar can be spectacular. The Polaris, the revolving bar at the top of the Regency-Hyatt House in Atlanta, had sales of close to $100,000 a month with only one bartender on duty. F&B profit for that bar would have to be at least $50,000 for the month. In fact, the average hotel can expect a departmental profit of 50 percent on beverage sales.

The sale of beverages in the usual hotel runs about 25 percent of the dollars of food sold. One rule of thumb reads:

Hotel sales—100 percent

Food sales—50 percent

Bar sales—25 percent

In other words, bar sales represent about half of food sales. Bar sales run at a much higher percentage in many hotels because of several lounges that are independent of or only partially dependent on the restaurants. Cocktail parties also increase the proportion of beverage sales to total sales.

The bar must be located near the heart of the hotel; otherwise, patrons feel out of touch, which is exactly what they do not want. Robert Sage, president of the Fenway Motor Hotels of Boston, found that moving a bar from the back of one of his motor hotels to the front increased sales by 250 percent.

PROFITABILITY OF F&B

The knowledgeable general manager knows that as much as two-thirds of the F&B business must come from people who are not guests of the hotel. Guests are not captive diners; they want to go out of the hotel for some of their meals. One study found that 69 percent of the people questioned ate none of their luncheons in the hotel where they were staying, while 52 percent ate none of their dinners there. Robert Sage noted that if a guest stays three days in one of his properties, he or she will eat in the hotel the first day and eat out on the other two. However, if the hotel has several specialty restaurants, the guest staying a few days may try more than one of them.

No longer can the GM or director turn over the F&B operations to an executive chef and hope for the best. Instead, the F&B director must be experienced and knowledgeable in food prepara-

TABLE 7-1 ABC Motor Hotel, Profit and Loss in the Food Department

	Current	Percent	Year to Date	Percent
Food sales	$49,430	100.0	$577,600	100.0
Cost of food sold	18,903	36.0	207,936	36.0
Salaries & wages	17,882	34.0	196,710	34.0
Employee meals	1179	2.2	12,960	2.2
Payroll taxes & benefits	2260	4.3	27,147	4.7
Total payroll & related expenses	21,321	43.1	236,817	41.0
Other expenses				
Cleaning supplies	248	0.5	3466	0.6
Guest supplies	93	0.2	1400	0.2
Laundry	27	0.1	400	0.1
China, glass, & silver	670	1.4	8795	1.5
Kitchen supplies	54	0.1	650	0.1
Linen supplies	211	0.4	2750	0.5
Uniforms	107	0.2	1500	0.3
Decorations	50	0.1	650	0.1
Printing & office supplies	80	0.2	1200	0.2
Telephone	50	0.1	600	0.1
Miscellaneous			150	
Exterminating & waste removal	130	0.3	1560	0.3
Contract cleaning			560	0.1
Total department expense	41,944	84.9	468,434	81.1
Food department profit	7486	15.1	109,166	18.9

TABLE 7-2 ABC Motor Hotel, Profit and Loss in the Beverage Department

	Current	Percent	Year to Date	Percent
Beverage sales	$24,727	100.0	272,000	100.0
Cost of beverage sold	4657	18.8	55,216	20.3
Salaries & wages	3398	13.7	40,800	20.0
Employee meals	142	0.6	1642	0.6
Payroll taxes & benefits	430	1.7	5590	2.1
Total payroll & related expenses	3970	16.1	48,032	22.7
Other expenses				
Cleaning supplies	33	0.1	398	0.1
Guest supplies	27	0.1	358	0.1
China, glass, & silver	557	2.3	2,785	1.0
Bar supplies	62	0.3	463	0.2
Uniforms	29	0.1	267	0.1
Decorations	85	0.3	185	0.1
Licenses			600	0.2
Miscellaneous	400	1.6	496	0.2
Total departmental expense	9820	39.7	108,800	45.0
Beverage department profit	14,907	60.3	163,200	55.0

TABLE 7-3   Accounting Classifications for Hotel & Beverage Operations (Uniform System of Accounts, American Hotel & Motel Association, 1985)

Total revenue	_____
Cost of sales	
Cost of food consumed	
Less: cost of employee meals	_____
Net cost of food sales	
Cost of beverage sales	
Other cost of sales	_____
Net cost of sales	_____
Gross profit	_____
Expenses	
Salaries and wages	
Employee benefits	_____
Total payroll and related expenses	_____
Other expenses	
China, glassware, silver, and linen	
Contract cleaning	
Laundry and dry cleaning	
Licenses	
Music and entertainment	
Operating supplies	_____
Uniforms	
Other	
Total other expenses	_____
Total expenses	_____
Departmental income (loss)	_____

tion and service, as seen in Tables 7-1, and 7-2, as well as marketing. Much of the property's reputation depends on its F&B operation. Its restaurants add to or detract from its total image. Hotels become known for their good food or lack of it. Impressed with the food and ambience, a customer may refer other travelers to the hotel.

To increase sales, the F&B manager works closely with the director of sales and the GM. The chain hotel can usually expect help from the corporate office. Often, a vice president is in charge of food and beverages, a professional who helps establish policy, quality control, and standards for the entire chain. There may also be a corporate-level executive chef who is on hand at the hotel openings, is available for consultation, and fills in when needed.

Guidelines and formats for F&B accounting are laid down in the *Uniform System of Accounts for Hotels*,[1] the most recent revision of which was

---

1. *Uniform System of Accounts for Hotels* (New York: AH&MA) 1986.

written in 1985. Accounting classifications and the format for compiling F&B accounting information are seen in Table 7-3. Separate statements should be made for each F&B facility in the hotel. Common expenses, such as administrative and kitchen wages, are allocated among facilities. The allocations can be based on any reasonable measure, such as customer count or a time and motion study.

The consolidated statement as seen in Table 7-3 is supported by detailed statements for each restaurant or lounge, using the same format as that in the consolidated statement. The *Uniform System* suggests that the information in the finan-

TABLE 7-4   Recommended Statistics for Comparative Purposes

Restaurant facilities
  Number of seats
  Meal period statistics
Meal period Covers Average check
Breakfast
Lunch
Dinner
    Total
  Beverage sales % of food sales
  Combined F&B sales per seat
Lounge facilities
  Number of seats
  Sales per seat
Room service
  Total sales per occupied room
Banquet
  Total square feet
  Banquet sales per square foot
  Covers and average check statistics (see restaurant facilities)
Inventory turns and number of days of inventory on hand
  These inventory statistics are calculated as follows for both F&B inventories:
  Inventory turns
  Monthly cost of goods consumed, divided by average inventory (opening inventory plus closing inventory divided by 2)
    Number of days of inventory on hand
    Number of days in the month, divided by the inventory turns, equals the average number of days it takes to turn over the inventory

cial statement be analyzed to produce statistics that can provide operational insights and be used for comparative purposes with statistics from other comparable properties. The kinds of statistics recommended are seen in Table 7-4.

Constraints on Hotel Food and Beverage Operations

There are several reasons why hotel restaurant operations have not been more profitable:

1. In the past, too often the GM knew too little about menu planning, food purchasing, preparation, and service, and so was happy to turn over the restaurants to an experienced executive chef. The chef, jealous of the GM's prerogatives and special knowledge, was not interested in educating him or her. The GM might visit the kitchen periodically, but it was more like a tour or state visit. The chef told the manager what he or she wanted to know; the manager's dignity and status remained intact; everybody was happy. Fortunately, this state of affairs has changed as chains have taken over much of the business and more trained F&B personnel have become available through the universities.

2. Also in the past, many hotels built in the 1920s had old-fashioned dining rooms unable to keep up with changing public tastes. The menu was likely to be high-style and costly and the service rather slow. To make major changes was expensive; often, the restaurant had to be relocated for immediate access to the street. Hotels reacted by adding coffeeshops at the street level and hoped for the best.

3. Older properties are often saddled with inefficient layouts that were designed when labor costs were low and knowledge of work flow little understood. Their kitchens are sometimes half a block from the point of service.

4. Restaurants were often located in spots so remote or hard to find that as one F&B director said, "A seeing-eye dog was needed to find them." This has changed dramatically as architects and other planners have become knowledgeable about hotel economics and operations.

5. Hours of hotel foodservice operation must be provided for guests even if some of those hours might produce very low volume and be unprofitable.

6. A number of hotels continue to offer room service, one of the hallmarks of a first-class hotel. The service is almost inevitably a loss operation because of the long distances involved in transporting food from the kitchen to the guest's room, the labor costs involved in such movement, and the special equipment and space required.

7. If the hotel is an old one and has acquired a certain image, it is very difficult to add a fun type of restaurant and expect people to patronize it. It will remain part of the larger, perhaps gloomy, original image.

8. F&B management personnel in a hotel may not be as strongly motivated as those in a conventional restaurant. Employees may lack the drive to succeed that is characteristic of the entrepreneur.

9. Because of the greater costs of a hotel restaurant, prices are likely to be higher than in a comparable place outside the hotel, which may result in a lower volume of sales than required for profitability.

10. As explained elsewhere, the *Uniform System of Accounts for Hotels* does not allocate true costs to the F&B operation. The restaurant manager may have a false feeling of accomplishment when he or she sees a 15 percent departmental profit. Actually, a 15 percent departmental profit may mean a loss for the restaurant.

11. Banquet sales usually involve a low F&B cost. That may be thrown into the overall cost for the entire F&B operation, which again may mislead management into feeling that it is more successful than is actually true.

Questions

1. In what way is the "city ledger" related to the F&B department operation?

2. The catering department of the hotel is charged with what primary function?

3. Does hotel management ever turn to outside foodservice specialists for the operation of any restaurants within a hotel? Explain.

4. Beverage costs in hotel bars are likely to run about what percent of sales?

5. Hotels very often break even or lose money on their food sales. Can you give five reasons why it is difficult to operate hotel restaurants profitably?

6. Why is it that banquet menus tend to be relatively few in number?

7. Why is the banquet department in a hotel likely to be more profitable than the restaurant operation?

8. Generally speaking, bar sales should run about what percentage of food sales in a hotel?

9. Give at least three reasons why large hotels are turning to the buffet breakfast rather than typical table service.

10. Would you guess that room service is a very profitable operation within a hotel? Explain.

Discussion Questions

1. Several of the larger hotel coffeeshops are introducing buffet luncheons. Under what circumstances would this arrangement be appropriate? What labor cost percentage could be expected?

2. As an F&B director of a 400-room hotel, you are asked to draw up a marketing plan. How would you go about this and in what sequence?

3. What changes do you foresee for hotel foodservice? Why?

4. Why or why not would you prefer work in a hotel F&B department as compared with an independent restaurant?

J. Willard Marriott

(1900–1985)*

Large numbers of innkeepers and restaurateurs have been on the list of the 200,000 millionaires said to be in the U.S. A few have been included in that even more select group of those with over $100 million; however, only one in the latter group has also been a bishop of his church and chairman of the inauguration committee of a president of the U.S. He is J. Willard Marriott, founder and chairman of the board of the Marriott Corporation.

Responsibility came early for Bill Marriott. At 14, he was sent on a long railroad trip to San Francisco along with several carloads of sheep. At 18, he had already served two years as a Mormon missionary. Educated at Weber College and the University of Utah, he sold woolen underwear to miners and loggers during summer vacations. By his junior year, he had a territory of seven states and 45 students were working for him.

The Marriott Corporation started with root beer. On graduation from the University of Utah in 1926, Bill bought a franchise for $2000 to sell A&W root beer from a stand in Washington, D.C. During the first summer in Washington, the chief root beer maker was Bill's new bride, Alice.

"The restaurant business was born of desperation," said Marriott. When root beer sales dropped sharply in the fall, Marriott and his partner, Hugh Coulton, tried to sublease their stores. No luck, so they added hot food: chili con carne and hot tamales. Hamburgers were not on the menu because at the time they were déclassé.

The change from a root beer stand to restaurant was made literally overnight. The big orange A&W barrel came out of the front window. Stools went in front of the counter. A steam table was placed under the counter, and the name "Hot Shoppes" went on the front of the store. The name had been suggested by a customer who had jokingly asked: "When are you going to open your hot shops?"

*Robert O'Brien, *Marriott: The J. Willard Marriott Story* (Salt Lake City, Utah: Deseret Book Company), 1977, pp. 265–267.

Bill bought out his partner the same year. When spring came, he opened one of the first drive-in restaurants in the nation. He literally built the restaurant, taking up hammer and nails himself; he had no architect. The design was a simple rectangle, the building painted orange with black trim.

Employees did not just cook or serve food; they painted, washed windows, did carpentry, and on occasion acted as bouncers. The drive-in turned into a big money maker. Profits from the place were used to finance other restaurants.

By 1930 there were five Hot Shoppes and nine years of the Depression ahead. Profit margins were small, but with full value given to customers, the business prospered. Bill and Alice Marriott began laying plans for expansion. Characteristically, they had an unshaken belief that prosperity would return.

In 1933 Bill became desperately ill with what was diagnosed as Hodgkins disease. Five doctors were unanimous in telling him that he had but one year to live. Frightened, he took a much-needed vacation trip. Amazingly, on his return the disease was found to be gone. It was at this time, Marriott stated, that he realized the importance of having an organization behind him, one not dependent on any single individual.

Marriott had several close calls with death, including bouts with hepatitis, San Joaquin Valley fever, a stroke, and several heart attacks. He was convinced that his prayers, those of his friends in the Mormon Church, and his sense of mission pulled him through. He deeply believed in his Mormon faith, his family, and good health habits. Good habits in general, he said, lengthen our lives and prepare us for death. "Life after death? I'm certain there is one—just as certain as I am that I'm alive at this moment."

Like most Mormons, he tithed. In addition, he gave $2 million to Brigham Young University to be used for a library and an activities center.

Like Ernest Henderson before him, Marriott laid down a number of "guideposts."

1. Keep physically fit, mentally and spiritually strong.

2. Guard your habits—bad ones will destroy you.

3. Pray about every difficult problem.

4. Study and follow professional management principles. Apply them logically and practically to your organization.

5. People are number one—their development, loyalty, interest, team spirit. Develop managers in every area. This is your prime responsibility.

6. Decisions: Men grow making decisions and assuming responsibility for them.
   a. Make crystal clear what decision each manager is responsible for and what decisions you reserve for yourself.
   b. Have all the facts and counsel necessary—then decide and stick to it.

7. Criticism: Do not criticize people, but make a fair appraisal of their qualifications with their supervisor only (or someone assigned to do this). Remember, anything you say about someone may (and usually does) get back to them. There are few secrets.

8. See the good in people and try to develop those qualities.

9. Inefficiency: If it cannot be overcome and an employee is obviously incapable of a job, find a job he or she can do or terminate *now*. Do not wait.

10. Manage your time:
    a. Short conversations—to the point.
    b. Make every minute on the job count.
    c. Work fewer hours—some of us waste half our time.

11. Delegate and hold accountable for results.

12. Details:
    a. Let your staff take care of them.
    b. Save your energy for planning, thinking, working with department heads, promoting new ideas.
    c. Do not do anything someone else can do for you.

13. Ideas and competition:
    a. Ideas keep the business alive.
    b. Know what your competitors are doing and planning.
    c. Encourage all management to think about better ways and give suggestions on anything that will improve business.
    d. Spend time and money on research and development.

14. Do not try to do an employee's job for him or her—counsel and suggest.

15. Think objectively and keep a sense of humor. Make the business fun for you and others.

Diversification came early, but was introduced in measured steps. In 1934 the sandwich menu was enlarged to include full-course meals. In 1937 the company became the first airline caterer, putting up meals in cardboard boxes for American and Eastern airlines passengers out of Washington, D.C. By 1969 Marriott In-Flight Services was supplying 50 airlines from 20 domestic flight kitchens and 19 overseas airports.

Early into World War II, Marriott moved into in-plant foodservice. Lunch wagons roved around five war plants and foodservice was offered in the cafeteria of the Naval Communications Annex. After the war, the takeout market was tapped with the opening of the Pantry Houses. Their slogan was "Take home food for the family."

In 1957 lodging operations were added to the food business. A 360-room motel was built in Washington, D.C. Its design and location made it an instant success.

To a greater extent than most hotel and restaurant chains, Marriott is family-oriented. Alice Marriott continued to be active in the business (except for periods when her children were small), serving as treasurer. In 1931 brother Paul joined the organization as general manager. Woodrow and Russell, the other two brothers, joined the company in 1933. Woodrow Marriott served as senior vice president. Today, J. Willard Marriott, Jr., is chairman of the board. Brother Paul is executive vice president in charge of architecture and construction.

The company has the largest centralized personnel department of any in the field. Annual employee parties began in 1938. Group insurance, Christmas gifts, length-of-service gifts, a credit union, and a suggestion system are evidence of the interest in employee relations. Since 1953, when the stock was offered to the public, employees have been encouraged to buy into the company. Marriott has been an industry leader with its company profit-sharing plan.

Marriott was an early believer in a centralized commissary operation. In 1930 certain food items were prepared centrally for distribution to the other stores. Raw food items such as vegetables were graded but not cooked. Meat, fish, and poultry were graded and portioned. All were later cooked at the stores. All baked items, ice cream, and sherbets were made in the commissary. So, too, were soups, stocks, and gravies. In 1941 production, administration, personnel, and accounting functions were all moved into a new three-story building.

The Marriott Corporation might be called a conglomerate, in that it is a multifaceted organization built around the production of food and hospitality. It serves food in almost every possible manner: via vending, table service, and counter service. The restaurant group comprises four categories of food service: fast foods, coffeeshops, cafeterias, and family-style restaurants. The company prepares food, and usually serves it, in industrial plants, business offices, schools and colleges, public cafeterias, and turnpike restaurants. It serves airlines (by 1985 Marriott had 90 flight kitchens operating on four continents) and has specialty restaurants, drive-ins, and coffee shops. It operates in the hotel business in a big way, with more than 677 hotels, resorts, and franchised inns, totaling nearly 155,000 rooms.

Undoubtedly, many people have grown rich with the Marriott family. The company has been one of the industry's biggest winners.

It will probably be some time before the Marriott Corporation becomes a bureaucracy. Marriott was an entrepreneur in the old-style American way, a style that is highly competitive and driving, that brutally absorbs the individual engaged in it and moves the organization ahead to whatever goals the person thinks important. Marriott himself became a disciplinarian, a stickler for perfection, a person who put the customer first.

He was not particularly industry-oriented and did not follow some of the business's traditional practices. Until late in life, J. Willard read every complaint card personally and was incensed at any sign of carelessness in a Marriott facility.

The company has moved into a variety of ventures, and the Marriott empire has the thrust for continued expansion. Bill Jr. has introduced more corporate-level staff and spread responsibilities further down the line than did J. Willard. It took a J. Willard, however, to perceive the existence of the drive-in and in-flight markets and to have the tenacity and drive to develop those markets—fuzzy and indistinct as they were at the time. Business pioneers somehow foresee markets and dedicate themselves to their development. Marriott was one such person.

By 1987 the company had moved into the mid-priced hotel market with its Courtyard Hotels. These two-story, 150-room suburban hotels compete directly with Holiday Inns and Ramada Inns. Marriott Suites, the all-suite hotels, were also being built. In addition the company went into vacation condominium time-sharing and life-care community development.

The Marriott Corporation employs 200,000 people and operates in 47 states and 26 countries.

In 1986 Marriott acquired the Howard Johnson restaurants, with the intention of converting many of them to Bob's Big Boy units. The company quickly sold off the Howard Johnson's motor lodges and franchise system. Marriott also purchased about 98 percent of the Saga Corporation, one of the largest contract food and restaurant operators.

Marriott manages many of its hotels, but does not own them. They are usually sold to limited partnerships or institutions. The company also franchises and owns some of the hotels under its label.

Marriott Hotels are run by the book, literally. More than a dozen tomes detail operations down to how to remove hair from bathroom sinks. The company is heavy with management personnel.

J. Willard Marriott died in 1985 at the age of 84. Son Bill Jr. has rapidly expanded the company: With his brothers he owns 25 million stock shares.

The 1989–1990 recession caught the Marriott Company with about $2 billion of unsold hotel properties, part of its strategy of building hotels, selling them to investors, and negotiating management contracts to operate them. In 1990 Marriott put up for sale more than 1000 of its foodservice outlets, including Roy Rogers, Howard Johnson's, and Bob's Big Boy units. By 1994, the Marriott Company had recovered from the recession and was a leading hospitality firm.

8

The Resort Business

As said earlier, The American Automobile Association defines a resort as a hotel with extensive recreational facilities, which means it could be a casino hotel in Las Vegas, a motel sitting on the beach in Florida, or any one of 110 villages operated by Club Med in such locations as the Ivory Coast in West Africa, Tunisia, the Turks and Caicos in the Caribbean, Beijing, Bali, or Copper Mountain, Colorado. Most of the large resorts in the U.S. depend heavily on convention and association meeting business to offset social guest occupancy, which makes their markets part business, part leisure. Traditionally, resorts were classified as beach, mountain, or ski resorts.

The traditional resort hotel most often was a stately old building surrounded by broad acres of trees or fronting on a lengthy section of beach or other scene of natural beauty. It usually had large rooms, a multitude of staff, and a bounteous table.

The traditional mountain or sea resort is still around: Such places as the Biltmore in Phoenix, the Boca Raton in southern Florida, the Del Coro-

nado in San Diego, the Greenbrier in West Virginia, and the Broadmoor near Colorado Springs represent the grand resorts of the early part of the century in the hotel world of today.

The vacation hotel, which encompasses the bulk of the vacation hotel business today, is more often a high-rise building in an urbanized setting, a hotel found among dozens of hotels on Miami Beach, the Strip in Las Vegas, or Waikiki Beach, Honolulu.

The old resort hotels were independently owned and operated. By the mid-1980s that situation had changed. The big-name hotel chains decided that resort hotel keeping—especially in the American South, Hawaii, and the Caribbean—was not just a seasonal business. With management contracts rather than ownership, their risks were small. Westin, Hilton, Hyatt, Radisson, and the Ritz-Carlton became prominent resort operators. The Club Corporation of America, the largest of the club contract operators, also entered the resort business by forming a resort arm, CCA Club Resorts.

Figure 8-1 The Arizona Biltmore, opened in 1929, is one of the classic American hotels. Located on the edge of Phoenix, it has received the Mobil Five-Star rating for resorts every year since those awards have been made. Frank Lloyd Wright, America's premier architect, designed the hotel, using precast concrete blocks as the primary interior and exterior building material. The property is managed by Westin Hotels and Resorts.

The newer, larger resorts are centerpieces for land-development schemes, land and condos being sold as part of the resort atmosphere. Japanese investment has spurred the construction of resorts that have brought a new dimension in scale and scope to resort keeping. The Westin and Hyatt properties in Maui are examples. The Westin Kauai, owned by the Bass brothers of Texas and the Aoki Company of Japan, set a new standard and adds another dimension to resort-keeping. Betore was the place breathtaking in imaginative grandeur. After leaving the port, co-chère guests descended on an escalator to be greeted by eight marble horses cavorting amidst torrential spray in a huge reflecting pool that is 210 feet in diameter. Water was cannoned out of the mouths of huge stone fish. Water cascades from walkways above. Millions of dollars of oriental art are displayed throughout the property. Guests are transported by carriages, pulled by some 106 Percheron, Belgian, and Clydesdale horses. A massive hurricane almost destroyed the property.

Since World War II, business and pleasure traveling have tended to commingle. Much convention business takes place in vacation hotels in Hawaii, Las Vegas, Florida, and the Caribbean. The resort hotel caters to both the social guest and group business—meetings, conventions, trade shows, package tours.

It is becoming to make a distinction between business and pleasure traveling. Much business travel takes on elements of pleasure travel. The spouse may go on a business trip, and the business trip may be extended a few days to include a vacation.

Business is still listed as the number-one reason for travel to American hotels, however; 71 percent of the travel to Sheraton Corporation hotels is for business purposes, 29 percent for pleasure. Some of the larger airlines have found that the mix is about 50-50. For purposes of this chap-

Figure 8-2 Mexico's Cancún resort enclave has several spectacularly designed resort hotels. The seven-story Cancún Sheraton suggests a terraced Mayan temple. Built with stone stained to simulate the golden limestone of Mayan cities, six levels are bordered by hanging gardens. Cancún International Airport is 1 hour and 20 minutes by plane from Miami.

Figure 8-3 Pool of the Westin Kauai, three-quarters the size of a football field, suggests the glamor and lavishness of the resort.

Photo by Media Systems, Hawaii.

ter, the tourist is defined as the pleasure traveler, more specifically, the person on vacation.

The interlocking nature of the hotel and travel business was underscored in the 1960s when a number of oil companies and airlines bought or built hotel and restaurant chains. Pan American Airways started the pattern back in 1947 by setting up Intercontinental Hotels, Inc., a wholly owned subsidiary. Until about 1960 its growth was fairly slow and restricted to Latin America and the Caribbean. It then became international, with hotels in most major capital cities. Because of financial problems, Pan Am sold Intercontinental to a British concern, Ladbroke, a large betting house and conglomerate.

In 1967 Trans World Airways startled the hotel world by buying Hilton International. Whereas the travel agent, hotel, and airline had previously operated independently, TWA merged the three activities, selling travel and hotel space as a package. Travel and vacationing began to be seen more clearly as two sides of the same coin. In 1987 TWA sold Hilton International to Allegis, parent company of United Airlines.

The year 1968 saw the vacation business being integrated even further when ITT bought Sheraton Hotels. U.S. Steel built the convention complex at Disney World in Florida that contains 5000 rooms. Alcoa owns the Century-Plaza, which is part of a living-entertainment-hotel complex in Beverly Hills. MCA owns the Yosemite and Curry Company, and Amfac the Fred Harvey Company. All of these companies are conglomerates.

SEASONAL QUALITY

Most resort hotels have one thing in common: seasonal business. New England resorts typically open about June 20 and close on Labor Day, or soon after. Tropical and subtropical resorts have both a peak season, which lasts from about Christmas through March, and a summer season, with lower occupancies and reduced rates.

Spring and fall are the low points (so-called "shoulder seasons") in California, Arizona, Florida, and the Caribbean. Until the 1960s, many re-

Figure 8-4 Ahwahnee Hotel, Yosemite National Park, Calif., is one of the "grand" old resort hotels.

Figure 8-5   The Ritz-Carlton in Laguna Niguel, Calif., carries on in the Ritz tradition of elegance and service. The hotel employs 13 full-time concierges, some of whom, with the title of conference concierge, report to a conference manager. Total staff numbers 720. There are 393 guestrooms, 31 of which are suites. The four-story structure is reminiscent of a classic Mediterrean villa with its tiled courtyards, fountains, and French doors in each guestroom that open onto a private balcony. The Ritz-Carlton Company is operated by W. B. Johnson Properties, headquartered in Atlanta. It operates five of the Ritz-Carlton hotels in this country and licenses the other two.

sort operators could make a profit operating on a 90- to 110-day season. Compared to the present day, labor and food costs were low; the fixed expenses of taxes and insurance were also low. These expenses are now high; many resorts are surrounded by towns in which taxes have risen. The constant effort on the part of the resort operator is to extend the season, usually by bringing in convention groups at the beginning and end of the peak time of year. October has become a popular month in the Poconos, White Sulphur Springs, and parts of New England.

Each resort area tends to develop a particular market or markets. New York City and the surrounding area make up a principal tourist market. New Yorkers themselves are perhaps the biggest resorters. In season New Yorkers popu-

late the beachfront hotels of the Caribbean Islands. In Hawaii, Las Vegas, and Mexico, however, Californians are the largest group.

DIFFERENT PLACES FOR DIFFERENT PEOPLE

Obviously, travelers select destinations for different reasons, such as climate, historical or cultural appeal, available sports, entertainment, and shopping facilities. A major appeal of England for Americans is its history and culture. American Express[1] found that travelers to Flor-

1. Jonathan N. Goodrich, "Benefit Bundle Analysis: An Empirical Study of International Travelers," *Journal of Travel Research* (Fall, 1977).

ida, California, Mexico, Hawaii, the Bahamas, Jamaica, Puerto Rico, the Virgin Islands, and Barbados were attracted by the following, in descending order:

Scenic beauty

Pleasant attitudes of the local people

Suitable accommodations

Rest and relaxation

Airfare cost considerations

Historical and cultural interests

Cuisine

Water sports

Entertainment (e.g., night life)

Shopping facilities

Golf and tennis

Many resorts seek to attract only a particular type of guest; others welcome just about anybody who can pay the tab. Larger resort hotels

that rely on conventions may have a medical group one week and the plumbers' union the next.

The manager of a resort that relies heavily on social guests is usually concerned with having a fairly homogeneous guest list. He or she recognizes that most people enjoy being with those of a similar background and social position in a resort setting, but the manager also recognizes that deep in the heart of most people lies a snob. The origin of the word *snob* itself explains a great deal. It comes from the Latin *sine nobilitas*, originally reserved for students at Oxford who were "without nobility"—in other words, commoners. Those without nobility, of course, would like to have it, and the abbreviation of the two words, "s-nob," has come to mean a person with the desire to associate with those considered to be of a higher class and to exclude those considered to be of a lower class. Snobbery is to be reckoned with in the nonconvention hotel.

At beach resorts, the pool is the focal point. A tan is a vital part of the experience; it is evidence

Figure 8-6 Wentworth-by-the-Sea, a resort near Portsmouth, N. H., was built in the grand style. It opened in 1874, and various owners have spent many millions of dollars in expansion and maintenance. The Wentworth achieved international fame in 1905 when the Russians and Japanese met there to decide the Treaty of Portsmouth. Many of the greats or near-greats of the world have stopped there over the years. In 1981 the hotel was purchased by a Swiss firm and New England–style townhouses were built and sold under a time-share plan. When not occupied by the owners, the rooms are part of the hotel room inventory.

that the guest has been on vacation. The tan is sought at all costs, come cold weather, sweltering sun, or sunburn. How else would the folks back home know that the traveler has been to Florida, Arizona, or Nassau? The pool is the great leveler. The isolated guest cries for friendship and gets it. Persons who in everyday life have little in common suddenly develop an appreciation for each other. The pool is the body of warmth, the altar of sun worship. Here, the currents of humanity flow, revitalizing the tired, soothing anxieties, and bringing peace of mind.

VACATIONING IN HISTORY

The urge to vacation is deep-seated. It expresses itself today in the weekend rush to the beach, the pell-mell trip to the mountains to ski, the 10-day junket to the Caribbean, or the European tour. Vacationing brings change, excitement, and, for some, relaxation. It may be a way of acquiring a prestige tan during the winter. Going to the "in" place and mixing with the best people may be important. For a number of older people, it may be an escape from loneliness. For the young man or woman, it can be a flight to find the perfect mate. For others, a vacation is the series of slides to show neighbors.

The urge to vacation has existed for a long time. The Ancient Romans, with summer villas in Herculaneum and Pompeii, were vacationing when Mt. Vesuvius erupted and covered them and their houses completely in lava, hot mud, and volcanic ash. In the U.S. history does not record exactly when the first resort appeared, but many who attended the first Continental Congress of 1774 and 1775 "escaped the heat and humidity" of Philadelphia by traveling to Germantown, where they leased homes or stayed with local residents.

The first American resort advertisement, it is said, appeared as a broadside dated May 20, 1789, telling of the "genteel and plentiful table" of Gray's Ferry, Pennsylvania. "Guests could expect free concerts weekly and fishing tackle…to those who may be fond of that amusement." Transportation between Gray's Ferry and the city would be provided twice daily, announced the proprietor, by "a handsome State Waggon mounted on steel springs, with two good horses…."

Resorts as vacation spots satisfy at least four basic human needs: social, recreational, health, and prestige. Different resorts have specialized in satisfying particular needs. Health and therapeutic springs were the vogue before 1850, some of them in operation since before the Revolution. Previous to 1900, nearly 2000 spas were attracting the American health seeker.

The hundreds of sporting camps in this country, built first for fishermen and hunters in the nineteenth century, later became camps and lodges for vacationers. More recent lodges still follow the pattern of the lumber camp, with a central lodge and dining hall surrounded by a cabin colony. Today, Maine alone has over 5000 hotels, camps, and tourist homes where visitors, mostly from the East and Canada, come to eat, hunt, fish, canoe, climb mountains, and just enjoy the pleasantly cool summers.

In the Alleghenies just before the Civil War, going to the various hot springs became a necessity for both health and social prestige. A grand tour of the springs became the established summer "must" for people of means. It covered 170 miles and about a dozen resorts. Colonel Job Fry, proprietor of one of the springs, described the tour when he told his guest, "Go get well charged at the White, well salted at the Salt, well sweetened at the Sweet, well boiled at the Hot, and then return to me and I will Fry you."

Numerous glasses of the usually unpleasant spring water were drunk, and at some of the springs better-tasting mint juleps and food were floated out on trays to the soaking resorters. Mint julep itself was created in 1858 at the Old White Springs: French brandy, old-fashioned cut-loaf sugar, limestone water, crushed ice, and young, hand-grown mountain mint. It was at the Old White that the governor of South Carolina is reported to have said to the governor of North Carolina, "It's a long time between drinks."

Today, two famous resorts are left of the dozen that operated there at the turn of the century: the Homestead at Hot Springs, Virginia, and the Greenbrier in West Virginia (Figs. 8-7 and 8-8). The Greenbrier, owned by the Chesapeake and Ohio Railroad, is now an elegant grand convention property, a lavish hotel with 700 rooms, no two identical in decor. Conference guests comprise 65 percent of occupancy. Prices are in keeping with the style.

Figure 8-7 Lobby of one of the great classic mountain resorts, the Homestead in Hot Springs, Va. The resort sits in 6,000 acres of the Allegheny Mountains. It offers golf, tennis, riding, and, of course, hot mineral springs.

The Coming of the Railroad

The coming of the railroad was as much of a boon for the resort business as it was for the city hotel. People could travel long distances quickly and reach areas that formerly were relatively inaccessible. When the railroad went into the mountains or other potential recreational areas, resorts soon followed.

The Delaware Water Gap region in Pennsylvania offers a good example of what happened. Around the turn of the nineteenth century, summer visitors to the region braved the trip by stagecoach and canal boat and stayed in the spare rooms rented out by local residents. When the Delaware, Lackawanna, and Western Railroad came, visitors arrived in such numbers that hotels were built by the score. Today, the Gap area has about 500 summer hostelries.

One of the oldest tourist establishments in the Gap region, the Swiftwater Inn, took pains to reassure travelers that everything would go well with them there. Its sign might well serve as a motto for all good innkeepers (Fig. 8-9).

The railroad saw the logic of building and operating resorts that could be reached easily by their trains. The relationship was clear enough, but railroad management for resorts was (and remains) almost uniformly lacking in imagination and efficiency. Consequently, the marriages between railroads and resort hotels may have been blissful but costly. The Chesapeake and Ohio was originally involved in the Homestead and now completely owns the Greenbrier, both famous resorts in the Blue Ridge Mountains.

The Romantics and the Catskills

The Romantic movement of the nineteenth century modified the Puritan tradition of utilitarianism in America. The new religion of nature, as expounded by the Romantics and abetted by Thoreau's "return to simplicity," was hardly needed to get people out of the industrial centers. "Go to the mountains," said the brochures of the time, for "deep reflections, leading to wisdom and happiness." Before this time, Americans

Figure 8-8 The Greenbrier, a mountain spa at White Sulphur Springs, W.Va. Surrounded by a 6500-acre estate, the resort is a perfect setting for golf, tennis, horseback riding, skeet and trap shooting, hiking, and numerous other sports, all available at the resort.

Figure 8-9 Sign at the Swiftwater Inn.

never thought of going to the mountains and countryside for vacations. Most of them were already there.

The Catskills became an early resort center. The Catskill Mountain House opened July 4, 1823. The elite of American society began patronizing the place its very first season. By 1843 one could choose from a selection of burgundies and madeiras, French dishes, and French dances.

The Catskills, romanticized by Washington Irving as Rip Van Winkle country, became a symbol of the American Romantic movement in paintings and literature. Nature paintings by such people as Winslow Homer and Thomas Cole helped to heighten the aura of desirability of a return to nature.

In the 1880s and 1890s, converted farmhouses allowed the summer visitor to enjoy the illusion of rural existence without facing its hardships. Farmhouses could accommodate 10 to 25 paying guests. By 1905 there were at least 900 hotels, farmhouses, and boardinghouses accommodating about 25,000 guests in the Catskills.

The Catskills are about 100 miles north of New York City and easily reached by highway. The region stands as an exception to the poor showing of most mountain resort areas. Known as the Borscht Belt, it drew most of its guests from metropolitan New York. They went to frolic, look for marriage partners, and, as one wit put it, seek exhaustion.

In Sullivan County, where most of the Borscht Belt hotels are located, the first resorts were ramshackle farm buildings of 20 to 40 rooms. Each had a communal kitchen for workers from New York's lower East Side who were determined to capture the pleasures of rural life. The 1920s boom brought Tudor architecture and stuccoed four- or five-story hotels. Most of the Catskill hotels were built at this time.

Before air conditioning and airplane travel, spending the summer or part of it in the cool mountains was the social thing to do, and a pleasant way to escape the heat of the city. In 1891 the White Mountains of New Hampshire had some 60 resort hotels with more than 11,000 guest rooms. By 1959 the number of guest rooms had dropped to about half as many, and today the number is considerably less. In 1890 the mountain resorts were the center of the summer social season and presented a way of life unique for both the guests and operator, an aspect of Americana overlooked by most history books (Fig. 8-10).

Early New England Resorts

New England's resort business had several beginnings: farmers taking in summer tourists, old inns gradually merging into the resort business, and hunting/fishing camps gradually assuming

Figure 8-10 The Mountain View House in Whitefield, N.H., one of the stately, elegant mountain inns of New England, still survives. The resort began taking "summer boarders" in 1866. Farmer William Dodge ran the farm that supplied the milk, cream, chickens, eggs, pork, fresh fruits, and vegetables for the table. He also took the boarders for rides in his mountain wagon and to church on Sundays. By the 1890s, the original farmhouse had disappeared and part of the present building, with the cupola, had been built. The resort includes some 3000 acres with a heated swimming pool, a golf course, and an auditorium with a seating capacity of 450. The Mountain View House is the oldest resort in the country remaining in the hands of descendants of the original owners.

the character of resorts. Big farm families were naturals for the resort business. The large families meant plenty of cheap help, big houses that could accommodate city folks during the summer, and plenty of chickens, eggs, and vegetables to feed visitors.

The wonderful mountain scenery was free. All that was necessary was a ledger book with a big "Guest Register" scrawled across it and a potato in which to stick a pen for use by the city folks in writing their names and home addresses. As business grew, families added wings here and there until they finally had a moderate-sized summer resort.

In Maine, the first "tourists" were Native Americans from inland and Canada who spent their summers along the seacoast, fishing and feasting. The first summer boarder came to Old Orchard Beach in 1837, and by 1850 Maine's tourist business was well underway, accompanied by promotional leaflets and handbills.

THE TRAVEL AGENT ARRIVES

In England, Thomas Cook started the travel agency business in 1841 when he arranged a railroad trip for a temperance-group meeting in Leicester, 15 miles from his home in Market Harborough. Soon he was arranging trips for groups all over the British Isles and later in Europe, the U.S., and the Near East.

Today, the tour business is said to be the fastest growing segment of air travel. The traveler gets convenience, reservations, and often arrangements for food, drinks, sightseeing, and entertainment.

Package tours have had a tremendous effect on the vacation business. The first in America was offered by the Pennsylvania Railroad in the 1890s, when Pullman excursion trains were dispatched from New York City to Jacksonville, Florida, as part of a package plan that included railfare, hotel room, and meals. Eastern Airlines started the first package tours to Miami in the winter of 1951. They helped make Miami both a summer and winter resort and have been responsible for filling thousands of empty seats on the airlines.

Tour packages in the U.S. are assembled by some 300 tour wholesalers, who sell the tours to some 37,000 travel agencies, which retail them to people who do not want to take the trouble, or do not know how, to arrange their own travel, accommodations, and entertainment.

For their trouble, tour operators receive a 20 percent discount on everything they package, except air fare. If a hotel room rate is $60 a day, the packager may get it for $40 or less. If a tourist attraction charges $10, the tour operator gets it for $8. The 20 percent discount applies at restaurants and nightclubs as well. The packager keeps about half of the discount and passes the other half on to the travel agent.

Resort hotels are usually delighted to be a part of a tour package; some hotels could not survive without being on some regular itineraries. The airlines are pleased; the travel agent is pleased; the restaurant operator is pleased. Everybody is pleased—except the traveler, who may sometimes feel part of a nameless crowd being herded from one attraction to another. Others, of course, would not want it otherwise. The sophisticated traveler may join a tour group because of its economy and leave it for part or most of the schedule. Tours can save tremendous time and effort in making arrangements, and in many cases a considerable amount of money as well.

DETERMINING THE REAL VALUE OF A RESORT

What is a resort worth? What is its fair market value? What price will a willing buyer pay and a willing seller sell for, both of whom have the facts and neither of whom is under pressure to act?

The fair value is hard to come by for several reasons. Much resortkeeping is tied to psychic income, pride of ownership, and the pleasure the owner or prospective buyer has or may get from owning a resort on a beautiful lake or beach. More practically, tax considerations are often a major factor. Wealthy resort owners may expect operating losses that can be used as deductions against other income; many resorts have been built or bought by such individuals in the past. Special circumstances—estate settlement or partnership disagreement, for example—may also distort the real market value.

According to the Helmsley-Spear Company, one of the largest real estate brokers in the country, the traditional approach to determining fair value has three aspects:

1. Value as compared with comparable properties

2. Reproduction cost, separating the value of the land from that of the buildings

3. The capitalized value of the property, what the property will produce in profit on a free and clear basis

The approach most commonly used is the one based on the capitalization of earnings: what the property will yield.

From the profit viewpoint, a resort is as valuable as the net income it can generate. For a new property, a pro forma profit and loss statement is drawn up that projects revenues, expenses, taxes, depreciation, and expected net profit. For the established property, profit and loss statements for preceding years are a guide to future profits or losses.

In the late 1980s the devalued U.S. dollar made American-owned properties a decided bargain for foreign buyers and dozens of hotels were purchased by Japanese, British, Dutch, Indian, and others at prices that to Americans appeared highly inflated, but which to the foreign buyers with strong currencies appeared cheap as explained in Chapter 4. Based on the income flow, the old rules of thumb, earnings multiplied by price, were no longer applicable. The Beverly Hills hotel was reported to be sold for $1 million a room. At this price, the average room rate, according to the Hubbart formula, would be $1000 a day. A number of hotels were built at reported costs of $200,000 or more a room (total cost divided by number of rooms).

Estimating Potential Earnings

The potential earnings of a property take into consideration the land value itself, its setting, the environment, and such things as riparian rights, easements, and special circumstances relating to the property. In the past, a rule of thumb was to multiply the income of the property for 1 year by 7 or 8. Of course, such a figure is only a starting point to be checked against all the factors that bear on the net profit figures for the future.

Potential earnings may not be the same as what has been produced in the past. Many large resorts are tied to land development and the sale of condominiums. The hotel itself might be viewed as the activities center of the land development, profits coming from land and condominium sales and not necessarily hotel operations.

The earnings of many resorts are linked almost directly to the convenience of reaching the place by air or highway, as is the relationship of the property to present and proposed interstate highways, air routes, and airfares. The relations that an owner or prospective owner may have with tour operators and travel agents can be highly important.

Important to financing is whether or not the resort can be connected with a nationwide referral system or will be part of a franchise plan. Institutions are more favorably disposed toward lending money for an operation that is part of such a system.

The resort business is a highly specialized business, quite separate from the commercial hotel and restaurant business. There is a separate body of knowledge and practices that, combined with good judgment, make for expertise. In apparent contradiction to this statement are the numerous entries into the field by outsiders such as conglomerates, airlines, and oil companies. However, the outsiders bring their own financial and managerial know-how, which they add to the specialized management skill of the seasoned operator.

The question of "the highest and best use" of the property should always be asked. Many resorts have been best used by being torn down and the land sold as building lots. Others have been turned into private clubs and still others into schools or colleges. In Las Vegas, the hotel is only a setting for the gaming rooms and restaurants, a place to sustain guests until they can get back to the business at hand—gambling or being entertained.

Resort Profits

What about profits? They vary tremendously, depending on management, location, investment, and, for the summer resort, weather. Casino hotels, discussed later, can produce huge profits.

Rain and cold are the bane of the summer resort manager. Guests soon complain about the food, personnel, and management. *Does it always rain here, Mr. Hoyt?* is the title of a book recounting the miseries of a summer resortkeeper during poor weather. The title is apt. Most resorts, above all else, are selling their climate and scenery. Bad weather for one season can ruin a lightly financed property. What is one man's poison is another man's food: Cold, rainy weather may dry up business in the Poconos, whereas the same weather may fill other resort areas to capacity—"We'll go to the Caribbean to get warm."

Length of season is a critical factor for profitability in Northern resort hotels. In some areas it gets shorter each year. The day after Labor Day finds most summer resorts everywhere deserted. The Cape Cod season does not get underway until about June 20. The Southeast and Southwest have fairly long seasons and are developing into year-round resort areas with lulls during May and September.

Seasonal Resorts Face High Operating Costs

With short seasons and many fixed costs, like insurance, taxes, and maintenance and repairs, seasonal resorts must charge rates that may seem inordinately high. There are good reasons for this. Labor is not hard to find in many areas, since college students clamor for jobs in locations where it will be pleasant to spend the summer. The Glacier National Park Hotels, as an illustration, received 12,000 applications in one year, but had only 600 positions open. College students usually turn out to be excellent employees, but for many the romance of the resort begins to wear thin by early August. A multitude of reasons are found why they must return home—grandmother is dying, mother's demands, necessary shopping for school clothes, and many similar stories. To guard against this mass exodus, nearly all summer resorts pay bonuses to those who remain for the full season. Many of the bonuses in reality are wages withheld to insure compliance with employment agreements.

Since employees sometimes came cheap, owners in the past tended to overhire. With analysis and tighter scheduling, the number of resort employees can often be drastically reduced. Each employee, even though he or she may be paid little and does little, eats three meals a day

and requires linen and supervision. Such expenses add up fast.

Another way to reduce payroll costs in resorts is to schedule employees more closely to fit the season. Many resorts open June 15, but have only 20 to 30 percent occupancy until July 1. By contracting for something less than half of the entire crew during June, payroll is reduced, cost of employees' meals is less, and employee morale is higher. A small crew is easier to train and forms a nucleus of experience on which to build when the rest of the employees arrive in July. Personnel are kept busy, which is especially important for tip employees.

Combining jobs is another way of reducing payroll. Strange job combinations are possible: an 18-year old at a resort served as lifeguard in the morning, switchboard operator during the afternoon, and busboy in the evening. The boy still found time to ring the fire bell in the wee hours of the morning, causing the guests no small alarm.

Resorts spend roughly 6 to 8 percent of their income on repairs and maintenance. The well-kept ones may expend 10 percent. Without constant rehabilitation, resort hotels are like MacArthur's old soldiers: "They just fade away."

ADVERTISING

What about advertising? Resort operators must be promoters or have an imaginative, alert promoter working for them, either on the staff or in an advertising agency. The best advertising has been, and probably always will be, the enthusiasm of present guests. However, they too must be resold during each visit and between visits.

Nearly every resort has a brochure with copy that often overdoes the superlatives. If the descriptions of what the guest can expect were true, the poor guest would die from pure ecstasy—either that or relax so much that revival would be impossible. Here is a description of the Boom Boom Room in a Miami Beach resort:

Calypso…voodoo…the cool, cool joy of a jungle cave…French-Haitian darkness lit with primitive primary colors and the flickering glimmer from hammered-copper oil lamps. Sip a rum and let your pulse respond to the beating drums…the offbeat rhythms…the dark, glistening movement of Calypso!

Direct Mail

Direct mail, sending letters and literature to former guests and prospects, is a major part of resort promotion. It can be an art. A few operators rely on it completely, spending nothing on paid advertising.

RESORT MEALS

Food—and plenty of it—has long been the hallmark of the American Plan resort. French wines and French cuisine were offered at a few of the resorts before 1850 and have been since, the American Plan hotel dining room has catered to the typical American appetite. Each hotel had to have an array of fresh baked goods. The baker might be a professional from the city or, more frequently, one of the local citizens with a flair. The distinctively American food at a resort can be seen from the menu offered by the Atlantic House in Rye, New Hampshire, on July 27, 1859, and a breakfast menu offered on January 18, 1887, by the Raymond in South Pasadena, California. Note the wide selection of items, including pigs' feet, tripe, steak, and liver (Fig. 8-11). Diet be damned. Eat hearty and well. Frozen and bake-and-serve items have reduced the demands for a baker on premise.

American Plan resort operators have more or less buried the cost of food in the total daily cost. Suppose the guest pays $100 a day; the operator arbitrarily allocates part of the rate to cover the cost of meals. Many resorts offer meals to nonregistered guests for a flat charge. Hotels operate on several meal plans:

EP (European Plan): no meals included in the room rate

AP (American Plan): all meals as part of the room rate

MAP (Modified American Plan): breakfast and dinner as part of the room rate

Continental Plan: a limited breakfast included in the room rate

In the United Kingdom and parts of Europe, bed-and-breakfast (B&B) plans are offered that include breakfast in the rate. In parts of England, Ireland, and Scotland, the breakfast is lavish, including bacon, eggs, cereal, and beverage. B&Bs

are widespread in several parts of this country as well. In France and Spain, the continental breakfast is likely to be rolls, jam or honey, and a beverage.

Accommodations listed as "hotel garni" mean only breakfast, no regular restaurant service otherwise.

The MAP is growing in popularity. It reduces food cost for the hotel and is helpful to those guests who are diet-conscious. The plan permits the guest to have lunch at some other place than in the hotel, perhaps combining it with sightseeing.

A continuing problem in operating a resort is feeding employees. Chefs, eager to hold down food cost or indifferent to employee appetites, are prone to run a few menu items over and over.

CASINO HOTELS

A strange phenomenon occurs in a few places in the U.S.: People from all parts of the country and many from abroad converge in these places, bringing money. Most leave a part of it and return home, some the sadder, some the richer, none the wiser. Las Vegas epitomizes this phenomenon and accounts for the largest aggregation of first-class and glitzy hotel rooms in the world. Some 21 million visitors occupy 86,000 hotel rooms, incidental to being lavishly fed, entertained, and placed at risk at hundreds of slot machines and crap, poker, blackjack, and roulette tables. The most sedentary individuals can play keno. The state of Nevada is delighted with all of this, since gaming tax revenues account for 40 percent of the state budget. Most hotel owners are happy. In 1991 visitors to Las Vegas stayed an average of 3.5 nights, which held hotel occupancy at 89 percent, one of the highest in the world.[2]

Casino hotels, originally casinos with guest rooms, have become a ménage à trois—casino, hotel, and entertainment—legitimized by much of America, stigmatized no longer by doubts of the evils of gambling. Sin is out; entertainment is in. New jobs and tax revenues created by gaming are overcoming lingering doubts about the morality of gambling (except in Hawaii and Utah).

A survey of the American gambling market showed that half of all adults had at least entered

2. *Lodging Hospitality*, (April 1991).

ATLANTIC HOUSE
Rye Beach
Rye, New Hampshire

Wednesday, July 27, 1859

Soup
Fish
Leg of Mutton with Capers
Chickens, Pork, Corned Beef, Ham, Tongue
Entrees:
Macaroni, Mutton Cutlets, Corned Veal, Lobsters, Escalloped Oysters
Croquettes of Rice, Chicken Pies
Roast of Veal, Beef, Lamb and Chicken
Vegetables:
Pastry:
Dessert: Almonds, Apples, Fruit, Pecans, Oranges, Blanc Mange
Wines:

THE RAYMOND,

SOUTH PASADENA.   CALIFORNIA.

C. H. MERRILL, MANAGER.

BREAKFAST.

FRUIT.

OOLONG TEA.   ENGLISH BREAKFAST TEA.   COFFEE.   CHOCOLATE.   MILK

OATMEAL.   FRIED INDIAN PUDDING   HOMINY.
HOT ROLLS.   GRAHAM ROLLS.   GRAHAM BREAD.
MUFFINS.   DRY TOAST.   DIPPED TOAST.
CREAM TOAST.   CORN CAKE.

FISH.

BROILED BASS.   FRIED COD.
SMOKED SALMON.   FRIED OYSTERS.

BROILED OR FRIED TO ORDER.

SIRLOIN STEAK.   LAMB CHOPS.   MUTTON CHOPS
PORK CHOPS.   HAM.   BEEF LIVER.
BREAKFAST BACON.   TRIPE.   SAUSAGES.   RUMP STEAK
VEAL CUTLETS.   PIG'S FEET.

STEWED KIDNEYS   FRICASSEE OF CHICKEN.

EGGS.

OMELETTES, PLAIN, WITH CHEESE OR ONIONS.
BOILED.   POACHED.   FRIED.   SCRAMBLED.

POTATOES.

BAKED WHITE AND SWEET.   SAUTE.   STEWED.
SARATOGA CHIPS.

BUCKWHEAT CAKES.   GRIDDLE CAKES
MAPLE SYRUP   HONEY.

TUESDAY, January 18th, 1887.

Figure 8-11   These hearty offerings are typical of the American Plan menus featured in early resort dining rooms.

a casino some time in their lives. Casino gambling was legal in 16 states in 1994.

In Las Vegas entertainment shares billings with gaming and hotel rooms. Bring the family. Circus Circus, as its name implies, offers circus acts. Treasure Island offers an hourly sea battle fought by actor buccaneers aboard two full-size ships, located, of course, just outside the gaming rooms. The same owners built the Luxor, an Egyptian fantasy that includes a food, entertainment, and merchandise mall. The Luxor visitor can enjoy rides within the hotel that rival Disneyland's. The place has reached beyond the hunched over blackjack player to attract the whole family.

The MGM Grand hotel and casino (Fig. 8-12), also in Las Vegas, is not only the world's largest hotel (5005 guest rooms), but includes a 33-acre park to keep the kids happy (for at least 2 days). Its theme park includes 12 attractions, one a special effects show that puts the audience into movie scenes. The MGM Grand was built at a grand cost, something just over $1 billion dollars. To help insure that the high rollers get to the casino, there is the MGM Grand Air Charter service. Championship boxing matches and other planned events are held in the MGM Grand's 15,000-seat arena. It was projected to generate revenue approaching $700 million in its first year of operation. Each of the 3500 slot machines were expected to clear as much as $135 a day. (Kerkor Kerkoran, who owns 73 percent of the casino, was a junior high school dropout.)

Another billion-dollar hotel/casino/theme park is in the planning stage for Las Vegas, this one to be part of ITT Sheraton.[3]

The new hotels create employment for thousands of people. Between them, the Luxor and Excalibur, with some 7500 guest rooms, have about 7000 employees, or about one employee per guest room. The MGM Grand has 5005 guest rooms and 8000 employees (although the number of employees will decrease as the hotel shakes down).

Las Vegas hotels are as much spectacle as lodging establishments. The Excalibur, a 4032-room hostelry, is a Disney-like castle. The Mirage treats the visitor to volcanic eruptions every few minutes with a 54-foot manmade volcano spewing forth a piña-colada–scented smoke column. Las Vegas, it is said, is where nothing succeeds like excess. Figure 8-13 attests to the rapid growth in Las Vegas casino hotels.

3. *Los Angeles Times* (Dec. 12, 1993).

Figure 8-12 The MGM Grand, hotel and casino in Las Vegas complete with 5005 rooms, there is also a 33-acre theme park. (Courtesy of MGM Grand)

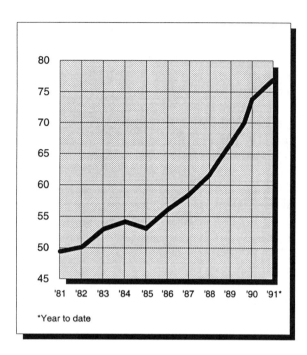

Figure 8-13 Las Vegas hotel room inventory (in thousands).

Source: Las Vegas Convention Visitors Authority.

Reno is also a casino hotel town, but on a more modest scale than Las Vegas. Sitting on the Colorado River, Laughlin, Nevada, appeals to another market. About a fifth of its 3 million visitors come by bus on "gamblers' specials," buses that originate in Los Angeles and Orange counties. The ride is free, but the riders are expected to gamble a certain number of hours.[4]

Atlantic City runs a poor second place to Las Vegas. It caters to the working man and the retiree and has only 13,000 guest rooms. Of the 30 million visitors to the city in 1993, two-thirds are daytrippers who arrive by bus, car, or train. People who are bused in from nearby cities see Atlantic City as a break from everyday routine, a chance for a little excitement and change, an opportunity for an inexpensive meal and entertainment, as well as having the fun of dropping quarters into slot machines. The average length of stay is 6 hours. In one month, that of December 1990, the Taj Mahal, largest of the Atlantic City casino hotels, bused in 120,000 patrons.[5]

Gambling and resorts have an affinity going back a long time. Gambling was a part of the appeal of the watering spots of Europe. Bath and Baden-Baden attracted the elite for fun, as well as health reasons. The "gambling hells" of England predated Vegas in providing free liquor, free food, magnificent rooms in which to gamble and women for the big bettors. In the 1700s English club owners figured to keep 25 percent of the money gambled. Las Vegas gives slightly better odds. The casino operators keep 18 to 20 percent.[6]

Monaco, the semi-independent principality on the French Riviera, was built largely around its casino. Baden-Baden in Germany also became what it is largely because of its casino.

Casino gambling laid out with gaudy entertainment and lavish food and beverage spreads have brought huge profits to some operators and spawned a unique kind of hotelkeeping, the casino hotel. Las Vegas is the prototype, but it is a resort anomaly: It is neither near the sea nor in the mountains; rather, it is in a desert. What makes it all possible is that it has legalized casino gambling, and it is close by air to the population centers of California. Half the visitors are from one city, Los Angeles. The 2249 miles from New York City becomes 4 hours and 25 minutes by nonstop jet.

Las Vegas

Gambling was legalized in Nevada in 1931. Its reputation has not always been the best. One of its early and more notorious developers, Bugsie Siegel, built the Flamingo Hotel on the Strip and named it after his girlfriend, Virginia Hill, whom he called his "flamingo." Bugsie was able to build the hotel just after World War II, even though materials were scarce, because it was considered unhealthy not to deliver them. He was later shot in the head, reportedly by his associates. Mafia connections in Las Vegas have been reported from time to time.

Las Vegas began as a resort in 1941 when Tommy Hull, then of the Hollywood Roosevelt Hotel, had a flat tire a few miles out of town. While his companion went for help, Hull began counting cars, counted for two days, and then

4. *Los Angles Times* (Feb. 10, 1993).
5. *Lodging Hospitality* (April 1991).

6. Mario Puzo, *Inside Las Vegas* (New York: Grosset & Dunlap) 1976.

went back to Hollywood and persuaded the owners to erect the 80-room El Rancho Vegas (later renamed the New Frontier). One of the early developers of Las Vegas, William Clark, left San Diego at the age of 16, got a job as a bellboy in San Francisco, and later learned the gambling business in Reno.

Until the late 1950s, Vegas meant gambling, girls, and gangsters, but they were not enough to keep the hotel rooms filled or the dice tables jammed year-round. In 1959 the city opened a $10 million convention center on a 67-acre site, one of the most modern in the country, financed by a tax on hotel rooms. Almost every major hotel has also added convention halls and meeting rooms. The range of groups picking Las Vegas is wide: from the National Council of Catholic Women to the American Dental Association.

The city of Las Vegas is a paradox: It acquires most of its income from gambling, yet there are 143 churches and 159 Boy Scout troops. *Time* magazine calls the place the most vulgar of resorts, where an estimated 1000 prostitutes are at work, while in "the carpeted clockless confines [of the casinos], nothing seems real: time stands still and $100 is just a black gambling chip."[7] The magazine went on to point out that, because of the low rainfall, the tourist influx has brought the water table down so much it has caused the whole town to sink three feet in the past 30 years.

The Visitors.   The hotelier, says a veteran observer, looks at three different visitor markets:

1.   Those who seek momentary diversion from their regular routine on their days off

2.   Those who are on vacation

3.   Those who are members of the professional and social groups holding meetings in Las Vegas[8]

Each group is further separated into "grinds," the small bettors, and "premiums," the large bettors. What disturbs the pit bosses to no end are the "walkers," those who leave the entertainment rooms and walk right through the ca-

sino with nary a nod at the alluring extraction devices. It turns out that junk dealers are one of the favored betting groups. They, like those in other high-risk speculative businesses that suffer from relatively high bankruptcy rates, are high rollers. Others who produce large casino drops are people in construction, real estate developers, tract home and highway builders, and major contractors.

Income alone is not enough to signify whether a group will be premium gamers. Doctors, dentists, attorneys, bankers, accountants, and insurance salespeople may have incomes well above $100,000 a year, but are not top clients.

Neither can dress be used as an infallible index of affluence. Pit bosses and others who grant credit have been fooled by sartorial elegance, or the lack of it. Once, an eccentric millionaire lost $100,000 on a single roll of the dice while wearing worn boots, a torn sweater, and old Levis held up with a knotted rope. The same gentleman left Las Vegas after 4 months minus $3.2 million.

After slots, which are favored by women, blackjack is the most popular form of gambling, followed by dice, keno, poker, and roulette. The vast majority of Las Vegas's visitors, according to another expert observer, are from middle-income groups who can afford the trip there, but are not particularly disposed toward gambling—the "grinds." They seem hypnotized by the slot machines and are overwhelmed by the clanging of large bells and airplane beacons, which go off every time a machine registers a jackpot. Stands on the slot machines that hold the payoff trays are hollowed out so that each tray reverberates with loud clangs as the coins bounce into them, and someone screams the amount of every jackpot over a public address system. Since several of the casinos have as many as a thousand machines, a lot of excitement is generated for those who respond to this noise level.

The Junket.   Casinos and jet travel form a happy marriage: the "junket" casino business. A gaming junket is a group put together by a "junket master," who entices a group of persons to fly from cities all over the country to a particular casino. The whole idea is to arrange for people to lose money graciously. To that end, the airplanes and motorcoaches are loaded with people who are under the illusion that they are getting an all-expenses paid vacation to Las Vegas or Atlantic City. They pay no

7. "Las Vegas: The Game Is Illusion," *Time* (July 11, 1969).
8. Bill Friedman, *Casino Management* (Secaucus, N.J.: Lyle Stuart), 1974.

airfare and the hotel's rooms and food may be free and of the best quality, but only serious gamblers are invited under this arrangement. Mr. or Ms. Average is reimbursed for his or her fare, quite naturally in the form of poker chips.

Junket members are carefully selected: Each player commits himself or herself to gamble a certain minimum sum of money. Credit is extended to each member depending on financial standing and resources. The gamblers seem to consist largely of middle- and upper-middle-income groups, but there are still some high rollers who make gambling a profession or are completely addicted to it and play for high stakes. The junket promoter receives a commission based on the quality of the "action" demonstrated by his or her group.[9]

Gaming is a magnet for thousands of people, especially when it is done in pleasant, respectable, and safe surroundings. It offers a sense of adventure usually missing in ordinary life and a small chance for winning money. It also offers a way to ruin, since, when money changes hands as quickly as it does over the gaming tables, its value departs.

The gambler in Las Vegas experiences an exciting, romanticized version of life in the Old West with its flavor of derring-do; it all takes place in air-conditioned surroundings. The threat of physical violence or hardship is removed.

Hotels host guests, but Las Vegas casino hotels offer the professional host—an employee whose job is to get gamblers to come to the hotel and once they are there to make them happy in every way possible. The host arranges show tickets, compliments of the house. He or she arranges special dinners and parties, such as golf or gin parties, and luxury transportation for sightseeing and shopping trips, and can raise the client's credit limit. The host will even arrange special discounts at hotel gift shops and provide unusual gifts. Some hosts even have "the pencil," the power to sign off on all of a customer's expenses at the hotel.

For many years, the food and beverage operations of the Strip hotels were not expected to make money. They existed merely as adjuncts to the casinos. Beginning in the early 1960s, however, food and beverage operations began to be tightly controlled.

Apparently, control is a key word among casino and hotel operators. Certainly, the odds on slot machines are controlled in favor of the management. They can be set for practically any odds in favor of the house. In the game of blackjack, the dealer has a theoretical advantage of 2.5 percent over the player, but most players do not bet wisely, which increases the house odds considerably. In roulette, the casino has a 5.26 percent advantage. Most of the other games offer even better house odds.

One reason the major hotel chains are so keen on Las Vegas is the tremendous amount of profit possible in an "in" hotel. The expected rate of return on casino income fluctuates between 20 to 30 percent. Of course, costs can be tremendous, such as uncollectible accounts, salaries and wages, and the high cost of entertainment, which can be exceedingly lavish.

The major hotels spend considerable sums of money in advertising and promotion, decor, and other incidental amenities as they compete with each other. And each year there seems to be a new, bigger, and better casino hotel built.

Some Las Vegas Statistics.

> The average stay is 4 days, during which time visitors attend 1.5 shows.
>
> In 1990 more than 21 million people visited Las Vegas, half from the West.
>
> Fridays and Saturdays are the heaviest days; Tuesday is the lightest.
>
> About 30 percent of the visitors are repeaters.
>
> Some 96 percent say they enjoyed their visit.
>
> A number of southern Californians travel to Las Vegas on a regular basis, some as often as once a month. The average visitor to the place makes the trip twice a year.
>
> About 500,000 people arrive by plane each month.
>
> Too bad everyone does not own a slot machine in a Vegas setting. Some machines make a profit as high as $250,000 a year.[10]

---

9.   Alberto Caballero and R. B. Taylor, "A Growing of Gaming in America," *L & H. Perspective* (Spring/Summer 1977). Published by Laventhol & Horwath, Philadelphia.

10.   Somerset R. Waters, *Travel Industry World Yearbook—1993–94* (New York: Childs & Waters, Inc.), 1993.

Profitability of Casino Hotels

As said, casino hotels can be enormously profitable. Hilton Hotels reported in 1993 that gambling would continue to provide most of its profits. Its owned-and-operated properties include five hotel casinos in Nevada and it operates casinos in Australia and Turkey. (Hilton owns 21 hotels, partly owns 14 and manages or franchises 207 others, including resorts.)[11]

Operating a profitable casino hotel is complicated by the fact that many of the guest feel challenged to cheat the house, and feel no compunction in doing so. Hence, security in the form of plain clothes police and hidden cameras are omnipresent.

Current Trends

The general sentiment against gambling seems to be fading as a number of states promote their lotto games and make deals to permit native American Indian tribes to operate casinos. Five states permit casino gambling. Mafia influences are being contained and gambling as a hobby and as entertainment is increasing. The number of retired people who casino gamble is rising in part because the casinos provide inexpensive all-you-can-eat buffets. Las Vegas has some 40 of them.

Several of the Las Vegas casino hotel properties have widened their markets to include families with children. The MGM Grand's theme park with its real and "virtual reality" rides is the best example. Opponents of gambling say that it can be just as addictive as tobacco, or more so, placing not only the addicted gambler but the whole family at risk.[12]

THE SKI BUSINESS

Each winter millions of skiers take to the mountain slopes of New England, Pennsylvania, Colorado, California, Nevada, Washington, and wherever else snow falls or can be made. There is even a ski resort at Gatlinburg, Tennessee, in the Great Smoky Mountains. There are about 3000 ski resorts worldwide.

In many places, the state involved has helped to finance ski areas. The financing may take several forms, from building access roads to complete construction, as was done by the state of New Hampshire at Sunapee. Skiing offers challenging athletics and lively socializing. Skiing also offers resort operators the opportunity for a two-season operation, summer and winter. Numerous hotels, motels, and an assortment of lodges accumulate around the ski area. The economics of the ski business are not clearcut. A few ski areas are highly profitable and may have seasons running from November into June. The new $2.4-billion Denver International Airport, covering 53 square miles, sees pleasure seekers from around the world coming in for a few days of skiing. Aspen attracts the rich and famous skiers in numbers that surpass those found in Switzerland, making tourism Colorado's largest industry.

Mt. Snow in Vermont, one of the largest ski areas in the world, is extremely busy on weekends with good snow. Like most ski areas, however, business drops sharply on weekdays. Mt. Snow is said to be profitable.

Skiing can bring a great deal of money into an area: construction money and payroll money for lodges, restaurants, and grocery and liquor stores. Ski facilities also stimulate the building of private lodges and year-round homes. Real estate values jump, and, to some extent, the community as a whole prospers.

The origins of the ski business as known today are debatable, but it is known that in 1931 the Boston and Maine Railroad sent its first snow train to Warner, New Hampshire, with 197 winter enthusiasts aboard. The skier at that time was regarded as a hardy eccentric willing to tolerate the cold and hardship for a day or weekend on narrow ski trails. In 1934 a Model T engine was placed at the base of a hill in Woodstock, Vermont. At the end of the driveshaft, turned by the engine, was a wheel. Over this wheel, held in position by a flange, a rope was set going; it was the first uphill tow. The spectacular Sun Valley, Idaho, resort opened in 1936, built by the Union Pacific Railroad for the purpose of creating new business.

Today, enclosed gondolas travel for miles up mountains. Plush lodges with European cuisine may be scattered around the foot of the slopes. The typical skier, however, does not stop at such lodges. He or she travels by auto from a population center (usually for a weekend) and eats from

11. *Ibid.*, p 141.
12. Vogel, Harold L., *Entertainment Industry Economics*, 2nd edition, (New York: Cambridge University Press) Chapter 9, 1990.

Figure 8-14 A heated swimming pool in the midst of a ski resort—this one at Sun Valley, Idaho, was probably the first to be built. It was installed in about 1950. Though few people use such pools at ski resorts, they do add glamour, novelty, and decorative value.

a cafeteria line or vending machine. The usual fare is hot dogs, hamburgers, beef stew, and soups.

As a part of the ski operation, there are usually one or two orthopedists with X-ray machines and plenty of plaster for making casts for broken legs.

The ski business is an adjunct to the hotel and restaurant business; however, for the skiing addict in the business, the lodge can be a sideline to the principal purpose in life, getting onto the slopes.

By the 1960s skiing had moved into the realm of big business. Some of the more than 600 ski areas are controlled by big corporations like Twentieth-Century Fox, Ralston-Purina, Apex Oil, and Solon Automated Services. Many ski areas now cater to the family, offering deluxe accommodations and the American Plan tied in with ski lessons and use of the slopes. Mom and Dad struggle into strange clothes and equipment to join ski classes with their grammar-school-age sons and daughters. Hundreds of thousands of students and young couples dash off on Friday afternoon for several hours at a ski area.

The lodge and ski-tow operators enjoy it while it lasts. Most operate at the whim of the weather. Good snow means big crowds; storms and warm weather cause business collapses. Although snowmaking equipment is becoming a must in many places, temperatures above freezing drain away the snow (made during the night), and the profits go with it. Even so, the ski business is likely to continue its mad growth. In 1994 about 85 percent of the major ski resorts had snow-making equipment.

Lodges and restaurants in ski areas depend on snow conditions. The lodges at Mt. Snow may be filled to capacity one weekend and have almost no guests the next. Any summer resorts near ski areas have everything to gain, since they can do business at least on skiable weekends. Typically, hotels close to a ski resort run close to 100 percent occupancy on weekends and anywhere from 50 to 80 percent during the week.

Big ski resorts are getting bigger, smaller ones being closed. Big resort operators such as Vail Associates, Aspen Skiing Company, S-K-I Ltd., and Ralston Purina continue to buy up resorts. More than 200, or about a quarter of the small ones were closed between 1984 and 1994.[13]

In New England only 69 ski resorts remain as compared to 107 two decades earlier. Many experienced excessive debts because of speculative condominium building and unseasonably warm winters.[14]

The major ski resorts target specific markets. To attract summer business several ski resorts include health spas, tennis courts, golf courses and hiking trails. Vail, Colorado themed its ski resort as a European-style alpine ski center catering to the affluent during both the summer and winter.

Condominium sales play a large part in ski resort finance and their owners are frequent buyers of season ski passes.

U.S. spending on skiing in the 1989-90 season totaled $7 billion, a figure that is likely to hold steady during the 1990's in part because of demographics: fewer people in the 15 to 24 age bracket.[15]

Factors Affecting Profitability

In analyzing profitability—or the lack of it—in ski operations, several factors become apparent: The large, heavily invested ski operation with a diversity of activities and attractions has a greater appeal to the general public than the traditional ski operation with a few tows and cafeteria-style foodservice. The large corporation with access to large sums of money can extend the season by introducing indoor tennis courts, a disco, and a variety of restaurants. Some operations have metamorphosed into year-round resorts.

Most successful ski operations are part of a larger concept involving land development, with condominium and land sales for private homes. Perhaps as much profit or more is made via the land development as the ski operation itself, which becomes the focal point and major appeal of the larger concept. Merely operating ski lifts and hoping for snow are not enough.

The ski operation has a much better chance of success if it is within a few hour's travel time of a population center of 50,000 or more. Mammoth Mountain in California, said to attract more skiers than any other area, is a little over 4 hours driving time from Los Angeles.

The climate should be such that there are at least 105 days of snow. The possibility of little or no snow, even in areas where large snowfalls are normal, means that most ski areas should take out insurance, in the form of snowmaking equipment.

A major factor in the break-even point of a resort is the uphill ski lift capacity available—the number of skiers that a resort can move to the top of a mountain. Skiing historically begins in most ski areas at Thanksgiving, when the snow pack is suitable and continues through Easter.

Summer ski camps are one way of extending the season. Two-week blocks can be sold to groups interested in body conditioning through hiking and skill improvement via movies, professional indoor instruction, and classroom-type lectures. Summer operations can include backpacking tours, fishing camps, health seminars, and related sports and health activities.

Installation of a convention center and emphasis on selling group business during off-peak seasons have long been a means of extending the resort season. Ski resorts may enter the convention business to extend the season.

Cluster resorts seem to add to the appeal of the individual resort, just as "restaurant row" is more than the sum of its parts. The avid skier enjoys moving from one ski area to another if they are relatively close together. The cluster resort can also support a greater variety of restaurants and evening entertainment than the individual property.

Larger ski resorts maintain year-round marketing programs, which include circulars and advertising in magazines and newspapers and on radio and occasionally TV. Periodic mailings are sent to travel agents, groups, and individuals. Primary marketing is done via ski shows. Ski-club councils are also contacted and presentations made for them.

Ski resorts remain a high-risk business that requires heavy capital investment in lifts and land (some resorts lie on land leased from the National Forest Service). Ski resorts carry massive third-party insurance. They represent a substantial gamble in that they may be highly profitable one year and financially disastrous the next. Generally, profits are reinvested in the property rather

---

13. *Wall Street Journal*, Jan. 20, 1994.
14. Somerset R. Waters, *Travel Industry World Yearbook—1993–94* (New York: Childs & Waters, Inc.) p. 19.
15. "Diversifying to Counter a Slump on the Slopes," *New York Times*, Jan. 6, 1994.

than distributed to the owners. An average of 220 inches of snow each year permits Mamouth Mountain in California a long ski season, from November sometimes through July. Its principle market is Southern California.

Ski resorts must continue to innovate, and some are doing so. For example, Squaw Valley maintains an extensive babysitting program. Other resorts sponsor races and exhibitions during slack periods of the ski season.

A ski resort depends heavily on seasonal employees. The free seasonal ski pass is a big inducement for such employees, because the salary range is usually low compared to city pay standards.

U.S. ski resort operators look to foreign markets to increase their business. About 80 percent of the world's 60 million skiers live outside the U.S. Most ski in Europe, in the mountains of Austria, Switzerland, and France. About 12 million Japanese are skiers with limited ski facilities at home, they are thus big spenders while abroad. The Australians and British are another target ski market. In 1990 about a half million foreign skiers visited the U.S., only about 3 percent of the total number of skiers on American slopes, a figure that will undoubtedly increase with promotion and advertising.[16]

VARIETY IN RESORT AREAS

It is misleading to think of the vacation business as confined to the traditional resort areas, such as the mountains of New England, the seacoast of New Jersey, or the ski slopes of Colorado. By far the largest concentrations exist in places like New York City, London, Paris, San Francisco, Honolulu, and Las Vegas. The traditional vacation cities remain—such as Paris, Rome, Copenhagen, Salzburg, and Vienna—and continue to attract many more people than glamour spots such as the Greek Isles or Canary Islands.

New resort destinations are developing on the southern coast of Spain, the Algarve in Portugal, and several locations in Mexico—Cancún on the gulf coast, and Puerto Vallarta, Ixtapa, and Mazatlán, and Acapulco on the west coast. After Oahu, the island of Maui is second largest in tourism in the Pacific basin.

---

16. *Wall Street Journal* (Nov. 26, 1991).

Time-Sharing

Time-sharing allows an individual or group to purchase the right to use or own one or more unit(s) of a resort property, almost always a condominium, for a specified period of time, usually in increments of one week. Units are usually studio, one-bedroom, and two-bedroom apartments. Hotels that convert to time-sharing typically must convert two or three hotel rooms into one unit.

Time-sharing started as recently as 1967, and it has proved highly popular. By 1985 there were some 1000 time-share resorts. Time-sharing has proved profitable for many hotel owners and developers, but there have also been failures. In some destinations, it competes with traditional hotelkeeping.

Provided there is good management and reasonable management and maintenance fees, the time-share owner gets vacation accommodations at relatively low cost and can participate in the appreciation (if any) of the property.

Management of these properties is similar to, but simpler than, hotel management. A number of hotel companies, including Holiday Inn, Marriott, Sheraton, and Westin, offer time-share plans.

The "numbers" look good for the time-share converter or developer. Each apartment can be sold 52 times, once for each week of the year. If each week is sold for $9000, total revenue for the apartment is $468,000. Suppose that the cost to the developer is $200,000 for the apartment and that marketing costs are $75,000 for each apartment. This leaves a gross profit of $193,000 per unit. Little wonder that tremendous sales efforts are made to sell these shares. Time-sharing arrangements permit resort developers to finance without the need of conventional long-term financing. Owners of existing resorts may be able to expand or pay off mortgages. Nevertheless, it should not be forgotten that several such projects have failed.

Time-shares are often bought as real estate investments. Some have done well; others have gone bankrupt. Marketing costs have been high, 35 to 45 percent, according to the *Wall Street Journal*. This sharply reduces resale value. A $10,000 unit may have a resale value of only $7000. However, the time-share may appreciate over time to make for a good investment.

A possible disadvantage exists: Time-share management can push up the management and maintenance fees so high that the cost to the owner is comparable to that of rental accommodations in a resort hotel.

Time-sharing has been extended from real estate to houseboats, cruise ships, yachts, ski and beach houses, and even converted railway cars.

Time-sharing takes two principal forms: right to use and interval ownership.

Time-sharing ownership (TSO) units are purchased outright by several owners, but the unit is shared. Each owner may use the apartment, room, or cottage for a specific length of time each year. Title to each undivided interest is conveyed through a warranty deed, including an agreement of use for a particular time period each year. The buyer, in effect, becomes a part owner of a condominium and must pay a prorated share of maintenance, taxes, and utilities. The part owner can sell, transfer, or bequeath his or her interest as with any real property ownership.

The part owner has the pride of ownership, may participate in a rental pool together with the other owners, and also has a vacation unit for part of the year. The investment is relatively small, and if the property appreciates, the individual has made a profit.

The original owner or developer has his or her money back and perhaps a management contract to operate the establishment. One disadvantage exists: The cost of marketing to the large number of owners is likely to be high.

Some of the units may be kept for traditional resort use and rented to vacationers. TSO units may also be rented when not occupied by the owners.

It is sometimes possible to exchange ownership or the right to use from one property to other properties. Resort Condominiums International, founded in 1974, is the largest agency for that purpose. A member "deposits" his or her time-share in the agency's "space bank" and requests an equivalent withdrawal of time at a resort listed in a directory published annually. A rival company, Interval International, was started 2 years later. The directories of both companies contain photographs and descriptions of time-share resorts.

Interval International, however, operates differently. Owners put up their time-shares for exchange and then select a condominium from those available, or their requests are placed on a waiting list. Exchanges arranged by both companies are made on the basis of space, not cost. An efficiency apartment is exchanged for an efficiency apartment, for example, even if the building-cost difference between two areas of the world results in doubling the price.

What's Ahead?

The package tour takes on major importance because of economies made possible by selling blocks of airline seats, rooms, sightseeing, and entertainment tickets. In the off-season, blocks of hotel rooms are sold to wholesalers for 25 to 50 percent below the published rate; airlines also discount their tickets. Packages hasten what was already a firm trend toward mass travel.

Hotel management and convention and visitor bureaus will work together much more closely; hotel and bureau representatives will travel together to sell vacations.

Resortkeeping has taken on the character of big business and spread across much of the world. Conglomerates may play an even larger role in the vacation business as they expand. The major chains are heavily involved in vacation destinations like Hawaii, Las Vegas, San Juan, and Mexico and will continue to be so. The Japanese are investing heavily in the resort business and will undoubtedly influence it.

Huge resort complexes, especially those featuring casino gambling, are being built on a scale that overshadows the traditional resort. The jet has opened up resorts in formerly remote and unfamiliar locations, such as Fiji, Cancún, and Aruba. The adventuresome vacationer may pop into Turkey, or the Seychelles. Time-sharing and the exchange of time-shares are almost certain to increase, adding another dimension to the world of travel and tourism. Tourism in Asia is coming to life as its millions of people acquire discretionary income and become domestic and international travelers.

THE VACATION HOTEL BUSINESS OF THE FUTURE

The vacation hotel business is seen as merging with a number of other businesses or becoming a part of them. Traveling for pleasure has become

Figure 8-15 The Desert Springs Resort and Spa. This deluxe convention resort in southern California desert has 892 rooms. It is distinguished by a lobby that features two waterfalls and an indoor lake that serves as a docking area for boats carrying guests to restaurants, lounges, and recreational facilities. Among the facilities are two 18-hole golf courses, 16 tennis courts, areas for lawn games, and a spa that contains a medical suite. The spa employs a full-time, registered dietician, said to be the first in the hotel business. Built in 1987 at a reported cost of $250 million, the resort is part of a development that will include 91 homes. Marriott manages the property and employs some 1500 persons.

one of the world's great businesses, involving vacation planning, the means of travel, accommodations en route and at the destination, and entertainment during the entire process.

Economic forecasters predict greater discretionary income for the average person. That means more interest in vacationing and travel in the future. The growth will continue as airline travel becomes easier and relatively less expensive.

The vacation business is often inextricably bound with land development. Hotels add luster and value to newly developed communities, to entertainment complexes such as Disney World, and to related projects in Hawaii, Spain, Sardinia, the Carribbean, California, Mexico, and elsewhere.

The rapid growth of rent condominiums as vacation apartments may have a marked effect on the economics of hotelkeeping in resort areas. At one time, Hawaii had the largest number. On the island of Maui, some 8000 condo units were for rent as hotel apartments in 1979, while the island had only about half that number.

Questions

1. The classic resort hotel of the turn of the century was usually a fairly remote, independently operated mountain or beach resort. How has the resort business of today changed in location and character?

2. Name three prestige resort hotels.

3. Name at least one conglomerate that is active in the resort business.

4. In the context of seasonality of the resort business, define "shoulder periods."

5. In the early days of the American resort, what relationship existed between the growth of resorts and the railroad?

6. As a resort destination Atlantic City had been fading, but was brought back to life because of what legislative change?

7. What do the words "hotel garni" signify when used in a European hotel?

8. Which hotel is now the largest?

9. Generally speaking, is the ski business a highly profitable one for a resort operator?

10. How does time-sharing affect the hotel business?

11. Why has the American Plan of meal service faded in this country?

12. Are state and national parks in direct competition with the resort business? Why or why not?

13. Hawaii gets about the same number of visitors as Americans who visit Europe. Why is Hawaii so popular?

Discussion Questions

1. Where do you think the next big resort development will take place? Give your reasons.

2. How are the markets for Las Vegas and Atlantic City different?

3. What will happen to the resort business if casino gambling is permitted in such states as New York, California, and Florida?

4. What dangers, if any, do you see in the heavy investments by the Japanese in the American resort business?

5. Are there any dangers in the rapid growth of casino hotels to the investors? To society?

Conrad N. Hilton

(1887–1979)*

Conrad Hilton was the best-known hotelman in the world, the first truly international hotelkeeper, and the most durable. At age 90, he was still nominally active as Chairman of the Board of Hilton Hotels Corporation, which owned, managed, or franchised 105 hotels with 46,746 rooms.

According to a Hilton Hotels' release, efficiency in Hilton Hotels is predicated on six factors: time and method studies, job analysis, job standards, safety programs, budgetary control, and pricing programs. Hilton believed that costs must be controlled every day, every week, every month.

With the help of the leading accounting firms, Hilton introduced industrial methods of forecasting and control not previously used in the hotel business. Each of the larger Hilton Hotels sets up the position of operations analyst, charged with coordinating the system. A forecasting committee predicts the number of rooms and covers that will be sold a month, a week, and three days in advance. These forecasts are based on the reservations on hand and experience for the same month in previous years.

Employees are then scheduled to fit the volume of business forecast. Deviations from the number of employees scheduled must be approved in advance. Department heads are informed if they are over or under the number needed according to the forecast.

The hotel business fluctuates widely from day to day and between seasons; the forecasting system correlates sales demand and labor needed. Payroll costs are reduced dramatically because only the needed number of employees are on hand to service the number of hotel and restaurant guests that had been forecast.

Each hotel prepares a detailed daily report summarizing revenues, expenses, profit and loss for the day and for the month to date, and a comparison of these figures with the preceding month and preceding year.

Hilton also employs corporate forecasting control. The annual forecast is prepared well before the first of the year.

Though the Hilton organization is decentralized in the sense that pride is taken in developing a personality for each hotel, accounting and control are highly centralized. Reports reach the Beverly Hills main office each day from every hotel. They are also funneled into the divisional offices daily so that the top operating executives know exactly what is transpiring.

"Digging for gold" is another Hilton idea, the gold being unused space. Hilton became a master at identifying areas that could be made revenue producers. He could walk through a hotel and within a few minutes locate places for new restaurants and bars in the lobby area or project the installation of a lower ceiling in the lobby so that a new floor could be added.

The Waldorf-Astoria is a case in point. The hotel was under the management of Lucius Boomer from the day it opened until Boomer's death. Boomer, a highly respected and knowledgeable hotelman, could never make the Waldorf-Astoria very profitable, even during World War II. Hilton extracted a million dollars in profit from the Waldorf-Astoria the first year (1949) his company operated it. By renting small areas and display cases in the lobby, he made $42,000 a year. The laundry was moved from Manhattan to New Jersey to free space, and his "digging for gold" operation produced a number of new revenue-producing bars and restaurants.

The Palmer House in Chicago had been a money-maker. When Hilton bought it for a little over $19 million in 1945, it became a gold mine. His goal was to increase the operating profit by $50,000 a month over

---

*Thomas E. Dabney, *The Man Who Bought the Waldorf* (Duell, Sloan & Pearce), 1950.

the preceding year. Actual increase during the first year was $1,450,000. All restaurants were converted to 7-day operations; locker-room space was converted into 60 additional guest rooms; and nightclubs added photographic departments that yielded $20,000 in profit the first year. Store rentals brought in $950,000 per year.

Hilton noted that some 4000 persons passed through the lower arcade every day with no bar facilities to serve them. He converted a bookstore (rental of $250 a month) into the successful Town and Country Room, which produced $490,000 in revenue its first year.

The subrentals plus the revenue from food and beverage sales were said to pay all the operating expenses of the entire 2200-room hotel—the first time in history that a bonafide hotel had a perfect break-even point.

When Hilton bought the Statler Hotels, they were among the most efficient of hotel operations. He was able to produce an additional $3 million in profit each year. One-third of that was the removal of $1 million a year in payroll from the central office.

One thing most Hilton Hotels have in common is that they were bought at bargain prices. The Palmer House cost $25,837,000 to build in 1929; Hilton paid $19,385,000 in 1945. The Stevens was built in 1925 at a cost of $30 million; he got it for $7,500,000. It had been a white elephant, yet Hilton obtained a net profit of $1,730,242 the first year. In 1985 it was renamed the Chicago Hilton after being completely renovated.

Hilton's home in Beverly Hills provided an example of his keen sense of a bargain. It cost $250,000 in 1949. In 1979, after his death, the asking price was $15 million, the highest-priced private home in California up to that date. (Proceeds of the sale were placed in a charitable trust.) The furnishings alone, which he acquired with the home, were worth more than what he paid for the entire 8-acre estate, which was so large that 18 servants were required to maintain it. Most of the time Hilton lived alone with the servants in this "palace."

Perhaps Hilton's background explains his character. He was born in San Antonio, New Mexico, in 1887, a time when the state was a bonafide frontier. Conrad's father, Gus, was a financial plunger, well-fixed part of the time and in bad straits at other times.

During one of Gus's lean periods after the financial panic of 1907, Conrad jumped into the breach and began as a hotel operator. He was up at 3 AM to meet the incoming train and rent some of the family rooms in the back of his father's store to traveling salesmen. The tariff was $2.50 for a room and three bountiful meals served by Hilton's mother and sisters.

It was not until 1919, after being a state legislator, a banker in a small way, and having served in the army during World War I, that Hilton bought his first hotel, almost by chance. Hilton went to Cisco, Texas, intending to buy a bank; he backed out of the deal when the price was raised abruptly. Instead, he bought a hotel from an owner who had caught oil fever—the Mobley, one of the first of several mints that were converted into hotels. Cisco was a boomtown short of hotel rooms, and Hilton found himself many nights with the dubious gratification of sleeping in a leather chair in his office, having rented all the rooms. His investment was $5000.

The Mobley was the first of a Texas chain, which by 1929 included seven properties. Hilton expanded as fast as his profits and credit would allow. His first reverse came during the construction of the Dallas Hotel. He ran out of money and ended up operating it on a lease.

The Depression struck him hard. At one point, he was so short of funds that $300 was pressed on him by one of his bellmen for "eatin' money." During another period, he was $500,000 in debt. Despite everything that could be done—taking out room telephones, renting out entire floors as storage space, saving on lights and heat—he still could not meet his obligations.

During this phase of his career, Hilton learned to operate economically, one of the keys to his future success. He managed to hold on to five of his eight hotels. It was not until 1937 that he was again able to relax, hold up his head, and begin buying hotels once more.

With an unshakable faith in the American economy, he acquired the famed Sir Francis Drake in 1938 and for the first time attracted national attention. Hilton was 51 years of age. From then on, his progress was steadily up and up. Three times he experienced temporary setbacks, but he always bounced back.

In 1946 Hilton Hotels Corporation was formed. In 1949 controlling interest in the Waldorf-Astoria was acquired, and in 1954 all the Statler Hotels were purchased in a grand acquisition representing $111 million.

An indication of Hilton's daring and skill can be seen in the Statler purchase. Hilton Hotel Corporation obligated itself to raise about $110 million by a certain date or forfeit $8 million. The $8 million was payable as damages pro rata to each Statler stockholder in case the deal was not closed. The $77.5 million in cash necessary was raised by organizing a new company and offering securities to the stockholders of the existing Hilton Hotels Corporation. The new company, Statler Hotels Delaware Corporation, raised the money to purchase Statler Hotels. The Equitable Life Assurance Society of the United States lent $49.5 million and the First National Bank of Boston $20 million. More than 100 lawyers in all parts of the country worked on the deal, plus many people in banks, insurance companies, and investment banking houses.

With the new company, there was a stepped-up base for the depreciation of fixed assets, both building and equipment. By adopting a plan of complete liquidation of the old company and the distribution of the assets to the stockholders, a capital gains tax was avoided. The benefits of the sale-and-lease-back plan were also exploited by using the new corporation. After the sale was completed, securities of the Hilton Hotels Corporation in the form of convertible debentures were offered to the stockholders of the Statler Company. Some of the debentures carried a 4.5 percent interest rate, others 4.75 percent, and were convertible into Hilton common stock. The warrants for the convertible debentures were oversubscribed.

Hilton International began in 1949 when Hilton was given the contract to operate a hotel that eventually became known as the Caribe Hilton. The Puerto Rico Industrial Development Company was looking for an operator of their planned hotel and wrote to seven hotel executives in the U.S. asking if they were interested in the project. Only Hilton was gracious enough to reply, and in Spanish, starting "Mi estimade amigo." The Caribe Hilton is one of the most successful hotel ventures of all time. For a number of years it made a profit of something like $3 million a year, one-third of it going to the Hilton organization.

The contract between Hilton and the Puerto Rican government set a pattern for later international hotels. The land, buildings, and usually the furnishings and equipment are financed in each country by local capital (government or private), whereas the corporation operates the hotels under a long-term percentage rental agreement with renewal options. Generally, two-thirds of the gross operating profits go to the owners, the remaining one-third to Hilton International.

The Hilton International Company cannot lose; the owners are usually pleased because they obtain the advantage of Hilton know-how and become a part of the huge international referral and promotion system. Like most hotel people, Hilton was slow to recognize the value of franchising and only in the middle 1960s began franchising the Hilton name. In 1967 Hilton International Company, now owner of 38 hotels, was purchased by Trans World Airlines and merged into the TWA corporate structure as a subsidiary. In 1975 Hilton sold a 50 percent interest in six of its larger hotels to the Prudential Insurance Company for $83.3 million, retaining a management contract by which the company receives 3 percent of the gross revenues and one-half the profits.

The move made Hilton less vulnerable to falling occupancies and enabled the company to reduce its long-term debt to $150 million. By using $26 million of the sum to buy one million shares of its own stock, 87-year-old Conrad Hilton was left with 29.5 percent of the ownership. Prudential liked the deal because hotel properties tend to be more inflation-proof than other investment properties with long-term leases.

What kind of a man was Hilton? He was energetic, capable, and an incurable optimist. Not one to hide his light under a bushel, he was said to carry around in his pocket a roll of newspaper clippings concerning his own activities. Two biographies have been written about him: *The Man Who Bought the Waldorf*[*] and *Silver Spade*.[†] In addition, he has written an autobiography, *Be My Guest*.[‡]

A *Time* magazine article noted that he was very conscious of his appearance.[§] The fact that he was 6 feet, 2 inches tall and had an outdoor look make him a handsome man by most standards. He abhorred fat men, said *Time*, to the point where he did not even like to do business with them.

One biographer explained that the night life of which he was fond was undertaken as a doctor's prescription. Hilton could not forget work even after working hours. He was told that at six o'clock he should squire a beautiful woman to a fine restaurant and dance the evening away. This, together with swinging a golf club during office hours, may partly account for his longevity.

Hilton preached the value of God and country. According to his biographer, he prayed regularly, and before and after acquiring another property. One public relations ad in *Time*, which cost $50,000, was built around the image of Uncle Sam down on his knees in prayer. Testimony to his strong belief in God and the Catholic Church is the fact that he bequeathed 27.4 percent of his Hilton stock to his private foundation, set up primarily to benefit Catholic nuns worldwide. By 1987 the stock was worth $612 million.

The *Time* article had this to say about Hilton's philosophy of innkeeping:

Hiltons are assembly-line hostelries with carefully metered luxuries—convenient, automatic, a bit antiseptic. Conrad Hilton's life is rooted in the belief that people are pretty much equal, and that their taste and desires are, too. His hotels have made the world safe for the middle-class travelers, who need not fear the feeling of being barely tolerated in some of the older European hotels. At a Hilton all they need is a reservation and money.

If this is an indictment of Hilton, it is also a commentary on the American traveling public. Many complain about and resent Hilton, but continue to patronize his hotels.

In 1969 Hilton joined Statler in having his name closely associated with a school of hotel administration. A gift of $1.5 million made by Hilton to the School

[†]Whitney Bolton, *Silver Spade: The Conrad Hilton Story* (Plainview, N.Y.: Books for Libraries), 1974.

[‡]Conrad N. Hilton, *Be My Guest* (Englewood Cliffs, N.J.: Prentice Hall), 1957.

[§]*Time* (July 19, 1963).

of Hotel Management at the University of Houston was used to pay for part of a new continuing education and hotel administration building; the name of the Houston school was changed to the Conrad N. Hilton School of Hotel Management. later, the grant was increased by the Hilton Foundation by another $20 million.

The star property of the Hilton empire is the Las Vegas Hilton, the 3120-room resort hotel, which in some years created as much as 40 percent of the corporation's total profits.

"Each Hilton Hotel and Inn is an individual, a unique and special place, free to do what it does best."

That, according to Barron Hilton, Hilton's son and current CEO of Hilton Hotels, is the Hilton difference. Barron runs the Hilton empire. An aviation buff, each year he hosts an annual retreat for top glider pilots at his Flying M ranch in Nevada, 780 square miles of it. He is also an aerobatics enthusiast, not afraid to take risks in the air as well as in business. He owns 6 million shares of the chain, valued at over $400 million.

Conrad Hilton's name has again come to the fore as Hilton is building international hotels under the Conrad International Hotels name. The first of that chain opened as the Conrad International Hotel and Jupiter's Casino in 1986 in Queensland, Australia.

9

Tourism

The abstraction *tourism* is an umbrella term that includes all of the hotel and motel business and that part of the restaurant business serving the traveling public. A complex of interrelated businesses, tourism links the travel modes, restaurants, lodging, and much of the entertainment away from home. Travel retailers and wholesalers, convention centers, the airlines, buses, cruiseships, rental cars, and passenger railroads come together in the same overall business: serving people away from home.

The common dictionary definition of tourism is "the business of providing tours and services for tourists." Broadly defined, in 1993 tourism contributed 6 percent or $3.2 trillion to the global economy.

Definitions of who a traveler is and who a tourist is are not uniform. Domestic travel is generally considered to be any travel away from home that involves at least 25 miles. The definition, however, excludes travel for the purpose of commuting to work. The World Tourist Organi-

zation, an affiliate of the United Nations, defines "tourists" as anyone who crosses a national boundary and remains out of his or her home country for a period of at least 24 hours. This includes travel for business as well as pleasure, but excludes the military, immigrants, resident students, diplomats, nomads, border workers, and refugees. People working away from home are not tourists. Neither are those millions of people who cross borders and remain less than 24 hours.

The traveler is provided a means of travel (auto, air, rail, bus, rental car) by travel "suppliers." His or her trip is assisted and expedited by travel agents who act as brokers between the traveler and the supplier. Influencing travelers in their destination choice are the destination marketers (regional, national, and local tourist offices). The Pacific Area Travel Association (PATA) and European Travel Commission are examples of regional destination marketers. Nearly every country has a national tourist office (NTO) with the principal purpose of attracting more visitors to it. States and provinces have state offices with a

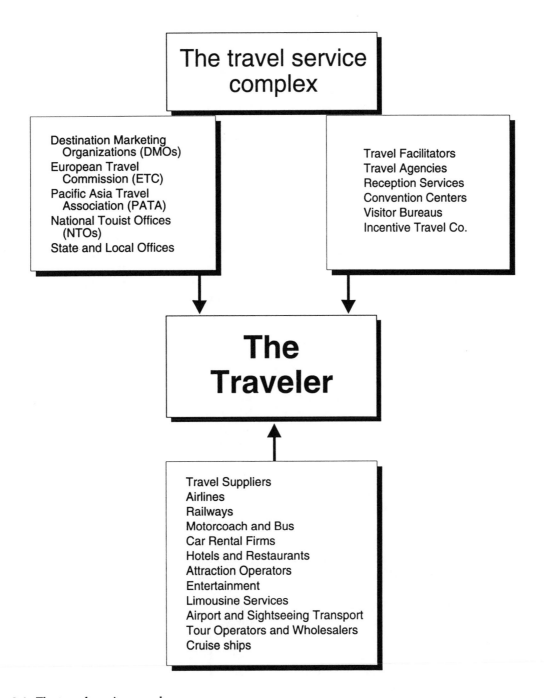

Figure 9-1 The travel service complex.

similar purpose. The more than 330 convention centers in this country attract hundreds of thousands of people who might not otherwise visit the convention center location. Figure 9-1 shows the traveler being influenced by destination marketing organizations, his or her travel being facilitated by the travel agency, reception service companies, convention centers, visitors' bureaus, and incentive travel firms.

About 25 percent of domestic hotel reservations are made with the assistance of a travel agent. For overseas travel, the percentage may be as high as 90. In 1992 the 32,147 travel agencies in the U.S. booked $51 billion in air ticket sales.[1] Hotels pro-

1. Somerset R. Waters, *Travel Industry World Yearbook—1991*, (New York: Childs & Waters, Inc.), 1991.

vided discounted room rates for travel agents. Commissions on room sales are paid on room sales booked by travel agents. The usual commission is 10 percent, but hotels at times have paid commissions of as much as 20 percent. Hotels may offer complimentary rooms to travel agents when they take part in familiarization (fam) trips sponsored by a destination marketing organization, such as a state or national tourist office.

SYMBIOTIC RELATIONSHIPS

Hotels are dependent on travel retailers, the travel agents and tour operators, to varying degrees. Some resort hotels receive as much as 90 percent of their business via tours and agents. Larger hotels may get 25 to 30 percent of their reservations through travel agents and another 20 percent from tour operators. Some hotels could not survive without tour business. Certain restaurants may acquire half or more of their business from the traveler. The foreign traveler to the U.S. spends close to $6 billion in hotels and restaurants each year. The cruise ship is both competitor and partner to the hotel and restaurant. The cruise traveler may spend one or more days in a hotel before and after a cruise.

A few astute and enterprising businesspeople, recognizing the symbiotic nature of the components of tourism, have established travel conglomerates that sell cruise travel, air travel, rental car service, and food and accommodations. Carlson Travel, headquartered in Minneapolis, is a network of travel agencies, tour wholesalers and operators, and an incentive travel house. Carlson Travel, in turn, is owned by the Carlson Hospitality Group, which includes TGI Friday's and Country Kitchen restaurants, Colony Resorts, and Radisson Hotels. Numerous airlines own or are affiliated with a hotel chain.

Swissair is an example of the intermarriage of travel business segments. In a joint venture with Nestlé of Switzerland, the airline owns Swisshotel, which is an international chain. Swissair also controls Resiburo Kuoni, parent of Kuoni Travel, which in turn owns Kuoni Hotel Management, a company that concentrates on managing hotels in the Caribbean and Mediterranean.

Marriages between airlines and hotels would seem logical as their services are advantageous both to them and the traveler. In fact, they have been taking place since the 1940s, when Pan American World Airways was asked by the U.S. government to assist Latin American development by arranging for first-class hotels in the major Latin American capitals. Pan Am obliged by setting up Intercontinental Hotels. The company operated and took equity positions in several Latin American cities in Venezuela, Columbia, Brazil, Chile, and elsewhere. Airline ownership of hotels helped market airline tickets and also assured travelers of American-style accommodations.

International hotels seldom can go it alone in promotion and advertising. The airlines advertise destinations heavily, at no expense to destination hotels. Hotel advertising insofar as it promotes a destination also stimulates air travel. Since hotels are part and parcel of destination marketing, however, they should do their share in the community, state, and regional marketing.

Research conducted by tourist authorities provides traveler profiles and travel trends that are very valuable to hotels (and restaurants), particularly since trends may change rapidly. An example: Travelers to the United States from Australia appeared suddenly one year and became a prime market for Los Angeles hotels, bringing a new market that could be exploited by those who were informed.

Frequent flyer bonus plans illustrate how ideas flow between airlines and hotels. Seeing how effective these plans were in attracting passengers to the airlines, nearly every major hotel chain began offering frequent-guest plans, starting with the Holiday Corporation in 1983. Participants won points on the basis of the number of times they were guests of the chain. Subsequently, most such programs were based on the amount of money spent by the guest, rather than number of stays. Marriott offered air trips, car rentals, and accommodations after a stipulated amount was spent with the company. The programs were, and are, especially appealing to business travelers, who spend so much time on the move.

Many hotels around the world also contract with an airline to accommodate the line's flight crews and block out sizable numbers of rooms at a special rate. Such contracts help assure a breakeven occupancy level.

Airline schedules are closely related to the occupancies of some hotels, especially those located in or near a busy airport. Remote destinations such as Fiji, American Samoa, or Tonga are utterly dependent on airline service. A change in flight schedule or cancellation of service by an airline directly affects occupancy on the island. Within the U.S., the hub-and-spoke system has increased flights to hub cities, and reduced flights to non-hub cities. Chicago, Atlanta, and Denver are examples of hub cities where airlines collect passengers from a region via smaller planes and transfer them to larger planes for longer flights. Airport hotels in the vicinity benefit, but are overbooked when bad weather cancels or delays flights.

AIR TRAVEL AND TOURISM

Air travel has shaped the hotel and restaurant business dramatically. Prior to World War II, most travel was done via the car or train, and hotels and restaurants were often located to best serve them. Now most long-distance travel is by plane; many hotels with thousands of guest rooms are located in or near airports. Airport hotels enjoy occupancy levels above the national average. Large city hotels rely heavily on the business traveler, who is very likely to travel by air. Almost all the guests at resort destinations like Hawaii come by plane.

Direct flight by jet is a very important factor in tourism. The time and cost of getting to a destination form a primary influence. Advertising then comes into play. Independent hotels cannot afford to reach mass markets through advertising. The airlines can and do; the chains can also; and travel articles help. The fact that a friend or neighbor went to Saint Martin last year may be critical in making that island next year's vacation choice.

Eastern Airlines was probably the biggest single determinant in the growth of Miami Beach. American Airlines and the other lines serving the Caribbean were of similar importance for the West Indies. United Airlines has been significant in Hawaiian tourism.

Another decisive factor in the growth of tourism in the islands is the introduction of large management and franchise hotel systems: Hilton, Intercontinental, Sheraton, and Holiday Inns. Their extensive referral systems bring the islands to the attention of hundreds of thousands of people. These far-away and exotic places suddenly become safe and appealing when there is a Holiday Inn or Hilton Hotel in which to stay. The food, housekeeping, and security can be counted on to be as travelers would find them in the U.S.

Commercial airlines can be classified according to the markets being served. Commuter airlines serve people flying short distances; regional lines, serve a particular part of the country; national airlines serve the entire country; and international airlines fly across national borders. Another way to classify airlines is by sales volume per year: anything over $1 billion in sales ranks the airline as a major.

Following deregulation, which began in 1978 and was completed in 1984, the airlines were largely freed of restrictions from buying one another. By 1992 a "Big Five" of airlines had emerged: Continental, United Airlines, American Airlines, Northwest Airlines, and Delta.

INTERNATIONAL TOURIST TRAVEL

International travel is spurred by "the endless fascination of the unknown," by the need for challenge and change, the desire to compare others with ourselves.

As a phenomenon, it ebbs and flows as political, economic, and other conditions and circumstances change.

The strength of a country's currency affects travel: A cheap dollar brings visitors, a strong dollar reduces the number. A strong British pound means fewer overseas visitors to the United Kingdom; a weak pound attracts more vacationers. A principal reason for the some 40 million visitors to Spain each year was the deliberate government policy of keeping wages and prices low, which made the country an inexpensive tourist mecca for millions of English and Europeans. (Prices have now climbed, however.)

Some 49 million visitors came to this country in 1992 and spent $71.2 billion, leaving the U.S. with a travel surplus of $20 billion. The Japanese and Canadians represent America's most important visitors from abroad, followed by those from Europe and Mexico. The Japanese spent more than any other country in visiting the U.S. ($13.7 billion) in 1992, followed by Canada ($9.3 billion) and Mexico ($6.4 billion).

The U.S. Travel and Tourism Administration, part of the U.S. Department of Commerce, is actively engaged in attracting trade shows to the U.S. and providing assistance to individual states and private organizations in overseas marketing.

ECONOMIC IMPACT OF TOURISM

As would be expected, the various states attracted foreign tourists at widely different rates. For example, Canadian tourists who visit the U.S. favor New York, Florida, Washington, Michigan, Maine, and California with the most visits. California received the most overseas tourists, followed by New York, Florida, Hawaii, and Nevada.[2]

Tourism spending creates direct jobs, those that service visitor needs directly, such as taxi drivers, airline personnel, hotel staff, travel agents, waiters, and service station personnel. Indirect jobs are created among bank employees, real estate offices, accountants, companies that manufacture hotel equipment, aircraft, car rentals, and other tourist-related industries. Eastman Kodak, for example, is such a company, its sale of photographic equipment and film is affected by traveler purchases. Other jobs are created by the spending of wages earned by those employees directly or indirectly by tourism spending.

California, for example, the state with an amazing out-of-state visitor spending of $70.5 billion, found that tourism created 2.18 million jobs, representing 15.5 percent of the state's civilian work force. Tourism is Florida's largest industry. Nevada's economy is also largely based on tourism. And Hawaii's tourism industry is by far its largest source of income. In 1990 visitor arrivals in Hawaii reached almost 7 million. A Bank of Hawaii economic model showed that a 10 percent drop in visitor arrivals would cause a $570 million decline in retail sales, an amount that would exceed the total annual value of the state's sugar industry.[3]

Many poor areas turn to tourism as a realistic way to raise themselves from the poverty level. The tourist dollar, it is maintained, is more valuable than the dollar generated and spent within the local economy. Much tourist money goes to pay for the services of people in constructing and operating vacation facilities. It is fresh money, brought in from outside the local economy, that triggers several rounds of spending, thus stimulating the economy.

The U.S. Department of Commerce states that the tourist dollar turns over an average of 3.27 times during a year. In other words, a tourist dollar is received and spent more than three times in the course of one year. This multiplier effect varies with the degree of self-sufficiency of the local economy. If food has to be imported, for example, the money that goes to pay for the food is immediately shipped out of the community and does not take part in the multiplier effect. For the U.S. economy as a whole, the multiplier effect is about 2.

A study of the multiplier effect of tourism on the economy of New Hampshire found that within a year what the visitor spent was respent several times. As each round of spending took place, additional value accrued to the people of New Hampshire. Leakages, in the form of savings, federal tax payments, and purchases made outside the state, reduce the amount left for the next round.

The multiplier effect has less impact in the less developed countries. Much construction material, furnishings, equipment, and food must be imported. In the Caribbean, for example, a study found that for every tourist dollar spent on an island, only 18¢ remained on that island. Several projects are underway in the Caribbean to increase the local component of the tourist product. Realistically many areas have few alternative job-producing industries.

Many states conduct their own tourism impact studies. California, for example, finds that tourism generates more than $50 billion to the state's economy each year. For 1989, Florida estimated that spending by in-state and out-of-state travelers reached $49.3 billion, an amount that generated about 1.5 million jobs and accounted for 24 percent of the state's civilian labor force.

NATIONAL TOURIST OFFICES

More than a hundred countries have tourist offices that, like state and local tourist offices, are set up to attract more visitors to their respective countries. In a sense, they compete with each other. The visitor who travels to the Orient this

---

2. U.S. Travel and Tourism Administration.
3. Somerset Waters, *op. cit.*

year is probably not going to Europe any time soon. The Swede who goes to the Greek isles is not likely to visit America this year. Each tourist office produces promotion literature, sometimes a travel film or two, and encourages writers and media people to visit and write or film something favorable about its country. National tourist offices (NTOs) budgets range from tiny to some that exceed $50 million a year. The size of the country is unrelated to the size of the budget. The Bahamas NTO has had an $50 million budget in 1991; the U.S. travel office, about half that amount.

NTOs often work closely with their country's national airline, which provides free transport for travel writers and others who it is believed will publicize the country's charms.

NTOs conduct research and send the results to organizations and companies, such as hotels and restaurants, that can make good use of the information. To which states and attractions do visitors go? What kind of lodging and food service appeals to them? What special services are required? Is it necessary to employ staff who speak their languages? What special menu items should be offered?

Japanese visitors, for example, enjoy fresh fruit for dessert and are a little overwhelmed at the size of a 12-ounce steak. They are pleased with the price, however, because steak at home costs $30 a pound or more. Orientals generally do not like to be touched. Upper-class Latin Americans expect more deference from the staff than is usual in this country. When being introduced to a Japanese man, should the hotel manager offer his business card first? Who offers his hand for a handshake, the manager or the visitor? Who averts his eyes, the manager or the visitor? (Normally, men do not shake hands with Japanese women.) These and other questions are important when dealing with the international visitor.

STATE TOURIST OFFICES

State tourist offices are among the big spenders in attracting visitors to their states, and as such they are close allies with the hotel and restaurant business. In the year 1990–1991, U.S. state travel offices had budgets totaling almost $356 million. Illinois led the list with a travel office budget of $31.9 million. Hawaii was second, with a budget

of over $22 million. Texas, Pennsylvania, Michigan, New York, Florida, Tennessee, and Alaska each had budgets of over $10 million in the 1990–1991 year. Every state had a tourist office budget; the average amount was $7,199,230.[4]

The Hawaii Visitor's Bureau (HVB) is funded by the state government general budget and the hospitality businesses in the state. The HVB is divided into five divisions: marketing, visitor satisfaction, research, finance, and membership.

State tourist offices are charged with bringing more visitors into the states and convincing them to stay longer and spend more. State tourist offices conduct research to identify their visitors demographically and psychologically. Some of the findings can be surprising. During he month of July, Germans and Swiss were second in numbers using the Alaska Highway, the 1490-mile road from Dawson Creek, British Columbia, to Fairbanks, Alaska. (The trip takes 7 days.) The largest number were Californians. With this kind of information, tourist offices can pinpoint their potential markets and aim their advertising to reach the people most likely to be enticed to the state.

Once hotel and motel operators realize that tourism profitability can unify businesses involved in it, they lobby for larger tourism budgets.

Room Taxes. Lodging room taxes can be onerous, a hidden charge in the room rate, but perceived by the guest as part of the rate. More and more areas are levying this tax as an easy way to increase revenues. It excites opposition from no one except hoteliers. Existing room taxes are being increased. The authority imposing the tax usually promises that the income will be used to promote tourism. Often, it is not. Vigilance and pressure from hotel and restaurant groups are necessary to insist that the room tax money be used as promised. The AH&MA found that hotel-occupancy rates decline an average of 3.1 percent for every 10 percent increase in room taxes or room rates.[5]

HOTELS AND TRAVEL ATTRACTIONS

An obvious relationship exists between the hotels of an area and the travel attractions in the vicinity.

4. Somerset Waters, *op. cit.*
5. Reported in *Meeting News* (Oct. 1991).

Orlando would be a sleepy southern town without Disney World and have little need for the 70,000 guest rooms in the area. Universal Studios in Hollywood adds occupancy to Los Angeles hotels. Travel attractions and theme parks drew 249 million visitors in 1988. The top 8 U.S. attractions in 1992 were:[6]

Park & Location	Attendance (in millions)
Walt Disney World/Epcot (Lake Buena Vista, Florida)	30.2
Disneyland (Anaheim, California)	11.6
Universal Studios Tour (Universal City, California)	4.1
Knott's Berry Farm (Buena Park, California)	3.9
Sea World of Florida (Orlando, Florida)	4.1
Sea World of California (San Diego, California)	4.0
Busch Gardens—The Dark Continent (Tampa, Florida)	3.1
Kings Island (Kings Island, Ohio)	3.3

The larger theme parks exemplify the interconnections of the tourist business, attracting millions of people and providing guest rooms, food service and a variety of entertainment including thrill rides and theater. Many theme parks combine entertainment and education. Led by the Disney company the theme parks are kept scrupulously clean and safe. Tens of thousands of jobs are created and large tax revenues generated. In the high season Disney World in Florida has some 30,000 employees; Disneyland about half that number.

The MGM Grand Hotel Resort and Theme Park and the Excalibur hotel in Las Vegas demonstrate a move to combine casino gambling with a theme park. Nearly all of the 50 U.S. theme parks have added one or more big simulator rides, rides which cost about a million dollars each, or are planning one. Sophisticated hydraulic or electrically driven platforms form a base for most of these thrill rides. Virtual reality rides are being built that are reprogrammable so that customers will return for a different experience.

In 1990 attraction receipts were estimated at $3.4 billion. Water parks that combine water slides and wave pools are among the fastest growing attractions. As of 1992 there were 78 major water parks and some 500 smaller ones in the U.S.[7]

Sea World's Marine Life Park in San Diego attracts about 4 million visitors and the San Diego Zoo some 3 million. Along with other attractions in the area, they help make tourism San Diego's number-one business and provide guests for the 43,000 hotel rooms in San Diego County.

Orlando, Florida, is now a metropolis, with some 80,000 guest rooms and dozens of restaurants serving up to 30 million visitors to Disney World each year. Hearst Castle in California, built by William Randolph Hearst and given to the state, offers another example. It is the number-two attraction in California and gives life to dozens of motels and restaurants in the vicinity, along with creating a travel urge in the general public that influences tourism in much of the state.

Casino gambling is the appeal of Las Vegas and Atlantic City. Twelve to 14 million people visit Las Vegas annually. Atlantic City, once a prime destination in the Eastern seaboard, was slowly dying until revived by casino gambling. Without its casinos, Las Vegas would probably be just another little dry, dusty desert town, and Atlantic City just another decaying resort.

Sporting activities also stimulate tourism expenditures. Millions of sports fans travel, sometimes great distances, to watch their teams play. Fortunate are the hotels/motels in the general area of a Superbowl game. The Los Angeles Visitors and Convention Bureau determined that the average fan to a Superbowl spends $600. It was estimated that visitors to the Pasadena Superbowl in 1986 occupied up to 50,000 guest rooms, some as far as 75 miles from the game site. For the period of the game, the hotels obliged by raising rates as much as 50 percent.

6. *Amusement Business.*

7. Somerset Waters, *op. cit.*

CONVENTION CENTERS AND VISITOR BUREAUS

Convention centers are facilities designed to provide exhibit and meeting space (Fig. 9-2). Most operate independently or semi-independently of the convention and visitor bureaus. Some, as in Las Vegas, operate under the same management. Twenty-two of the largest centers each have exhibit and meeting space exceeding 300,000 square feet. A few have a million square feet of space and can service the extremely large conventions. The largest centers are in New York City and Chicago.

Since the mission of visitor and convention centers is to attract free-spending visitors to their areas, they are natural allies of the hotel and restaurant operator. Some conventions arranged through them reserve every hotel room available in the city and places nearby. Across the country these centers and their cousins, the visitor and convention bureaus, are constantly engaged in marketing and public relations to make the areas they represent appealing to all sorts of visitors.

Convention and visitor bureau management has come to be a highly specialized field of work. Those engaged in it have many traits and problems in common with hotel managers. Like them, to move up in their careers, they usually must move on to larger centers. The job is highly political in that there are several constituencies to please.

San Diego, California's second largest city, has two convention centers. The newer and larger one cost well over $150 million and is funded by the San Diego Port Authority. The other one obtains its support from a city and county tax of 7 percent levied on guest room sales. The two centers are managed independently of each other

Figure 9-2 The San Diego Convention Center. Funded by the San Diego Unified Port District, it will be operated as a nonprofit corporation. Like numerous other convention centers in the United States, it is designed to handle major trade shows and meetings in addition to consumer shows and special events. Cost is about $150 million.

and are not formally joined with the San Diego Convention and Visitor Bureau, although the bureau considers itself the marketing arm for the centers.

The San Diego Convention and Visitor Bureau employs some 60 full-time employees and uses an additional 45 part time to help with visitor registration. Several of the full-time employees are salespeople who visit trade shows and call on groups who can be motivated to come to San Diego. The most important for this purpose is the American Society of Association Executives, the members of which influence thousands of travel decisions. The San Diego Bureau is headed by a 70 member board of directors. Its 1500 members are made up of people from government, the hotel and restaurant business, and others interested in San Diego tourism.

Hotel managers and marketing directors work closely with their convention office staff, jointly planning budgets, promotional trips, and future efforts. Hotel and restaurant owners and operators are prominent on the centers' boards of directors. Hotel and restaurant people can extend and magnify their marketing efforts by working with and through the office. The offices mobilize and focus the components of tourism, thereby helping to fill guest rooms and restaurant seats. These centers can attract literally thousands of people who probably would not otherwise come to the city or area.

Most of the larger offices belong to the International Association of Convention and Visitor Bureaus, an organization with some 300 members, including 22 from other countries. Even small communities, which do not have visitor bureaus, have one or a few people assigned to promote visitor spending, usually as a part of the local chamber of commerce. The Association has developed a computerized database listing more than 7700 associations. The database, called INET, allows members access to information covering associations and their past meetings.

As of 1992, convention centers were being built in so-called second-tier cities like Providence, Rhode Island, and Columbus, Ohio, to attract some of the annual 10,000 trade shows, which according to the Trade Show Bureau had doubled during the previous decade.

Some 330 convention centers were in operation to attract the average trade show delegate who, according to the International Convention

and Visitors Bureaus, spends more than $900 during his or her stay in town.

The huge convention centers were expanding their space to handle even larger groups, such as 65,000 Alcoholics Anonymous members who will attend their meeting at the San Diego Convention Center in 1995. Note that they were also serving smaller groups. The San Diego Center hosts stockholder meetings, high school proms, banquets, and dozens of Christmas parties.

Most or all of the convention centers run a financial deficit, made up directly from city budgets or by a special tax on guest rooms in the area.[8]

PLEASURE CRUISING

Pleasure cruising it is said has emerged as the fastest growing segment of tourism, a business largely focused on the Caribbean and Mediterranean seas as a place where more than 4.5 million passengers cruise for fun and relaxation. Some passengers favor relaxation; others, like most of the Carnival cruise line passengers, opt for razzle dazzle. Cruise ship foodservice and other services are usually of high quality. Cruise lines employ about one worker for every two passengers. The work entails long hours with few breaks.

Cruise lines depend almost exclusively on travel agencies for booking tickets; the agencies are happy to comply because cruise sales are big ticket items with travel agency commissions of 15 percent or more. Some agencies specialize in cruise sales; others engage in cruise sales only. Cruise sales for two people can run as high as $100,000 for a long cruise. Cruises are getting shorter, however, as the market has moved to reach more people under age 50.

Cruise ship economics are such that bigger ships mean greater profits: bigger ships translate into larger casinos. The $300-million cruise ship *Sensation*, a Carnival Cruise Line ship, carries 228 slot machines and other gaming equipment in a club, appropriately called Club Vegas. Carnival, largest of the cruise lines, is building a 95,000-ton vessel capable of carrying 3,300 passengers, a moving hotel that places travel in a self-contained capsule, mobile, free of hassle and most travel

---

8. "The Latest-Municipal Malady: Convention Center Fever," *New York Times* (Feb. 24, 1991).

problems. One cruise ship inconvenience for many people is the size of the cabins, most of them smaller than 186 square feet, including a tiny shower. (The fly-cruise package lessens travel hassle in that almost everything is included in the price: flight, cruise, and food. Not included are tips and liquor.)

The cruise ship is competition for hoteliers and restaurateurs. Hotels and restaurants do get some business from cruise ship passengers before and after the cruise. The Disney Company has its own cruise affiliation.

American hotel and restaurant graduates find relatively few positions among cruise lines. Shore-based marketing and administrative positions are exceptions. Most cruise ship personnel are not U.S. nationals but represent dozens of countries. Ship officers are likely to be Europeans. And nearly all cruise ships operate under foreign flags that allow lower labor and other costs than permitted by U.S. law., To fly the American flag, a ship must be built in the U.S. where ship-building costs are about 50 percent higher. (Some ship construction is subsidized by governments.)

Like the U.S. airlines, cruise ships are being dominated by only a few large companies.

MIAMI BEACH

Resort destinations rise and fall. Miami Beach is an excellent example. In 1977 Miami Beach was being supplanted by destinations as far away as Europe. Cancún, Hawaii, Acapulco, and Caribbean resorts. A major factor in the decline of Miami Beach was the bright and shiny new Disney World, located in Orlando in the middle of Florida, cutting off a visitor from the north "at the pass." Things were so bad that local hoteliers went to Washington to seek federal backing for low-cost refurbishment loans refused by South Florida banks.

The Fontainbleau Hotel, largest of the beach hotels, thought it had a way out: It advertised a plan for singles that included nude sunbathing in the solarium and videotaped dating services. Outraged citizens in Miami quashed that idea. The once proud Fontainbleau Hotel, largest of the Miami Beach hotels, was sold in 1977 in bankruptcy court. It is now operated by Hilton Hotels and doing well.

Figure 9-3 The Americana on Miami Beach. Note the guest room balconies, so arranged that they all face the Atlantic Ocean. The Americana was one of the first large resort-convention complexes to be built on the beach. It combines guest rooms, food and beverage facilities, convention facilities, and cabanas.

Figure 9-4 The Americana—another view. The swimming pool in the subtropical and tropical resort is the center of most activity. The Americana's food and beverage business is close to the pool, where a large part of the luncheon business at today's resort takes place.

Miami Beach's problems are said to have stemmed from not only outside problems, but also poor management and lack of maintenance. When profits were made, the money was siphoned off without a thought for tomorrow. Hotels were built close together along the beach, making them invisible from the street and causing beach erosion. In the 1980s Miami Beach developed the British market with inexpensive packaged tours.

In 1993 the murder of several British and German tourists in Florida focused the state government's attention on the importance of tourism to the state and its need to protect visitors from criminal assaults.

Questions

1. Define tourism.

2. Hotels, motels, and restaurants constitute a large part of tourism. So too do the airlines. Point out at least three ways that the two segments are interrelated.

3. Name three prominent resort destinations almost entirely dependent on air travel for survival.

4. The multiplier effect is referred to when explaining the economic benefits of tourism to a destination. How does the multiplier effect increase the value of tourism to an area?

5. Suppose the value of the U.S. dollar increases sharply. What is the likely effect on foreign visitor travel to this country?

6. How does the value of the British pound affect the hotel business of New York City?

7. As a restaurant owner, what factors could influence you to become a member of your local visitor and convention bureau?

8. As a hotel owner, under what circumstances would you favor a lodging room tax?

9. Who should fund your state tourism office: private enterprise or the state government?

10. Name two states that receive huge numbers of international visitors from out of state.

11. Which two countries provide the largest numbers of foreign visitors to the U.S.?

Discussion Questions

1. Several airlines are owners of hotel chains. What factors discourage the airlines from buying more hotels?

2. Many restaurant owners believe themselves not to be a part of an area's tourist business. Is such a belief sometimes justified?

3. Can travel and tourism grow to the point of being self-destructive? Explain.

4. Tourism development affects the residents of a destination area in several different ways. What groups do not necessarily benefit from tourism development?

5. Tourism is often cited as a positive force for world peace. Take a position for or against this idea.

6. What can be done to reassure visitors, especially foreign visitors, that your city or state is safe for them to visit?

Christopher B. Hemmeter

(1940–)

Christopher B. Hemmeter has raised the size, scope, and investment of the destination resort to a new high. As John Portman introduced the 70-story city hotel and inaugurated the huge atrium design in hotels, so Chris Hemmeter has changed the magnitude and opulence of destination resorts.

Hemmeter, with the help of a burgeoning tourist business in Hawaii and hundreds of millions of dollars of mostly Japanese money, has created resorts on Kauai and the big island of Hawaii that set a pattern for beauty and dramatic style of resort facilities for the future.

Primarily a promoter/developer, Hemmeter has solid hotel and restaurant operating experience as well. As a newly minted graduate of Cornell's Hotel School in 1962, his first job was as assistant manager at Honolulu's Royal Hawaiian Hotel. Two years later, he was in business with two partners managing the food and beverage operations of the newly opened Illikai Hotel. In 1968 the operation contract was lost when the hotel was sold. The partners then bought Don the Beachcomber's restaurant, which soon after burned to the ground. Associated Innkeepers, the partnership, went on to develop restaurants in Hawaii and the mainland U.S.

In 1968 at the age of 28, he sold out for $1.5 million in stock, which quickly increased in value to $3 million. The buying company then proceeded to go bankrupt, leaving Hemmeter with no assets.

The scarcity of funds lasted for only a short time as he was able to save the development of the Hawaiian Regent Hotel by changing the design from steel to concrete and, with his immense enthusiasm, to arrange its financing. The same skills enabled him to borrow enough to build the Hyatt Regency Waikiki.

His trademark properties followed:

The Hyatt Regency Maui (1976)

The Westin Maui (1987)

Westin Kauai (1987)

The Hyatt Regency Waikoloa (1988)

The Westin Kauai, now owned by the Bass brothers of Texas and a Japanese construction company, illustrates the kind of eloquent architectural statement of which Hemmeter is capable. Everything is on a bigger or grander scale. From the port cochere, the guest descends via an escalator on three levels, encountering a breathtaking reflecting pool, with an island in the center from which eight marble stallions leap and cavort in mist from three fountains rising six stories high. The swimming pool, three-fourths the size of a football field, recalls the magnificent pool that graces the Hearst Castle in California. The oriental art seems endless, located in the lobby, all corridors, around the pools, on the grounds, even on the beach, which is situated on a protected cove.

Huge horses, all Percherons, Belgians, and Clydesdales, are used to pull the guest carriages around the property. One of the horses is the world's largest, standing over 19 hands and weighing some 3000 pounds.

Hemmeter built the resort using an older hotel as a base and, when completed, will have 10 restaurants and lounges and 200 acres of lawns and botanical gardens, all sitting on 520 acres along a half-mile expanse of white sand bay. Also, there will be 10 miles of waterways negotiated by gondola.

Hemmeter believes that the public wants "fantasy" in a resort hotel, something larger than life. In his design and furnishings, he tries to comply with this wish. The public thinks of a Chinese porcelain horse as something to place on a living room mantle. He provides a life-size horse. The public is accustomed to seeing a normal-size riding horse. He provided huge Belgians to pull the carriages of his Westin Kauai hotel. The olympic-size swimming pool is too small. Double or triple the pool size. Bigger is better. Expect a large vase in a hotel lobby? Hemmeter provides one 6 feet tall. The "Ooh-Ah-Wow" reaction is part of what he seeks from his guests. For some guests, it is simply overstatement, but not for most. Unfortunately much of the Westin Kauai was destroyed in a hurricane and is being rebuilt.

The Hyatt Waikola, a 1244 room property located on the dry side of the big island of Hawaii, is expected to cost $360 million. Sixty acres is being carved out of jagged lava. A 700-foot water-filled atrium is part of one of three towers and contains 10 small islands with banyon trees and tropical birds. A 7-acre lagoon, stocked with colorful reef fish, will be available for snorkelers.

One reason Hemmeter is able to raise hundreds of millions for his projects is his hotel and restaurant experience and, according to his chief architect, Herbert T. Lawton, the uncanny ability to see a rocky piece of land in 3-D technicolor. Without the benefit of marketing studies or other aids, Hemmeter sketches complete buildings and layouts, drawing on a photographic memory of architectural details observed in world travel. Once made in a few hours, the designs need rarely be changed. For these reasons, though lacking formal architectural training, Hemmeter was chosen by Jimmy Carter to design the $25 million Carter Presidential Center in Atlanta.

An article in *Aloha*, the Aloha Airlines Magazine, says that Hemmeter dreams big, talks big, and charged across the slow-to-react island landscape in a big way.

Dreaming big is an understatement. Hemmeter proposed building seven pyramids in Atlantic City, each larger than the Great Pyramid at Giza, outside of Cairo. Each pyramid would rise 70 stories and be sheathed in golden glass. "Lighted at night," says Hemmeter, "you'd be able to see the pyramid for hundreds of miles." In 1988 he was planning turnkey resort fantasies on the U.S. mainland, in the Caribbean, and in Pacific Rim countries.

His personal lifestyle is equally flamboyant. He has a converted Boeing-727 for personal travel and an eight-bedroom home in Aspen, as well as plans for a 25,000 sq. ft. Honolulu beachfront home.

Thanks to the incessant urge of the Japanese to own Hawaiian real estate and the burgeoning numbers of tourists to Hawaii, the Hemmeter projects have paid off handsomely to the developers. Hemmeter netted about $188 million when he sold the Hyatt Regency Maui and his Waikiki Beach hotel. Another $72 million came from the 12.5 percent equity he retained in the hotels, along with various concessions and ground leases he kept in Waikiki.

His formula is to conceive a plan on a grand scale, promote the financing, build and sell the project for a handsome profit, and move on to other projects already in the planning stage.

Christopher B. Hemmeter, the premier destination resort developer in Hawaii, has used his formula successfully in the past with the Westin Kaui, the Hyatt Regency Waikoloa, and the Hyatt Regency Maui, properties whose scale and appointments will influence destination resorts for years to come. Currently, he is planning to build billions of dollars of grandstyle, huge resort complexes at other locations in the Pacific Rim, the U.S. mainland, the Caribbean, and Australia.

10

The Restaurant Business

The pleasures of the table belong to all times and all ages, to every country and every day; they go hand in hand with all our other pleasures, outlast them, and remain to console us for their loss.

—Brillant-Savarin

The restaurant business, says the National Restaurant Association (NRA), is the third largest of all businesses in the United States. One of every three meals eaten in this country is eaten away from home, constituting 42 percent of the consumer food dollar. The percentage of food dollars spent has been increasing since World War II.

The restaurant business as we know it today emerged out of World War II, as millions of Americans, men, and women, went to war and work and ate meals provided at the workplace or in the military. Eating habits changed and people who had some discretionary income for restaurant meals and who had never eaten in a public foodservice, liked the experience. The number of restaurants and the volume of sales

began a steady rise that extended into the 1980s, leveling off in the 1990s. World War II was the watershed period that made eating away from home a habit to be enjoyed by millions of people and thought of as a necessity by other millions. Since World War II, a number of social and economic trends have favored the restaurant business. The most important has been the rise in family income, the principal source of which has been the working woman. The more disposable income available, the greater the likelihood of eating out.

Lifestyle changes have also been important for restaurant sales. Millions at work or traveling eat away from home at restaurants out of necessity, foregoing a brown bag. Despite economic cycles, many people perceive restaurant eating to be something deserved or even a different kind of necessity.

The tremendous increase in divorce and the number of singles living alone, coupled with smaller living quarters, favors dining out as an escape from loneliness and boredom. For many, the great desire to own such things as a home, cars, or a boat has been replaced by a need for "experience." Dining out is one of them. The number of households made up of singles and unrelated roommates has been growing, and according to the Census Bureau, these "nonfamily" households represent 29 percent of all households in the U.S. in 1990.

The Government Bureau of Labor Statistics has provided information as to which groups spend the largest share of their food budget on eating out. Employed persons living alone spend the highest percentage, an average of 55 percent. Households headed by persons under 25 years old are not far behind: 43 percent of their food money goes to restaurants. High-income households spend 42 percent, the total dollar amount exceeding that of any one of the other groups.

In 1990 the $139 billion commercial restaurant market had slowed its growth to something less than 3 percent a year, a drop from 8 percent growth in 1983 for fast food and a little over 4 percent for full-service restaurants. Takeout food from grocery stores or delis has cut into sales; convenience-store food increased in popularity because of its cheaper price.

Expansion abroad, mainly via franchising, still presents many opportunities. McDonald's, for example, has 25 percent of its units outside the U.S., and its most popular stores are in Moscow and Beijing. In 1992, it received about 40 percent of its $21.9 billion in revenues from abroad. KFC is in more than 60 countries, and Pizza Hut is in some 65 countries. Dunkin Donuts is the world's largest coffee and doughnut shop, with over 100 of them in Japan. Altogether more than 30 international restaurant chains, mostly fast-food–oriented, have their home base in the U.S.[1]

Although an individual restaurant may cater almost exclusively to local trade, travelers in the U.S. spent an estimated $76 billion consuming food and beverages in 1990. International visitors to this country are another sizable market segment. In 1991 these visitors spent over $8 billion in food and beverage and accounted for about

274,000 foodservice jobs and a payroll of $2.3 billion.[2]

The overall foodservice business is divided between establishments operating for profit (the usual restaurant) and non-profit places such as schools, hospitals or the military (usually called institutional foodservices). The distinctions between the two hold only partially. The number of "institutional" foodservices operated for profit are increasing as schools and collages contract their foodservices to outside for-profit firms, many of which are huge companies employing thousands of personnel.

Commercial foodservice establishments can be divided about equally between fastfood (quick service), places which are largely self-service, and all of the others providing various levels of service. Fastfood represented by McDonalds has had phenomenal growth and bee the most profitable. Independent (non-chain restaurants) are at a comparative disadvantage in finance, marketing, and economy of scale. Until the rapid growth of fastfood restaurants, the independently owned restaurant was typical. The fastfood franchise and the corporately-owned restaurant chain are now the dominate players.

EARLY HISTORY OF EATING OUT

Eating out has a long history. Taverns existed as early as 1700 B.C. The record of a public dining place in Ancient Egypt in 512 B.C. shows a limited menu—only one dish was served, consisting of cereal, wildfowl, and onion. Be that as it may, the ancient Egyptians had a fair selection of foods to choose from: peas, lentils, watermelons, artichokes, lettuce, endive, radishes, onions, garlic, leeks, fats—(both vegetable and animal)—beef, honey, dates, and dairy products, including milk, cheese, and butter.

Women were not permitted in such places then. By 402 B.C., however, women became a part of the tavern atmosphere. Little boys could also be served if accompanied by their parents. Girls had to wait until they were married.

The ancient Romans were great eaters-out. Evidence can be seen even today in Hercu-

1. *Wall Street Journal* (Jan. 29, 1990).

2. U. S. Department of Commerce, U.S. Travel and Tourism Administration, 1991.

laneum, a Roman resort town near Naples that in A.D. 70 was buried under some 65 feet of mud and lava by the eruption of Mt. Vesuvius.[3] Along its streets were a number of snack bars vending bread, cheese, wine, nuts, dates, figs, and hot foods. The counters were faced with marble fragments. Wine jugs were imbedded in them, kept fresh by the cool stone. Mulled and spiced wines were served, often sweetened with honey. A number of the snack bars were identical or nearly so, giving the impression that they were part of a group under single ownership.

Bakeries were nearby, where grain was milled in the courtyard, the mill turned by blindfolded asses. Some bakeries specialized in cakes. One of them had 25 bronze baking pans of various sizes, from about 4 inches to 1.5 feet in diameter.

After the fall of Rome, eating out usually took place in an inn or tavern, but by 1200 there were cooking houses in London, Paris, and elsewhere in Europe, where cooked food could be purchased but with no seating.

The coffeehouse, which appeared in Oxford in 1650 and 7 years later in London, was a forerunner of the restaurant of today. Coffee at the time was considered a cure-all. As one advertisement in 1657 had it: "…Coffee closes the orifices of the stomach, fortifies the heat within, helpeth digesting…is good against eyesores, coughs, or colds…." Lloyd's of London, the international insurance company, was founded in Lloyd's Coffee House. By the eighteenth century, there were about 3000 coffeehouses in London.

Coffeehouses were also popular in Colonial America. Boston had many of them, as did Virginia and New York. Both the words café, meaning a small restaurant or bar, and cafeteria come from the single word café, French for coffee.

The first restaurant called by that name where food was served at tables carried this inscription over the door: "Venite ad me omnes qui stomacho laboratoratis et ego restaurabo vos." Few of the Parisians who saw this sign in 1765 could read French, let alone Latin, but if they could, they knew that Monsieur Boulanger, the proprietor, had said, "Come to me all whose stomachs cry out in anguish and I shall restore you."

Boulanger called his soup "le restaurant divin," divine restorative. It was quite an improvement over the bitter herb and vegetable mixtures brewed by the medieval physicians as restoratives. A richly delicious bouillon, it attracted fashionable folk who would not patronize the public taverns, where eating ran a poor second to drinking. Boulanger's Restaurant Champs d'Oiseau also charged prices sufficiently high to make it acceptably exclusive, a place where ladies and gentlemen would enjoy being seen.

Boulanger lost no time in enlarging his menu, and thus was this new business born. Soon the word restaurant was established, and chefs of repute who had worked only for private families either opened their own restaurants or were employed by a new group of small businessmen—restaurateurs.

The word restaurant came to America in 1794 via a French refugee from the guillotine, Jean Baptiste Gilbert Paypalt. Paypalt set up what must have been the first French restaurant in this country, Julien's Restorator in Boston. Here he served truffles, cheese fondues, and soups. The French influence on American cooking was felt even earlier: Both Washington and Jefferson were fond of French cuisine, and several French eating establishments were opened in Boston by the Huguenots, who fled France in the eighteenth century to escape religious persecution.

The restaurant generally credited as the first full-fledged one in this country was Delmonico's in New York City, opened in 1827.[4] This claim may be disputed by the Union Oyster House in Cambridge, Massachusetts, opened in 1826 by Atwood and Bacon and still operating.

Delmonico's

The name Delmonico once stood for what was best in French-American restaurants. The story of the restaurant and its proprietors is a fascinating one. It epitomizes much of the history of family-operated restaurants in this country. Few family operations last more than a generation, but four generations of the Delmonico family were involved in nine restaurants from 1827 to 1923. The last of the family-owned Delmonico restaurants, at 44th Street and Fifth Avenue in New York City,

3. Joseph J. Deiss, Herculaneum, Italy's Buried Treasure (New York: Thomas J. Crowell Co.), 1969.

4. Thomas Lately, Delmonico's, a Century of Splendor (Boston, Mass.: Houghton Mifflin), 1967.

closed its doors in humiliation and bankruptcy during the early Prohibition year of 1923. The family had gathered acclaim and a fortune, but finally the drive for success and the talent for it were missing in the family line. As has happened with most family restaurants, the name and the restaurants faded into history.

John Delmonico, the founder, was a Swiss sea captain who retired from ship life in 1825 and opened a tiny shop on the Battery in New York City. At first, he sold only French and Spanish wines, but in 1827 with his brother Peter, a confectioner, he opened an establishment that also served fancy cakes and ices that could be enjoyed on the spot.

New Yorkers, apparently bored with plain food, approved of the petits gateaux (little cakes), chocolate, and bonbons served by the brothers Delmonico. Success led in 1832 to the opening of a restaurant on the building's second story, and brother Lorenzo Delmonico joined the enterprise. Lorenzo proved to be the restaurant genius. New Yorkers were ready to change from a roast-and-boiled bill of fare to *la grande cuisine*—and Lorenzo was ready for New Yorkers.

A hard worker, the basic qualification for restaurant success, Lorenzo was up at 4:00 AM and on his way to the public markets. By 8:00 AM he appeared at the restaurant, drank a small cup of black coffee, and smoked the third or fourth of his daily 30 cigars. Then home to bed until the dinner hour, when he reappeared to direct the restaurant show. He set high standards for himself and Delmonico employees. He also set them high for Delmonico patrons—no guest could entertain behind closed doors, not even a married couple.

Guests were encouraged to be as profligate with food as they could afford. In the 1870s a yachtsman gave a banquet at Delmonico's that cost $400 a person, astronomical at that time. Before every guest was a small yacht basin 20 inches in diameter, and in each floated a perfect model of the host's yacht, complete in detail to a tiny gold bar. A 30-foot artificial lake was created at another banquet, and in it swam four swans. Golden cages full of birds added to the decor.

Delmonico's pioneered the idea of printing the menu in both French and English. The menu was enormous—it offered 12 soups; 32 hors d'oeuvres; 28 different beef entrees, 46 of veal, 20 of mutton, 47 of poultry, 22 of game, 46 of fish, shellfish, turtle, and eels; 51 vegetable and egg

dishes; 19 pastries and cakes; plus 28 additional desserts. Some 24 liqueurs and 64 wines and champagnes were listed. The highest-priced entree was canvasback duck fed on sherry.

Except for a few items temporarily unobtainable, any dish could be called for at any time, and it would be served promptly, as a matter of routine. What restaurant today could or would offer 371 separate dishes to order?

Delmonico's expanded to four locations, each operated by one member of the family. Lorenzo did so well in handling large parties that he was soon called on to cater affairs all over town. Delmonico's was *the* restaurant. In 1881 Lorenzo died, leaving a $2 million estate. Charles, a nephew, took over, but in three years he suffered a nervous breakdown, brought on, it was believed, by overindulgence in the stock market. Other members of the family stepped in and kept the good name of Delmonico's alive.

The senior chef, Charles Ranhofer, also acquired his own reputation, one of the few chefs in this country to do so. His book, *The Epicurean*[5] was considered authoritative. (Lobster à la Newburg was invented at Delmonico's by a Mr. Wenburg. Cruelly, Wenburg was deprived of gastronomic immortality when, after an altercation with one of the Delmonicos, the first three letters in the dish were transposed—lobster à la Wenburg was lost forever.)

Oscar of the Waldorf, whose full name was Oscar Tschirky, got his start at Delmonico's in 1887 as a waiter. Shortly before the old Waldorf opened, enterprising Oscar composed a letter of recommendation for himself on Delmonico's stationery and collected eight pages of signatures from Delmonico's regular customers. It was sufficiently impressive to win him the job of headwaiter at the Waldorf.

In 1910 the last male member of the Delmonico family to run the restaurants died of a heart attack, and Delmonico's began its final slow decline.

The Typical American Style

Although Delmonico's restaurant is to be admired for its subtlety, grace, and service, it will probably remain more of a novelty on the Ameri-

---

5. Charles Ranhofer and R. Ranhofer, *The Epicurean* (New York:), 1900.

Figure 10-1 The dining room of Le Pavillon in New York City. This was considered by many to have been the finest restaurant in the country, some say in the world. The restaurant was created by Henri Soule, who came to America to manage the restaurant in the French exhibit area during the 1939 New York World's Fair. House specialties included poached striped bass, duckling aux pêches, and plume de veau. Unfortunately, the restaurant closed in 1972.

can scene than the norm. While they won the kudos of the day and were the scene of high-style entertaining, there were hundreds of more typical eating establishments transacting business. It has been so ever since.

Only a few cities in this country could, or would, support the kind of high cuisine and prices of Delmonico's. Restaurants in the same tradition, such as Spagos, Antoine's, the Four Seasons, Ernie's, and the Blue Fox, exist only in sophisticated and sizable metropolitan cities. New York City, New Orleans, and San Francisco are the centers of such cookery. These restaurants, of course, influence American cooking, but they constitute a minute part of the U.S. restaurant business.

The gourmet writers are fond of disparaging the average American restaurant, calling it a vulcanizing plant and extolling in contrast the expensive restaurant in the French tradition. It should be pointed out that there is also an American style in restaurants; in fact, several American styles. These are the coffeeshops, fast-food restaurants, cafeterias, family-style restaurants, and good, solid table-service restaurants, all now being copied around the world. They meet the taste,

timetable, and pocketbook of the average American and increasingly that of others elsewhere.

After about 1850, much of the fine eating in this country was found on the riverboats and in railroad dining cars. Dining-car service was among the most elegant and the most expensive, both to the customer and the railroads. The least expensive item on a cross-country train during the middle of the Depression was three stewed prunes priced at 50¢, very high for that time.

Dining service on some of the crack trains was indeed deluxe. Each meal cost the railroad between $1 and $1.50 because of the high labor costs and inefficiency of the dining-car operation. But as on the ocean liners, food service on some of the railroads was considered a prestige operation and promotion cost.

The better known resort hotels and private clubs have always set a fine table, food costs being buried in the cost of the American Plan rate. Many of the finer city hotels were also known for their excellent foodservice.

The public restaurant business grew steadily, but even as late as 1919 there were still only 42,600 restaurants in this country. For the average family in small cities and towns, dining out was an occasion. The workingman's restaurant and the boardinghouse were strictly meat and potatoes. In 1919 the Volstead Act prohibited the sale of alcoholic beverages and forced many restaurants that depended on their liquor sales for profit out of business. It also forced a new emphasis on food-cost control and accounting.

CLASSIFICATION OF RESTAURANTS

There is a great variety of restaurants, and most vary in terms of their:

- Menu items offered and quality of food,

- Menu prices,

- Service, and

- Ambiance.

For example, service in a particular restaurant may include table service, counter service, self-service, takeout service, and/or delivery service.

The NRA classifies all eating establishments into three categories: commercial foodservice, institutional foodservice (the topic of the next chapter), and military foodservice (Table 10-1). Commercial foodservices are distinguished from the others by the fact that they strive to make a profit. Institutional foodservice is a broad segment of business, educational, governmental, or institutional organizations that operate their own foodservice. As compared to commercial foodservice, institutional foodservice does not aim to make money; it simply strives to provide a service. Military foodservice is the smallest segment, with about 1000 foodservice units.

Foodservice contractors (also called contract foodservice companies) are companies that specialize in running the foodservice department of an organization, such as those found in manufacturing and industrial plants. Foodservice contractors usually operate in institutional settings (such as schools and employee foodservice), where they provide a needed service and try to make money. They operate (as of 1991) approximately 80 percent of B&I foodservices, 55 percent of college and university foodservices, 40 percent of healthcare foodservices, 8 percent of school foodservices, and 60 percent of recreation foodservices.

Foodservice contractors operate much like restaurant chains; several are part of commercial

TABLE 10-1   Eating Establishments

Group I—Commercial foodservice

Eating places
Restaurants, lunchrooms
Limited-menu restaurants, refreshment places
Commercial cafeterias
Social caterers
Ice cream, frozen-custard stands
Bars & taverns

Food contractors
Manufacturing & industrial plants
Commercial & office buildings
Hospitals & nursing homes
Colleges & universities
Primary & secondary schools
In-transit foodservice (airlines)
Recreation & sports centers

Lodging places
Hotel restaurants
Motor-hotel restaurants
Motel restaurants
Retail host restaurants
Recreation & sports
Mobile caterers
Vending & nonstore retailers

Group II—Institutional foodservice—Business, educational, governmental, or institutional organizations that operate their own foodservice

Employee foodservice
Public & parochial elementary, secondary schools
Colleges & universities
Transportation
Hospitals
Nursing homes, homes for aged, blind, orphans, and the mentally & physically disabled
Clubs, sporting & recreational camps
Community centers

Group III—Military Foodservice

Officers' & NCO clubs ("Open Mess")
Foodservice—military exchanges

Source: National Restaurant Association

chains. Contractors employ many hospitality program graduates; other graduates may establish their own companies after gaining experience and seek institutional contracts from corporations and educational institutions. Companies like Canteen, ARA, and Marriott are prominent in the field, employing tens of thousands of people. Marriott, for example, which had been largely concerned with hotels and restaurants, has moved into institutional foodservice in a big way through acquisitions of established companies.

ARA Services, the largest of the institutional foodservice companies, experienced $4.2 billion in sales in 1990. In its present form, it is the result of a leveraged buyout by management that took place in 1984. Eighteen percent of the equity went to a 62-man Executive Corps. Based in Philadelphia, the company has 135,000 employees who work in nearly all 50 states. Food and refreshment services account for more than 60 percent of the company revenues. ARA also provides health and education services, periodicals and book distribution, maintenance service, leisure services, and uniform and linen rentals.

Management attributes much of its success to its employee ownership plan, which places the employee in the position of winning or losing along with the fortunes of the company. A retirement plan further joins the employee's interest with that of the company. ARA matches employees' contributions.

The company is expanding into Europe and is the largest foodservice contract company in Japan. In 1990 ARA had a $1.2 billion debt.

Marketing people divide restaurants into three groups according to prices: quick service (about 65 percent), midscale (about 25 percent), and upscale (about 15 percent). Midscale, in turn, is broken down into family style, as represented by Big Boy's, Denny's, and Country Kitchen, and cafeterias, such as Morrisons, Wyatts, and Furrs; so too are most Mexican restaurants and "upscale" hamburger places like Ground Round and Fuddrucker's. Midscale restaurants attract small-householders of age 25 and up who are likely to have had some college education. Such restaurants probably provide a salad bar; guest checks are dropped off at the same time as food, something not done in the usual dinner house.

Another restaurant classification has appeared in the restaurant press, casual dining. This may mean double the price for a "gourmet hamburger" and funky decor, or it could mean something approaching the traditional dinner house but with more pizzazz, à la TGI Friday's. Casual dining probably caters to the 21 to 40-year-old market, has bar sales of 40 percent or more of total

sales, and offers a fairly extensive menu and an imaginative liquor list. Casual dining features quick service compared to the dinner house, a little camp, and some novelty.

Fast service typified by McDonald's has been the steady gainer following World War II and in 1992 comprised more that two-thirds of total restaurant sales. Fast-service domination of the restaurant business, according to NPD Crest, the market research firm that does most of the research for the NRA is changing. The Crest breakdown of restaurant sales is seen in Figure 10-2. In its surveys of the restaurant business in 1991, Crest found fine dining and midscale dining dropping off slightly, with casual dining on the upswing.[6]

So-called value pricing (reduced pricing) kept PepsiCo (Taco Bell, Pizza Hut, KFC) the largest restaurant company in the world in terms of the growing number of units. McDonald's remained the most profitable. Take-out food, even faster than fast food, was taking a healthy bite out of fast-service restaurants. With lower prices, service was self-service. Fine dining (luxury service) was reserved for top executives, representing a special occasion for the general public.

Fast-service chains are indeed big business. For 1991 systemwide sales of the five largest chains in billions of dollars were:

McDonald's	$19.6
Burger King	6.2
KFC	6.1
Pizza Hut	5.3
Hardee's	3.6

The percentage of restaurants operated by the companies themselves varied widely. At McDonald's it was 20 percent compared with 60 percent at Taco Bell. Pizza Hut operated half of its stores and KFC 35 percent. Profits for McDonald's in 1992 topped $1 billion.[7]

Compared to the chains, the independent restaurant is not necessarily small in size or sales volume. *Restaurant and Institutions* magazine in 1987 listed 60 independents that had annual sales exceeding $5 million; 10 had sales of over $10 mil-

6. *Wall Street Journal* (Aug. 15, 1992).
7. "Some High Hurdles Loom for PepsiCo's Fast Food Hotshots," *New York Times* (Feb. 16, 1992).

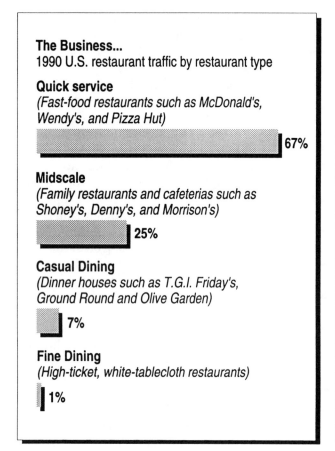

The Business...
1990 U.S. restaurant traffic by restaurant type

Quick service
(Fast-food restaurants such as McDonald's, Wendy's, and Pizza Hut)
67%

Midscale
(Family restaurants and cafeterias such as Shoney's, Denny's, and Morrison's)
25%

Casual Dining
(Dinner houses such as T.G.I. Friday's, Ground Round and Olive Garden)
7%

Fine Dining
(High-ticket, white-tablecloth restaurants)
1%

And the Performance
U.S. restaurant traffic growth rates, by restaurant type, in percent

	1990
Quick service	2%
Midscale	1
Casual Dining	5
Fine Dining	6
Total	2

Figure 10-2 Eating out in America.
Source: NPD Crest, National Restaurant Association.

lion. The Hilltop Steak House in Saugus, Massachusetts, does about $27 million in annual sales.

Various types of eating establishments, offering a continuum of services (Fig. 10-3), will now be discussed.

Fast-food Restaurants

Fast food as defined by the dictionary is simply "food prepared and served quickly." Dispensing food on request, fast and hot, is nothing new. The ancient Romans did it at Pompeii and Herculaneum; the roadside diner did it, the Automats in New York and Philadelphia did it. But it took the franchise, the automobile, and plenty of parking space to make the fast-food business the 1960s phenomenon of the restaurant industry.

The fast-food restaurant, with parking lots and walk-up service, surged during the 1960s and well into the 1980s. McDonald's and KFC led the way with limited menus and national TV advertising. McDonald's advertising suggested that the hamburger was love, family, fun, pure ecstasy. Later, fish sandwiches, cheese sandwiches, and other items were added to its menu.

Many entrepreneurs who flocked to the fast-food banner have been suitably rewarded with millions of dollars. Franchised chains exist within chains, hamburger barons within the hamburger realm. But those who would support king hamburger must not come empty-handed. There are many candidates; few are chosen. Something like $1.2 million is needed to invest in a Burger King or McDonald's.

Chapter 13 covers fast food and franchising in more detail.

The Coffeeshop

Coffeeshops are related to fast-food restaurants in that speed of service is emphasized and they are usually located on or close to a busy highway.

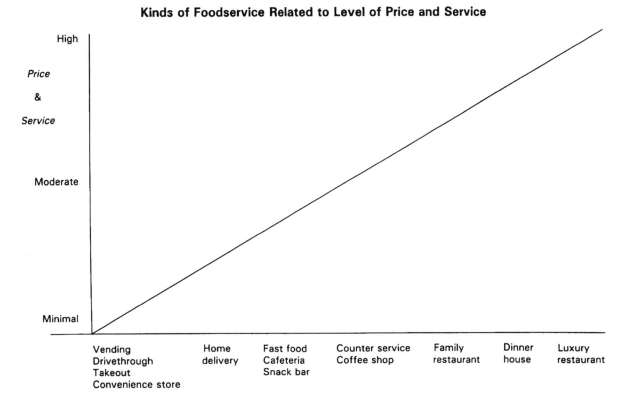

Figure 10-3 Foodservices can be placed on a continuum in terms of the kinds and amounts of service offered and the menu prices charged. The more service given, usually the higher the prices. Price and service also tend to characterize the type of establishment. Walkup, takeout, home delivery, convenience store, and vending are almost devoid of service, which make low menu prices possible. They are not restaurants in the usual sense of the word. Luxury restaurants provide maximun service accompanied by the highest menu prices. In between in price and service are fast-food places, cafeterias, snack bars, and counters. The coffee shop is a combination of counter and booth service. Family restaurants usually offer table service. Dinner houses and luxury restaurants offer white tablecloth service and high prices.

Bob's Big Boy restaurants, the prototype of the coffeeshop, served food from counters and booths as early as 1939 in Glendale, California. Many coffeeshops offer 24-hour service. Late-evening and early-morning trade is slow, but the staff is ready to serve travelers, night workers, or anyone who wants food, drink, or escape from loneliness or boredom at any hour. The night-shift staff is small in number. Average seat turnover is three or four per meal period.

Unlike fast-food places, coffeeshops offer a fairly extensive menu, as well as table, counter, booth, and hostess service. Waiters and waitresses often bus their own tables. There are cooks or cook managers, no chefs. Kitchen employees are usually minority-group members. In the Southwest, California, and Florida they are typically Hispanic, in the South mostly black.

Some coffeeshops are large and can seat up to 200 patrons. The usual one seats between 100 and 150 customers. With more than 1000 stores, Denny's is the largest coffeeshop chain.

Dining areas have a higher level of illumination than the usual full-service restaurant. Built-in, counter-model cooking equipment with refrigerated drawers below and high-velocity ventilators above are characteristic. Elevator-type dispensers for china and automatic coffee brewers are common. Pastries and other desserts are often merchandised in illuminated wall-hung display cases with mirrored backs, usually arranged to face counter seating. Usually, a cashier/hostess station is placed near the entrance so that patrons can be greeted and seating controlled.

Coffeeshops feature the 24-hour breakfast menu: pancakes, eggs, ham, bacon, sausage, and of course, coffee. For lunch and dinner, perhaps seven or eight entrees are featured, mostly grilled items. Some always feature desserts, especially pies.

Coffeeshop markets vary. Some appeal to the affluent, others to the less monied. Depending on location, a particular coffeeshop can cut across several markets. For example, business travelers select coffeeshops after atmosphere and specialty restaurants.

Wendy's, the fast-food hamburger chain that muscled into the limited-menu, fast-service territory, represents the transition from hamburgers, frostys, and fries to something approaching a coffeeshop. The menu was expanded to include fresh salads, specialty sandwiches, dinner platters, and stuffed baked potatoes. The dining area was opened up and wood, brass trim, and hanging plants added. One prototype featured a greenhouse as part of the dining area. A superbar features three all-you-can-eat sections: salad, pasta, and Mexican food bars.

Carl's Jr. is another example of the fast-food *cum* coffeeshop transition. It is also an example of how a transition can go wrong. Carl Jrs. introduced steaks, which complicated the preparation and service so much they had to be withdrawn from the menu. They have since successfully introduced pancakes, broiled chicken breast sandwiches, and salads.

The T.J. Applebee's chain is positioned somewhere between a fast-food operation and a family-style restaurant. Each unit employs about 135 and has annual sales of $1.4 million. Alcohol accounts for 40 percent of sales. Experience is not a factor in hiring. Labor costs, including benefits, stand at a low 20 percent. Service is fast.

Cafeterias

Commercial cafeteria service is highly popular in the South and Midwest. Comparatively little is found in New England, the Mid-Atlantic states, and the West. It is now typically found in industrial foodservice and in schools and colleges.

Vending machines are also widely found in institutional foodservice. A recent trend has been to combine vending with a short cafeteria line to avoid depersonalizing foodservice entirely; customers are likely to find a room that contains only vending machines a lonely place to eat.

The speed at which customers move through a cafeteria is also determined by the way cashiering is done. In a commercial cafeteria, a cashier can handle a maximum of six to eight transactions per minute, usually fewer. A food checker who totals the bill before the customer arrives at the cashier station may double the number of transactions per minute. Free-flow systems, with duplicate sections serving the same foods but separated from each other, allow the free movement of patrons to the least crowded section or where the desired food is located.

There are several basic cafeteria designs, as follow.

Straight-Line System. The straight-line system (Fig. 10-4) is the least expensive small-cafeteria operation and the slowest. Speed of service is determined by the slowest-moving person in line. Attempts have been made to place the customer on a conveyor belt that moves past the counter, but customers have resisted such mechanization. When the line is curved or turned at a 90-degree angle service is slowed even further, but room design often requires the line to be bent one or more times. The speed of any cafeteria line is largely influenced by that of the cashier at the end of the line.

Bypass Line. The serving counter in a bypass line comprises three sections. The first may offer salads, cold sandwiches, and condiments. The recessed center section can be devoted to hot foods. The third may offer desserts and beverages. The bypass line is a variation of the straight line or the sawtooth and keeps customers from becoming part of a slow-moving line by allowing them to move from one section to another at will.

Sawtooth. The sawtooth design (Fig. 10-5), a series of counters set diagonally, made its appearance in the mid-1960s. Each counter serves a particular group of items. It allows customers to bypass the line and move directly to the area of their choice. The design is especially good for a long, narrow room. More than one cashier can be used to speed patron flow.

Free-flow systems. Before the 1930s cafeterias and counters were all straight line in design. The free-flow cafeteria, also called the shopping-center or scramble cafeteria (Fig. 10-6), was intro-

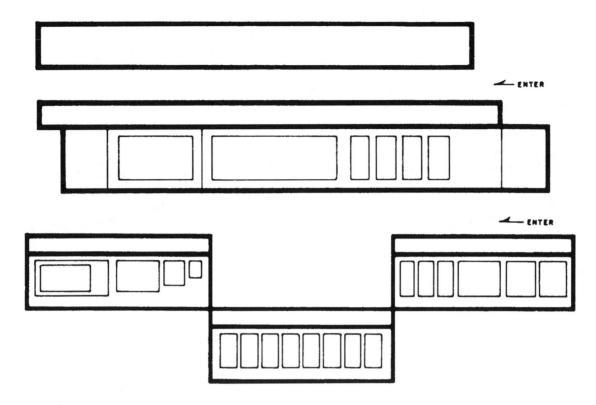

Figure 10-4 Floor plans of two straight-line systems.

duced in the 1930s by the Colonnade Cafeterias and the Grace Smith Restaurants in Toledo, Ohio. In 1947 a scramble cafeteria was introduced at the student union building of Michigan State University. The Western Electric plant in Winston-Salem, North Carolina, offered one of the first shopping-center cafeterias for industrial foodservice in 1951. Since then, the shopping-center cafeteria has become widely used.

In a given amount of square feet, more people can be served in the free-flow cafeteria than in a straight-line operation. Customers are not forced to travel at the speed of the slowest person in the line; they can move about, going to the counter that is least crowded. Once patrons become accustomed to the free flow, they usually like it.

The shopping-center system is like a giant U, or open square. Three sides are serving counters: hot foods on one side, salads and desserts on another, and sandwiches and beverages on the third. Snack bars may be included as part of the scramble. Speed of service is largely determined by the number of cashiers; there should be enough to permit rapid egress from the system. The free-flow system requires greater total area than other systems mentioned.

Cafeterias have been particularly well received by senior citizens, who enjoy selecting only a few items from a great array of foods for a particular meal. The fact that many cafeterias avoid tipping by offering complete self-service is an additional attraction for the eater on a fixed income or low budget.

Successful public cafeterias usually prepare most of their food on the premises, especially those with high sales volume. A number have sales in excess of $2 million a year. Often, a cafeteria does its own baking; a baker begins at 6:00 AM and has its goods ready for service at 11:00 AM. The key to good food is management's insistence that it be freshly cooked in relatively small quantities so that it does not have to remain in the steam pans on the line long enough to dry out and lose quality. Gelatin desserts and salads are not allowed to remain so long on the line that they become rubbery. This can also mean that vegetables are being prepared by pressure steamers more or less continuously during service hours.

Frozen entrees have not been especially popular in cafeteria service because food quality was perceived by customers to be less desirable than that of freshly prepared food. One promi-

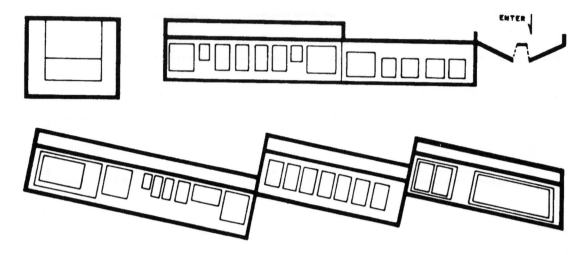

Figure 10-5 Floor plan of a sawtooth system.

nent California chain withdrew from the field after trying to prepare meals in a commissary, freeze them, and serve them later in a number of their cafeterias; they failed.

The Convenience Store

A close relative to the standard fast-food restaurant is the booming convenience-store food service, even faster than a fast-food restaurant. Once confined to selling take-out packaged food, by 1988 30 percent provided in-store dining space for patrons.

Convenience stores began offering a few items in the 1960s. 7-Elevens installed Slurpee machines and then self-service beverage stations. Do-it-yourself milkshakes followed. Now the stores go after the same customers as the fast-food restaurants, offering deli sandwiches, chicken, hot dogs, pizza, and hamburgers. In some stores, sandwiches prepared ahead of time gave way to freshly prepared ones. Some stores have joint-ventured with Church's Fried Chicken.

Moving into the restaurant business, from selling packaged snacks to preparing a few items on premises, has made convenience-store management much more aware of cost accounting than it used to be. Employee scheduling has changed from a shift basis to hourly scheduling.

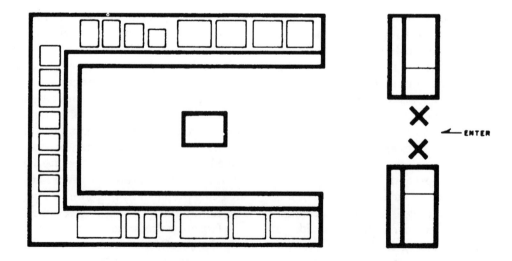

Figure 10-6 Floor plan of a free-flow system.

Extra employees are needed during rush periods and for the minimal food preparation required.

Competition between convenience stores and conventional fast-food restaurants is likely to increase as the fast mover, the impulse buyer, and the person who does not want to cook at home purchases food where it is most easily available and least expensive.

Take-out Service

Full-service restaurants are partially meeting the challenge of foodservice provided by convenience stores, supermarkets, and drive-through restaurants by offering take-out service. They use their present equipment, often the same employees, make little or no additional investment; some have doubled sales volume and increased profit margins. Menu items are those not easily prepared at home; they are different or even upscale from items that can be served easily to guests invited to a home. The take-out meal from a fast-food restaurant may be superior to a frozen dinner bought at the supermarket.

Not ordinarily thought of as a separate style of service, takeout grows in importance as families become smaller, more people live as singles, and the number of two-income families increases. The fast pace of life makes eating in a car or taking precooked food home increasingly acceptable. Microwave ovens in the home render reheating quick and easy.

Take-out service is nothing new. It is as old as the snack bars of ancient Rome. Certainly, the cooking houses of thirteenth-century London and Paris were take-out houses. Short-order restaurants—the drive-in and diner—all evolved in the take-out tradition. Chicken restaurants—notably, KFC—have popularized takeout. By the 1980s almost every fast-food hamburger restaurant had installed a drive-through window, which increased its total sales without requiring significant additional capital investment. One of the reasons for pizza's popularity is that it can be ordered by phone and picked up by one person, taken home, and served to any number of people, still fairly hot and tasty.

From the operator's viewpoint, takeout has a number of advantages:

1. The patrons supply their own seating and dining room space, either in their car or at home.

2. Kitchen space is minimized because of the characteristically limited menu offering.

3. Labor cost is low compared to places offering more service.

4. Few food and beverage skills are required.

5. Because of its simplicity, the restaurant with a limited take-out menu is comparatively easy to manage and maintain with teenaged employees.

6. The capital investment required is minimal compared with a full-service restaurant.

7. In areas of high security risks, having only a take-out window reduces the possibility of robbery. (Some restaurants close their doors to seating during late evening hours.)

Good take-out locations are not cheap. Mall locations are not that convenient for the customer, and good freestanding locations are expensive.

The customer sees takeout as meeting the requirements of economy, speed, and diversion. (The family can sit down together for a meal.) The working wife, it is said, experiences less or no guilt in taking home a cooked meal.

The major drawback of takeout is the fact that once food is cooked it falls off rapidly in quality. The longer it is held, the less appetizing it becomes. One of its positives—no tipping—is lost when it is delivered to the house because the delivery person, like the waiter or waitress, expects a tip.

Takeout is probably more expensive than similar food bought from a supermarket freezer. It is no substitute for the dining experience, where one is served by attentive and attractive waiters and waitresses. Unless the menu offers more than a few items, the food available can quickly become boring. How often does anyone want fried chicken, spaghetti, or pizza?

The popularity of take-out food for certain markets is well established. It has moved from being limited to fried chicken and hamburgers to include extensive, expensive meals that can be put on a credit card, as well as a variety of ethnic foods, such as Japanese sushi and French escargot.

Home Delivery

What happens when a person arrives home from work too tired to cook, but is hungry and wants to stay at home and perhaps watch the TV or a tape? Enter home delivery.

Home delivery has probably been around before corned beef and cabbage was delivered to Irish workmen in Boston about 1850, but it remained for Domino's Pizza to show its true potential. Tom Monaghan, the founder, spent 25 years finetuning his system of home delivery. He then astonished the restaurant world by building sales that in 1987 exceeded $2 billion. The company has about 10,000 stores in the U.S. and Canada; two-thirds are franchised, the rest company owned and operated. The keys for home delivery success are speed of delivery, food quality, and employee spirit. Domino's delivers in about 23 minutes. Food quality is monitored and tested continually. Company spirit is evidenced in its slogan, PEP: passion, enthusiasm, and pride.

"Mystery shoppers," members of the general public, evaluate and record the pizza's temperature and taste and note the delivery time on a form, which is sent to the Ann Arbor, Michigan company headquarters. These mystery shoppers receive a free pizza per month for their services.

The rapid growth of the chain is aided by encouraging employees, typically 18 to 24 years old, to take on a franchise. The franchise fee is low, and the company will help finance it. Franchisees must serve as a manager for a year. Another factor in rapid growth is that stores can be located anywhere, since the customer never sees them.

Successful home delivery requires as much or more of a system and simplicity than a regular restaurant. Time is on the side of a system, and time governs home delivery: order-taking, food preparation, routing instructions for delivery, and cash management. At Domino's all of these functions are accomplished in less than 30 minutes. Personnel organization is minimal; pizza crews are divided into five basic jobs: order-taker, pizza maker, oven-tender, router, and driver. If you cross-train all your employees, you begin to see how a 30-minute deadline is possible.

The number of elements crucial to home delivery is smaller than in a full-scale restaurant, and each element is worked and reworked to maximize customer satisfaction and minimize production and delivery time. Domino's tested more than 50 different designs for delivery boxes. The choice was an "ortabox," an eight-sided box that uses 10 percent less cardboard, costs 1¢ less, and holds the pizza 2 to 3 degrees warmer. It is easier to discard because it has no sharp points protruding. The Domino's menu is simplicity itself: pizza and cola. Storage space in Domino's stores is kept to a minimum by the delivery of supplies three times a week from a commissary.

Home delivery has recently taken a new turn: the delivery of complete meals by companies that do not prepare the meals. Several companies have been set up that contract with existing restaurants to home-deliver their meals. The restaurants make no investment; the sales from home delivery are merely add-ons to regular sales. Delivery trucks usually have separate heated and refrigerated sections. Hot food is undercooked at the restaurant and continues to cook at 1858F en route to the customer. Home delivery is especially appealing during bad weather—appealing to customers because they do not have to leave home, appealing to the restaurant that participates and might otherwise experience low sales volume.

Luncheon delivery to corporate offices is another market. Luncheon delivery is popular if no in-house foodservice is offered. Even when in-house foodservices are available, luncheon delivery is popular for a change of pace or special meetings and events.

RESTAURANT ORGANIZATION AND FUNCTIONS

A restaurant, be it a one-man snack bar or a luxury restaurant with 100 employees, must perform these functions:

Purchase food and beverages

Receive, store, and issue food and beverages

Prepare food

Serve food and beverages

Directing, coordinating, and supporting these functions are:

Management

Accounting and control

Marketing and public relations

These functions and activities can be related to each other and brought together to form a simple restaurant organization chart, an example of which is seen in Figure 10-7.

In a large restaurant the functions are further divided among more jobs, as seen in Figure 10-8.

WHY PEOPLE EAT OUT

People eat out for a variety of reasons: to satisfy hunger, social needs, and ego and self-fulfillment needs. The most popular theory of motivation, that proposed by A. H. Maslow, states that humans are wanting animals. As soon as one need is satisfied, another appears to take its place, moving from the need for safety or security up the scale through social, ego, and self-fulfillment. People go to restaurants to satisfy not only hunger but also self-esteem, self-respect, self-confidence, and prestige needs. They select a restaurant because of particular psychological needs at the moment, the way they are feeling about the money they have to spend, the prices of a restaurant, its service, how the restaurant is perceived in terms of its aesthetics, social status, and the kind of people that can be expected to be there (patrons, management, and employees).

A person may eat at a stand-up snack bar to satisfy a hunger or physiological need, but will select varying styles of restaurants to meet social needs, and finally will go to the high-priced places for reasons of self-esteem and self-fulfillment.

Disposable Income and Restaurant Sales

Aside from all of the reasons why people find pleasure in eating out, there is the problem of having the money to do so. Discretionary income is the key here. It is the income left over after expenses are met that can be used as one sees fit. As disposable income increases, so too does the amount of money spent in eating and drinking places. The greater the family income, the greater the proportion of it that is spent in restaurants.

As more women have entered the work force and increased both family income and disposable income, restaurant visits have increased.

RESTAURANT CHAINS

Fast-food restaurants, those offering simplified menus and highly standardized service, training, and decor, are dominated by chains. One source

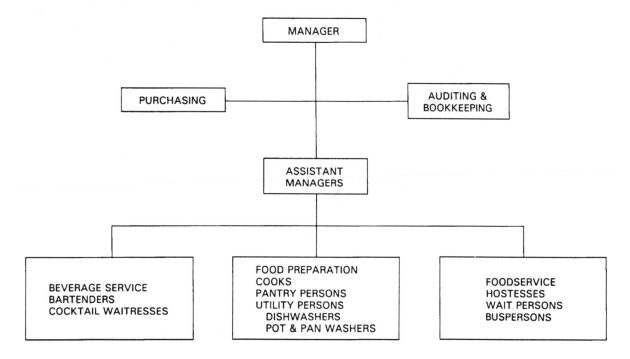

Figure 10-7 Basic organization of a restaurant.

PURCHASING AGENT AND STOREROOM SUPERVISOR Orders, receives, inspects, and stores all food for distribution to the different food departments. Must be capable of managing an inventory and keeping track of current market prices. This job is sometimes the responsibility of the manager or chef.

FOOD PRODUCTION MANAGER Responsible for all food preparation and supervision of kitchen staff. Must have thorough knowledge of food preparation and good food standards. Should know how to work with and supervise people.

PANTRY SUPERVISOR Supervises salad, sandwich, and beverage workers. Should be able to create attractive food arrangements. May be in charge of requisitioning supplies and supervising cleaning crew.

CHEF AND COOK Prepares and portions all foods served. In large restaurant operations, job can be highly specialized with individual cooks or chefs responsible for a single product category such as vegetables, cold meats, soups, sauces, and short orders.

BEVERAGE WORKER Prepares hot beverages such as coffee, tea, or hot chocolate. May assist in the pantry and help others in the kitchen during rush hours. It is a good beginning position.

KITCHEN HELPER Assists the cooks, chefs, and bakers by performing supervised tasks. It is a good entry job for the individual who wants to learn food preparation, because the kitchen helper is busy measuring, mixing, washing and chopping vegetables and salad ingredients.

SANDWICH MAKER Does basically what the name implies, but also is involved in preparing fillings and dressings. This position is an opportunity for a quick, careful worker who may find the job has a touch of creativity. Skills acquired here will help the individual to move to a better-paying position.

SANITATION/MAINTENANCE WORKER Maintains clean cooking utensils, equipment, walls, and floors. In most modern restaurants, dishwashers and other machines simplify part of the job. This behind-the-scenes position allows the individual to study the various kitchen duties before choosing a particular job or direction for the future. This category includes porters, dishwashers, and potwashers.

PASTRY CHEF AND BAKER Bakes cakes, cookies, pies and other desserts. Bakes bread, rolls, quick breads. In some restaurants, must also be skilled in cake decorating.

RESTAURANT MANAGER Coordinates and directs the entire operation to assure efficient quality, courteous food service. Works through supervisory personnel, but in smaller restaurants may directly supervise kitchen and dining room staffs. Must know all of the details involved in every restaurant job.

BOOKKEEPER Audits guests' checks. May compute daily cash intake, operating ratios, deposits money in bank, and maintain financial records.

ASSISTANT MANAGER Performs specific supervisory duties under the manager's direction. Generally takes over in the manager's absence. Must be thoroughly familiar with the entire operation and have good management skills.

DINING ROOM MANAGER Coordinates dining room activities, trains and supervises host/hostess, waiters, waitresses, busboys and busgirls. Should possess leadership qualities, objectivity, and fairness.

CASHIER Receives payment for food and beverage sold. May total check. Must be personable, quick at mental arithmetic, and completely honest.

HOST/HOSTESS Takes reservations. Keeps informed on current and upcoming table reservations. May present menu and introduce waitperson. Should be attractive, friendly, able to maintain composure when restaurant is busy.

WAITER-CAPTAIN Supervises and coordinates activities of dining room employees, performing in a formal atmosphere. May be responsible for scheduling hours and shifts and keeping employees' time records and assigning work stations.

WAITPERSON Takes food orders and serves the foods to customers. These key employees must like people, be poised and have good self-control, be able to coordinate and respond to many requests made at almost the same time. The individual must move quickly and accurately. Many people make this a career position.

BUSPERSON Clears the table, resets it with fresh linen and eating utensils, fills water glasses, and helps in other housekeeping chores in the dining area. A fine way to start learning the business.

estimates that they control about 90 percent of hamburger sales. Over 80 percent of pizza and ice cream sales are in the hands of the chains.

Chain participation in the full-menu segment of the market is much less, and for a fairly obvious reason. The more complex the menu, the more difficult it is to standardize and control and the more managerial knowledge and skills are needed. It is comparatively simple to develop a fast-food concept for hamburgers or pizza, lay out the plans and format of operation, and train relatively inexperienced managers and workers to operate it. A full-service restaurant is something else. It requires a greater range of knowledge and managerial know-how.

America's first big chain operator was Fred Harvey, originally from England. His first eating house opened in Topeka, Kansas, in 1876. By 1912 he was operating a dozen large hotels, 65 railway station restaurants, and 60 dining cars. He provided foodservice for the Santa Fe Railroad.

A man of enterprise and imagination, Harvey sent an envoy to Guaymas and Hermosillo in Mexico to get fruit, green vegetables, shellfish, and other foods. Turtle steaks and green turtle soup were a house specialty; sea celery was used for salad. A contract was made with the chief of the Yaquí Indians to supply green turtles and sea celery. The price was right. The Indians were paid $1.50 for each turtle weighing 200 pounds and full of eggs.

The Fred Harvey restaurants were models of efficiency; train passengers were served well in minimum time. When patrons disembarked, they were immediately asked their choice of beverage. Waitresses placed a coded cup on the table and a "drink girl" followed, "magically" pouring the patron's preferred beverage without his or her even asking.

The Fred Harvey Company had one unexpected major impact in the Southwest—Fred Harvey Girls, who had been brought to the area as waitresses, married there, and settled down.

John R. Thompson was another early large-chain operator. Thompson, a young storekeeper, and his wife left the little town of Fithian, Illinois, in 1893 with $800 and purchased a small restaurant in Chicago; soon he owned three units. Like every successful entrepreneur, Thompson cast about for a better way of doing things. He switched from the service-style restaurant to a one-arm dairy lunch, one of the first self-service restaurants. Customers walked up to a serving counter where they picked up their food and carried it back to a schoolroom type of chair, the arm used as a tray. By 1926 there were 126 one-armed dairy lunches in the Midwest and South. By the 1940s the dairy luncheons had changed to straight-line cafeterias or were sold.

Thompson was probably the first restaurateur to use a central commissary for the preparation of food; delivery was by electric truck. Part of his success can be accounted for by the fact that the labor cost of the day was 15 percent of gross sales.

Another chain that began in the nineteenth century was Horn & Hardart Restaurants in New York City and Philadelphia, two separate corporations. Joe Horn, with $1000 in capital, and Tom Hardart, a luncheon waiter, started the business in 1888. In 1898 they introduced the Automat, paying $30,000 for the German invention. These were a kind of grand vending machine; Automats had their day and are now closed.

Child's restaurants was the largest chain in the world during the 1920s. It pioneered food-cost analysis, breaking down all food purchases into categories and developing standard ratios for each category. Centered in New York City, the chain operated 150 units and did about $28 million in sales. Then, in the 1930s, Child's president became fascinated with vegetables because of their health value and low cost. The public was less fascinated, and the chain did not change with the times. By the 1950s the chain almost went bankrupt and was bought, largely as a tax-loss investment, by A. M. Sonnabend, principal owner of Hotel Corporation of America (now called Sonesta).

Stouffer's, a well-known table-service restaurant chain in the country, started in 1924 as a $12,000 lunch counter in Cleveland. Mother Stouffer baked the pies that were sold. Dad and his two sons helped run the restaurant.

The company operates restaurants situated on the uppermost floor of large buildings in major cities. It also operates Stouffer's hotels and a prepared frozen-food division. Today, it is a subsidiary of Nestlé, a Swiss-based corporation, and the Stouffer family is no longer a part of management.

The Marriott Corporation and Howard Johnson's company, covered earlier in this book, both started in the 1920s.

Advantages of the Chain

Once it has established itself, the chain has several advantages over the independent operator, advantages that chain management often neglects to use. With its larger resources, the chain can more readily establish credit and take out long-term leases on land and buildings. Perhaps the biggest advantage is that it can afford to make more mistakes than the independent operator; one serious error and the independent is likely to go bankrupt.

Manufacturers and Food Processors Enter the Business

Beginning in 1967 a number of large food manufacturers and processors entered the restaurant business. It is only surprising that they had not done so before. Most of the large food manufacturers have separate divisions set up especially to market their products to the institutional food trade, which includes restaurants.

The Pillsbury Company bought Burger King Corporation and itself is now British-owned. Pet, Inc. bought the Schrafft's Restaurants and Motor Inns. The company also runs the Steak and Ale chain.

General Mills owns over 500 Red Lobster Inns and York Steakhouses. Quaker Oats has the Magic Pan Restaurants.

In 1977 PepsiCo bought Pizza Hut for $300 million in stock and in 1986 bought KFC, making it the largest in number of units of all restaurant chains.

In the 1970s chain acquisition grew rapidly. Large conglomerates bought dozens of established restaurant chains. Some of the purchases by food companies, however, have not worked out well; one was a disaster. In 1972 General Foods reported that it had lost $89 million, mostly on Burger Chef since its acquisition in 1968. The reasons were lack of knowledge about the fast-food field, rapid expansion, and excessive prices paid for some Chef locations.

The food manufacturing companies' entrance into foodservice marks a decided change in the character of the restaurant business: These companies bring capital, management know-how, and computer technology with them.

The restaurant business provides these companies with controlled sales outlets for their products. Their restaurants can be used as testing stations for food products. Even more important, the food companies have access to capital for acquiring sites for new restaurants and buying existing ones.

Foreign Ownership

In the 1970s foreign-owned companies began buying U.S. restaurant chains. Nestlé Alementana of Switzerland bought Stouffer's, the Rusty Scuppers, and the Jaques Borel Group. Trust House Forte of England bought Colony Kitchens and Hobo Joe's. Howard Johnson's was purchased by the Imperial Group Ltd., also of Great Britain, and later sold to Marriott, who also sold it. The ice cream chain of Baskin-Robbins was bought by another English firm, the huge J. Lyon & Co. Ltd. of London. Interstate United Corporation was acquired by Hanson Trust of Great Britain.

In the past, a large number of U.S. restaurant companies expanded into Canada. In the 1970s the Canadians returned the favor and about 20 Canadian restaurant firms expanded into the U.S. The Swiss are represented in ownership by Wienerwald Holding, a company that acquired Lum's, the International House of Pancakes, Ranch House, and Love's Copper Penny. By 1991 more than 100 U.S. foodservice companies were operating abroad.[8]

A major difference exists between U.S. restaurant representation abroad and foreign operation in this country. U.S. companies license and rarely invest; risk is minimal or nill. Foreign representation exist here in the form of investment—and the risk can be high.

A HIGH-RISK BUSINESS

One of the riskiest of businesses, many more commercial restaurants fail than succeed. The NRA reports that about 50 percent of new restaurants fail in their first year, 65 percent within 2 years. According to the Small Business Administration, only one of ten persons who start as restaurant owners are in business after 5 years.

Behind every person who likes to cook, enjoys being with people, and wants to make money lurks a would-be restaurateur. The restau-

---

8. *Arizona Hospitality Trends* (Winter 1990–1991).

rant business exerts a fatal fascination on hundreds who should never consider being restaurant owners or operators. The roads and streets of America are dotted with former restaurants that held the hopes and aspirations, and sometimes the fortunes, of such people. Every potential operator should consider that he or she is more likely to fail than succeed.

The independent restaurant operator is hard put to compete with the huge resources of several of the chain restaurants. The Olive Garden restaurant chain, an Italian concept owned by General Mills, is a case in point. Planning for the Olive Garden began in 1979, but the concept did not spread nationally until 1986 or report a profit until 1989. In 1990 it had 173 units and was growing at 50 units a year.

The large chains can afford to reduce prices, even take a loss, in order to gain market share and often squeeze out competitors. PepsiCo Inc.'s Taco Bell chain in 1990 dropped taco prices to 49¢ or 50¢ depending on the market, from 79¢, which forced its competitors to reduce prices at a rate many of them could simply not afford.

It is clear that the restaurant business keeps in step with the economy, especially the local economy. The big financial winners have been the chains, including the franchisors, with regional and national marketing clout and programs for purchasing, cost controls, and personnel training. Television advertising has had widespread and potent influence in marketing success.

NUTRITION AND RESTAURANTS[9]

Nutritional concerns, especially those known to be related to heart disease, some types of cancer, high blood pressure, and being overweight, are seen in menu modification. Figure 10-9 visually demonstrates current dietary guidelines. Studies conducted by the National Restaurant Association showed that the percentage of customers who want menu items served in restaurants that contain reduced fat, sugar, and cholesterol is increasing. Demand for chicken and seafood items continues to rise. In fact, two-thirds of all seafood is eaten in restaurants. Seafood is expected to con-

tinue its popularity in restaurants partly because most of it is low in cholesterol and sodium and, compared to other animal foods, low in fat and rich in the highly polyunsaturated omega-3 fatty acids, which may prevent heart attacks. Public awareness of what constitutes healthful food has prompted restaurants to offer more broiled, poached, and steamed items. Kentucky Fried Chicken changed its name to KFC, to divert attention from the word *fried* in its original name. Animal fats being used were changed to "100 percent vegetable oil." McDonald's also changed its cooking oil for potatoes from animal fat, high in cholesterol, to 100 percent vegetable oil, which is cholesterol free.

McDonald's also publishes a nutritional breakdown of all of its menu items. (This is somewhat ironic in that McDonald's has for years paraded the "billions" of hamburgers served in its restaurants over the years; some nutritionists claim that the hamburger is America's number one nutritional offender with its highly saturated fat content.) Ecologists point out that cattle are ecological disasters because they require excessive amounts of food to produce a pound of meat.

In McDonald's favor it must be said that it has tried offering a hamburger with only 9 percent animal fat, a product that has not proved popular.

A National Restaurant Association survey found that adults surveyed could be divided into three groups, each with its own characteristics. First there are the "unconcerned," who eat whatever they want and account for 32 percent of consumers. This group is likely to be males, 18 to 24, single, average income earners, and living in the Midwest. They tend to choose fast-food restaurants for eating out.

The next group is the "committed," those customers who are concerned with health and make healthy food choices. Representing 39 percent of consumers, they are likely to be females, 35 to 54, college graduates, high-income earners, and living in the Northeast or on the West Coast. Table-service restaurants tend to be their choice for eating out.

The last group is the "vacillators," customers who say they are health and nutritious conscious, but who don't generally make nutritious food choices. They represent about 29 percent of consumers and are slightly more likely to be female, over 65, below-average income earners, and living in the southeastern and southwestern states.

9. Sections are excerpted from Karen Eich Drummond, *Nutrition for the Foodservice Professional, 2nd Ed.* (New York: Van Nostrand Reinhold), 1993.

The Food Guide Pyramid
A Guide to Daily Food Choices

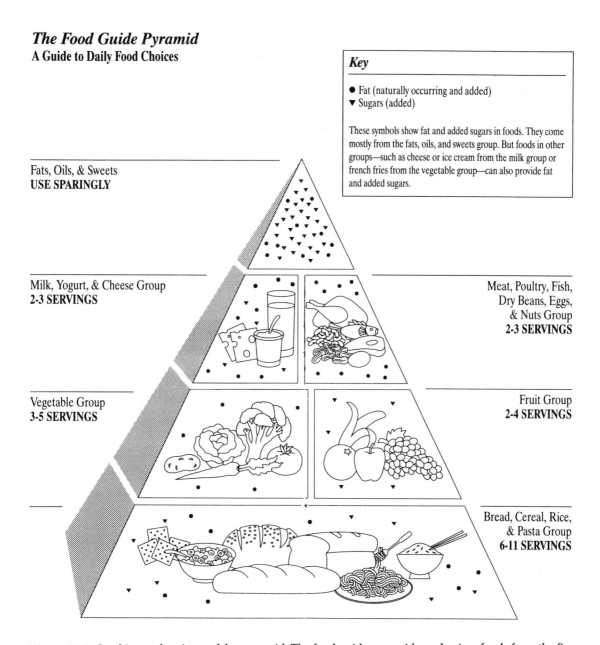

Key

● Fat (naturally occurring and added)
▼ Sugars (added)

These symbols show fat and added sugars in foods. They come mostly from the fats, oils, and sweets group. But foods in other groups—such as cheese or ice cream from the milk group or french fries from the vegetable group—can also provide fat and added sugars.

Fats, Oils, & Sweets
USE SPARINGLY

Milk, Yogurt, & Cheese Group
2-3 SERVINGS

Meat, Poultry, Fish,
Dry Beans, Eggs,
& Nuts Group
2-3 SERVINGS

Vegetable Group
3-5 SERVINGS

Fruit Group
2-4 SERVINGS

Bread, Cereal, Rice,
& Pasta Group
6-11 SERVINGS

Figure 10-9 Looking at the pieces of the pyramid. The food guide pyramid emphasizes foods from the five major food groups shown in the three lower sections of the pyramid. Each of these food groups provides some, but not all, of the nutrients you need. Foods in one group can't replace those in another. No one of these major food groups is more important than another—for good health, you need them all.

Source: USDA and U.S. Department of Health and Human Services.

Survey results clearly show that interest in nutritious dining is not a fad. Demographics also explains the interest in nutrition. With the graying of America, there are more older restaurant customers, traditionally more health and nutrition conscious. The baby boom generation has also had a greater-than-average interest in nutrition when dining out.

A growing number of foodservice operators are offering nutritious choices in their restaurants. A National Restaurant Association survey showed that almost all table-service restaurants will alter the preparation method on request, serve sauce or salad dressing on the side, cook without salt, and cook with vegetable oil or margarine instead of butter or shortening. Almost half the adults surveyed said they were comfortable asking for specially prepared foods when they go out to eat.

Most operators offer sugar substitutes, diet beverages, and caffine-free beverages. Half of the operators or more offer fresh fruit for dessert, whole grain breads or crackers, and margarine. Table 10-2 shows some nutritious choices being offered by quick-service and family-dining restaurants in 1990.

Operators generally have three choices in developing nutritious menu items:

- *Use existing items on your menu.* Certain menu selections, such as fresh vegetable salads or roasted chicken, may already meet U.S. Dietary Guidelines.

- *Modify existing items to make them more nutritious.* For example, offer fish broiled with a small amount of vegetable oil or margarine rather than butter, or use herbs and spices instead of salt to season vegetables. In general, modification centers around decreasing fat (which also decreases calories), cholesterol, and sodium.

- *Create new selections.* Currently, there are many light and nutritious cookbooks on the market, mostly for the consumer. There is even a *Cooking Light* magazine!

TABLE 10-2   Nutritious Choices Offered by Quick-Service and Family-Dining Restaurants

Menu Items	1990 Results (of Restaurants Surveyed)
Decaffeinated coffee	89%
Entree salads and/or salad bars	78
Skinless poultry items	78
Reduced- or low-calorie salad dressing	74
Margarine	67
Grilled chicken sandwich	59
Whole-grain breads or muffins	48
Fresh fruit (including on salad bars)	48
Decaffeinated soda	41
Low-fat frozen yogurt	33
Low-fat/low-cholesterol mayonnaise	30
Low-fat/low-calorie fruit-based dessert	30
Egg substitutes	22

Source: National Restaurant Association

An example of a successful nutritious dining program is St. Andrew's Cafe, located at the Culinary Institute of America in Hyde Park, New York. St. Andrew's Cafe is a 60-seat public restaurant featuring healthful eating. All complete meals (including appetizer, salad, roll, butter, entree, dessert, and beverage) contain less than 900 calories and are lower in fat, cholesterol, and sodium than most meals in white tablecloth restaurants. All C.I.A. students are required to work in St. Andrews for 7 days, both in the front and back of the house.

St. Andrew's Cafe takes a low-key marketing approach with regard to its nutrition program. The only mention of it to customers is on the back of the menu. The approach, which has been quite successful, is designed to position the restaurant as upscale.

Several rules with regard to food preparation at St. Andrew's are:

Use ingredients that are fresh.

Meat is lean and well-trimmed.

Healthful cooking techniques, such as steaming and broiling, are used.

Most interesting, almost all foods are used, including butter and cream, but in moderation. For example, for chocolate bread pudding, just enough cocoa is used to give the dessert a chocolate flavor, and a small amount of whipped cream garnishes it. Attractiveness and taste are of prime concern, as is the job of ensuring a nutritious dining experience.

Successful nutritious dining programs, such as St. Andrew's, follow some basic guidelines:

1. Nutritious menu items need first to be delicious, second to be attractive, and only third to be nutritious. In other words, if the food does not taste delicious and look out of this world, then no matter how nutritious it may be, it is not going to sell.

2. Nutritious selections need to blend with and complement the menu concept. For example, a self-service salad bar with plenty of fresh vegetables and reduced calorie salad dressings may be appropriate for a fast-food or family restaurant or institutional cafeteria, but probably not for a white tablecloth operation. Nutritious items should not dominate a

menu, as only a minority of customers will order from it.

3. Menu items need to be creative and convey a desirable image. The old-fashioned diet plate of a hamburger, no roll, with cottage cheese and a canned pear is neither novel, desirable, or nutritious!

4. A successful restaurant nutrition program starts with only two to four entrees and one to two appetizers and desserts. Start simply, with only a few quality items. Then evaluate the success of the program to see if it is worth expanding. On the average, 15 to 20 percent of orders come from this section of the menu, and selection of rich desserts has been increasing.

5. Luncheon customers who are businesspeople are likely to be interested in low-calorie foods. Dinner customers may be out for social reasons and want to indulge in a heavier meal.

6. All new recipes need to be tested and evaluated by staff and management.

7. Nutritious menu selections have to make money just like every other selection on the menu. A thorough cost analysis should be done on each item and prices set accordingly.

The move towards the "healthier" calorie-counting menu has been relatively slow in making its appearance across the country, and its popularity may never be great in places like truck stops and the typical working man's restaurant, where calories are a sissy word. Athletes may consume 6000 calories a day, and growing adolescents seem to have bottomless stomachs. The hamburger—the most popular food in America—is likely to be around for some time. The least the restaurant operator can do is to include one or two items that are low fat and low cholesterol on the menu; items can be starred that are recommended by the American Heart Association. As the mass media carries information about the association of nutrition and disease, more customers will appreciate restaurants that offer at least a few "healthy" choices. The mass media and food advertising will probably continue to

market "light," non-fat, low-fat, and low-cholesterol products that heighten interest in the menu items with these qualities. Who knows where "light" foods will go now that there is a non-fat margarine?

TRADE AND PROFESSIONAL RESTAURANT ORGANIZATIONS

Numerous state and local trade and professional organizations relating to the foodservice industry have been formed over the years. Some are specialized, such as the American Culinary Federation, whose members are primarily chefs. Others are more general in character, such as the Food Service Executives' Association, with chapters here and abroad. Membership represents supervision, management, and ownership in the foodservice industry.

Some organizations are concerned primarily with fraternal social functions; others have been formed largely to deal with unions. Still others, such as the NRA and the various state associations, are concerned with affecting legislation favorable to the industry and in preventing passage of unfavorable legislation. The NRA, headquartered in Washington, D.C., conducts an active educational program, including seminars offered around the country and the operation of an active book department and research library.

The various state restaurant associations are not affiliated with the NRA. Some are very strong and effective, such as the California Restaurant Association. The strength and effectiveness of the associations depend in a large part on their funds. Those that must rely completely on membership fees are not very effective. The NRA, on the other hand, receives much of its funding from profits made by conducting an annual trade show in Chicago. The California Restaurant Association receives similar funding from trade shows held in Los Angeles and San Francisco. Trade shows make possible the exhibition of new food products, kitchen equipment, and a vast array of other products of interest to the foodservice operator. The fact that the expenses of attendance can be written off for tax purposes adds to the attractiveness of the shows.

Other professional foodservice associations are listed on page 359 and 360.

THE RESTAURANT: FOR THE ENTREPRENEUR

Despite the massive growth of the restaurant chain, the restaurant business is still a stronghold of free enterprise in the U.S. Few businesses can be entered so easily with so little capital, and success or failure be seen so quickly. Operators who have assessed the market correctly and put together the right menu and format of operation win big; those who are wrong, fail.

There are plenty of chains and franchisors, but anyone can join them with determination, know-how, and luck. The restaurateur, the small businessperson, is still free to come up with a new design, a new recipe, or a new market approach and must do so periodically to win.

An advertising slogan of Jack-in-the-Box's, "Watch out, McDonald's," can be applied to hundreds of restaurant owners. What goes well in the East may fail in the West, and vice versa. A restaurant flourishes, may proliferate into a chain, become stagnant, and be overtaken by a fresh format, a better market fix, a different sandwich, or a menu mix better tuned to a particular market. The restaurant business in the U.S. is challenging and changing—bringing wealth or vast disappointment to its practitioners.

Questions

1. Would you say that restaurants with sales in excess of $3 million a year are a rarity? Explain.

2. List at least three principal reasons why the restaurant business has grown so much since World War II.

3. It has been said that there are fewer restaurants today than there were 20 years ago. Is this true? Explain.

4. About 30 percent of all the employees in the restaurant business are teenagers. What does this imply for restaurant management and labor costs?

5. What was the original meaning of the word "restaurant"?

6. Fred Harvey, an Englishman, figures in the history of the American restaurant in what way?

7. Name at least two advantages and two disadvantages of being part of a chain.

8. Most recent hotel and restaurant graduates tend to shy away from institutional foodservice. What advantages does such foodservice offer over a commercial restaurant unit or chain?

9. What advantages does the free-flow system have over other styles of cafeteria service?

10. Why is it that hospital foodservice is so much more complicated than that in a restaurant?

11. What is the name of the trade association that represents restaurants nationally?

12. All the various state hotel associations automatically belong to the American Hotel and Motel Association. Do the state restaurant associations automatically belong to the national association?

13. If we refer to Maslow's theory of motivation, a person who patronizes a very expensive restaurant does so to satisfy what basic needs?

14. According to the same theory, a person patronizing a coffeeshop does so for what reasons?

15. If you had to identify but one factor that correlates most highly with the number of people eating out in the U.S., what would that factor be: disposable income, unemployment rate, or rate of savings?

16. Which of these factors probably accounts for more of the increase in eating out than any other: the working woman, smaller family, smaller living spaces for the family, or more self-indulgence on the part of Americans?

Discussion Questions

1. Relatively few luxury restaurants exit. What is the future of the luxury restaurant? Give you reasons.

2. Of the several types of restaurants, which will be the big money maker of the 1990s? What will it be like? What menu will it offer?

3. Why is the restaurant failure rate so high in this country?

4. Institutional food service is often overlooked by the hotel and restaurant graduate. Why?

Louis Szathmary

Few American chefs have been in the public eye long enough or written extensively enough to leave a lasting mark on the foodservice industry. Louis Szathmary, proprietor of the Bakery restaurant in Chicago, is an exception. A culinary bibliophile, he has collected one of the largest such libraries anywhere. He is the most colorful of the current generation of chef/restaurant operators.

Chef Louis, at various times actor, journalist, and psychologist, immigrated to this country from Austria in 1951. After a few futile attempts to find a job elsewhere, Szathmary accepted an offer from the New England Province of the Jesuit order to cook in a retreat house for semiretired priests on Manresa Island off Norwalk, Connecticut. The salary was low and the hours 6 AM to 6 PM, but room and board came with it. For Szathmary it represented a great offer. He was the only Hungarian on an island where no one spoke anything but English and he was forced to learn it as quickly as possible. He also had to learn and master the differences between European and American cooking.

In the mid-1950s, Chef Louis (as he was called by all who could not pronounce his Hungarian family name) became the private dining-room chef for Thomas O'Neill, president of the Mutual Broadcasting System. His job was to give small, intimate lunches for VIPs from every segment of American society.

Compared to the 6 AM to 6 PM shift with the Jesuits coupled with his night job at a diner, this five-day-week, six-hour-day job preparing lunch for four or six people seemed like heaven. It also gave Szathmary a great opportunity to roam the streets of Manhattan and read every menu posted outside restaurants; to browse through the frozen-food sections of all the supermarkets; and to talk to hundreds of salesmen and other chefs, as well as anyone who could offer any information on food processing, canning, freezing, or foodservice.

Chef Szathmary still had ample time on his hands. Thanks to the recommendations of top Mutual Broadcasting executives, he began home catering, from the most elegant Manhattan apartments to rambling estates in Connecticut and New Jersey owned by the giants of entertainment and broadcasting, writers, actors, and politicians.

Still, the dream of owning his own restaurant lingered in his mind. When a management decision closed the Mutual executive dining room, Tom O'Neill offered Szathmary another opportunity. O'Neill had recently bought the well-known Humpty Dumpty Restaurant in Old Greenwich, Connecticut. It was one of the original "hamburger places" that became the prototype of many later copies. The hamburgers weighed eight ounces uncooked, ground from fresh beef in front of the customer, served on a toasted, freshly baked bun, and put in a paper bag.

Louis and his brother, Geza, bought the place, expanded the menu, and built a large clientele. Everything went well until one night squirrels, chewing through wires in the main building, started a fire. The venerable restaurant burned to the ground. Despite insurance money, Chef Louis could not stand his idleness after two months. He took a job in a small Italian restaurant that enabled him to try actual "field tests" in what he was planning to do with frozen foods.

After a few months of experimenting, by sheer chance he met a wealthy young socialite who thought it would be an interesting experiment to fill the catering needs of affluent young suburbanites by offering frozen single or double portions and casseroles for four or six, of entrees such as beef Burgundy, beef Stroganoff, and coq au vin rouge. After tasting some of the dishes Chef Louis had developed, the young socialite quickly hired him as plant superintendent and partner in his company, Reddy-Fox Catering.

Shortly after a new Reddy-Fox plant and retail store opened in Darien, Connecticut, a customer introduced himself as Harve Hearl, director of packaging development for Continental Can. He asked Chef Szathmary if he would be interested in packing his frozen dishes in special aluminum trays with aluminum-coated cardboard covers that Continental had developed for the restaurant industry.

At the urging of Harve Hearl, Szathmary developed numerous dishes for the companies that were pioneering the field of frozen prepared entrees—Dulany, Seabrook Farm, and Stouffer, to name a few. Chef Louis met with Mrs. Stouffer and her son, Vern, and developed formulas for their first line of frozen food.

New starches were developed at his suggestion. Among the first was a rice flour, waxy rice, by the California Ricegrowers Association. As sample introductory dishes for his clients, Louis packed frozen chicken paprikash with spaetzels, Hungarian goulash with egg barley, and Hawaiian chicken breast with fried rice, all using the flour. The first experiments did not work out. The starch soaked up all the sauces. The dishes had little shelf life and, after reheating, turned into a sad mess.

To counter this, Louis applied heat seals to the middle of these flexible pouches. He packed the noodles, rice, egg barley, or potatoes on one side and then, after sealing the center of the pouch, filled the other end with the sauce and meat. The double pouch was born, making it possible to take from freezer to serving platter, in 12 to 14 minutes, individual portions of some 40 items.

In the late 1950s Chef Louis developed Armour's Continental Cuisine, American Fare, Hospital Fare, and several other lines of institutional products. In 1960 he became Armour's product-development manager and continued in that capacity until the end of 1963.

Having more and more nationwide contact with restaurants, lecturing at Cornell University and at industry seminars, and learning more and more about the hospitality industry, Chef Szathmary felt the urge to demonstrate the validity of his ideas in a restaurant of his own.

He firmly believed in certain principles. He felt that gimmicks, promotions, and decor can lure people into a restaurant, but only good food and good service would bring them back. He believed that location is not of primary importance if the product is desirable and of high quality. He felt that it was not necessary to have wall-to-wall carpet, huge menus, or sparsely clad waitresses selling drinks.

The media quickly became aware of the new restaurant, The Bakery Restaurant. In the first two years, more than 200 articles appeared about it. Guests came to the establishment from London, Tokyo, and Sydney, as well as New York, New Orleans, and Montreal.

Working for a leading diversified international corporation was a great help to Chef Louis in developing his analytical skills. At Armour he learned the importance of sampling, collecting, and processing statistical data. He applied these techniques in directing the Bakery. During its first year of operation, the restaurant added 131 main-course items to its menu. From the very first day, a daily accounting was analyzed on every single item sold. More than half were dropped in the second year, some of which Louis and his wife, Sada (an equal partner in management decisions), originally had high hopes for.

Chef Louis thought that sweetbread dishes, high-quality shrimp items, and veal creations would be bestsellers, but they never moved. From the sixth month on, it became increasingly evident that individual filets of Beef Wellington in the form created at Armour would be the star of the menu. From the seventh month on, beef Wellington became, and remained after more than two decades, not only the number one seller, but also accounted for more than 50 percent of all main-course items ordered.

Instead of guarding the secret of this successful dish, he published the recipe in the 1965 issue of *The Cornell Hotel and Restaurant Administration Quarterly*. The article was the most frequently requested reprint in the history of the *Quarterly*. John Sexton & Company ordered 10,000 reprints from Cornell to distribute to its white-tablecloth restaurant customers throughout the U.S.

Chef Szathmary is very involved in educational activities and is a frequent speaker or demonstrator at regional conventions, shows, exhibits, and educational meetings. The book department of the NRA has sold thousands of his books over the years through its mail-order catalog.

Now retired from active restaurant operation, Chef Louis lives in Chicago and spends part of his time as a consultant to Johnson and Wales College.

11

Restaurant Operations

A person considering the restaurant business has several career and investment options. He or she can:

Manage a restaurant for someone else (individual or a chain).

Purchase a franchise and operate the franchise restaurant.

Buy an existing restaurant.

Build a new restaurant and operate it.

The advantages and disadvantages of each style of operation should be analyzed closely and the potential risks and rewards of each option carefully considered.

The individual should assess his or her own temperament, ambitions, and ability to cope with frustrations (Table 11-1). Buying a restaurant may satisfy a personal desire; if the restaurant is a success, the rewards can be very high. If it fails, the financial loss is also high, but usually not as high as if the investment had been made in a new build-

ing. Franchising reduces risk all along the line, but may also reduce the potential reward because of franchise fees. No financial risks are ordinarily attached to being a manager, but the psychic cost of failure can be high.

There are some people who have gone into the restaurant business with almost no experience, built a restaurant, and been successful from day one. Such examples are relatively rare. When buying an existing restaurant that has failed or is for sale for some other reason, the purchaser has some information that the former owner lacks. The buyer may know that the original restaurant was not successful because of location or that a certain menu or style of management was not the right one. Such information could cut risks somewhat. On the other hand, the buyer may find it difficult to overcome a poor reputation acquired by the previous operator over a period of time.

As a general rule, it is best to learn a format of operation thoroughly before buying or building a restaurant. The franchisee is partially protected because he or she usually has completed a man-

TABLE 11-1 Buy, Build, Franchise, or Manage: Advantages and Disadvantages

Original Investment Needed	Experience Needed	Potential: Personal Stress	Psychic Cost: Failure	Financial Risk	Potential Reward
Buy	medium	high	high	high	high
Build	highest	high	high	highest	highest
Franchise	low to medium	low	medium	medium	medium
Manage	none	medium to high	medium	medium	none

agement training course before opening a franchised restaurant. The franchisor should be just as eager to avoid failure as the franchisee, a plus for the latter. Of course, franchised restaurants also fail, and the prospective franchisee must be careful to select a reputable franchisor with an excellent track record.

MARKETING TO THE FORE

Marketing as a discipline has become more important for restaurant success. The business has always been competitive. To make a restaurant stand out from its competitors, a restaurant is "positioned"—a clear picture is presented to the consumer of what the restaurant offers, and its unique points in comparison with competitors are emphasized. Positioning strategies stress such things as atmosphere, personal service, signature foods, convenience price, value, quality, atmosphere, celebrity clientele, and so on.

The place and the product are aimed at a particular market. This is done by considering the kind of people who will be attracted to the location, the product, the prices, and the general ambience. McDonald's is positioned to attract the masses; Fuddruckers, a gourmet hamburger chain with prices four times those of McDonald's, attracts a more discriminating clientele.

Part of the overall image of a restaurant is created by advertising and public relations. Advertising usually exists in the form of purchased radio, TV, or print messages and understood by the viewer as advertising. Public relations also has costs, but the message is more subtle, projected indirectly in a variety of forms such as by news releases, the creation of newsworthy events, complimentary meals for newsmakers, public

services donated by the restaurant owner, and actions taken to build good will. All add up to the image of the restaurant in the eyes of consumers.

Market Segmentation

Market segmentation is another marketing concept. It is an effort to identify precisely the particular group of people—the market segment—that is likely to patronize the restaurant. They can be identified in terms of income, eating-out habits, age, proximity to the restaurant, credit rating, and so on.

Marketing segmentation can also be expressed in spending terms—low-end, midrange, and luxury markets, meaning groups of consumers who buy inexpensive, midprice, or luxury products, respectively. Each group would go to the appropriately priced restaurant.

Pricing for Market Penetration

To establish a foothold in a market or increase a market share, restaurant operators often undercut their competitors by lowering prices on selected items or reducing prices with coupon promotions and various other gimmicks. New-restaurant prices are often reduced below those of the competition and then raised once a clientele has been established.

Supermarkets are well known for offering "loss leaders," items sold at or near cost that create a loss but bring in buyers for other products. Restaurant operators, especially those in fast food, do something similar when they offer such promos as "two tacos for the price of one" or a "free medium-sized Coke with a burger." The expectation is that total sales will increase.

Econometric Models for Sales Predictions

Econometric models, which combine economics and mathematics, began to be used in the 1930s for other businesses. The models were first devised for restaurants in 1966 by Francis R. Cella at the University of Oklahoma.

The Oklahoma Restaurant Restaurant Association gave Cella a contract for the development of restaurant models. Using a computer, he was to simulate a restaurant operation and determine potential sales. Initially, models were built for five types of foodservice operations: general, cafeteria, drive-in, specialty, and hamburger. The needed information was developed from the experiences of Oklahoma residents. Cella has said his models can predict restaurant sales within 5 percent, plus or minus, 95 percent of the time. (The Oklahoma Restaurant Association has since taken over Cella's computer analysis program and sharply reduced the claims of what the program can do.)

The theory is simple: If the importance of the various factors that determine the sales of a restaurant can be pinpointed and weighted according to their effect, then by using the computer, it is a matter of a few minutes to derive a forecast of what sales that restaurant should produce. The more obvious factors that bear on restaurant sales are the population in the vicinity, income of that population, number of competitors in the area, volume of traffic passing the location, ability of the restaurant manager, amount of advertising, and appearance and kind of structure that houses the restaurant.

According to Cella, a minimum of 16 factors affect sales volume, a number that rises to 30 for some kinds of restaurant operations. Subsequently, models for other restaurants have been developed and numerous models built for chain operations.

Without the use of computers, the mathematics of correlating the effects of the factors on gross sales and each other would be very time-consuming. According to Cella, without a computer it would take 40 clerks 6 months to manually make the calculations necessary for one model.

The construction of the model cannot be done by a beginner, since some of the factors involved that affect restaurant sales are negative and some are nonlinear. Decisions as to whether a factor is important enough to warrant inclusion in the model requires judgment as well as reference to the experience of a number of operations.

Carl Karcher Enterprises has come up with a model for site selection for the Carl's Jr. fast-food restaurants. It is a multiple-regression formula that correlates various factors with sales volume to evaluate a potential site by predicting sales on the site. The model compares the characteristics of the site with existing successful restaurants. The information needed includes:

Daily traffic count on surrounding streets

Total number of existing seats in comparable restaurants in the area

Proportion of blue-collar households in the area

Estimated number of office workers within a 10-minute drive of the site

Number of single-member households in a 10-mile radius

Total population within a 10-mile radius

Mean age of area population

The same company has also found from experience that their most successful restaurants have these factors in common:

The area contains less than 1200 fast-food seats.

Some 75 percent of the area's population live in blue-collar households.

The mean age of the area's population is between 26 and 32 years old.

Some 10,000 office workers are within 10 minutes of the site.

This information was put together in a mathematical equation. This theoretical equation considers four key pieces of information and weights them based on the experience of existing restaurants.

Other uses. In addition to being able to predict the volume of business for a potential site, the econometric models can be used to determine whether a particular location is being put to its best use. The location of an unsuccessful drive-in was found to be good for a hamburger stand. The change was made and, after a shakedown period, the business made more money in one month as a hamburger stand than it had in the previous 12 months as a drive-in restaurant.[1]

The models can also be used to make management decisions. If the advertising budget is increased by 5 percent, a forecast can be made of the additional sales that would be generated. How much additional business can be expected if the restaurant is refurbished? Would it be better to divide an investment among a combination of factors or to concentrate it on a single factor? How much additional business can be expected if a more experienced manager is employed? All these projected courses of action can be tested by simulation.

In the past, each expert has been able to prove that his or her specialty is the all-important factor affecting total sales. The sales manager feels that advertising is the all-important factor; the production person feels sure that the quality of the product is most important; the designer feels that building design or appearance is what attracts customers. With an econometric model, the size of each factor's contribution can be determined with a greater degree of accuracy.

LOCATION

Generalizations about restaurant location are much more difficult to make than those relating to hotels and motels. Perhaps the following statements are valid:

1. Restaurants catering to the luncheon trade must be reasonably convenient to the clientele. Other than the expense-account restaurants, the luncheon restaurant must be within a few minutes' walk or drive of its market. Most luncheons eaten away from home are consumed during a specified lunch break that usually lasts from 30 to 60 minutes. For the shorter quickie luncheon, the restaurant must be close to the place of work, preferably in the same building. The business luncheon usually lasts much longer than an hour and often includes liquor. The business luncheon can take place farther away, but the restaurant must be convenient to reach by taxi or private car.

2. The highway restaurants on the main thoroughfares that cater to the traveler must be readily accessible. Even a 5-minute drive from the highway may be disastrous for the restaurant.

3. Fastfood restaurants are most successfully located adjacent to a main thoroughfare, in a busy shopping mall, or an apartment/condominium area.

4. Locations for the atmosphere, theme, or special-occasion restaurants can be less convenient for their intended market than others. The clientele will search them out. One of the most successful in the world in terms of sales volume is Anthony's Pier 4 Restaurant in Boston. It is relatively difficult to reach, but its harborside location adds glamour, and people go out of their way to eat there. In Marina del Rey, near Los Angeles, some 35 restaurants are concentrated. The public comes to think of the area as a place to go for both the sake of fun and eating out.

Menu price goes with location. A luxury restaurant in a high seat-turnover location would fail, and a fast-food operation in a luxury area might also fail. Some leading restaurants are found in highly unlikely locations. This is not to say that they might not be even more successful if they were more conveniently and pleasantly located.

Some restaurant developers have a very simple plan for site selection. They go where McDonald's goes. Others stick with the mall developers, feeling that if a developer believes enough in a location to invest several million dollars in a regional center, the same location is also desirable for a restaurant.

The character of the restaurant—its tempo, decor, noise level, and personnel—must be appropriate to a location. In a congested downtown area, people do not seem to mind being processed rather than served. Often, customers in such places are required to push their way to the serving counter, stand while eating, and are then expected to leave in about 10 minutes. Young people especially seem to relish this type of eating behavior. They will spend little more than a few minutes eating, even in college and university dining halls that are luxuriously equipped, carpeted, and lighted.

Dinner, however, is something else, especially for the middle-aged and older person. That

1. Francis R. Cella, *Retail Site Selection*, 1970 (printed privately).

individual, unlike the one who is satisfied to sit on a stool just inches away from somebody else at lunch, wants a chair with arms on it and at least 15 square feet per customer while eating dinner.

A critical factor in the location of a restaurant is the minimal size of the market needed; in other words, what size population is required to support a particular kind of restaurant.

KFC personnel say that their restaurants can do about $200,000 in sales in a community of 10,000 people. Population requirements for a McDonald's were once placed at 30,000; later, the company found that in heavily urbanized communities McDonald's restaurants could be located 3 miles apart. A Polynesian restaurant, serving food that is relatively exotic for the average American palate, may require a market of 500,000. (Fried chicken and hamburgers are considered a regular part of the U.S. diet; sweet and sour pork is not.)

The factor of "competition" also requires close scrutiny. Three restaurants side by side may complement rather than compete with each other. Numerous "restaurant rows" have experienced added business for each restaurant as other restaurants are added. A fried-chicken outlet, hamburger joint, and steak house may not compete with each other if the total available market is large enough. Three hamburger restaurants on the same block almost certainly will compete with each other. An additional hamburger restaurant will necessarily reduce the market of the established ones.

Restaurants that are on the top of a tall building did not become popular until the 1960s. They have a special appeal. Stouffer's now has 13 "tops," all of them successful. The Top of the Prudential Center in Boston, 52 stories in the sky, grosses more than $3 million a year in sales. The diner gets not only good food and drink, but also a marvelous view of Boston Harbor and metropolitan Boston. The top restaurant in the John Hancock Building in Chicago stands 95 stories in the air; the World Trade Center in New York serves food at an even greater height. Currently, "tops" restaurants exist around the world: London, Brussels, Rotterdam, Frankfurt, Montreal, Cairo, Tokyo, and Hong Kong, among the many.

The Space Needle at the Seattle World's Fair brought wide publicity for its revolving top restaurant. Such revolving restaurants turn on donut-shaped turntables around a stationary core.

Figure 11-1 Indicative of a trend to luxurious appointments in cafeterias is the Holiday House, a John R. Thompson Cafeteria in St. Louis. Note the wall-to-wall carpeting, the rich leather upholstered chairs, and decorative lighting fixtures. Note also the fact that the dining area has been broken up into several rooms.

The turntables may have a diameter as large as 132 feet. Believe it or not, only 2.75 horsepower motors are needed to revolve a restaurant weighing some 200,000 pounds and filled with over 300 diners. Obviously, revolving restaurants are expensive. However, since the supporting structure is usually built for some other reason, the cost of the restaurant itself may not be excessive. Some problems in operating revolving restaurants exist: lingering customers, trouble finding one's seat after going to the restrooms, and motion sickness.

Kemmons Wilson of Holiday Inns favored the revolving restaurant, and was quoted as saying, "At a revolving restaurant the food is terrible, the price is high, and the service slow, but the people are lined up to get in."

Most give diners one complete turn around the building in the course of an hour. They can buy a drink or two, look down on the little people, sit eye-level with a passing airplane, and become detached from it all. At the end of the hour's merry-go-round, the restaurant hopes the guests will depart contented, relaxed, and minus $20 or more.

THE MENU

The menu, to a large extent, determines what markets can be reached. Therefore, the selection of menu items and method of presentation are critical. The hamburger-fried-chicken-milkshake menu reaches teenagers and young marrieds. The steak menu is for the more affluent middle-aged market. The Polynesian menu must be aimed at the "special occasion" market and those people who want a "different" atmosphere. The French menu and individual French menu items are for the more sophisticated, widely traveled affluent market. The meat and potatoes menu may be right for the people who eat out day after day and expect to eat more or less the same things that they would have eaten at home. The sandwich menu apparently reaches just about everyone, at least for lunch, from the club member to the vacationer on the thruway.

The restaurant operator is not wise to try to change tastes. He or she may discover that a market exists for tacos and other Mexican food. If so, well and good, but the operator must not try to force tacos or anything else down anybody's throat. For example, liver may be an excellent item nutritionally, but it cannot be served more than about once a month in a college foodservice—few people will eat it.

It is quite possible, however, to modify existing tastes—to add an embellishment to a basic, popular food. Chicken, for example, can be served in hundreds of ways.

Menu-making is often considered an art, but it is becoming a science. Research done at Tulane University under a grant from the National Institute of Health pointed the way for menu construction using the computer. Several hospitals now plan menus with a computer. The problem is to select items that are popular, low cost, and together form a nutritious meal, the solution to which can be expedited by computers.

The first step is to place into a computer's memory all the relevant data concerning available foodstuffs. One hospital, for example, has on file 800 recipes and 19 nutritional factors for each of 2500 foodstuffs. The cost of these foodstuffs must be included and the computer programmed so that the combinations of foods selected are eye-appealing—the computer has been known to turn out menus that are all bland, all soft, and all white. Restraints must also be placed on the computer so that the same items do not appear too often.

Recent Food Trends

In the past, the American restaurant public liked beef. Of the 600 pounds of food that the average American ate each year, more than 100 was beef. However, beef consumption is declining. Pork consumption is going down; chicken is rising, as is turkey; cheese is going up fast; lamb and mutton consumption is down. Fish and other seafood are climbing fast.

Ham or bacon and eggs are most preferred at breakfast, but after these, a Gallup poll showed that young people like fancy pancakes and sweet or Danish rolls.

Among foreign and specialty foods served in restaurants, the same poll found that Italian food was the leader, followed by seafood. Coffee is still the most popular restaurant beverage, but, especially among young people, cold drinks are gaining.

Nutritional information had a marked effect on menus in the 1980s. Deep cold-water fish, it was learned, may help reduce cholesterol, as well as waistlines. They and shellfish, though the latter is high in cholesterol, contain fatty acids, primarily those labeled omega-threes, that appear to be even more effective than polyunsaturated vegetable oils in helping to reduce the risk of heart disease. Especially desirable are shellfish like mussels, oysters, and scallops. The result has been a surge in fish and seafood on restaurant menus.

Animal fats, highly saturated and high in cholesterol, gave way to vegetable oil in fast-food restaurants; calcium has been added to some foods; and more broiling rather than frying is done.

The now prominent trend of healthy eating was anticipated with the introduction of a few salad bars in the 1960s. By the early 1980s salad bars, like the Sunday brunch, became a feature in thousands of restaurants, from fast-food establishments to dinner houses. Variety and versatility are the name of the salad bar game. Items can be easily changed, new items tried, others omitted. Some become indistinguishable from buffets, offering hot foods as well as cold dishes, breads, desserts, and fresh fruit. Salad bar versatility permits the restaurant operator to reflect ethnic food trends. If Mexican food becomes popular in the area, cilantro, peppers, tomatillos, and other Mexican foods can be added, either as discrete items or for flavor and garnishment. If tapas bars become popular, tapas bar items can be added, either interspersed or in an identified section of the salad bar.

Quality food items and tight control of safety and sanitation are needed with salad bars. If they are lacking, the bar becomes a liability, reflecting negatively on the entire restaurant. Wilted lettuce, food displays allowed to become unsightly, or employees seen handling salad ingredients with their bare hands are absolute no-no's. Food poisoning resulting from some foods remaining out too long or left unrefrigerated can destroy a restaurant. Failing to cook hamburgers to at least 160 degrees F. has caused illness, and even death, from food poisoning.

There seems to be a growing preference for foods that are more acidic, probably because of the vast amount of carbonated drinks being consumed, most of which are on the acidic side. Almost all kinds of snacks are increasing in popularity.

Some of the most popular new menu items are those that stimulate a number of senses—smell, taste, feeling—all at once. A hot fudge sundae sets off sensory responses for something hot, cold, sweet, and bitter. Nuts add a desirable chewiness. Even pain elicited by red pepper has a role in the favorable response to foods. One reason for the popularity of Creole cooking is the bite of hot pepper sauce. The gas in carbonated beverages acts on the pressure senses in the mouth. Noise, in the form of the "snap, crackle, and pop" of some foods, is appreciated.

Preference for that old Italian favorite, tomato sauce, is growing, as can be seen in the rapid growth of the consumption of pizza, and pasta dishes.

Pizza in its many variations has become a favorite not only for home delivery, but also in upscale restaurants. Goat cheese has replaced dairy cheeses. Several cheeses are mixed to produce different flavors. Mexican food is increasing in appeal, which makes the restaurant operator happy because of the comparatively low food cost of rice, beans, corn, ground beef, and chicken. Instead of using lard as the cooking fat, smart Mexican food operators have substituted canola oil, lowest of all oils in saturated fatty acids.

Chicken in its many variations is gaining in popularity because of relatively low fat content. Boneless, skinned chicken breast with a choice of several sauces is growing in popularity and appears on fast-food menus, as well as in mid- and upscale restaurants. Chicken may well replace the hamburger in terms of preference. Because chicken can be raised in about eight weeks and thrives on soybean feed, it is always available and relatively inexpensive.

Menu internationalization keeps pace with world travel and culture globalization. Creative chefs mix cuisines, serve chicken with a Thai peanut sauce, substitute raddichio for lettuce, or combine French and Chinese dishes. In the more expensive restaurants, artistic food presentation may take precedence over the food itself.

A severely limited menu may be satisfactory in a new market until competition moves in. Then other items may have to be added to reach additional people. McDonald's added fish sandwiches to its menu, twin-patty hamburgers, and breakfast to its menu and continues to include new food items.

The menu determines the kitchen equipment needed: Broiled items on the menu require a broiler or grooved griddle; fried items need a deep-fat fryer. One successful group of fish and chips restaurants has no equipment in its kitchens except deep-fat fryers.

Prestige Foods

What constitutes a prestige food changes with the times. Brillat-Savarin, the famous gourmet of the early nineteenth century, ranked truffles and turkeys as the twin jewels of gastronomy. Turkeys have lost out; truffles remain, and like caviar, they still have high status, probably because of rarity and cost.

Terrapin turtle, once on nearly every important menu, disappeared almost completely when sherry and Madeira, needed for cooking it properly, were outlawed by Prohibition. Canvasback duck was largely eliminated when an army ordinance seized the bird's favorite feeding grounds in Chesapeake Bay; the bird lost its favorite wild celery and so lost its distinctive flavor and thus its popularity.

High-status dishes today, at least those served in the prestige restaurants in New York City, use fresh and often exotic ingredients. In many cases, traditional center-of-the-plate entrees such as beef, are being upstaged by pasta, grains, and legumes.

Much wine snobbery has a flimsy basis; the "authority" happens to know a little more than somebody else. One thing that can give a particular wine its reputation as extremely good is its price; the higher the price, the better the wine. Taste tests conducted so that the brand name, price, and origin are unknown often produce startling results; less expensive wines are frequently selected as best. The same wine placed in different bottles sets off arguments as to which is better. But much of dining is romance, and who is the nasty fellow who would dare destroy romance?

Among the status wines today are Romanee-Conti, considered by many to be the greatest red wine of Burgundy; Le Montrachet, usually conceded to be the greatest white wine of Burgundy; and Chateau d'Yquem, the "great" sauterne of Bordeaux.

Signature Items

The search for menu items that uniquely characterize the restaurant, like a personal signature, continues in all evolving properties. These signature items may be conversation pieces served by only one or a few restaurants. Preferably, they are low in cost.

A cafeteria chain discovered that they could tenderize and country fry a flank steak, which was very inexpensive at the time. Until other restaurants picked up the idea and it lost its specialness, the country fried steak was a big winner, both in popularity and profit. The Velvet Turtle restaurants found that by cutting up a large squid into bit-sized pieces, pounding it to make it tender, and then frying it, they had another winner. The squid was about one-tenth the price of abalone, but after cooking it tasted much like abalone. The name given it on the menu was "calamari sauté," a much fancier name than squid.

Even chicken, ever cheap and plentiful, can be served in one of dozens of ways to become a signature item.

Banquet Foods

The banquet-menu planner is severely limited by the fact that relatively few foods are universally liked, even within a given community. Another limiting factor is the time required for preparation. Items that need long preparation are precluded when large numbers of people must be served in a hurry.

Pork and fish items seldom appear on banquet menus because pork is taboo to several religious groups and in any sizable group a number of people do not like fish. Fowl items are popular, but duck and goose are expensive. Common chicken items are considered just that, too common. Veal is popular, but it too is expensive.

Certain items become fashionable and then go out of style. Rock Cornish game hen was a popular banquet item, but it is relatively expensive and cumbersome to eat as a whole bird. Unless prepared carefully, a game hen is likely to be dry and lacking in flavor. Its day seems to be over.

Menu Strategies: Leftovers

Consideration of the use of leftovers is important in menu planning. Can the leftover item be incorporated into another dish? Can it be served tomorrow? Can it be frozen and held for later use? How long can it be held without having to be discarded? The "chef's special" has three advantages: It is a way of using leftovers; it offers the chef a creative outlet; it offers the customer variety.

A restaurant serves shoulder roast one night; the next day the leftovers are cooked further and served as pot roast: no leftovers. Leftover steak can appear as country fried steak or steak, country style.

A tour de force in menu planning is the hamburger not served as hamburger. For example, those patties that stay on the griddle too long and dry out appear in chili, Wendy's "leftovers" big seller. This represents excellent planning on the part of management.

Other examples of leftover dishes: beef stroganoff, beef strips in pepper sauce, and, of course, varieties of hash—leftover meat and cooked potatoes. Goulash also makes use of leftover beef, as do shepherd's pie and stuffed peppers.

Chicken can appear with a fresh face as escalloped chicken, chicken pot pie, chicken croquettes, or chicken chow mein. Enchiladas can wrap up leftover chicken or beef. Cooked chicken or veal can be fricasseed and appear as a new dish. Crabcake is often made from leftover crab, although care must be taken that it is not contaminated. Leftover fish may appear in chowder or seafood manicotti. Leftover sausage can be wrapped in dough and baked as a "pig in blanket."

A few basic principles must be remembered. Leftover fresh foods can be rejuvenated by adding moisture by some means, such as a sauce, or by using the food as part of a soup. (The "soup of the day" may more honestly be called the "soup of yesterday," made up of bits and pieces of vegetables and meat from the day before.) Cooking in wine enhances flavoring, restores moisture, and adds interest. Seasonings enhance flavor. A la king sauce can be added to ham, veal, chicken, or turkey. Creamed ham or chicken are good items. Adding barbeque sauce to beef or ham can be delicious. Putting chunks of meat or chicken in gelatin is a possibility, and flesh food—fish, fowl, beef, veal, even pork—can be chopped or ground and made into loaves or croquettes.

A flesh food can be made attractive by serving it with noodles or macaroni. Stir-frying vegetables and adding leftover pieces of meat is a good idea. So, too, is serving bits and pieces of meat with rice or potatoes. The hot roast beef sandwich, a favorite in many Midwestern restaurants, can be made with leftover beef slices placed on a slice of bread and hot gravy poured over the top.

Fancy dishes can also be produced from leftovers. Chicken divan can use already cooked chicken, as can numerous other "gourmet" dishes. One chain, which features fried chicken, pulls any that is held for more than an hour and uses it for pot pies and soup. A bland food could be used again by adding a curry or any other zesty sauce.

When the exact quantity of meat needed is not known, it should be cooked to a rare stage only. If all is not used, it can be reheated to a medium or well-done stage and served as is or modified. If a banquet has leftover breast of chicken or veal cordon bleu, each serving can be cut in half, a sauce added, and served as a luncheon entree.

Almost any leftover can be at least used partially. Crab meat can be taken from a tortilla; pie filling can be scooped out and used for a cobbler; chicken can be cut up for chop suey; tomatoes removed from a salad; and so on. All this requires time and labor. Usually, the leftover is sold at a lower price than the original dish. The more expensive the food item left over, the more important that portions be used. Today's seafood Newburg is tomorrow's seafood chowder. The only other option is to throw the item away.

Restaurants that change menus frequently should make provisions for appending clip-ons or inserts to the menu so that they do not cover print and will stand out. Such clip-on items usually feature seasonal foods or specially made dishes (often with leftovers from the day before). Many dinner-house operators prefer that the servers announce the chef's special or catch of the day, believing that clip-ons are tacky.

Changing Menu Items

Depending on the style of restaurant, the menu can be relatively fixed or it can change seasonally or even more often. The fast-service restaurant is likely to have the most rigidly fixed menu: hamburger, milkshake, french fries, coffee, and soft drinks. Even here, the menu must be changed to excite new markets, retain old ones, or keep abreast of competition. A hamburger restaurant adds a fish sandwich, fried chicken, and a breakfast item. The pizza parlor adds a deep-dish pizza amidst great fanfare. Then out comes a personal pizza, prepared within five minutes and just enough for one person. The fried chicken outlet adds barbecued ribs, barbecued chicken, and corn on the cob. Management continually monitors the competition and thinks of new ways to reach new customers.

A dinner-house menu is relatively fixed, especially if the clientele is known to visit the establishment only once a month or every few months. Items are likely to change infrequently. For several years, Gulliver's, in Southern California, featured one item—roast beef—on its dinner menu and did extremely well. Steak and lobster houses, of course, feature steak and lobster consistently.

Restaurants with fixed images and fixed menus may have excellent management and still experience gradual erosion of business simply because the market has changed.

The coffeeshop menu is relatively fixed, but if the clientele is made up of regulars, they too want some change. The chef's special may be on a cycle, changing daily for seven or more days and then starting over.

No matter how well a menu may fit a market, the market will change because of the mobility of society in general, the aging of the clientele, and youngsters growing up and becoming a new part of the market. Few restaurants can maintain the same menu over a long period of time. The coffeeshop that opened with a limited breakfast menu offered over most of the day, or even 24 hours a day, may have to change as more choices are offered to the same market by competition. The coffeeshop may find itself moving into the family-restaurant business by necessity of its changing market, all by trial and error—a Polish dish is offered and it goes well; a Mexican dish is offered and it goes well; a Belgian waffle begins to sell better than the American-style pancake—and so it goes. The coffeeshop is no longer a coffeeshop in the traditional sense. It has moved into family trade.

Introducing new items can be a tricky business, especially when it requires new equipment or new skills to produce. Even an experienced chef has a limited repertoire of recipes and skills.

Will it interfere with the work flow of established menu items? In a high-volume luncheon restaurant, will the introduction of omelettes overcrowd the griddle and slow service? Since they have to be cooked to order, this is a possibility. It may be a good idea to use the leftover chicken for chow mein, but will the cooks have time to prepare it? The introduction of any baked product, such as cinnamon rolls and biscuits, may be a great idea, but is there the space, equipment, time, and skill available to do so?

Fast-food kitchens have been carefully planned, so there is almost no spare space. Will the new item need additional equipment and space? McDonald's spends months, even years, testing a new item before introducing it chain-wide.

The menu of one restaurant in an area affects the others in that area. When McDonald's began promoting and advertising breakfast and its McMuffin sandwiches, breakfast business increased in other restaurants as well. The heavy advertising made the public more amenable to a restaurant breakfast.

Portion Size Psychology

A hot dog chain offered two sizes of hot dogs: large and small. More than 60 percent of their sales were for the small size. The operator decided to add a third hot dog size, one larger than the large one on the old menu. The sales pattern changed dramatically. Few patrons ordered the new large size, but the hot dog that formerly was the large size jumped in sales and accounted for about half the total sales volume. Apparently, customers were reluctant to treat themselves to a "large" hot dog. The result of the menu change was that sales volume increased sharply.

Telephone Audits

A way to conduct a market audit of current customers is to have a host or hostess hand customers cards inviting them to participate in an audit. The card requests them to write in their names and telephone numbers and offers a reward for those who participate, typically a free dessert or discount on the next meal after a phone interview.

The phone interview can be used to learn whether the restaurant's concept is clear in the customer's mind, what food items should be added or deleted, how the patron feels about the location. In one instance, customers felt that the restaurant was dirty. It turned out that the restaurant itself was clean, but the exterior badly needed paint and the parking lot repaving. The work was done and on the next survey the restaurant scored high on cleanliness.

As a result of phone surveys, some restaurants have been found to project an ambiguous image. An upscale Mexican restaurant failed to offer such standard items as burritos and enchiladas, which most customers expected. Adding those items strengthened the Mexican image and met customers' menu expectations.

MENU ANALYSIS

Restaurateurs are forever examining their menu to see if it fits their clientele and to determine if each item is profitable. Menu items might be classified as:

Popular and profitable

Popular but unprofitable

Unpopular but profitable

Unpopular and unprofitable

Unprofitable items are usually dropped unless there is some good reason for retaining them. A menu may include a few seldom sold, unprofitable prestige item as window dressing for the menu. Chain restaurants will have none of this kind of thinking and stay with the items that are fast movers and preferably long on profit.

The Air Force *Manual for Operating Clubs* recommends careful analysis of a menu to determine exactly what each item contributes in the way of profit to the enterprise. Figure 11-2 shows the analytical device used to identify the cost of each item and the contribution it makes to total sales. (Prices have not been updated and the percentages are illustrative only.)

In the example, the total food cost percentage is 43 percent. But as the menu is broken down, it is seen that different items have widely different costs:

1 percent: food cost 25 percent

10 percent: food cost 30 percent

10 percent: food cost 35 percent

15 percent: food cost 40 percent

23 percent: food cost 45 percent

32 percent: food cost 50 percent

9 percent: food cost 55 percent

Item Contribution

What does each item contribute to profit? In Figure 11-2 the T-bone steak, selling for $13.50 an order, contributes $472.50. It has a high food cost of 50 percent, but never mind that, the contribution is the thing. The T-bone steak is a star on this menu.

The chef's salad is something else again. It is time-consuming to prepare and is probably a loss item when the labor cost is added to the food cost. Lobster tails might well be retained, since there is little preparation involved other than broiling them, and they can easily be stored in a frozen state.

The cherry or apple pie might look like a good item to retain or promote, since it has only a 30 percent food cost. Yet it might be dropped unless the pie has been purchased from a baker and entails little labor in serving. Labor cost in making such a pie would be considerable. On the other hand, cherry pie may be a menu leader and should be retained. Strawberry pie, freshly made daily, has proved to be a leader in a number of coffeeshops, no matter what the cost. Ice cream has almost no labor cost.

For reasons related to these, menu planners almost always include chicken items. They cost relatively little and are readily available. It takes less than 8 pounds of food, mostly inexpensive soybeans, to raise a chicken to 4 pounds in 8 weeks. The feed-to-meat ratio for chickens—two pounds of food produce one pound of meat—is far superior to that of other animals. Soybeans, with their 36 percent protein content, can be produced in almost every agricultural region of the world where there is water. So both the animal and what it eats are inexpensive, a major factor in the chicken's popularity. Chickens are mass-produced—the 20 largest mass producers turn out up to 5 million birds per week—another factor that brings down price.

Pricing

One of the more important management decisions is determining the selling price of each food item so that it will be both acceptable to the market and profitable to the restaurateur. Factors that go into this decision include the following:

What is the competition charging for a similar item? What is the cost of food that goes into the item?

What is the cost of labor that goes into the item?

What other costs must be covered by whatever is sold?

What profit is expected?

If food and labor costs plus a profit cannot be covered by a menu, the restaurant should not be in operation. A proposed venture should be cancelled or an existing one changed to make profit possible.

SCATTER SHEET

SALES PRICE	MENU ITEM	TIMES SOLD	TOTAL	SALES VALUE
	25% Cost			
$ 1.25	Hamburger	ꞁꞁꞁ ꞁꞁꞁ ꞁꞁꞁ ꞁꞁꞁ - ꞁꞁꞁ ꞁ	26	$ 32.50
1.00	Cheese Sandwich	ꞁꞁꞁ - ꞁ	6	6.00
1.50	Egg Salad Sandwich	ꞁꞁꞁ - ꞁꞁꞁ	10	15.00
1.00	Jello Salad	ꞁꞁꞁ	5	5.00
	30% Cost			
1.25	Pie, Cherry & Apple	ꞁꞁꞁ - ꞁꞁꞁ - ꞁꞁꞁ	13	16.25
1.00	Ice Cream	ꞁꞁꞁ - ꞁꞁꞁ - ꞁꞁꞁ	15	15.00
1.75	Cheeseburger	ꞁꞁꞁ - ꞁꞁꞁ - ꞁꞁꞁ - ꞁꞁꞁ - ꞁꞁꞁ - ꞁꞁꞁ	30	52.50
2.00	Ham Sandwich	ꞁꞁꞁ - ꞁꞁꞁ - ꞁꞁꞁ	15	30.00
1.50	Waldorf Salad	ꞁꞁꞁ - ꞁꞁꞁ - ꞁꞁ	12	18.00
7.00	Baked Ham Dinner	ꞁꞁꞁ - ꞁꞁꞁ - ꞁꞁꞁ - ꞁꞁꞁ - ꞁꞁꞁ	25	350.00
5.75	Fried Chicken Dinner	ꞁꞁꞁ - ꞁꞁꞁ - ꞁꞁꞁ - ꞁꞁꞁ	20	115.00
	35% Cost			
2.75	Pork Sandwich, Hot	ꞁꞁꞁ - ꞁꞁꞁ	10	27.50
2.75	Beef Sandwich, Hot	ꞁꞁꞁ - ꞁꞁꞁ - ꞁꞁꞁ - ꞁꞁꞁ	20	55.00
4.50	Shrimp Salad	ꞁꞁꞁ - ꞁꞁꞁ - ꞁꞁꞁ - ꞁꞁꞁ - ꞁꞁꞁ - ꞁꞁꞁ	30	135.00
6.00	Turkey Dinner	ꞁꞁꞁ - ꞁꞁꞁ - ꞁꞁꞁ - ꞁꞁꞁ - ꞁꞁꞁ	25	150.00
6.50	Pork Chop Dinner	ꞁꞁꞁ	5	32.50
1.30	Ice Cream, Sundae	ꞁꞁꞁ - ꞁꞁꞁ - ꞁꞁꞁ - ꞁꞁꞁ - ꞁꞁꞁ	25	37.50
	40% Cost			
6.00	Lobster Cocktail	ꞁꞁꞁ - ꞁꞁꞁ - ꞁꞁꞁ - ꞁꞁꞁ	20	120.00
3.75	Club Sandwich	ꞁꞁꞁ - ꞁꞁꞁ - ꞁꞁꞁ - ꞁꞁꞁ - ꞁꞁꞁ - ꞁꞁꞁ - ꞁꞁꞁ	35	131.25
6.50	Pork Tender, Dinner	ꞁꞁꞁ - ꞁꞁꞁ - ꞁꞁ	12	78.00
8.50	Filet Mignon, Dinner	ꞁꞁꞁ - ꞁꞁꞁ - ꞁꞁꞁ - ꞁꞁꞁ - ꞁꞁꞁ	25	212.50
2.00	French Pastry	ꞁꞁꞁ - ꞁꞁꞁ - ꞁꞁꞁ	15	30.00
	45% Cost			
6.00	Oyster Cocktail	ꞁꞁꞁ - ꞁꞁꞁ - ꞁꞁꞁ - ꞁꞁꞁ	20	120.00
4.50	Fruit Salad, Plate	ꞁꞁꞁ - ꞁꞁꞁ - ꞁꞁꞁ - ꞁꞁꞁ - ꞁꞁꞁ	23	103.50
7.00	Rib Steak, Dinner	ꞁꞁꞁ - ꞁꞁꞁ	10	70.00
7.25	Rainbow Trout, Dinner	ꞁꞁꞁ - ꞁꞁꞁ - ꞁꞁꞁ - ꞁꞁꞁ - ꞁꞁꞁ - ꞁꞁꞁ - ꞁ	31	224.75
9.75	Prime Rib, Dinner	ꞁꞁꞁ - ꞁꞁ	7	68.25
.50	Coffee	ꞁꞁꞁ - ꞁꞁꞁ - ꞁꞁꞁ - ꞁꞁꞁ - ꞁꞁꞁ - ꞁꞁꞁ - ꞁꞁꞁ - ꞁꞁꞁ - ꞁꞁꞁ - ꞁ	46	23.00
.50	Milk	ꞁꞁꞁ - ꞁꞁꞁ - ꞁꞁꞁ - ꞁꞁꞁ - ꞁꞁꞁ - ꞁꞁꞁ - ꞁꞁꞁ	35	17.50
	50% Cost			
2.00	Asparagus Tip Salad	ꞁꞁꞁ - ꞁꞁꞁ - ꞁꞁꞁ - ꞁꞁꞁ - ꞁꞁꞁ - ꞁꞁꞁ	30	60.00
5.00	Prime Rib Sandwich	ꞁꞁꞁ - ꞁꞁꞁ - ꞁꞁꞁ - ꞁꞁꞁ	19	95.00
13.50	T-Bone Steak, 16 oz.	ꞁꞁꞁ - ꞁꞁꞁ - ꞁꞁꞁ - ꞁꞁꞁ - ꞁꞁꞁ - ꞁꞁꞁ - ꞁꞁꞁ	35	472.50
12.50	New York Cut Steak, 12 oz	ꞁꞁꞁ - ꞁꞁꞁ - ꞁꞁꞁ - ꞁꞁ	17	212.50
2.25	Strawberry Shortcake	ꞁꞁꞁ - ꞁꞁꞁ - ꞁꞁꞁ - ꞁꞁꞁ - ꞁꞁꞁ - ꞁꞁꞁ - ꞁꞁꞁ	35	78.75
	55% Cost			
3.50	Chef's Salad Bowl	ꞁꞁꞁ - ꞁꞁꞁ - ꞁꞁꞁ - ꞁꞁꞁ - ꞁꞁꞁ	25	87.50
6.25	Calf's Liver Dinner	ꞁꞁꞁ - ꞁꞁꞁ - ꞁꞁꞁ - ꞁꞁꞁ - ꞁꞁꞁ - ꞁ	26	162.50
12.50	Lobster Tails	ꞁꞁꞁ - ꞁꞁ	7	87.50

$3550.75

A "SCATTER-SHEET" IS A VALUABLE MANAGEMENT TOOL.

"Scatter Sheet" RECAP

ITEMS	25% Cost	30% Cost	35% Cost	40% Cost	45% Cost	50% Cost	55% Cost	TOTALS
Cost % to Sales	0.4%	4.1%	4.4%	6.4%	9.8%	13.7%	3.9%	42.7%
% of Food Cost	1 %	10%	10%	15%	23%	32%	9 %	100%

Figure 11-2 Scatter sheet.

The cost of preparing any individual menu item must be considered in pricing. Those items with a high labor cost might better be omitted from the menu. Harry Pope of Pope's Cafeterias, headquartered in St. Louis, has pioneered the previously mentioned concept of prime cost, the combination of labor and food cost of a menu item.

Pope has pointed out that many menu items may have a low food cost but a high labor cost. Ingredients for soup, for example, may cost only a dime a portion, but the cost of making the soup is appreciable. Most establishments today buy soup in canned or dehydrated form because they cost less to prepare.

Consider each factor. In the dynamic marketplace represented by the foodservice industry, competition continually changes. Individual and chain restaurants rise and fall. New restaurants are constantly being opened, old ones closed. New marketing concepts are always in the making or being introduced. New management plans, new building designs, new advertising, and, more slowly, newer modified foods are forever appearing.

How the hamburger is priced, for example, depends on such factors as whether it is self-served or table-served, its size, its garnish, and the atmosphere and convenience of the restaurant. No one expects to get a hamburger served on a white tablecloth at the same price as one served in a drive-through restaurant. The same goes for a steak or any other food item. A walk-up, select-your-own steak may cost a third less than one served at a table in a quiet, attractive diningroom. Competition, however, usually determines menu price more than any other factor.

Food cost must be reflected in pricing, but usually it is overemphasized. The reason is fairly obvious: The cost of food varies with the volume of sales. Stated as a percentage of sales, its cost provides a simple target for management, a barometer of profitability.

Traditionally, menus were priced by a fixed markup or multiple of food cost. The system worked fairly well, in that other costs tended to be fairly predictable in a well-managed restaurant with a steady market. If, for example, 40 percent of sales was used as a food-cost target and other costs were steady, main food items were multiplied by 2.5 to arrive at a sales price. A number of items, such as coffee, tea, cola, desserts, and soups, were sold at a much lower food-cost percentage, balancing off the costs of employee meals and waste and making it possible for the target of 40 percent to be achieved.

Steak houses came along, and their operators saw that the traditional factor markup did not apply. Steaks could be purchased precut and sold at a price that would permit a 50 percent food cost or higher, and still the operation was successful. The reason was that labor costs in preparing and serving steak ran 15 or 20 percent or even less as a percentage of sales.

Operators began using food and labor costs as a combination target. If the two combined totalled something less than 70 percent of sales, a 10 percent profit, at least, showed up.

(Customers have no idea of traditional restaurant markup practices. The perception of value by the customer is not necessarily based on the actual cost of the item. Rather, it is likely to be based on pricing in comparable restaurants in the same region. For example: A $20 luncheon at the Moana Kea Hotel in Hawaii is seen as a value, whereas a $25 luncheon in the local hashery may be seen as a rip-off.)

Average markups in a Texas study were reported as shown in Table 11-2. These were made after all costs had been figured: food-ingredient costs, direct costs, controllable costs, and fixed costs. The Texas operators were able to price appetizers and desserts to make a much higher profit than they did on entrees. Gelatin desserts, carbonated drinks, and tea were long-profit items.

Pricing may also be determined by setting volume leaders—the food most often sold—at a higher food cost, and the slower-moving items—those that are more subject to waste, spoiling, becoming leftovers, or being pilfered—at a lower food cost. The latter represent a greater risk. When the leading items, for example, roast beef, hamburgers, and chicken, are in direct competition with those of nearby restaurants, there is

TABLE 11-2   Traditional Restaurant Markups

Appetizers	20–50 percent
High-priced entrees	10–12 percent
Fast-moving entrees	15–18 percent
Slow-moving entrees	22 percent
Desserts	35 percent

more reason to price these high-volume items at a higher food cost.

Some vegetables cost only a few cents per pound. Cabbage is almost always much cheaper than lettuce, is high in vitamin C, and can often be substituted for lettuce. Coleslaw is a popular cabbage dish. Noodles and desserts are low-cost items. Most of the year carrots, beets, and grapefruit are also cheap. Most puddings are low-cost, as are cereal dishes such as oatmeal or boiled rice. Anything made of wheat or other grains is likely to be relatively cheap. Pastas are inexpensive. So, too, are potato items—french-fried, baked, boiled, or otherwise.

COSTS

A logical way to arrive at a desired food-cost percentage is to produce a pro forma array of percentages, starting with the desired profit percentage. For example, suppose the operator feels it is possible to achieve a 15 percent net profit on gross sales before taxes. The following figures might be arrived at:

Desired profit percentage: 15

Expected labor cost percentage: 30

Occupancy cost percentage: 10

All other overhead costs percentage: 10
Total: 65

The total percentages except for food: 65

100 − 65 = 35 left for food cost

For a 15 percent profit, the food cost would have to be 35 percent. The operator prices the menu to achieve that result, recognizing that some items have a higher food cost percentage than others and allowances must be made for slippage in the computation. If the employees are receiving their meals or a meal allowance, that too has to be reflected in the computation. Usually, employees' meals run between 2 and 5 percent of sales.

Any system to arrive at a targeted food-cost percentage can only be used as a guide; the market calls the shots.

The Influence of Beverage Sales on Costs

Restaurants serving liquor generally expect around 25 percent of total sales to be from the beverage sales. The bar sales of some equal 50 percent, but these are usually more bars than restaurants. Many operators are not concerned if food costs alone rise to 38 percent or even higher. What does concern them is the combined food and bar costs. The lower bar costs in restaurants—25 percent—factor in to produce a satisfactory combined total of 34 percent or less. The greater the ratio of beverage to total sales, the lower the combined food and bar cost.

Sales Mix and Cost

The ideal food cost of a restaurant, of course, depends on how much of each menu item is sold, the sales mix. In a fast-food restaurant, the ideal food cost can be computed fairly easily because the menu is limited and the number of each food item sold can be recorded as part of a cash register procedure, or it can be tallied by hand on a tally sheet. Some of the newer cash registers (costing several thousand dollars each) function as mini-computers and store such information as the sales transaction takes place.

This simplified example of two restaurants, each with the same three menu items, shows the effect of sales mix. Each store sold $300 worth of food on a given day.

Restaurant A		Restaurant B	
200 orders of cod	$200	50 orders of cod	$50
75 orders of chicken	$75	200 orders of chicken	$200
100 orders of Coca Cola	$25	200 orders of Coca Cola	$50
	$300		$300

Suppose the cost of cod per portion was $.50, the cost of chicken was $.333, and the cost of cola was $.05.

The costs for Restaurant A would be:

Cod	$100.00
Chicken	$25.00
Coca Cola	$5.00
Total	$130.00

Costs for Restaurant B would be:

Cod	$25.00
Chicken	$66.67
Coca Cola	$101.67

Both the restaurants took in $300 for the day. Yet Restaurant A's food cost was $130, whereas Restaurant B's was only $101.67. Expressed as a percentage of sales, Restaurant A's food cost was 43.3 percent, Restaurant B's a little over 34 percent.

Which manager was the more effective? It is hard to know. Perhaps the market controlled the sales mix, and both managers were effective. It might be a good idea if the manager of Restaurant A tried to change the sales mix to sell more chicken and Coke.

Changing Prices

How often should menu prices be changed? The answer depends on the costs of the items served. They also must reflect labor costs. When inflation reached a double-digit level, some restaurants changed prices every 2 months to keep up with changing food prices. The alternative to increasing prices is to offer smaller portions, substitute less expensive items, and remove items that have become so costly that customers refuse to buy them. Lobster, for example, has continued to increase in price to the point that some restaurants have removed it from the menu. Salmon, at one time a "poor man's" food, is now a rich man's food. One reason for the huge success of the Mexican restaurant has been the relatively low-cost menu prices that the lower-priced foods permit.

When can prices be raised without losing customers? Experts propose that, when a market audit reveals that 95 percent of the customers feel that menu prices are not out of line, it is time to raise prices. Of 100 people who patronize a particular restaurant, it is hardly likely that all of them will be satisfied with the prices. But if as much as 10 percent are dissatisfied, prices should not be raised, according to the experts.

Decoy Menu Items

According to one restaurant operator, some menu items are added for the effect they have on establishing a price reference for other items on the menu. A steak house might offer three steak choices, two of them more expensive per ounce than the third. By comparison, the third choice looks like a bargain even though it also offers a good profit margin. "Decoy" items are placed on the menu primarily to make other items by comparison appear to offer a better "price value."[2]

The Proper Food Cost

What constitutes a proper food cost depends on the costs of service, atmosphere, and other factors that are offered together with the food. In a luxury restaurant, the food cost may be only 28 percent, but the cost of labor may more than offset the low figure, running as high as 35 to 40 percent. In "atmosphere" restaurants, customers necessarily pay for the atmosphere and, in most cases, are willing to do so.

In city and country clubs, food costs run 40 to 55 percent. The members want it that way; dues paid make up the deficits. A family restaurant might have a high food cost, 40 percent or more, but its labor cost could be 25 percent or less.

A fast-turnover steak house might run a food cost as high as 45 percent of sales and still make a good profit if labor cost is 25 percent or less of sales.

In fast-food restaurants, the cost of paper goods is often figured as part of the food cost.

One hamburger chain has a food cost of 37 percent. The reason: The chain features a roast beef sandwich, a three-ounce portion of roasted knuckle on a roll that sells for 69¢. Though the food cost of the sandwich is about 43 percent, the cost of labor involved in preparing the sandwich is low, about 15 percent. One cost balances the other.

Patterned like a teeter-totter, as labor costs go up, food costs go down. In other words, customers get less food for their money.

How can a hamburger chain sell a hamburger for only $1.20? Easy. If hamburger sells for $1.28 a pound and a two-ounce patty is served, food cost for the patty is about 16¢. The bun costs 8¢. Garnish might add another 4¢, for a total cost of 30¢. The selling price, $1.20, is divided by the cost, 30¢, which gives a food cost percentage on the hamburger of about 25 percent.

Beverages such as Coke and orange drink have a food and paper cost of 20 percent or less, which brings down the overall food cost.

---

2. Stowe Shoemaker, "Decoy Menu Items Can Enhance Margins Revenues," *Restaurant & Institutions* (Dec. 1990).

The foodservice business uses an odd accounting practice to compute food cost. Usually, that is expressed as the total cost of food consumed divided into the food sales, including the food eaten by employees. Other businesses would compute employee meals separately or include them as part of the cost of labor.

Food costs in specialty restaurants are likely to vary widely, depending on the menu, atmosphere, and prices. Polynesian restaurants—actually Chinese restaurants in a Polynesian setting—have low food costs, usually under 34 percent. The reason: lots of inexpensive rice. Beverage costs are also low: lots of rum at high prices. Mexican restaurants run food costs of about 30 percent or less because of their plenitude of cheap corn, rice, and beans.

Food cost cannot be considered apart from labor cost. As noted previously, if one goes up, the other must inevitably come down. When labor costs rise, the food cost must come down, and the customers pay a little more for a little less. The only way to avoid raising menu prices is to become more efficient or have the customers help by serving themselves. This is what happened in the rapidly expanding fast-food and cafeteria restaurants.

Food and Labor Costs Are Functions of Each Other

It helps to look at food and labor costs as interacting variables, one necessarily affecting the other. Ordinarily, other costs do not exceed 20 percent of sales. If combined food and labor can be kept below 65 percent, a 15 percent sales profit is possible. In other words, par for the course is 65, as seen in Table 11-3. If food and labor can be kept below that figure, as is often the case, then 15 percent profit should be forthcoming.

Exceptions exist. Turnpike and airport contracts for food service are awarded to the highest bidder. The successful bidder may pay 15 percent or even more "off the top" to the authority operating the turnpike or airport. To meet such fees, the operator must raise prices. Food costs come down to below 30 percent; beverage costs drop to below 25 percent.

Some rather amazing food and labor cost combinations can exist. A pizza chain had a food cost of 25 percent and a labor cost of 25 percent, for a combined total of 50 percent. The Little Red Hen, Inc., surprisingly, had a combined total of 52 percent: 43 percent food and 9 percent labor.

It is common practice in the restaurant business to establish food and labor cost targets that will ordinarily result in profit. In a family-style table service restaurant, a typical cost combination might be:

Food cost as a percentage of sales: 40

Labor cost as a percentage of sales: 25
  Balance: 65

If other costs did not exceed about 15 percent, the operation would produce a 20 percent profit before taxes.

The combination of food-cost percentage and labor-cost percentage has come to be known as prime cost. If the prime cost does not exceed 70 percent, the restaurant ordinarily produces a 10 to 15 percent net profit on sales.

The usual "other costs" would not exceed about 15 percent.

There are exceptions. Occupancy costs ordinarily run 5 to 10 percent but can go as high as 15 percent in some choice locations, such as in an airport or on a turnpike.

On the other hand, occupancy cost can run as low as 2 percent of sales in a low-rent area or if the owner has taken over an old building and remodeled it. Also, sometimes a restaurant location will have failed several times in succession and the owner is quite ready to offer a very low-cost lease.

Food and labor costs can vary widely as long as the total does not exceed 70 percent. Some possible combinations follow:

Steak house
  Food costs: 50 percent
  Labor costs: 20 percent
  Total: 70 percent

Mexican fast-food restaurant
  Food costs: 30 percent
  Labor costs: 20 percent
  Total: 50 percent

Coffeeshop
  Food costs: 38 percent
  Labor costs: 26 percent
  Total: 64 percent

A dinner house featuring roast beef when it is low in cost has:

Food costs: 48 percent
Labor costs: 20 percent
Total: 68 percent

Restaurants with sizable bar sales can sometimes afford to be less concerned about food and labor costs as long as the combined average of the food/labor/bar cost comes out to be less than 40. For example, these are the costs of a fine dinner house with a sales volume of $1.8 million a year:

Food costs: 46 percent
Labor costs: 32 percent
Bar costs: 22 percent
Total: 100 percent
Average: 33 percent

Influence of Preparation and Service Style

Labor costs are greatly influenced by the style of service and the amount of food preparation done on premises. A fast-food restaurant, with its limited menu and minimal preparation, has a lower labor cost than a table-service restaurant. Bonanza, a chain, has a labor cost of only 18 percent, which permits a higher food cost of 42 percent.

Labor costs in cafeterias might be expected to be somewhat lower than in table-service restaurants, because the customers largely serve themselves. Much of the servers' labor cost is borne by the customer in the form of tips. Forum Cafeterias, a large midwestern chain, has a food cost of 33 percent and labor cost of 35 percent, not much different than could be expected in a table-service restaurant.

The food and labor equation also varies regionally. When wages are high, in northern cities and the West, food costs necessarily must be lower. If labor costs in California average 34 percent, food cost is 34 percent or lower. In the South, with its low labor costs, food costs are higher. If labor cost in a Mississippi restaurant is 20 percent, food costs may be 40 percent or higher.

Fast-food labor costs range in the area of 12 to 20 percent of sales; other kinds of restaurants have costs ranging from about 28 percent to 42 percent of sales. The 10 to 20 percent labor-cost advantage makes it possible for fast-food operators to spend as much as 7 percent on advertising and still retain 10 to 20 percent as profit before taxes.

As has been pointed out, "You don't bank percentages." This means that overemphasis on maintaining a particular food- or labor-cost percentage may divert management's attention away from its true purpose: maximizing profits.

One way to maximize profits is to sell high-priced items, if patrons will buy them. Steak may have a food cost of 50 percent and sell for $15.00. A half-chicken might be sold for $5.00 and have a food cost of 33 percent. The gross profit on the steak would be $7.50, compared to only $3.35 for the chicken. Increasing the average check is a fast way of increasing profit, because ordinarily the item priced higher will bring a disproportionately large contribution of profit, even though the food cost may be higher.

Wage and Salary Cost

Many of the jobs in a restaurant are entry positions, those requiring little or no previous experience or training. At least 30 percent of the employees in the restaurant business work part time, a factor leading to instability in the labor force and contributing to a poor image of the industry.

Perhaps more important as a factor influencing the image are the low hourly wages paid in the industry, usually hovering near the minimum allowable by law.

Salaries paid cooks in northeastern cities, Los Angeles, Chicago, and San Francisco are largely controlled by union contract; the chef in a southern restaurant with no union receives much less and works longer hours. The salaries of top chefs range from about $40,000 to $55,000 a year. Many experienced and knowledgeable chefs are found in private clubs; some leave the restaurant industry to work as research chefs for food manufacturers.

Management salaries, as might be expected, also show a wide range. Management trainees just out of college in 1992 started at about $22,000 a year in the large restaurant chains. Managers in units of chain restaurants were paid from about $25,000 to about $60,000 a year in a large restaurant. The incomes of managers who share in profits and/or receive bonuses can exceed $100,000 a year.

Foodservice wages lag behind other industries. *Restaurant & Institutions* reported in 1990 that hourly wages in eating and drinking places were about half those found in all other industries, a fact partly accounted for by the relatively high hourly wages offered in the manufacturing sector.[3]

Tips and Tip Reporting

Reviled and praised, the practice of tipping provides incentives for servers, problems for restaurant patrons, and cost savings for operators. Without tipping, the work staff in dinner houses would have to be paid much more than the minimum wage they now receive. If tips did not exist, hundreds of college students would not line up to work as waiters and waitresses when a new dinner house opens. Tips can far exceed wages paid. One hundred dollars an evening for wait staff or cocktail servers in a name restaurant is not unusual.

Back in the kitchen where the work is equally demanding and the working conditions far less pleasant, there are no tips for cooks and utility personnel. Servers in fast-food restaurants are seldom tipped, probably one of the reasons for their rapid personnel turnover.

Some operators insist on a policy of tip pooling and distribution to all personnel, including bus personnel. In other places, tip sharing is informal and a matter of custom.

In theory, a tip corresponds in size to the quality of service. The equation is complicated by custom, attitudes, and other factors. One of those factors is the attractiveness of the server. Highly attractive waitresses receive significantly higher tips than less attractive waitresses, even though attractive servers may provide poor service and the less attractive provide excellent service.[4] It was not what Dr. Samuel Johnson had in mind in the eighteenth century when he handed the server in the London coffeehouse a slip of paper with coins attached. On the paper was written "To Insure Promptness," the origination of the word "tip."

Group size affects the size of the tip. Single parties and parties of two tend to tip more than larger groups on a per person basis. Men squiring women are big tippers. Geography and custom, in part, determine the amount. New Yorkers are big tippers, for example, whereas Midwesterners and people from small towns tip less. Dinner-

house patrons tend to tip at least 12 percent and go up to 20 percent. The customer unaccustomed to eating in an expensive restaurant may be intimidated and overtip.

Gamesmanship for a higher tip is played by some wait staff. The server radiates good will and concern and plays to the customer's ego. The pretty waitress implies that the middle-aged male she serves is irresistible. It is the waiting game skillfully played. Tips are the stakes of the game.

Management cannot force tipped employees to report their tip income to the Internal Revenue Service (IRS). The NRA says that "it's the government's job to collect them, not the restaurants." However, if employees in larger restaurants (25 or more employees) do not report tips totaling 8 percent or more of gross receipts to the IRS, the employer must allocate an amount equal to the difference between that 8 percent and the amount reported to them by employees. The Tax Equity and Fiscal Responsibility Act (TEFRA) of 1982 requires larger restaurants to file Form 8027 annually, which requires figures on gross receipts from food and beverage, the amount of charge receipts to which the tip was also added, the aggregate amount of tips shown on the charge receipts, and reported tip income.

Total tip income reported in 1984 was $2.2 billion, 127 percent over that reported in 1982. The percentage of restaurant employees who reported tips doubled from 16 percent to 32 percent.

Under the revised 1984 tax law, it is possible for restaurateurs to use a tip-reporting and allocating formula as low as 2 percent of sales. To use the lower formula, the operators must petition the district office of the IRS, providing proof that tips in their establishments are well below the 8 percent level. Detailed descriptions of the business, nature of the restaurant, style of service, and type of clientele must be submitted. Other information required includes how the customer pays the check, whether alcohol is served, and the size of the average check.

Variation in Restaurant Costs by Restaurant Type and Sales Volume

Some costs vary with the type of restaurant. Fast-food properties typically have lower food and labor costs than table-service restaurants, while fast-food occupancy costs are usually higher. As might be expected, as sales volume increases, the

---

3. *Restaurant & Institutions* (April 18, 1990).
4. Joanne M. May, "Looking for Tips: An Empirical Perspective on Restaurant Tipping," *Cornell Hotel and Restaurant Administration Quarterly* (Feb. 1980).

percentage of gross profit also increases. In other words, the large-volume restaurants generate higher gross profits and a higher profit percentage as well. Restaurant costs and profits, of course, differ around the country.

Occupancy costs vary widely. They depend on the arrangement between the operator and owner of the land or restaurant. Many restaurateurs try for a 5-year lease to avoid being tied to a location that could prove unsuitable. Leases are paid in one of several ways:

1. Minimum sum plus (or against) a specified percentage of the gross

2. Straight percentage of gross (usually 5 to 8 percent)

3. Percentage with no minimum sum, which will vary depending on how much the lessee makes

4. A flat monthly sum

Other arrangements are not uncommon. The lease trade-off is one of these: The more improvements the landlord makes, the higher the rent; the more improvements the operator makes, the lower the rent. Trade-offs are particularly important when the operator is beginning a new restaurant or plans extensive remodeling.

The turn-key lease is another possibility: The restaurant, completely furnished, is turned over to an operator for a flat sum.

A restaurant grossing $1 million needs about 80 employees. These average figures mean little, however, since in very efficient restaurants the productivity per employee may exceed $50,000 a year in sales.

As sales increase, the cost of food consumed tends to go down. In one study, the cost of food and beverages, including employees' meals, ran 40.2 percent in establishments doing less than $100,000 a year in sales. As sales increased, food cost went down, until finally, in restaurants doing between $500,000 and $1 million in sales, food cost dropped to 36 percent.

RESTAURANT PROFITABILITY

Handsome profits have been made in the restaurant business, many failures have also taken

TABLE 11-3   The Restaurant Industry Dollar

Where it came from:	
Food sales	76.2
Beverage sales	23.2
Other income	0.6
Where it went:	
Cost of merchandise sold	
Food	31.6
Beverage	6.1
Total	37.7
Payroll and related expenses	
Payroll	26.6
Employee benefits	3.8
Total	30.4
Direct operating expenses	5.4
Music and entertainment	0.7
Advertising and promotion	1.8
Utilities	2.2
Administrative and general	4.7
Repairs and maintenance	1.7
Occupation costs	
Rent, property taxes, and insurance	5.7
Interest	0.7
Depreciation	2.2
Other deductions	0.6
Net income before income tax	6.2

Source: National Restaurant Association

place over the years. Amateurs have "made it big," but not often. Even the professionals make mistakes in projecting a style of restaurant for a particular market, and most of the larger chains have had their share of losers. General Mills, which has restaurant sales exceeding $1 billion a year, could afford to spend $20 million in developing its Olive Garden restaurants, even after suffering losses and having to sell three other restaurant chains. The chain can afford to lose on a few places; the individual cannot. The individual can be out of business after only a few months of losses.

Consider the profits possible with a big winner. Some restaurants gross $14,000 to $20,000 per seat each year, even while the national average is less than $5000 per seat. Seat turnover can be as high as 7 per hour, or 60 customers per day. In dinner houses, seat turnover is more like 1 per hour or more, whereas the average restaurant gets less than 2 or 3 per hour.

Restaurant corporations seldom report net profit as a percent of sales exceeding 12 percent.

Nationally, the figure is below 5 percent. Corporations are not eager to show high profits on which they must pay taxes. Of course, many restaurant operations are pleased to show any profit at all.

Restaurant profits vary widely, depending on a number of factors: check average; seat turnover; costs of food, labor, occupancy, advertising, and other elements. The fast-food outlet, such as McDonald's, has a relatively low labor cost because mostly teenagers are hired and paid minimum wages. Some table-service restaurants reduce occupancy costs by remodeling old stores, barns, and houses. Food costs are considerably lower in a Mexican restaurant than a steak house, though both may be highly successful. The coffeeshop may have a check average of $3.00 compared with one of $20 for a gourmet restaurant, yet the coffeeshop may be much more profitable because of greater seat turnover and lower food and labor costs.

Restaurant Ideal

As an ideal, one might set up a model restaurant that costs $4000 per seat. With 100 seats, the restaurant's total cost should be $400,000. Ideally, sales should be $10,000 per seat per year, or $1 million. Also ideally, net profit before taxes should be 20 percent, or $200,000 a year.

Capital cost 100 seats at $4000 per seat	$400,000
Sales per year 100 seats at $10,000 per seat	$1,000,000
Profit before taxes: 20 percent of sales ($1,000,000)	$200,000

Of course, only a handful of restaurants in high-income, high-density locations have such a record. As might be expected, restaurants serving liquor usually have slower seat turnover and fewer sales per seat. The higher profit on liquor tends to compensate for the lower total sales.

Chain restaurants and franchise restaurants usually gross at least $600,000 annually. To be really profitable, they must gross more than $1 million. Such operations are growing in number each year.

If a restaurant is a winner, the return on investment can be very high. A restaurant doing sales of $1 million a year may make as much as

$200,000 net profit before taxes. Such a restaurant might cost $1 million to build. Return on investment (ROI) could be 20 percent before taxes. A good restaurant today costs between $3000 and $5000 per seat to build and equip, depending on size, cost of land, and appointments. A 100-seat restaurant would run between $300,000 and $500,000 in cost. Such a restaurant should gross between $400,000 and $600,000 in sales per year. If it nets 8 percent before taxes, profits would be $32,000 to $48,000 a year.

Break-Even Points

Like most businesses, profits are not a direct straight-line percentage of sales. Each restaurant has a break-even point at which the income pays for all the operating costs and fixed costs. In other words, a point is reached where income equals outgo. Until the restaurant reaches and then passes the break-even point, no profit at all has been made.

Once the break-even point in sales has been passed, profits may rise on an accelerated scale (Fig. 11-3). For example, the break-even point for a restaurant is $1000 in sales a day. If the sales are $1500, profit may be 10 percent on every dollar beyond $1000. When sales pass the $1500 mark, the profit may jump to 20 percent. When sales go beyond a certain figure, the operation reaches the point of diminishing returns and profit begins to fall off, efficiency falls off, the place becomes overcrowded, service is poor, and so on.

Break-even points vary widely. It may be only $200 or so a day for a family-operated restaurant. On the other hand, the Four Seasons, a luxury restaurant in New York City, was said at one time to have a break-even point of $6000 a day.

In Figure 11-4 the break-even point is $150 in sales per day.[5] If sales rise to $250 a day, profit would be the difference between S1 and P1, or about $50. If sales go to $350 in one day, profit would be close to $100. The point of diminishing returns would be reached when a line representing cost began trending upward and paralleled the sales line.

Typically, a company's officers look 2 years ahead setting sales, unit, and profit goals. Some

5. "Using Break-Even Analysis in Food Service Establishments," Food Management Program Leaflet No. 13 (Amherst, Mass.: College of Agriculture, University of Massachusetts).

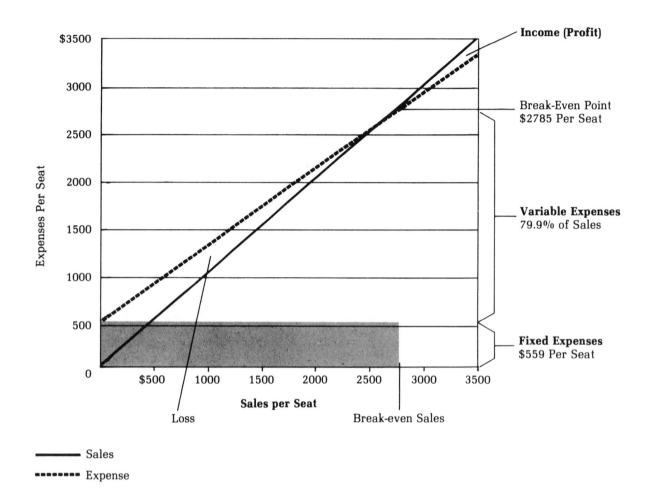

Figure 11-3 Daily break-even chart.

companies set 1-year goals in consultation with all managers above a certain level. Five-year horizons are necessarily less clear and may entail entry into new markets, new restaurant concepts, or major menu changes.

STRATEGIC PLANNING[6]

In setting long-range objectives (the strategic planning process), restaurant owners should consider both financial and nonfinancial objectives, as well as risk constraints. The most common types of financial objectives are those that deal with profitability, growth, and shareholder well-being.

Hospitality companies typically use return on equity or capital as their profitability measure and annual earnings per share increase as their growth measure. An objective of a 15 to 20 percent annual growth in earnings per share has been a fairly common target for companies involved in lodging, restaurants, and institutional foodservice—and many have achieved this target over a number of years.

As a measure of shareholder well-being, companies traditionally have used the market value of their common stock. Gyrations in the stock market have raised questions in the minds of many as to the practicality of this measure.

Some believe that dividend payout could be used as a measure of shareholder well-being and

---

6. Much of this section appears courtesy of James Crownover, formerly corporate planner, Saga Corporation.

as a financial objective, together with profitability and growth targets.

Two types of nonfinancial objectives are increasingly being used. First, companies are making specific statements regarding their role with respect to employees. Saga, for example, has a bill of rights for employees. Other companies state objectives in the area of maximizing personal development for employees.

Companies also establish objectives regarding their role with respect to society. In recent years, some hospitality companies have begun to define their role with respect to the conservation of resources.

Limits and Guidelines

Companies should consider risk at the same time they are establishing financial objectives. Typi-

cally, a company may be able to achieve higher financial objectives if it is willing to assume greater risk. For example, by borrowing larger sums of money or acquiring greater numbers of businesses, a company might achieve relatively higher financial objectives; however, greater risk is involved.

Some companies set specific risk limits beyond which they will not go to achieve financial objectives. In limiting the dependence on borrowed funds, a company sometimes uses a debt ceiling based on a minimum ratio between after-tax earnings and fixed-interest requirements. For example, if a company mandated that fixed-interest requirements would remain less than one-half of current after-tax earnings, this would insure that a 50 percent drop in company earnings would not leave the company unable to meet its debt requirements.

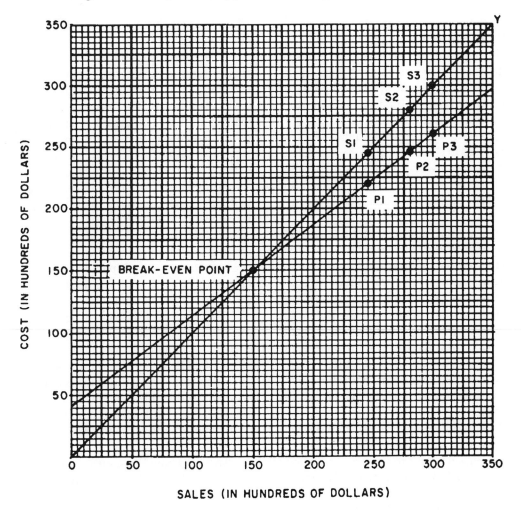

Figure 11-4 Break-even point.

TABLE 11-4   Estimating Long-Range Financial Results

Markets	Volume	× Price	− Cost	+ Investment
College feeding	1% annual enrollment decline 20 net new accounts per year	No increase due to competitive pressures	5% increase per year More extensive unionization	Minimal
Hospital feeding	2% annual increase in hospital census 15 net new accounts per year	Etc.	Etc.	Etc.
Business and industry feeding	4% annual increase in HQ populations 15 net new accounts per year	Etc.	Etc.	$100 K per year for vending

Source: James Crownover, Saga Corporation.

Some companies specify the maximum number of new businesses that they can become involved in during the year. This limitation is based on the belief that the top management structure can handle only so many new businesses per year before the current ongoing business suffers from a lack of management attention.

Finally, a company may set guidelines for the mix of businesses in which it will be involved. For example, a company with both institutional and restaurant foodservice businesses may set a limit on the size of the restaurant business as a percentage of the total.

The institutional foodservice business requires little capital and, consequently, has little risk associated with it, but its growth rate is relatively slow. In contrast, restaurants require considerable financial exposure as a result of long-term lease commitments, but the potential growth is large. By setting a limit on the overall size of the restaurant foodservice business as a percent of the total, a company can limit its overall risks. Most of the larger hotel chains limit risk by foregoing investment and seeking management contracts.

The strategic planning process includes an estimate of the long-range financial results (Table 11-4) that a company can produce, by assuming "business as usual." In developing this base case financial projection, a company should make a thorough evaluation of each market it currently serves and should analyze trends in each aspect

of the profitability equation: volume, price, cost, and investment.

The company then makes its base case projection, assuming current levels of efficiency and the continuation of current market trends. The difference between the base case projection and the objective in each financial area is called the performance gap. For example, the earnings performance gap is a measure of those additional earnings that will have to be produced to meet the long-range earnings objectives, either through better performance in current businesses or entry into new business areas.

At this stage of the strategic planning process, a check should be made to be sure that the risk constraints developed in conjunction with long-range objectives have not been violated by the base case projection.

The chief executive officer or principal owner (or owners) of a business usually strongly influences the strategic planning process. Highly ambitious CEOs in the restaurant business have a tendency to overexpand, building or otherwise acquiring more units than the company can operate well. The result: financial failure, tremendous tension within the company, and often the departure of the CEO.

The CEO may insist on a strategic tack that is wrong for the company or existing conditions. The company is acquired by another company that changes objectives. Often, the CEO or the board chairman is forced out and the new management changes corporate goals. Examples of restaurant companies that have experienced sharp changes in policy are Howard Johnson's, Holiday Corporation, and Saga.

NO MAGIC FORMULA

A wide variety of menu formats has been successfully merchandised in this country. The modified and upgraded railroad-car diner that serves foods right off the grill is favored by the highway traveler in parts of the East. It is especially popular in New Jersey, where most of the "dining cars" have been built. These diners were originally railroad dining cars that were taken out of service and revamped; now they are mostly structures patterned after such a car. New diners are lavish indeed and expensive.

Nondescript restaurants have been known to succeed for a time, perhaps because of good location and the personality of the operator. Funky restaurants with oddly assorted themes often succeed, whereas the more traditional restaurant does not. Specialty restaurants have had a greater chance of success because of that specialization. Deluxe restaurants come and go. Fashions in decor change.

If a restaurant meets a need or evokes excitement, glamour, or adventure, it will succeed if it is well managed. The big money-makers seem to be those that either offer a menu familiar to a particular market or that glamourize a familiar menu. The milieu should be impressive, pleasing, or exciting. For the teenager and patrons in their twenties, the noise level must be much higher than in a restaurant catering to older clientele. Loud, rhythmic music—even noise—tends to please a teenager and person in his or her early 20s. They seem to enjoy a higher tension level. Yet a buffet served with the same tension level in a country club would be a failure.

The decor must be pleasing or impressive to a particular market. Something that is known to be expensive or has status impresses most people. Patrons have stood in line to stay overnight at Woburn Abbey and breakfast with the Duke and Duchess of Bedford. The tariff was $200 per person.

Food is only one aspect of a restaurant. All hamburger chains sell hamburgers, one not much different from the other. The setting and advertising account for much of the success of one hamburger operation over another.

If there is a formula for success in the restaurant business, it goes something like this:

1. Identify a potential market.

2. Develop a menu that will appeal to that market.

3. Build a restaurant around the menu that will also appeal to the market.

4. Locate the restaurant as conveniently to the market as possible.

5. Merchandise the total restaurant to the market.

6. Cater to the chosen market.

7. Be ready to modify the menu or restaurant concept as the market calls for such changes.

8. Design the restaurant with style or to meet a fashion.

9. Set moderate menu prices.

10. Be aware of competition and restaurant trends.

Questions

1. Which kind of operation represents the highest financial risk: buying an existing restaurant, building one, franchising one, or managing one?

2. Of the various kinds of restaurants, which one of these could be least conveniently located for the clientele: a luncheon restaurant, a highway-restaurant, a fast-food

restaurant, or an atmosphere/theme restaurant?

3. The econometric model, one combining economics and mathematics, can be used in choosing the location for a particular style of restaurant. Can you explain what is involved?

4. Restaurants of the same chain and type should not be located too closely together. McDonald's management feels that there needs to be how many miles between each of its restaurants?

5. Suppose someone says that there are universal food preferences; some foods will always be liked. What kind of a response do you have to that statement?

6. Give two reasons why certain foods are prestigious at a given time in history.

7. In what way does seat turnover affect sales and profit? (Consider the seat-turnover ratio in relation to the average check.)

8. Some cost ratios are worth memorizing as benchmarks. About what percentage of sales are these costs in a table-service restaurant:

Payroll

Utilities

Advertising and promotion

Occupation costs

Food costs

Beverage costs

9. Although the usual restaurant probably makes a profit of about 5 percent of sales, how high can profitability go in terms of percentage of sales?

10. Why is it important to know the break-even point of sales per day?

11. In terms of the break-even chart, profit is measured by the distance between what two lines?

12. Which is better to sell, a steak at $7 with a food cost of 40 percent, or chicken at $4 with a food cost of 33.3 percent?

13. Why is it that the prices are so high at an airport restaurant?

14. Why is it that menu prices are likely to be lower in Alabama than they are in California or New York?

15. Which of these foodservices would you expect to send the most for advertising and promotion: fast food, pancake house, atmosphere restaurant, coffeeshop?

16. Which of these restaurants would you expect to have the lowest food cost as a percentage of sales: Mexican, coffeeshop, dining restaurant, fast food?

17. The term "prime costs" as related to a restaurant include what two costs?

18. Can you think of some good reasons to retain an item on the menu even though its sales account for less than 2 percent of the total?

19. Give two reasons why making a frequency distribution of guest checks is valuable.

20. Are tips considered a part of income by the IRS?

21. Give three examples of fixed restaurant costs and three expenses that are usually considered to be variable and controllable.

22. In setting up a restaurant, you note that the occupancy cost will run 10 percent of sales. Is this about right?

23. Larger companies are likely to set up long-range plans; a typical one establishes plans for how many years in the future?

24. In considering an investment, the higher the risk, the higher the __ that should be expected.

25. Diversify the corporation. Is it possible to diversify too much within a given period of time? What are the factors involved?

Discussion Questions

1. Under what circumstances would it be possible to have a 10 percent labor cost in a restaurant?

2. A break-even point is difficult to establish precisely. Why?

3. What factors will favor more takeout in the future?

Howard Dearing Johnson

(1898–1972)

Howard Johnson is one of the best-known names in the restaurant business. The name reflects the driving ambition of an individual, a desire for a kind of excellence, and the prescient perception that the American public would be auto-borne and would want ice cream, sandwiches, and relatively simple meals while traveling. The name evokes images of white buildings, orange roofs, and rich ice cream. It is synonymous with restaurants that offer a choice of counter or table seating, and quick service of hamburgers, hot dogs, fried clams, chicken, and steaks.

Originally, Johnson was a tobacco salesman for his father. After his father died in 1925, Johnson dropped out of school after the eighth grade, borrowed $500, and took over a small drugstore in Wollaston, Massachusetts. The drugstore also served as a newspaper distributorship. Though it was highly profitable, Johnson feared that he might lose the newspaper franchise and decided to sell ice cream as well.

Instead of using synthetic vanilla, he used the true vanilla bean. He called on an expert to help produce a quality ice cream, and soon he had 10 hand-turned freezers of the ice and salt variety making flavors of ice cream no one had heard of before. When he got to 28 flavors, he felt that he had them all and developed the trademark, "28 Flavors," something like Heinz's "57 Varieties."

At the outset, Johnson vowed to make good quality and control that quality.

In the summer he built little shacks along the Massachusetts beaches and hired boys to sell big ice cream cones and frankfurters for a dime: Business boomed. As Johnson put it, "If I was at all bright, it was the fact that I realized that I had an idea that worked, and I followed it and kept following it; and I follow the same pattern today, except that we have improved a lot."

He pioneered franchising in the 1930s, insisting that the franchisee purchase and sell only specified food items. By 1935 there were 25 Howard Johnson's restaurants; by 1940 there were 100.

The franchise enabled Howard Johnson to expand rapidly. In effect, the franchise purchasers were his bankers, providing money to build restaurants that merchandised the Howard Johnson name and products.

With the coming of World War II, the highway restaurant business collapsed; 90 of the 100 Howard Johnson stores were closed. The war brought gasoline and tire rationing, and people would not go 50 feet from the center of town.

He contracted to serve food in colleges that were training the military, to shipyards, and to other military units. When the war ended, he returned to the highway restaurant, refurbished the ones that he had, and built more.

It is a tribute to Johnson's drive and ingenuity that he came out of the war in better financial condition than he was at the beginning. Part of this was possible because of his prewar production of ice cream, which gave him large quotas of sugar and cream, valuable since sugar and cream were strictly rationed and in short supply.

Highway location, cleanliness, high-quality ice cream, and sandwiches served in clean, attractive, and easily identifiable buildings were keys to the Howard Johnson success story. In the 1950s and 1960s the company bought many of the franchises back, arguing that the franchise holders were not maintaining Howard Johnson standards.

In the 1950s Johnson pioneered convenience frozen foods. Quietly and without publicity, he built companies in Boston and Miami where many of the Howard Johnson menu items were produced on a production-line basis and frozen. Huge refrigerated trucks left the commissaries, carrying frozen turkey pies and other preportioned and precooked foods. At the time (and even today, to some extent), it was wiser to say nothing about such commissary and frozen-food operations. Many people considered frozen foods inferior to freshly prepared ones.

Johnson went about distributing and reheating his frozen foods quietly, while professional foodservice organizations debated the merits, economics, and feasibility of serving frozen meals.

Commissary freezing was a milestone in large restaurant operations. It permitted impressive labor economies. As early as 1953, Howard Johnson supervisors were being told that it was no longer necessary to hire cooks; only "food warmers" were needed. Food preparation in Johnson's restaurants was restricted to grilling, frying, and baking.

No intricate recipes needed to be followed for preparing food and no chef's salaries paid—just the minimum wage paid for a kitchen preparation staff and the teenaged griddle and fry cooks. If a food warmer decided to leave, another person could be trained in a few days to take his or her place.

The company continually sought to simplify equipment, standardize preparation methods, and control portions. In the New England Division, all of the coffee-making machines were leased from one individual, who also contracted to maintain them. When Clyde "Sam" Weithe put together a continuous conveyor belt dishwasher in his garage in Newton, Massachusetts, he took it to the Howard Johnson Company. It was not long before all new Howard Johnson restaurants were installing the Weithe Adamation machine. One person could operate the washer, both loading and unloading. One teenager could operate it, keep the restrooms clean, and if necessary fill in at the food preparation station as part of one job.

The Howard Johnson menu was aimed directly at the American middle-class traveling public. Ice cream was the principal appeal, as well as meat in the form of hamburgers, hot dogs, and steaks. No frills, just solid American food, served in comparative luxury, with decor that was cheerful and contemporary in the fountain area and carpeted and chandeliered in the table area.

What kind of a manager was Johnson? What made him tick? How was he able to accomplish so much in one lifetime? As Johnson himself said, his business was his life. He had no hobbies and participated in no sports; when he was at a party he ended up talking business. He drove himself and others. His method of motivation was to needle, constantly check, and forever urge people to greater effort.

Stores were open from seven in the morning to midnight, and, at any of these hours, he might be found driving up, observing the store from a distance, then inspecting it closely inside. He observed everything—a smudge on the front door, a piece of paper in the parking lot, a stain on the wall. He did not wait to send a memo telling what he found.

The Howard Johnson Company's developmental stage was not one for the young graduate of hotel schools, even less for the Harvard Business School graduate. Johnson hired those people who would do what he told them with energy and persistence and without attention to the number of hours worked. Johnson believed in certain things, wanted certain things, and bent all of his energies and those of the people around him to obtaining those things.

Few college graduates were happy in the Howard Johnson organization while Howard D. Johnson ran the show. Little stock was placed in theory or in the needs of staff personnel. All managers were their own personnel manager, and the ideas they carried out were those laid down by Johnson and a few people close to him at the top.

Managers could not be distinguished from workers. They wore the same little hat and white coat as the fountain personnel and could be found dishing up ice cream, unloading supplies, or operating the cash register. The pressure was forever on to cut labor cost, and the working manager was one way to achieve that. Bonuses were paid on the basis of labor and food cost, little else. Managers were expected to work until the job was done; the 6- and 7-day week were commonplace for them.

Salaries for Howard Johnson store managers were not particularly good compared with those of unit managers in other chains. Supervisors with responsibility for several stores were expected to step in and relieve unit managers whenever necessary.

Most of the higher echelon unabashedly stood in some fear of Johnson. All respected him. All executives knew that, regardless of rank or salary, they could expect to hear from Johnson by telephone, and frequently. When abroad, Johnson called his executives daily to check on operations, costs, and new developments.

Johnson continually worked at standardizing his operations. He probably standardized foodservice to a greater extent than had been done before on a large scale. Statler standardized the foodservices of Statler Hotels long before Johnson was active, but Johnson did it differently. He produced a menu, commissary-prepared food, and a method of reheating and serving food that was followed almost exactly in all Howard Johnson restaurants.

In about 1955 a hotel student at Florida State University did a study that showed that the average ice cream cone being served in Howard Johnson restaurants in Florida cost the company 8.5¢ and was sold for 10¢. That meant the 10¢ cone was sold at a loss. Cone prices were raised shortly thereafter. (The dippers made it difficult to serve a larger than called for portion.)

The number of seats in a Howard Johnson restaurant varied as new stores were built, but gradually there evolved a standard building with standard seating and equipment. Eventually, all Howard Johnson's stores might have rolled off an assembly line. Each could have been operated by a system of signals in which the manager was the signal caller.

In 1954 the company opened its first motor lodge. Early ones were small, but they were built at strategic locations and with an architectural style that allowed for easy expansion. Johnson credits the idea of the motor lodge to his son, Howard Brennen Johnson, who at the time was only 21.

In about 1953 Johnson underwent a serious operation and decided to begin phasing out of the day-to-day management of the company. In 1959 he installed his son Howard as president and told him to "make it grow."

Johnson died at the age of 74 in New York City in June 1972. He was a pioneer in restaurant franchising, the person who saw the need for the highway restaurant and set about meeting that need so that his name became a household word.

Howard B. Johnson was 28 years old when he took over and in many ways he was the opposite of his father. The new president surrounded himself with experts to whom he gave responsibility and from whom he expected expert advice. The company was divisionalized and a large number of people added at staff levels.

The Howard Johnson company of 1985 could be described as an example par excellance of missed opportunity. In 1965 Howard Johnson sales exceeded the combined sales of McDonald's, Burger King, and KFC. In 1979 it was sold, then sold again to Marriott in 1986. What went wrong?

The motel and restaurant market were incompatible. The motor lodges attracted travelers who did not want the ice cream and sandwiches served in the Howard Johnson's restaurants next door. According to a *Forbes Magazine* article, the company became overly conservative, too cash- and control-conscious, short on market analysis and entrepreneurial spirit.* Instead of conducting full-fledged market analysis, the company relied on guest-comment cards for its market database. Instead of borrowing money to expand, the company built up a huge cash reserve.

The stockholders did well, however, when in 1979 the company was sold to the Imperial Group, a British conglomerate, for $630 million. That company could not turn their purchase around and 6 years later they sold out to Marriott for $300 million, retaining the 210 Ground Round restaurants that were part of Howard Johnson's. Marriott, in turn, sold the hotels, motor lodges, and franchise system to another company, Prime Motor Inns.

---

*John Merwin, "The Sad Case of the Dwindling Orange Roofs," *Forbes Magazine* (Dec. 30, 1985).

12

Restaurant Finance and Control

This chapter deals briefly with the numbers of the restaurant business, the ways to finance a restaurant and the need to establish an accounting and control system that insures that income is not wasted or stolen. Finance is discussed briefly from the viewpoint of the beginning entrepreneur, with observations about what is happening on the corporate restaurant scene. Nothing said is final because laws, particularly tax laws, are complex and subject to change. All financial and accounting moves should be done only after receiving expert and up-to-date advice.

Accounting has three major aspects: bookkeeping (the clerical aspect), analysis, and control. Bookkeeping functions to record and summarize business transactions in monetary terms, a systematic and efficient collection of information about financial transactions. Its presentation in standardized form, financial statements, is an accounting function, done by hand or with a computer.

Analysis compares budget forecasts with actual performance to learn if targets have been

met. Variances from the target figures are noted and explanations sought. If necessary, the controls in use are questioned and improved if possible. Analysis depends on the experience and judgment of the accountant.

Controls operate via rules and procedures imposed on employees by management to help insure that revenue due a restaurant is collected and that losses by theft or oversight are avoided.

To summarize these terms, bookkeeping is the practice of recording the financial transactions of a business. Accounting functions take bookkeeping information and put it into financial statements (profit and loss, and balance sheets). The purpose of cost accounting is to analyze the costs of food and beverage, labor, and other expenses. Controls are restrictions placed on personnel to insure that what belongs to the owner goes to him or her. Several controls may be treated as a system and called a food and beverage cost-control system, check-control system, or cash-control system. In addition, similar control

271

systems covering other parts of the business may be set up.

Accounting and control are, therefore, two sides of the same coin. They are parallel functions with the purpose of keeping track of financial transactions and ordering the actions of people to see to it that money and other assets are dealt with systematically and honestly. Control is about people rather than things, the regulation and restraints placed on people for the benefit of the restaurant.

Standards are set by management, specified measures of quality and quantity so that all concerned have reference points for judgment and performance.

Since standards are set in terms of expected results rather than actual ones, management can compare the actual with the potential. The difference between what actually happened and what was expected is called variance.

Bookkeepers record and process a constant flow of financial information. In its briefest form, the elements of the flow are:

Voucher

Journal

Ledger

Financial statement

The voucher, the original source of information, takes a variety of forms: food check, cash register tape, or time card. More and more, the primary bit of information is conveyed in the form of a computer entry backed up by a printout or voucher in some form.

The flow of data then moves to a ledger or ledgers, where it is posted, entries following the classifications carried in the journals. Finally, ledger entries are summarized and presented in a standardized format of the various financial statements:

Balance sheet

Income statement

Change in financial position

Capital statement

Cash flow statement

All this effort takes place during an accounting period, usually a month. The same cycle is repeated period after period.

Independent restaurant operators often work with private accountants in their area, auditing guest check totals and doing the accounts payable and accounts receivable in-house, having the outside accountants do the monthly financial statements and prepare tax reports.

UNIFORM SYSTEM OF ACCOUNTING FOR RESTAURANTS

To be sure that financial accounting is understood by everyone, the reports are based on common definitions and a common accounting system. For restaurants, these are found in the *Uniform System of Accounts for Restaurants*,[1] published by the NRA. The book presents standardized formats and terminology that all sizes and types of restaurants can follow, whether the accounting is done in-house or by an outside accounting firm. The content of each commonly used account in a restaurant is clearly established, making it possible to compare financial results between similar restaurants and allowing broad industry comparisons as well. The guidelines help ensure that the same items are included in a particular account.

For example, into which account should the cost of food consumed as employee meals be placed? The *Uniform System* treats them as an employee benefit along with social security taxes, medical insurance, and other employee benefits. Some operators include employee meal costs in the cost of food consumed. The *Uniform System* recommends that hotel restaurants deduct the cost of employee meals from the cost of food consumed and charge it against the respective departments whose employees are served. Since employee meals can be of considerable cost, their accounting is important when the owner of one restaurant compares costs with those of similar restaurants.

When operators get together, a favorite question is, "What is your food cost?" The follow-up question is then, "Is that before or after employee meals?" If all operators followed the *Uniform System*, the follow-up question would be unnecessary.

---

1. *Uniform System of Accounts for Restaurants*, 6th ed. 1990. Prepared by Laventhol & Horwath for the National Restaurant Association. The *Uniform System of Accounts for Restaurants* was first published in 1958.

The *Uniform System* is a manual of terms and guidelines. The *How to Use the Uniform System of Accounts for Restaurants* is a companion volume that explains the system in greater detail.[2]

Record Keeping

Sad to say, record keeping is a part of finance, a part that can be onerous, time-consuming, and boring. Nevertheless, it is necessary.

Being in business means keeping records, for anywhere from 2 years to "indefinitely." Indefinite records include tax returns and property records. The latter are needed to establish the basis for payment of capital gains taxes if and when the property changes hands. The American Institute of Certified Public Accounts (AICPA) recommends keeping the following records indefinitely:

Audit reports and financial statements

Canceled checks for taxes, capital purchases, and important contracts

Capital stock and bond records

Cash books

Contracts and leases in force

Copyrights, patents, and trademark registrations

Corporation charter, minute books, and by-laws

Correspondence on legal and tax matters

Deeds, mortgages, easements, and other property records

General ledgers and journals

Insurance records

Property appraisals

Tax returns and work papers, including records to support carrybacks and carryovers

With most tax data, the statute of limitations runs out 3 years after a return is due or filed. There are exceptions: If there is an omission of gross income of 25 percent or more, the statute of limitations is 6 years. In cases of fraud, there is no time limitation.

To be on the safe side, the AICPA recommends keeping employee withholding tax statements and employee disability benefits records for 6 years. Personnel files on terminated employees should be retained for 3 years. So too should expired insurance policies that have no residual values.

COST CONTROL

Few businesses exact the attention needed for controlling costs as much as a restaurant. Cost control is a never-ending, demanding exercise. Costs are put in perspective by dividing them into those that are controllable, those that are fixed, and those that are relatively variable. Fixed costs include:

Taxes

Occupancy costs (rent, lease costs, amortization)

Licenses

Insurance

Of course, no costs are immutable. Rents can be renegotiated, real estate taxes questioned, insurance policies changed.

Some expenses are semi-variable (or semi-fixed):

Repairs and maintenance

Utilities (heat, light, power, water)

Telephone charges

Phone companies charge a fixed minimum, but long distance charges are additional and variable. A certain amount of utility charges are fixed as well as variable.

Other expenses usually considered variable and controllable are:

Food and beverage consumed

Administrative and general payroll

Employee benefits

Bookkeeping expenses

Advertising and promotion

---

2. Douglas Keister, *How to Use the Uniform System of Accounts for Restaurants* (Washington, D.C.: National Restaurant Association), 1983.

Music and entertainment

Laundry and linen

China, glassware, and silver

Cleaning and cleaning supplies

Paper and guest supplies

Service contracts

Parts of even these "controllable" costs and expenses are likely to be fixed. A cadre of key employees must remain on the payroll even though business is slow, which also constitutes a fixed cost. But by separating costs into those that are fixed and those that can be at least partially controlled, management focuses its attention on them and can keep them in line.

Food and beverage costs are the perennial problem children; they can wreck a restaurant in a short time if not controlled. Other costs can be disastrous as well. Suppose, for example, that utility costs suddenly jump to 10 percent of gross sales when they should be running at about 2 percent. The 8 points lost could wipe out any and all profit.

Ratio Analysis

Without a knowledge of what each expense item should be as a ratio of gross sales, the manager is at a distinct disadvantage. The manager should know, for example, that utilities ordinarily do not run more than 4 percent of sales in most restaurants; that the cost of beverages for a dinner house ordinarily should not exceed 25 percent and could be much less; and that occupancy cost should not exceed 6 to 8 percent in most cases.

Of course, ratio analysis must be in terms of what is appropriate for a particular style of restaurant: coffeeshop, fast-food, club, or hotel. Moreover, the ratios must be appropriate for the area. Restaurant labor costs, for example, are usually comparatively low in the South and high in northern cities. (In other words, restaurant patrons get more food for their money in the South because of the lower wages paid restaurant personnel and, in some places, the cost of food is less.)

Reducing Theft and Accidental Loss

A number of systems have been established to reduce theft. Among them are:

1. Storerooms are kept under lock and key. Supplies are issued to each station only at the beginning of a watch according to a par stock (the amount needed for the day or other set time period at the station).

2. Tight key control. All keys are signed out by name and must be returned by name. If an employee leaves, the paycheck is withheld until keys are returned. When a manager leaves, all locks are changed.

3. Shopping reports. An independent shopping company is employed to "shop" the restaurant, to observe and report on every employee at regular intervals. Among the factors observed are whether or not all sales are recorded on sales slips. Items like candy bars are purchased at the cash register to see if the sale is rung up. Checklists with questions like the following are completed by the shopper:

Was your guest check added correctly?

As you approached the cash stand, how many patrons were ahead of you? Was payment taken in a reasonable length of time? How long?

Was the cashier working with the cash drawer open?

Were the numerals on the cash register window plainly visible?

Did the cashier call back the amount of sale and the amount tendered?

Was the change correct?

Guest Check Accountability

A great temptation exists by wait personnel if guest checks are not strictly accounted for. The waiter or waitress may bring in his or her own checks, present them to the customer, and pocket the payment. Guest checks can be altered and substitutions made if they are not numbered and accounted for.

To avoid such situations, most restaurants require that the wait personnel sign for checks as received and return unused ones at the end of the shift, their numbers conforming to the record. Checks may be issued by book, 150 to a book. For tight control, every guest check is audited, addition on each checked, and every check accounted for by number. Chains often audit guest checks in a central office, independents in someone's home.

Many restaurants use a duplicate check system. The second copy is handed to the cook in return for the food. No check, no food. Every food item ordered is recorded on a guest check, even if the order is only a cup of coffee.

The Robbery Business

Restaurant robbery has become so commonplace that if it were organized, it would almost constitute a separate business. Employees are threatened, some are brutalized. Customers are terrorized and millions in cash stolen. The average take is $500, but there are millions of dollars in personal injury suits in the aftermath.

According to a *Restaurant & Institutions* report, the fast-food industry is the big target, a robbery occurring every 27 minutes somewhere in this country.[3] Fast-food restaurants are replacing gas stations and convenience stores in robbery statistics.

Fast-food restaurants are convenient targets. Many are located in or near high-crime areas, accessible to robbers, open late at night, and manned by young, unsophisticated employees. Lone female employees are favorite victims.

The robbers tend to be young and on drugs or alcohol. Robberies are comparatively easy to pull off. One young man in Chicago held up 35 fast-food operations in a period of 2 months before being caught. Unfortunately, only 26 percent of the robbers are apprehended.

What has robbery to do with management? The restaurant is charged with providing security for employees and customers. The lack of that security, or if it looks lacking, results in those expensive personal injury suits. Things that can be done to ensure security, say the experts, include keeping cash on hand low, especially during late evening hours, and letting it be known that little cash is there. Excess money can be kept in a safe equipped with a time-delayed lock on a top-drop mechanism that prevents employees from opening it. Currency is dropped into the safe, which

the employee is unable to open until a certain amount of time has elapsed.

The building plan itself is a factor in security. Cashier areas should be placed in well-lighted and highly visible locations. All windowless outside doors should be equipped with peepholes and locks (in accordance with local fire regulations).

Closing procedures should prevent anyone from either remaining inside or gaining entry after the door is locked. No one should be permitted into the restaurant after that. Cash counting takes place only after the entire building and the office door are locked. Employees should not open rear doors to remove trash until all money is placed in the safe.

COMPUTER ASSISTANCE

Compare being hunched over a desk with an adding machine to tally yesterday's guest checks with pushing a button and having a video screen light up with all of the figures wanted! In the past, computers have fascinated, beguiled, bewildered, and frustrated. Today, they are becoming indispensible for high-volume restaurants. Restaurant computerization has not been easy, inexpensive, or free of problems. Computer jargon continues to obfuscate everyone but the experts. A major problem stems from the fact that specialized computer programs have been created by companies other than those who have manufactured the computers themselves. Optimistic restaurant operators have taken on the challenge of doing their own programming—only to learn that a program may take as long as 2 years to produce. Cost is another problem. Tens of thousands of dollars are invested in equipment in 1 year. A year or two later that equipment may be obsolete and sells at a fraction of the cost.

Point of Sales Terminals (POS)

Is it a cash register, a minicomputer, or part of a computer system? The point of sales terminal (POS) can be all three. The terminals are being installed in a number of restaurants, especially chain operations. As commonly used, service personnel punch ordered items in on a small computerlike console with a number of keys, each of which represents a particular menu item.

---

3. "The Business End of the Gun Is Your Business," *Restaurants & Institutions* (Oct. 30, 1985).

The information is kept in that machine, unless it is part of a larger system. In that case, the information is transferred electronically to a master computer, which is in another location (perhaps miles away). The individual terminal feeding the master computer is called a "slave."

In some systems, as an order is introduced by waiters or waitresses, a printer in the kitchen or bar prints out the order on a guest check, which is also totaled by the machine. This saves time and avoids errors. The system increases seat turnover by speeding the delivery system. Because drink orders are relayed electronically to the bar from the dining area, they are ready for pickup in moments. Service personnel need not enter the kitchen or bar until the already printed order is ready for them.

Information captured at the point of sale can be called up in the form of daily, weekly, and monthly sales. The machine can tally the number of each menu item sold, valuable information in deciding if an item should be dropped because of low sales.

Some systems eliminate the need to reconcile duplicate checks, a time-consuming practice. Management can track each waitperson's sales and evaluate his or her sales performance.

On the negative side, the systems are fairly expensive. They are vulnerable to electrical power fluctuations. Brownouts and blackouts can cause minicomputers to lose part or all of their memories, irretrievably losing important information.

TAX CONSIDERATIONS

Everyone in business has a partner: Uncle Sam. That gentleman is represented by the tax collector, the Internal Revenue Service, who is interested in every dollar transaction, waiting to skim off a portion for the good of the nation. The businessperson operates knowing that the IRS is looking over his or her shoulder. Being a good citizen, the businessperson wants to pay his or her fair share of taxes. What is fair is interpreted differently according to how the business is set up. Some pay a great deal more than their fair share; others pay little or nothing because they have been shrewd enough to have a tax consultant structure the business so as to avoid much or all of the taxes.

Tax laws and their interpretation continually change, so that what is said here can only be suggestive, not final.

Depreciation and Cash Flow

As a business generates income—the cash flow—and pays its immediate expenses, including taxes, the money left over is not all profit. Theoretically at least, money must be set aside to replace the building, furnishings, and kitchen and dining room equipment. These items depreciate in value year after year until they finally have no, or only salvage, value. The money that is set aside is called the depreciation allowance. (Actually, this money is seldom set aside, and very often the building appreciates rather than depreciates in value. This is dealt with in greater detail elsewhere in this book.)

The depreciation allowance is taken as a tax deduction by the owner/operator, since it is considered money lost to him or her as the buildings and items lose their value and eventually need replacement. The idea is to maximize depreciation so as to pay the least amount of taxes possible, especially during the first several years of operation. The restaurant owner receives the depreciation allowance. The owner of the land on which the restaurant sits gets none. Land is a nondepreciable item; other tangible assets are, because they have a life span. The matter of depreciation can be quite important in the success of a restaurant and is especially important to whoever owns the building.

Restaurants are often owned by a corporation that, in turn, owns another corporation, which owns the land. Still another corporation owns the restaurant building and equipment.

Easing the Tax Bite

Tax experts recommend putting all real estate and equipment into an asset company. This company should be retained by the restaurant. It owns the building, land, and operating equipment.

The equipment and building can be depreciated. Therefore, the best idea is to buy the building and allocate as much expense as possible to any item that can be legally depreciated: carpets, trees, fences, roses, garbage cans, dust pans, brooms, vacuum cleaners, dishmachines, stoves, and so on. The bigger the depreciable tax base, the better. Then, say the experts, depreciate it all as fast as possible. Those depreciation dollars are essentially tax-free dollars.

An operating company should also be established. As quite distinct from the asset company, it can carry a great load of expenses, which again are tax-free: a company automobile, a medical/dental plan for the officers, travel expenses, life insurance, entertainment expenses. The individual does not pay for those—the operating company does—and they are tax-free for him or her.

Restaurant owners with families should seriously consider setting up trusts for their children. Each trust carries a tax exemption.

There are other ways to lighten the tax burden. For example, a corporation owned by you and maybe one or two others leases a piece of land to you. You, the lessee, in turn erect a restaurant on the land and then lease the building back to the corporation. Thus, the lessee also becomes, in effect, a lessor. Put simply, it works like this. You, the individual, have leased the land from the corporation. You, the individual, have then erected the building and leased it back to the corporation. And you, the individual, own the restaurant and are able to take advantage of the depreciation on the building and draw money from the corporation in the form of lease payments.

GETTING STARTED: FINANCING

No one knows the real rate of restaurant failure because so many restaurants, like MacArthur's old soldiers, just fade away. Capitalization is all too often insufficient to cover contingencies that pop up like macabre jack-in-the-boxes to shock the unsuspecting novice operator.

Starting on a shoestring is the stuff of the American dream and sometimes works in the restaurant business—but usually not. Restaurant start-ups do not usually sail off into financial success. There are plenty of surprises. Some unpredictables pop up to foil the best efforts and plans. Menus must be changed to meet the market, there are personnel problems, and revisions must be made in marketing strategy.

One of the safest ways to become a restaurant owner is to buy an existing profitable restaurant after working there for a number of months, long enough to feel comfortable with its methods, personnel, and style. The buyer's best bet is to agree

to pay over time out of earnings generated by operations. The current owner may wish to phase out of operations and retire. Family restaurants lend themselves to such a transition.

Most small restaurants never have a chance. They are too isolated from their markets, too small, too unimpressive to compete with established restaurants. On the other hand, most of the successful operators of today started in very modest establishments, lacked formal training, and had little financial backing. A comprehensive study of failure in the restaurant business would be enlightening and valuable to the industry.

No matter how it is reached, financing the enterprise is one of the first major steps toward ownership.

Family Financing

Traditionally, restaurants have been financed by a family pooling its resources, both people and money, renting space, and opening a restaurant manned largely by family members. Members of the extended family may often be called on to help. Some end up as silent partners. Mom or Dad mans the kitchen, an in-law is at the counter or in the dining room, and the kids help out where needed. Such a modus operandi goes back to the New England tavern of colonial days.

Before World War II, hundreds of restaurants were operated by Greek immigrants. The story is repeated in thousands of different ethnic restaurants today.

Many of the big-name restaurant chains began as Mom and Pop operations. The small family ventures were bought out by corporate giants after they had proved successful. KFC, the Magic Pan, Stouffer's, and Marie Callendar's are examples of this "let the little guy prove a concept, then buy him out" philosophy.

How many restaurant success stories have been financed by borrowing against a family home, putting it on the line to get enough capital for a foothold in the foodservice business? Carl Jr.'s began as a hot dog cart, money for which came from a loan against the family car (much to the consternation of the spouse). A highly successful cafeteria chain got off the ground when two friends mortgaged their homes.

Numerous restaurants started when a small group of friends decided they could do better than existing ones. The Cask-N-Cleaver chain began this way, making it through the first several months only because the principal retained his job as an accountant and managed the restaurant at the same time. (This is a course of action predisposed to cardiac arrest.)

A well-known restaurateur got his start by inviting a group of wealthy people to a party at a friend's home, where he explained his proposed concept and asked for participation in a $100,000 limited partnership. It worked: He got his start-up capital.

No doubt, acquaintance with wealthy people helps. Some of them like the idea of being part owner of a name restaurant. Real estate developers, successful entertainers, lawyers, and physicians often enjoy the notion of having a place "of their own" in which to entertain. Tax write-offs soften the cost of failure to the investor.

Start-up Capital Investment

Too often a would-be restaurateur allows optimism to override financial resources and acumen. Too little capital investment, too little working capital, too little market analysis, or too little experience make for too much disappointment when profits fail to appear.

Although several millionaire restaurant operators started with small restaurants and were

successful from the day they opened, most restaurant operators have a rough time financially for the first several months. Many lose all of their investment because of lack of working capital. The time period required to break even in a restaurant is usually much longer than anticipated by the owners.

The start-up investment requirements of a hypothetical table-service restaurant have been developed by the *Small Business Reporter* and can be seen in Table 12-1. Too often, the capital is insufficient to reach a break-even point.

PARTNERSHIPS

Numerous restaurant ventures are syndicated and set up as limited partnerships, with the operator as the general partner.

Limited Partnerships

Restaurant partnerships have all the ingredients for misunderstanding and rancor. Responsibilities and rights should be spelled out initially, or a Subchapter S corporation, which is explained later, should be considered.

When things go wrong, it is the other partner's fault, and almost inevitably the day comes

TABLE 12-1   Initial Investment Requirements for a Hypothetical Table-Service Restaurant

Annual gross sales: $200,000–$350,000
Floor space: About 3000 sq ft
Seats: 100

Opening costs:	*Range*
Leasehold improvements (wiring, plumbing, air conditioning, painting, labor and materials at $50 to $90 a sq ft)	$150,000–270,000
Fixtures and equipment in dining area	5000–10,000
Kitchen (500 sq ft at $60 to $100 a sq ft)	30,000–50,000
Lease deposit (first and last month)	4000–8400
Food inventory (at opening)	2000–8000
Operating costs (first three months):	
Payroll	
Manager's salary	$6000–8400
Employees (4 servers, 2 cooking staff, 1 part-time cleanup)	23,000–25,600
Food supplies	30,000–40,000
Taxes and licenses	1000–2000
Professional services (legal and accounting)	1000–1500
Insurance	600–800

Source: Adapted from *Small Business Reporter.*

when the partnership must be dissolved. Partnerships with spouses can be very sticky, especially in case of a divorce, which can result in the forced sale of the restaurant to reach a settlement. In either scenario, when property is divided by judge or jury, the results can be bizarre. They hinge on how smart, competent, or maybe crooked each client's lawyer is.

General partners establish the terms of the agreement and are careful to protect themselves. In some cases, the fine print permits the general partner to borrow, if necessary, to keep his or her yield on the same level as that of the limited partners.

Limited partners should read the fine print to learn exactly the amount of control exercised by the general partner or partners. Some agreements give the general partner an inordinate degree of control, requiring as many as 90 percent of the limited partners to block any proposal by the general partner. An "overcall provision" is dangerous to the limited partners' financial health: It allows the general partner to call on limited partners for more cash. If the limited partners fail to ante up, their equity is usually reduced.

Limited partners who want to sell may have a tough time. Disputes over a restaurant's value are common. A usual provision in the limited partnership gives the general partner the right of first refusal when limited partners want to sell. This tends to discourage potential buyers because the general partner has the right to match any bid that is made.

Often a fractional interest in a restaurant is worth very little, especially if the success of the place has depended on the ability and personality of one of the partners. When a financially pressed partner wants out, the other may propose that a value be named for the restaurant and that one or the other must accept that figure. The financially pressed partner then is over a barrel: He has no money to buy so he must accept the figure presented.

General partners are the syndicators; it is they who, with legal help, initiate the partnership and manage it. At the end of each calendar year, the general partner is responsible for providing a K-1 form, which contains the amount earned and the amount of write-off allowed the limited partner. Fees, commissions, and other expenses can eat up as much as 20 percent of the investment.

The Tax Reform Act of 1986 removed the large deductions formerly available.

Buy-Sell Agreements

When a partnership is set up, the partners are advised to look ahead to the day when the relationship will be dissolved—a certainty over time—caused by ill health, death, retirement, or other reasons. A buy-sell agreement is providential and simply good business. It can save much ill will and misunderstanding. The agreement simply says: Either you buy my interest for a price I offer, or I buy your share at the same offering price. Such an agreement, however, may not be fair if one partner is unable to come up with the money, but still does not wish to sell. The other partner may know that such is the case and take advantage to buy at a below-value price.

An idea that does seem eminently fair may be called "You divide and I'll choose." When a division of assets is required, one person is asked to divide up the assets in any way that he or she wishes—but the other person has the right to choose which half to take.

The "you divide and I'll choose" arrangement can be written into the partnership agreement. It can be used in divorce settlements as well. It is hard to feel short-changed under such an agreement. It can avoid ill feelings that can last a lifetime.[4]

Master Limited Partnerships

A variation on the limited partnership is the master limited partnership (MLP). Ownership can be traded on a stock exchange, and like all partnerships, it avoids the corporation tax. Earnings go directly to limited partners. MLP dividends can be used to offset losses an investor realizes from existing tax shelters. Income to the limited partner is defined as passive when it was not earned by active participation in a business. Under the 1986 Tax Reform Act, passive losses to an owner can only be offset by passive income to that owner.

A decided advantage of the MLP is that because shares can be traded publicly—which

---

4. Michael D. Traktman, *What Every Executive Better Know About the Law* (New York: Simon & Schuster), 1987. Contains suggestions and ideas useful to restaurant operators.

makes ownership more liquid—they are more easily bought and sold. Among the hospitality companies that have made MLP offerings are Pillsbury, Perkins Restaurant, Prime Motor Inns, and Days Inns.

Burger King Corporation in 1986 offered what is called a captive MLP, which combined $85 million of real estate leases covering existing franchises for Burger King stores. Franchises started after the offering were not included, which meant that the value of the partnership's leases may not fully share in Burger King's growth.[5]

The Subchapter S Corporation

The restaurant with fewer than 35 owners should seriously consider the modified type of corporation known as the Subchapter S corporation. Unlike the standard corporation, the S corporation is treated as a partnership for tax purposes. All income, deductions, and credits flow directly through to the individual owners/shareholders and are reported by them. Moreover, the Subchapter S corporation has the same limited legal liability features as the standard corporation. Under the Tax Reform Act of 1986, corporate tax rates are higher than individual tax rates; the S corporation avoids the double taxation required under a standard corporation.

Avoiding corporate taxes can create significant savings. For example, in 1985 the percentage rate of pretax earnings was 44.6 percent for McDonald's, 47.5 percent for Dunkin' Donuts, and 40.6 percent for TGI Friday's.

LEVERAGED BUYOUTS

Restaurant corporate finance follows the same twists and turns as other corporate finance. Current interest rates, tax laws, and finance fashions are all a part of the scene. In the mid-1980s corporate raiding and leveraged buyouts (LBOs) dominated the corporate restaurant news as they did in the business world at large.

In an LBO, a group of investors buys a publicly owned company and takes it private. A group buys a controlling interest in a company at a price considerably higher than the current selling price of the company's stock. Very little of the buyer's own money is used; most is borrowed, usually by selling junk bonds. Cash flow and asset sales are often used to pay down the debt. "Leveraged" in this sense means that a little equity is used to borrow heavily. Denny's, largest of the coffeeshop chains, was acquired by its own management in this way.

The key to the buyout is the source of the tender-offer money, the "junk bond." These are bonds that pay interest at a considerably higher rate than the bond market as a whole. The current stockholders of the company, offered a premium price for their stock in this way, usually sell. The takeover group then gains control. Now, of course, the takeover group owes an inflated debt in terms of deliberately overpriced stock and debt that must be serviced from profits, leaving little or no money to pay stockholders dividends or interest to the owners of the junk bonds. The group may have made millions on the takeover by giving themselves a large block of the stock as part of the takeover proposal. Takeovers by management groups are often a defensive maneuver to obviate takeover attempts by outside "raiders" who, once in control, install their own management and often sell parts, or all, of the company. Denny's management obtained control of the company with something over $700 million of junk-bond financing.

Another major LBO occurred in 1987 when W. R. Grace sold out for $536.7 million to a management-led group, the Restaurant Enterprises Group, Inc. The LBO included sale of Coco's Carrow's, and JoJo's restaurants; casual dining units including Houlihan's, Old Place, Darryl's and Baxter's, Rueben's, Charley Brown's, and Charley's Place (dinner houses); Bristol Bar and Grill, Devon Bar and Grill, and Gladstone's 4-Fish (seafood restaurants). So too was the El Torrito chain. The new company employs more than 50,000 people. It was a "friendly" buyout in that W. R. Grace itself purchased $100 million of the new company's preferred stock and bonds, plus warrants, which gave W. R. Grace a 47 percent common equity interest in the new company.

Marriott illustrated another facet of takeover tactics by buying Howard Johnson's and then selling off the motels for close to the total purchase price. (Parts of a company may be worth more, sold as parts, than the whole.) Marriott also

5. "Some Master Limited Partnerships Offer High Yields but Post Poor Total Returns," *Wall Street Journal* (March 19, 1987).

acquired Saga Corporation and promptly divested itself of the commercial restaurants, keeping the contract foodservice for itself.

The LBO was the divestment choice of a restaurant company controlled by one family that wants to have control passed on to people whom they know, trust, and respect. Trans/Pacific Restaurant, Inc., for example, was started in 1946 by the Salisbury family. It had grown to become a 56-unit chain operating under nine concepts. The company was taken over in 1986 by key executives, who acquired 85 percent of the stock.

The impact of the LBO has had a lasting effect on the restaurant business, one that overall has been negative. The professional restaurant manager usually becomes secondary in the scheme of LBOs. Profits are paramount, and because the LBO results in huge debt increases, pressure is put on management to increase profits. In a down economy this is often impossible.

In the typical LBO, the price of the stock is increased at least temporarily, and stockholders expect dividends to be maintained even though much of the earnings are being used for debt service. The real beneficiaries of the takeover turn out to be the insiders who engineered the LBO and the buyout specialist who arranges the debt and equity financing necessary to purchase the common stock.

An example of a foodservice LBO was that done by ARA Services. Members of ARA's management who participated in that company's LBO received 31 percent ownership of the company by putting up only 2 percent of the capital. The rest was borrowed using ARA's assets for collateral.

Foodmaker, parent of the Jack-in-the-Box fast-food chain, is another example of how insiders have profited greatly by engineering LBOs. In 1985 the chief executive officer of Foodmaker, Jack Goodall, bought the chain from Ralston-Purina for $430 million. In early 1987 Foodmaker sold 4 million shares to the public at $13.50 each, a move that tripled the market value for the LBO partners. In 1988 the company went private again in a new management-led LBO for $247 million.[6] In other words, Jack-in-the-Box management got for $247 million what Ralston Purina was paid $430 million.

Another instance of a leveraged buyout that did not benefit employees, or over the long pull, the stockholders, was that of Flagstar Cos., a Spartanburg, S.D. company that owns or franchises five restaurant chains, of which 1000 Denny's restaurants are their largest holding. In 1989, Coniston Partners bought controlling interest in the company, which in 1994 was controlled by Kohlberg Kravis Roberts & Co. At that time $1.5 billion was paid for the nebulous asset called goodwill which was part of the huge debt of $2.4 billion incurred in the buyout. Goodwill is the excess over book value that a company pays for a company's assets. In 1994 Flagstar took a $1.5 billion write-off for the loss in the value of its goodwill.[7]

LBO proponents argue that old, incapable management is swept out and replaced by new management who can realize the firm's potential. Sometimes this happens.

Needless to say, taking part financially in any restaurant venture can be a tricky business, fraught with implications that may not be immediately apparent. A smart lawyer and an equally smart accountant are essential. Regardless of the amount of good will and trust present, initially "putting it in writing" can avoid a lot of misunderstanding and rancor if and when things do not work out as expected.

SELLING A RESTAURANT OR CHAIN

A discussion of restaurant finance is not complete without some mention of what happens when the restaurant owner sells. The desire to sell can be completely profit-motivated, or it can be the result of necessity—a death in the family, a divorce, declining health, or the plain fact that the owner wants a change. The owner may want to retain an interest in the restaurant or be associated with it on a part-time basis or as a consultant.

A straight cash sale is generally the simplest way to sell. A corporation buying the restaurant or chain, however, often prefers using its company stock in lieu of cash. The worth of the stock may be actually higher than the monetary value of a cash sale. The reason for this is simple: The

6. Elias S. Moncarz, "Leveraged Buyouts in the Hospitality Business: Five Years Later," *FIU Hospitality Review* (Spring 1991).

7. "Flagstar Loss Is $1.65 Billion In Big Charge," *Wall Street Journal*, 1/25/94.

former restaurant owner is restricted from selling the stock for a few years and assumes the risk that the price of the stock could fall during that time. He or she, in effect, is being "rewarded" for taking on that risk. (The restriction is made because selling a large block of stock generally drives down the market price.) If the stock climbs in value over that time, of course, the seller profits. He or she incurs the capital gains tax only when the stock is sold.

Another choice of sale is the "earn-out." The seller contracts to stay on for a few years and share in the company's profits over the time of the contract; the buyer pays for the company out of earnings.

In family-operated restaurants another option, the installment sale, has worked well in avoiding estate taxes. It has the advantage of allowing the owner to continue control of the business. The owner's heir sets up a corporation that buys the restaurant and then hires the present owner as president, with a noncancellable lifetime employment contract. This provides the present owner full control, plus long-term income as long as the restaurant is profitable. The heir buys out the parent's business over 10 to 20 years, using cash flow to make the payments. The donor parent can include a clause in the agreement that cancels the buyout if the donor changes his or her mind or tax laws change. In a family restaurant the heirs may already be involved in the operation; the long-term buyout is a work incentive for them. Over time they acquire complete ownership.

Restaurant corporation takeovers are facilitated when the chief executive officer is given a "golden parachute," often a sum in the millions of dollars, for his or her acquiescence in the sale. The golden parachute is a term used to describe an arrangement whereby the CEO (and certain other highly compensated employees) receives large sums as compensation for being removed from control of the company. It is a way of buying off the CEO, guaranteeing that he or she will not fight the acquisition. It does add to the price of the takeover.

CEOs have also been bought off with agreements in which they are given large sums of money to act as consultants over a specified period of time. The CEO may look forward to playing an important role in the acquiring company. Often, however, the consultancy is an empty title: the consultant is never consulted, is not even given an office; he or she just gets the money.

Questions

1. What is the distinction between bookkeeping and accounting?
2. In accounting terms, what is a guest check?
3. Name two financial statements.
4. How can you buy a copy of the *Uniform System of Accounts for Restaurants*?
5. Why is it desirable to set up the financial records of a restaurant following the recommendations made in the *Uniform System*?
6. Why are accounting and control so closely associated?
7. In accounting language, what is a "variance"?
8. Point of sales terminals (POSs) play an important part in the accounting and control systems of many restaurants. Explain.
9. What is meant by "ratio analysis"?
10. Fast-food restaurants are routinely robbed. What can be done to prevent this from happening?
11. During the early years of a restaurant, would you take the maximum depreciation allowable? Why or why not?
12. What are the advantages of operating a restaurant as a partnership? The disadvantages?
13. The master limited partnership (MLP) is a new form of limited partnership that avoids corporate taxation and has what other advantage?

Discussion Questions

1. Is the leveraged buyout (LBO) a good thing for the restaurant industry?

2. Could you justify selling your friends limited partnership shares in your restaurant venture?

3. As a student who has taken courses in hotel and restaurant accounting, would you set up your accounting system by yourself?

4. The LBO is sometimes said to be beneficial for business because it may force out inept management and replace it with leaner, more aggressive management. The stock price may go up. This can happen, but who usually benefits most from an LBO?

James A. Collins

(1926–)

The magnates of the hospitality business have come in a variety of shapes, sizes, and appearance. Conrad Hilton was Mr. Suave. Ray Kroc was the fiesty little fighter. Ellsworth Statler was a small dynamo. Jim Collins in his sixties looks like Jack Armstrong, the All-American boy as an adult. He projects an attitude of "The world out there is okay and I'm going to make it better." Clearly, he is not the scheming driver out to get his and then some. The world is not a rat race. It is a place in which to achieve, have fun, and enjoy yourself.

Like most hospitality industry winners, Collins has paid his dues. At age 25, his first self-service, fast-food restaurant, Hamburger Handout, called for 16-hour days, 7 days a week. His first restaurant format was patterned after the original MacDonald Brothers' "hamburger, french fries, and milkshake" operation; hamburgers for 19¢, 11¢ french fries, and 20¢ shakes. "Two-for-ones" and half-price specials were used to attract new customers and let them sample the product.

An innovator, he changed the budget steak house, the Sizzler, into a pseudo–dinner house, adding lobster, shrimp, salad bars, and beer and wine, but he retained a semi–self-service concept. He also ran with the franchise concept, both as the major franchisee and franchisor.

His background is truly that of the All-American boy: college at UCLA, a strong interest in sports, especially track and field, a major in civil engineering, and two years of work in the profession. At 25, a strong determination to be in business for himself found expression in a self-service drive-in. Huge sales enabled him to open three smaller stores, Hamburger Handout Jrs. The year 1960 was a turning point in that he met Colonel Sanders and began selling Kentucky Fried Chicken (KFC). Two years later, the colonel assigned Jim all of Southern California as a franchisor/franchisee.

Another major turning point came in 1967. Jim and some associates bought the Sizzler Family Steak Houses for $899,000. A year later the Sizzler and Kentucky Fried Chicken restaurants (33 KFCs and 156 franchised Sizzlers) were taken public. Some 300,000 shares were sold at $18 a share.

The original Sizzler was a minimal-service steak house. Salad bars, seafood, and service in an open dining area were added over time. The average check increased and the restaurants shifted to become a midscale chain. By 1983 there were over 500 Sizzlers in 39 states and franchised operations in Japan, Guam, Kuwait, and Saudi Arabia. Some 240 KFC units are under the Collins Foods International banner, headquartered in Los Angeles. About half of the Collins' KFCs are in Southern California, the others in Florida, Illinois, Oregon, Texas, and Queensland, Australia. Five distribution centers assure franchised stores a reliable source of uniform-quality food.

Three words have loomed large in the lexicon of fast-food success: timing, marketing, and value. Collins capitalized on trends by using mass marketing techniques and always keeping the price/value concept before the public.

On top of and anticipating trends, Collins and his associates see their Sizzler restaurants as an evolving concept and do not hesitate to gradually reposition them to reach new markets.

Unlike most hospitality magnates who are too busy or too individualistic to take part in the hospitality trade organizations, Collins has taken a very active role in both the California Restaurant Association and the National Restaurant Association. As chairman of a fund-raising drive, he helped raise $2 million for a Center for Hospitality Management at California State Polytechnic University, Pomona, $1 million of which he donated himself.

Sitting in a meeting chaired by Collins, the observer sees a highly integrated and organized person in action, a man with definite, well-planned goals. Meetings start on time, are brief, to the point, and effective. Obviously, he is a person who thrives on challenge. Many of the challenges he takes on are for the benefit of the industry and society as a whole. If he is the adult version of the All-American boy, it is only to be hoped that others will emulate him.

13

Franchising and Fast Food

It was not her sex appeal but the obvious relish with which she devoured the hamburger that made my pulse begin to hammer with excitement.
—Ray Kroc (1902–1984)

Fast food simply means food prepared and served quickly. The fast-food restaurant was explained by one wit as "where the fleet meet to eat."

The single factor creating the greatest change in the restaurant industry since World War II has been the franchise. Applied to the fast-food business, it has permitted hundreds of small entrepreneurs to enter the restaurant business because it starts them out with a fixed, limited menu, standardized building and operational format, and already established image, market plan, and financing scheme.

The fast-food franchise has had an impact on the restaurant business in a way few dreamed possible, stimulating billions of dollars in sales, bringing millions of new customers, and changing the face of the restaurant business. The phenomenon has been, in part, responsible for making multimillionaires of a number of franchisors and at least small fortunes for hundreds of entrepreneurs.

Fast-food franchising builds on three well-established business phenomena: product standardization, economies of scale, and mass marketing. Every established franchise chain has exact standards for buying, processing, preparing, and serving its product. The potatoes, the hamburger, and other menu items have been carefully specified, the preparation method controlled by training and the use of selected equipment. The "cookie cutter" approach to building and operating a franchised unit reduces costs and partially controls quality. A good cookie cutter (standardized everything) is worth a fortune and can stamp out units ad infinitum if locations are good and other conditions are right.

Economies of scale brought about by the mass purchasing of food, equipment, and advertising means that the large franchisor can assure the franchisee of reduced costs in everything from

286

building blueprints to the cost of a patty of butter. Economies of scale carry over to *mass marketing* and *merchandising*, which are critical in meeting the competition with the best advertising firms, TV advertising, and imaginative promotional schemes. The independent fast-food operator is playing against considerable odds.

Howard Johnson, who founded the Howard Johnson's restaurant chain, is credited with being the first restaurant franchisor. His first store was an ice cream parlor opened in 1925. In 1928 he had convinced a friend to build a restaurant and sell Howard Johnson's ice cream. Johnson's profit arose from selling Howard Johnson's ice cream to the restaurant. By 1939 there were 107 Howard Johnson's restaurants operating in six states. The Howard Johnson's motor lodge chain was started in 1958 and had grown to 391 lodges by 1969. Of these, 90 percent were franchises.[1] Restaurant franchising did not expand much until the 1950s, when it revolutionized the restaurant business.

By 1987 franchised restaurant chains were doing more than $54 billion in sales, close to half of the total of restaurant sales. Fast-food restaurants numbered 86,000, half of them controlled by about 11 companies.

Originally, fast-food restaurants opened at about 11:00 AM and offered extremely limited menus. Led by McDonald's, they extended opening hours and offered breakfast. The limited menu was expanded. Hamburger stores added chicken and steak sandwiches. Several of the chains introduced salad bars. Mexican food items suddenly appeared on menus around the country.

Some fast-food establishments have begun to seem like fast-service restaurants with partial table service. Patrons still stand in line to place their order, but once that order is taken and paid for, the patron is given a numbered table tent of plastic (folded to be self-standing) and seats himself. In a minute or so, the food is ready and delivered to the table by a service person.

Competition is heating up. Convenience stores are offering even faster food by having the customer serve him or herself, and the prices are lower. Supermarkets are offering packaged meals that require no refrigeration and are ready to be zapped by a microwave.

---

1. Charles L. Vaughn, *Franchising* (Lexington, Mass.: Lexington Books) 1974.

HISTORICAL BACKGROUND

The word *franchise* comes from the old French word *francer*, meaning "to free." During the Middle Ages it was used to refer to franchises granted by the Catholic Church to friendly persons to serve as tax collectors, who then took a sizable cut for themselves before sending the rest to the Pope. Franchising appeared in the U.S. just after the Civil War, in 1865. Singer Sewing Machine dealers were the first to be offered such an arrangement. Toward the end of the century, soft drink manufacturers, brewers, and oil companies had spread the franchise concept. Franchising in the food business goes back to the late 1920s and the 1930s, when A&W Root Beer and Howard Johnson's franchised some of their units. The field developed little momentum until hundreds of soft ice cream stores appeared in the 1950s. The number of franchisors expanded rapidly in the 1960s, cashing in on the country's general prosperity and the desire of many individuals to own their own businesses with a relatively small investment.

In the late 1960s fast-food franchising took a new turn. Major food manufacturers bought established chains or built their own. Between 1967 and 1969 Pillsbury Company acquired Burger King; General Foods bought Burger Chef; Consolidated Foods Corporation, Chicken Delight and Big Boy restaurants; Ralston-Purina, Jack-in-the-Box; Pet Milk Company, Stuckey's; and AMK Corporation's United Fruit Company, A&W Root Beer. Pepsico, General Mills, and Green Giant also entered the picture. These companies, with their access to large amounts of capital and resources, give the franchise business a new stability.

WHAT IS A FRANCHISE?

A franchise as used in the hotel and restaurant business is an agreement between one party, the franchisor, and another party, the franchisee. The franchisor grants the franchisee the right to market certain goods and services under prescribed conditions and within a certain territory. Cost controls, promotional plans, buying advice, and, usually, tested operating methods are sold as part of the package.

It combines the managerial know-how of big business with the personal incentive of the individual owner. It allows the small-business person to acquire an instant image, extend economic power, and gain relative assurance of success.

Federal and state legislation has been enacted to supervise the sale of franchises and the post-contract relationship between franchisor and franchisee more closely than in the past. Several states regulate the conditions under which a franchisee may terminate or fail to renew a franchise, and a number of states closely regulate registration and disclosure of information pertinent to the purchase of franchises.

Usually, the franchisees must agree to buy and erect a particular sign and follow a list of operational practices. In many cases, they have been expected to buy certain foods and kitchen equipment from the franchiser and to follow particular preparation and operational procedures. Other agreements allow franchisees to buy foods where they like, but they must follow purchase specifications laid down by the franchisor.

A recent trend in franchising could be called "standardized flexibility." For example, the Lum's restaurant corporation offered plans A, B, and C, or combinations of the three options. The franchisee could use the exterior of plan A with the interior of the B or C plan. Standardized flexibility has to be carefully controlled to keep up the overall image that the franchisor needs to maintain identity and quality.

Most fast-food companies have several building types. Wendy's range in size from 3000 to over 4000 square feet to fit specific sites. Their new store development costs range from $700,000 to $1 million or more and cover land, building, and equipment. Land cost is the most significant.

Those wishing to buy a franchise find that the cost ranges widely, from very little to start a Domino's Pizza to $1.2 million per unit for a McDonald's franchise. McDonald's owns the property and improvements in many instances, which are leased to franchisees at 8.5 percent of investment costs per year. In addition, the franchisee pays a royalty of 3 percent of sales for services provided by McDonald's. There is also a fee of 3.5 percent of sales for advertising and promotion. Well-established companies like Domino's and McDonald's are not interested in passive investors. Rather, the companies want experienced restaurant people who will take an active role in managing their franchised operations.

Franchising is a potential big winner for the franchisor. Business can be expanded straight across the country by merely signing up hundreds of franchisees. The company can expand as rapidly as the franchisees buy. The two principal franchisor problems are (1) to maintain the quality and standard of the product and services franchised, and (2) to see to it that few, if any, of the franchisees fail.

Franchisers were originally so keen on acquiring franchisees that long-term planning was sometimes overlooked and the franchisee was not required to periodically update his or her property. KFC now requires the franchisee to remodel every 7 years to stay competitive and insists that new products be introduced as proposed by KFC. The company has also eliminated a guarantee that each franchisee will normally be the only outlet within a 1.5-mile radius and will not permit a franchisee to go public or sell out to a public company.

Subway, a sandwich and salad fast-food franchiser, headquartered in Milford, Connecticut, has taken a different route. The franchise fee for Subway is only $7500 for the first store, $100 per additional franchise. The low initial fee attracts many who lack a higher initial fee or would not risk investing in a higher initial payment.

To speed franchise sales, "development agents" sell franchises and share in the initial franchise fee and part of the 8 percent fee of franchisee sales. Speeding the growth of franchises is the low total investment needed, $60,000 to $70,000, much smaller than that with other franchise formats. In 1989 Frederick Deluca, age 42, founder and CEO of Doctor's Associates, Inc., Subway's formal company name, had made it big: 4000 stores and 1000 new franchisees a year. Royalties were some $52 million a year. By 1993 the number of franchisees had reached 7900. However, complaints were rising about franchised units being sold so close to existing units that they cannibalized each other. Numerous franchisees said they had lost thousands of dollars on their Subway investments.

FRANCHISE FAILURES

Lest the franchise idea be oversold, it should be pointed out that not only many franchisees fail each year, but also many franchisors. *Restaurant*

& *Institutions* magazine reports that about 20 percent of new franchise concepts fade from the scene each year. According to one writer, the well-known franchised restaurants have a failure rate of under 5 percent a year.[2]

There are several reasons for failure are several: franchisee inexperience, too many of the same concept in a given territory, insufficient capitalization, excessive lease or purchase prices, and successful new competition. Franchisors have often been people inexperienced in the restaurant business who see the possibility of a public stock offering with quick profits. The promoter who wants to become a franchisor may retain 20 percent or more of the stock personally with little or no personal investment. But as a general rule, selling franchises to people who have never been in the business is a mistake. Ex-athletes, retired military personnel, and the like may not be ready for the long hours and dedication needed to make the franchise productive. The restaurant business soon is seen as too confining and the owner/manager feels incarcerated.

Franchisor/franchisee relations have often turned acrimonious. To maintain good franchisor/franchisee relations, many franchisors employ franchise relations personnel. They also arrange for franchisee groups to meet regularly with company representatives to discuss common problems and seek solutions to them.

The franchisor may insist that all products used by the franchisee be purchased from the franchisor, often at prices the franchisee feels are excessive. *Forbes* magazine reported the case of one Agostine Malerba. In 1980 he owned 12 Arthur Treacher's Fish & Chips franchisees in Philadelphia, with sales of almost $9 million a year. By 1984 he had closed all of them and had lost $2.5 million. The original Treacher's franchisor had sold the company to Mrs. Paul's Kitchens, who told the franchisees that they could use no product other than that sold by their firm. Their products, said Malerba, were below restaurant standards. The company said, "Either do it or get out." Malerba got out. All told, said Forbes, more than 50 Arthur Treacher's franchises went bankrupt.[3]

---

2. Tom Powers, *Introduction to Management in the Hospitality Industry* (New York: John Wiley & Sons), 1993.
3. *Forbes* (Dec. 15, 1986).

THE FASTFOOD FRANCHISE

What Franchisees Pay

Fastfood franchisees may expect to pay several charges. They include:

1. An initial franchise fee

2. Continuing royalty fees ranging from 5 to 7 percent of the unit's gross sales

3. Advertising assessments of about 1.3 to 4 percent of gross sales

4. Equipment purchase price or rental cost

5. Rent

Initial investment required for an established franchise operation is much more than the uninitiated expect. The cost of land can range from $200,000 to over $1 million. Building costs can range from $150,000 to $500,000, equipment from $150,000 to $300,000. Organization costs add another $10,000 to $30,000. There may be other requirements as well. Burger King, for example, requires that the net worth of the owners exceed $500,000, not including their primary residences. The debt/equity ratio cannot be more than 1.5:1. The owner must be 100 percent involved in the operation and have no other business commitments.

The majority of the chains are categorized as fast-food establishments and have these characteristics:

High-speed service, mostly to walk-up customers

Immediate service of food or assignment of a number for pickup

High customer turnover

Limited menu

Low check average

Assembly-line food production

Strict purchasing and portion control

Disposable plates, cups, and utensils

Special training programs for managers and workers

Franchise operators know the value of market research and promotion. They spend up to 7 percent of their gross sales on promotional gimmicks and TV and other advertising. Millions are spent on ads to publicize only one or two food items.

What Franchisees Get

A prospective franchise buyer has a wide range of choices, according to the cash he or she can raise and the style and size of operation desired.

The franchisee can expect from a reputable and established franchisor an established name and image maintained by advertising and a complete promotion package. This includes roadside pylons and a logo or signature on take-out boxes, bags, coffee cups, napkins, matchbooks, and just about everything else that the customer sees.

The fastfood chains take advantage of their size to negotiate purchasing advantages impossible for the independent restaurant operator. Purchasing can be centralized, or agreements can be made with purveyors to produce items to specification and delivered to the restaurants.

The franchisee can also expect quality control in purchasing and operations (which franchisees may resent and resist). Perhaps most important of all, if the parent company is not overly hungry for new outlets or money, the franchisee receives careful location analysis and a certain amount of financial advice (and even help with financing in some cases). It can be expected that eventually many franchise plans will include a central accounting service.

Nearly all franchisors provide some kind of initial training—at a Hamburger University, a Mr. Donut College, or a similar center. Following that training, both franchisee and operation are watched over by an area supervisor or field coordinator. The franchisee's books are set up and audited by the franchisor in one way or another to assure that the correct fees are paid, most based on sales.

McDonald's: Many Are Called, Few Are Chosen

Some 2000 people apply to become McDonald's franchisees in the U.S. each year. Only about 150 are chosen. McDonald's executives say they want people with "ketchup in their veins"—outgoing, high-energy people who are leased to put in 12- to 18-hour days learning the business and continuing that regimen as franchisees. Those between the ages of 35 and 45 with at least 10 years' business experience are preferred.

Once selected for a franchise, the company sees to it that the restaurant is a success. If there are problems, field consultants are sent in. Rents may be lowered, or, if necessary, those not making it are bought out. Franchisees that are successful (most of them are) are rewarded by being given first call on an additional franchise location. The average number of restaurants per licensee is a little over three.

Fast-Food Restaurant Employees

A typical successful fast-food restaurant has gross sales of about $750,000 annually, is managed by someone under the age of 30, and has perhaps 75 employees, most of whom work part-time and are students under 25. Wages are low; most employees are hired at close to the minimum wage.

Demographers forecast a decline in student numbers through 1995, which could mean fewer job applicants or higher starting wages. There will be an increase of older or semiretired persons, those age 60 and up, but relatively few are attracted to the fast pace and low wages of the restaurant. Tens of thousands of newly arrived immigrants are a labor source eager for jobs. A potential problem is that they cannot afford to live in the areas where many of the restaurants are located.

High personnel turnover is the norm in a fast-food restaurant; one study places the average stay at 4 months. This does not particularly disturb the restaurant owner because it keeps labor cost low. Few employees earn even $6 an hour, and short tenure means few pay raises; those 10¢-an-hour increases add up. The simplicity and standardization of operation reduce training time and costs, and new employees quickly become productive. Pension expenses are negligible, since few employees stay long enough to become eligible for one. Total labor costs are 22 percent of sales or less, one of the reasons for fast-food profitability.

High turnover has another advantage: It becomes, in part, a self-screening process by which unmotivated people leave of their own accord.

Operators who want to reduce turnover have several options. Some are listed here:

Pay higher wages.

Provide transportation by van from inner-city areas where high unemployment exists.

Offer flexible schedules.

Give paid time off after big-volume days.

Overstaff somewhat to make the work less strenuous and provide better service.

Consider cross-training those employees who can handle it or want it.

Build a list of on-call, part-time employees and pay them a premium wage per hour.

Many older persons may want such part-time work.

Consider hiring the disadvantaged, recent immigrants, and other people who really need the job.

Controversy exists over who and who is not a supervisor, because supervisors are not subject to the federal minimum wage law. Some companies hire people as management trainees and require them to work 50 or more hours a week. They receive a salary that can actually be less on an hourly basis than the minimum wage.

The Department of Labor has established several conditions to be met if a person is to be defined as a manager or supervisor:

The first and primary duty is the management of a company, department, or subdivision of a store.

The manager or supervisor regularly directs the work of at least two other employees.

He or she has authority to hire and fire, or recommends hiring and firing, transfer, and promotion.

The manager or supervisor regularly exercises discretionary powers in making operating decisions.

Nonmanagerial duties take up no more than 40 percent of the work time.

The employee who is in sole charge of a restaurant is considered exempt from federal minimum wage law, even though 40 percent of the work is nonmanagerial. In other words, the person in charge of a snack bar would do much of the physical work, but would still be exempt.

Interpretations of these company provisos change, as do laws relating to discrimination in pay on the basis of sex, race, or age; they must be checked periodically. Hospitality operators must be quite careful in drawing up their employment application forms to avoid including items or wording that violate these federal, state, or local laws. The NRA and the local state restaurant associations are good sources for information on current legal understanding of the various rules that apply to employees of the restaurant business.

The Menu

The hamburger sandwich, a meat patty on a bun, has become the star of the fast-food business. The hamburger is pattied, garnished, and eulogized by the smartest advertising people in the business. The American public has been conditioned by advertising to salivate at the thought of the Big Mac, the Whopper, and other anthropomorphized forms of the sandwich. The hamburger goes to college at Whopper College, training camp for those who aspire to greatness in the Burger King chain. At Hamburger University, players are drilled for wealth and status in the McDonald's Empire. For a food little known in the restaurant business until 1930, the hamburger has come a long way.

Indeed, it has virtues: Most grass-fed animals, including old cows, can be ground up and served. Inexpensive, imported boneless beef, raised on grass and containing only 10 to 12 percent fat can be mixed with domestic beef to produce a patty containing 18 to 20 percent fat, which is the desired level.

Hamburger history goes back to medieval times. Merchants from the German town of Hamburg traveling in Baltic areas adopted the Tartar habit of scraping and eating raw meat (steak à la tartar is still fancied by some). Later, the meat was browned before eating. The hamburg was brought to this country by immigrants and German sailors.

In England in 1888, a physician, Dr. J. H. Salisbury, promoted a variation of the burger as a wonder food, which he was certain would cure an assortment of diseases, including colitis, rheumatism, gout, and hardening of the arteries. This was the Salisbury steak, a large-patty version of the hamburger.

The St. Louis Exposition in 1903 served the hamburger in a bun. Later, in 1921, the White Castle chain added onions to a flattened meatball and cooked it on a griddle. That hamburger sold for 5¢.

Hundreds of people are examining the hamburger to improve it. No other food item in history has received such minute but widespread attention. Should it be broiled or grilled? Should it be garnished with a tomato? What kind of lettuce should be used with it, shredded or leaf? Should it be dressed with onions, mayonnaise? Should the bun have poppy seeds, caraway seeds, or something else? Should it be prepared and held ready to hand to the customer or made to order? Should it have 20 or 18 percent fat? Must the meat come only from the chuck, or can it come from the whole animal? Should cheek meat be used? What percentage of meat trimmings are allowable? These and other questions have led to the fine tuning of the hamburger.

Although the hamburger itself is king, its courtly companions also bear close scrutiny. Does the crown prince of fast food, the fried chicken, add to or detract from the regal might of Big Mac? Fries, shakes, and in some locations even Mexican food (the burrito and taco) are acceptable at court.

Just when the fast-food business seems to have stabilized its product and format, along comes Domino's Pizza, which takes an old idea, home delivery, sharpens it, and burgeons with over 5,000 stores. A simple improvement made a big difference—free home delivery of pizza in less than 30 minutes. Simplicity of operation is one of the keys to its unprecedented growth.

Fast food has gone Asiatic, with fast-fish Japanese items such as sushi and sashimi and Chinese food such as beef and noodles. Chicken appears as nuggets (white chunks or deep-fried), broiled with a Mexican flavor (asado), and as strips. Taco Bell and dozens of other fast-service Mexican restaurants serve tacos, fajitas, and a number of Mexican items most North Americans never heard of a few years ago. There is also Middle Eastern fast food, mostly made with chickpeas and lamb.

Nutritional Concerns

In 1986 the hamburger was indicated by no less an organization than the American Heart Asso-

ciation. The hamburger, said the association, was the major offender in causing heart disease in the U.S. Since heart disease is the number-one cause of death in this country, the indictment is certain over time to remove the hamburger from its preeminent position on the American restaurant menu and drastically change the fast-food business built around it. The cattle industry here and in those countries that export beef to America will be affected. Steak houses and other restaurants featuring beef will also be affected by the interdiction.

Nutritionists also point out that the animal fats used in deep frying are saturated, a factor in clogging the vascular system (Coconut and palm oil are also offenders.) Fast-food operators are guilty of using too much salt, an ingredient that complicates high blood pressure in certain people. Fast-food menus generally lack fiber, believed to be important in avoiding various kinds of cancer.

Fast-food operators were slow to respond to the indictments, many no doubt feeling, "We are in the business of pleasing our customers by giving them what they want." Yet by 1986 it was obvious that large numbers of customers were interested in healthier foods. Some fast-food operators proceeded to change their ingredients and cooking methods.

McDonald's and Burger King switched their cooking oil for chicken, fish, and pies from animal fat to vegetable oil. They also fortified their sesame seed bun with calcium. Wendy's placed its chicken on a multigrain bun and offered a low-calorie dressing at its salad bar. A Wimpy's in England produced a spicy vegetarian burger made from ground onions, peppers, carrots, chili peppers, and kidney beans.

No doubt there will be further changes in the future.

Computers in Fast Food

Fast food means just that; the intent is to reduce the time between order giving and order delivery. Portable order-entry terminals are being used to permit even faster, more accurate service. With a terminal on hand, an employee can take an order from a customer either standing in line or from one in a line of cars. The order is transmitted to a cash register and the production line, where it appears on a viewing screen.

Chain operators are linking personal computers located in each store to divisional and corporate offices, where such time-consuming chores as crew scheduling and inventory monitoring can be done more efficiently, which allows store managers to concentrate on customer service, personnel relations, and store cleanliness.

Drive-Through Service

Drive-through service reduces service time and space. By hooking a computer up to a window, Naugles shoots for a 20-second transaction time. In and Out Burger operates with double drive-through customer windows and limited or no seating; it gets by with a tiny store of 1000 square feet or less. Church's Fried Chicken does the same. Part of Wendy's success is attributed to the drive-through window. Many fast-food restaurants have determined that as much as 40 percent of their sales come through that window.

White Castle, a pioneer fast-food operator, has added a drive-through, a double-window system that can be attached to any side of the restaurant and process up to 100 cars an hour.

In a way, the drive-through is a return to the curb service of the old drive-in places that predated the fast-food restaurants. The big difference between them is speed of service: The customer now receives his or her order directly from a windowserver.

The stand-alone drive-through competes head to head with the convenience store. Occupying as little space as 14 by 14 feet, it can lease the odd-sized lot that is too small for the usual retail store. The drive-through puts its dining room in the customer's car, thereby cutting its occupancy cost to the bone and permitting it to underprice the standard fast-food restaurant. The severely limited menu of burger, fries, shakes, and soft drinks reduces investment and labor costs and limits the skills needed to operate successfully.

The mainstay for the drive-through is the middle-income, 18- to 38-year-old. The young families among them would rather the kids mess up the car than the restaurant. Young singles can eat on the run, as it were, in their cars, or later at home.

Child's Play

At more than 2000 McDonald's units throughout the world, children are treated to Playland and helpings of McDonald's fantasy world. Rather than use generic recreational equipment, McDonald's reinforces its own image in its play areas. Ronald McDonald is there. Garden burgers grow beneath the double-faced apple pie tree. Children sit on mushroom stools or eat from flower tables. In Atlanta, a Ronald McDonald robot can sing "Happy Birthday" and a number of other tunes composed by the McDonald's advertising agency. Other fast-food chains—Burger King, Hardee's, Dairy Queen, Arby's, and Whataburger—have followed suit, but without the same effect.

Vans

A close relative to the drive-through is the van that brings food to places of work. These mobile restaurants take their menus to customers and move from one group of customers to another as conditions warrant. The van completely eliminates the costs of land and a permanent structure. Some chains have engineered vans that can offer approximately the same menu as their regular restaurants.

Fast-Food Architecture and Interior Design

Fast-food restaurants have been both the inspiration and bane of architects. Called on to create economical and eye-catching structures, they have outdone themselves in designing buildings that strain credulity. During the great expansion of 1946–1980, fast-food restaurants mushroomed along highways leading into cities and produced a visual free-for-all that frequently looked garish. Huge neon signs designed to catch the speeding motorist's eye often overpowered the restaurants themselves. As the business matured and began attracting customers other than young people, designers muted the buildings by softening signage, using earth colors, and landscaping where space allowed.

Many chains change their restaurant design incrementally, adding or subtracting seats to find the optimal number, adding soft seats, and trying to make the architecture fit the region. Recent building codes in many locations have limited sign heights, outlawed the more outlandish structures, and in general checked designs so that they better fit the environment. The flimsy little buildings and tacky decor that characterized "fast food" until about 1970 have all but disappeared.

Criticism of the architecture has abated somewhat, and a few champions have appeared pronouncing fast-food architecture as pop art. The oldest extant McDonald's, built in 1953, has been included in the Department of the Interior's National Register of Historic Places.[4]

It is generally accepted that to hasten seat turnover the restaurant planner should use bright lighting, bright colors, and hard seats so customers do not become too comfortable and stay too long. The restaurants generally meet such specifications admirably. The hard seats also serve another purpose: They make it easy to clean up after children.

Unexpected Locations

Fast-food outlets have popped up in places that would have been considered strange a few years ago. A guest at Day's Inn in Atlanta can call room service and receive a Wendy's hamburger in a bag. Department stores, casinos, and corporate headquarters now have fast-food restaurants. The Field Museum of Natural History in Chicago serves Big Macs just a few halls away from Egyptian mummies. At the Columbus, Ohio, Zoo, a visitor can see gorillas busily watching visitors eating Wendy's burgers. Military bases provide some of the longest lines at fast-food emporiums. A McDonald's at the Great Lakes Naval Training Center has sales exceeding $4 million a year. Numerous budget and mid-priced motels have invited fast-food operators into their lodges or arranged to have them build nearby. A few hospitals have decided to join the club, but nutritionists have protested the usual fast-food menu.

Today's TV Advertising

TV advertising drives the fast-food business. It is exemplified by the battle among such fast-food titans as McDonald's, Burger King, KFC, Wendy's, and Domino's Pizza. Who can miss the deluge of McDonald's TV advertising, which is fueled by a fee of 3.5 percent imposed on McDonald's nationwide sales of billions of dollars?

---

4. For a comprehensive review of restaurant architecture, see Philip Langdon, *Orange Roofs, Golden Arches* (New York: Alfred A. Knopf), 1986.

Fast-food advertising reaches into the American psyche in ways other than traditional advertising. Young people and young families are the target markets, since in about one of six families, children are the single most significant factor in the selection of a new restaurant. Each fast-food operation appeals to a particular market, one that can fade or become ripe for further development.

Restaurants may appeal to different markets by meal—breakfast customers differ from luncheon customers, and yet another group arrives in search of food between 2:00 PM and closing. Advertising both aims at the market and helps create it.

By 1979 it was clear that single units of a franchise operation operated at a disadvantage in promotion and advertising. The single unit did not have enough money to compete with chain units that advertised as a group. As a consequence, some franchise companies would not sell fewer than five units, clustering them so that newspaper advertising and television time could be purchased en masse. Three or more units are needed to be competitive with any similar chain operation nearby.

New Competition

Fast-food restaurants are being beset by something new: the convenience store. They beat out fast-food restaurants on price and delivery time. Food quality is something else. Arco stations offer two hamburgers for 99¢. They are precooked and placed in a stainless steel merchandising unit that keeps them warm until a customer picks them up. As many as 60 are heated within eight minutes, with a convection oven located in the store. As for labor cost, one employee can do it all: reheat, wrap, distribute, and clean up. Other Arco self-serve foods include cheeseburgers, croissants, and french fries. In 7-Eleven Stores, hot dogs rotating on a ferris-wheel cooker are a standard item.

Some convenience stores ventured into foodservice with well-known operators. The joint ventures provide additional income for the store that helps to offset the high cost of the real estate. Seven-Eleven has installed Hardee's units and Church's Fried Chicken units in St. Louis. Circle K uses Dunkin' Donuts and Winchell's donuts. Circle K has also tried another tactic: It licenses the foodservice operation and sets up a portion of the store for that use, but bears no responsibility for cost or the operation.

Fast-Food Abroad

Some 5000 restaurants operate outside the U.S. carrying the imprimatur—owned or franchised—of American chains. McDonald's and KFC each have more than 1500 units abroad. Established fast-food chains—McDonald's, KFC, Pizza Hut, and Mr. Donut—have done well in Japan and Europe. Denny's have been in Mexico, Japan, Hong Kong, Australia, and Singapore for some time. Wendy's is in ten foreign countries.

The temptation to operate abroad is strong. How glamorous to own or operate a restaurant in Tokyo, London, or Paris. Glamorous, yes, but one with plenty of problems unless the operator knows the territory. Going into a foreign market on one's own can be fraught with a number of unforeseen obstacles. For example, few foreign markets have the disposable income found in America. Purveyors may regard the American company as a lamb ready to be shorn. Local zoning authorities can and do refuse to approve building plans or permit the erection of restaurant signs. Class consciousness in England presents its own special problem. Outside the big English cities, if a restaurant attracts working-class customers, the other classes will stay away.

Probably the best way to franchise abroad is by joint venture with a foodservice company already well established in the country. Franchisees have in several cases refused to live up to their agreements or maintain standards of cleanliness and product. The franchisor has been forced to buy back the franchise and operate as owner.

Foreign fast food in America also grows apace; the most notable being the purchase in 1989 of Pillsbury by Grand Metropolitan, a London-based hotel/restaurant chain. The 5600-unit Burger King chain is a part of Pillsbury. The most remarkable of the fast-food chains abroad is that of the Canadian McDonald's in Moscow, which opened in 1990. There were 30,000 patrons on opening day.

Two of the Winners

Colonel Sanders (1890–1980). Perhaps the most colorful of the franchise stories involves the origi-

Figure 13-1 "Colonel" Harland Sanders, pioneer in fast-food franchising. At the age of 65 he used his $105 social security check to start franchising his "finger lickin' good" chicken dinners, later incorporated as Kentucky Fried Chicken (KFC). Restaurant operators paid five cents an order for his merchandising format, his preparation technique, and his secret seasoning mix of eleven herbs and spices. KFC is now a part of the Pepsico conglomerate. In later life, the Colonel became a devout Christian and philanthropist.

nator of Kentucky Fried Chicken, "Colonel" Harland Sanders. He had been a farmhand, carriage painter, soldier, railroad fireman, blacksmith, streetcar conductor, justice of the peace, salesman, and service station operator. At the age of 65, he found himself operating his own Kentucky restaurant/motel with little business because a new interstate highway had bypassed it by 7 miles. His only income was a social security check of $105 per month.

He had previously experimented with frying chicken in his restaurant and found that preparing it in a home-sized pressure cooker produced an especially tender product. He had also assembled a zesty coating for the chicken. He set off on a trip around the country to sell restaurant operators a franchise to produce what he now called

Kentucky Fried Chicken (KFC). Since it was a promotion package and procedure only for cooking chicken, the franchise could be used in an existing restaurant. The initial investment was low, only enough to buy a few needed pieces of cooking equipment. The franchisee would pay the Colonel 5¢ for every order served.

Sanders would stop at a restaurant, demonstrate his frying process, stay on a few days without pay until customers began to react to the chicken, and then move on. He traveled from city to city, often sleeping rolled up in a blanket in his car.

Sanders put on a television cooking show in Salt Lake City with his first franchisee, Pete Harmon. To add color, he decided to turn into a full-fledged Kentucky colonel with pure white suit and goatee. "You got to remember," he said, "I didn't have no money for advertising and promoting, so I had to do the best I could." The Colonel's thoughts on marketing: "If you have something good, a certain number of people will beat a path to your doorstep; the rest you have to go and get."[5]

Within 3 years, restaurant operators were coming to him for a franchise. But it was 29-year-old lawyer/promoter John Brown, Jr. who put KFC on the map and incidentally made millions for himself. He and an associate changed the chicken shop into a standardized red-and-white building and streamlined the operations. A $5000 investment in KFC stock in 1964 was worth $3.5 million five years later. (Brown later married a national beauty queen contest winner and became governor of Kentucky.) The Colonel received $2 million in cash, retained the KFC franchises in Canada, and was hired under contract as a public relations image-builder. His "finger-lickin' good" recipes were changed. In the Colonel's words, they became "slop."

In 1971 KFC was bought from Brown by Heublein, a liquor company, for a reported $267 million. In 1974 Sanders filed a $222 million suit against the corporation for trying to interfere with his plans to develop a new franchise operation. They settled out of court.

KFC is the number-one chicken franchisor in the world. By 1985 sales exceeded $3 billion. Two

building plans were offered franchisees (the more popular a 24- by 65-foot unit). The recommended lot location was 126 by 125 feet, preferably on a corner or on a "going home" section of road. At least 16,000 cars should pass the site each day. These criteria remain in effect today.

Unlike many of the franchisors who insist that their units be located in sizable population centers, KFC has found that its operations can gross up to $250,000 annually in communities as small as 10,000 people.

Working for Heublein, the Colonel made television and personal appearances around the country, always dressed in white with the black-string tie, white mustache, and goatee.

Always a tither for his church, the Colonel became a devout Christian at 79 after his conversion at an evangelistic meeting. Trying to live up to his new standards, he said his hardest problem was to give up cussing, a practice at which he had few peers. God, he said, was responsible for curing him of what looked on X-rays like malignant cancer of the colon.

Always generous, he became a philanthropist. His personal charities included churches, the Salvation Army, a city mission, and a number of schools. All his stock in Colonel Sanders Kentucky Fried Chicken of Canada, Ltd., was donated to a Toronto foundation, which gives all profits to charity. In addition, each Canadian franchisee allocates a portion of profit to a charity of his or her choosing.

Of all the people who have received the Horatio Alger Award, few deserved it more than the Colonel. Few people have experienced more vicissitudes in a lifetime and overcome more adverse circumstances. His pressure-fried chicken seasoned with 11 secret herbs and spices is seen in almost every community in this country and dozens of other countries around the world.

Like Ellsworth Statler, Sanders was forced to drop out of school at an early age to help support his family. Like Statler, he had the indomitable will to succeed and the stamina, perseverance, and ability to do so. He happened to be a good friend of Ray Kroc, the founder of McDonald's, and it is easy to see why.

Sanders died in 1980 at the age of 90, well-respected and an ornament to the foodservice industry.

KFC is now part of the Pepsico food conglomerate, which paid $850 million for it. That ac-

5. Colonel Harland D. Sanders, *Finger Lickin' Good* (Carol Stream, Ill.: Creation House), 1974.

quisition made Pepsico the world's largest restaurant group, with 14,000 units and sales of $7 billion.

Tom Monaghan (1937–). The title of Tom Monaghan's autobiography is *The Pizza Tiger*, which seems particularly apt.[6] He is president and chairman of the board of Domino's Pizza, the privately held pizza chain that in 1987 had more than 4000 stores and sales exceeding $2 billion. The goal is 10,000 stores by 1990. Monaghan is the personification of the gung-ho, optimistic American entrepreneur who made it big after early years of adversity. It is particularly appropriate that his autobiography was written with Robert Anderson, the same person who co-authored *Grinding It Out*, Ray Kroc's autobiography.

Like Kroc, Monaghan follows the old military acronym, KISS (keep it simple, Stupid). The essence of Domino's is simplicity—give the customer only two sizes of pizza to choose from (but a choice of 10 toppings) and one beverage, a cola. Deliver the pizza and cola, Monaghan exhorts his personnel, within 30 minutes. Thirty is the magic number. In fact, the tower in the company's headquarters building has 30 floors.

The store organization is simple, pizza delivery only; two job titles exist: pizza maker and deliveryman. Pizza makers start at close to minimum wage; deliverymen get a percentage of sales plus a car mileage payment and tips. The company will lease a store to anyone who qualifies. Motivation is high because a person who does well and has managed a store for at least a year can then apply for a franchise. The cost of the franchise and opening of a store is comparatively low, from about $50,000 to $100,000.

Thus, it is possible for a person with little or no capital to work as a manager for 1 year and end up the owner of a franchised store that may gross $200,000 or more a year. Since food costs are in the mid–20 percent range, profits can exceed 20 percent of sales, or $40,000 or more. Not bad for someone in his early 20s. He or she can also buy other Domino's franchises. Ten or 12 of them could produce a profit of $400,000 a year.

Monaghan works tirelessly on maintaining and improving quality. The cheese for the pizza is

Figure 13-2 Thomas Monaghan, "the Pizza Tiger," president and chairman of the board of Domino's Pizza, Inc., a spectacular growth company in the fast-food business.

a blend. The sauce is a blend of spices and tomatoes. "Cheesing" the pizza is a skill—grab the right amount of cheese in the hand and spread it uniformly, right up to the edge of the sauce. One spoonful of sauce goes on a small pizza, two on a large. If spread too thin, the pizza tastes bland; if too thick, the spices are overpowering. A master saucer spreads it exactly to within one-half to five-eighths of an inch from the rim. Tossing or spinning the dough overhead looks good, but it can create thin spots in the center.

Monaghan is fervent about physical fitness. He starts the day by doing 150 consecutive push-ups, followed by a 6.3-mile run. He weighs himself daily and diets should his weight exceed 163 pounds. Dessert is a treat he permits himself but 11 times a year. To interest a company vice president in his health, Tom offered him $50,000 to complete a 26-mile marathon. The man ran it and received the check at the end. The new $300 million corporate headquarters contains a complete

6. Tom Monaghan with Robert Anderson, *The Pizza Tiger* (New York: Random House), 1986.

physical fitness center and running track. Reflecting his sports enthusiasm is his ownership of the Detroit Tigers, for which he paid $53 million.

Monaghan is a devout Catholic, attending mass every day. On his list of priorities, "spiritual" is at the top. Other priorities in order of importance are social, mental, and physical. "Financial" comes last on the list. Charities include gifts of medical care to poor Honduran children brought to this country in one of Monaghan's planes.

Monaghan is enraptured with architecture, especially that of Frank Lloyd Wright. The buildings of Domino's headquarters are designed in the Frank Lloyd Wright style more so than any other kind of building. Antique cars are another passion; his collection stars a 1934 Duesenberg.

All of this is a long way from his early life. His father died when he was four years old. An orphanage, foster homes, a failure as a seminarian, a stint in a detention home, and a stint in the Marine Corps followed. It seems like really started in 1960 with a $500 investment in a pizza store. Despite several setbacks since then, pizza and an unquenchable exuberance have made Monaghan a fast-food phenomenon.

Questions

1. Who originated the McDonald's concept of restaurant operation?

2. One of the keys to the success of the fast-food franchise is the standardized format of operation. Looking at the development of McDonald's, would you say that design should be fixed and never changed?

3. Someone says, "With a franchise you completely avoid a chance of failure in a fast-food restaurant." What is your response?

4. Name at least three of the top 10 fast-food franchisors in this country.

5. Give at least three advantages to buying a franchise over operating a private enterprise.

6. Restaurants generally spend less than 2 percent of their sales for advertising; fast-food restaurants, however, spend about what percent of sales for advertising and promotion?

7. One of the more colorful characters in the fast-food business was Colonel Harland Sanders. What were the keys to his success?

8. Some of the franchisors sell only groups of franchises at a time—several in a state or large area. What does this have to do with advertising and promotion?

9. What are the food and beverage costs of a typical fast-food restaurant?

Discussion Questions

1. Fast-food restaurants have been adding menu items. Will they eventually become like coffeeshops in nature? Give reasons for your answer.

2. Supermarkets and convenience stores are adding deli sections and even snack bars. How much of a threat are they to fast-food restaurants?

3. What menu changes in fast-food restaurants do you foresee over the next decade?

4. Why is it that few hotel and restaurant degree program graduates elect to go into the fast-food business?

Ray Kroc

(1902–1984)*

Of all hospitality entrepreneurs, none have been more financially successful than Ray Kroc. The business has seen many millionaires, like Howard Johnson and Conrad Hilton, but no one has approached the financial pinnacle reached by Kroc. In 1982 he was senior chairman of the board of McDonald's, an organization intent on covering the earth with hamburgers.

Among the remarkable things about him is that it was not until the age of 52 that he even embarked on the royal road to fame and fortune. The accomplishment is all the more astounding because Kroc invented nothing new. In fact, the concept was leased from two New Hampshire brothers named McDonald who had set up an octagonal-shaped, fast-food hamburgatorium in San Bernadino, California. Kroc was impressed with the property's golden arches, the McDonald's sign lighting up the sky at night, and the cleanliness and simplicity of the operation. Even more fascinating was the long waiting line of customers.

In 1961 the brothers Dick and Maurice sold out to Kroc and his associates for $2.7 million. They had sold 21 McDonald's franchises and opened 9 restaurants before Kroc arrived in 1955 and was hired by them as a franchise agent.

Kroc's genius came in the way of organizational ability, perseverance sparked with enthusiasm, and an incredible talent for marketing. His talents extended to selecting equally dedicated close associates who added financial, analytical, and managerial skills to the enterprise.

The McDonald's Corporation is the projected image of one man, entrepreneur par excellence, who believed with a passion that business means competition, dedication, and drive. The empire was built in good part as a result of his arch-competitiveness, best illustrated by his reply to this question: "Is the restaurant business a dog-eat-dog business?" His reply: "No, it's a rat-eat-rat business."

Some of the operational guidelines followed by Kroc included the concept of KISS, Keep It simple, Stupid. It lends itself beautifully to the fast-food operation, the franchise business and QSC&V (quality, service, cleanliness, and value). McDonald's menu illustrates the simplicity concept well. The original menu comprised hamburgers (containing one-tenth of a pound of meat) at 15¢, a slice of cheese on it at 4¢ more, soft drinks at 10¢, 16-ounce milkshakes at 20¢, and coffee at 5¢. French-fried potatoes were also a big seller and high-profit item, as they are today.

It takes 50 seconds at a McDonald's to serve a hamburger, shake, and french fries. There are precise specifications for everything: a 3.5-inch bun, one-quarter ounce of onions, and so on. A 385-page operations manual details it all.

Any changes in menu, restaurant design, and layout come slowly, and only after much experimentation, market testing, study, and consultation.

What pleased Kroc as much as anything else was to see a McDonald's crew working together at fever pitch, tied together by the rhythm and flow of business and a carefully planned kitchen layout.

Kroc had a fierce determination to maintain a family image for McDonald's. He allowed no jukeboxes, no vending machines, and no pay telephones in any of his restaurants; such items create unproductive traffic and encourage loitering, he believed. "McDonald's," said Kroc, "is kind of synonymous with Sunday School, the Girl Scouts, and the YMCA."

What could be more American than hamburg-

---

*Most information is based on a personal interview and the following books: Ray Kroc with Robert Anderson, *Grinding It Out, The Making of McDonald's* (Chicago: Regnery Co.), 1976 and Max Boas and Steve Chain, *Big Mac, The Unauthorized Story of McDonald's*, (New York: E. P. Dulton), 1976.

ers, french fries, apple pie, and milkshakes—the heart of the McDonald's menu? Attempts at sophisticating the menu often failed. A hula-burger, two slices of cheese with a slice of grilled pineapple on a toasted bun, was a giant flop. As one customer said, "I like the hula, but where is the burger?"

The Filet-O-Fish did work, and so did the breakfast sandwich. The sandwich is an egg with yolk broken fried in a teflon circle and dressed with a slice of cheese and grilled Canadian bacon placed on an open-faced, toasted, buttered English muffin. It changed the breakfast business not only for McDonald's, but also brought in breakfast trade for competing restaurants as well.

Other restaurant concepts also failed; the pie shops and Raymond's, a high-style hamburger shop, proved to be too sophisticated.

When McDonald's first appeared and standardized everything, including the red and white building and golden arches, it was following principles of success already laid down by Howard Johnson. Identity and visibility were essential. The American public, sanitation-conscious, was pleased to accept uniformity in exchange for immunity from salmonella and staphylococci. Also, the price was right.

The downtown McDonald's of today would not be recognized by the patron of the 1960s. Anything a franchisee wants within certain parameters is now acceptable to the design department. Some of the units provide saddles for little people on which to ride the range while eating hamburgers. There are hamburger mannikins in the shape of policemen. On the walls there may be pictures of an old Spanish mission like the one at San Juan Capistrano. At Port Hueneme a stylized surfboard flanked by beach scenes graces the wall. In Chula Vista a tree is reminiscent of the Wizard of Oz. On Wilshire Boulevard a fountain sparkles not with water, but lights. McDonald's has jumped on the Disneyland bandwagon with a vengeance. Inside the prestigious Water Tower complex in Chicago, hamburgers are grilling in McDonald's and the place is jumping.

Kroc believed in running a lean team with a minimum number of executives and levels of authority between himself and unit management. He also believed in owner participation. He said that he could have been overwhelmed with absentee investors, but would have none of them. A favorite saying—"McDonald's is for the needy, not the greedy"—meant that he wanted no investors as such, only active franchisees who showed up every day at the store and provided leadership.

An arch-defender of private enterprise, Kroc believed that doing what one enjoys is the way to be happy. "Find out where your talents lie and then do whatever you are doing better than anybody else. But be willing to pay the price of accomplishment." He told a story to illustrate the point. A woman approached a

great pianist and said, "I would give anything to be able to play like you!" The pianist replied, "No, you wouldn't." The point is that few people will pay the price of excellence.

There is no doubt about McDonald's quality. Extensive research has resulted in a good product and innovative equipment with which to prepare and serve it. Fish is one of the highest specification. The control on the basket for frying the fish is keyed to the weight of the fish—more weight, longer cooking time. And it is true that a hamburger held more than 10 minutes is thrown out. The patty itself is 19 percent fat; the french fries are cut small to absorb a lot of oil, meeting teenager taste. The buns have a little sugar, and a great deal of loving attention has gone into their formula. Meat patties are frozen for both convenience of handling and to hold down the bacteria count.

Kroc always wanted McDonald's to be in locations that are little subject to loitering or becoming hangouts. He would rent a plane and fly over a community, looking for schools and church steeples. After getting a general picture from the air, he followed up with a site survey. A computer in Oakbrook, Illinois, McDonald's headquarters, is programmed to make real estate printouts, but in the final analysis the top executives make their own judgments about the desirability of a location. They drive around in a car, go to the corner saloon and then the neighborhood supermarket. "Mingling with the people," said Kroc, told him what he needed to know about how well a McDonald's store would do.

Starting out, Kroc was not above checking out the garbage cans of competitors and counting wrappers to estimate their sales volume. He called himself "the location and griddle man." Like so many men of great determination, Kroc was blessed with endurance and surrounded himself with enduring people, he averaged not more than 6 hours sleep a night. Many times, said Kroc, he got 4 hours or less. "But I slept as hard as I worked." He did not believe that intelligence necessarily makes for restaurant success; rather, it is application, dedication, and hard work.

What are the keys of McDonald's success? They are the system, simplicity of format, menu, sanitation and cleanliness, and attractive architecture. Yet other chains have these same qualities. How then is McDonald's any different from the others? What unique contribution did Kroc bring to the enterprise?

Enterprises like McDonald's are not built without the dedication, some would say fanaticism, of at least one person like Kroc, who, as a promoter and salesman, was fired with daring unquenchable ambition and supreme confidence in the American future. His guiding principles are sound ones for any merchandising effort—give quality and value in pleasant surroundings, not the least of which are pleasant people. Offering quality has been an abiding principle. As Kroc put it, "We had principles when we were poor."

Even these are not enough without marketing and advertising, in which Kroc fervently believed. The name McDonald's itself is significant. Kroc believed that name had more advertising appeal than his own name and stuck with it. As a result, he is relatively unknown to the general public, whereas the McDonald's name is a household word. Television advertising has been remarkably effective. "We do it all for you"; the wholesome, beaming teenagers eager to serve; the corny, catchy names of the products, "Big Mac," "Egg McMuffin," and "McFeast"—all have proved spectacularly effective in motivating the under-30 crowd to move en masse to the nearest McDonald's. And, of course, there is the ever friendly Ronald McDonald.

McDonald's owns the land and buildings of many of the units. Although the capital investment required to purchase the land and construct the buildings runs into the millions and keeps the earnings of the company relatively low, the market value, the real equity position of the company, becomes stronger. Moreover, the well-located sites continue to appreciate in value.

Once the break-even point has been passed in the restaurant business, profits accelerate at a greater rate than sales. McDonald's units average over $1.3 million in annual sales volume alone.

Like many restaurant chains, McDonald's paid no dividends for several years. The company preferred to plow earnings back into expansion.

Critics of Kroc say that he made millions by working teenagers hard at the lowest possible wage. "Assistant managers," also teenagers, receive a little more, but not much. Also, he did not favor hiring women. (This is a far cry from what is true today, about half of all the company-owned restaurants managed by women.)

Kroc was a 5-foot, 8-inch dynamo. Part of the reason for his exuberance no doubt is that, like many very rich people, he could do pretty much as he pleased. A personal assistant traveled with him and acted as a chauffeur and valet. A $4.5 million jet that seated 17 passengers was ready when Kroc was. People eagerly responded to his wishes both because of his power and prestige and because most of the time he came across as a very likable person who loved what he was doing. Ray Kroc died in 1984. Much of his vast fortune, estimated to be upward of $2 billion, was willed to medical research. His wife's estate was estimated at between $700 million and $1 billion.

14

Institutional Foodservice

Hotel and restaurant students are often surprised at the size and opportunities offered by institutional management. Part of the reason lies in the term *institutional*, which carries lackluster connotations and lacks clear-cut definition. Institutional foodservice is usually offered in a facility whose primary mission is not food service. It is provided as a convenience or service for employees in business and industry; students at schools, colleges, and universities; travelers on planes, trains, ships, and other forms of transportation; patients in hospitals, nursing homes, and retirement residences; people in prisons and guests at clubs; and the general public while attending sporting events, camps, and community centers. Institutional foodservice becomes an omnibus term, a catch-all for foodservice outside the better-known commercial foodservice set up for profit making.

More and more hotel and restaurant school graduates and employees have been attracted to institutional food service in part because they are likely to work a 40-hour week rather than the longer hours characteristic of commercial foodservice. Institutional foodservice is also more apt to offer stable employment and more fringe benefits, especially more health insurance and paid time off, than is usual in the commercial area. Institutional foodservice managers also tend to work fewer weekends and holidays.

In the past, institutional foodservice salaries were lower than in commercial establishments; this has changed. Salaries in a number of institutional segments compete with those of commercial ventures.

The typical hotel and restaurant program, although it may not offer courses specifically called "institutional management," does offer personnel, marketing, finance, management, food preparation, and other courses quite relevant to institutional management. More schools, such as Pennsylvania State University and Johnson & Wales University, offer college degrees in institutional management.

This chapter explains in more detail the operations of various institutional foodservices.

BUSINESS AND INDUSTRY FOODSERVICE

Foodservice operations in business and industry provide meals and snacks to people who are working. Business and industry (commonly referred to as B&I) foodservices provide meals, for example, in light and heavy manufacturing plants, financial and insurance companies, service companies (such as electric companies), and high-tech businesses. Foodservices may provide breakfast, lunch, and supper meals, although supper is not always provided or else vending may be used instead. Typical offerings for lunch (the big meal of the day) include salad bar, deli, soup bar, sandwich bar, dessert bar, and takeout.

B&I sales come from foodservice (sometimes called manual foodservice), vending, and catering. Foodservices are usually provided using, at the minimum, a cafeteria (often using a scatter system). Some foodservices also provide executive dining rooms that provide restaurant-style service and/or are used for catering in-house functions.

B&I foodservice has undergone many positive changes over the years, and sales have increased dramatically. Drab dining facilities have been taken out of the basement, brightened up, and located in more central and larger spaces. Serving areas often look like a food court, and dining rooms rival many restaurants. Menus have gone far beyond meat loaf every Monday and feature fresh foods, healthy selections, self-service, and lots of variety. Creative menus are marketed and merchandised with flair in B&I foodservice. Many foodservices do one or more promotions a month, such as Mexican day, during which Mexican foods are highlighted, employees may be dressed in Mexican outfits, and the serving and dining areas are appropriately decorated. The stimulus for these changes is simple: B&I foodservice managers recognized the need to be innovative to compete effectively with restaurants in the area. At the same time, many companies realized the positive effects of a pleasant dining room and good food on its employees: increased morale and increased productivity.

An example of a B&I foodservice is that offered by a well-known New York bank. Foodservices provide a grill area; a hot food station with four or five entrees daily and special international entrees to break up the monotony; a carved

sandwich station; a barbecue area for fresh barbecued beef, chicken, and spare ribs; a premade salad and dessert station; a self-serve salad bar; a make-your-own ice cream bar; and hot and cold beverage stations, including gourmet coffees.

Besides providing just meals and snacks to be consumed in the dining facilities, foodservices often offer take-home foods, carts that bring food to employees at their desks, and nutrition education. Take-home foods might include dinner entrees, pizza, and bakery items and are usually put out for sale late in the afternoon before employees leave for home. Carts often sell popular snack foods, prepackaged lunch items, and beverages. Nutrition education may take the form of table tents, a regular nutrition publication, calorie and fat information on the menu or at point of purchase, and/or nutrient-oriented information on the reverse side of weekly menus.

Typically, 65 percent or more of employees utilize the foodservices offered. This percentage is referred to as the participation rate and indicates how many of the total employees purchase food and/or beverages in the service.

B&I foodservices often charge very reasonable prices. In many cases the company subsidizes the cost of the operation. What this means is that the revenue brought in by foodservice does not completely cover the costs. The company then kicks in whatever money is needed to operate the service. In the past the amount of the subsidy was often about 35 percent of annual sales. Many companies subsidize foodservice in order to provide inexpensive meals to their employees and provide a fringe benefit, convenience (instead of having to go out to eat), and productivity booster. Due to the recession of the early 1990s and the resulting belt tightening in many American companies, as well as changes in the federal tax code that made meal subsidies a taxable benefit, there have been substantial cuts in or elimination of subsidies. Now, instead of B&I foodservices losing money, more are trying to break even and be self-sufficient or even be profit centers.

SCHOOL FOODSERVICE

The National School Lunch Act of 1946 provided federal funding for lunch meals. The federal subsidy usually requires matching state or local funds. Today's program provides lunches to about 24 million students daily. Students pay for meals based on the family's ability to pay. In this manner, disadvantaged children are targeted for assistance. About half the lunches provided under this program are free or provided at a reduced price. Even students who must pay full price are still getting a bargain.

Lunch menus for the school lunch program follow the pattern in Table 14-1. Studies have shown that children who eat the school lunch receive more nutrients than children who eat a bagged lunch. (Bagged lunches tend to have less variety, with favorite foods being packed and repacked.) A number of California schools are testing (as a 6-year pilot) an alternative to the current school lunch pattern. California's Nutrient-Based Menu Planning System (NBMPS) has been greeted as being more flexible and easier to use in school meals to meet dietary guidelines. It involves using computerized nutrient analysis programs to determine the actual amount of nutrients in each meal. The revised meal pattern emphasizes leaner servings of meat and nonmeat protein sources and increased fruits and vegetables.

In addition to the school lunch program, some schools operate breakfast programs and after-school snacks to meet state mandates and/or parent requests. In Ohio, schools that provide more than 33 percent free lunch meals must provide a breakfast program.

Some of the concerns in school foodservice are as follows:

1. Excessive paperwork—To participate in the school lunch program requires the completion of so much paperwork that some schools have actually left the program.

2. Less government-subsidized foods—In the past the federal government would purchase food surpluses nationwide and distribute them to nonprofit schools (and other institutions as well) at a very low cost to the schools. Referred to as government commodities, these foods have been used heavily by school lunch programs, particularly cheese for pizzas and hamburgers. Fewer government commodities have been available for schools to use, forcing schools to purchase these foods at full cost or change the menu.

3. Budget slashing by school districts—As school districts have been trying to lower costs, foodservice budgets have been cut. A 1992 survey of school foodservices showed that half of all school districts spent less money on food purchases and that per-meal costs were dropping.

In some cases, some schools are bringing in revenue by providing meals for senior citizens, prisoners, and the homeless.

TABLE 14-1 School Lunch Program

Food Group	Grade K–3	4–6	7–12
Meat or meat alternate			
1 serving			
Lean meat, poultry, or fish	1½ oz.	2 oz.	3 oz.
Cheese	1½ oz.	2 oz.	3 oz.
Large egg	1½	2	3
Cooked dry beans or peas	¾ cup	1 cup	1½ cups
Peanut butter	3 tbsp.	4 tbsp.	6 tbsp.
Vegetable and/or fruit			
2 or more servings, to total	½ cup	¾ cup	¾ cup
Bread or bread alternate servings	8 per week	8 per week	10 per week
(1 serving is 1 slice of whole-grain or enriched bread or a whole-grain or enriched biscuit, roll, muffin, and so on; or ½ cup cooked pasta or other grain.)			
Milk	1 cup	1 cup	1 cup

HEALTHCARE: HOSPITALS AND NURSING FACILITIES

Healthcare foodservice includes foodservices in hospitals and nursing facilities. Nursing facilities include primarily nursing homes and also other long-term care facilities, such as those for the disabled. Although the food provided in healthcare operations has not always enjoyed a great reputation, the picture is definitely improving. More restaurant-style chefs are being employed in healthcare foodservices, not only to make good food but to make attractively presented dishes. Foodservices in hospitals are responsible for serving patient meals, but they also run employee cafeterias (much like in B&I) and provide catering services within (and sometimes outside) the hospital.

The cook-serve system is the traditional method of preparing patient food in health care facilities. Most foods are prepared from raw ingredients the day they are to be served. Foods are heated or chilled prior to service. Entrees, salads, and desserts are often made from scratch. Frozen vegetables and potatoes are commonly used. Baked goods are usually bought already prepared. Although this system is labor-intensive, the dietary manager often feels that he or she has better control over food quality and menu selection. Skilled cooks are needed for this system, as well as many types and sizes of equipment.

In the cook-freeze or cook-chill system, foods are prepared and chilled or frozen a day or more before service, and then reheated just before serving. In this manner, more food items can be cooked during a normal 40-hour workweek and labor cost is reduced. Disadvantages include greater opportunities for bacterial problems, additional expense for special equipment such as blast freezers, and changes to recipes to maintain food quality despite freezing.

However patient food is prepared, it must be transported by individual trays to the patient's room. Hot food can be kept hot using pellets or insulated trays. These two systems tend to be the most popular. The pellet system requires heating of a metal base in a hot oven before use. Some manufacturers have designed a special oven to hold and heat the pellets. The cover may be constructed of stainless steel or structural foam.

The insulated tray is generally a rectangular tray with indentations for food. The idea is to hold hot foods hot and cold foods cold.

A third temperature maintenance system is a hot/cold cart. A section of the cart is refrigerated; the other section is kept hot.

Patient menus are often 1- or 2-week cycle menus. Figure 14-1 is a sample 1-day menu for patients on low-fat and low-cholesterol diets. In some cases, hospitals offer a restaurant-style menu. This type of menu is the same every day except that it often features a different entree ("Chef's Special") at lunch and supper in addition to a selection of standard entrees. For example, one hospital offers five alternate entrees—spaghetti, hamburger, chef's salad, sliced turkey on croissant, and fruit and cottage cheese plate—for lunch and dinner. Restaurant-style menus tend to be easier to produce due to less variety than cycle menus.

Competition among hospitals for patients is keen, and patient stays are shorter due to federal regulations for controlling healthcare costs. To cut costs and increase revenue, hospital foodservices are looking for new sources of revenue, such as take-home food for employees and gourmet meals for patients. It is not unusual to see a fast-food outlet, such as McDonald's or Burger King, inside a hospital. It can be financially advantageous to rent out portions of a hospital's foodservice floor to chains that have strong brand and operational clout. Hospitals that lack capital to finance kitchen renovation or dining room expansion can do so by asking a branded operator to make the necessary investment. The chains benefit because they often get long-term leases at attractive square footage rates.

To save money, foodservice directors are being asked to oversee other hospital support services, such as housekeeping, laundry, and even the mailroom. Foodservice directors are taking advantage of computerization, cook-chill production systems, and group purchasing. Group purchasing involves combining needs from several facilities to increase purchase in quantity and get cost savings because of volume purchase discounts.

Nursing Home Foodservice

There are currently about 19,000 nursing homes in the U.S. with 1.6 million beds. The Omnibus Budget Reconciliation Act of 1987 (OBRA) imposed sweeping changes in nursing home regula-

Good Morning

LO FAT LO CHOL   **LO FAT LO CHOL**

Chilled Fruits and Juices
Orange Juice   Grapefruit Juice
Apple Juice   Grape Juice
Prune Juice   Fresh Banana

From the Granary. . .
Corn Flakes   Raisin Bran
Special K   Puffed Wheat
Rice Krispies   Puffed Rice
Shredded Wheat   Bran Flakes
Cream of Wheat Cereal

White Toast   Wheat Toast
Rye Toast   Margarine
Jelly

Breakfast Entrees
Scoop of Cottage Cheese   Scrambled Egg Beaters

Beverages and Condiments
Maxwell House Coffee   Skim Milk
Sanka   Tea
Decaffeinated Tea   Lemon Packet
Non Dairy Creamer   Sugar Substitute
Catsup Packet   Regular Seasoning Kit

For Lunch

LO FAT LO CHOL   **LO FAT LO CHOL**

Appetizer Selections
Tomato Juice   Fresh Fruit Cup
Cranberry Juice   Chicken Noodle Soup
Saltine Crackers

Entrees
Hot Roast Beef Sandwich   Turkey Casserole
Chef's Salad

Complements to the Entree
Steamed Corn   Steamed Broccoli Spears
Mashed Potatoes

Salads
Tossed Salad   Molded Peach Salad
Carrot Salad

Sweet Endings
Pineapple Chunks   Fresh Fruit
Homestyle Rice Pudding   Rasberry Sherbet
Orange Jello   Fresh Banana

Breads
White Bread   Dinner Roll
Wheat Bread   Margarine
Rye Bread   Jelly

Beverages and Condiments
Maxwell House Coffee   Skim Milk
Sanka   Tea
Decaffeinated Tea   Non Dairy Creamer
Lemon Packet   Sugar Substitute
Catsup Packet   Mustard Packet
Estee Mayonnaise   Estee Italian Dressing
Estee French Dressing   Estee 1000 Island Dressing
Regular Seasoning Kit

Dinner Meal

LO FAT LO CHOL   **LO FAT LO CHOL**

Appetizer Selections
Tomato Juice   Fresh Fruit Cup
Cranberry Juice   Chicken Noodle Soup
Saltine Crackers

Entrees
Baked Fish Fillet with Lemon Wedge
Salisbury Steak with Sauce Chef's Salad

Complements to the Entree
Noodles   Spinach
Stewed Tomatoes   Mashed Potatoes

Salads
Tossed Salad   Molded Peach Salad
Carrot Salad

Sweet Endings
Pineapple Chunks   Fresh Fruit
Homestyle Rice Pudding   Rasberry Sherbet
Orange Jello   Fresh Banana

Breads
White Bread   Dinner Roll
Wheat Bread   Margarine
Rye Bread   Jelly

Beverages and Condiments
Maxwell House Coffee   Skim Milk
Sanka   Tea
Decaffeinated Tea   Non Dairy Creamer
Lemon Packet   Sugar Substitute
Catsup Packet   Mustard Packet
Estee Mayonnaise   Estee Italian Dressing
Estee French Dressing   Estee 1000 Island Dressing
Regular Seasoning Kit

Figure 14-1 Hospital menu.

Source: Brandywine Hospital and Trauma Center.

tions, emphasizing the rights of nursing home residents. OBRA placed more significance on the medical role of nutrition and on the social role of meals for residents. The emphasis of nursing home foodservice is patient feeding. Employee feeding and catering may not be provided and is largely dependent on the size of the facility.

The Role of Registered Dietitians

A key person in healthcare foodservice is the *registered dietitian*. In the U.S. the largest and most visible group of professionals in the nutrition field are the over 50,000 registered dietitians (RD), most of whom belong to the America Dietetic Association. Registered dietitians are recognized by the medical profession as the legitimate providers of nutrition care. They have specialized education in human anatomy and physiology, diet therapy, foods and food science, the behavioral sciences, and foodservice management. Registered dietitians must complete at least a bachelor's degree, an internship or equivalent experience, and a qualifying examination. Continuing education is required to maintain RD status. RDs work in private practice, hospitals, nursing homes, wellness centers, business and industry, and many other settings.

COLLEGES AND UNIVERSITY FOODSERVICE

Colleges and universities have provided meals (and rooms) for students for many years. Whereas only one or two meal plans (usually two meals daily or three meals daily) were offered 20 years ago, there is much more flexibility in meal plans today and more options available. Most schools offer students the options of 10, 15, or 20 meals per week and price them accordingly. College and university food services normally serve 20 meals total each week. (There are only two meals served on Sunday: brunch and dinner.)

For example, at Tufts University six meal plans are available. There are 20-, 14-, and 5-meal-per-week programs in addition to the 140-meals-per-semester or 105-meals-per-semester plans. Students may use any of the university's six food-service operations for their meals. Students may also purchase an all-point meal plan, at a cost of $500 per semester and are given a magnetic card with 50,000 points (each point is worth one cent). Students may add to their balances at any time

during a semester. Points can be spent in any of Tufts' food services as well as some non-food-service outlets, such as the bookstore or copy center. Points are taken off the card by card readers installed at the appropriate locations. Under this plan students don't pay for meals not eaten.

In addition to the growing variety of meal plans offered to students, the variety of foods found in dining halls has increased tremendously. Gone are the days of only one or two entrees, vegetables, and starches. If a student does not wish to have the main entree, there's probably a grill, self-service sandwich bar, salad bar, and soup bar available. More students than ever are asking for hamburgers, pizza, tacos, and other fast foods because these are the foods they grew up with.

Many students ask for nutritious food selections including vegetarian dishes and low-fat, low-cholesterol offerings. Some operations offer nutritional analysis of menu items as well as leaflets and newsletters on nutrition topics. Many of the larger colleges and universities have registered dietitians on staff who might counsel individual students on nutrition concerns, develop nutrition leaflets, table tents, or other printed material for general circulation, survey students' needs, or work with cooks to develop nutritious recipes.

Developing menus and providing food for college students is a challenge. They come from diverse backgrounds and have differing lifestyles; many are from foreign countries. Menus need variety because most students eat at the same dining hall and soon the food becomes boring. Forecasting the amount of food to produce is difficult because several meal plans are generally available, and students can usually eat in any foodservice (including the student union) on campus.

Concerns felt by managers in college and university foodservice include:

- Budget cuts—Cuts are more acute at state-run institutions than private institutions, but all campuses are feeling the pinch. Due to budget cuts, managers have to reduce staffing, work longer hours, and do without much needed equipment and repairs.

- Declining enrollments—There are fewer college-age students in the country today than at any time in the last 20 years.

- Increasing food and labor costs—Food costs continue to inch upwards along with hourly wages.

With decreasing enrollments, foodservices are having to deal with less revenue. To make up for lost revenue, many are developing new ways to make money, such as in-house branding (a brand name is developed and used on certain foods), use of commercial branded concepts, development of food courts, on-campus food and pizza delivery, operation of campus convenience stores, catering at university stadium and sports events, and declining balance meal programs (pay for only the meals consumed) for faculty, staff, and commuting students.

An example of in-house branding is a line of pre-made deli sandwiches in black containers that are identified as "Bow Tie Deli" sandwiches at California State Polytechnic University. Likewise, items coming from the university's bakery have similarly been branded and marketed with the "Enchanted Bakery" logo. In-house branding gives foodservices an opportunity to present in-house products on the same level as those being sold commercially and to hopefully sell more, increasing revenue and profit.

Some university foodservices have brought in national brands, such as Burger King or Little Caesar's Pizza, who lease space and pay the foodservice department a percentage of gross sales (or sometimes a minimum financial return).

TRANSPORTATION

In-flight foodservice is a major segment of foodservices provided to people during transportation. Per-passenger spending was $6.16 for 1992, with a total of $2.54 billion spent by airlines to provide foodservices. Foodservice is generally considered an airline's fifth-largest expense. In-flight foodservice is highly specialized. It is managed largely by hotel and restaurant-trained persons. Tens of thousands of meals must be prepared and delivered to planes for in-flight service. Scheduling is particularly important to avoid flight delays. Major airports have huge kitchens designed as food-production factories for the planes.

The Marriotts began putting up meals in cardboard boxes in 1937 for American and Eastern Airlines out of Washington, D.C. American Airlines, through its subsidiary, Sky Chefs, began providing meals for airplane passengers in about 1941. Later, Host International and the Dobbs House secured large-scale foodservice contracts for serving a number of airlines. Marriott Food Service is the largest of the airline caterers, having bought Host International, also an in-flight foodservice pioneer.

Many airlines now offer fare from commercial foodservice chains. United Airlines and McDonald's, American Airlines and Pizzeria Uno, and Continental and Subway have all entered agreements that launch select restaurant menu items skyward.

Airline caterers negotiate to provide foodservice for airlines and airports. Short cafeteria-style service was standard until about 1985, when fast-food operators like McDonald's, Burger King, and Roy Rogers units were introduced. They fit well in the grab-it-and-run spirit of the crowded airports. Snack services provide such items as tacos, omelettes, Belgium waffles, pizza, and specialty ice cream to satisfy the desires of people waiting for flights or arrivals.

ELDERCARE FOODSERVICE

America is rapidly aging—12 percent of the U.S. population is age 65 or older; in 30 years the figure will be closer to 20 percent. Eldercare foodservice provides meals to older Americans in a variety of settings:

- Nutrition programs for home-bound elderly (called Meals on Wheels).

- Meals for seniors at congregate dining sites.

- Continuing care retirement communities (CCRCs).

Home-delivered meals and congregate dining site programs have grown 48.5 percent from 1980 to 1990. These programs are federally funded under the Older Americans Act. CCRCs are quite different, being financed entirely by occupants. About 800 CCRCs are located in the U.S. and service about 220,000 residents. Traditionally run by non-profit religious groups, the number of for-profit communities is growing. Among the newest for-profit players in eldercare are Marriott and Hyatt.

Also called lifecare communities, CCRCs offer retirees their own housing and a variety of services, including meals, recreational facilities, golf courses, beauty salons, and transportation to nearby libraries, churches, and shopping. Housing could be a private house, cottage, or apartment. Most lifecare communities feature 24-hour-a-day nursing assistance for residents in independent-living apartments, assisted-living housing for those residents who need help performing daily routines, and a skilled nursing facility for the chronically or acutely ill.

To live in a lifecare community, residents often pay a substantial entry fee and monthly rental/maintenance fees, although some communities only charge rental fees. Rental fees often include meal plans, nursing care, and housekeeping.

Foodservices in CCRCs are varied and can be quite elegant. The primary focus of the CCRC is serving residents, restaurant style, in the dining room, where they take their meals (often it is just lunch and/or dinner). The dining room is usually the centerpiece of the community and is designed for leisurely dining. In addition to daily meals for residents in independent-living, foodservice also makes and delivers meals to residents in assisted-living and skilled nursing facility. As much as possible, these residents are encouraged to eat in dining rooms. Foodservices also often offer elaborate catering, room service, and theme dinners for residents.

THE PRIVATE CLUB

Private clubs are, in several respects, similar to hotels, and many hotel managers move from hotel operations to that of clubs. Food and beverage operations are common to both. If anything, club food and beverage operations call for a higher standard, especially in the leading city and country clubs. Management stress can be less in a club because there is usually less emphasis on profit, and business volume may be more variable. Some clubs are busy only on weekends and may be more seasonable than hotels.

The two principal categories of private clubs are country and city clubs. Golfing is central to most country clubs, dining operations to city clubs, which may also have membership based on profession, athletic interest, university affili-

ation, or social interest. Yacht clubs, fraternal membership, and military clubs are other club categories. In 1992 it was estimated that clubs operated by professional managers numbered about 10,000. The managers of about 3000 of the larger clubs are members of the Club Managers Association of America (CMAA). Some of these also belong to the National Club Association, an organization mainly for club presidents and directors.

While most country and private clubs are operated on a non-profit basis, others are proprietory-operated for profit. The largest of the for-profit clubs is the Club Corporation of America, based in Dallas, which operates some 200 country and city clubs. Twenty are operated under management contract; the rest are company-owned.

Most clubs have higher payroll and related costs, partly because sales volume fluctuates widely and club members expect good service. These costs typically run as much as 50 percent of total costs, as compared with less than 40 percent in hotels. Food and beverage costs in a club as a percentage of sales are usually higher in the non-profit clubs than in hotels and commercial restaurants. Membership dues and assessments help defray deficits in food and beverage and other departments.

The CMAA reports that the average club belonging to its Association had 90 employees with a payroll of just over $1 million. CMAA managers serve 2.8 million club members and in 1991 had a gross revenue of over $7.4 billion, of which just over $3 billion, or 40 percent, was food and beverage revenues.

Of interest to hotel and restaurant college students is the fact that 37 percent of these clubs had internship programs.[1]

PROFESSIONAL ASSOCIATIONS

Professional associations representing institutional foodservice managers perform very useful member functions. Following is a list of several of these associations.

---

1. Report on a telephone survey conducted by the CMAA 1991 Economic Impact Survey, Alexandera, Va.

Employee feeding: Society for Foodservice Management (SFM)

Schools: American School Food Service Association (ASFSA)

Hospitals: American Society for Hospital Foodservice Administrators (ASHFSA) (a Society of the American Hospital Association)

Colleges/universities: National Association of College and University Food Service (NACUFS)

Nursing homes: Dietary Managers Association (DMA)

Corrections: American Correctional Food Service Association (ACFSA)

These associations (except for the Society for Foodservice Management) include mostly members from self-operated units. In other words, there are few members who work for contractors.

Membership in most of these associations varies from 500 to 2000, except for the ASFSA (with about 66,000 members) and DMA (with about 14,000 members). In addition, *registered dietitians* work in many of the institutional segments.

Professional associations generally provide its members with:

- Educational programs and activities, designed to foster continued education and development of management skills,

- A medium for the exchange of information related to foodservice management,

- A network of peers to foster growth and professional development, and

- Professional standards and ethics.

Several associations also provide a means for certifying its members through a combination of training and testing.

Questions

1. What are the advantages and disadvantages of working as a manager of an institutional foodservice operation as compared with a hotel, resort, or commercial restaurant?

2. Why might it be more advantageous for a manager to work for a foodservice contract company than directly for an institutional employer? Why might it be advantageous to work directly for an institutional employer?

3. Under what conditions would a job as director of a large school foodservice be of interest to an experienced graduate of a hotel and restaurant management program?

4. What factors favor the growth of hospital foodservice? What factors are restricting its growth?

5. What roles do graduates of hotel and restaurant programs play in in-flight foodservice?

15

The Commercial Kitchen

What is the commercial kitchen? The definition depends on a number of factors and who describes it. Over the years, it has been likened to hell on earth, stashed away in the nether regions of a hotel or tacked onto a free-standing restaurant; a hot, humid place best forgotten; a place of long working hours, hard floors, and puddles of dirty water; a place where youths are tyrannized by the chef, where workers grow old before their time, burned out by the flames of their stoves and the pressures of their environment.

The kitchen also has been likened to an orderly processing plant with controlled temperature, well managed by people of expertise and compassion; a place of spotless stainless steel with great machines to wash pots and serving ware, huge kettles that cook food by a mere turn of a valve; a place of respect and a joy in which to work.

Perhaps both descriptions are correct.

The modern commercial kitchen can be and often is air conditioned, well ventilated, spotless, and a pleasant place to work. In other kitchens,

however, the temperature may reach 120 degrees, and they are anything but pleasant.

The history of the kitchen reflects the social history of the time; it reveals the esteem (or lack of esteem) with which the society held a cook and other kitchen personnel. In 1526 Henry VIII found it necessary to decree that scullions, the kitchen helpers of the day, "shall not goe naked or in garments of such vileness as they doe...nor lie in the nights and dayes in the kitchens...by the fireside...." The social standing of the chef has waxed and waned, as has that of the staff. Their position has largely depended on the availability of labor and the class of the kitchen.

Before 1930 the large hotels in New York City customarily recruited their entire kitchen brigades from France. Communication with kitchen personnel occurred through the chef, and very often he controlled the lives and destinies of those under him. A dispute with him might mean loss of the entire brigade, and the chef himself was almost certain to time his departure in the middle of an important meal.

A few chefs have achieved a degree of fame—men like Carème, who is credited with founding classical cookery; Soyer, chef to the Reform Club of London and the only chef included in the *Dictionary of National Biography*, the British equivalent of *Who's Who*; and Escoffier, "Chef to kings and king of chefs." The millions of cooks and kitchen helpers throughout history who have also served are largely forgotten.

In the past, people disadvantaged in one way or another have usually filled the unskilled ranks in the kitchen. Newly arrived immigrants traditionally have manned the kitchens along the eastern seaboard, on the West Coast, and in the Southwest. In New York City, the language heard is likely to be Spanish. Hotels and restaurants of today are being called on to take in and train the hardcore unemployed and learning disabled whenever possible.

The cook, who formerly grew up in the business and was probably of European extraction, is being replaced by native-born Americans who learned their skills on the job or have attended a vocational school. Kitchen management personnel were likely to be drawn from those who had learned on the job, but more recently they come from 2-year technical schools or community colleges that offer hotel and restaurant courses.

A BRIEF HISTORY OF KITCHEN EQUIPMENT

Primitive man cooked food by holding it over a fire. Early American tavernkeepers relied heavily on an open fire and a few pots and pans. With the aid of heated stones, early California boiled food in tightly woven baskets. Kitchen equipment has an interesting history of development. The Roman tavernkeeper used round and oval frying pans, service pans with handles for serving hot foods in the dining room, saucepans resembling our modern chafing dishes, stewpots with covers, and colanders.

The open hearth served as a range, but there was also a *craticula*, a combination broiler and stove. A movable apparatus, it usually rested on top of a brick oven fueled by charcoal. Pans rested over the coals on sliding rods, and special openings at the rear held stewpots. The *thermospodium* was a charcoal-heated hot-drink urn similar to a coffee urn. It was used in the dining room and by snack bars specializing in hot drinks.

The Medieval Kitchen

The medieval kitchen was cluttered with fowl lying on the floor, vegetables in baskets, and a half bag on the table. The fireplace lacked draft; the room was smoky. The place had plenty of cooks, scullions, and serving maids—and maybe a small dog.

The dog was used to turn the spit over the fire. He ran in a wicker cage with a hot coal in it to insure his interest. (Basset hounds were particularly favored in England; the remains of their cages can be seen at Oxford.) If the dog failed, a small boy, not in a basket, would do nicely as a substitute turnspit.

Over in one corner, a crew of people ground up food with mortars and pestles. Without refrigeration, plenty of spices were a necessity. When sugar became available from the West Indies, it was used with abandon. There were no chefs' uniforms here. Kitchen helpers were low men on the social totem pole.

The Colonial Kitchen

The colonial kitchen was a room with a hearth and a few blackened iron pots and kettles. Until late in the seventeenth century, cooking pots were scarce and precious. Handed down from generation to generation, iron pots were commonly listed with valuables in wills.

A crude spit—a short iron rod with a handle on one end resting on crossed iron uprights—some stewpans, iron skillets, and copper mortars and pestles were the principal cooking tools. The Dutch oven, a shallow iron pot with a tight, flat iron cover designed so that it could be covered with coals, was also used.

Some of the taverns and larger homes had a surprising array of handmade gadgets: cheese presses, sausage stuffers, butter presses, cabbage shredders, waffle and wafer irons, grinders, warmers, and mechanically turned spits. Pewter dishes with hollow bases were filled with hot water to keep the contents warm.

An Eighteenth-Century Genius

Most people in the foodservice field have never heard of Count Rumford, even though he was born an American and is credited with being the first person to study kitchen equipment scientifically. Born Benjamin Thompson in 1753, in Woburn, Massachusetts, he lived a full life as a military man, inventor, and administrator.

Perhaps he is so little known because he picked the wrong side in the American Revolution. He married for money, and when the war came, he was appointed a Tory colonel, fighting Washington's troops. After the war, he headed for England and then on to Bavaria, where he was made inspector general of the artillery and aide de camp to mad King Ludwig. Soon he had Bavaria on a regimen calculated to put everyone to work. Beggars were rounded up and placed in jobs in workhouses. He invented several cheap, nutritious soups for the poor, some of which are still served in Europe.

Rumford studied combustion and designed stoves, roasters, and pots and pans that absorbed maximum possible heat from fuel. Until his invention of a kitchen stove, open ranges were installed in ordinary fireplaces. His stove was a complete cooking unit set into the kitchen; only the back was used as a flue. With its lids and cov-

ers, it was much like the old-fashioned coal range of Grandma's kitchen. His roasters with their two cooking levels can still be found in some old New England houses.

Steam-jacketed kettles were also invented by Rumford, as well as the double boiler. The first to make a drip coffeepot, he also designed a single-cup device for those who could not afford the pot. He devised a fireplace with a smoke shelf and throat that separated the warm and cool air into orderly convection currents. Before Rumford, chimneys were merely large holes or flues connecting a fireplace to the roof above.

Rumford also anticipated kitchen planning. His large ranges for military hospitals were oval in shape; the cook did not have to walk around his pots, but could watch them from the central work area.

The Turn of the Century

By the turn of the century, some of the new hotels had large, airy, well-equipped kitchens. The

Figure 15-1 The kitchen of the Old Palmer House Hotel, Chicago, about 1890. It is departmentalized and not too different from some of the kitchens seen in old resorts today. Women cooks were very much in evidence by that time.

kitchen in the original Waldorf in New York was the most prestigious of the new hotels.

Delmonico's, one of the other two or three prestige restaurants in New York at the time, was more picturesque. The kitchen was reached by a flight of shabby stairs and a narrow, dimly lit passage:

into a big, low-ceilinged underground room, so divided by partitions and so blocked off by innumerable tables and refrigerators and storage closets as to be a veritable labyrinth to the stranger. The ranges extend the length of the room, and opposite them are stoves, for the vegetables, leaving an aisle sacred to the use of the forty-five cooks in caps and aprons upon whose final efforts depends Delmonico's fame.... When this gloomy, crowded, busy kitchen, dark with smoke, and brilliant with polished copper pots hanging from every rafter, is assailed by a swarm of eager waiters, wonderful indeed is the clash of tongues and orders and clash of dishes.... The pen into which the waiters are allowed to come is necessarily very small and is accessible to the kitchen proper only through two openings in the wire gratings that separate. In this the hubbub of waiters is appalling. The crowd pushes and jostles each other, in a mighty scramble for the best attention of the cooks. Here and there, rush the chef's assistants, giving orders; and the chef himself, with his thoughtful, kindly face, emerging from the tiny closet office where he concocts his menus and invents his masterpieces of cookery, walks up and down, and keeps all moving smoothly.[1]

THE MODERN KITCHEN

A kitchen can be anything from a one-burner stove to a complex, elaborate food-processing plant. Kitchen consultant, Richard Flambert, pointed out that a kitchen is a warehouse, a factory, a distribution point, a processing plant, a testing laboratory, an artists' studio, a sanitation establishment, a waste treatment plant, sometimes a retailer and bank, a place of diverse skills and trades, and often a boulevard of broken dishes and dreams.

Flambert went on to say that it is the only kind of establishment where a product is purchased, received, stored, processed, served, and consumed every day. Foodstuffs arrive at the back door, whether fresh, chilled, canned, boxed,

or frozen and then are placed in some form of holding. Vegetables are placed on dry slatted racks a few inches above the floor. Dairy products are refrigerated at a temperature between 38 and 40 degrees F. Fresh fish and meat are placed under slightly colder refrigeration, fresh fruits and vegetables at a slightly higher temperature. Flour, cereals, and pasta products are placed off the floor in a cool room at a temperature between 50 and 65 degrees F. Frozen foods are sent to freezers between -10 and $+5$ degrees while canned and boxed foods are shelved in a dry storeroom on a first-in, first-out arrangement.

Perhaps a kitchen can be better visualized via the flowchart in Figure 15-2.

Precision in Cooking

Cooking is growing more precise as technical knowledge about the process increases. The fisherman's platter, combining a fillet of fish, scallops, oysters, and french fries, is not likely to be cooked all at once, as it has been in the past. Each item requires a different cooking time; if they are all dumped into the deep fryer at once, some are overcooked and some are underdone. To avoid overcooking, items are dropped into a deep fryer, item by item, according to the length of time required to cook them.

Richard Keating, a foodservice equipment manufacturer, tells us that, although all parts of a chicken are usually cooked at 350 degrees, the time and temperature should be something different for each part. At 350, the leg and wing of a 2.75-pound chicken require 10 minutes to be cooked to complete doneness; the breast of the same chicken requires 12 minutes; the thigh, 13 minutes. This means that, if the chicken parts are all placed in a fry basket at the same time, the leg and wing will be 30 percent overcooked. Shrinkage and flavor loss are the result. In most fried chicken orders, the leg looks as though it had come from a different and smaller bird. Timing is even more exact with microwave cooking; seconds count.

The cook today needs more than skill with a knife to cook well. Slicing onions may not have to be done at all, if dehydrated onions are used, which are lower in cost, require less labor, and for many dishes are just as tasty as a fresh onion. The quality of instant potatoes varies widely, and the cook must be somewhat of an analyst to deter-

1. Thomas Lately, *Delmonico's, A Century of Splendor* (Boston, Mass.: Houghton Mifflin Co.), 1967.

mine which are best from a cost and quality standpoint.

The cook takes on some of the character of a food technologist and comes to understand a little food chemistry and physics as they relate to cooking.

MODERN COOKING EQUIPMENT

Today's restaurant keepers have a wide choice of cooking and sanitizing equipment from which to choose. Specialized equipment, such as fryers, broilers, griddles, ovens, steamers, steam-jacketed kettles, and microwave ovens, are available.

Restaurant magazines parade the virtues of particular equipment, and the restaurant manager can be kept up to date at the annual restaurant trade shows, especially those sponsored by the NRA each spring in Chicago, the California Restaurant show in August, and the International Hotel/Motel and Restaurant Show in New York City.

Restaurateurs are challenged to cook food so that it will be enjoyed by their patrons. The equip-

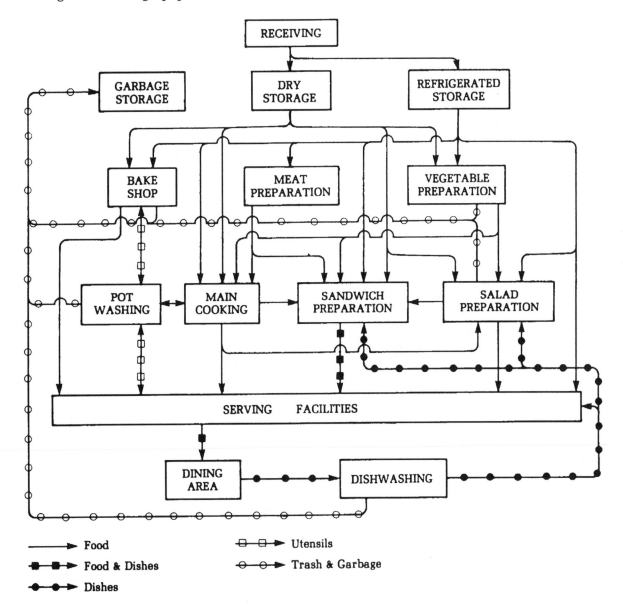

Figure 15-2 Kitchen work-flow chart.

Source: Commercial Kitchens, The American Gas Association, New York City 1962 edition, p. 134.

ment used and how it is used plays a part in making the food pleasing to the eye and palate. The restaurant operator also has the inescapable public-health responsibility of providing food that is safe, for serving it on sanitized ware, and for doing everything practicable to prevent the spread of disease. Heat used in the cooking process and in sanitizing ware destroys harmful germs, viruses, and the various parasites that can infest animals. Heat also inactivates enzymes, changes food textures and flavors, and in some instances makes the food more digestible.

Kitchen equipment can be anything from a pot for boiling water on a one-burner stove to a multimillion-dollar highly engineered food-production factory. A fast-food operation may need only deep fryers and use only disposable serviceware. A large dinner house with an extensive menu may use an array of cooking equipment plus a sizable warewashing facility. A commissary can be like a small food-processing plant.

The restaurateur's choice of cooking equipment, largely determined by the menu, includes ovens, broilers, fryers, griddles, ranges, steam cookers, and warmers. He or she also needs a warewashing facility, refrigerators, and freezers. Typically, a kitchen has one or several range tops, griddles, and broilers. Range tops and griddles are similar in that they transfer heat from a heating element through a cooking surface to food. The range top can consist of open, individually controlled burners or hot plates—heavy-duty, open-top ranges equipped with tubular coils that can be used to cook up to 40 quarts of food.

The gas burners or electric coils on enclosed or solid-top ranges and griddles are positioned beneath the solid cast-iron or stainless-steel tops. Controls permit either the entire top or one or more sections to be heated at one time. Griddles and range tops are used to fry and sauté. Institutional kitchens are often larger and have more cooking and other equipment than necessary. Institutional kitchen planners are prone to specify extra equipment recognizing that, once money has been budgeted for a kitchen, additional money may be hard to come by. It is better to have standby equipment on hand. Another explanation for excessive equipment is that most professional kitchen planners are paid a percentage of the total cost of the kitchen—the higher the cost, the greater the fee. For the unscrupulous, that is a

great temptation. A brief description of standard items of kitchen equipment commonly used in the American commercial kitchen follows.

Frying Equipment

Deep-fat frying became widespread following World War II, when thermostats were designed that controlled fat temperature and prevented it from reaching the flash point by mistake. New kettles are available with self-cleaning coils, cool spots in which to collect food particles, gravity-feed grease strainers, and with rapid heat recovery.

Frying under pressure was introduced with the Henny Penny fryer and the Broaster in the 1950s. With a lid on a fry kettle, some pressure soon builds up in a fry kettle, created by the steam produced by the frying food itself. If the lid is tight, high pressures are soon created, and some of the steam must be released to avoid dangerous levels. Pressure in the Henny Penny is held at 9 pounds per square inch; the Broaster goes higher.

Increased pressure cuts frying time in about half. It reduces the steam formed by cooking food and cuts the amount of cooling that takes place when steam evaporates. At one point, Colonel Sanders' Kentucky Fried Chicken used a pressure cooker similar to the home-style pressure pot.

The frying operation has long been associated with kitchen and hotel fires. More fires are started in kitchens by burning fat than from any other cause. The flash point of fat is 625 degrees F; combustion is sustained at 675 degrees F. Most foods are fried at a temperature of 350 degrees F. Should the cook turn away from the frying pan for a few minutes or the thermostat on a fry kettle fail, flames are soon soaring to the ceiling. Should the flames reach the exhaust hood, the building may soon be on fire, for many exhaust hoods are lined with layers of accumulated grease, which also catch fire. Exhaust ducts may extend for several stories and carry the flames to the top of the building.

Throwing water on a fat fire spreads the fire; the water forms steam pockets that explode, spewing burning fat around the kitchen. The fire should be covered with a sheet pan to deprive the flame of oxygen, or a CO_2 extinguisher should be used.

The emphasis on healthful foods and the belief that excessive fat is linked to some forms of

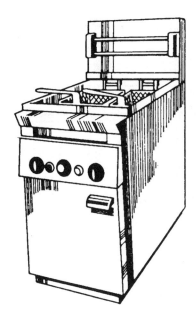

Figure 15-3 Deep-fat fryer.

cancer and assorted other diseases have scarcely dented the fried-food market.

Switzerland, France, Germany, and Scandanavia will not permit overused frying oil to be used in food service. Two ways to avoid overusing oil is to keep frying temperatures at the lowest practical temperatures and to select fryers of a size matched to quick consumption of the cooking oil. Foods cooked in oil absorb the oil. If a third of the oil in the fryer can be absorbed daily, if the fat is filtered and not exposed to unnecessary heat, the buildup of polymers and contaminants is not excessive and the oil need not be discarded.

Deep-fat (French) fryers. These are electric or gas-fired kettles for holding fat or oil in which baskets of food can be immersed for frying. Temperature usually can be controlled in a range of 325 to 400 degrees F.

Fryer models range in size from 12-pound capacity table models to 80-pound floor models. The large models are more efficient for heavy production, the smaller models less costly to operate when demand is low.

Convection fryers. These are conventional fryers that have an added pump that circulates the oil in a continuous closed-loop flow, past a cluster of heat exchangers. The exchangers, heated by gas, pass heat into the oil. Speeding the oil around the heat exchangers increases the rate and efficiency of heat exchange. At least one manufacturer provides a screen that filters the oil as it circulates.

Pressure fryers. These are deep-fat fryers with tight lids that act to create pressure within the fry kettle. The increased pressure reduces cooking time by as much as one half, mainly because less evaporative cooling takes place in the cooking process. Some pressure fryers include moisture-injection systems; the water injected turns to steam.

Tilting skillets. Essentially, these are large frying pans that can be tilted. They are also called *braising pans* or *griddle skillets*. As with any frying pan with a cover, they can be used to stew, sauté, simmer, and even roast. Because the temperature can be reduced and held at as little as 150 degrees F, the tilting skillet can be used for holding already prepared foods. This is a highly versatile piece of equipment that, because of temperature control, can be used to braise or roast meat, cook pancakes, scramble or fry eggs, simmer, prepare roux, and fry chicken. It can serve as a grill, hot top, range, or oven; with a lid it can become a steamer.

Ovens

Conventional ovens. Standard or range ovens heat the air in a closed chamber. This air surrounds food and cooks it.

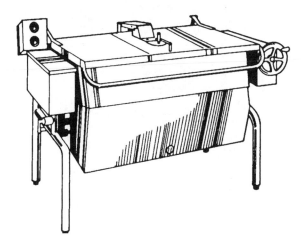

Figure 15-4 Tilt skillet (closed).

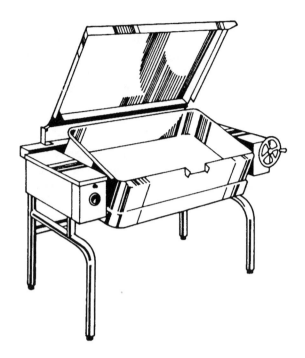

Figure 15-5 Tilt Skillet (open).

Deck oven. This is the same as the conventional oven, except that the chambers are long, deep, and usually rectangular. There are several chambers, or "decks," each stacked on top of another. The sections can be operated separately and at different temperatures.

Convection ovens. These are similar to conventional ovens, except that a fan or rotor, usually lo-

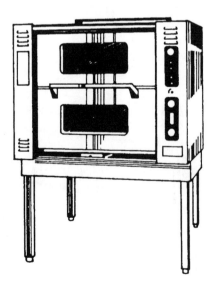

Figure 15-6 Conventional oven.

Figure 15-7 Deck oven.

cated in the back, makes for rapid circulation of the air and considerably quicker preheating and cooking times. Directions for baking with a convection oven must be followed exactly, otherwise some foods, such as flat sheet cakes, will dry out excessively on top. A pan of water can be placed in the oven to humidify the oven air and reduce moisture loss in the food.

Cook-and-hold oven. Several ovens are specially designed for slow cook and hold. Sold as modular units, these ovens can be stacked, placed on counters, or mounted on wheels. Thermometers in the form of probes act to control oven tempera-

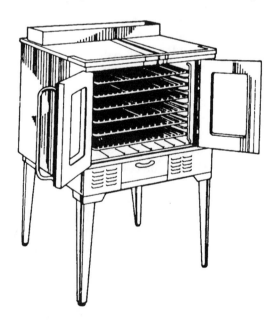

Figure 15-8 Convection oven.

tures and shift from cook to hold modes. Cooking is done over long periods at lower than usual temperatures; reducing shrinkage in large cuts of meat can be reduced to as little as 5 to 10 percent. (Slow cooking allows the meat's own enzymes to activate as temperatures rise to above 45 degrees F. The enzymes break down the meat's cell structure and tenderize it. Rapid cooking, at meat temperatures above 130 degrees F, inactivates these enzymes, and the meat is tougher.)

Humidity differs in these ovens. High-humidity ovens reach the 90 to 95 percent level. (Convection ovens reach 30 to 60 percent because the air is circulated rapidly.) The long cooking time means that the ovens can be operated untended overnight, when energy rates are lowest.

Microwave ovens. In these, the cooking chamber is usually small and the capacity much less than that of larger ovens. Magnetrons, usually in the top of the oven, emit microwaves. These penetrate foods in the chamber, agitating the water and fat molecules all food contains to produce heat, which is conducted to the area around them, thus cooking the food from inside out. No preheating is needed, since once the microwaves are produced, they travel at the speed of light and enter the food to heat it almost instantaneously. The ovens cannot cook large quantities of food like standard ovens. However, they are excellent for reheating small quantities.

The microwave oven developed from the use of radar during World War II, in which electromagnetic waves were used to detect far-away objects, "see" objects at night, and locate those behind clouds.

In 1947 the Raytheon Company began marketing a microwave oven known commercially as the RadaRange. Electromagnetic waves of 915 megacycles and 2450 megacycles penetrate and are absorbed by the moisture in food. Strangely, some materials are transparent to the waves and are not heated by them. Glass, china, and paper containers do not absorb the waves. Metal reflects them, so metal containers are not used.

Since microwaves are absorbed preferentially by water, cooking is not uniform. Instead of heat being applied to the surface of the food and then being conducted slowly into the interior of the food, as in conventional cooking, microwave energy heats the food under the surface first and

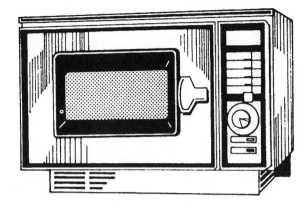

Figure 15-9 Microwave oven.

then moves outward. The surface is left unbrowned and relatively cool.

Such a revolutionary form of cooking was certain to stir the imagination. It also raised the hope that the ovens would replace conventional cooking equipment. Hundreds were sold, but later discarded because their limitations were not recognized. The early ovens were excellent for heating single or few portions of food, but were not useful for large-quantity food production.

However, microwave cooking has several advantages over conventional methods. First, the energy can be directed; there is no heat loss to the kitchen from the oven. Second, the cooking speed is amazingly fast for small quantities of food. Microwave cooking's principal use will probably be in reheating already cooked frozen foods. It has little value for producing baked dough items or any food that requires a leavening action.

In 1994 microwave ovens were being used in restaurants primarily for reheating precooked foods and defrosting frozen ones. A Burger King, for example, typically contains one or two microwave ovens used mainly to melt cheese on sandwiches, freshen buns, and finish cooking bacon that has been received already 90 percent cooked. Microwave ovens in most hotels are regarded as a piece of backup equipment to quickly heat a bowl of soup or warm up a roll.

The most common sizes of microwave ovens in use in Burger King restaurants are either the 1200-watt or 1400-watt size. Combination models include thermal heat units that introduce temperatures of up to 550 degrees F, some include a fan.[2]

---

2. "The Wave of the Future," *Restaurant & Institutions* (April 18, 1990).

Infrared Cooking Equipment

Infrared cooking equipment made its appearance in the 1950s. Like microwave energy, infrared waves are transmitted at the speed of light. They can penetrate the vapor blanket that surrounds moist food when it is heated. (Hot air takes longer.) Infrared wavelengths used for cooking are only microns in length. Those of about 1.4 to 5 microns are said to be the most effective for cooking.

Quartz crystal, calrod units, lava rock, man-made ceramics, cast iron, or stainless steel are heated to 1750 degrees F. These materials emit the proper wavelengths to be classified as infrared. Glowing charcoal also gives off infrared waves.

The overhead heating lamps seen frequently in service areas to keep plates warm use infrared waves.

Broilers and Grills

Broilers are sometimes called overhead broilers to avoid confusing them with grills. Broilers generate heat from above the food; grills generate heat from below.

Charbroiler. These use charcoal briquettes. When ignited, the charcoal gives off heat.

Open-hearth broilers. These produce heat from gas flames or electric rods that focus heat directly onto meats from above or below.

Oven-fired broilers. Such broilers produce heat over the racks holding the meat. Some models produce infrared heat once temperatures of 160 degrees F or more are reached. Preheating time is eliminated.

Salamander or back-shelf broilers. These are usually used in conjunction with an oven to hold or finish cooking food. They are sometimes used to create a crust on food or apply quick heat to a sauced food.

Ceramic grills. These use ceramic chips that are brought to high temperatures and give off heat.

Charcoal grill. This kind of grill again is gaining in popularity, partly because it adds interest to a restaurant when in view of the customers and partly because of the flavor created in food from such woods as mesquite when they are used for fuel.

Moving Cookers

Conveyor cooker. As on an assembly line, uncooked food is put in on one end, moved past and through the heat source, and removed at the other end, cooked. Time and temperature are easily controlled in such a system. Cooking time is controlled by setting the speed of the conveyor belt in its movement through the heated tunnel. All the food gets exactly the same amount of time and heat in the heat tunnel. This eliminates the need for judgment, and cooking is "deskilled." Most conveyors use chain-link belts to transport the food, but one model uses rotating rollers instead.

Unlike a griddle, where heat reaches the food placed on it via conduction, the conveyor cookers rely on radiant heat applied from the top and bottom simultaneously. The food need not be turned. Both electric and gas conveyor cookers are available. Some models use heat jets to cook the food, in effect becoming convection ovens. Pizzas cooked in these can be baked at a much lower temperature and in far less time than in a conventional pizza oven.

The portion-controlled hamburger patty (uniform size and thickness) was the logical candidate for cooking in a conveyorized broiler. Several fast-food chains used such broilers. Pizza is another popular candidate for conveyor cooking. Conveyorized cooking works best on foods of uniform thickness, such as cookies, biscuits, muf-

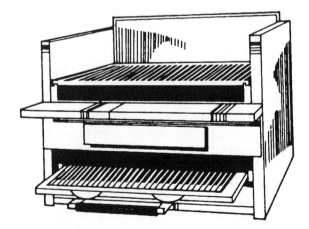

Figure 15-10 Grill.

fins, or sausage. Already plated Mexican meals or casseroles can be heated just prior to serving.

Turntable cooking. Related to the conveyor concept is the turntable. A pizza turntable has four quadrants, one exposed for loading and unloading; the remaining three are closed, forming the ovens where the pizza is cooked.

Griddles

Griddles, the heated flat surfaces used for the fast cooking of such items as hamburgers, eggs, and pancakes, have long been a principal cooking device for fastfood restaurants (Figs. 15-11 and 15-12). Some can be heated in sections.

Griddles are relatively energy inefficient. Surfaces not covered by food radiate energy into the kitchen. More recently, the grooved griddle has been widely used in many fastfood restaurants, where it has replaced the broiler. The griddle ridges produce marks on the steak similar to a broiler and the grooves allow fat and juices to drain off, thus avoiding the smoke created by the conventional broiler. Because the food is in direct contact with the surface, the grooved griddle cooks faster than a broiler. It also uses less fuel than a broiler. Hamburgers cooked on this surface are less likely to be burned than with a hot broiler, where it takes only a minute or two for the hamburger to become a charburger.

Steam Cooking

Steam cooking equipment transfers heat to food more efficiently than hot air. Each pound of steam

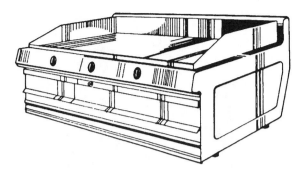

Figure 15-12 Countertop griddle.

contains 970 more BTUs than the same pound of boiling water. The latent energy of the steam is given off as the steam condenses back into water. If the steam is pressurized, its temperature goes up, which increases cooking speed.

Steam-cooking equipment is likely to be found where large quantities of soups, sauces, or anything cooked in a liquid must be prepared. Institutional kitchens—in hospitals, schools, colleges, correctional institutions, and so on—make wide use of steam-jacketed kettles for soups, stews, puddings, meats, and vegetables. Pressure steamers are also used in cafeterias and restaurants.

Stouffer's pioneered the use of the pressure steamer for cooking small batches of vegetables quickly, prepared to order. The speed of cooking permits "progressive cookery," the preparation of small quantities as needed. This is a big improvement over the large steam-jacketed kettles, which resulted in overcooking and excessive holding times.

Steamers, steam-jacketed kettles, steam frying pans, and steam pressure cookers are almost universally used in large-quantity kitchens and

Figure 15-11 Stand-alone griddle.

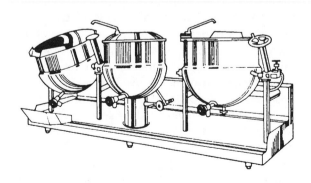

Figure 15-13 Steam kettles.

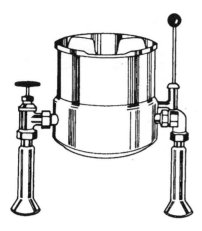

Figure 15-14 Trunnion kettle.

commissary operations. Their major disadvantage is that crisped or browned surfaces are not possible.

Steam-jacketed kettles.   These kettles can range in size from about 1 to 500 gallons (Figs. 15-13 and 15-14). They are surrounded by a shell into which steam is introduced. The steam does not come into contact with the food, but heats it through the shell. If the steam is under pressure, its temperature can go above 212 degrees F.

Steam-jacketed kettles were on the scene as early as 1874. The John Van and Company in 1879 was urging multiple use of steam kettles and sold "any size" for coffeemaking in "large public institutions." The copper jacketed and seamless cast-iron jacketed kettles of the 1870s would not look too much out of place in today's kitchen.

Combination oven/steamers.   Combination convection oven/steamers have been in use in Europe for some years. They are now available in this country (Fig. 15-15). Regarded as one of the most flexible and useful cooking devices available, the combination oven/steamer can steam, bake, or bake and steam at the same time. Steam can be introduced while roasting is done, which reduces meat shrinkage, or used to produce hard crusts on breads. Set at lower temperatures, frozen foods can be defrosted or foods reheated. Combination oven/steamers are available in various sizes.

Bain marie.   Literally, "Marie's bath," this is the forerunner of the steam table. It is a table containing hot water into which pots, crocks, and pans holding food are directly inserted, to keep warm.

Steam tables.   These are large tables into which tanks are placed and filled with about 3 inches of water, which is heated by steam, gas, or electricity. Pans holding food are inserted into the rectangular openings and held slightly above the water, which keeps the food warm.

Some so-called dry steam tables do not use water at all, but instead heat the air surrounding the pans to keep the food hot. Steam tables are intended to hold food rather than cook it, although cooking can take place whenever temperatures rise much above 140 degrees F.

Food Processing Equipment

Dough mixers.   Machines used for mixing flour, water, and other ingredients to form doughs. Special pie dough mixers are available.

Blenders.   These electrically driven blenders come in a variety of sizes. In a few seconds, they can cut food materials into minute sizes or blend them into liquid if enough water is present in the food.

Vertical mixers.   So-called vertical mixers are actually large blenders that can chop vegetables and other foods into small sizes or blend them into liquid form. They can be used for chopping vegetables into salad-sized materials. First made in Germany, the vertical mixer was originally called the *Schnell* (quick) cutter.

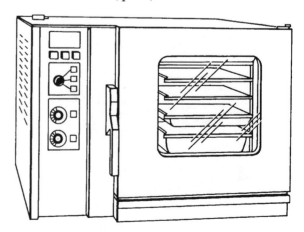

Figure 15-15 Combination convection oven and steamer.

Dough rollers. Machines that roll out dough for bread or pie crusts.

Slicing machines. A variety of machines are available for slicing vegetables by hand. Those that use machine-driven rotary knives are used to slice almost every food material.

WAREWASHING MACHINES

Build a machine and let it do your work. Why not also avoid dishpan hands? A tenacious gentleman, Haskins by name, started making dishwashing machines in the 1880s. A few were used in hotels, but dish crews struggled both with the dishes and the machine. At one stage of development, the machine was called "The Niagara," but when one hotelman said it was aptly named because it took a Niagara of water to run it, the name was changed to "Columbia." Another version did perfect washing, but wore the enamel off the edges of the dishes. Finally, after several failures, the machines were thrown out and hand dishwashing resumed. The patents for the machines were bought by G. S. Blakeslee about 1890.

The first machines merely consisted of baskets lowered into and raised from tubs or tanks of water by means of hand-operated cranks. Their circulating pumps were large and cumbersome, driven by steam or gasoline engines. Because of the large size of the machines—one used four by fours as supporting beams and stood 10 feet high—remodeling the kitchen was often necessary to install them.

Finally, water sprays were introduced. Electric motors and design for various sizes of operations came by 1910. By the 1920s, a new metal called ascoloy, was used for hoods, doors, and tanks. It was the forerunner of today's stainless steel. Not until the 1930s did the equipment manufacturers learn how to weld, bend, draw, or break stainless steel.

Many improvements have come with the years—and well they might, for most operators agree that the major foodservice problem area is the scullery. Even though there may be a china inventory three times the place settings needed, a breakdown of the dish machine throws the entire operation into a panic. It is not long before there are no clean dishes.

It is the wise operator who knows his or her

dish machine in detail, how to maintain it, how to operate it, and how to train others to operate it. At one time or another, it will be necessary to replace a part, tighten a valve, or do other repairs.

Few people are interested in making a career of dishwashing; even fewer can be found who are willing to stand over a hot sink, washing pots and pans by hand.

In the 1950s, Clyde R. Weithe experimented in his garage to produce a conveyorized machine that could be operated by one person. The Adamation machine that emerged (named after Adams Street in Newton, Massachusetts, where it was first manufactured) is widely used today. It has a revolving circular table attached that permits a merry-go-round of racks of dishes to move in and out of the machine. Soiled dishes are loaded onto the rack. The same person can wait for the rack to return with the now-clean ware and unload it. The table can be extended into the dining room, and the machine operated from there by a waiter or waitress, if necessary. At first, other dishmachine builders were not impressed by the machine, but later came to develop similar "rotary table" machines.

In 1969 the G. S. Blakeslee Company of Chicago produced a rotary table machine with a conveyor, which carries either racks or can be random-loaded with plates, glasses, or cups. Random loading eliminates the need for the presorting of soiled ware required for racking.

The Blakeslee machine has sensors built into the final rinse tank that both activate and turn off the hot final-rinse water. The water goes on only when dishes are passing through the machine, thereby saving hot water and rinse additive and reducing detergent dilution in the wash tank.

Today, huge dishwashing machines are in service that can sanitize dishes for thousands of persons each day. Cushioned conveyors carry the dishes between four top and bottom sprays, and then through an air drier. Machines come in one, two, three, and four tank sizes. They can exceed $35,000 in cost.

Dishwashing Layout for a High-Volume Restaurant[3]

The machine pictured in Figure 15-16 is a loading flight type. Tableware is loaded into racks, and

3. Courtesy of Planned Economics Laboratory, Inc., St. Paul, Minn.

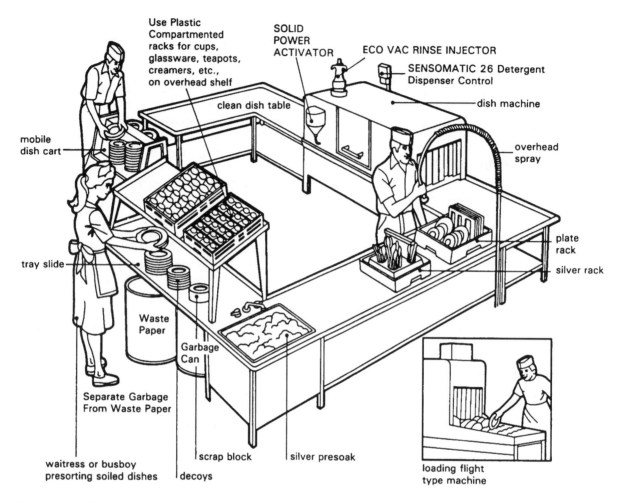

Figure 15-16 Dishwashing layout for a high-volume restaurant.

the racks are moved into the dish machine. They are then transported by conveyor through the machine. The system includes a presoak tank for loosening soil on silver. An overhead spray flushes off most soil from the tableware. Detergent is metered into the wash water, and an additive introduced into the rinse water to prevent water spots and film from forming on glasses and dishes.

Low-Temperature Machines

With costs of heating water increasing, new machines have entered the market that eliminate the need for the 180 degrees F water required for sanitization. A chemical bactericide added to the rinse allows 95 degrees F water to be used for this purpose. Some restaurant operators have reported

dishwashing costs cut in half with chemical agents. In bars where hot-water hookups are not very practicable, only cold water is used and sanitization is done completely with chemical agents.

Low-temperature dishwashers add a chlorine sanitizer, sodium hypochlorite, to detergent to sanitize serving ware. A necessarily well-engineered device adds only 50 parts per million into the rinse. Too much more than that, and it can be tasted by the patron. Water pressure during the wash cycle must be high to clean effectively.

Low-temperature machines not only save energy, but also reduce water consumption as well. Some machines recycle the wash water. No steam is produced by these machines; hence, no exhaust or ventilating system is necessary. Their cost is less than that for the conventional hot-water dishwasher.

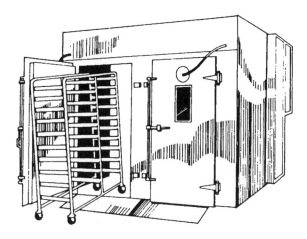

Figure 15-17 Roll-in refrigerator.

Low-temperature dishwashers can be rented; a counter on the machine adds up the number of racks cleaned, and the operator pays a few cents per rack. The rental machines are single-tank versions, and the operator is more likely to wash only full racks than with large machines. The latter are often kept running without dishes, or partially filled racks are sent through. The machines have been available for several years, but were relatively unnoticed until energy and water costs increased.

REFRIGERATORS AND FREEZERS

A refrigerator or freezer can be thought of as two boxes, one inside the other, separated by insulation. Heat is withdrawn from the inside box by a cooling system. The insulating material is usually polyurethane foam. Refrigerators require a minimum of 2 inches, freezers 3.

The cooling system consists of a compressor outside the refrigerator or freezer that contains a liquid freezing agent held under pressure. When this agent enters the interior, it expands and turns into a gas, which cools the interior. A valve allows the expanded gas to escape into an evaporator and returns it to the compressor, where it is once again a liquid. This cooling cycle is continuous.

For efficient functioning, coils within the refrigerator that carry the coolant must be kept defrosted and deiced. Otherwise, the cooling system cannot pick up heat within the box and transport it away.

If the compressor and evaporator are built as part of the refrigerator or freezer, the heat removed is carried into the room, usually the kitchen. When practical, compressors are located in a basement or outside the restaurant, where the heat and noise produced by them is less of a problem.

Large restaurants need large refrigerator and freezer space, usually large enough for a person to walk into, thus called walk-in boxes. Refrigerator drawers and undercounter units permit storage at the point of use. The smaller reach-in refrigerators conserve energy, both in cooling and in the absence of large doors.

Refrigerators and freezers are part of every restaurant's armamentarium against spoilage and the spread of germs. Temperatures below 40 degrees F immobilize most germs so that they cannot multiply. Refrigerators are set to hold food at 32 degrees F; most frozen food is best held at 0 degrees F or lower.

Broadly speaking, refrigerators and freezers are either "walk-in" or "reach-in." Walk-ins are large enough for a person to enter; reach-ins are too small to be entered. Walk-ins are often located adjacent to food-receiving areas, whereas reach-ins are more likely to be near a cook's station and used as cook's storage.

Walk-in freezer units are often built adjacent to a refrigerator or as part of a combined freezer-refrigerator, the freezer placed most remotely from the refrigerator door. Care must be taken to insure that doors can be opened from the inside, to avoid trapping anyone inside. Pass-through refrigerators, a third type, have doors both on the front and back, so that food can be received at one side of the box and taken out on the other. Some refrigerators, roll-ins are built to handle a complete wheeled rack (Fig. 15-17). Display refrigerators have glass doors for quick inspection or merchandising appeal. Undercounter units are examples of point-of-use equipment, placed to be immediately accessible to cooks or servers.

Sales volume, cost of storage, and the availability of food delivery by vendors determine the refrigerator/freezer capacity required.

Multiple-rack storage units on wheels permit maximum storage and save energy in moving food in and out of refrigerators. See-through glass or plexiglass doors reduce the need for frequent opening.

Kitchen planners recommend the following amount of refrigerator space on a per-meal basis for a luxury restaurant:

Meat and poultry	0.030 cu ft
Dairy products	0.015 cu ft
Produce	0.040 cu ft

Blocks of frozen foods, such as turkey, chicken, and cuts of meat, are best brought to lower temperatures by being placed in a refrigerator for several hours before being cooked. Refrigeration cost is reduced by using this method, rather than thawing at room temperature, or by being placed in running water. The frozen food in a refrigerator reduces the temperature of the holding space.

ICE MACHINES

Restaurants need at least one machine to produce ice for water and for alcoholic and nonalcoholic beverages. Some machines can produce ice as cubelets, which are ideal for tall drinks and make them look even taller. Standard cube-sized ice is good for beverages served at banquets; the larger-sized ice melts slowly and lasts longer. Crushed ice drops the temperature of a beverage most quickly. It is used as the cooling foundation for salad bars, oyster bars, and juice displays.

The hotter the climate, the more ice capacity is needed. A hundred-seat restaurant with a bar would probably need an ice machine capable of producing 400 pounds of ice and with a storage capacity of 540 pounds.

Some experts advise against buying one large central machine; that will leave the restaurant without ice if it breaks down. Rather, they recommend two or more smaller machines located near their points of use. A bar often has its own ice machine.

KITCHEN ORGANIZATION AND PLANNING

The old prints of kitchens in the royal palaces show huge, unpartitioned, high-ceilinged rooms. During the time of Napoleon, the French chef was seen wearing a long, floppy cap on the order of a nightcap as a symbol of his authority. At the other end of the status spectrum came the lowly plongeur, the dishwasher. Carême is credited with devising the tall starched hat that identifies the chef or chief. The height of the toque blanc is supposed to correlate with rank in the kitchen.

Auguste Escoffier, the famous French chef and César Ritz associate, is credited with synchronizing the kitchen staff's operation.

For example, under the old system, eggs Meyerbeer, a dish consisting of eggs, lamb, kidneys, and truffle sauce, required 15 minutes to prepare. Escoffier placed a chef at each station— an entremetier baked the eggs in butter, a rotisseur grilled the kidney, while a saucier prepared the truffle sauce. The result was that the dish was prepared in a fraction of the time.

At the turn of the century and for some time after that, most hotel builders placed their kitchens in the basement, where space was less valuable. Kitchens were large. The Astor Hotel in New York City opened in 1904 with a kitchen 231 feet long and an average width of 150 feet.

Of course, the planners had not reckoned with the cost of operating the kitchens, of moving people, food, and dishes from one level to another and within the kitchen. These costs are built in and continue for the life of a building.

Ellsworth Statler was one of the first to see the merits of placing the kitchen on the same level as the dining areas. In 1917 the kitchen of the St. Louis Statler was placed on the same floor as all of the dining facilities, which were built around three sides of the kitchen. This layout made it possible for one kitchen to serve the dining room, the coffeeshop, and a café more efficiently. The plan has been used several times since. One of the most dramatic examples is in the Beverly Hilton Hotel, where the kitchen is circular and the various dining facilities surround it.

Many high-rise buildings, especially where land is a major cost, cannot afford to place kitchen and serving areas on the same level. At the New York Hilton, for example, the kitchen and warewashing facilities are located in a central core of the building and occupy several floors, connected by elevator to each other and the restaurants.

When the kitchen is built in the shape of a square, equipment is frequently placed around three walls, forming an open square or U. The first station as the waiter enters is apt to be the dish room, and the last station before entering the dining room is the pantry, or coffee and dessert station.

The practice of placing a number of preparation stations side by side behind a pickup counter is used by most commercial kitchens that prepare

Figure 15-18 The layout of the McDonald's kitchen has evolved over the years. The kitchen is compact on the large griddle and garnished on the rotary table across the aisle.

food for a large and complicated menu. The Waldorf-Astoria kitchen, for example, stretches a long distance, with station after station placed side by side. The waiter enters the kitchen and drops off parts of his order at each station, returning later to pick up the prepared food.

Some kitchens in the larger hotels are immense, the distances walked by the waiters in placing and picking up orders prodigious. Waiters and waitresses in huge American Plan resort hotels must develop into track athletes by the end of the busy season.

Cooking equipment is arranged in an island in the center of the room at some institutional kitchens. They are not as likely to be as departmentalized as commercial kitchens. The equipment in one place permits all of it to be under one exhaust hood, which can draw off the hot air and vapors created by the equipment that much more efficiently.

Professional Planners

Many professional kitchen planners are associated with restaurant equipment houses. The larger equipment firms employ layout specialists who are called on to plan new kitchens, their services being included in the contract for the purchase of the kitchen equipment.

Following World War II, a few foodservice consultants set themselves up in business, offering their kitchen planning skills for a fee. In the 1950s a group of independent consultants formed the Food Facilities Engineering Society. Another group, including both independent consultants and kitchen planners employed by equipment houses, formed the International Society of Food Service Consultants. The two groups are now merged into one, the Food Facilities Engineering Society.

Because the number of possible arrangements in any given kitchen is astronomical, no two kitchen consultants plan a kitchen alike. Each has developed preferred patterns that have worked satisfactorily over the years.

Kitchen planning essentially revolves around the amount of space allocated or available. In expensive locations, the kitchens are often miniscule, one employee working almost on the back of another. Surprisingly, such small kitchens turn out to be more efficient than the large ones because of the need to plan each work station in detail and the elimination of steps required when foodservice workers move from station to station, station to storeroom, and within a station. In most cases, reducing the size of the menu also improves kitchen efficiency.

A Prizewinning Design

An example of a restaurant kitchen designed for function and speed of operation is the prize-winning kitchen in Eddy's Restaurant in Kansas City. The floor plan is shown in Figure 15-20.

The serving person flow is a loop that starts with the dish pantry, just six steps inside the door from the diningroom. The loop continues past the meat and fish station, vegetable station, salad station, and on to the pantry station. From there it passes the service bar and food checker. There is no cross-traffic, nor long distances between stations.

Preparation units buttress the serving stations and are set up so that food passes from one department to the next on its way to the serving line. Each employee is trained in two jobs; as work runs out at one station, he or she moves to another point of service. Multicolored lights signal waiters when orders are ready. Refrigerated drawers directly opposite the broilers and ranges keep food at the chef's elbow.

Figure 15-19 Another section of the McDonald's kitchen, showing how the paper service is arranged for most efficient use. Hamburgers are bagged and held for up to ten minutes. If after that time they are not sold, they are discarded. Paper cups are separated in size and held upside down.

All equipment, including ranges, is elevated 8 inches above the floor for easy cleaning. Interiors and shelves are removable for complete cleaning. Self-leveling plate coolers and warmers are used. Ledges that accommodate two tiers of trays facilitate the assembling of orders.

Here is a case where the kitchen was planned first and the building constructed around it. Most kitchens must conform to the building, and the result is a poor layout, making process flow analysis all the more needed.

Two Problems

In or Out? Points of debate in kitchen planning revolve largely around whether serving personnel should enter the kitchen and what they should do once there. Some operators require servers to make salads and toast and do other pantry work. Others believe that the less time servers are in the kitchen, the better. They arrange for soiled ware to be carried into the kitchen via a conveyor belt or use the merry-go-round rotary rack system, described earlier, that extends into the diningroom.

How much time servers should spend in the kitchen is partly determined by the speed of the diningroom. If breakfast and lunch are relatively slow, servers might well be used in the pantry and elsewhere in the kitchen. If turnover is fast, they can be more efficiently used in the diningroom.

Kitchen floors. Kitchen floors are characteristically covered with quarry tile that is easy to clean, relatively impervious to water, and durable. Quarry tile is also extremely slippery when wet, however, which is probably the greatest cause of accidents in the hospitality business. Whoever has experienced a fall on tile, hitting his or her head on the floor, will never forget it—or perhaps he or she will.

A few kitchens have installed carpets. As an alternative, a Washington, D.C., cafeteria operator provides each employee with a small rag rug for his or her station and has found both safety and cleanliness increased.

Open Kitchens and Display Kitchens

How much of the kitchen can be assigned to the diningroom? That is, will there be a section for display cooking, dessert carts wheeled about for the delectation of the patron, a salad bar, tableside cooking using gueridons (carts for finish cooking and flaming foods)? A few restaurants have the kitchen completely open to the view of diners. Who has not seen the pizza maker twirling and tossing pizza dough in the front window of a pizza parlor, making it part of the place's excitement?

Open kitchens and display-cooking sections have taken several forms, from the open-pit barbecue to the completely open kitchen where the customer can "participate" visually in kitchen activity. The traditional chef's garb of checked pants, white starched jacket, and high white hat are part of the restaurant drama.

One word of caution is in order: A display-cooking section left unused is a negative; it must

be occupied and busy to provide the feeling that the restaurant is a going concern.

An open kitchen saves kitchen space. The usual kitchen requires two traffic aisles, one outside the kitchen and one inside. With an open kitchen the service aisle is in the diningroom.

Many theme or specialty restaurants incorporate display kitchens in the diningroom. They either must be supported by an auxiliary kitchen elsewhere or an extremely limited menu used. In the Charlie Brown restaurants, the chef and his supporting equipment are installed in the diningroom. The Rib Room display kitchens are built around a limited menu featuring roast beef,

EDDYS' RESTAURANT   KANSAS CITY, MISSOURI
ARCHITECTS: GENTRY & VOSKAMP
FABRICATED & INSTALLATION:
GREENWOOD'S, INC.   SOUTHERN EQUIPMENT CO.

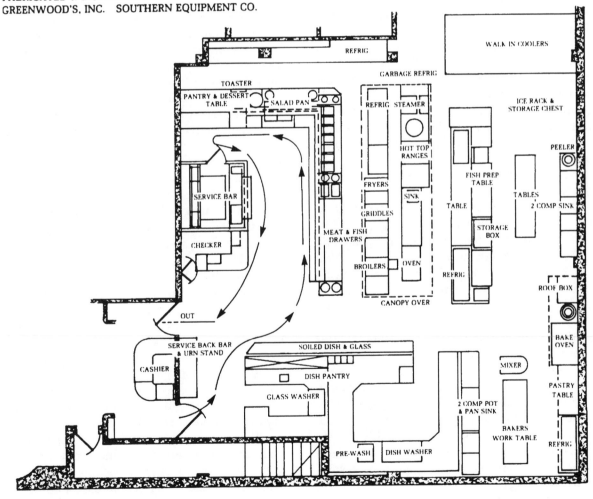

Figure 15-20 "Custom-built by Southern." Given an Award of Merit.

Source: Institutions/Volume Feeding.

baked potatoes, and tossed salads. In some Japanese-style restaurants, the guests sit around a large griddle, and the wait personnel acts as both cook and server.

Among the most efficient restaurant operations are the Friendly Ice Cream Shops in New England. All food preparation is done on an island surrounded by counters and stools. The menu is limited to a few grill items, soup, and ice cream so that every employee can grill, as well as act as waiter or waitress. The distance between preparation area and serving area is a matter of a few steps. Most of the food is already prepared. The wait personnel merely hands it to the customer across a counter.

The Work Environment

The value of color in the kitchen is becoming recognized. Instead of the customary antiseptic white, walls and ceilings are painted peach and yellow, colors found to be pleasant to work in. Adequate lighting is especially needed at the pickup area of the dish machine and at food-preparation stations. Lighting must be bright enough so that employees can see whether the dishes are clean on the one hand and watch the results of their handiwork in garnishment and plate arrangement on the other.

According to Arthur Avery, a well-known foodservice consultant, the dishwashing area should be lit to a level of 20- to 30-foot candles. At the clean end of the washer, lighting should be raised to 40- to 50-foot candles. (Egg white and white cereal residues are hard to see without that much light.) The hot dishroom can be "cooled," from a psychological standpoint, by the use of cool blue and blue-green colors on the wall.

Air conditioning increases productivity by 10 to 15 percent. It also reduces accidents and improves quality control.

The kitchen is usually much too noisy, especially the dishroom. Plastic racks reduce clatter. Coating the underside of dish tables with a mastic material or the use of plastic or rubber mats on the tables decreases decibels. Acoustic tile on the walls and ceilings also help. Acoustic paint can be used, and so can an acoustic honeycomb system of baffles hung from the ceiling.

Sinks in kitchens are almost always too low; having to bend constantly can create fatigue and back problems. It is to be hoped that someday sinks will be adjustable to fit the height of a worker.

All dials should be at eye level, so that they can be read easily. Aisles are often too narrow or too wide. Industrial designers say that aisle space should be at least 30 inches; 36 to 38 inches where items are retrieved from under a counter; 45 inches when kneeling is necessary. When two employees must work on either side of an aisle, 48 inches should be allowed.

Gas or Electric?

The competitive situation being what it is between the electric and gas utility companies, the kitchen planner is beset by claims of superiority for gas on the one hand and electricity on the other.

Since most chefs have learned the trade using gas, the tendency is for them to favor it as a cooking fuel. They feel gas, for top-of-the-stove cooking, is more controllable than electric heating elements. The gas flame responds instantaneously to a turn of the knob and is visible.

The electric utility companies point out that burning gas consumes oxygen, and if there is not a constant source of fresh air, the carbon monoxide level can rise dangerously. Proportionately, more institutional kitchens use electric cooking equipment than commercial ones.

The cost of cooking fuel is a major consideration. The American Gas Association readily admits that it takes 1.6 BTU of gas to equal 1 BTU of electricity. The reason is that much of the heat produced by gas is carried out the ventilation system, along with the noxious fumes produced by gas combustion. But, say the gas people, when present rates are applied to this ratio, electric cooking in typical cities in the U.S. costs from two to ten times as much as gas. (In a few areas where hydroelectric power is cheap, electricity for cooking is cheaper than gas.) The gas people also argue that their product is more fail-safe, in that the gas supply is not likely to break down, which happens periodically with electricity.

The gas vs. electricity decision need not be made in favor of one or the other, but rather in terms of specific pieces of cooking equipment. Either gas or electricity can be used to produce the hot air needed in ovens, the stove-top temperatures of 3000 degrees F or more, and steam and infrared energy.

Electricity must be used for microwave ovens. Gas broilers seem to be more effective than electric ones; electric deep fryers, in which the heating units are immersed in the fat, seem to be more effective than gas fryers, in which the heat is concentrated on the bottom of the kettle. Some electric equipment is more attractive in appearance and better insulated than comparable gas equipment. Gas is more hazardous than electric fuel because of its combustibility.

Computer Assistance

It had to come: computer-assisted kitchen planning. The optimal arrangement of equipment in a kitchen may appear to be a fairly simple problem. The mathematics of the problem, however, are formidable. A kitchen can be thought of as a system of interacting components.

A major problem in kitchen design is to arrange the work stations so as to minimize the steps between stations, equipment, and storage areas. George Conrad, staff member of the AH&MA Educational Institute, has estimated that, if there were ten stations in a kitchen, the paper-and-pencil calculations required to arrive at the best possible layout would require 3 years. With a computer, the calculations can be made in a matter of minutes.

A computer model is used to evaluate the number of employees needed to handle any given sales volume based on the layout of the kitchen, sales mix, and percentage of drive-through customers. The model also suggests the most effective positioning of employees. By reference to charts developed from the computer model, managers know when to shift employees to overloaded stations, such as cash registers, the preparation board, or drink stations.

Burger King uses the computer to project sales levels at which kitchen counters will need to be extended and point-of-sales terminals and fry stations added. Information fed into the computer includes customer arrival patterns, manning strategies, customer/cashier interactions, customer ordering characteristics, production time standards, stocking rules, and inventory. The goal was to continue to serve the customer within 3 minutes and utilize personnel and equipment to the maximum. Computer-assisted analysis reduced labor costs by 1.5 percent.

The analysis also resulted in lengthening drive-in serving area and the addition of a second drive-through window.

Burger King was able to keep labor costs to 16 percent of sales. Computer analysis is credited with helping to make this possible.

COMMISSARY FOOD PRODUCTION

Much or all of the food preparation for a multi-unit food service can be centralized in one or more production kitchens, rather than carried out in the kitchen of each individual foodservice unit. The resulting systematization reduces costs and increases quality.

Economies of scale are possible with centralization. Serving units require no food-preparation equipment. All purchases are made by a specialized food purchaser. Large bulk purchases are warehoused and moved efficiently with forklifts and conveyor belts. Jobs can be specialized and simplified. Large-volume, heavy-duty food-preparation equipment can be purchased. Salaries can be paid that attract qualified candidates for commissary manager.

Some commissaries have been highly effective over the years; others have not. Foodservice specialists disagree as to the merits of centralization. Some ardently favor it; others are vehemently opposed. Those who favor the commissary point to the value of operating the kitchen like a factory, using standardized recipes and labor-saving equipment. They recommend operating the commissary very much like a food-processing plant.

Those who oppose the commissary maintain that the intricacies of relating the commissary to the unit are overly complicated. Whenever food is prepared in one location and delivered to another, energy costs are involved. Holding food in any form after it is cooked requires energy—energy to chill or freeze it and energy to reconstitute (reheat) the food. Food produced in the commissary and finally delivered to the unit, they say, is of a less desirable quality than can be produced in the unit itself. Food can be of top quality to start with, but once the item is cooked, quality usually declines the longer it is held.

In-flight foodservice almost proves the last criticism. Prepared in a central commissary, the food must be refrigerated, kept heated at relatively low temperatures, or frozen before it is brought to the plane. In the plane, it must be brought up to serving temperature. Almost everyone concerned with in-flight foodservice agrees that it is most difficult to produce a meal for the passenger's tray that measures up to the quality of one produced from scratch in a restaurant and served immediately. If they are honest with themselves, food experts almost unanimously agree that the best food is prepared and served that way. Quality inevitably declines the longer food is held from its fresh state.

The debate over commissaries is particularly relevant to college and university foodservices. Most of the larger schools, with a number of student houses or a dining commons, have the option of centralizing part or all of food preparation. Smith College has some 30 houses, each with its own kitchen and preparation team, which personalizes the foodservice. The college administration recognizes that centralization would reduce costs, but they are willing to pay extra for food prepared in each kitchen. Michigan State University, on the other hand, operates from a central commissary, as do a number of other universities.

Centralization at Work

Centralization of the public-school foodservice program began in the late 1950s, and by the 1960s many school systems had followed suit. Food is centrally prepared by industrial methods and machinery and then distributed by truck to the individual school. Fewer employees are needed than when each school operates its own kitchen, but part of the savings in labor is offset by the cost of transporting the food.

Centralized commissaries for commercial restaurants go back at least to the 1890s. The John R. Thompson Company of Chicago operated a central commissary for three restaurants and later distributed the food to the individual units by electrically driven vans. The Marriott Corporation began commissary operation in the early 1930s by centralizing some of the food preparation in one of their stores and distributing it to the others. In 1941 a large centralized commissary building and headquarters was built near Washington, D.C. This was enlarged several times, and in 1967 a brand new commissary building was completed.

The Marriott operation is highly automated. Purchase orders from the individual stores are telephoned into the commissary via data-phone. The caller inserts a properly punched card, and the order is transmitted via a code. A computer at the receiving end compiles the orders and prints them out.

A number of companies have elected to prepare only some foods in their commissaries, producing only those in which economies of scale are involved and that are as good or better in quality than that produced on restaurant premises or purchased from a supplier. Items like soups, chili, dressings, and teriyaki and barbecue sauce can be made in a commissary and distributed without any loss in quality.

Many small restaurant chains have compromised on the commissary concept by centralizing all baking and heavy meat roasting, sauce making, and soup making, whereas salad making and all frying are done on the unit's premises.

Commissaries have not always been successful. It is reported that the Horn and Hardart Baking Company of Philadelphia installed a multimillion-dollar commissary, only to find that its capacity was much too great for the volume of food that could be sold in the individual units. Other companies have tried commissaries and abandoned them for a variety of reasons.

Whether or not the central commissary is economical and effective depends on its design, the menu it produces, the number of units it serves, and the geographical spread of the units. If an individual unit has a high enough volume of sales, it can, in effect, operate its own food-processing plant on the premises. If the unit is large enough to achieve that economy of scale, there is no need to turn to a commissary to produce the same item and transport it to the unit.

One factor in commissary operation is the distance involved in transporting food from the commissary to the individual unit. At some point, it becomes necessary to introduce another commissary or produce locally because of transportation costs. The Teamsters union has been another factor in driving up transportation costs.

Efficiency and Quality

It costs money to freeze and reheat. It is not necessary to freeze if the food does not have to be held for extended periods.

A large hospital contract foodservice company refrigerates cooked food in five-portion quantities in vacuum-sealed bags. Its technique is based on the Swedish Nacka food system, named after the Nacka hospitals in Stockholm where it originated. The food is processed and packaged at various stages of doneness. Stewed items, such as meat or chicken pot pie, are completely cooked. Broiled items, such as chopped steak, are grilled just long enough to give surface color. Other foods are packaged raw and completely cooked within the pouch.

The food is portioned uncooked and packaged under vacuum. It is then cooked to desired doneness in a hot-water bath. Quick chilling is done in cold water, and the food stored in a refrigerator. Shelf life is said to be at least 60 days. When the food is to be readied for serving, it is placed in a hot-water bath for 30 to 40 minutes, until it reaches an internal temperature of 160 degrees F. It is then plated and placed briefly in a microwave oven before service.

Such low-temperature cooking reduced meat shrinkage by as much as 20 percent. Batching of production, producing a number of the same items at one time, permits greater economy and efficiency. Seven-day requirements can be produced in a 5-day, 40-hour week.

Many foods need not be refrigerated at all, if the temperature can be held at 140 degrees or higher without damaging quality. A chain of Georgia cafeterias transports round ribs of beef from a central commissary some 50 miles to various service cafeterias. The food is undercooked initially, and additional cooking takes place during transportation, finishing off the process.

Items like soups, sauces, gravies, and heavy roasts can be held for 48 hours or longer at temperatures that will not permit bacterial growth. Most items lose some flavor, but a few actually improve.

Salad greens can be prepared and held for several hours in a moist, cool environment. Salad dressings, however, cannot be added until just before serving without severe quality loss. Many salads with or without dressings cannot be held on the cafeteria line for more than a few minutes without quality deterioration. A flat statement can be made about fried items: Their quality falls off rapidly, and none should be held for more than about 15 minutes before serving.

ENERGY CONSERVATION

Energy costs in the kitchen have always been important, but little attention was given to them until the energy crisis of the 1970s, when those costs doubled in some areas. Since the typical kitchen consumes 40 percent or more of the total energy used in the restaurant, the NRA, the AH&MA, and several hospitality chains began to examine ways to reduce the costs of heating water for dishwashing, pot and pan washing, cooking, and heating and cooling the kitchen.

Ideas for conserving energy include constructing thick walls on the western and southern exposures of a restaurant, limiting the size and number of windows, using fluorescent lighting in other than dining areas, installing devices on equipment to reduce peak electricity load at any one time (electricity rates are based on maximum consumption for any 15-minute period, plus the total amount consumed; the overall rate charged per kilowatt hour is determined by measuring the highest demand for a 15-minute period; a high demand for that period sets an overall rate higher than if the demand for that 15-minute period were lower), and installing wrap-around heat-recovery devices on incinerator stacks and using the hot air generated for heating purposes.

The Heating, Ventilation, and Air-Conditioning System (HVAC)

Ordinarily, the kitchen HVAC system should operate independently of the other rooms. Fumes must be exhausted by fans through filters that trap grease and odors and force the dirty air directly to the outside. Air in the kitchen is kept at a slightly negative pressure by the use of fans so that it will not move into the dining room. As a result, there is a slight air movement from the dining and other rooms into the kitchen and out the exhaust ducts over the cooking and dishwashing equipment.

Since air is continually being exhausted out of the ducts by fans, makeup or fresh air is often pumped directly into the kitchen, which helps to cool it in the summer. The makeup air can be heated during cold periods.

Air pressure for the entire restaurant must be slightly positive, meaning that the amount of fresh air should be slightly greater than the

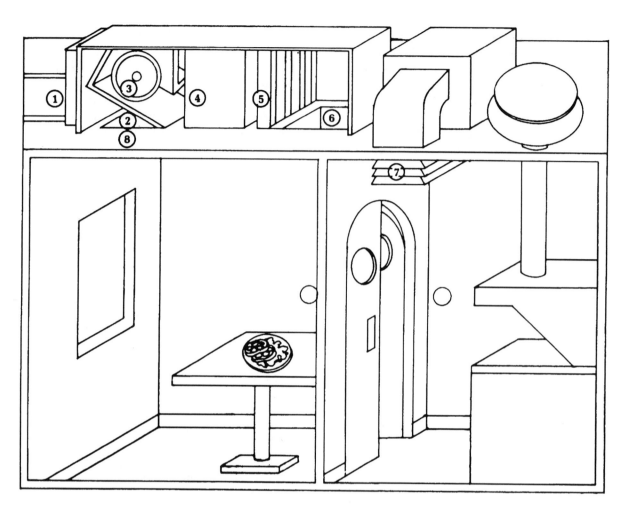

Figure 15-21 A "typical" HVAC system and kitchen make-up unit.

amount exhausted. When doors and windows are opened, air gently flows out; outside air does not rush in.

Terminal reheat systems distribute air through the ducts at the temperature needed by the room with the greatest cooling requirement— the main dining room. Small heaters or fans inside the ducts that are controlled by thermostats in each room reheat or cool the air as required.

Variable volume systems deliver the same temperature air to all rooms, but dampers inside the ducts controlled by individual room thermostats regulate the amount and temperature of air delivered.

Most restaurant operators will never engineer an HVAC system, but all should look into how such a system works. They should follow out the ducts from where the air is taken in to

where it is exhausted. They should know the location of each blower, heater, and chiller. The Department of Energy includes in its *Guide to Energy Conservation for Food Service* a number of simplified drawings that show how kitchen equipment and HVAC systems operate. Figure 15-21 is taken from that publication.

A PARTING NOTE

Today's foodservice operator has a wide choice of equipment from which to choose, equipment that is easy to use and clean, is durable and compact, and that will cook and otherwise prepare food quickly and efficiently. Today's kitchen can provide a relatively pleasant environment in which to work, provided that proper heating, ventilation, and air conditioning are installed and if kitchens are properly planned and laid out to maximize work flow and minimize labor. Like most areas of specialization, kitchen planning and equipment selection are fairly complex. The restaurant operator can gain valuable assistance from food facilities engineers.

Questions

1. Name three pieces of kitchen equipment used in ancient Roman kitchens and the colonial kitchens of the U.S.

2. What is the name of a prestige restaurant that operated before 1900 in New York City?

3. Count Rumford, a gentleman who was born in Massachusetts, achieved some fame as a kitchen inventor. Can you name one of his inventions?

4. Who is the famous chef given credit for first organizing the kitchen into departments?

5. Why is a kitchen called a food-processing plant?

6. The tilting skillet (or braising pan) can be used to cook several ways. Name three such ways.

7. Fires in the kitchen before about 1950 were frequently caused by overheated frying fat. What device has helped to limit such fires?

8. How is a forced convection oven different from the conventional oven?

9. Define a magnetron and its use in the kitchen.

10. Name three advantages and three disadvantages of microwave cooking.

11. Define a salamander.

12. What is the advantage of using a grooved griddle over a flat griddle?

13. Define bain marie.

14. Dishmachines that use a rotary table have what advantage over flight-type machines?

15. Is it necessary to place a dishwashing room close to the dining room? Explain.

16. What is the great disadvantage of using gas over electricity?

17. Is there one best way to plan a kitchen? Explain.

18. Kitchen floors are normally covered with quarry tile. What is the advantage of quarry tile? A big disadvantage?

19. Why is it not a good idea to fry all the parts of a chicken at the same time in a deep-fry kettle?

20. Name three or four items that can be easily prepared in a commissary and distributed without loss of quality.

21. Name two food items that are difficult to prepare in a commissary and distribute without loss of quality.

22. Name a major disadvantage of freezing prepared food before distributing it.

23. Energy management is a consideration of a number of restaurant operators. Name three ideas that can be incorporated into a restaurant to reduce energy demand.

24. Air pressure in a restaurant dining room must be slightly positive. Why?

25. Which uses less energy: fluorescent or incandescent lighting?

26. Why not use fluorescent lighting throughout a restaurant?

27. Why is it so important to spread out the demand for electricity as much as possible throughout a day?

28. Suppose you installed solar collectors on the roof of your restaurant. How would the heat collected in them be transferred and used in the restaurant?

29. Conveyorized cooking equipment has what advantages?

Discussion Questions

1. What will the commercial kitchen be like in the year 2000?

2. Will highly trained chefs become more valuable? Or will they fade in importance because of equipment and systems advances?

3. How will nutritional changes in our diet be reflected in the commercial kitchen?

4. Which pieces of kitchen equipment will be less widely used in the future than now?

Georges Auguste Escoffier

(1846–1935)*

Georges Auguste Escoffier, called King of Chefs, Chef to Kings, is the most respected culinary personality of our times. He is almost a cult figure among chefs.

Only a few chefs have known international fame: Vatel, maître d'hotel to the Prince de Conde; Alexis Soyer, master chef to the Reform Club in London; and Antonine Carème, chef to kings.

To become outstanding in any métier usually requires tremendous devotion and energy; Escoffier had these in abundance. Although married, he lived most of his off-working hours by himself in hotel apartments in London and Paris while his wife lived in Monaco. They had no children. Every day (except Sundays) for the better part of 75 years was spent on his work. His day typically started with breakfast in his office, after which he would walk around the kitchen, supervising personnel and overseeing food preparation. No detail was overlooked, including personal behavior (no indulgence in alcohol, smoking, vulgarity, or fits of temper).

At 11:00 AM he joined the restaurant manager and the headwaiters, and together they discussed the likes and dislikes of the VIPs coming for the day's meals.

During lunch he tasted and supervised food preparation, and after lunch went for a walk, taking the same route every day. So well known did he become on his walks that friendly police stopped traffic for him to cross the street; whereupon, with great deliberation, Escoffier would reward the gesture with a sixpence. A brief nap followed, and then he went back to the kitchen at 6:00 PM where he worked until 9:00. Like many illustrious chefs, he eschewed the rich foods of the trade, preferring a little rice and fruit for supper. The day ended at midnight. Then he oversaw the col-

*Information adapted from Eugene Herbodeau and Paul Thalamas, *George Auguste Escoffier* and *Pupils and Literary Executors of Maître Escoffier* (London: Practical Press), 1955 and Edward B. Page and P. W. Kingsford, *The Master Chefs* (London: Edward Arnold), 1970.

lection of leftovers, which were given to a religious organization for distribution to the poor.

Perhaps Escoffier's greatest achievement was his book *Le Guide Culinaire* (called in this country *The Escoffier Cookbook*), prepared in collaboration with several of his friends, also culinary experts. A collection of his menus appeared in *Le Livre des Menus*, a complementary volume. The *Guide* has been called "the new testament of contemporary cookery," but, of course, food and cookery research has been extensive since 1902, and Escoffier's book should be regarded as a collection of the best cooking knowledge available at the turn of the century.

The *Guide* was an attempt to end the age of guesswork in cooking, with cooks following the practice of a pinch of that and a spoonful of this. Escoffier prescribed exact weights and measures and set the stage for modern cookbook writing.

Much of Escoffier's effectiveness can be traced to his role as executive chef of the famous Ritz-managed hotels. Madame Ritz said of the association: "The collaboration of Ritz and Escoffier must be counted as one of the most fortunate events of their lives." Escoffier held forth in the back of the house with a brigade of some 60 or more cooks, while Ritz managed the front of the house. Both men were perfectionists, complementing each other perfectly.

It was only natural that Escoffier, artistically sensitive and creative, would bend his talents to pleasing the great patrons of the day—the rich, the powerful, and those in the entertainment world. He was probably only partly joking when he said, "My success comes from the fact that my best dishes were created for ladies." An opera devotee, he was particularly successful with opera stars. Several of his more famous dishes were created especially for opera stars.

Great chefs are expected to produce works of art as well as cook, and Escoffier excelled at producing baskets of flowers and birds from wax and icing sugar, and swans from huge blocks of ice. His pêches Eugènie is an example of his artistry: Monreuil peaches, stones and skins removed, are placed on a silver dish interspersed with wild strawberries, and the whole sprinkled with sugar, kirsch, and maraschino. Just before serving, the peaches are covered with iced champagne-flavored sabayon, the wine-custard dessert.

His associates always thought of him as kindly, thoughtful, and helpful. His personal life was one of order and simplicity. He is credited with bringing new status to the vocation of chef, insisting that the cooks and chefs change to respectable street clothing when leaving the kitchen for home. In the kitchen he demanded discipline and a curb on temper. The rush hour, he said, was not the signal for a rush of words, and under his management the *aboyeur* (barker) who barked out orders from the dining room gave way to the *annonceur* who called them out.

He has been called the father of the modern menu and creator of the kitchen system as we know it today. A contemporary of Frederick Winslow Taylor, the efficiency expert, Escoffier was similarly interested in quality and speed of service. He reduced the number of items on the menu and simplified preparation whenever possible. The French kitchen had been departmentalized before him, but he integrated and coordinated it. Under him each order was taken in triplicate, one copy going to the cashier, one to the kitchen, and one kept by the waiter. The guest's name was written on the check so that Escoffier could include in the dishes any refinements of which he knew the guest was particularly fond. The announcer called the order in the kitchen and the chef of each department or *partie* began the preparation of that part of the meal for which he was responsible. When the entire course was ready, it was brought to a hot plate where Escoffier reviewed it before it was served to the customer.

Escoffier also had faults. According to David Ogilvy, a chef who worked under Escoffier at the Savoy Hotel in London saw Escoffier signing receipts for cartloads of beef that were then delivered to his brother Robert's sauce factory on Tottenham Court Road.[*] Escoffier grew rich and, in Ogilvy's view, looked in his later years like a Victorian banker.

It is doubtful if in this day of chain restaurants and highly standardized menus, any one chef can ever emulate Escoffier in international acclaim. There are too many excellent television food commentators, home economists, and others showing homemakers how to cook, and too many food entertainers and cookbook writers for any one person to be needed to perform the kind of culinary overview that Escoffier provided.

Of all national groups, the French probably respect fine food preparation and service the most, and it was not surprising when the French government gave public recognition to Escoffier's genius. Escoffier was awarded the Legion of Honor and later made an officer in that honorable company.

---

[*]David Ogilvy, *Blood, Brains and Beer* (New York: Atheneum), 1978, p. 46.

16

Management of People

There are two major functions involved in managing human resources in an organization:

1. *Personnel function.* In a formal organization, this is the division that is responsible for the actuarial and policy function of personnel. This includes maintaining employee records, setting up training programs, coping with labor unions, providing employee counseling, establishing and managing hiring procedures, and dealing with government employee regulation forms.

2. *Employee management function.* At the work place, this task is performed by the operational manager, supervisor, or foreman. This function is concerned with planning the work objectives of a group, assembling teams, seeing to it that the necessary tools and equipment are in place, setting goals and objectives, and ensuring that these objectives are met. It involves the manager's under-

standing, the entire daily give and take of the complicated interactions that are the workplace.

Since many readers will become supervisors and/or managers, this chapter is concerned primarily with providing an introduction to the second aspect of the human resources management function.

The management of individuals and groups has been occurring for a long period of time. Some of the earliest records of supervision hark back to the construction of the pyramids in Egypt around 2000 BC. The task for the supervisor then was the same as it is now. The supervisor was expected to plan the work so as to obtain the highest possible productivity from each worker and team of workers as they performed the tasks. In ancient Egypt, if a worker was not doing his job well, he was flogged on the spot. If he continued to do unsatisfactory work, his head was cut off and hung on a pole for other workers to see. This represents extreme discipline. Yet for many years, even today, supervisors, while not engaged in flogging or cutting off heads, are often measured by their ability to force employees to work.

Fear is the most frequently used motivator. Managers threaten to fire employees, dock their pay, lay them off for a period of time, give them undesirable jobs to do, or deny them opportunities for advancement. We ought to know better. Later on in this chapter, we will talk about newer and better ways to manage people. Unfortunately, many managers and supervisors learned autocratic and punitive forms of persuasion. They worked for others who used this style. Slave owners in the South learned it was an effective form of supervision, particularly if short-term results were the objective. As we shall see, there are serious shortcomings to this style. In modern profitable organizations, effective supervision depends on the supervisor possessing a great array of knowledge and skills that do not include how to handle a whip. Supervision of other workers is a highly complex, demanding task.

REQUIREMENTS OF THE MODERN MANAGER

Just think of what the modern supervisor/manager needs to be able to do: He or she must know the technical requirements for the job. With these in hand, the supervisor must be able to plan the work of the group and then organize them into teams of individuals who can perform the tasks needed; he or she must see to it that the workers have the skills to perform the tasks, training them him or herself if necessary; he or she must constantly correct and oversee production once it is underway; in addition, he or she must know company, government, and union rules and regulations, be able to work with specialists when needed, and, with his or her own managers and peers, coordinate the group's work within the whole system. To do all of this, he or she must be able to communicate, interview, counsel, motivate, train, and discipline. In other words, a supervisor has to be an expert in interpersonal relations, as well as a technically competent individual. All this is particularly true of supervisors in the hospitality industry.

GROWTH TO THE PRESENT DAY

The modern industrial and service organization is a product of the Industrial Revolution of the late 1700s and early 1800s. During this period, large groups of people came from farms into urban areas to produce manufactured goods. Initially, the owner/managers were interested in the men at the workplace as individuals. Their primary focus was how men related to the tools and machines that were used to produce the factory's products. The management style was autocratic, sometimes benevolent, most times not. The owner/manager had a rather simple view of humans at work. The owner had machines that needed to be operated to produce goods that could be sold to make money. (By analogy, the hotel/restaurant owner had a facility that needed to be operated to provide services to customers, so he or she could make money.) The assumption was that the average worker was motivated by economic needs to make money. The owner would pay "A fair day's pay in return for a fair day's work." If the worker did not work, he or she did not get paid and, if the work continued to be unsatisfactory, was fired. Since the owner also wanted to make money, the desire for profit was the common bond between them.

Since it was the owner who was paying the worker, the owner felt that he or she could make any demands he or she wanted. The worker had little choice but to do what he or she was told. The worker's "contribution" was little more than to operate machines and also provide the physical labor that machines could not be built to perform. The individual was treated like a machine. A person was hired to "work," not think. Workers were closely supervised and told what to do every minute of the day. This style assumes that work is unpleasant (and under these circumstances, it undoubtedly was). There were no freedoms, even in terms of how the work was to be done. It was assumed that, unless the worker was told what to do and how to do it, he or she would do as little as possible, and what was done would be done poorly or in a slipshod fashion. This required continuous follow-up by the supervisor and finally resulted in elaborate checks and cross checks. The "inspector" became an important part of the production facility. To this day, most hotels have a person (often the floor supervisor) check each room after the room attendant has cleaned it and made it up, supposedly ready for occupancy.

It is important to realize that hotels and restaurants are significantly different than most of industry in terms of what is expected of the employee and, in turn, the manager or supervisor. Visualize a long row of sewing machines in a factory. At each is an operator sewing up seams on coveralls or some other garment. A supervisor or foreman sees to it that the machines are working properly and the unfinished materials are available for each worker. If a problem occurs, the supervisor is available to handle it immediately. The supervisor goes down the line sampling the work of the operators. The finished garments are then taken to a line of inspectors, who go over each garment quickly but carefully. When a flaw is detected, the garment is set aside to be repaired or sold as a second. The operator who caused the error is notified, and the cause of the error is investigated and corrected.

This is *not* the situation in the hospitality industry. The major "product" in the hospitality industry is "service"—service in the form of clean rooms, available when the guest checks in. Of course, food is a product of a restaurant, but there are few assembly-line setups, and the service that accompanies the product is often the difference between failure and success. To provide the services that go with a hotel and/or restaurant, people are needed. The hospitality industry is very, very labor-intensive. At the same time, the hospitality industry is different from other industries in that the labor force is for the most part *unsupervised* at the time this service is delivered.

For instance, the bell captain (supervisor) is at the bell desk at the time the bell person (line employee) is escorting guests with their luggage to their rooms. Upon arrival at the room, the bell person ("bell" for short) explains to the guest how the TV works, how the room temperature may be controlled, where the ice machine is, and so on. The bell also quickly scans the room to make sure it is clean and picked up and that there is soap and the proper number of towels in the bath. In addition, this unsupervised individual also tries to make the guests feel welcome and secure. The manager does not know how well this job is being performed unless a complaint is filed by a guest.

This is true throughout the hotel for employees who make guest contact as a part of the job. Desk receptionists, cashiers, wait staff, and room

attendants are all largely unsupervised at the moment the most important part of their job is being performed. For other employees also, the inability to supervise them closely requires special management consideration. A hotel-restaurant is in a way like a city. People are off in various parts of it, repairing, preparing, observing, painting, cleaning—doing their jobs without immediate supervision. All of this means the hotel or restaurant employee must be carefully selected, well trained, and properly managed, so that he or she is skilled enough to provide the product—service. This individual must be able to "think." This also means that the management of these individuals must be different since these "hotel people" operate independently at the time they are providing their most critical services.

GROWTH OF THE HOTEL INDUSTRY

In the history of hotels and restaurants, the advent of the major multiproperty chain is fairly recent. In earlier years, hotels and restaurants were for the most part privately owned and operated. Many were "family run." Europe was the model. Hotels initially were small. As they grew in size, management styles did not change a great deal. They were still owned and operated by a single individual. As a result, the development of management styles other than owner/autocratic has been slow to emerge. The move to more modern styles of management has lagged behind the changes that have occurred in other industries. In those hotels that are not part of major hotel groups, the nonowner manager has continued in many instances to maintain an autocratic style. He behaves as the surrogate owner and is "King of the Castle." The manager is by far the highest paid individual in the hotel and usually has many prerogatives as well as fringe benefits. It was not until the advent of the hotel or restaurant chain that management styles changed significantly.

The Personnel Function

The personnel division came into being as a result of the growth of industry during and following the Industrial Revolution.

Industrial organizations grew to mammoth proportions. Factories employed thousands of workers under one roof. Organizations became multifunctional. For example, an automobile company assembled cars, but also manufactured parts and even made its own steel. Some of these organizations had factories or divisions in many parts of the country. These organizations found it necessary to keep track of employees in some fashion. Gradually, a personnel department emerged, which kept employee records, managed the hiring function, and handled employee complaints. As organizations became larger and more formalized, the government became more active in controlling them. Government involvement in regulating some employee matters meant more record keeping and reporting to be handled by "personnel." In this fashion, the personnel office became well established. Similar events occurred in the hospitality industry, but later in time, since the growth of large chains generally lagged behind industry.

Several events have occurred over recent years to generate a need to enlarge the personnel department further. The creation of strong labor unions made it necessary for organizations to have a professional staff to deal with them. This has usually become part of the personnel function. Jobs also have become more complicated, with greater skills required. This has created a need to organize more formal training programs. The personnel office has also taken over this function, training employees at all levels. This does not mean that all training is done by the personnel department. They train the trainers in many instances. In this way, supervisors are trained to train the employees in their own sections.

In the 1930s, research conducted by F. J. Roethlesberger and W. J. Dickson at the Hawthorne Plant of the Western Electric Company just outside of Chicago had a major and long-term impact on the personnel department and personnel function.[1] The research was designed to determine the effects of temperature, noise, and lighting on worker productivity. A group of workers in the relay assembly department were set up in a special room where the environmental factors could be controlled. Lighting levels, for example, were varied, and output was measured under the different lighting conditions.

As lighting levels were increased, productivity grew in number. Then the lighting level was lowered and productivity *increased* further. The researchers soon realized that the workers were not only responding positively to better lighting, but also their productivity was increasing, because they felt they were part of a special group. The nature of supervision in the "laboratory" was different. There the staff was asked questions about its working conditions. Supervisors took an interest in the concerns expressed. They formed work teams that had different relationships than those on the factory floor. If problems arose, they were handled differently than in the past. These workers had been singled out by the very act of being part of a research effort and had responded favorably to this treatment by increasing their production.

The experimental employee counseling program that resulted from this research was so successful that it became an integral part of Western Electric's personnel policy. Counseling thus became another facet of the personnel function. In this fashion, over time, the personnel department has taken on more and more functions.

Today, in all major hotel and restaurant organizations, there is a personnel department. These departments are professionally staffed and cover a wide range of support functions. The personnel department is the first point of contact for an employee with an organization, and it maintains this contact over time by various means. Thus, a modern, properly operating personnel department is crucial to the successful operation of a viable hotel or restaurant. It is important to realize, however, that the presence of a properly functioning personnel department does not eliminate the manager's and/or supervisor's responsibilities in hiring and other personnel matters. It may alleviate some of the record keeping and processing, but the day-to-day responsibility for motivating, directing, and supervising is part of the management function.

A chart suggesting the scope of the personnel function in a large hotel organization is given in Figure 16-1.

Despite the importance of this function, it has only been in recent years that the personnel manager has become a part of the hotel's executive committee. The executive committee of a large hotel is usually comprised of the top five or six functional managers or area directors in the prop-

1. F.J. Roethlesberger and W.J. Dickson, *Management and the Worker* (Cambridge, Mass.: Harvard University Press), 1939).

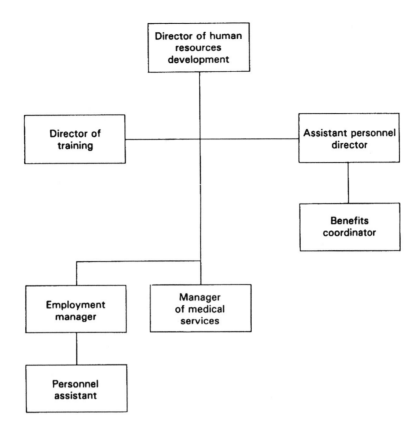

Figure 16-1 Organizational chart for human resources department

erty. Most often included are the food and beverage manager, rooms division manager, comptroller (or finance director), sales manager, and engineering manager. The Personnel Director is usually included, but this is a quite recent development. For many years it was thought that anyone could carry a tray, take an order into the kitchen, make up a room, carry a suitcase, and the like. It has only been in the past few years that management has realized that the waitperson is, in truth, a salesperson and that what is sold from the menu is quite often determined by the individual taking the order. Similarly, the bellperson is not just a luggage carrier, but also a receptionist, a greeter, and the first point of contact with the hotel. The desk receptionist (formerly called room clerk) is also a receptionist/salesperson.

The story is often told of the guest who walks out the front door of the hotel and asks the doorman, "Where is a good place to get a steak around here?" The doorman then replies, "Three blocks down the street turn right and halfway down the block is a great steakhouse." A well-trained and satisfied doorman employee, on the other hand, will say, "Inside the hotel at the foot of the escalator is 'The Plank,' and I honestly believe you won't find a better steak in town." Of course, if the guest now says, "Well, we've been in the hotel all day at a meeting and want to go somewhere for a change," then the well-trained doorman will refer the guest down the street. It has been a combination of several factors that have made the personnel function of critical importance:

1. Increasing government laws and regulations requiring reports and observance and compliance

2. The increasing number of functions involving personnel that need to be managed

3. The realization that the people in the organization need to be carefully selected and trained to provide the services guests expect.

Such expected services cannot be provided by casual workers who come in off the street looking for a quick "couple of bucks." The painful problems this approach creates is illustrated by an event that occurred in New York City a few years ago. A large bus tour came into the city before Christmas to see a Broadway show and the decorated stores, have a couple of interesting nights on the town, and then return home. After the tourists returned home, two of them contracted typhoid fever. The disease was traced to a large popular restaurant, where the tour group had enjoyed dinner one night. A close check of all restaurant employees failed to discover the carrier because five employees who worked that particular night were unaccounted for. The restaurant did not even know their names. They had been hired off the street to wash dishes, clean floors, or bus trays to the kitchen. This is a stern reminder that a properly run organization needs well trained, carefully selected, long-term employees who can be counted on to work effectively and efficiently. If part-time employees are needed, they should be called in from a pool of previously selected and trained workers, so that their part-time status does not mean poorer service.

MANAGEMENT OF PEOPLE AT THE WORKPLACE

In years past, the hotel owner/manager, operating without a formal personnel organization to keep records and hire and train, did most of this work him or herself with the help of supervisors. Supervisors hired individuals as they saw fit and managed their departments in a manner that they had learned from their bosses before they were promoted. It was a "be tough, let them know who's boss" style of leadership. Even the early research done by Frederic Taylor reflected this notion of dealing with workers.

Taylor was interested in finding out the optimum amount of work (productivity) an individual could perform. For example, what was the optimum size of a coal shovel for a worker unloading coal cars? His notions of what came to be called "scientific management" became quite popular. He and others developed techniques for observing and measuring worker output. They became so sophisticated that a new specialty "time and motion study" was born. Using motion pictures and elaborate timing devices, expected output was determined before individuals were hired to perform the tasks.

Although time and motion studies are not common in the hotel and restaurant industry, they can be of value when large quantities of one item need to be prepared. Fast-food companies have used time and motion studies to determine the layout and materials handling in their stores. Similarly, airline feeding operations and large banquet facilities have used time and motion economy to advantage. The idea is to make certain that necessary materials are conveniently available in the sequence they are used and that the proper tools exist for the employee's use. The employee is then trained to assemble the materials into the finished product using the fewest possible motions. Unnecessary movements are eliminated. Benches or tables are designed to be at the right height for optimum work. Stools are provided if the employee can best perform while seated. In other words, the task to be performed is analyzed in detail by experienced planners and the best (usually this means the fastest) way of performing the task is determined. From then on, this is the manner in which it is done.

The problem with these methods is that they are concerned almost exclusively with worker *output*. Very little if any consideration is given to worker *input*, or the cost to the worker of doing the task. The cost of work to the worker includes not only the effort and energy the worker expends, but also many other factors, such as the extent to which the work may be unhealthy, how dangerous the work is, and what the likelihood of accidents is. (In the hospitality industry, falls, injuries from heavy lifting, kitchen burns, and cuts are common.) It perhaps should include as a cost employee dissatisfaction, created by poor leadership or an unsatisfactory workplace environment. Any adverse effect on the work may be considered part of the cost of doing work, since these factors lead to discontent, absenteeism, and ultimately employee turnover.

Of course, it is difficult to add up the various "costs of work" because it is like adding apples and oranges. Nevertheless, the consideration of employee effectiveness/efficiency should not be based on productivity alone, but must include at least estimates of "what the cost to the worker is" in doing the work. If a new cutting tool increases production, the question must also be asked,

"Does the new tool increase accidents?" If so, the increase in production may not be worth it.

Employee efficiency is described by the equation $E = O \div I$ (i.e., efficiency equals output divided by input). Both the numerator and denominator of the equation must be considered. Another failure is that it fits in ideally with the autocratic notion of the leadership function, and that money is the sole reason people work. Produce more and you will earn more. There is one best way to do each task, and management will figure it out. Once that has been determined, employees are paid to work in that manner. There are many managers today who believe this to be true and more who wish it were true.

Research, however, has shown that the reasons people work, and the best ways to work, are a lot more complicated than this simplistic view of a need for money being the motivation and that there is only one best way to do the task. There are many motivators in the workplace, and employee motivation is not the only determinant of performance. The nature of the work and the ability of the worker to perform it are important factors. The materials and tools available also enter into the equation. Perhaps most important is the ability of managers and supervisors to coordinate the work effort of individuals and work teams.

The Psychological Contract

As was pointed out earlier, the original notions of management were based on simple conceptions of why people worked and what it took to make them productive. A lot of research over the last 70 years has made our models of behavior far more complicated. It follows that the management of people has also become more complicated. We have come to realize that people have many needs, not just a need for money. These needs change over time, and many of them can be satisfied in the workplace.

Young people out of high school may be more than willing to work long hours as a waiter or waitress because of the high wages it brings for relatively unskilled labor. Ten years later, these same individuals will want job security. In addition, they may want to be trained at jobs that will use more of their potential. Ten years after that, they may want leadership positions, so they can assume a different role in an organization.

Organizations, for their part, have learned that individuals have a much greater influence on the organization than merely supplementing the work of a machine. In the hospitality industry, in particular, many jobs were thought of as being simple manual labor: carrying a suitcase or tray, washing a dish, scrubbing a floor, making a bed.

The waiter does carry food on a tray from the kitchen to the customer (the labor function). But what does the waiter say when he delivers the food? How does the waitress handle the complaint of the customer who discovers the food to be cold (the human relations function)? At the time the food is ordered, does the waitperson become involved as a salesperson or is the individual merely a recorder? The organization has come to realize that it needs to gather data to determine whom to promote. It has learned that it has to understand and meet the expectations of the people in the organization if it wants to keep them and keep them productive.

The employee, on the other hand, has to learn what the organization expects, in turn. Most organizations expect the employee to be at work on time, to do an agreed upon amount of work, and to be loyal to the organization. The list can go on. Very few of these expectations on the part of the employer or employee are written down. Rather, they become what is called a psychological contract. An understanding of what each will get and give in return is arrived at: wages in exchange for loyalty, promotion in exchange for hard work, bonuses in exchange for high productivity. There are obviously many possible combinations of these, and they are not necessarily the same as stated here.

The point is that an extremely important interrelationship is established that determines what the worker will get from the organization in exchange for what is given. It works both ways. The organization establishes what it feels it should get from the worker in exchange for what it gives. The worker, in turn, has expectations of what the organization will do in exchange for his or her services.

Several years ago, the manager of a major New York City hotel realized that each member of the work force of the hotel had the potential to become a salesperson for the hotel. They would not be a member of the formal sales force, rather, if each worker perceived every guest as a possible point of sale for the services of the hotel, if not at that moment but some future time perhaps, then hotel employees might approach guests in a different way. He decided it was a matter of convincing employees that they were salespeople and that they should act accordingly. He chose as a slogan, "It's a matter of strawberries," exploiting the notion that selling services was not really much different than selling strawberries and that each employee was, in truth, a "strawberry salesman." Small "strawberries" were sewn onto the uniform lapels of housekeepers, room attendants, front office receptionists, and other workers in the back of the house. Instructional programs, including films and film strips, were shown to all employees, suggesting how they were, in truth, sales personnel. It caught on! The behavior of employees changed in terms of the manner in which they greeted and dealt with guests. Sales increased. In addition, employees started to sell the hotel's services to their friends and relatives. For example, employees would arrange to have family wedding parties at the hotel or celebrate birthdays in the dining room.

For its part, the hotel discounted employee-sponsored events and gave cash rewards for "sales efforts" employees made. Very little of this was written down; no formal agreements were made. It was a matter of a clever idea being implemented and a psychological contract being established. This new psychological contract brought about a significant change in the hotel, in the form of not only increased sales, but also something just as valuable. The employees felt that they were a part of the team; they were contributing to the hotel's and, in turn, their own success. The psychological contract added a new dimension to what it meant to be an employee.

Thus, the psychological contract is interactive and changes through influences on each side over time. The "contract" must constantly be established and reestablished through an informal bargaining process as time goes on. Things change within the hotel or restaurant. The individually owned restaurant is sold and becomes part of a chain. The psychological contracts of each employee must be renegotiated. If a hotel is sold to a Japanese purchaser, the contract will undoubtedly be different. Even simple factors, such as a menu change or the departure of a supervisor, requires renegotiation of the psychological contract.

It can be said that everything the organization does vis-a-vis its employees has some impact on the psychological contract. Similarly, everything the employee does on the job has some influence on it.

The remainder of this chapter can be viewed as a discussion of how the psychological contract is established and amended. It also attempts to describe the ideal psychological contract.

Why People Work

People work to achieve many different goals, economic as well as ego-relevant ones. In selecting where they work and what work they do, they choose a situation in which they are most likely to achieve the best possible psychological contract. They choose a situation that is most likely to satisfy their economic and ego-relevant goals. Of course, the economic situation prevalent at the time, an employee's own background (skills, education, age, etc.), and many other factors determine what work may be available to them. Within the situational framework, however, employees will choose the job that they think provides the most favorable psychological contract.

For many people the hospitality industry provides many different means for fulfilling the psychological contract. In fact, the hotel and restaurant business is unique, and many workers can find satisfactions there that they cannot find anywhere else.

The hospitality industry can meet economic needs in many ways. Because services are often provided 24 hours a day, 7 days a week, workers can frequently arrange to work shifts of their own choosing or part time while going to school. Many hotel and restaurant positions require a lot of common sense, but not much formal education or very complicated skills. Good on-the-job training and supervision can provide the skills necessary for relatively unskilled workers to perform their work and earn a good income. Waiting tables is a good example of this. A relatively unskilled but intelligent employee can learn on the job the sales skills and serving skills necessary to earn a good income. An additional advantage is being able to choose a wide range of working hours. And the job of waiting tables in a restaurant can satisfy a great many other needs as well. Many of these needs can be considered ego-relevant. Recognition for doing the job well can come from customers as well as supervisors. Immediate rewards in the form of tips for a job well done provide quick feedback. Included in the total reward structure are the following:

1. Satisfaction of social needs via working closely with other workers or in teams and getting to know regular customers

2. Self-satisfaction in knowing that a difficult situation was handled well, such as handling more than the regular number of tables because of an unexpected rush or the illness of a fellow worker

3. Status and prestige from being able to train new service employees, explain to a customer how a particular menu item is prepared, or describe a wine on the wine list and explaining what types of food it might accompany

The reader might find it interesting to study and think about which of these needs might be served by various occupations within the hospitality industry.

CLASSIFICATION OF HUMAN NEEDS

It is certain that, in addition to the income used to satisfy innate needs, the many acquired social and egoistic needs can be at least partially satis-fied by being an employee at various levels within a well-run hotel or restaurant. This is particularly true if a good psychological contract has been established.

Managing People Day After Day

Several years ago, a most important study was completed at Ohio State University.[2] In an effort to study the preferred styles of leadership, researchers broke down leadership into two key dimensions. One was the task of providing leadership to get the job done, identifying the tasks that the group must accomplish, and making sure the work was scheduled properly and that the right tools and materials were available. This dimension was named the *initiating* structure within leadership. The second dimension was genuine concern for people in the group (e.g., making sure the rules are enforced fairly, being certain that good personal relations exist within the group and between the manager and his or her subordinates, and, perhaps most important, creating a sense of approval for work properly done). This dimension was labeled the *consideration* structure. These two factors, initiation and consideration, certainly describe a very large portion of the set of responsibilities we call leadership.

---

2. E.A. Fleishman, E.F. Harris, and H.E. Burth, *Leadership and Supervision in Industry* (Columbus, Ohio: The Ohio State University) 1955.

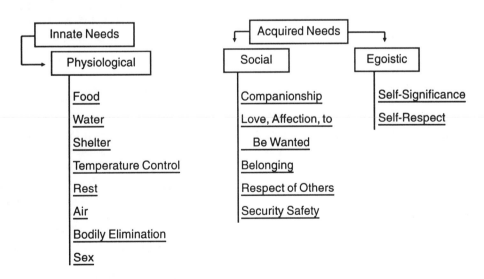

Figure 16-2 Classification of Human Needs.

Source: Dale S. Beach, Personnel: The Management of People at Work, 4th ed. (New York: Macmillan), p. 430, Fig. 18-1.

The researchers described these two dimensions to a number of workers and asked them which kind of leadership emphasis they preferred—someone whose primary emphasis was consideration of the workers in his or her group (position A in Figure 16-3) or someone whose focus was on getting the job done? Or would the same employee prefer a third style of manager who places a strong emphasis on consideration of subordinates, while at the same time, as a true professional, seeing to it that the job is satisfactorily completed (position C in Figure 16-3)? In the survey, most workers preferred a leader who would operate at position C. That is, they wanted a manager who knew and did what was needed to get the job done, *while at the same time* being extremely considerate of all workers in the group.

What is of particular interest is the fact that, when surveyed, highly placed executives came up with a different preference for supervisory leadership style than other employees. They selected someone who would operate at position D on the chart. That is, they wanted someone who was high on getting the job done, but relatively low on consideration. Their rationale was that they preferred a supervisor whose paramount interest was completing the job; they did not want someone who showed a lot of consideration for their employees. They were afraid that such a

leader would not be "tough enough." Being considerate, in their minds, apparently meant being unable to discipline or motivate.

This difference in preference for supervisory style is a major potential source of conflict. Even before the training, the provision of the workplace, and all the other factors that go into creating the psychological contract, a basic disagreement exists in terms of what kind of supervisory style is preferred. Employees want someone who is considerate, but also knows how to get the job done. Management, on the other hand, does not want someone who is "too concerned about employees." This is typical of the autocratic form of management. It reflects a sense of distrust on the part of management, an instinctive feeling that, if you show "them" too much consideration, they are going to "get away with murder." Employees cannot be trusted to work for the best interests of a company unless a manager/supervisor is tough. It is these attitudes that have created problems in the hospitality industry and that must be changed if the hotel and restaurant business is to be successful in providing the quality of services that guests expect.

A great deal of research has been done in recent years that shows it is not sufficient for a supervisor/manager to be primarily an initiator. The same manager must also be capable of providing *support* for his or her subordinates. The supervisor demonstrates support by showing concern for each individual in the group, exhibiting trust, and giving credit for a job well done. Perhaps the most important factors are involving employees in decision making and ensuring that they are treated fairly and squarely.

Some Examples of Managing Day to Day

A large hotel, a member of an international chain, had a problem. We will label the problem "high absenteeism on Wednesday." It arose in this fashion. A group of hotel employees were interested in having a bowling league that would involve competition among teams from various departments of the hotel. They approached the personnel department, which thought it was a good idea, a means of fostering friendship and acquaintances in the various departments. It was also a means for developing team spirit and departmental pride. Personnel approached management, who agreed to "sponsor" the league,

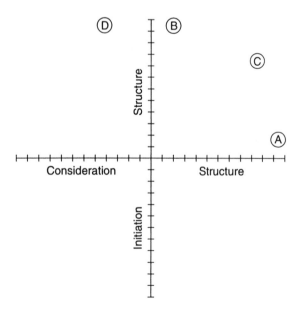

Figure 16-3 Initiation vs. consideration.

believing it would be good for morale. They, therefore, agreed to provide inexpensive "team" shirts to team members, trophies, and an annual bowling banquet.

All went well for a while. The participants enjoyed the bowling and appreciated the support of hotel management. The bowling leagues bowled on Tuesday nights on their own time, of course. Each participant paid his or her own bowling fees and supplied his or her own equipment. Several of the teams represented some of the food outlets at the hotel, and, as a result, they were forced to bowl late because of dinner and banquet service in the hotel. After several months, a number of supervisors and restaurant managers noticed that a small but significant number of employees were not reporting to work on Wednesdays. Further investigation showed that most of the Wednesday absentees were bowling participants.

The question was, "What to do about it?" The problem posed was a serious one for several reasons. Absenteeism in itself is an expensive matter. The loss of productivity is very costly. In addition, Wednesday is the busiest day in most commercial hotels, and high absenteeism on Wednesdays is particularly damaging. Also, the fact that the bowling league was supported by the hotel as a "morale builder" made the negative result particularly troublesome. Managers also discovered that the bowling lanes served alcoholic beverages and that a lot of drinking was done by team members. This, in turn, increased the probability that certain workers would not show up for work on Wednesday.

This case was made a problem for discussion in several management training sessions. It stimulated a lot of interest, as well as a great number of ideas for addressing the problem.

One of the most frequent suggestions was to stop supporting the bowling league. The idea, of course, was that, if the league was not supported, it would in all likelihood die. The problem with this "solution" was that management initially supported the league to boost morale; now the program had backfired. If support was withheld, management became the "bad guy." The good intentions of supporting the league would turn into a source of employee unhappiness, and management would be to blame. Furthermore, withdrawing support represented punishing all the participants when only relatively few were not

reporting for work on Wednesday. This obviously was not a realistic solution, particularly if one considers the psychological contract the organization was trying to maintain.

Another frequent suggestion was to "change the bowling night to Friday." The thinking here was that Saturday is a much quieter day in a commercial hotel and, therefore, some absenteeism would not be as harmful. Additionally, many participants would not be scheduled to work on Saturday. But could management change the bowling night? The employees were bowling on their own free time. They originally selected Tuesday because it was the most convenient day of the week *for them.* Friday night is more typically a time used for other activities: dates, family gatherings, entertaining, dining out. It was doubtful that the employees would want to change the night. It was also very likely that employees would resent the suggestion if it were made. Urging or insisting on the change would be resisted strongly, and management again would be the "bad guy."

Another suggestion was to insist that the bowling lanes not serve alcohol when the hotel's teams were bowling. This, of course, represented one more instance in which the hotel would come out looking poorly, and, in addition, the request would undoubtedly be refused by the lane operators, for whom liquor sales was a source of profit.

Yet one more frequent response was to suggest that management urge supervisors and unit managers to participate in the bowling leagues. In this way, managers could try to serve as models by not drinking and reporting to work on time the next day. It was thought that such behavior might even embarrass workers into showing up for work on Wednesday. However, this "solution" also demonstrated an attempt to use power and authority to coerce people to come to work. In addition, like all the rest of the schemes, it was a device that imposed itself on every participant in the bowling league, not just those who were frequently absent on Wednesdays. Perhaps the participants in the bowling team did not want a group of supervisors around when they bowled. Where then did a solution lie?

The foundation for a solution should have been established in having *good managerial practices in place* long before the bowling leagues were started. It is essential that every organization have reasonable work rules in place. All hotels and restaurants and their employees recognize the need for rules governing various facets of behavior in the workplace. There must be rules governing the drinking of alcoholic beverages at work, condition of uniforms and appearance, sexual harassment, working hours, absenteeism, tardiness, discipline, and so on. Not only do organizations acknowledge the need for rules, but also employees realize that a well-run hotel or restaurant must have rules and standards. As a matter of fact, a great many well-managed hospitality organizations have rules that have been created and agreed on jointly by management and workers. In this way, the rules are accepted as reasonable and are more likely to be observed. It is only logical that, if the rules and discipline to enforce them have been created jointly by a committee representing both workers and management, they will be viewed as more acceptable. With reasonable rules in place and proper disciplinary procedures applied, the problem of high absenteeism on Wednesday (or any other day) is simply a routine matter of "enforcing the rules." According to this approach, not all the bowlers would be disciplined, but only those who were frequently absent on Wednesday. The hotel does not become "the bad guy," and the bowling team can continue as a potential morale booster.

The hotel's solution was to make certain that proper work rules were in place and that everyone knew what the rules were and understood the consequences of infractions. The rules included regulations concerning absenteeism and what disciplinary procedures were to be followed if employees were absent without proper cause. The rules were then applied to those who failed to show up for work on Wednesday or on any day for any reason. Absenteeism on Wednesday attributed to bowling on Tuesday night was not singled out as a special problem, but dealt with routinely. The bowling continued, and absenteeism on Wednesday was significantly reduced.

This raises an important people management problem. What constitutes good disciplinary practice, and how is it used? The answer to this question becomes particularly important if one is concerned with establishing a good psychological contract.

Disciplinary measures are something management has to have in place, although it undoubtedly would prefer not to use them. Ideally,

rules are generated (preferably jointly by workers and management) and disciplinary procedures worked out, *but* then it is expected (or at least hoped) that everyone will obey the rules and discipline will never have to be enforced. What has been suggested as a good device for making this ideal situation a reality is called the "red hot stove rule."

Think about a red hot stove for a minute. If you touch it, you know that you are going to be burned. The rule is do not touch a red hot stove; the discipline is that you will be burned. Furthermore, there are other factors that make the red hot stove rule important to the concept of rules and discipline. *Everyone* who touches the stove gets burned; there are no exceptions. The punishment is exactly the same for all; also, it is immediate. Break the rule, get burned. This simple analogy can be applied to the proper management of rules and discipline in the workplace. An acronym helps one to keep it in mind:

KISS

　Know

　Immediate

　Same

　Sure

Know what the rule is and what the punishment is for breaking it. There is *immediate* discipline for breaking the rule—not tomorrow, next week, or at performance review time, but now. Discipline is the *same* for anyone who breaks the rule, whether it be the boss's son, wife, girlfriend, husband, or boyfriend. The discipline is *sure* to be applied. The consequences of breaking the rule are absolutely certain. Touch the stove; a burn is sure to result. There are no exceptions, no excuses. In this way, rules can be enforced equitably. A manager can establish a reputation for fairness and dealing promptly with a situation when it arises. This reinforces the sort of management style about which we have been talking. It also helps establish a favorable and workable psychological contract.

One of the cleverest devices for helping to reduce absenteeism involved a deck of cards and a little knowledge of poker. The astute supervisor of a hotel department that had relatively high absenteeism as well as lateness (and turnover, which goes hand in hand with absenteeism) instituted the following game. Each employee who arrived for work on time was allowed to draw a card from a deck of cards. This occurred every day. The employee with the best five-card stud poker hand at the end of the five-day work week won a small prize (e.g., a bottle of wine). A card was given only if the employee reported to work on time. If the employee had only four cards (i.e., was absent or late one day), participation was not permitted. Absenteeism and turnover were significantly reduced by this simple but insightful device. It is this kind of "soft discipline" that is most successful. In this instance, the "prize" was relatively insignificant; it was playing the game and winning it that became important.

Compliments Rather than Discipline

One should not emphasize rules and discipline too much. Rather, one should emphasize complimenting and rewarding the employee for good work instead of disciplining for improper performance. Managers tend to be "error-oriented." They are trained to look for things that are wrong, or for mistakes. The room attendant can maintain rooms on a hotel floor for weeks without a single complaint from guests. But let one guest report nutshells under a bed or cigarette butts in an ashtray, and the wrath of the manager comes down on the same attendant. During the weeks of satisfactory performance, it is doubtful that any positive feedback was provided. No one told the worker "thanks for a job well done." Yet this is exactly what is needed. Managers must learn to seek out and acknowledge good performance and not just wait for errors to occur. As Blanchard and Johnson suggest,[3] "try to find something nice to say to your employees." The psychological reason behind this is that research has shown if proper behavior is rewarded (reinforced positively), it is more likely to occur again. Punishment or discipline (negative reinforcement) will reduce the likelihood of poor behavior recurring, but the one administering the punishment or discipline becomes feared or disliked. Fear of punishment tends to reduce the scope of one's

performance. It particularly limits the initiative that is truly needed by employees in the hospitality industry.

Importance of Employee Initiative

Employee initiative is of critical importance in the hospitality industry because *most guest contact by employees goes unsupervised*. It is this factor alone that makes hospitality service management different from all other management. The waitperson at a guest's table is unsupervised while orders are taken, menu items explained, or the wine list questioned. The bellperson escorts guests to their rooms, explains the workings of a room, adjusts temperatures, checks for cleanliness, and so on, all while completely unsupervised. The same holds true throughout the hotel or restaurant. This means that these employees must be *trained* to act on their own. They must have the confidence to take initiative and know what to do in a great variety of unplanned situations. Proper responses and creative initiative are less likely to occur if the waitperson, hallperson, or any other employee is afraid that they will be disciplined or "chewed out" if the manager/supervisor does not exactly agree with the initiative taken.

A very successful consultant to many industries, most notably in Japan, W. Edwards Deming,[4] has long touted "empowerment," the idea of urging, training and giving the opportunity to employees to take the initiative and act on their own. The basis of empowerment is, as Tom Peters says, "the bone-deep belief in the dignity and the worth and creative potential of each person in their organization."[5] *Empowerment* encourages employees to solve problems, improve a situation, and satisfy a customer's complaint, *without* checking with higher management.

One restaurant owner established empowerment as the means for fulfilling a guarantee of customers' YEGA, an acronym for "your enjoyment guaranteed always." In trying to make good on the guarantee, the owner, Timothy W. Firnstahl, "empowered" his 600 employees to

3. Kenneth Blanchard and Spencer Johnson, *The One Minute Manager* (New York: Morrow), 1982.

4. Y.K. Snetty and V.M. Buehler, eds., *Productivity and Quality Through People: Practices of Well Managed Companies* (westport, Conn.: Quorum Books), 1985.
5. Ibid.

make good on the promise of the guarantee at once and on the spot. Firnstahl

instituted the idea that employees could and should do anything to keep the customer happy. In the event of an error or delay, any employee right down to the busboy could provide complimentary wine or desserts, or pick up an entire tab if necessary.[6]

The view here is that "customer complaints are company failures and require immediate corrections." Firnstahl then kept track of the costs for treating customers in this fashion. He dubbed them system-failure costs (not employee failure costs) and conducted investigations, staff meetings, and the like to understand what caused the system failures. Correcting them led to dramatic cost savings, while at the same time customer satisfaction remained extremely high.

An example is taken from his paper:

Our search for the culprit in a string of complaints about slow food service in one restaurant led first to the kitchen and then to one cook. But pushing the search one step further revealed several unrealistically complex dishes that no one could have prepared quickly....

This kind of problem solving is popular with employees. Since the object of change is always the company, employees don't get blamed for problems beyond their control.

Firnstahl goes on to end his article by saying,

People often ask us where we find such wonderful employees. While it is true that we screen carefully, I believe our employees are better than most because they have the *power* and the *obligation* to solve customer problems on their own and on the spot. Giving them complete discretion about how they do it has also given them pride.

To make empowerment work, good company management practices must be in place. Empowerment will not work if items are overpriced, poor-quality raw materials are provided, or the physical plant is run down (i.e., if things employees cannot control are not working well). As implied in the Firnstahl article, empowerment requires well-selected employees who are trained and managed well. It requires the existence of a good psychological contract.

EMPLOYEE PERFORMANCE EVALUATION

One of the means management has used over the years to train, motivate, and influence employees is an employee evaluation system. Often called "performance appraisal," it is customarily one of the standard tools used in the management of human resources. In recent years, it has come under attack and even been abandoned by some major companies, although at the same time it has been embellished and formalized in others and made the center of an employee motivation system called management by objectives (MBO).

W. Edwards Deming, cited earlier as a strong proponent of empowerment, speaks vehemently against "performance evaluation." In his article, "Transformation of Western Style Management,"[7] he lists as one of the major "forces causing the decline" the "personal review system or evaluation of performance, merit rating, annual review, or annual appraisal, but whatever name, for people in management, the effects of which are devastating." Later in the article, he goes on to state,

It nourishes short term performance, annihilates long term planning, builds fear, demolishes team work, nourishes rivalry and politics. It leaves people bitter, others despondent and dejected, some even depressed...unable to comprehend why they are inferior. In particular, it works against the effectiveness of employee "empowerment."

In spite of Deming's strong stand against all forms of performance evaluation, the fact remains that workers' *performances are going to be evaluated*. It cannot be avoided. All of us are constantly evaluating the performance of one another, and it is extremely important, perhaps more than any other factor. The ideas that employees and managers have about each other and how they are transmitted influence the psychological contract.

To discuss the impact of performance evaluation on the psychological contract, it makes sense, however, to divide the topic of how management and workers assess each other's behav-

6. Timothy W. Firnstahl, "My Employees are My Service Guarantee," *Harvard Business Review* (July/Aug. 1989).

7. W. Edwards Deming, "Transformation of Western Style Management," in Y.K. Shetty and V.M. Buehler, *op. cit.*

ior or performance into two separate parts. The first portion is the day-to-day interaction at the workplace as supervisors and managers interface with the workers and make judgments and come to some conclusions about each other's performance and, in turn, the psychological contract. The second part involves the formal action or process of "performance appraisal" that occurs up and down the line, with superiors formally evaluating and recording the work performance of those individual workers who report to them. This event usually occurs as a matter of organizational routine at least once (often more) each year.

The Influence of Day-to-Day Interaction

In the workplace, it is unavoidable that one employee observes and evaluates the performance of another. The employee sees a coworker doing his or her job and makes a judgment. The employee sees how his or her supervisor handles a particular situation and makes a judgment. A bellperson evaluates the performance of the other bellpersons with whom he or she works. The bell captain evaluates the bellpersons being supervised. The wait captain evaluates the performance of the waiters and buspeople. A formal performance appraisal form is not filled out, but their performance is being observed and recorded (if only mentally). It is unavoidable. In fact, the very existence of each of us depends to some extent on our ability to judge others. Whom we choose for friends, whom we like to work for, whom we like working for us, whom we vote for to lead us, and so on are based on the "people judgments" we make. In turn, we are constantly being judged by others, and our futures depend to a large extent on how we are judged. We rely on our ability a great deal, and some individuals believe that they are quite expert in judging people or situations.

Therefore, it behooves us to attempt to improve our ability to assess the performance of others. The key problem with judging other's performance is that most assessments are based on judgments for which we often have little data, and, as such, they are influenced by personal prejudices and opinions, some of which are based on myth rather than fact. We frequently act on the opinions of others (rumor), but whatever the source, we do make judgments. As we all are aware, each of us has a personality, and each per-

son's personality is different from that of another. As we meet people and get to know them, we grow to understand and react to their personalities. This is particularly true in the workplace. We spend 8 hours a day, 5 days a week, working side by side with others. We would like to be able to get along with them, to even get to like them. We must, in many instances, become dependent on them and they in turn on us. We come to know how someone responds to a problem, to being asked to do something "special" not part of the routine. These same persons, in turn, get to see how we respond to various situations. In this way, we come to "know" each other's personalities. Based on this "knowledge," we make judgments. Is he or she fair, honest, hardworking, decent, or impulsive? Does he or she discourage easily? And so on. In other words, we learn about other employees and are able to predict to a certain extent how they will react in a particular situation.

Having learned to make these types of judgments, we go one step further and begin to wonder about these same employee's personality development, goals, or motivations. Some individuals may identify their goals and then proceed to behave in ways that make us suspicious. Nevertheless, we attribute certain purposes, intentions, or goals to others. Then we make judgments about these goals. Are they reasonable? Are they realistic? At the workplace, we might question whether these employees are achieving their goals at our expense? Even more serious then is any judgment we make on whether the personality we observe and the goals we discern are those of a "normal" person. All of these thoughts that are part of the process by which we observe and judge others in the workplace (and by which they, in turn, judge us) are an integral part of forming the psychological contract.

Fortunately, individuals are adaptable and willing to make compromises. Managers and supervisors, however, must be constantly aware that this process is going on and that errors in hiring a person who does not fit in or putting together teams in which certain members are incompatible can bring disaster. Counseling programs, training, and good selection and assignment procedures can be of help. Supervisor knowledge, awareness, and concern are the key factors, however.

Formal Performance Appraisal

It is important to discuss the process of formal employee performance appraisal for several key reasons. The manner or style of it and the fairness with which it is accomplished have a major effect on the psychological contract and, in turn, the performance of individuals in the workplace. In addition, the Equal Employment Opportunity Commission (EEOC), a federal agency, requirements cover any evaluation process that affects employment decisions. This includes transfer and promotion as well as hiring. In other words, the EEOC is concerned with any procedure that affects an employee's career.

As was pointed out earlier, since personnel judgments will be made anyway, the task is to make them more objective and relevant to the job. This means making them less subjective and prone to the many types of judgment errors that can arise. Moving in this direction will also help overcome the fact that neither the person doing the rating nor the person being rated like the process very much. Many supervisors find performance appraisals one of the most onerous of all the tasks they perform. Yet it can also be one of the most important. Employees do not like being rated or appraised because no one likes being criticized for their performance. If you do not know your shortcomings, however (or at least what are perceived by others to be your shortcomings), you do not know how or what to change to improve your performance. Feedback is essential if one is to improve one's work.

A simple example will illustrate the point. Many of us tend to be somewhat casual about time. Some feel that arriving at work at 8:05 or 8:10 AM is perfectly OK, even though 8:00 AM is the announced starting time. We rationalize, instead of planning to arrive at 7:55 so we will be "on time." We feel rush-hour traffic can be avoided by delaying our departure 10 or 15 minutes, thus arriving 5 or 10 minutes after the appointed hour. This may well be acceptable to some managers or supervisors, particularly if you stay beyond the quitting time, also to avoid rush-hour traffic. *But it may not be acceptable* to some supervisors who want all their staff to be ready to start work at the same time. It is essential that the employee know this. It is incumbent on the supervisor to let an employee know that getting to work on time is of critical importance.

Simple feedback to the employee on this matter should correct any problem.

The dean at a prominent northeastern hotel school used a very simple but effective feedback device. When the time came for the start of a meeting in his office with students or faculty, he would shut and lock the door. Any latecomers would be forced to knock; they would thus be embarrassed by the dean himself having to come to the door open it. Most individuals soon learned to arrive on time.

The halo effect is only one of the many sources of error that can creep into judgments on performance. There are supervisors who view chronic lateness as a personality flaw. They then view the late employee as one who is unsatisfactory in other areas as well, even though his or her performance may truly be above average. The judgment of the supervisor is negatively influenced by one factor. This influence may be overlooked if the supervisor happens to be favorably impressed by one stellar performance. A favorable letter from a guest, for example, may diminish a history of weak performance. This kind of judgmental error is dubbed the "halo effect."

There are other judgmental errors that need to be corrected. It is common to make performance appraisals every 6 or 12 months. A common error is to make judgments based on the most recently observed performance. We have a tendency to not take into account or remember behaviors over a long period of time. This is clearly unfair (whether the recent performance is good or bad) because a supervisor is really interested in behavior over the long term. Recent bad performance might be due to a temporary illness or personal problem. The good performance might have been due to luck. However, we remember and are influenced by the most recent event.

There are many other sources of error in the evaluation of performance, but the most important one is based on inadequate information. At rating time, supervisors are required to evaluate the employees under their supervision. Yet it frequently occurs that supervisors do not know enough about their employees' performance to rate them fairly. Perhaps they have not kept adequate records of performance. Perhaps newer employees have not been observed often enough. The supervisor may have had a special project to complete and did not have the time to spend with his or her employees. Many potential reasons exist, but the fact remains that supervisors frequently do not have enough information on which to base their evaluations.

This crucial source error and many types of bias error can be eliminated by the establishment of a well-designed, professionally developed evaluation system and the training of supervisors and other raters in the proper use of that system.

Critical to the preparation of good performance appraisals is the maintenance of good records by each supervisor/manager. These records should make note of the instances of exemplary behavior as well as below-average or poor performance. A small notebook in a pocket will do. When good performance on the part of an employee is observed, make a note of it along with the date. Similarly, if a less than desirable performance is noted, record it. These notes then become the basis of the *objective* evaluation of performance. An evaluation is designed to help the employee improve his or her overall performance. This is far superior to subjective overall performance descriptions, such as "favorable" or "unfavorable" attitudes or a comment like "strongly motivated" or "poorly motivated." These general characteristics so stated are meaningless and cry out for definition. They require instances or descriptions of events to substantiate them. What did the employee *do* to lead you to the conclusion that he or she was poorly motivated?

Other techniques can make the act of performance appraisal more effective and valuable. Since the purpose of performance appraisal is to make it the center of an evaluation feedback procedure, make it a routine, rather ordinary, fairly frequent, expected performance. Do not turn it into a once-a-year major event tied to wage increases. You want the employee to pay attention, to discuss with you what is expected and how to improve performance. If appraisal is tied to an annual wage change, then the matter of wages becomes most important. Performance evaluation is ignored or becomes a source of argument and disagreement if the individual employee feels your appraisal had an immediate direct impact on salary for the coming year.

This is not to say that employee performance has nothing to do with salary determination. It has a lot to do with a raise, but salary is determined by many other factors, including the state of the economy and how well the organization is doing in that economy, the cost of inflation, the budget or profit that year, and so on. Discuss salary increments and rates for the coming year openly and honestly. Mention overall performance as a part of that discussion, but save a detailed performance appraisal and discussion until another time.

Performance appraisals can actually be done casually, rather frequently, *if* you do not make a big deal out of them. Short, easily prepared forms to record objective data is the goal. Long multi-page forms requiring a lot of preparation are cumbersome and fearsome to both the appraising manager and the employee being appraised.

THERE IS NO ONE BEST WAY

Managing the employee in the workplace requires a lot of managerial attention and skill. There is no single means available to a manager/supervisor that will guarantee success. There are many "systems" or "techniques" that are available and may be helpful: "management by objectives," "empowerment," "the Scanlon plan," "the managerial grid," "systems 4 management," "Sensitivity training," and "quality control circles," to name but a few well known ones. (For further information, see the references at the end of the chapter.) However, in many instances, organizations have adopted one of these and then gone "overboard" in promoting it to the exclusion of other possibilities, with very mixed results.

Some of the above-mentioned techniques, in the hands of trained and dedicated personnel, may be influential and helpful, but none are a panacea. All of these require common sense, honesty, dedication, sincerity, and time to make them work. There is no simple easy route to follow. There is not a single formula that will solve the problem of managing other human beings. One cannot read a book, hear a lecture, take a course, follow a computer program and become a successful manager of others. It takes all of these things, plus more. It is a fallacy to practice the teachings of one guru who may be popular at the moment and then conclude that your people management problems are solved. The fact is that being a good manager requires the ability to do as a good juggler does: keep many balls in the air at the same time. To keep some of the balls in the air requires that the manager know his or her job and product in detail; the other balls require the manager to know enough about people and what motivates them to be able to show consideration, empathy, and understanding.

SUMMING UP

An article in a recent newspaper[8] discussed what a senior professional football coach and others had to say about a former college coach who was recently named the head coach of a major pro team. "He's a gentleman, he's bright, he's very dedicated. I saw good personal qualities in him, and he knew his stuff when he went to the blackboard. He was organized, he was cautious, he got along well with others, all those things." A professional quarterback who in his college days had played for this coach was asked if he would like to play under him again. He responded, "I'd love to." He went on to describe the coach as one with sound theories, a surpassing knowledge of the game, and an ability to motivate players. In short, he prepared his team for football games. No stone was left unturned. The coach was a guy the players could respect because of the principles for which he stood. He was very honest and direct with his players. He was consistent in his behavior and they respected him. This is what people management takes: a combination of initiating action to get the job done and consideration of the people who work with you and for you to do the job over the long haul.

It cannot be said often enough or too strongly that the key responsibility in managing people in a hotel or restaurant is to discover the set of working conditions that permit an integration of the goals of the organization with the satisfaction of the needs of the individual employees. This responsibility is best met by a manager who is oriented toward getting the job done while also realizing that the job is done largely by others (often working in teams) who must derive some real and significant satisfaction from the work they are doing.

---

8. *San Diego Union* (Jan. 8, 1992). Jerry Mayee, "Ross Has Right Stuff"

In Conclusion

The hotel and restaurant business is action-oriented, fast-paced, and highly competitive. Managers need excellent health, a high level of energy, and a readiness to serve the public. Management of a sizable hotel or large restaurant can come early in a person's career, quicker than is true for many other industries.

The amount of travel and the overall economy are the bases on which the hotel and restaurant business is built. Over the long haul, both domestic and international travel will increase as it has in the past. The amount of discretionary income correlates highly with travel for pleasure. Convenience of travel and the absence of such travel inhibitors as airport congestion, high travel costs, and safety problems are also factors in travel growth. Technological advances in rail, air, and road travel can make travel safer and more enjoyable.

The transnationalization of hotel and restaurant ownership and operation is accelerating. Hotel and restaurant managers are now more likely to face transnational ownership and greater cultural diversity. The management contract has helped to divorce hotel ownership from operation and taken names like Hilton, Sheraton, Westin, and Holiday World around the world. Referral and marketing organizations, such as Best Western, make hotelkeeping more uniform as standard accounting and marketing systems spread. The largest hotel chain in number of units, Accor, S.A., is French-owned. Holiday Worldwide is a British company. The Japanese own a majority of Hawaiian hotels. The hotel manager of the future may be an American working in a Hong Kong–owned hotel with employees drawn from a dozen ethnic groups. Continued consolidation and globalization mean fewer large hotel companies with greater capital assets.

Restaurant franchising has accomplished the same end by introducing marketing and operating systems with such names as McDonald's, KFC, and Pizza Hut to places like Moscow, China, and South America. The restaurant executives of the future may oversee dozens of restaurants located in a number of countries.

Financial success in the hotel business will continue to depend as much on financial know-how as on operational competence. Cyclical overbuilding, the consequence of tax laws, the cost of borrowing money, and the amount of debt will continue to impact on profitability.

Individual restaurants will rise and fall. Based on past experience, however, most will last fewer than 5 years. Chain restaurant operations that rely heavily on franchising will no doubt continue to control the fast-food segment and will expand into the midscale category of restaurants. There will always be room, however, for the new restaurant, the new method of food preparation and service, and the new way of marketing and delivery. Lastly, some restaurants will expand and make millionaires of their owners.

The manner of operations of hotels will change depending on the availability and cost of money, the legal environment, and the adaptability of hotel and restaurant owners and operators. The real estate investment trust is again popular in hotel finance and a new job to the hotel business has been introduced, the asset manager. This person, hired by the hotel owners who have become reluctant hotel owners because of loan default, turn to the asset manager for assistance in dealing with hotel management contractors, for advice in repositioning a hotel in the marketplace, and for help in a hotel sale or purchase. The asset manager works directly with the owner and may also have an overview of the hotel's financial performance. Restaurant chains that have relied heavily on expansion via the franchise may prefer ownership if they are well financed. Who knows? Public nutrition concerns may even unseat the king of restaurant menus, the hamburger.

Appendix A

Hotel and Restaurant Trade Associations

ASSOCIATIONS

American Bed and Breakfast Association (ABBA)
16 Village Green, Suite 203
Crofton, MD 21114

American Hotel & Motel Association (AH&MA)
1201 New York Ave., N.W., Suite 600
Washington, DC 20005

American School Food Service Association (ASFSA)
1600 Duke St., 7th Floor
Alexandria, VA 22314

American Society for Hospital Food Service
Administrators (ASHFSA)
c/o American Hospital Association
840 N. Lake Shore Drive
Chicago, IL 60611

American Society of Travel Age
1101 King St.
Alexandria, VA 22314

Association of Corporate Travel I
P.O. Box 5394
Parsippany, NJ 07054

Association of Group Travel Executives
c/o Arnold H. Light
A. H. Light Co., Inc.
424 Madison Ave., Suite 705
New York, NY 10017

Association of Retail Travel Agents
1745 Jefferson Davis Hwy.
Arlington, VA 22202

Club Managers Association
7615 Winterberry Place
Bethesda, MD 20817

Cruise Lines International Association (CLIA)
500 Fifth Ave., Suite 1407
New York, NY 10110

Council on Hotel, Restaurant, and Institutional
Education (CHRIE)
1200 17th St., N.W.
Washington, DC 20036

Hospitality Lodging and Travel Research
Foundation (HLTRF)
c/o Raymond C. Ellis, Jr.

American Hotel & Motel Association
1201 New York Ave., N.W.
Washington, DC 20005

Hotel-Motel Greeters International (HMGI)
P.O. Box 20017
El Cajon, CA 92021

Hotel Sales and Marketing Association (HSMAI)
1300 L St., N.W., Suite 800
Washington, DC 20005

International Association of Hospitality
Accountants (IAHA)
Box 27649
Austin, TX 78755

International Caterers Association (ICA)
220 S. State St., Suite 1416
Chicago, IL 60604

National Association of Catering Executives (NACE)
5757 W. Century Blvd., #512
Los Angeles, CA 90045

National Association of Concessionaires (NAC)
35 E. Wacker Dr., Suite 1545
Chicago, IL 60601

National Bed-and-Breakfast Association (NB&BA)
P.O. Box 332
Norwalk, CT 06852

National Restaurant Association (NRA)
1200 17th St., N.W.
Washington, DC 20036

Travel and Tourism Research Association (TTRA)
P.O. Box 58066
Salt Lake City, UT 84158

Travel Industry Association of America (TIA)
Two Lafayette Center
1133 21st St., N.W.
Washington, DC 20036

U.S. Travel Data Center
Two Lafayette Center
1133 21st St., N.W.
Washington, DC 20036

PERIODICALS

Annals of Tourism Research
Pergamon Press (Journals)
Maxwell House, Fairview Park
Elmsford, NY 10523

Club Management
Club Managers Association of America
Commerce Publishing Company
408 Olive Street
St. Louis, MO 63102

Convention World
63 Great Rd.
Maynard, MA 01754

Cooking for Profit
P.O. Box 267
Fond Du Lac, WI 54935

Cornell Quarterly
327 Statler Hall
Cornell University
Ithaca, NY 14853

FIU Hospitality Review
Florida International University
N. Miami, FL 33181

Hospitality Education and Research Journal
Council on Hotel, Restaurant and Institutional
Education
311 First St., N.W.
Washington, DC 20001

Hospitality Educator
CHRIE
311 First St., N.W.
Washington, DC 20001

Hotels
1350 East Touhy Ave.
Des Plaines, IL 60018

International Journal of Hospitality Management
Pergamon Press (Journals)
Maxwell House, Fairview Park
Elmsford, NY 10523

Journal of Travel Research
College of Business and Administration
University of Colorado
Campus Box 420
Boulder, CO 80309

Lodging Hospitality
Penton Publishing
P.O. Box 95759
Cleveland, OH 44101

Lodging Magazine
American Hotel & Motel Association
1201 New York Ave., N.W.
Washington, DC 20005

Nation's Restaurant News
Lebhar-Friedman
305 Madison Ave., Suite 535
New York, NY 10165

Restaurant Business
Circulation Department
633 Third Ave.
New York, NY 10017

Restaurant Hospitality
Penton Publishing
P.O. Box 95759
Cleveland, OH 44101

Restaurants & Institutions
Cahner's Publishing Company
270 St. Paul St.
Denver, CO 80206

Restaurants USA
National Restaurant Association
1200 Seventeenth St., N.W.
Washington, DC 20036

Sales & Marketing Management
P.O. Box 1025
Southeastern, PA 19398

School Food Service Journal
5600 S. Quebec St., Suite 300-B
Englewood, CO 80111

Successful Meetings
633 Third Ave.
New York, NY 10017

Tour and Travel News
600 Community Drive
Manhasset, NY 11030

Travel Agent Magazine
825 Seventh Ave., 3rd Floor
New York, NY 10019

Travel Digest
1654 S.W. 28 Ave.
Ft. Lauderdale, FL 33312

Travel Trade
6 East 46th St.
New York, NY 10017

Travelage
888 Seventh Ave., 29th Floor
New York, NY 10106

Appendix B

Suggested Readings

Starr, Nona, *Viewpoint, An Introduction to Travel, Tourism and Hospitality*, Houghton Mifflin, Boston, 1993.

Powers, Tom, *Introduction To Management In the Hospitality Industry*, Fourth Edition, John Wiley & Sons, New York, 1992.

Nebel, Eddystone C. *Managing Hotels Effectively*, Van Nostrand Reinhold, New York, 1991.

Index